THE **CDEV** SOLUTION

Print + Online

CDEV² delivers all the key terms and core concepts for the **Child and Adolescent Development** course.

CDEV Online provides the complete narrative from the printed text with additional interactive media and the unique functionality of **StudyBits**—all available on nearly any device!

What is a StudyBit™? Created through a deep investigation of students' challenges and workflows, the StudyBit™ functionality of **CDEV Online** enables students of different generations and learning styles to study more effectively by allowing them to learn their way. Here's how they work:

COLLECT WHAT'S IMPORTANT
Create StudyBits as you highlight text, images or take notes!

WEAK

FAIR

STRONG

UNASSIGNED

RATE AND ORGANIZE STUDYBITS
Rate your understanding and use the color-coding to quickly organize your study time and personalize your flashcards and quizzes.

StudyBit™

TRACK/MONITOR PROGRESS
Use Concept Tracker to decide how you'll spend study time and study YOUR way!

85%

PERSONALIZE QUIZZES
Filter by your StudyBits to personalize quizzes or just take chapter quizzes off-the-shelf.

CORRECT

INCORRECT

INCORRECT

INCORRECT

CENGAGE
Learning®

CDEV²

Spencer Rathus

Sr. Vice President, General Manager:
  Balraj Kalsi
Product Manager: Clinton Kernen
Content/Media Developer: Sarah Keeling
Product Assistant: Eli Lewis
Sr. Marketing Manager: Andrew Ginsberg
Marketing Coordinator: Quynton Johnson
Content Project Manager: Darrell E. Frye
Manufacturing Planner: Ron Montgomery
Production Service: SPi Global
Sr. Art Director: Bethany Casey
Internal Designer: Joe Devine, Red Hangar
Cover Designer: Lisa Kuhn, Curio Press,
  LLC/Trish & Ted Knapke, Ke Design
Cover Image: Comstock/Stockbyte/Getty
  Images, plherrera/E+/Getty Images
Special Page Images: Computer and tablet
  illustration: iStockphoto.com/furtaev;
  Smart phone Illustration: iStockphoto.
  com/dashadima; Feedback image:
  Rawpixel.com/Shutterstockcom
Intellectual Property Analyst:
  Alexandra Ricciardi
Intellectual Property Project Manager:
  Carly Belcher

For product information and technology assistance, contact us at
Cengage Learning Customer & Sales Support, 1-800-354-9706

For permission to use material from this text or product,
submit all requests online at **www.cengage.com/permissions**
Further permissions questions can be emailed to
permissionrequest@cengage.com

Library of Congress Control Number: 2016963473

Student Edition ISBN: 978-1-337-11694-7

Student Edition with Online ISBN: 978-1-337-11692-3

Cengage Learning
20 Channel Center Street
Boston, MA 02210
USA

Cengage Learning is a leading provider of customized learning solutions with employees residing in nearly 40 different countries and sales in more than 125 countries around the world. Find your local representative at **www.cengage.com.**

Cengage Learning products are represented in Canada by Nelson Education, Ltd.

To learn more about Cengage Learning Solutions, visit **www.cengage.com**

Purchase any of our products at your local college store or at our preferred online store **www.cengagebrain.com**

Printed in the United States of America
Print Number: 02   Print Year: 2018

SPENCER A. RATHUS
CDEV²

BRIEF CONTENTS

Comstock/Stockbyte/Getty Images, plherrera/E+/Getty Images

CONTENTS

rubberball/Getty Images

1 | History, Theories, and Methods

Image Source/Alamy Stock Photo

LEARNING OUTCOMES

After studying this chapter, you will be able to…

1-1 Relate the history of the study of child development

1-2 Compare and contrast theories of child development

1-3 Enumerate key controversies in child development

1-4 Describe ways in which researchers study child development

After you finish this chapter, go to **PAGE 21** for **STUDY TOOLS**

This book has a story to tell. An important, remarkable story—your story. It is about the amazing journey you have already taken through childhood, and about the unfolding of your adult life. Billions of people have made this journey before. You have much in common with them. Yet you are unique, and things will happen to you, and because of you, that have never happened before.

> You are unique, and things will happen to you, and because of you, that have never happened before.

1-1 THE DEVELOPMENT OF THE STUDY OF CHILD DEVELOPMENT

Developmental psychology is the discipline that studies the physical, cognitive, social, and emotional development of humans. It focuses on the many influences on behavior, including the effects of the person's physical, social, and cultural environment, and how these factors interact to influence the developments that occur over time.

Scientific inquiry into human development has existed for little more than a century. In ancient times and in the Middle Ages, children often were viewed as innately evil and discipline was harsh. Legally, medieval children were treated as property and servants. They could be sent to the monastery, married without consultation, or convicted of crimes. Children were nurtured until they were seven years old, which was considered the "age of reason." Then they were expected to work alongside adults in the home and in the field.

The transition to modern thinking about children is marked by the writings of philosophers such as John Locke and Jean-Jacques Rousseau. Englishman John Locke (1632–1704) believed that the child came into the world as a *tabula rasa*—a "blank tablet" or clean slate—that was written on by experience. Locke did not believe that inborn predispositions toward good or evil played an important role in the conduct of the child. Instead, he focused on the role of the environment or of experience. Locke believed that social approval and disapproval are powerful shapers of behavior. But Jean-Jacques Rousseau (1712–1778), a Swiss-French philosopher, argued that children are inherently good and that, if allowed to express their natural impulses, they will develop into generous and moral individuals.

During the Industrial Revolution—a period from the late 18th century through the 19th century when machine-based production replaced much manual labor—family life came to be defined in terms of the nuclear unit of mother, father, and children rather than the extended family. Children became more visible, fostering awareness of childhood as a special time of life. Still, children often labored in factories from dawn to dusk through the early years of the 20th century.

In the 20th century, laws were passed to protect children from strenuous labor, to require that they attend school until a certain age, and to prevent them from getting married or being sexually exploited. Whereas children were once considered the property of parents, laws now protect children from abuse by parents and other adults. Juvenile courts see that children who break the law receive treatment in the criminal justice system.

Various thoughts about child development coalesced into a field of scientific study in the 19th and early 20th centuries. G. Stanley Hall (1844–1924) is credited with founding child development as an academic discipline and bringing scientific attention to

> **developmental psychology** the discipline that studies the physical, cognitive, social, and emotional development of humans.

TRUTH OR FICTION?

WHAT DO YOU THINK? FOLKLORE, COMMON SENSE, OR NONSENSE? SELECT T FOR "TRUTH" OR F FOR "FICTION," AND CHECK THE ACCURACY OF YOUR ANSWERS AS YOU READ THROUGH THE CHAPTER.

T	F	During the Middle Ages, children were often treated as miniature adults.
T	F	Nail biting and smoking cigarettes are signs of conflict experienced during early childhood.
T	F	Research with monkeys has helped psychologists understand the formation of attachment in humans.
T	F	To learn how a person develops over a lifetime, researchers have tracked some individuals for more than 50 years.

focus on the period of adolescence. French psychologist Alfred Binet (1857–1911), along with Theodore Simon (1872–1961), developed the first standardized intelligence test near the beginning of the 20th century. Binet's purpose was to identify public school children who were at risk of falling behind their peers in academic achievement. By the start of the 20th century, child development had emerged as a scientific field of study. Soon major theories of the developing child were proposed by theorists such as Arnold Gesell, Sigmund Freud, John B. Watson, and Jean Piaget.

1-1a WHY DO RESEARCHERS STUDY CHILD DEVELOPMENT?

Curiosity and love of children are two key motives for studying child development. There are other motives as well:

▶ To gain insight into the nature of human nature—whether children are aggressive or loving, whether children are conscious and self-aware, whether they have a natural curiosity that demands to unravel the mysteries of the universe, or whether they merely react mechanically to environmental stimulation.

▶ To gain insight into the origins of adult behavior—the origins of empathy, of antisocial behavior, of special talents in writing, music, athletics, and math?

▶ To gain insight into the origins of gender roles and gender differences.

▶ To gain insight into the origins, prevention, and treatment of developmental problems such as fetal alcohol syndrome, PKU, SIDS, Down syndrome, autism, hyperactivity, dyslexia, and child abuse.

▶ To optimize conditions for development in areas such as nutrition, immunizations, parent–child interaction, and education.

1-2 THEORIES OF DEVELOPMENT

Give me a dozen healthy infants, well-formed, and my own specified world to bring them up in, and I'll guarantee to train them to become any type of specialist I might suggest—doctor, lawyer, merchant, chief, and, yes, even beggar and

behaviorism Watson's view that science must study observable behavior only and investigate relationships between stimuli and responses.

Developmental psychologists and educators attempt to sort out the influences of heredity (maturation) and the environment (experience) in development. John Watson would have argued that this girl's preferences and skills are shaped by experience. Arnold Gesell might have preferred to focus on the expression of her inborn ability.

thief, regardless of their talents, penchants, tendencies, abilities, vocations, and the race of their ancestors.

—*John B. Watson (1924, p. 82)*

TRUTH

(T) F During the Middle Ages, children were often treated as miniature adults.

It is true that during the Middle Ages, children were often treated as miniature adults. This does not mean that they were given more privileges, however. Instead, more was expected of them.

Theories are formulations of apparent relationships among observed events. They allow us to derive explanations and predictions. Many psychological theories combine statements about behavior (such as reflexes), mental processes (such as whether a reflex is intentional or not), and biological processes (such as maturation of the nervous system). A satisfactory theory allows us to predict behavior. For example, a theory about a reflex should allow us to predict the age at which it will drop out or be replaced by intentional behavior. John B. Watson (1878–1958), the founder of American **behaviorism**, viewed development in terms of learning theory. He generally agreed with Locke that children's ideas, preferences, and skills are shaped by experience. There has been a long-standing nature–nurture debate in the study of children. In his theoretical approach to understanding children, Watson came down on the side of nurture—the importance of the physical and social environments—as found, for example, in parental training and approval.

Arnold Gesell expressed the opposing idea that biological **maturation** was the main principle of development: "All things considered, the inevitability and surety of maturation are the most impressive characteristics of early development. It is the hereditary ballast which conserves and stabilizes growth of each individual infant" (Gesell, 1928, p. 378). Watson was talking about the behavior patterns that children develop, whereas Gesell was focusing mainly on physical aspects of growth and development.

Theories such as behavioral theory and maturational theory help developmentalists explain, predict, and influence the events they study. Let's consider theories that are popular among developmentalists today. They fall within broad perspectives on development.

According to John B. Watson (1878–1958), the founder of American behaviorism, a theory about a reflex should allow us to predict the age at which it will drop out or be replaced by intentional behavior. Here Watson is demonstrating the grasp reflex of a newborn infant.

Courtesy of the Ferdinand Hamburger Archives of The Johns Hopkins University

1-2a THE PSYCHOANALYTIC PERSPECTIVE

A number of theories fall within the psychoanalytic perspective. Each owes its origin to Sigmund Freud and views children—and adults—as caught in conflict. Early in development, the conflict is between the child and the world outside. The expression of basic drives, such as sex and aggression, conflict with parental expectations, social rules, moral codes, even laws. But the external limits—parental demands and social rules—are brought inside or *internalized*. Once internalization occurs, the conflict takes place between opposing *inner* forces. The child's observable behavior, thoughts, and feelings reflect the outcomes of these hidden battles.

Let's consider Freud's theory of **psychosexual development** and Erik Erikson's theory of psychosocial development. Each is a **stage theory** that sees children as developing through distinct periods of life. Each suggests that the child's experiences during early stages affect the child's emotional and social life at the time and later on.

SIGMUND FREUD'S THEORY OF PSYCHOSEXUAL DEVELOPMENT Sigmund Freud's (1856–1939) theory of psychosexual development focused on emotional and social development and on the origins of psychological traits such as dependence, obsessive neatness, and vanity. Freud theorized three parts of the personality: the *id*, *ego*, and *superego*. The id is present at birth and is *unconscious*. It represents biological drives and demands instant gratification, as suggested by a baby's wailing. The ego, or the conscious sense of self, begins to develop when children learn to obtain gratification consciously, without screaming or crying. The ego curbs the appetites of the id and makes plans that are in keeping with social conventions so that a person can find gratification but avoid social disapproval. The superego develops throughout infancy and early childhood. It brings inward the wishes and morals of the child's caregivers and other members of the community. Throughout the remainder of the child's life, the superego will monitor the intentions and behavior of the ego, hand down judgments of right and wrong,

FREUD'S THEORY OF PSYCHOSEXUAL DEVELOPMENT

Sigmund Freud's (1856–1939) theory of psychosexual development focused on emotional and social development and on the origins of psychological traits such as dependence, obsessive neatness, and vanity. According to Freud, there are five stages of psychosexual development:

▶ **oral**

▶ **anal**

▶ **phallic**

▶ **latency**

▶ **genital**

maturation the unfolding of genetically determined traits, structures, and functions.

psychosexual development the process by which libidinal energy is expressed through different erogenous zones during different stages of development.

stage theory a theory of development characterized by distinct periods of life.

and attempt to influence behavior through flooding the person with feelings of guilt and shame when the judgment is in the negative.

According to Freud, there are five stages of psychosexual development: *oral, anal, phallic, latency,* and *genital*. If a child receives too little or too much gratification during a stage, the child can become *fixated* in that stage. For example, during the first year of life, which Freud termed the *oral stage*, "oral" activities such as sucking and biting bring pleasure and gratification. If the child is weaned early or breast-fed too long, the child may become fixated on oral activities such as nail biting or smoking, or even show a "biting wit."

FICTION

T (F) Nail biting and smoking cigarettes are signs of conflict experienced during early childhood.

Actually, there is no evidence that nail biting and smoking cigarettes are signs of early childhood conflict. The statement must therefore be considered "fiction."

In the second, or *anal*, stage, gratification is obtained through control and elimination of waste products. Excessively strict or permissive toilet training can lead to the development of anal-retentive traits, such as perfectionism and neatness, or anal-expulsive traits, such as sloppiness and carelessness. In the third stage, the *phallic stage*, parent–child conflict may develop over masturbation, which many parents treat with punishment and threats. It is normal for children to develop strong sexual attachments to the parent of the other sex during the phallic stage and to begin to view the parent of the same sex as a rival.

By age five or six, Freud believed, children enter a *latency stage* during which sexual feelings remain unconscious, children turn to schoolwork, and they typically prefer playmates of their own sex. The final stage of psychosexual development, the *genital stage*, begins with the biological changes that usher in adolescence. Adolescents generally desire sexual gratification through intercourse with a member of the other sex. Freud believed that oral or anal stimulation, masturbation, and male–male or female–female

psychosocial development
Erikson's theory, which emphasizes the importance of social relationships and conscious choice throughout eight stages of development.

sexual activity are immature forms of sexual conduct that reflect fixations at early stages of development.

Evaluation Freud's views about the anal stage have influenced child-care workers to recommend that toilet training not be started too early or handled punitively. His emphasis on the emotional needs of children has influenced educators to be more sensitive to the possible emotional reasons behind a child's misbehavior. Freud's work has also been criticized. For one thing, Freud developed his theory on the basis of contacts with adult patients (mostly women) (Hergenhahn & Henley, 2014), rather than observing children directly. Freud may also have inadvertently guided patients into expressing ideas that confirmed his views.

Some of Freud's own disciples, including Erik Erikson, believe that Freud placed too much emphasis on basic instincts and unconscious motives. He argues that people are motivated not only by drives such as sex and aggression but also by social relationships and conscious desires to achieve, to have aesthetic experiences, and to help others.

ERIK ERIKSON'S THEORY OF PSYCHOSOCIAL DEVELOPMENT Erik Erikson (1902–1994) modified Freud's theory and extended it through the adult years. Erikson's theory, like Freud's, focuses on the development of the emotional life and psychological traits, but Erikson focuses on social relationships rather than sexual or aggressive instincts. Therefore, Erikson speaks of **psychosocial development** rather than of *psychosexual development*. Furthermore, Erikson places greater emphasis on the ego, or the sense of self. Erikson (1963) extended Freud's five stages to eight to include the concerns of

ERIKSON'S THEORY OF PSYCHOSOCIAL DEVELOPMENT

Erik Erikson (1902–1994) modified Freud's psychosexual theory and extended it through the adult years. Erikson's theory, like Freud's, focuses on the development of the emotional life and psychological traits, but Erikson focuses on social relationships rather than sexual or aggressive instincts. He expanded Freud's five stages to eight, to include the stages of adult development.

Erik Erikson was concerned with the development of our sense of identity—who we are and what we stand for. He was especially concerned with the crisis in identity that affects adolescents in our culture. How would you describe this adolescent's apparent sense of identity?

adulthood. Rather than label his stages after parts of the body, Erikson labeled them after the **life crisis** that people might encounter during that stage.

Erikson proposed that social relationships and physical maturation give each stage its character. For example, the parent–child relationship and the infant's dependence and helplessness are responsible for the nature of the earliest stages of development.

Early experiences affect future developments. With parental support, most children resolve early life crises productively. Successful resolution of each crisis bolsters their sense of identity—of who they are and what they stand for—and their expectation of future success.

Erikson's views, like Freud's, have influenced child rearing, early childhood education, and child therapy. For example, Erikson's views about an adolescent **identity crisis** have entered the popular culture and have affected the way many parents and teachers deal with teenagers. Some schools help students master the crisis by means of life-adjustment courses and study units on self-understanding in social studies and literature classes.

WATSON: THE FOUNDER OF AMERICAN BEHAVIORISM

John B. Watson (1878–1958) is considered the founder of American behaviorism. He was a major force in early 20th century psychology, arguing that psychologists should study only observable behavior, not thoughts, fantasies, and other mental images. He viewed development in terms of learning theory. He generally agreed with Locke that children's ideas, preferences, and skills are shaped by experience. In the long-standing nature–nurture debate in the study of children, his theoretical approach to understanding children comes down on the side of nurture.

Evaluation Erikson's views are appealing in that they emphasize the importance of human consciousness and choice. They are also appealing in that they portray us as prosocial and helpful, whereas Freud portrayed us as selfish and needing to be compelled to comply with social rules. There is also some empirical support for the Eriksonian view that positive outcomes of early life crises help put us on the path to positive development (Gfellner & Armstrong, 2012; Marcia, 2010).

1-2b THE LEARNING PERSPECTIVE: BEHAVIORAL AND SOCIAL COGNITIVE THEORIES

During the 1930s, psychologists derived an ingenious method for helping five- and six-year-old children overcome bed-wetting from the behavioral perspective. Most children at this age wake up and go to the bathroom when their bladders are full. Bed wetters, though, sleep through bladder tension and reflexively urinate in bed. To address this problem, the psychologists placed a special pad beneath the sleeping child. Wetness in the pad closed an electrical circuit, causing a bell to ring and waking the sleeping child. After several repetitions, most children learned to wake up before they wet the pad. How? They learned through a technique called *classical conditioning*, which we explain in this section.

The so-called bell-and-pad method for bed-wetting is a more complicated example of learning theory being applied to human development. Most applications of learning theory to development are found in simpler, everyday events. In this section, we consider two theories of learning: behaviorism and social cognitive theory.

BEHAVIORISM John B. Watson argued that a scientific approach to development must focus on observable behavior only and not on things like thoughts, fantasies, and other mental images.

life crisis an internal conflict that attends each stage of psychosocial development.

identity crisis according to Erikson, a period of inner conflict during which one examines one's values and makes decisions about one's life roles.

FIG.1.1 | SCHEMATIC REPRESENTATION OF CLASSICAL CONDITIONING

Before conditioning, the bell is an unlearned or unconditioned stimulus (UCS) that elicits waking up, which is an unlearned or unconditioned response (UCR). Bladder tension does not elicit waking up, which is the problem. During the conditioning procedure, bladder tension repeatedly precedes urination, which in turn causes the bell to ring. After several repetitions, bladder tension has become associated with the bell, making bladder tension into a learned or conditioned stimulus (CS) that causes the child to awaken. Awakening in response to bladder tension is a learned or conditioned response (CR).

Classical conditioning is a simple form of learning in which an originally neutral stimulus comes to bring forth, or elicit, the response usually brought forth by a second stimulus as a result of being paired repeatedly with the second stimulus. In the bell-and-pad method for bed-wetting, psychologists repeatedly pair tension in the children's bladders with a stimulus that awakens them (the bell). The children learn to respond to the bladder tension as if it were a bell; that is, they wake up (see Figure 1.1).

classical conditioning a simple form of learning in which one stimulus comes to bring forth the response usually brought forth by a second stimulus by being paired repeatedly with the second stimulus.

operant conditioning a simple form of learning in which an organism learns to engage in behavior that is reinforced.

reinforcement the process of providing stimuli following responses that increase the frequency of the responses.

positive reinforcer a reinforcer that, when applied, increases the frequency of a response.

negative reinforcer a reinforcer that, when removed, increases the frequency of a response.

extinction the cessation of a response that is performed in the absence of reinforcement.

SKINNER AND BEHAVIORISM

B.F. Skinner (1904–1990) picked up the behaviorist mandate from John Watson. Behaviorists argue that much emotional learning is acquired through conditioning. Skinner introduced the key concept of positive and negative reinforcement in operant conditioning. He was interested in popularizing his views on psychology and wrote a novel, *Walden Two*, which supported his views and achieved a sort of cult following.

Behaviorists argue that much emotional learning is acquired through classical conditioning. In **operant conditioning** (a different kind of conditioning), children learn to do something because of its effects. B. F. Skinner introduced the key concept of **reinforcement**. Reinforcers are stimuli that increase the frequency of the behavior they follow. Most children learn to adjust their behavior to conform to social codes and rules to earn reinforcers such as the attention and approval of their parents and teachers. Other children, ironically, may learn to misbehave because misbehavior also draws attention. Any stimulus that increases the frequency of the responses preceding it serves as a reinforcer.

Skinner distinguished between positive and negative reinforcers. **Positive reinforcers** increase the frequency of behaviors when they are *applied*. Food and approval usually serve as positive reinforcers. **Negative reinforcers** increase the frequency of behaviors when they are *removed*. Fear acts as a negative reinforcer in that its removal increases the frequency of the behaviors preceding it. Figure 1.2 compares positive and negative reinforcers.

Extinction results from repeated performance of operant behavior without reinforcement. After a number of trials, the operant behavior is no longer shown. Children's temper tantrums and crying at bedtime can often be extinguished by parents' remaining out of the bedroom after the children have been put to bed. Punishments are aversive events that suppress or *decrease* the frequency of the behavior they follow. (Figure 1.3 compares negative reinforcers with punishments.) Many learning theorists agree that punishment is undesirable in rearing children for reasons such as punishment does not in itself suggest an alternative acceptable form of behavior; punishment tends

FIG.1.2 POSITIVE VERSUS NEGATIVE REINFORCERS

Procedure	Behavior	Consequence	Change in behavior
Use of positive reinforcement	Behavior (studying)	Positive reinforcer (teacher approval) is **presented** when student studies	Frequency of behavior **increases** (student studies more)
Use of negative reinforcement	Behavior (studying)	Negative reinforcer (teacher disapproval) is **removed** when student studies	Frequency of behavior **increases** (student studies more)

Reinforcers, by definition, increase the frequency of behavior. In this example, teacher approval is a positive reinforcer because it increases the frequency of behavior when it is *applied*. Teacher disapproval functions as a negative reinforcer because *removing* it increases behavior—in this case, studying. But teacher disapproval can backfire when other students show strong approval of a student's disobeying the teacher.

to suppress behavior only when its delivery is guaranteed; and punishment can create feelings of anger and hostility.

Research suggests that when teachers praise and attend to appropriate behavior and ignore misbehavior, studying and classroom behavior improve while disruptive and aggressive behaviors decrease (Coffee & Kratochwill, 2013; Jenkins et al., 2015). By ignoring misbehavior or by using *time out* from positive reinforcement, we can avoid reinforcing children for misbehavior.

In using time out, children are placed in drab, restrictive environments for a specified time period such as ten minutes when they behave disruptively.

Operant conditioning is used every day in the *socialization* of young children. Parents and peers influence children to acquire behavior patterns they consider to be appropriate to their gender through the elaborate use of rewards and punishments. Thus, boys may ignore other boys when they play with dolls and housekeeping toys but play with boys when they use transportation toys. Many children are thus taught to engage in behavior that may please others more than it pleases themselves.

SOCIAL COGNITIVE THEORY Behaviorists tend to limit their view of learning to conditioning. **Social cognitive theorists** such as Albert Bandura (1986, 2011, 2012) have shown that much learning also occurs by observing other people, reading, and viewing characters in the media. People may need practice to refine their skills, but they can acquire the basic know-how through observation.

Observational learning occurs when children observe how parents cook, clean, or repair a broken appliance. It takes place when adults watch supervisors sketch out sales strategies on a blackboard or hear them speak a foreign language. In social cognitive theory, the people after whom we pattern our own behavior are termed *models*.

FIG.1.3 NEGATIVE REINFORCERS VERSUS PUNISHMENTS

Procedure	Behavior	Consequence	Change in behavior
Use of negative reinforcement	Behavior (studying)	Negative reinforcer (teacher disapproval) is **removed** when student studies	Frequency of behavior **increases** (student studies more)
Use of punishment	Behavior (talking in class)	Punishment (detention) is **presented** when student talks in class	Frequency of behavior **decreases** (student talks less in class)

Both negative reinforcers and punishments tend to be aversive stimuli. Reinforcers, however, increase the frequency of behavior. Punishments decrease the frequency of behavior. Negative reinforcers increase the frequency of behavior when they are removed.

social cognitive theory a cognitively oriented learning theory that emphasizes observational learning.

BANDURA AND SOCIAL COGNITIVE THEORY

Albert Bandura (b. 1925), a leading social cognitive theorist, emphasized the role of social learning—that is, learning by observing others—as a key element in learning theory. He labeled the people after whom we, as children and adults, pattern our behavior "models." While behaviorists tend to limit their view of learning to conditioning, social cognitive theorists focus on modeling behavior.

EVALUATION OF LEARNING THEORIES Learning theories allow us to explain, predict, and influence many aspects of behavior. The use of the bell-and-pad method for bed-wetting would probably not have been derived from any other theoretical approach. Many of the teaching approaches used in educational TV shows are based on learning theory.

1-2c THE COGNITIVE PERSPECTIVE

Cognitive theorists focus on people's mental processes. They investigate the ways in which children perceive and mentally represent the world, how they develop thinking, logic, and problem-solving ability. One cognitive perspective is **cognitive-developmental theory**,

cognitive-developmental theory the stage theory that holds that the child's abilities to mentally represent the world and solve problems unfold as a result of the interaction of experience and the maturation of neurological structures.

scheme an action pattern or mental structure that is involved in the acquisition and organization of knowledge.

adaptation the interaction between the organism and the environment, consisting of assimilation and accommodation.

assimilation the incorporation of new events or knowledge into existing schemes.

advanced by Swiss biologist Jean Piaget (1896–1980) and further developed by many theorists. Another is information-processing theory.

COGNITIVE-DEVELOPMENTAL THEORY

During his adolescence, Jean Piaget studied philosophy, logic, and mathematics, but years later he took his Ph.D. in biology. In 1920, he obtained a job at the Binet Institute in Paris, where research on intelligence tests was being conducted. Through his studies, Piaget realized that when children answered questions incorrectly, their wrong answers still often reflected consistent—although illogical—mental processes. Piaget regarded children as natural physicists who actively intend to learn about and take intellectual charge of their worlds. In the Piagetian view, children who squish their food and laugh enthusiastically are often acting as budding scientists. They are studying both the texture and consistency of their food, as well as their parents' response.

Piaget used concepts such as *schemes, adaptation, assimilation, accommodation,* and *equilibration* to describe and explain cognitive development. Piaget defines the **scheme** as a pattern of action or mental structure that is involved in acquiring or organizing knowledge. For example, newborn babies might be said to have a sucking scheme (others call this a *reflex*), responding to things put in their mouths as "things I can suck" versus "things I can't suck."

Adaptation refers to the interaction between the organism and the environment. According to Piaget, all organisms adapt to their environment. Adaptation consists of assimilation and accommodation, which occur throughout life. Cognitive **assimilation** refers to the process by which someone responds to new objects or events according to existing schemes or ways of organizing knowledge. Two-year-olds who refer to horses as

PIAGET'S COGNITIVE-DEVELOPMENTAL THEORY

Cognitive theorists investigate the ways in which children perceive and mentally represent the world, how they develop thinking, logic, and problem-solving ability. One cognitive perspective is cognitive-developmental theory, advanced by Swiss biologist Jean Piaget (1896–1980). Piaget's early training as a biologist led him to view children as mentally assimilating and accommodating aspects of their environment.

Piaget used concepts such as schemes, adaptation, assimilation, accommodation, and equilibration to describe and explain cognitive development. In 1963, Piaget hypothesized that children's cognitive processes develop in an orderly sequence, or series, of stages. He identified four major stages of cognitive development: sensorimotor, preoperational, concrete operational, and formal operational.

"doggies" are assimilating horses into their dog scheme. Sometimes a novel object or event cannot be made to fit into an existing scheme. In that case, the scheme may be changed or a new scheme may be created to incorporate the new event. This process is called **accommodation**. Consider the sucking reflex. Infants accommodate by rejecting objects that are too large, that taste bad, or that are of the wrong texture or temperature.

Piaget theorized that when children can assimilate new events into existing schemes, they are in a state of cognitive harmony, or equilibrium. When something that does not fit happens, their state of equilibrium is disturbed and they may try to accommodate. The process of restoring equilibrium is termed **equilibration**. Piaget believed that the attempt to restore equilibrium lies at the heart of the natural curiosity of the child.

PIAGET'S STAGES OF COGNITIVE DEVELOPMENT

Piaget (1963) hypothesized that children's cognitive processes develop in an orderly sequence, or series, of stages. Piaget identified four major stages of cognitive development: *sensorimotor, preoperational, concrete operational*, and *formal operational*. These stages are discussed in subsequent chapters.

Because Piaget's theory focuses on cognitive development, its applications are primarily in educational settings. Teachers following Piaget's views actively engage the child in solving problems. They gear instruction to the child's developmental level and offer activities that challenge the child to advance to the next level. For example, five-year-old children learn primarily through play and direct sensory contact with the environment. Early formal instruction using paper and workbooks may be less effective with this age group.

Evaluation Many researchers, using a variety of methods, find that Piaget may have underestimated the ages when children are capable of doing certain things. It also appears that many cognitive skills may develop gradually and not in distinct stages. Nevertheless, Piaget has provided a strong theoretical foundation for researchers concerned with sequences in cognitive development.

INFORMATION-PROCESSING THEORY Another

face of the cognitive perspective is information processing (Brigham et al., 2011; Calvete & Orue, 2012). Many psychologists and educators speak of people as having working or short-term memory and a more permanent long-term memory (storage). If information has been placed in long-term memory, it must be retrieved before we can work on it. Retrieving information from our own long-term memories requires certain cues, without which the information may be lost.

Thus, many cognitive psychologists focus on information processing in people—the processes by which people encode (input) information, store it (in long-term memory), retrieve it (place it in short-term memory), and manipulate it to solve problems. Our strategies for solving problems are sometimes referred to as our *mental programs* or *software*. In this computer metaphor, our brains are the *hardware* that runs our mental programs. Our brains—containing billions of brain cells called *neurons*—become our most "personal" computers. When psychologists who study information processing contemplate cognitive development, they are likely to talk in terms of the *size* of the person's short-term memory and the *number of programs* she or he can run simultaneously.

The most obvious applications of information processing occur in teaching. For example, information-processing models alert teachers to the sequence of steps by which children acquire information, commit it to memory, and retrieve it to solve problems. By understanding this sequence, teachers can provide experiences that give students practice with each stage.

We now see that the brain is a sort of biological computer. Let us next see what other aspects of biology can be connected with development.

1-2d THE BIOLOGICAL PERSPECTIVE

The biological perspective directly relates to physical development: to gains in height and weight; development of the brain; and developments connected with hormones, reproduction, and heredity. Here we consider two biologically oriented theories of development, evolutionary psychology and ethology.

EVOLUTIONARY PSYCHOLOGY AND ETHOLOGY: "DOING WHAT COMES NATURALLY" Evolutionary

psychology and ethology were heavily influenced by the 19th-century work of Charles Darwin and by the work of 20th-century ethologists Konrad Lorenz and Niko Tinbergen. **Ethology** is concerned with instinctive, or inborn, behavior patterns. According to the theory of evolution, there is a struggle for survival as various species and individuals compete for a limited quantity of resources. The combined genetic instructions from parents lead to variations among individuals. There are also sharper differences from parents,

accommodation the modification of existing schemes to permit the incorporation of new events or knowledge.

equilibration the creation of an equilibrium, or balance, between assimilation and accommodation.

ethology the study of behaviors that are specific to a species.

caused by sudden changes in genetic material called *mutations*. Those individuals whose traits are better adapted to their environments are more likely to survive (that is, to be naturally selected). Survival permits them to reach sexual maturity, select mates, and reproduce, thereby transmitting their features or traits to the next generation. What began as a minor variation or a mutation becomes embedded in more and more individuals over the generations—if it fosters survival.

The field of **evolutionary psychology** studies the ways in which adaptation and natural selection are connected with mental processes and behavior. One of the concepts of evolutionary psychology is that not only physical traits but also patterns of behavior, including social behavior, evolve and are transmitted genetically from generation to generation. In other words, behavior patterns that help an organism to survive and reproduce are likely to be transmitted to the next generation. Such behaviors are believed to include aggression, strategies of mate selection, even altruism—that is, self-sacrifice of the individual to help perpetuate the family group. The behavior patterns are termed *instinctive* or *species-specific* because they evolved within certain *species*.

The nervous systems of most, and perhaps all, animals are "prewired" to respond to some situations in specific ways. For example, birds raised in isolation from other birds build nests during the mating season even if they have never seen a nest or seen another bird building one. Nest-building could not have been learned. Birds raised in isolation also sing the songs typical of their species. These behaviors are *built in*, or instinctive. They are also referred to as inborn **fixed action patterns (FAPs)**.

During prenatal development, genes and sex hormones are responsible for the physical development of female and male sex organs. Most theorists also believe that in many species, including humans, sex hormones can "masculinize" or "feminize" the embryonic brain by creating tendencies to behave in stereotypical masculine or feminine ways. Testosterone, the male sex hormone, seems to be connected with feelings of self-confidence, high activity levels, and—the negative side—aggressiveness (Hines, 2011; Nguyen et al., 2016; Rice & Sher, 2013).

Research into the ethological perspective suggests that instinct may play a role in human behavior. Two questions that ethological research seeks to answer are: What areas of human behavior and development, if any, involve instincts? How powerful are instincts in people?

1-2e THE ECOLOGICAL PERSPECTIVE

Ecology is the branch of biology that deals with the relationships between living organisms and their environment. The **ecological systems theory** of development addresses aspects of psychological, social, and emotional development as well as aspects of biological development. Ecological systems theorists explain development in terms of the interaction between people and the settings in which they live (Bronfenbrenner & Morris, 2006).

According to Urie Bronfenbrenner (1917–2005), for example, we need to focus on the two-way interactions between the child and the parents, not just maturational forces (nature) or child-rearing practices (nurture). Bronfenbrenner suggested that we can view the setting or contexts of human development as consisting of multiple systems, each embedded within the next larger context (Bronfenbrenner & Morris, 2006). From narrowest to widest, these systems are the microsystem, the mesosystem, the exosystem, the macrosystem, and the chronosystem (Figure 1.4).

The **microsystem** involves the interactions of the child and other people in the immediate setting, such as the home, the school, or the peer group. Initially, the microsystem is small, involving care-giving interactions with the parents or others, usually at home. As children get older, they do more, with more people, in more places.

The **mesosystem** involves the interactions of the various settings within the microsystem. For instance, the home and the school interact during parent–teacher conferences. The school and the larger community interact when children are taken on field trips. The ecological systems approach addresses the joint effect of two or more settings on the child.

evolutionary psychology the branch of psychology that deals with the ways in which humans' historical adaptations to the environment influence behavior and mental processes, with special focus on aggressive behavior and mating strategies.

fixed action pattern (FAP) a stereotyped pattern of behavior that is evoked by a "releasing stimulus"; an instinct.

ecology the branch of biology that deals with the relationships between living organisms and their environment.

ecological systems theory the view that explains child development in terms of the reciprocal influences between children and environmental settings.

microsystem the immediate settings with which the child interacts, such as the home, the school, and peers.

mesosystem the interlocking settings that influence the child, such as the interaction of the school and the larger community.

FIG.1.4 THE CONTEXTS OF HUMAN DEVELOPMENT

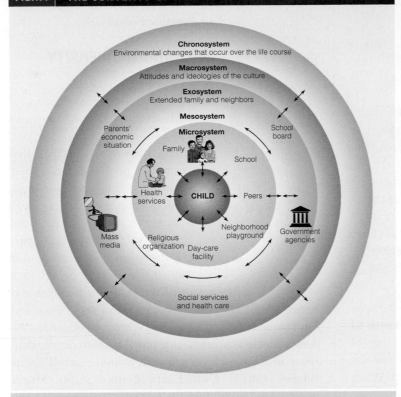

Chronosystem
Environmental changes that occur over the life course

Macrosystem
Attitudes and ideologies of the culture

Exosystem
Extended family and neighbors

Mesosystem

Microsystem

Parents' economic situation

School board

Family

School

Health services

CHILD

Peers

Mass media

Neighborhood playground

Government agencies

Religious organization

Day-care facility

Social services and health care

Psychologists and educators explain social and environmental influences on development in various ways. Urie Bronfenbrenner spoke of the importance of *ecological systems*, which affect development in various ways. The child's family, peers, and day-care facility, for example, are part of the child's microsystem and exert enormous influence. But the elements in the microsystem interact with other systems to influence the child. The parents' economic situation, for example, which is considered part of the child's exosystem, makes certain things possible for the child and rules out others.

The **exosystem** involves the institutions in which the child does not directly participate but which exert an indirect influence on the child. For example, the school board is part of the child's exosystem because board members put together programs for the child's education, determine what textbooks will be acceptable, and so forth. In similar fashion, the parents' workplaces and economic situations determine the hours during which they will be available to the child, and so on (Hong & Eamon, 2012; Tisdale & Pitt-Catsuphes, 2012). When some parents are unavailable, children may be more likely to misbehave at home or in school.

The **macrosystem** involves the interaction of children with the beliefs, values, expectations, and lifestyles of their cultural settings. Cross-cultural studies examine children's interactions with their macrosystem. Macrosystems exist within a particular culture. In the United States, the dual-earner family, the low-income single-parent

household, and the family with father as sole breadwinner describe three different macrosystems. Each has its lifestyle, set of values, and expectations (Bronfenbrenner & Morris, 2006; Lustig, 2011).

The **chronosystem** considers the changes that occur over time. For example, the effects of divorce peak about a year after the event, and then children begin to recover. The breakup has more of an effect on boys than on girls. The ecological approach broadens the strategies for intervention in problems such as prevention of teenage pregnancy, child abuse, and juvenile offending, including substance use disorders (Kaminski & Stormshak, 2007; Latkin et al., 2013).

1-2f THE SOCIOCULTURAL PERSPECTIVE

The sociocultural perspective teaches that people are social beings who are affected by the cultures in which they live. Developmentalists use the term *sociocultural* in a couple of different ways. One refers quite specifically to the *sociocultural theory* of Russian psychologist Lev Semenovich Vygotsky (1896–1934). The other addresses the effect of human diversity on people, including such factors as ethnicity and gender.

VYGOTSKY'S SOCIOCULTURAL THEORY

Whereas genetics is concerned with the biological transmission of traits from generation to generation, Vygotsky's (1978) theory is concerned with the transmission of information and cognitive skills from generation to generation. The transmission of skills involves teaching and learning, but Vygotsky does not view learning in terms of conditioning. Rather, he focuses on how the child's social interaction with adults, largely in the home, organizes a child's learning experiences in such a way that the child can obtain cognitive skills—such as computation or reading skills—and use them to acquire information. Like Piaget, Vygotsky sees the child's functioning as adaptive, and the child adapts to his or her social and cultural interactions.

exosystem community institutions and settings that indirectly influence the child, such as the school board and the parents' workplaces.

macrosystem the basic institutions and ideologies that influence the child.

chronosystem the environmental changes that occur over time and have an effect on the child.

VYGOTSKY'S SOCIOCULTURAL THEORY

Lev Semenovich Vygotsky (1896–1934) was mainly concerned with the transmission of information from one generation to another. He explained the social influences on children's development of knowledge and skills in terms of their zone of proximal development and scaffolding.

The zone of proximal development (ZPD) refers to a range of tasks that a child can carry out with the help of someone who is more skilled, as in an apprenticeship. A scaffold is a temporary skeletal structure that enables workers to fabricate a building or other more permanent structure. In Vygotsky's theory, teachers and parents provide children with problem-solving methods that serve as cognitive scaffolding while the child gains the ability to function independently.

Key concepts in Vygotsky's theory include the *zone of proximal development* and *scaffolding*. The **zone of proximal development (ZPD)** refers to a range of tasks that a child can carry out with the help of someone who is more skilled, as in an apprenticeship. When learning with other people, children internalize—or bring inward—the conversations and explanations that help them gain the necessary skills (Vygotsky, 1962; Poehner, 2012; Thompson et al., 2016).

A *scaffold* is a temporary skeletal structure that enables workers to fabricate a building or other more permanent structure. In Vygotsky's theory, teachers and parents provide children with problem-solving methods that serve as cognitive **scaffolding** while the child gains the ability to function independently. For example, children may be offered scaffolding that enables them to use their fingers or their toes to do

zone of proximal development (ZPD) Vygotsky's term for the situation in which a child carries out tasks with the help of someone who is more skilled.

scaffolding Vygotsky's term for temporary cognitive structures or methods of solving problems that help the child as he or she learns to function independently.

According to Vygotsky's theory, teachers and parents provide children with problem-solving methods that serve as cognitive scaffolding.

Brand X Pictures /Jupiter Images; Len Rubenstein/Photolibrary/Getty Images

simple calculations. Eventually, the scaffolding is removed and the cognitive structures stand alone.

1-2g HUMAN DIVERSITY

The sociocultural perspective asserts that we cannot understand individuals without awareness of the richness of their diversity (Markus, 2016; Russo et al., 2012). For example, people differ in their ethnicity (cultural heritage, race, language, and common history), their gender, and their socioeconomic status. Population shifts are under way in the United States as a result of reproductive patterns and immigration. The numbers of African Americans and Latin Americans (who may be White, Black, or Native American in racial origin) are growing more rapidly than those of European Americans (United States Census Bureau. (2015). QuickFacts, United States. http://www.census.gov/quickfacts/table/PST045215/00). The cultural heritages, languages, and histories of ethnic minority groups are thus likely to have an increasing effect on the cultural life of the United States, yet it turns out that the dominant culture in the United States has often disparaged the traditions and languages of people from ethnic minority groups. For example, it has been considered harmful to rear children bilingually, although research suggests that bilingualism broadens children's knowledge of the various peoples of the world.

Studying diversity is also important so that students have appropriate educational experiences. To teach students and guide their learning, educators need to understand children's family values and cultural expectations. Issues that affect people from various ethnic groups include bilingualism, ethnic differences in intelligence test scores, the prevalence of suicide among members of different backgrounds, and patterns of child rearing among parents of various groups.

Gender is another aspect of human diversity. Gender is the psychological state of being male or being female, as influenced by cultural concepts of gender-appropriate behavior. Expectations of females and males are often polarized by cultural expectations. Males may differ from females in some respects, but history has created more burdens for women than men as a result. Historically, females have been discouraged from careers in the sciences, politics, and business. Recent research, however, shows that females are as capable as males of performing in so-called STEM fields (science, technology, engineering, and math) (e.g., Brown & Lent, 2016). Women today are making inroads into academic and vocational spheres—such as medicine, law, engineering, and the military—that were traditionally male preserves. Today, most college students in the United States are female, but there remain many parts of the world in which women are prevented from obtaining an education (Yousafazi & Lamb, 2013).

Table 1.1 summarizes the theoretical perspectives on development.

Contemporary psychologists and educators recognize that we cannot understand the development of individuals without reference to their diversity—for example, their cultural heritage, race, language, common history, gender, and socioeconomic status.

Derek Latta/Getty Images

1-3 CONTROVERSIES IN DEVELOPMENT

The discussion of theories of development reveals that developmentalists can see things in very different ways. Let us consider how they react to three of the most important debates in the field.

1-3a THE NATURE–NURTURE CONTROVERSY

Researchers are continually trying to sort out the extent to which human behavior is the result of **nature** (heredity) and of **nurture** (environmental influences). What aspects of behavior originate in our genes and are biologically programmed to unfold as time goes on, as long as minimal nutrition and social experience are provided? What aspects of behavior can be traced largely to such environmental influences as nutrition and learning?

Scientists seek the natural causes of development in children's genetic heritage, the functioning of the nervous system, and in maturation. Scientists seek the environmental causes of development in children's nutrition, cultural and family backgrounds, and opportunities to learn about the world, including cognitive stimulation during early childhood and formal education.

Some theorists (e.g., cognitive-developmental and biological theorists) lean heavily toward natural explanations of development, whereas others (e.g., learning theorists) lean more heavily toward environmental explanations. Today, though, nearly all researchers agree that nature and nurture play important roles in nearly every area of development. Consider the development of language. Language is based in structures found in certain areas of the brain. Thus, biology (nature) plays a vital role. Children also come to speak the languages spoken by their caretakers. Parent–child similarities in accent and vocabulary provide additional evidence for the role of learning (nurture) in language development.

1-3b THE CONTINUITY–DISCONTINUITY CONTROVERSY

Some developmentalists view human development as a continuous process in which the effects of learning mount gradually, with no major sudden qualitative changes. In contrast, other theorists believe that a number of rapid qualitative changes usher in new stages of development. Maturational theorists point out that the environment, even when enriched, profits us little until we are ready, or mature enough, to develop in a certain way. For example, newborn babies will not imitate their parents' speech, even when parents speak clearly and deliberately. Nor does aided practice in walking during the first few months after birth significantly accelerate the emergence of independent walking. The babies are not ready to do these things.

nature the processes within an organism that guide it to develop according to its genetic code.

nurture environmental factors that influence development.

TABLE 1.1   CHILD DEVELOPMENT PERSPECTIVES AND THEORIES

Perspective	Theory	Core Concepts	Is Nature or Nurture More Important?
The Psychoanalytic Perspective	**Theory of psychosexual development** (Sigmund Freud)	Social codes channel primitive impulses, resulting in unconscious conflict.	Interaction of nature and nurture: Maturation sets the stage for reacting to social influences.
	Theory of psychosocial development (Erik Erikson)	People undergo life crises that are largely based on social relationships, opportunities, and expectations.	Interaction of nature and nurture: Maturation sets the stage for reacting to social influences and opportunities.
The Learning Perspective: Behavioral and Social Cognitive Theories	**Behaviorism** (John B. Watson, Ivan Pavlov, B. F. Skinner)	Behavior is learned by association, as in classical and operant conditioning.	Nurture: Children are seen almost as blank tablets.
	Social cognitive theory (Albert Bandura and others)	Conditioning occurs, but people also learn by observing others and choose whether to display learned responses.	Emphasizes nurture but allows for the expression of natural tendencies.
The Cognitive Perspective	**Cognitive-developmental theory** (Jean Piaget)	Children adapt to the environment via assimilation to existing mental structures by accommodating to these structures.	Emphasizes nature but allows for influences of experience.
	Information-processing theory	Human cognitive functioning is compared to that of computers—how they input, manipulate, store, and output information.	Interaction of nature and nurture.
The Biological Perspective	**Ethology and evolution** (Charles Darwin, Konrad Lorenz, Niko Tinbergen)	Organisms are biologically "prewired" to develop certain adaptive responses during sensitive periods.	Emphasizes nature but experience is also critical; e.g., imprinting occurs during a sensitive period but experience determines the object of imprinting.
The Ecological Perspective	**Ecological systems theory** (Urie Bronfenbrenner)	Children's development occurs within interlocking systems, and development is enhanced by intervening in these systems.	Interaction of nature and nurture: Children's personalities and skills contribute to their development.
The Sociocultural Perspective	**Sociocultural theory** (Lev Vygotsky)	Children internalize sociocultural dialogues in developing problem-solving skills.	Interaction of nature and nurture: Nurture is discussed in social and cultural terms.
	Sociocultural perspective and human diversity	Development is influenced by factors such as cultural heritage, race, language, common history, gender, and socioeconomic status.	Nurture.

Stage theorists such as Sigmund Freud and Jean Piaget saw development as discontinuous. They saw biological changes as providing the potential for psychological changes. Freud focused on the ways in which biological developments might provide the basis for personality development. Piaget believed maturation of the nervous system allowed cognitive development.

Certain aspects of physical development do occur in stages. For example, from the age of two years to the onset of puberty, children gradually grow larger. Then the adolescent growth spurt occurs as rushes of hormones cause rapid biological changes in structure and function (as in the development of the sex organs) and in size. Psychologists disagree on whether developments in cognition occur in stages.

1-3c THE ACTIVE–PASSIVE CONTROVERSY

Historical views of children as willful and unruly suggest that people have generally seen children as active, even if mischievous (at best) or evil (at worst). John Locke introduced a view of children as passive beings (blank tablets); experience "wrote" features of personality and moral virtue on them.

At one extreme, educators who view children as passive may assume that they must be motivated to learn by their instructors. Such educators are likely to provide a rigorous traditional curriculum with a powerful system of rewards and punishments to promote absorption of the subject matter. At the other extreme, educators who view children as active may assume that they have a natural

Here we have a clear example of the importance of maturation in development. Adolescents undergo a growth spurt that disrupts a pattern of gradual gains in height and weight that persisted throughout most of childhood. Girls, interestingly, spurt earlier than boys. The girl and boy shown here are actually the same age, even though the girl towers over the boy. But her height advantage is temporary; when he spurts, he will quickly catch up to her and surpass her in height.

Mark Richard/PhotoEdit

love of learning. Such educators are likely to argue for open education and encourage children to explore and pursue their unique likes and talents.

These debates are theoretical. Scientists value theory for its ability to tie together observations and suggest new areas of investigation, but scientists also follow an **empirical** approach. That is, they engage in research methods, such as those described in the next section, to find evidence for or against various theoretical positions.

1-4 HOW DO WE STUDY DEVELOPMENT?

What is the relationship between intelligence and achievement? What are the effects of maternal use of aspirin and alcohol on the fetus? What are the effects of parental divorce on children? What are the effects of early retirement? We may have expressed opinions on such questions at one time or another, but scientists insist that such questions be answered by research. Strong arguments or reference to authority figures are not evidence. Scientific evidence is obtained only by gathering sound information and conducting research.

1-4a GATHERING INFORMATION

Researchers use various methods to gather information. For example, they may ask teachers or parents to report on the behavior of children, use interviews or questionnaires with adults, or study statistics compiled by the government or the United Nations. They also directly observe children in the laboratory, the playground, or the classroom. Let us discuss two ways of gathering information: the naturalistic-observation method and the case-study method.

NATURALISTIC OBSERVATION Naturalistic-observation studies are conducted in the field, that is, in the natural, or real-life, settings in which they happen. In field studies, investigators observe the natural behavior of children in settings such as homes, playgrounds, and classrooms and try not to interfere with it. Researchers may try to "blend into the woodwork" by sitting quietly in the back of a classroom or by observing the class through a one-way mirror.

Naturalistic-observation studies have been done with children of different cultures. For example, researchers have observed the motor behavior of Native American Hopi children who are strapped to cradle boards during their first year. You can read more about this in Chapter 5.

THE CASE STUDY The **case study** is a carefully drawn account of the behavior of an individual. Parents who keep diaries of their children's activities are involved in informal case studies. Case studies themselves often use a number of different kinds of information. In addition to direct observation, case studies may include questionnaires, **standardized tests**, and interviews. Information gleaned from public records may be included. Scientists who use the case-study method try to record all relevant factors in a person's behavior, and they are cautious in drawing conclusions about what leads to what.

empirical based on observation and experimentation.

naturalistic-observation a scientific method in which organisms are observed in their natural environments.

case study a carefully drawn biography of the life of an individual.

standardized test a test in which an individual's score is compared to the scores of a group of similar individuals.

1-4b CORRELATION: PUTTING THINGS TOGETHER

Researchers use the correlational method to determine whether one behavior or trait being studied is related to, or correlated with, another. Consider intelligence and achievement. These variables are assigned numbers such as intelligence test scores and grade point averages. Then the numbers or scores are mathematically related and expressed as a **correlation coefficient**—a number that varies between +1.00 and −1.00.

In general, the higher people score on intelligence tests, the better their academic performance (or income) is likely to be. The scores attained on intelligence tests are **positively correlated** (about +0.60 to +0.70) with overall academic achievement (and income). There is a **negative correlation** between adolescents' grades and delinquent acts. The higher an adolescent's grades, the less likely he or she is to engage in criminal behavior. Figure 1.5 illustrates the concepts of positive and negative correlations.

LIMITATIONS OF CORRELATIONAL INFORMATION
Correlational information can reveal relationships between variables, but it does not show cause and effect. It may seem logical to assume that exposure to violent media makes people more aggressive, but it may also be that more aggressive people *choose* violent media. This research bias is termed a *selection factor*.

Similarly, studies report that children (especially boys) in divorced families tend to show more behavioral problems than children in intact families (Daryanani et al., 2016; Vélez et al., 2011). These studies, however, do not show that divorce causes these adjustment problems. It could be that the factors that led to divorce—such as parental conflict—also led to adjustment problems among the children (Hetherington, 2006). To investigate cause and effect, researchers turn to the experimental method.

1-4c THE EXPERIMENT: TRYING THINGS OUT

The experiment is the preferred method for investigating questions of cause and effect. In the **experiment**, a group of research participants receives a treatment and another group does not. The subjects are then observed to determine whether the treatment changes their behavior. Experiments are usually undertaken to test a **hypothesis**. For example, a researcher might hypothesize that TV violence will cause aggressive behavior in children.

INDEPENDENT AND DEPENDENT VARIABLES In an experiment to determine whether TV violence causes aggressive behavior, subjects in the experimental group would be shown a TV program containing violence, and its effects on behavior would be measured.

correlation coefficient a number ranging from +1.00 to −1.00 that expresses the direction (positive or negative) and strength of the relationship between two variables.

positive correlation a relationship between two variables in which one variable increases as the other increases.

negative correlation a relationship between two variables in which one variable increases as the other decreases.

experiment a method of scientific investigation that seeks to discover cause-and-effect relationships by introducing independent variables and observing their effects on dependent variables.

hypothesis a proposition to be tested.

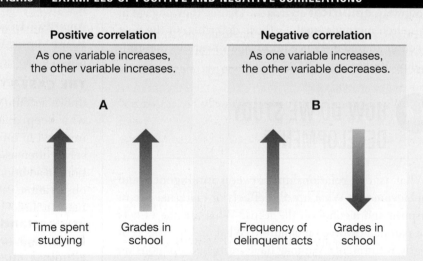

FIG.1.5 EXAMPLES OF POSITIVE AND NEGATIVE CORRELATIONS

Positive correlation
As one variable increases, the other variable increases.

A

Time spent studying — Grades in school

Negative correlation
As one variable increases, the other variable decreases.

B

Frequency of delinquent acts — Grades in school

When two variables are correlated positively, one increases as the other increases. Part A shows that there is a positive correlation between the amount of time studying and one's grades in school. In contrast, when two variables are correlated negatively, one decreases as the other one increases. As in Part B, a teenager's school grades are likely to decrease as he engages in more delinquent acts. But correlation does not show cause and effect. Do the teenager's grades fall off because of his engaging in more delinquent behavior? Do falling grades lead to more delinquency? Or could another factor explain *both* falling grades and increased delinquency?

TV violence would be considered an **independent variable**, a variable whose presence is manipulated by the experimenters so that its effects can be determined. The measured result—in this case, the child's behavior—is called a **dependent variable**. Its presence or level presumably depends on the independent variable.

EXPERIMENTAL AND CONTROL GROUPS Experiments use experimental and control groups. Subjects in the **experimental group** receive the treatment, whereas subjects in the **control group** do not. All other conditions are held constant for both groups. Thus, we can have confidence that experimental outcomes reflect the treatments and not chance factors.

RANDOM ASSIGNMENT Subjects should be assigned to experimental or control groups on a chance or random basis. We could not conclude much from an experiment on the effects of TV violence if the children were allowed to choose whether they would be in a group that watched TV violence or in a group that did not. A *selection factor* rather than the treatment might then be responsible for the results of the experiment.

Ethical and practical considerations also prevent researchers from doing experiments on the effects of many life circumstances, such as divorce or different patterns of child rearing. We cannot randomly assign some families to divorce or conflict and assign other families to "bliss." Nor can we randomly assign parents to rearing their children in an authoritarian or permissive manner. In some areas of investigation, we must settle for correlational evidence.

When experiments cannot ethically be performed on humans, researchers sometimes carry them out with animals and try to generalize the findings to humans.

TRUTH

 T **F** Research with monkeys has helped psychologists understand the formation of attachment in humans.

It is true that research with monkeys has helped psychologists understand the formation of attachment in humans. Researchers have exposed monkeys and other nonhuman animals to conditions that it would be unethical to use with humans.

No researcher would separate human infants from their parents to study the effects of isolation on development, yet experimenters have deprived monkeys of early social experience. Such research has helped psychologists investigate the formation of parent–child bonds of attachment.

1-4d LONGITUDINAL RESEARCH: STUDYING DEVELOPMENT OVER TIME

The processes of development occur over time, and researchers have devised different strategies for comparing children of one age with children or adults of other ages. In **longitudinal research**, the same people are observed repeatedly over time, and changes in development, such as gains in height or changes in mental abilities, are recorded. In **cross-sectional research**, children of different ages are observed and compared. It is assumed that when a large number of children are chosen at random, the differences found in the older age groups are a reflection of how the younger children will develop, given time.

LONGITUDINAL STUDIES The Terman Studies of Genius, begun in the 1920s, tracked children with high IQ scores for more than 50 years. Male subjects, but not female subjects, went on to high achievements in the professional world. Why? Contemporary studies of women show that women with high intelligence generally match the achievements of men and suggest that women of the earlier era were held back by traditional gender-role expectations.

Most longitudinal studies span months or a few years, not decades. For example, briefer longitudinal studies have found that the children of divorced parents undergo the most severe adjustment problems within a few months of the divorce, peaking at about a year. By two or three years afterward, many children regain their equilibrium,

independent variable a condition in a scientific study that is manipulated so that its effects can be observed.

dependent variable a measure of an assumed effect of an independent variable.

experimental group a group made up of subjects who receive a treatment in an experiment.

control group a group made up of subjects in an experiment who do not receive the treatment but for whom all other conditions are comparable to those of subjects in the experimental group.

longitudinal research the study of developmental processes by taking repeated measures of the same group of participants at various stages of development.

cross-sectional research the study of developmental processes by taking measures of participants of different age groups at the same time.

as indicated by improved academic performance and social behavior (Hetherington, 2006; Moon, 2011).

Longitudinal studies have drawbacks. For example, it can be difficult to enlist volunteers to participate in a study that will last a lifetime. Many subjects fall out of touch as the years pass; others die. The researchers must be patient or arrange to enlist future generations of researchers.

CROSS-SECTIONAL STUDIES Because of the drawbacks of longitudinal studies, most research that compares children of different ages is cross-sectional. In other words, most investigators gather data on what the "typical" six-month-old is doing by finding children who are six months old today. When they expand their research to the behavior of typical 12-month-olds, they seek another group of children, and so on.

A major challenge to cross-sectional research is the **cohort effect**. A cohort is a group of people born at about the same time. As a result, they experience cultural and other events unique to their age group. In other words, children and adults of different ages are not likely to have shared similar cultural backgrounds. People who are 80 years old today, for example, grew up without TV. Today's children are growing up taking iPods and the Internet for granted.

Children of past generations also grew up with different expectations about gender roles and appropriate social behavior. Women in the Terman study generally chose motherhood over careers because of the times. Today's girls are growing up with female role models who are astronauts and government officials.

In longitudinal studies, we know that we have the same individuals as they have developed over 5, 25, even 50 years or more. In cross-sectional research, we can only hope that they will be comparable.

CROSS-SEQUENTIAL RESEARCH Cross-sequential research combines the longitudinal and cross-sectional methods so that many of their individual drawbacks are overcome. In the cross-sequential study, the full span of the ideal longitudinal study is broken up into convenient segments (see Figure 1.6). Assume that we wish to follow the attitudes of children toward gender roles from the age of 4 through the age of 12. The typical longitudinal study would take eight years. We can, however, divide this eight-year span in half by attaining two samples of children (a cross-section) instead of one: four-year-olds and eight-year-olds. We would then interview, test, and observe each group at the beginning of the study (2018) and four years later (2022).

cohort effect similarities in behavior among a group of peers that stem from the fact that group members were born at the same time in history.

cross-sequential research an approach that combines the longitudinal and cross-sectional methods by following individuals of different ages for abbreviated periods of time.

FIG.1.6 EXAMPLES OF CROSS-SEQUENTIAL RESEARCH

Cross-sequential research combines three methods: cross-sectional, longitudinal, and time lag. The child's age at the time of testing appears in the boxes. Vertical columns represent cross-sectional comparisons. Horizontal rows represent longitudinal comparisons. Diagonals represent time-lag comparisons.

An obvious advantage to this collapsed method is that the study is completed in four years rather than eight years. Still, the testing and retesting of samples provides some of the continuity of the longitudinal study. By observing both samples at the age of eight (a **time-lag** comparison), we can also determine whether they are, in fact, comparable or whether the four-year difference in their birth date is associated with a cohort effect.

1-4e ETHICAL CONSIDERATIONS

Researchers adhere to ethical standards that are intended to promote the dignity of the individual, foster human welfare, and maintain scientific integrity. These standards also ensure that they do not use methods or treatments that harm subjects:

▶ Researchers are not to use methods that may do physical or psychological harm.

▶ Participants (and parents, if participants are minors) must be informed of the purposes of the research and about the research methods.

▶ Participants must provide voluntary consent to participate in the study.

▶ Participants may withdraw from the study at any time, for any reason.

▶ Participants should be offered information about the results of the study.

▶ The identities of the participants are to remain confidential.

▶ Researchers should present their research plans to a committee of their colleagues and gain the committee's approval before proceeding.

These guidelines present researchers with a number of hurdles to overcome before proceeding with and while conducting research, but because they protect the welfare of participants, the guidelines are valuable.

In this chapter we have defined developmental psychology, discussed its history as a discipline, explored theories of developmental psychology, and seen how developmental psychologists and educators conduct research into human development. In the next chapter, we return to the true beginnings of human development: heredity and prenatal development.

time-lag the study of developmental processes by taking measures of participants of the same age group at different times.

STUDY TOOLS 1

READY TO STUDY?

In the book, you can:

☐ Rip out the chapter review card at the back of the book for a handy summary of the chapter and key terms.

☐ Check your understanding of what you've read with the quizzes that follow.

ONLINE AT CENGAGEBRAIN.COM YOU CAN:

☐ Collect StudyBits while you read and study the chapter.

☐ Quiz yourself on key concepts.

☐ Find videos for further exploration.

☐ Prepare for tests with CDEV2 Flash Cards as well as those you create.

SELF-ASSESSMENTS

Fill-Ins

Answers can be found in the back of the book.

1. _____ believed that a child came into the world as a tabula rasa.

2. Freud theorized that the personality has three parts: the id, the ego, and the _____.

3. Erikson emphasized _____ rather than psychosexual development.

4. In the bell-and-pad method for treating bed-wetting in children, psychologists repeatedly pair tension in the _____ with a stimulus that awakens them.

5. According to Piaget, _____ is the process by which a person responds to new objects or events with existing schemes.

6. According to evolutionary psychologists, organisms can inherit _____-specific behaviors.

7. According to the ecological perspective, the _____ involves the institutions in which the person does not directly participate but which exert an indirect influence on the person.

8. The _____ Studies of Genius followed children with high IQ scores for more than 50 years.

9. There is usually a(n) _____ correlation between time spent studying and grades in school.

10. Cross-_____ research combines cross-sectional research, longitudinal research, and time-lag research.

Multiple Choice

1. **Which of the following is the correct order for the stages of psychosexual development?**
   a. anal, oral, genital, phallic, latency
   b. oral, anal, phallic, latency, genital
   c. genital, phallic, anal, oral, latency
   d. phallic, latency, oral, genital, anal

2. **In operant conditioning, extinction results from repeated performance of operant behavior in the absence of**
   a. the conditioned stimulus.
   b. punishment.
   c. time out.
   d. reinforcement.

3. **Negative reinforcers differ from punishments in that**
   a. negative reinforcers increase the frequency of behavior when they are removed.
   b. punishments increase the frequency of behavior when they are removed.
   c. negative reinforcers decrease the frequency of behavior when they are removed.
   d. punishments decrease the frequency of behavior when they are removed.

4. **According to Bronfenbrenner, the _____ involves the interactions of the child and other people in the immediate setting, such as the home, school, or peer group.**
   a. mesosystem
   b. macrosystem
   c. exosystem
   d. microsystem

5. **Which of the following kinds of theorists is likely to view development as continuous?**
   a. a psychoanalytic theorist
   b. a behaviorist
   c. a cognitive-developmental theorist
   d. a psychosocial theorist

6. **Which of the following is an example of development occurring discontinuously?**
   a. the adolescent growth spurt
   b. scaffolding
   c. acquiring social skills
   d. learning new vocabulary words

7. **In a _____ sample, each member of a population has an equal chance of being selected to participate.**
   a. random
   b. selection
   c. stratified
   d. free

8. **More aggressive people are more likely to watch violent TV shows. Which of the following is true about this statement?**
   a. It shows that violent TV shows cause aggressive behavior.
   b. It shows that aggressive behavior leads to a preference for violent TV shows.
   c. It shows a relationship between aggressive behavior and violent TV shows.
   d. It shows cause and effect involving several unknown factors.

9. **Which of the following is true of all experiments?**
   a. Participants are blind as to the treatment they have received.
   b. Experimenters deceive the participants.
   c. Equal numbers of participants are assigned to the experimental and control groups.
   d. There are independent and dependent variables.

10. **Dr. Liu was interested in testing the effects of violent television on six-year-old children. She showed a particularly violent episode of *Power Rangers* to one group and a short nonviolent episode of an old Bill Cosby show to another group. She then observed the groups in the playground and measured their behaviors. What is the dependent variable in this study?**
    a. Bill Cosby and his family
    b. violent or nonviolent TV show
    c. the behavior on the playground
    d. the amount of time watching TV

2 | Heredity

LEARNING OUTCOMES

After studying this chapter, you will be able to…

2-1 Describe the influences of heredity on development

2-2 Discuss chromosomal and genetic abnormalities

2-3 Discuss methods of prenatal testing for chromosomal and genetic abnormalities

2-4 Explain ways in which researchers sort out the effects of heredity and the environment in development

After you finish this chapter, go to **PAGE 34** for **STUDY TOOLS**

Perhaps it comes as no surprise that fish cannot learn to speak French or dance an Irish jig, even if you raise them in enriched environments and send them to finishing school. A fish's heredity makes it possible to swim, breathe underwater through gills, and do many other "fishy" things. But the fish's heredity also limits its

> The structures we inherit make our behavior possible and place limits on it.

physical and cognitive abilities. Similarly, our own heredity makes possible all things human and at the same time limits us, for example, by preventing us from breathing underwater (without special equipment) and flying (again, without special equipment). The field of biology that studies heredity is called **genetics**.

2-1 HEREDITY: THE BASICS

Genetic influences are fundamental in the transmission of physical traits, such as height, hair texture, and eye color. Heredity appears to be a factor in almost all aspects of human behavior, personality, and mental processes (Plomin & Asbury, 2005; Plomin & Haworth, 2009; Stone et al., 2012). Examples include sociability, anxiety, social dominance, leadership, effectiveness as a parent, happiness, and even interest in arts and crafts (Blum et al., 2009; Ebstein et al., 2010; Sirgy, 2012). Genetic factors are also involved in psychological problems such as schizophrenia, depression, and dependence on nicotine, alcohol, and other substances (Leonardo & Hen, 2006; Lewis et al., 2013; Viding et al., 2013).

2-1a CHROMOSOMES AND GENES

Traits are transmitted by chromosomes and genes. **Chromosomes** are rod-shaped structures found in cells. Typical human cells contain 46 chromosomes organized into 23 pairs. Each chromosome contains thousands of segments called genes. **Genes** are the biochemical materials that regulate the development of traits. Some traits, such as blood type, appear to be transmitted by a single pair of genes, one of which is derived from each parent. Other traits are **polygenic**, that is, determined by several pairs of genes.

Our heredity is governed by 20,000 to 25,000 genes (Gonzaga-Jauregui et al., 2012). Genes are segments of strands of **deoxyribonucleic acid (DNA)**. DNA takes the form of a double spiral, or helix, similar to a twisting ladder (see Figure 2.1). The "rungs" of the ladder consist of one of two pairs of bases, either adenine with thymine

(A with T) or cytosine with guanine (C with G). The sequence of the rungs is the genetic code that will cause the developing organism to grow arms or wings, skin or scales.

2-1b MITOSIS AND MEIOSIS

We begin life as a single cell, or zygote, that divides repeatedly. There are two types of cell division: *mitosis* and *meiosis*. In **mitosis**, strands of DNA break apart, or "unzip" (see Figure 2.2). The double

genetics the branch of biology that studies heredity.

chromosomes rod-shaped structures composed of genes that are found within the nuclei of cells.

gene the basic unit of heredity. Genes are composed of deoxyribonucleic acid (DNA).

polygenic resulting from many genes.

deoxyribonucleic acid (DNA) genetic material that takes the form of a double helix composed of phosphates, sugars, and bases.

mitosis the form of cell division in which each chromosome splits lengthwise to double in number. Half of each chromosome combines with chemicals to retake its original form and then moves to the new cell.

TRUTH OR FICTION?

T	F	Your father determined whether you are female or male.
T	F	It isn't possible for two brown-eyed parents to have a child with blue eyes.
T	F	You can carry the genes for a deadly illness and not become sick yourself.
T	F	When identical twins are reared by different families, their intelligence and personality traits become more different as they grow older.

helix then duplicates. The DNA forms two camps on either side of the cell, and then the cell divides. Each incomplete rung combines with the appropriate "partner" (i.e., G and C, A and T) to form a new complete ladder. The two resulting identical copies of the DNA strand separate when the cell divides; each becomes a member of a newly formed cell. As a result, the genetic code is identical in new cells unless **mutations** occur through radiation or other environmental influences. Mutations also occur by chance, but not often.

Sperm and ova ("egg cells") are produced through **meiosis**, or *reduction division*. In meiosis, the 46 chromosomes within the cell nucleus first line up into 23 pairs. The DNA ladders then unzip, leaving unpaired halves of chromosome. When the cell divides, one member of each pair goes to each newly formed cell. Each new cell nucleus contains only 23 chromosomes, not 46.

When a sperm cell fertilizes an ovum, we receive 23 chromosomes from our father's sperm cell and 23 from our mother's ovum, and the combined chromosomes form 23 pairs (see Figure 2.3). Twenty-two of the pairs are **autosomes**—pairs that look alike and possess genetic information concerning the same set of traits. The 23rd pair are **sex chromosomes**, which look different from other chromosomes and determine our sex. We all receive an X sex chromosome (so called because of its X shape) from our mothers. The father supplies either a Y or an X sex chromosome. If we receive another X sex chromosome from our fathers, we develop into females, and if a Y (named after its Y shape), males.

2-1c IDENTICAL AND FRATERNAL TWINS

Now and then, a zygote divides into two cells that separate so that each develops into an individual with the same genetic makeup. These individuals are identical twins, or **monozygotic (MZ) twins**. If the woman

---

FIG.2.1 THE DOUBLE HELIX OF DNA

A. The nuclei of cells contain chromosomes.

Cell

Nucleus

Chromosomes

B. Chromosomes are made up of DNA.

DNA

C. Segments of DNA are made up of genes.

From Weiten, *Psychology, 8E.* © 2011 Cengage Learning.

Your genetic code determines your species and all those traits that can be inherited, from the color of your eyes to predispositions toward many psychological traits and abilities, including sociability and musical talent.

---

mutation a sudden variation in a heritable characteristic, as by an accident that affects the composition of genes.

meiosis the form of cell division in which each pair of chromosomes splits so that one member of each pair moves to the new cell. As a result, each new cell has 23 chromosomes.

autosome a member of a pair of chromosomes (with the exception of sex chromosomes).

sex chromosome a chromosome in the shape of a Y (male) or X (female) that determines the anatomic sex of the child.

monozygotic (MZ) twins twins that derive from a single zygote that has split into two; identical twins. Each MZ twin carries the same genetic code.

TRUTH

 F Your father determined whether you are female or male.

It is true that your father determined whether you are female or male. Fathers supply either an X or a Y sex chromosome, which determines whether the baby is female or male.

FIG.2.2 MITOSIS

Bonds break

■ Adenine
□ Thymine
■ Cytosine
■ Guanine

a   b   c

(a) A segment of a strand of DNA before mitosis. (b) During mitosis, chromosomal strands of DNA "unzip." (c) The double helix is rebuilt in the cell as each incomplete "rung" combines with appropriate molecules.

produces two ova in the same month and they are each fertilized by different sperm cells, they develop into fraternal twins, or **dizygotic (DZ) twins**. DZ twins run in families. If a woman is a twin, if her mother was a twin, or if she has previously borne twins, the chances rise that she will bear twins (Fellman, 2013).

As women reach the end of their childbearing years, **ovulation** becomes less regular, resulting in a number of months when more than one ovum is released. Thus, the chances of twins increase with parental age (Fellman, 2013). Fertility drugs also enhance the chances of multiple births by causing more than one ovum to ripen and be released during a woman's cycle (Fellman, 2013).

2-1d DOMINANT AND RECESSIVE TRAITS

Traits are determined by pairs of genes. Each member of a pair of genes is termed an **allele**. When both of the alleles for a trait, such as hair color, are the same, the person is said to be **homozygous** for that trait. When the alleles for a trait differ, the person is **heterozygous** for that trait. Some traits result from an "averaging" of the genetic instructions carried by the parents. When the effects of both alleles are shown, there is said to be incomplete dominance or codominance. When a *dominant* allele is paired with a *recessive* allele, the trait determined by the dominant allele appears in the offspring. For example, the offspring from the crossing of brown eyes with blue eyes have brown eyes, suggesting that brown eyes are a **dominant trait** and blue eyes are a **recessive trait**.

If one parent carried genes for only brown eyes and if the other parent carried genes for only blue eyes, the children would invariably have brown eyes. But brown-eyed parents can also carry recessive genes

FIG.2.3 THE 23 PAIRS OF HUMAN CHROMOSOMES

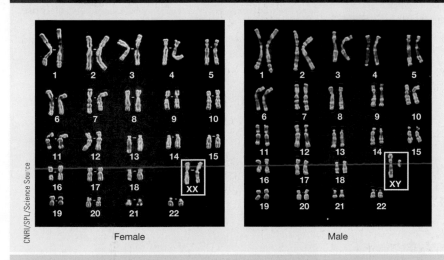

CNRI/SPL/Science Source

Female

Male

People normally have 23 pairs of chromosomes. Females have two X chromosomes, whereas males have an X and a Y sex chromosome.

dizygotic (DZ) twins twins that derive from two zygotes; fraternal twins.

ovulation the releasing of an ovum from an ovary.

allele a member of a pair of genes.

homozygous having two identical alleles.

heterozygous having two different alleles.

dominant trait a trait that is expressed.

recessive trait a trait that is not expressed when the gene or genes involved have been paired with dominant genes.

Identical twins. Monozygotic twins share 100% of their genes, whereas dizygotic twins share 50% of their genes. Identical twins are extremely close in appearance and also tend to share many psychological traits.

for blue eyes, as shown in Figure 2.4. If the recessive gene from one parent combines with the recessive gene from the other parent, the recessive trait will be shown. As suggested by Figure 2.4, approximately 25% of the children of brown-eyed parents who carry recessive blue eye color will have blue eyes. Table 2.1 shows a number of dominant and recessive traits in humans.

FICTION

T (F) It isn't possible for two brown-eyed parents to have a child with blue eyes.

If each parent carries a recessive gene for blue eyes, their children have a one in four chance of having blue eyes.

People who bear one dominant gene and one recessive gene for a trait are said to be **carriers** of the recessive gene. In the cases of recessive genes that cause illness,

carrier a person who carries and transmits characteristics but does not exhibit them.

FIG.2.4 TRANSMISSION OF DOMINANT AND RECESSIVE TRAITS

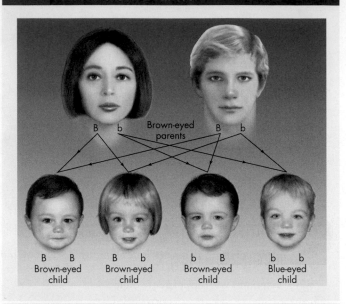

| B | b | Brown-eyed parents | B | b |

| B B | B b | b B | b b |
| Brown-eyed child | Brown-eyed child | Brown-eyed child | Blue-eyed child |

Did you know that you can have brown eyes but be carrying a gene for blue or green eyes? The genes for brown eyes are dominant—meaning that they are the ones that will be shown, and the genes for blue eyes are recessive. Here each of the two parents carries a gene for brown eyes (so they both have brown eyes) and a gene for blue eyes (which remain recessive, or hidden). Their children inherit the genes for brown or blue eyes by chance. Therefore, three out of four of their children will have brown eyes. Of the three, two will have a recessive gene for blue eyes as well as the gene for brown eyes. Only the fourth child, who inherits two genes for blue eyes, will actually have blue eyes.

TABLE 2.1 EXAMPLES OF DOMINANT AND RECESSIVE TRAITS

Dominant Trait	Recessive Trait
Dark hair	Blond hair
Dark hair	Red hair
Curly hair	Straight hair
Normal color vision	Red-green color blindness
Normal vision	Myopia (nearsightedness)
Farsightedness	Normal vision
Normal pigmentation	Deficiency of pigmentation in skin, hair, and retina (albinism)
Normal sensitivity to touch	Extremely fragile skin
Normal hearing	Some forms of deafness
Dimples	Lack of dimpling
Type A blood	Type O blood
Type B blood	Type O blood
Tolerance of lactose	Lactose intolerance

Alessandro de Leo/Alamy Stock Photo

carriers of those genes are fortunate to have dominant genes that cancel their effects.

2-2 CHROMOSOMAL AND GENETIC ABNORMALITIES

Chromosomal or genetic abnormalities can cause health problems. Some chromosomal disorders reflect abnormalities in the 22 pairs of autosomes (such as Down's syndrome); others reflect abnormalities in the sex chromosomes (e.g., XYY syndrome). Some genetic abnormalities, such as cystic fibrosis, are caused by a single pair of genes; others are caused by combinations of genes. Diabetes mellitus, epilepsy, and peptic ulcers are **multifactorial problems**; they reflect both a genetic predisposition and environmental contributors.

2-2a CHROMOSOMAL ABNORMALITIES

People normally have 46 chromosomes. Children with more or fewer chromosomes usually experience health problems or behavioral abnormalities. The risk of chromosomal abnormalities rises with the age of the parents (Desai et al., 2013; Sandin et al., 2012).

DOWN'S SYNDROME Down's syndrome is usually caused by an extra chromosome on the 21st pair, resulting in 47 chromosomes. The probability of having a child with Down's syndrome increases with the age of the parents. People with Down's syndrome have characteristic features that include a rounded face, a protruding tongue, a broad, flat nose,

and a sloping fold of skin over the inner corners of the eyes (see Figure 2.5). They show deficits in cognitive development and motor development (van Gameren-Oosterom et al., 2013) and usually die from cardiovascular problems by middle age, although modern medicine has extended life appreciably.

SEX-LINKED CHROMOSOMAL ABNORMALITIES A number of disorders stem from an abnormal number of sex chromosomes and are therefore called **sex-linked chromosomal abnormalities**. Most individuals with an abnormal number of sex chromosomes are infertile. Beyond that common finding, there are many differences, some of them associated with "maleness" or "femaleness."

Approximately 1 male in 700–1,000 has an extra Y chromosome. The Y chromosome is associated with maleness, and the extra Y sex chromosome apparently heightens male secondary sex characteristics. For example, XYY males are somewhat taller than average and develop heavier beards. For these kinds of reasons, males with XYY sex chromosomal structure were once called "supermales." However, XYY "supermales" tend to have more problems than XY males. For example, they are often mildly delayed in language development.

Approximately 1 male in 500 has **Klinefelter syndrome**, which is caused by an extra X sex chromosome (an XXY sex chromosomal pattern). XXY males produce less of the male sex hormone

FIG.2.5 DOWN'S SYNDROME

Michael Greenlar/The Image Works

People with Down's syndrome have characteristic features that include a rounded face, a protruding tongue, a broad, flat nose, and a sloping fold of skin over the inner corners of the eyes.

multifactorial problems problems that stem from the interaction of heredity and environmental factors.

Down's syndrome a chromosomal abnormality characterized by intellectual disabilities and caused by an extra chromosome in the 21st pair.

sex-linked chromosomal abnormalities abnormalities that are transmitted from generation to generation and carried by a sex chromosome.

Klinefelter syndrome a chromosomal disorder found among males that is caused by an extra X sex chromosome and that is characterized by infertility and mild intellectual disabilities.

testosterone than normal males. As a result, male primary and secondary sex characteristics—such as the testes, deepening of the voice, musculature, and the male pattern of body hair—do not develop properly. XXY males usually have enlarged breasts (gynecomastia) and are usually mildly mentally retarded, particularly in language skills (Skakkebaek et al., 2014). XXY males are typically treated with testosterone replacement therapy, which can foster growth of sex characteristics and elevate the mood, but they remain infertile.

Approximately 1 girl in 2,500 has a single X sex chromosome and as a result develops **Turner syndrome**. The external genitals of such girls are normal, but their ovaries are poorly developed and they produce little **estrogen**. Girls with this problem are shorter than average and infertile. Researchers have connected a specific pattern of cognitive deficits with low estrogen levels: problems in visual–spatial skills, mathematics, and nonverbal memory (Davenport et al., 2013). Yet a sample of women with Turner syndrome who are participating in a National Institutes of Health (NIH) study found that women with Turner syndrome were more likely to have a bachelor's degree and be employed than their age-mates in the general population (Gould et al., 2013).

Approximately 1 girl in 1,000 has an XXX sex chromosomal structure, *Triple X syndrome*. Such girls are normal in appearance but tend to show lower-than-average language skills and poorer memory for

> **GENETIC ABNORMALITIES**
>
> **Phenylketonuria**
>
> **Huntington's disease**
>
> **Sickle-cell anemia**
>
> **Tay-Sachs disease**
>
> **Cystic fibrosis**
>
> **Hemophilia**
>
> **Muscular dystrophy**
>
> © Image Ideas/Jupiterimages

recent events. Development of external sexual organs appears normal enough, although there is increased incidence of infertility (Lee et al., 2011).

2-2b GENETIC ABNORMALITIES

A number of disorders have been attributed to genes.

PHENYLKETONURIA The enzyme disorder **phenylketonuria (PKU)** is transmitted by a recessive gene and affects about 1 child in 8,000. Children with PKU cannot metabolize an amino acid called phenylalanine, so it builds up in their bodies and impairs the functioning of the central nervous system, resulting in mental retardation, psychological disorders, and physical problems. There is no cure for PKU, but children with PKU can be placed on diets low in phenylalanine within three to six weeks of birth and develop normally (Casey, 2013; Dawson et al., 2011).

HUNTINGTON'S DISEASE Huntington's disease **(HD)** is a fatal, progressive degenerative disorder and a dominant trait, affecting approximately 1 American in 18,000. Physical symptoms include uncontrollable muscle movements. Psychological symptoms include loss of intellectual functioning and personality change (van Dujin et al., 2014). Because the onset of HD is delayed until middle adulthood, many individuals with the defect have borne children only to discover years later that they and possibly half their offspring will inevitably develop it. Medicines can help deal with some symptoms.

SICKLE-CELL ANEMIA **Sickle-cell anemia** is caused by a recessive gene. Sickle-cell anemia is most common among African Americans. Nearly

testosterone a male sex hormone produced mainly by the testes.

Turner syndrome a chromosomal disorder found among females that is caused by having a single X sex chromosome and is characterized by infertility.

estrogen a female sex hormone produced mainly by the ovaries.

phenylketonuria (PKU) a genetic abnormality in which phenylalanine builds up and causes intellectual disabilities.

Huntington's disease (HD) a fatal genetic neurological disorder whose onset is in middle age.

sickle-cell anemia a genetic disorder that decreases the blood's capacity to carry oxygen.

MARKA / Alamy Stock Photo

Richard Burton and Elizabeth Taylor, the co-stars of the movie *Cleopatra*. Burton was diagnosed with hemophilia.

1 African American in 10 and 1 Latin American in 20 is a carrier. In sickle-cell anemia, red blood cells take on the shape of a sickle and clump together, obstructing small blood vessels and decreasing the oxygen supply. The lessened oxygen supply can impair cognitive skills and academic performance (Smith et al., 2013). Physical problems include painful and swollen joints, jaundice, and potentially fatal conditions such as pneumonia, stroke, and heart and kidney failure.

TAY-SACHS DISEASE Tay-Sachs disease is also caused by a recessive gene. It causes the central nervous system to degenerate, resulting in death. The disorder is most commonly found among children in Jewish families of Eastern European background. Approximately 1 in 30 Jewish Americans from this background carries the recessive gene for Tay-Sachs. Children with the disorder progressively lose control over their muscles, experience sensory losses, develop intellectual disabilities, become paralyzed, and usually die by about the age of five.

CYSTIC FIBROSIS Cystic fibrosis, also caused by a recessive gene, is the most common fatal hereditary disease among European Americans. Approximately 30,000 Americans have the disorder, but another 10 million (1 in every 31 people) are carriers (Cystic Fibrosis Foundation, 2014). Children with the disease suffer from excessive production of thick mucus that clogs the pancreas and lungs. Most victims die of respiratory infections in their 20s.

SEX-LINKED GENETIC ABNORMALITIES Some genetic defects, such as **hemophilia**, are carried on only the X sex chromosome. For this reason, they are referred to as **sex-linked genetic abnormalities**. These defects also involve recessive genes. Females, who have two X sex chromosomes, are less likely than males to show sex-linked disorders because the genes that cause the disorder would have to be present on both of a female's sex chromosomes for the disorder to be expressed. Sex-linked diseases are more likely to afflict sons of female carriers because males have only one X sex chromosome, which they inherit from their mothers.

One form of **muscular dystrophy**, Duchenne muscular dystrophy, is sex-linked. Muscular dystrophy is characterized by a weakening of the muscles, which can lead to wasting away, inability to walk, and sometimes death. Other sex-linked abnormalities include diabetes, color blindness, and some types of night blindness.

2-3 GENETIC COUNSELING AND PRENATAL TESTING

It is possible to detect genetic abnormalities that are responsible for many diseases. **Genetic counselors** compile information about a couple's genetic heritage to explore whether their children might develop genetic abnormalities. Couples who face a high risk of passing along genetic defects to their children sometimes elect to adopt or not have children rather than conceive their own. In addition, **prenatal** testing can indicate whether the embryo or fetus is carrying genetic abnormalities.

Although we discuss amniocentesis and chorionic villus sampling, it should be noted that their use tends to be declining because blood tests and ultrasound are becoming more sophisticated and used more frequently. By the time an amniocentesis is normally scheduled, a woman today may have had several blood tests and ultrasounds, which provide evidence of chromosomal as well as genetic abnormalities, and also provide reasonably clear pictures of the embryo and fetus.

2-3a AMNIOCENTESIS

Amniocentesis is usually performed on the mother at 14–16 weeks after conception, although many physicians now perform the procedure earlier ("early amniocentesis"). In this fetal-screening method, the health professional uses a syringe (needle) to withdraw fluid from the amniotic sac. The fluid contains cells that are sloughed off by the fetus. The cells are separated from the amniotic fluid, grown in a culture, and then examined microscopically for genetic and chromosomal abnormalities.

Tay-Sachs disease a fatal genetic neurological disorder.

cystic fibrosis a fatal genetic disorder in which mucus obstructs the lungs and pancreas.

hemophilia a genetic disorder in which blood does not clot properly.

sex-linked genetic abnormalities abnormalities resulting from genes that are found on the X sex chromosome. They are more likely to be shown by male off spring (who do not have an opposing gene from a second X chromosome) than by female offspring.

muscular dystrophy a chronic disease characterized by a progressive wasting away of the muscles.

genetic counselors health workers who compile information about a couple's genetic heritage to advise them as to whether their children might develop genetic abnormalities.

prenatal before birth.

amniocentesis a procedure for drawing and examining fetal cells sloughed off into amniotic fluid to determine the presence of various disorders.

Amniocentesis was once routinely recommended for women who become pregnant past the age of 35 because the chances of Down's syndrome and other chromosomal abnormalities increase dramatically as women—or their mates!—approach or pass the age of 40. Amniocentesis also permits parents to learn the sex of their unborn child through examination of the sex chromosomes, but most parents learn the sex of their baby earlier by ultrasound. Amniocentesis carries some risk of **miscarriage**, although the extent of the risk is unclear.

2-3b CHORIONIC VILLUS SAMPLING

Chorionic villus sampling (CVS) is similar to amniocentesis but is carried out between the 9th and 12th week of pregnancy. A small syringe is inserted through the vagina into the **uterus** and sucks out some threadlike projections (villi) from the outer membrane that envelops the amniotic sac and fetus. Results are available within days. CVS has not been used as frequently as amniocentesis because CVS carries a slightly greater risk of miscarriage. However, there is controversy as to how much amniocentesis and CVS increase the risk of miscarriage, and some health professionals assert that the risk of these procedures has been exaggerated (Akolekar et al., 2014; Ogilvie & Akolekar, 2013). Check with your physician for the latest information.

2.3c ULTRASOUND

Health professionals also use sound waves that are too high in frequency to be heard by the human ear—**ultrasound**—to obtain information about the fetus. Ultrasound waves are reflected by the fetus, and a computer uses the information to generate a picture of the fetus. The picture is termed a **sonogram** (see Figure 2.6).

Ultrasound is used to guide the syringe in amniocentesis and CVS by determining the position of the fetus. Ultrasound also is used to track the growth of the fetus, to determine fetal age and sex, and to detect multiple pregnancies and structural abnormalities. In the fourth and fifth months, ultrasound is usually used to perform complete anatomical scans of the fetus.

2-3d BLOOD TESTS

Parental blood tests can reveal the presence of genetic disorders such as sickle-cell anemia, Tay-Sachs disease, and cystic fibrosis. The **alpha-fetoprotein (AFP) assay** is used to detect neural tube defects such as spina bifida and certain chromosomal abnormalities. Neural tube defects cause an elevation in the AFP level in the mother's blood. Elevated AFP levels also are associated with increased risk of fetal death. Blood tests are also now testing for chromosomal abnormalities, and at three to four months of pregnancy they reveal the sex of the baby.

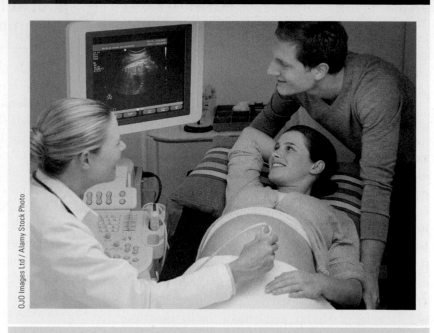

FIG.2.6 SONOGRAM

OJO Images Ltd / Alamy Stock Photo

The first baby pictures? In the ultrasound technique, sound waves that are too high in pitch for the human ear to hear are bounced off the fetus. A computer then assembles the information into a picture that enables health professionals to detect various abnormalities. Once the fetus reaches a certain age, the method also reveals its anatomic sex.

miscarriage the expulsion of an embryo or fetus before it can sustain life on its own, most often due to defective development.

chorionic villus sampling (CVS) a method for the prenatal detection of genetic abnormalities that samples the membrane enveloping the amniotic sac and fetus.

uterus the hollow organ within females in which the embryo and fetus develop.

ultrasound sound waves too high in pitch to be sensed by the human ear.

sonogram a procedure for using ultrasonic sound waves to create a picture of an embryo or fetus.

alpha-fetoprotein (AFP) assay a blood test that assesses the mother's blood level of alpha-fetoprotein, a substance that is linked with fetal neural tube defects.

HEREDITY AND THE ENVIRONMENT

In addition to inheritance, the development of our traits is also influenced by nutrition, learning, exercise, and—unfortunately—accident and illness. A potential Shakespeare who is reared in poverty and never taught to read or write will not create a *Hamlet*. Our traits and behaviors therefore represent the interaction of heredity and environment. The sets of traits that we inherit from our parents are referred to as our **genotypes**. The actual sets of traits that we exhibit are called our **phenotypes**. Our phenotypes reflect both genetic and environmental influences.

Researchers have developed a number of strategies to help sort out the effects of heredity and the environment on development.

2-4a KINSHIP STUDIES

Researchers study the distribution of a trait or behavior among relatives who differ in degree of genetic closeness. The more closely people are related, the more genes they have in common. Parents and children have a 50% overlap in their genetic endowments, and so do siblings (brothers and sisters). Aunts and uncles have a 25% overlap with nieces and nephews, as do grandparents with grandchildren. First cousins share 12.5% of their genetic endowment. If genes are implicated in a trait, people who are more closely related should be more likely to share it.

2-4b TWIN STUDIES: LOOKING IN THE GENETIC MIRROR

MZ twins share 100% of their genes, whereas DZ twins have a 50% overlap, just as other siblings do. If MZ twins show greater similarity on some trait or behavior than DZ twins do, a genetic basis for the trait or behavior is indicated.

MZ twins resemble each other more closely than DZ twins on a number of physical and psychological traits, even when the MZ twins are reared apart and the DZ twins are reared together (Bouchard & Loehlin, 2001). MZ twins are more likely to look alike and to be similar in height and weight (Dubois et al., 2012; Plomin et al., 2013). Heredity even affects their preference for coffee or tea (Luciano et al., 2005). MZ twins resemble one another more strongly than DZ twins in intelligence

> A potential Shakespeare who is reared in poverty and never taught to read or write will not create a *Hamlet*.

and personality traits (Hur, 2005; McCrae et al., 2000; Trzaskowski et al., 2013). MZ twins are also more likely to share psychological disorders such as **autism**, depression, schizophrenia, and vulnerability to alcoholism (Belmonte & Carper, 2006; Plomin et al., 2013; Ronald et al., 2006).

But one might ask whether MZ twins resemble each other so closely partly because they are often treated so similarly? One way to answer this question is to find and compare MZ twins who were reared apart. Except for the uterine environment, similarities between MZ twins reared apart would appear to be a result of heredity. In the Minnesota Study of Twins Reared Apart (McGue & Christensen, 2013), researchers have been measuring the physiological and psychological characteristics of 56 sets of MZ adult twins who were separated in infancy and reared in different homes. The MZ twins reared apart are about as similar as MZ twins reared together on measures of intelligence, personality, temperament, occupational and leisure-time interests, and social attitudes. Moreover, the similarities persist throughout life (McGue & Christensen, 2013). These traits would thus appear to have a genetic underpinning.

FICTION

T (F) When identical twins are reared by different families, their intelligence and personality traits become more different as they grow older.

Actually, the similarities in intelligence and personality between MZ twins tend to persist throughout life.

---

genotype the genetic form or constitution of a person as determined by heredity.

phenotype the actual form or constitution of a person as determined by heredity and environmental factors.

autism a developmental disorder characterized by failure to relate to others, communication problems, intolerance of change, and ritualistic behavior.

2-4c ADOPTION STUDIES

Adoption studies in which children are separated from their natural parents at an early age and reared by adoptive parents provide special opportunities for sorting out nature and nurture. When children who are reared by adoptive parents are nonetheless more similar to their natural parents in a trait, a powerful argument is made for a genetic role in the appearance of that trait.

Traits are determined by pairs of genes. One member of each pair comes from each parent in the process called conception, which we discuss next.

STUDY TOOLS 2

READY TO STUDY?

In the book, you can:

☐ Rip out the chapter review card at the back of the book for a handy summary of the chapter and key terms.

☐ Check your understanding of what you've read with the quizzes that follow.

ONLINE AT CENGAGEBRAIN.COM YOU CAN:

☐ Collect StudyBits while you read and study the chapter.

☐ Quiz yourself on key concepts.

☐ Find videos for further exploration.

☐ Prepare for tests with CDEV2 Flash Cards as well as those you create.

SELF-ASSESSMENT

Fill-Ins

Answers can be found in the back of the book.

1. _____ are the biological materials that regulate the development of traits.

2. We begin life as a single cell, which is called a(n) _____.

3. Reduction division is also known as _____.

4. Pairs of chromosomes that look alike and have information about the same set of traits are called _____.

5. Each member of a pair of genes is known as a(n) _____.

6. Dizygotic twins share _____ % of their genes.

7. About _____ % of children of brown-eyed parents who each carry recessive blue eye color will have blue eyes.

8. "Supermales" have _____ sex-chromosomal structure.

9. _____ -cell anemia is most common among African Americans.

10. When adopted children are more similar to their biological parents in a trait, we suspect that _____ plays a major role in the development of the trait.

Multiple Choice

1. **Which of the following is accurate about the age of the parents and possible health risks for a child?**
   a. Only the mother's age matters.
   b. The younger a female is, the greater the chances of a positive pregnancy outcome.
   c. Only the father's age matters.
   d. The age of both the mother and the father can matter.

2. **Which of the following is a sex-linked disease?**
   a. Tay-Sachs disease
   b. Huntington's disease
   c. hemophilia
   d. cystic fibrosis

3. **Girls with which one of the following disorders are infertile, have poorly developed ovaries, and attain shorter than average height?**
   a. Klinefelter syndrome
   b. supermale syndrome
   c. triple X syndrome
   d. Turner syndrome

4. **Which of the following is a dominant trait?**
   a. straight hair
   b. type O blood
   c. farsightedness
   d. lactose intolerance

5. **Which of the following is a fatal, progressive degenerative disorder?**
   a. Turner syndrome
   b. Huntington's disease
   c. cystic fibrosis
   d. Tay-Sachs disease

6. **Which of the following are least likely to be similar in appearance?**
   a. siblings
   b. MZ twins
   c. DZ twins
   d. children and adoptive parents

7. **Which of the following is a developmental disorder characterized by failure to relate to other people and intolerance of change?**
   a. Klinefelter syndrome
   b. muscular dystrophy
   c. autism
   d. down's syndrome

8. **Which of the following is a multifactorial problem?**
   a. diabetes mellitus
   b. Down's syndrome
   c. phenylketonuria
   d. Huntington's disease

9. **Which of the following disorders can be controlled by diet?**
   a. autism
   b. sickle-cell anemia
   c. Down's syndrome
   d. phenylketonuria

10. **Which of the following is usually caused by an extra chromosome on the 21st pair?**
    a. triple X syndrome
    b. Down's syndrome
    c. cystic fibrosis
    d. diabetes mellitus

3 Conception and Prenatal Development

LEARNING OUTCOMES

After studying this chapter, you will be able to...

3-1 Describe the process of conception

3-2 Discuss the causes of infertility and alternate ways of becoming parents

3-3 Describe what happens during the three stages of prenatal development

3-4 Discuss various environmental influences on prenatal development, including critical periods of vulnerability

After you finish this chapter, go to **PAGE 51** for **STUDY TOOLS**

Hill Street Studios/Blend Images/Getty Images

3-1 CONCEPTION: AGAINST ALL ODDS

Conception is the union of an ovum and a sperm cell. Conception, from one perspective, is the beginning of a new human life. From another perspective, though, conception is also the end of a fantastic voyage in which one of several hundred thousand ova produced by the woman unites with one of hundreds of millions of sperm produced by the man in the average ejaculate.

3-1a Ova

At birth, women have 300,000 to 400,000 ova in each ovary, although she will only ovulate some 500 of these during her lifetime (Adhikari & Liu, 2013). The ova, however, are immature in form. In addition to ova, the ovaries also produce the female hormones estrogen and progesterone. At puberty, in response to hormonal command, some ova begin to mature. Each month, an egg (occasionally more than one) is released from its ovarian follicle about midway through the menstrual cycle and enters a nearby fallopian tube. It might take three to four days for an egg to be propelled by small, hairlike structures called cilia and, perhaps, by contractions in the wall of the tube, along the few inches of the fallopian tube to the uterus. Unlike sperm, eggs do not propel themselves. If the egg is not fertilized, it is discharged through the uterus and the vagina along with the **endometrium** that had formed to support an embryo, in the menstrual flow.

Ova are much larger than sperm. The chicken egg and the six-inch ostrich egg are each just one cell, although the sperm of these birds are microscopic. Human ova are barely visible to the eye, but their bulk is still thousands of times larger than that of sperm cells.

TRUTH

T F   Approximately 120 to 150 boys are conceived for every 100 girls.

It is true that approximately 120 to 150 boys are conceived for every 100 girls. Sperm with Y sex chromosomes swim more rapidly, resulting in the conception of more boys than girls.

3-1b SPERM CELLS

Sperm cells develop through several stages. They each begin with 46 chromosomes, but after meiosis, each sperm has 23 chromosomes, half with X sex chromosomes and half with Y. Each sperm cell is about 1/500th of an inch long, one of the smallest types of cells in the body. Sperm with Y sex chromosomes appear to swim faster than sperm with X sex chromosomes. This difference contributes to the conception of 120 to 150 boys for every 100 girls. Male fetuses suffer a higher rate of miscarriage than females, however, often during the first month of pregnancy. At birth, boys outnumber girls by a ratio of only 106 to 100. Boys also have a higher incidence of infant mortality, which further equalizes the numbers of girls and boys.

The 150 million or so sperm in the ejaculate may seem to be a wasteful investment because only one sperm can fertilize an ovum, but only 1 in 1,000 sperm will ever approach an ovum. Millions deposited in the vagina flow out of the woman's body because of gravity. Normal vaginal acidity kills many more sperm. Many surviving

conception the union of a sperm cell and an ovum that occurs when the chromosomes of each of these cells combine to form 23 new pairs.

endometrium the inner lining of the uterus.

TRUTH OR FICTION?

T	F	Approximately 120 to 150 boys are conceived for every 100 girls.
T	F	Sperm travel randomly inside the woman's reproductive tract, so reaching the ovum is a matter of luck.
T	F	"Test-tube babies" are grown in a laboratory dish throughout their nine-month gestation period.
T	F	Newly fertilized egg cells survive without any nourishment from the mother for more than a week.
T	F	Fetuses suck their thumbs, sometimes for hours on end.
T	F	A father's age at the time of conception can influence the development of the fetus.

sperm then have to swim against the current of fluid coming from the cervix (see Figure 3.1).

Sperm that survive these initial obstacles may reach the fallopian tubes 60 to 90 minutes after ejaculation. About half the sperm enter the fallopian tube that does not contain the egg. Perhaps 2,000 enter the correct tube. Fewer still manage to swim the final two inches against the currents generated by the cilia that line the tube. It is *not* true that sperm travel about at random inside the woman's reproductive tract. Sperm cells are apparently "egged on" (pardon the pun) by a change in calcium ions that occurs when an ovum is released (Olson et al., 2011).

FIG.3.1 FEMALE REPRODUCTIVE ORGANS

Conception — Fallopian tube — Uterus

Ovum — Ovary

Cervix

Vagina

Sperm

The ovaries release egg cells (ova), which find their ways into fallopian tubes—exactly how is not fully known. Fertilization normally takes place in a fallopian tube. The fertilized ovum begins to divide while it travels through the tube into the uterus, where it becomes implanted in the wall and grows to term.

FICTION

T (F) Sperm travel randomly inside the woman's reproductive tract, so reaching the ovum is a matter of luck.

It is not true that sperm travel about at random inside the woman's reproductive tract. The direction in which sperm travel is influenced by a change in calcium ions that occurs when an ovum is released.

Of all the sperm swarming around the egg, only one enters (see Figure 3.2). Ova are surrounded by a gelatinous layer that must be penetrated if fertilization is to occur. Many of the sperm that have completed their journey to the ovum secrete an enzyme that briefly thins the layer, but it enables only one sperm to penetrate. Once a sperm cell has entered, the layer thickens, locking other sperm out.

The chromosomes from the sperm cell line up across from the corresponding chromosomes in the egg cell. They form 23 new pairs with a unique set of genetic instructions.

FIG.3.2 HUMAN SPERM SWARMING AROUND AN OVUM IN A FALLOPIAN TUBE

The Science Picture Company / Alamy Stock Photo

Hundreds of millions of sperm enter a woman during sexual intercourse. Thousands arrive in the fallopian tube with the ovum. Many attempt to enter the ovum, but only one succeeds because the surface of the ovum becomes impermeable to other sperm. It is believed that sperm locate the ovum through a rudimentary sense of smell.

3-2 INFERTILITY AND ALTERNATE WAYS OF BECOMING PARENTS

Approximately one American couple in six or seven has fertility problems (path2parenthood, 2016). The term *infertility* usually is not applied until the couple has failed to conceive on their own for one year. Infertility was once viewed as a problem of the woman, but it turns out that the problem lies with the woman in only 40% of cases. The problem lies with the man in about 40% of cases, and the other 20% have unknown origins (path2parenthood, 2016).

3-2a CAUSES OF INFERTILITY

A low sperm count—or lack of sperm—is the most common infertility problem in men. Men's fertility problems have a variety of causes: genetic factors, environmental poisons, diabetes, sexually transmitted infections (STIs), overheating of the testes (which happens now and then among athletes, such as long-distance runners), pressure (as from using narrow bicycle seats), aging, certain prescription and illicit drugs, and obesity (path2parenthood, 2016). Sometimes the sperm count is adequate, but other factors such as prostate or hormonal problems deform sperm or deprive them of their **motility**. Motility can also be impaired by the scar tissue from infections, such as STIs.

The most common problem in women is irregular ovulation or lack of ovulation. This problem can have many causes, including irregularities among the hormones that govern ovulation, stress, and malnutrition. So-called fertility drugs (e.g., clomiphene and pergonal) are made up of hormones that cause women to ovulate. These drugs may cause multiple births by stimulating more than one ovum to ripen during a month (path2parenthood, 2016).

Infections may scar the fallopian tubes and other organs, impeding the passage of sperm or ova. Such infections include **pelvic inflammatory disease (PID)**. PID can result from bacterial or viral infections, including the STIs gonorrhea and chlamydia. Antibiotics are usually helpful in treating bacterial infections, but infertility may be irreversible.

Endometriosis can obstruct the fallopian tubes, where conception normally takes place. Endometriosis has become fairly common among women who delay childbearing. Each month, tissue develops to line the uterus in case the woman conceives. This tissue—the endometrium—is then sloughed off during menstruation. But some of it backs up into the abdomen through the fallopian tubes. It then collects in the abdomen, where it can cause abdominal pain and lessen the chances of conception. Physicians may treat endometriosis with hormones that temporarily prevent menstruation or through surgery.

Let's consider methods used to help infertile couples bear children.

3-2b ARTIFICIAL INSEMINATION

Multiple ejaculations of men with low sperm counts can be collected and quickfrozen. The sperm can then be injected into the woman's uterus at the time of ovulation. This method is one **artificial insemination** procedure. Sperm from men with low sperm motility can also be injected into their partners' uteruses so that the sperm can begin their journey closer to the fallopian tubes. When a man has no sperm or an extremely low sperm count, his partner can be artificially inseminated with the sperm of a donor who resembles the man in

motility self-propulsion.

pelvic inflammatory disease (PID) an infection of the abdominal region that may have various causes and that may impair fertility.

endometriosis inflammation of endometrial tissue sloughed off into the abdominal cavity rather than out of the body during menstruation; the condition is characterized by abdominal pain and sometimes infertility.

artificial insemination injection of sperm into the uterus to fertilize an ovum.

LGBT Family Building

Not only heterosexual couples want children. So do singles. And so do members of the lesbian, gay, bisexual, and transgendered community.

Some LGBT people have children from previous marriages or other relationships. But if they don't, and if they want children, they have to decide how to make it happen. Transgendered individuals who have had genital surgery are also sterile, so they cannot father or bear offspring.

Lesbians, of course, can conceive through sexual intercourse with a friend or confidant, but many prefer not to do so. They can also conceive

They've got each other. How do they go about building a family?

through assisted productive technologies such as artificial insemination, intrauterine insemination (IUI), and in vitro fertilization (IVF). These methods require donor sperm, from either a known or an anonymous source. Artificial insemination is a low-technology method in which sperm are inserted directly into the uterus. If artificial insemination does not work, a woman may consider IVF.

Gay males will need a surrogate mother to become impregnated by their sperm and carry the embryo and fetus to term. The two potential fathers' sperm is analyzed, and either the sperm with the strongest likelihood to impregnate the surrogate are selected, or the sperm may be mixed so that the fathers do not know which partner actually fathered the child. Of course, actual fatherhood usually becomes clear enough in terms of the child's appearance and behavior as time goes on.

The American Fertility Association (www.theafa.org) invites all individuals who have fertility questions or issues to be in touch with them—heterosexual couples, would-be single parents, and lesbian, gay, bisexual, and transgendered couples.

physical traits. Some women who want a baby but do not have a partner also use artificial insemination.

3-2c IN VITRO FERTILIZATION

So called "test-tube babies" are not actually grown in a test tube but are conceived through **in vitro fertilization (IVF)**, a method of conception in which ripened ova are removed surgically from the mother and placed in a laboratory dish. The father's sperm are also placed in the dish. One or more ova are fertilized and then injected into the mother's uterus to become implanted.

IVF may be used when the fallopian tubes are blocked because the ova need not travel through them. If the

father's sperm are low in motility, they are sometimes injected directly into the ovum. A variation known as **donor IVF** can be used when the intended mother does not produce ova. An ovum from another woman is fertilized and injected into the uterus of the mother-to-be.

Because only a minority of attempts lead to births, it can take several attempts to achieve a pregnancy. Several embryos may be injected into the uterus at once, heightening the odds that one of the embryos will become implanted. IVF remains costly but is otherwise routine, if not guaranteed.

3-2d SURROGATE MOTHERS

Surrogate mothers bring babies to term for other women who are infertile. Surrogate mothers may be artificially inseminated by the partners of infertile women, in which case the baby carries the genes of the father. But sometimes—as with 60-year-old singer-songwriter James

in vitro fertilization (IVF) fertilization of an ovum in a laboratory dish.

donor IVF the transfer of a donor's ovum, fertilized in a laboratory dish, to the uterus of another woman.

Gary John Norman/Cultura/Getty Images

Taylor and his 54-year-old wife—ova are surgically extracted from the biological mother, fertilized in vitro by the biological father, and then implanted in another woman's uterus, where the baby is brought to term. Surrogate mothers are usually paid and sign agreements to surrender the baby.

3-2e ADOPTION

Adoption is another way for people to obtain children. Despite occasional conflicts that pit adoptive parents against biological parents who change their minds about giving up their children, most adoptions result in the formation of loving new families. Many Americans find it easier to adopt infants from other countries or with special needs.

3-2f SELECTING THE SEX OF YOUR CHILD

Today, there is a reliable method for selecting the sex of a child prior to implantation: preimplantation genetic diagnosis (PGD). PGD was developed to detect genetic disorders, but it also reveals the sex of the embryo. In PGD, ova are fertilized in vitro. After a few days of cell division, a cell is extracted from each, and its sex chromosomal structure is examined microscopically to learn of its sex. Embryos of the desired sex are implanted in the woman's uterus, where one or more can grow to term. However, successful implantation cannot be guaranteed.

3-3 STAGES OF PRENATAL DEVELOPMENT

The most rapid and dramatic human developments are literally "out of sight" and take place in the uterus. Within nine months, a fetus develops from a nearly microscopic cell to a neonate about 20 inches long. Its weight increases a billionfold.

We can date pregnancy from the onset of the last menstrual period before conception, which makes the normal gestation period 280 days. We can also date pregnancy from the assumed date of fertilization, which normally occurs two weeks after the beginning of the woman's last menstrual cycle. With this accounting method, the gestation period is 266 days.

Prenatal development is divided into three periods: the germinal stage (approximately the first two weeks), the embryonic stage (the third through the eighth weeks), and the fetal stage (the third month through birth). Health professionals also commonly speak of prenatal development in terms of three trimesters of three months each.

3-3a THE GERMINAL STAGE: WANDERINGS

Within 36 hours after conception, the zygote divides into two cells. It then divides repeatedly as it undergoes its three- to four-day journey to the uterus. Within another 36 hours, it has become 32 cells. The mass of dividing cells wanders about the uterus for another three to four days before it begins to implant in the uterine wall. Implantation takes another week or so. The period from conception to implantation is called the **germinal stage**.

A few days into the germinal stage, the dividing cell mass takes the form of a fluid-filled ball of cells called a **blastocyst**. In the blastocyst, cells begin to separate into groups that will eventually become different structures. The inner part of the blastocyst has two distinct layers that form a thickened mass of cells called the

germinal stage the period of development between conception and the implantation of the embryo.

blastocyst a stage within the germinal period of prenatal development in which the zygote has the form of a sphere of cells surrounding a cavity of fluid.

embryonic disk. These cells will become the embryo and eventually the fetus.

The outer part of the blastocyst, or **trophoblast**, at first consists of a single layer of cells, but it rapidly differentiates into four membranes that will protect and nourish the embryo. One membrane produces blood cells until the embryo's liver develops and takes over this function. Then it disappears. Another membrane develops into the **umbilical cord** and the blood vessels of the **placenta**. A third develops into the amniotic sac, and the fourth becomes the chorion, which will line the placenta.

The cluster of cells that will become the embryo and then the fetus is at first nourished only by the yolk of the egg cell. A blastocyst gains mass only when it receives nourishment from outside. For that to happen, it must be implanted in the uterine wall. Implantation may be accompanied by bleeding, which is usually normal, but bleeding can also be a sign of miscarriage. Most women who experience implantation bleeding, however, do not miscarry, but have normal pregnancies. Miscarriage usually stems from abnormalities in the developmental process. Approximately 10% to 20% of known pregnancies terminate in miscarriage. The actual figure is higher because many women miscarry before they knew they were pregnant (Miscarriage, 2016).

3-3b THE EMBRYONIC STAGE

The **embryonic stage** begins with implantation and covers the first two months, during which the major organ systems differentiate. Development follows **cephalocaudal** (Latin for "head to tail") and **proximodistal** (Latin for "near to far") trends. Growth of the head takes precedence over growth of the lower parts of the body (see Figure 3.3). You can also think of the body as containing a central axis that coincides with the spinal cord. The growth of the organ systems near the spine occurs earlier than growth of the extremities. Relatively early maturation of the brain and organs that lie near the spine allows them to play key roles in further development.

During the embryonic stage, the outer layer of cells of the embryonic disk, or **ectoderm**, develops into the nervous system, sensory organs, nails, hair, teeth, and outer layer of skin. At approximately 21 days, two ridges appear in the embryo and fold to compose the **neural tube**, from which the nervous system will develop. The inner layer, or **endoderm**, forms the digestive and respiratory systems, the liver, and the pancreas. A bit later, the mesoderm, a middle layer of cells, becomes differentiated. The **mesoderm** develops into the excretory, reproductive, and circulatory systems, the muscles, the skeleton, and the inner layer of the skin.

During the third week after conception, the head and blood vessels begin to form. Your heart started beating when you were only ¼ of an inch long and weighed a fraction of an ounce. The major organ systems develop during the first two months. Arm buds and leg buds begin to appear toward the end of the first month. Eyes, ears, nose, and mouth begin to take shape. By this time, the nervous system, including the brain, has also begun to

---

embryonic disk the platelike inner part of the blastocyst that differentiates into the ectoderm, mesoderm, and endoderm of the embryo.

trophoblast the outer part of the blastocyst from which the amniotic sac, placenta, and umbilical cord develop.

umbilical cord a tube that connects the fetus to the placenta.

placenta an organ connected to the uterine wall and to the fetus by the umbilical cord. The placenta serves as a relay station between mother and fetus for the exchange of nutrients and wastes.

embryonic stage the stage of prenatal development that lasts from implantation through the eighth week of pregnancy; it is characterized by the development of the major organ systems.

cephalocaudal from head to tail.

proximodistal from the inner part (or axis) of the body outward.

ectoderm the outermost cell layer of the newly formed embryo from which the skin and nervous system develop.

neural tube a hollowed-out area in the blastocyst from which the nervous system develops.

endoderm the inner layer of the embryo from which the lungs and digestive system develop.

mesoderm the central layer of the embryo from which the bones and muscles develop.

FIG.3.3 A HUMAN EMBRYO AT 7 WEEKS

Petit Format/Nestle/Science source

By the time this photo was taken, the embryo's heart had already been beating for about a month. By another week, all the major organs systems will have formed, and the embryo will enter the fetal stage.

develop. During the second month, the cells in the nervous system begin to "fire"; that is, they send messages among themselves. Most likely, it is random cell firing, and the "content" of such "messages" is anybody's guess. By the end of the second month, the embryo is looking quite human. The head has the lovely, round shape of your own, and the facial features have become quite distinct. All this detail is inscribed on an embryo that is only about one inch long and weighs 1/30th of an ounce. By the end of the embryonic period, teeth buds have formed. The embryo's kidneys are filtering acid from the blood, and its liver is producing red blood cells.

SEXUAL DIFFERENTIA-TION By five to six weeks, the embryo is only one-quarter to one-half inch long. At this stage of development, both the internal and the external genitals resemble primitive female structures. By about the seventh week, the genetic code (XY or XX) begins to assert itself, causing sex organs to differentiate. Genetic activity on the Y sex chromosome causes the testes to begin to differentiate. The ovaries begin to differentiate if the Y chromosome is *absent*. By about three months after conception, males and females show distinct external genital structures. Once the testes have developed in the embryo, they begin to produce male sex hormones, or **androgens**, the most important of which is testosterone. Female embryos and fetuses produce small amounts of androgens, but they are usually not enough to cause sexual differentiation along male lines.

THE AMNIOTIC SAC The embryo and fetus develop within a protective **amniotic sac** in the uterus. This sac is surrounded by a clear membrane and contains **amniotic fluid**. The fluid serves as a kind of natural air bag or shock absorber, allowing the embryo and fetus to move around without injury. It also helps maintain an even temperature.

THE PLACENTA The **placenta** is a pancake-shaped mass of tissue that permits the embryo (and, later on, the fetus) to exchange nutrients and wastes with the mother. The placenta is unique in origin. It grows from material supplied by both the mother and the embryo. The fetus is connected to the placenta by the umbilical cord. The mother is connected to the placenta by blood vessels in the uterine wall.

Mother and embryo have separate circulatory systems. The placenta contains a membrane that permits oxygen and nutrients to reach the embryo from the mother, and permits carbon dioxide and waste products to pass to the mother from the embryo. The mother then eliminates them through her lungs and kidneys. Some harmful substances can also sneak through the placenta, including various "germs," such as the ones that cause syphilis and German

A human fetus at 12 weeks. Note how oversized the head is in relation to the rest of the body.

A human fetus at 4½ months. The organ systems are maturing and the fetus is making dramatic gains in size. It also looks unmistakably human.

measles, but HIV (the virus that causes AIDS) is more likely to be transmitted via bleeding that occurs at childbirth. (Check with your physician as to how to minimize this risk.) Some drugs—aspirin, narcotics, alcohol, tranquilizers, and others—do cross the placenta and affect the fetus.

The placenta also secretes hormones that preserve the pregnancy, prepare the breasts for nursing, and stimulate the uterine contractions that prompt childbirth. Ultimately, the placenta passes from the birth canal after the baby; for this reason, it is also called the afterbirth.

androgens male sex hormones.

amniotic sac the sac containing the fetus.

amniotic fluid fluid within the amniotic sac that suspends and protects the fetus.

placenta the organ formed in the lining of the uterus that provides nourishment for the fetus and elimination of its waste products.

3-3c THE FETAL STAGE

The **fetal stage** lasts from the beginning of the third month until birth. The fetus begins to turn and respond to external stimulation at about the ninth or tenth week. By the end of the first trimester, the major organ systems have been formed. The fingers and toes are fully formed. The eyes and the sex of the fetus can be clearly seen.

The second trimester is characterized by further maturation of fetal organ systems and dramatic gains in size. The brain continues to mature, contributing to the fetus's ability to regulate its own basic body functions. The fetus advances from one ounce to two pounds in weight and grows four to five times in length, from about 3 inches to 14 inches. By the end of the second trimester, the fetus opens and shuts its eyes, sucks its thumb, alternates between wakefulness and sleep, and perceives light and sounds.

During the third trimester, the organ systems mature further. The fetus gains about 5½ pounds and doubles in length. During the seventh month, the fetus normally turns upside down in the uterus so that delivery will be head first. By the end of the seventh month, the fetus will have almost doubled in weight, gaining another 1 pound, 12 ounces, and will have increased another two inches in length. If born now, chances of survival are nearly 90%. If born at the end of the eighth month, the odds are overwhelmingly in favor of survival. Newborn boys average about 7½ pounds and newborn girls about 7 pounds.

FETAL PERCEPTION By the 13th week of pregnancy, the fetus responds to sound waves. Sontag and Richards (1938) rang a bell near the mother's abdomen, and the fetus responded with movements similar to those of the startle reflex shown after birth. During the third trimester, fetuses respond to sounds of different frequencies

fetal stage the stage that begins with the third month of pregnancy and ends with childbirth, during which organ systems mature and there are gains in size.

Did you develop your appreciation of Dr. Seuss before you were born? In a fascinating experiment, mothers read *The Cat in the Hat* aloud twice a day during the final month and a half of pregnancy. Their newborns showed a preference for hearing *The Cat in the Hat* rather than another book.

Vince Bucci/Getty Images Entertainment/Getty Images

TRUTH

(T) F Fetuses suck their thumbs, sometimes for hours on end.

It is true that fetuses suck their thumbs. Sometimes they do so for hours on end.

through a variety of movements and changes in heart rate, suggesting that they can discriminate pitch (Lecanuet et al., 2000).

An experiment by Anthony DeCasper and William Fifer (1980) is even more intriguing. In this study, women read the Dr. Seuss book *The Cat in the Hat* out loud twice daily during the final month and a half of pregnancy. After birth, their babies were given special pacifiers. Sucking on these pacifiers in one way would activate recordings of their mothers reading *The Cat in the Hat*, and sucking on them in another way would activate their mothers' readings of a book that was written in very different rhythms. The newborns "chose" to hear *The Cat in the Hat*. Fetal learning may be one basis for the development of attachment to the mother (DiPietro, 2010; James, 2010; Lee & Kisilevsky, 2013).

FETAL MOVEMENTS The mother usually feels the first fetal movements in the middle of the fourth month (Raynes-Greenough et al., 2013). By 29–30 weeks, the fetus moves its limbs so vigorously that the mother may complain of being kicked. The fetus also turns somersaults, which are clearly felt by the mother. The umbilical cord will not break or become dangerously wrapped around the fetus, no matter how many acrobatic feats the fetus performs. As the fetus grows, it becomes cramped in the uterus, and movement is constricted, so that the fetus becomes markedly less active during the ninth month of pregnancy.

3-4 ENVIRONMENTAL INFLUENCES ON PRENATAL DEVELOPMENT

The developing fetus is subject to many environmental hazards. Scientific advances have made us keenly aware of the types of things that can go wrong and what we can do to prevent these problems.

3-4a NUTRITION

It is a common misconception that fetuses "take what they need" from their mothers. However, maternal malnutrition has been linked to low birth weight, prematurity, retardation of brain development, cognitive deficiencies, behavioral problems, and even cardiovascular disease (Monk et al., 2013; de Souza et al., 2011). The effects of fetal malnutrition are sometimes overcome by a supportive, care-giving environment. Experiments with children who suffered from fetal malnutrition show that enriched day-care programs enhance intellectual and social skills by five years of age (Ramey et al., 1999). Supplementing the diets of pregnant women who might otherwise be deficient in their intake of calories and protein also shows modest positive effects on the motor development of infants (de Souza et al., 2011). On the other hand, maternal obesity is linked with a higher risk of **stillbirth** (Crane et al., 2013) and neural tube defects. Over the course of pregnancy, women who do not restrict their diet normally will gain 25–35 pounds. Overweight women may gain less, and slender women may gain more. Regular weight gains of about one-half pound per week during the first half of pregnancy and one pound per week thereafter are desirable.

> Maternal malnutrition has been linked to low birth weight, prematurity, retardation of brain development, cognitive deficiencies, behavioral problems, and even cardiovascular disease.

3-4b TERATOGENS AND HEALTH PROBLEMS OF THE MOTHER

Teratogens are environmental agents that can harm the embryo or fetus. They include drugs taken by the mother, such as marijuana and alcohol, and substances that the mother's body produces, such as Rh-positive antibodies. Another class of teratogens is the heavy metals, such as lead and mercury, which are toxic to the embryo. Hormones are healthful in countless ways—for example, they help maintain pregnancy—but excessive quantities are harmful to the embryo. Exposure to radiation can also harm the embryo. Finally, disease-causing organisms—also called pathogens—such as bacteria and viruses are also teratogens.

3-4c PERIODS OF VULNERABILITY

Exposure to particular teratogens is most harmful during **critical periods** that correspond to the times when organs are developing. For example, the heart develops rapidly in the third to fifth weeks after conception. As you can see in Figure 3.4 on page 42, the heart is most vulnerable to certain teratogens at this time. The arms and legs, which develop later, are most vulnerable in the fourth through eighth weeks. Because the major organ systems differentiate during the embryonic stage, the embryo is generally more vulnerable to teratogens than the fetus. Even so, many teratogens are harmful throughout the entire course of prenatal development.

Let's consider the effects of various health problems of the mother. We begin with sexually transmitted infections (STIs).

SEXUALLY TRANSMITTED INFECTIONS The **syphilis** bacterium can cause miscarriage, stillbirth, or **congenital** syphilis. Routine blood tests early in pregnancy can diagnose syphilis. The syphilis bacterium is vulnerable to antibiotics. The fetus will probably not contract syphilis if an infected mother is treated with antibiotics before the fourth month of pregnancy (Centers for Disease Control and Prevention, 2013). If the mother is not treated, the baby may be infected in utero and develop congenital syphilis. About 12% of those infected die.

HIV/AIDS (human immunodeficiency virus/acquired immunodeficiency syndrome) disables the body's immune system and leaves victims prey to a variety of fatal illnesses, including respiratory disorders and cancer. HIV/AIDS is lethal unless treated with a "cocktail" of antiviral drugs. Even then, the drugs do not work for everyone, and the eventual outcome remains in doubt.

stillbirth the birth of a dead fetus.

teratogens environmental influences or agents that can damage the embryo or fetus.

critical period in this usage, a period during which an embryo is particularly vulnerable to a certain teratogen.

syphilis a sexually transmitted infection that, in advanced stages, can attack major organ systems.

congenital present at birth and resulting from genetic or chromosomal abnormalities or from exposure to the prenatal environment.

HIV/AIDS HIV stands for human immunodeficiency virus, which cripples the body's immune system. AIDS stands for acquired immunodeficiency syndrome, a condition in which the immune system is weakened such that it is vulnerable to diseases it would otherwise fight off.

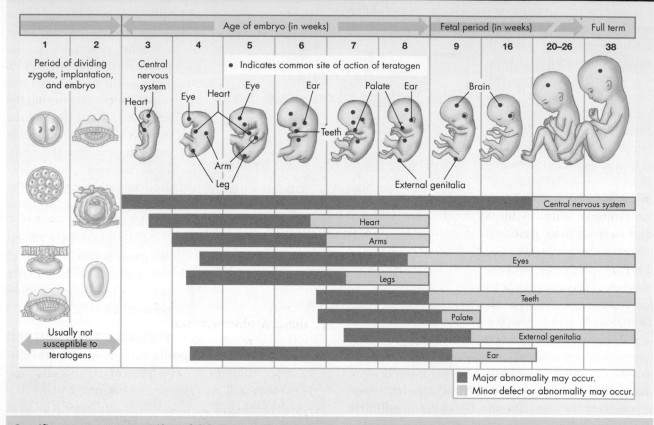

FIG.3.4 CRITICAL PERIODS IN PRENATAL DEVELOPMENT

| Age of embryo (in weeks) | | | | | | | | Fetal period (in weeks) | | | Full term |

Period of dividing zygote, implantation, and embryo

Central nervous system

• Indicates common site of action of teratogen

Heart, Eye, Heart, Eye, Ear, Palate, Ear, Brain, Teeth, Arm, Leg, External genitalia

Usually not susceptible to teratogens

Central nervous system
Heart
Arms
Eyes
Legs
Teeth
Palate
External genitalia
Ear

Major abnormality may occur.
Minor defect or abnormality may occur.

Specific teratogens are most harmful during certain periods of prenatal development.

HIV can be transmitted by sexual relations, blood transfusions, sharing hypodermic needles while shooting up drugs, childbirth, and breast feeding. During childbirth, blood vessels in the mother and baby rupture, enabling an exchange of blood and transmission of HIV. HIV is also found in breast milk. However, a majority of babies born to mothers with HIV/AIDS do not become infected themselves. It also appears that women can decrease the risk of their babies becoming infected with HIV by regular use of antiviral drugs such as Truvada (Callahan et al., 2015; Conniff & Evensen, 2016).

RUBELLA Rubella (German measles) is a viral infection. Women who are infected during the first 20 weeks of pregnancy stand at least a 20% chance of bearing children with birth defects such as deafness, intellectual disabilities, heart disease, or eye problems, including blindness.

Many adult women had rubella as children and became immune in this way. Women who are not immune are best vaccinated before they become pregnant, although they can be inoculated during pregnancy, if necessary.

About one-fourth of babies born to mothers infected with HIV become infected themselves. Maternal use of antiviral drugs decreases the likelihood of transmitting the virus. Check with your doctor about various ways of keeping the fetus and the birth process safe.

Ablestock/Jupiter Images

rubella a viral infection that can cause retardation and heart disease in the embryo. Also called German measles.

PREECLAMPSIA Preeclampsia (also called **toxemia**) is a life-threatening disease characterized by high blood pressure that may afflict women late in the second or early in the third trimester. Women with toxemia often have **premature** or undersized babies. Toxemia also causes some 15% to 20% of pregnancy-related maternal deaths (Bangal et al., 2012; Verlohren et al., 2012). Preeclampsia appears to be linked to malnutrition, but the causes are unclear. Women who do not receive prenatal care are much more likely to die from preeclampsia than those who do receive prenatal care.

RH INCOMPATIBILITY In **Rh incompatibility**, antibodies produced by the mother are transmitted to a fetus or newborn infant and cause brain damage or death. Rh is a blood protein found in the red blood cells of some individuals. Rh incompatibility occurs when a woman who does not have this factor—and is thus Rh negative—is carrying an Rh-positive fetus, which can happen if the father is Rh positive. The negative–positive combination occurs in approximately 10% of American couples and becomes a problem in some resulting pregnancies. Rh incompatibility does not affect a first child because women will not have formed Rh antibodies. The chances of an exchange of blood are greatest during childbirth. If an exchange occurs, the mother produces Rh-positive antibodies to the baby's Rh-positive blood. These antibodies can enter the fetal bloodstream during subsequent deliveries, causing anemia, mental deficiency, or death.

If an Rh-negative mother is injected with Rh immunoglobulin within 72 hours after delivery of an Rh-positive baby, she will not develop the antibodies. A fetus or newborn child at risk of Rh disease may receive a blood transfusion to remove the mother's antibodies.

3-4e DRUGS TAKEN BY THE PARENTS

Rh antibodies can be lethal to children, but many other substances can have harmful effects. Even commonly used medications, such as aspirin, can be harmful to the fetus. If a woman is pregnant or thinks she may be, it is advisable for her to consult her obstetrician before taking any drugs, not just prescription medications. A physician usually can recommend a safe and effective substitute for a drug that could potentially harm a developing fetus.

preeclampsia (or **toxemia**) a life-threatening disease that can afflict pregnant women; it is characterized by high blood pressure.

premature born before the full term of gestation. Also referred to as preterm.

Rh incompatibility a condition in which antibodies produced by the mother are transmitted to the child, possibly causing brain damage or death.

Drugs taken by the parents may be harmful to the embryo and fetus. Heavy drinking is connected with fetal alcohol syndrome (FAS), and there is no guaranteed safe small amount of alcohol. Cigarettes deprive the fetus of oxygen. Other drugs have other effects.

THALIDOMIDE **Thalidomide** was marketed in the 1960s as a treatment for insomnia and nausea and provides a dramatic example of critical periods of vulnerability to teratogens. A fetus's extremities undergo rapid development during the second month of pregnancy (see Figure 2.11). Thalidomide taken during this period almost invariably causes birth defects, such as missing or stunted limbs. The drug is no longer prescribed for pregnant women.

HORMONES Women at risk for miscarriages have been prescribed hormones to help maintain their pregnancies. **Progestin**—a synthetic version of naturally occurring progesterone—is chemically similar to male sex hormones and can masculinize the external sex organs of female embryos. **DES** (short for diethylstilbestrol), a powerful estrogen, often prescribed during the 1940s and 1950s to help prevent miscarriage, has been shown to have caused cervical, vaginal, and testicular cancers in some offspring. Among daughters of DES users, some 2% to 3% will develop cancer in the reproductive tract (Verloop et al., 2010, Gee et al., 2014).

VITAMINS Although pregnant women are often prescribed multivitamins to maintain their own health and to promote the development of their fetuses, high doses of vitamins A and D have been associated with central nervous system damage, small head size, and heart defects (Simpson et al., 2011; Wagner et al., 2014).

HEROIN AND METHADONE Maternal addiction to heroin or methadone is linked to low birth weight, prematurity, and toxemia. Narcotics such as heroin and methadone readily cross the placental membrane, and the fetuses of women who regularly use them can become addicted. Addicted newborns may be given the narcotic or a substitute shortly after birth so that they will not suffer serious withdrawal symptoms. The drug is then withdrawn gradually. Addicted newborns may also have behavioral effects, such as delays in motor and language development at the age of 12 months (Minnes et al., 2011).

MARIJUANA (CANNABIS) Smoking marijuana during pregnancy apparently poses a number of risks for the fetus, including slower growth and low birth weight. The babies of women who regularly used marijuana show increased tremors and startling, suggesting immature development of the nervous system (Minnes et al., 2011).

Research into the cognitive effects of maternal prenatal use of marijuana suggests that cognitive skills, including learning and memory, may be impaired (Huizink, 2013). One study assessed the behavior of ten-year-olds who had been exposed prenatally to maternal use of marijuana (Goldschmidt et al., 2000), and suggested that prenatal use of marijuana was significantly related to increased hyperactivity, impulsivity, problems in paying attention, and increased delinquency and aggressive behavior.

COCAINE Pregnant women who abuse cocaine increase the risk of stillbirth, low birth weight, and birth defects. Infants exposed to cocaine prenatally are often excitable and irritable, or lethargic; sleep is disturbed (Richardson et al., 2013). There are suggestions of delays in cognitive development, even among preadolescents (Richardson et al., 2013).

Children who are exposed to cocaine prenatally also show problems at later ages. One study compared 189 children at four years of age who had been exposed to cocaine in utero with 185 four-year-olds who had not (Lewis et al., 2004). The children exposed to cocaine had much lower receptive and expressive language abilities.

ALCOHOL Because alcohol passes through the placenta, drinking by a pregnant woman poses risks for the embryo and fetus. Heavy drinking can be lethal and is also connected with deficiencies and deformities in growth. Some children of heavy drinkers develop **fetal alcohol syndrome (FAS)** (O'Leary et al., 2010; see Figure 3.5). Babies with FAS are often smaller than normal, and so are their brains. They have distinct facial features: widely spaced eyes, an underdeveloped upper jaw, a flattened nose. Psychological characteristics appear to reflect dysfunction of the brain.

The facial deformities of FAS diminish as the child moves into adolescence, and most children catch up in height and weight, but the intellectual, academic, and behavioral deficits of FAS persist. Maladaptive behaviors such as poor judgment, distractibility, and difficulty perceiving social cues are common (Kooistra et al., 2010). Although some health professionals allow pregnant women a glass of wine with dinner, there is no guaranteed safe minimal amount of alcohol (Kelly et al., 2013).

---

thalidomide a sedative used in the 1960s that has been linked to birth defects, especially deformed or absent limbs.

progestin a synthetic hormone used to maintain pregnancy that can cause masculinization of the fetus.

DES diethylstilbestrol, an estrogen that has been linked to cancer in the reproductive organs of children of women who used the hormone when pregnant.

fetal alcohol syndrome (FAS) a cluster of symptoms shown by children of women who drank heavily during pregnancy, including characteristic facial features and intellectual disabilities.

FIG.3.5 FETAL ALCOHOL SYNDROME (FAS)

Small head

Flat face

Small eye openings

Short nose

Low nasal bridge

Underdeveloped jaw

Thin upper lip

Fetal Alcohol Syndrome

The children of many mothers who drank alcohol during pregnancy exhibit FAS. This syndrome is characterized by developmental lags and such facial features as an underdeveloped upper jaw, a flattened nose, and widely spaced eyes.

Gwen Shockey/Science Source

CAFFEINE Many pregnant women consume caffeine in the form of coffee, tea, soft drinks, chocolate, and nonprescription drugs. Some authors argue that research findings on caffeine's effects on the developing fetus have been inconsistent (Signorello & McLaughlin, 2004). However, some studies have found that pregnant women who take in a good deal of caffeine are more likely than nonusers to have a miscarriage or a low-birthweight baby (Bakker et al., 2010; Sengpiel et al., 2013). Ask your doctor.

CIGARETTES Cigarette smoke contains many ingredients, including the stimulant nicotine, the gas carbon monoxide, and hydrocarbons ("tars"), which are carcinogens. Nicotine and carbon monoxide pass through the placenta and reach the fetus. Nicotine stimulates the fetus, but its long-term effects are uncertain. Carbon monoxide decreases the amount of oxygen available to the fetus. Oxygen deprivation is connected with impaired motor development, academic delays, learning and intellectual disabilities, and hyperactivity (Minnes et al., 2011).

Pregnant women who smoke are likely to deliver smaller babies than nonsmokers (Anblagan et al., 2013). Their babies are more likely to be stillborn or to die soon after birth (Still-birth Collaborative Research Network Writing Group, 2011). Babies of fathers who smoke have higher rates of birth defects, infant mortality, lower birth weights, and cardiovascular problems (Misra et al., 2010).

3-4f ENVIRONMENTAL HAZARDS

Mothers know when they are ingesting drugs, but there are many other substances in the environment they may take in unknowingly. These substances are environmental hazards to which we are all exposed, and we refer to them collectively as pollution.

Prenatal exposure to heavy metals such as lead, mercury, and zinc may delay mental development at one and two years of age (Chen et al., 2014; Gorini et al., 2014). Polychlorinated biphenyls (PCBs), used in many industrial products, accumulate in fish that feed in polluted waters. Newborns whose mothers consumed PCB-contaminated fish from Lake Michigan were smaller and showed poorer motor functioning and memory defects (Jacobson et al., 1992). On the other hand, prenatal exposure to the low levels of metals that we now find in most developed countries may not be harmful (Foms et al., 2014).

Experiments with mice show that fetal exposure to radiation in high doses can damage the eyes, central nervous system, and skeleton (Buratovic et al., 2016; Hossain et al., 2005). Pregnant women exposed to atomic radiation during the bombings of Hiroshima and Nagasaki in World War II gave birth to babies who were likely to be intellectually disabled as well as physically deformed (Sadler, 2005). Pregnant women are advised to avoid unnecessary exposure to x-rays. (Ultrasound, which is not an x-ray, has not been shown to harm the fetus.)

3-4g PARENTS' AGE

What about the parents' age? Older fathers are more likely to produce abnormal sperm. The mother's age also matters. From a biological vantage point, the 20s may be the ideal age for women to bear children. Teenage mothers have a higher incidence of infant mortality and children with low birth weight (Save the Children, 2011). Girls who become pregnant in their early teens may place a burden on bodies that may not have adequately matured to facilitate pregnancy and childbirth (Save the Children, 2011).

ian nolan / Alamy Stock Photo

Women's fertility declines gradually until the mid-30s, after which it declines more rapidly. Women possess all their ova in immature form at birth. Over 30 years, these cells are exposed to the environmental slings and arrows of toxic wastes, chemical pollutants, and radiation, thus increasing the risk of chromosomal abnormalities such as Down's syndrome. Women who wait until their 30s or 40s to have children also increase the likelihood of having miscarriages (Khalil et al., 2013). With adequate prenatal care, however, the risk of problems in pregnancy is relatively small, even for older first-time mothers (Williams et al., 2011).

DO MEN REALLY HAVE ALL THE TIME IN THE WORLD? The artist Pablo Picasso fathered children in his 70s. Strom Thurmond, a longtime U.S. senator, fathered a child in his 90s. It has been widely known that women's chances of conceiving children decline as they age. The traditional message has been "Women, you'd better hurry up. Men, you have all the time in the world."

TRUTH

(T) F · A father's age at the time of conception can influence the development of the fetus.

It is true that a father's age at the time of conception can influence the development of the fetus. The older the father, the greater the risk of chromosomal abnormalities.

Not so, apparently. Older fathers are more likely to produce abnormal sperm, leading to fertility problems. But that's only the tip of the iceberg. University of Queensland researchers analyzed data from some 33,000 U.S. children and found that the older the father is at

FIG.3.6 AUTISM RISK INCREASES WITH PATERNAL AGE

Chance of autism spectrum disorder among 132,271 subjects, by paternal age:

6 in 10,000
15- to 29-year-old fathers

9 in 10,000
30- to 39-year-old fathers

32 in 10,000
40- to 49-year-old fathers

52 in 10,000
50- year-old fathers and older

conception, the lower a child's score may be on tests of reading skills, reasoning, memory, and concentration. The ages of 29 and 30 are something of a turning point for men, because children conceived past these ages are at greater risk for the psychological disorders of schizophrenia and bipolar disorder. Children born to men past 40 also have a greater risk of autism, as shown in Figure 3.6 (Reichenberg et al., 2006).

These findings do not mean that the majority of children born to men past their reproductive "prime" will develop these problems, but it does mean that men's age, as women's, is related to risks for their children.

Whatever the age of the mother and father, the events of childbirth provide some of the most memorable moments in the lives of parents. In Chapter 3, we continue our voyage with the process of birth and the characteristics of the newborn child.

SELF-ASSESSMENT

Fill-Ins

Answers can be found in the back of the book.

1. Sperm are apparently guided toward an egg cell (ovum) by changes in _____ ions.

2. Some women are infertile due to _____, which can obstruct the fallopian tubes.

3. The outer layer of the blastocyst is the _____.

4. The _____ is a pancake-shaped mass of tissue that permits the embryo and fetus to exchange nutrients and wastes with the mother.

5. _____ is a life-threatening disease characterized by high blood pressure that may afflict women late in the second or early in the third trimester.

6. Cigarette smoking by a pregnant woman is harmful to the fetus because it decreases the amount of _____ available to the fetus.

7. Newborn girls average about _____ pounds in weight.

8. The nervous system develops from the _____ tube of the embryo.

9. The organ called the _____ enables the embryo to exchange nutrients and wastes with the mother.

10. Fertility drugs are made up of _____ that cause the woman to ovulate.

Multiple Choice

1. The arms and the legs are most vulnerable to teratogens
   a. one to four weeks after conception.
   b. four to eight weeks after conception.
   c. eight to twelve weeks after conception.
   d. twelve to sixteen weeks after conception.

2. Which of the following is not likely to be transmitted to the fetus through the placenta?
   a. HIV
   b. aspirin
   c. narcotics
   d. alcohol

3. About _____ % of cases of infertility have unknown causes.
   a. 20
   b. 40
   c. 60
   d. 80

4. The period from conception to implantation is called the _____ stage of prenatal development.
   a. latency
   b. germinal
   c. fetal
   d. embryonic

5. _____ is a powerful estrogen that was often prescribed during the 1940s and 1950s to help prevent miscarriage. Since then, it has been shown to cause cervical, vaginal, and testicular cancers in some off spring.
   a. DES
   b. Progestin
   c. Vitamin A
   d. Thalidomide

6. In _____, antibodies produced by the mother are transmitted to a fetus or newborn infant and cause brain damage or death.
   a. preeclampsia
   b. Rh incompatibility
   c. spina bifida
   d. FAS

7. The most common infertility problem in men is
   a. endometriosis.
   b. sexually transmitted infections.
   c. use of illicit drugs.
   d. low sperm count.

8. Early in the germinal stage, the dividing mass of cells takes the form of a fluid-filled ball termed a
   a. blastocyst.
   b. embryonic disk.
   c. trophoblast.
   d. ectoderm.

9. The embryonic stage begins with
   a. differentiation of major organ systems.
   b. composing of the neural tube.
   c. implantation in the uterine wall.
   d. formation of the head.

10. Which of the following is least likely to pass to the fetus through the placenta?
    a. alcohol
    b. HIV
    c. oxygen
    d. germs that cause syphilis

CDEV
ONLINE

ACCESS TEXTBOOK CONTENT ONLINE—
INCLUDING ON SMARTPHONES!

Includes Videos & Other Interactive Resources!

Access CDEV ONLINE at www.cengagebrain.com

4 | Birth and the Newborn Baby: In the New World

LEARNING OUTCOMES

After studying this chapter, you will be able to...

4-1 Identify the stages of childbirth

4-2 Examine different methods of childbirth

4-3 Discuss potential problems with childbirth

4-4 Describe the postpartum period

4-5 Examine the characteristics of a neonate

After you finish this chapter, go to **PAGE 72** for **STUDY TOOLS**

During the last few weeks before she gave birth, Michele explained: "I couldn't get my mind off the pregnancy—what it was going to be like when I finally delivered Lisa. I'd had the amniocentesis, so I knew it was a girl. I'd had the ultrasounds, so all her fingers and toes had been counted, but I was still hoping and praying that everything would turn out all right. To be honest, I was also worried about the delivery. I had always been an A student, and I guess I wanted to earn an A in childbirth as well. Matt was understanding, and he was even helpful, but, you know, it wasn't him."

Nearly all first-time mothers struggle through the last weeks of pregnancy and worry about the mechanics of delivery. Childbirth is a natural function, of course, but so many of them have gone to classes to learn how to do what comes naturally! They worry

> Nearly all first-time mothers struggle through the last weeks of pregnancy and worry about the mechanics of delivery.

about whether they'll get to the hospital or birthing center on time. ("Is there gas in the car?" "Is it snowing?") They worry about whether the baby will start breathing on its own properly. They may wonder if they'll do it on their own or need a C-section. They may also worry about whether it will hurt, and how much, and when they should ask for anesthetics, and, well, how to earn that A.

Close to full **term**, Michele and other women are sort of front-loaded and feel bent out of shape, and guess what? They are. The weight of the fetus may also be causing backaches. Will they deliver the baby, or will the baby—by being born—deliver them from discomfort? "Hanging in and having Lisa was a wonderful experience," Michele said in the end. "I think Matt should have had it."

COUNTDOWN ...

Early in the last month of pregnancy, the head of the fetus settles in the pelvis. This process is called *dropping* or *lightening*. Because lightening decreases pressure on the diaphragm, the mother may, in fact, feel lighter.

The first uterine contractions are called **Braxton-Hicks contractions**, or false labor contractions. They are relatively painless and may be experienced as early as the sixth month of pregnancy. They increase in frequency as the pregnancy progresses and may serve to tone the muscles that will be used in delivery. True labor contractions are more painful and regular, and are usually intensified by walking.

A day or so before labor begins, increased pelvic pressure from the fetus may rupture blood vessels in the birth canal so that blood appears in vaginal secretions. Mucus that had plugged the **cervix** and protected the uterus from infection

becomes dislodged. About one woman in ten has a rush of warm liquid from the vagina at this time. This liquid is amniotic fluid, and its discharge means that the amniotic sac has burst. The sac usually does not burst until the end

term the typical nine-month period from conception to childbirth.

Braxton-Hicks contractions the first, usually painless, contractions of childbirth.

cervix the narrow lower end of the uterus, through which a baby passes to reach the vagina.

TRUTH OR FICTION?

T	F	The fetus signals the mother when it is ready to be born.
T	F	After birth, babies are held upside down and slapped on the buttocks to stimulate independent breathing.
T	F	Women who give birth according to the Lamaze method do not experience pain.
T	F	In the United States, nearly three of every ten births are by cesarean section.
T	F	It is abnormal to feel depressed following childbirth.
T	F	Parents must have extended early contact with their newborn children if adequate bonding is to take place.
T	F	More children in the United States die from sudden infant death syndrome (SIDS) than from cancer, heart disease, pneumonia, child abuse, AIDS, cystic fibrosis, and muscular dystrophy combined.

of the first stage of childbirth, as described later. Other signs that labor is beginning include indigestion, diarrhea, an ache in the small of the back, and cramps.

The fetus may actually signal the mother when it is "ready" to be born by secreting hormones that stimulate the placenta and uterus to secrete **prostaglandins** (Plunkett et al., 2011; Swaggart et al., 2015). Prostaglandins not only cause the cramping that women may feel before or during menstruation, they also excite the muscles of the uterus to engage in labor contractions. As labor progresses, the pituitary gland releases the hormone **oxytocin**, which stimulates contractions powerful enough to expel the baby.

4-1 THE STAGES OF CHILDBIRTH

Regular uterine contractions signal the beginning of childbirth. Childbirth occurs in three stages. In the first stage, uterine contractions **efface** and **dilate** the cervix, which needs to widen to about four inches (ten centimeters) to allow the baby to pass. Dilation of the cervix causes most of the pain of childbirth (see Figure 4.1).

The first stage is the longest stage. Among women undergoing their first deliveries, this stage may last from a few hours to more than a day. Subsequent pregnancies

prostaglandins hormones that stimulate uterine contractions.

oxytocin a hormone that stimulates labor contractions.

efface to become thin.

dilate to widen.

episiotomy a surgical incision between the birth canal and anus that widens the vaginal opening.

transition movement of the head of the fetus into the vagina.

take less time. The first contractions are not usually all that painful and are spaced 10 to 20 minutes apart. They may last from 20 to 40 seconds each. As the process continues, the contractions become more powerful, frequent, and regular. Women are usually advised to go to the hospital or birthing center when the contractions are four to five minutes apart. Until the end of the first stage of labor, the mother is usually in a labor room.

If the woman is to be "prepped"—that is, if her pubic hair is to be shaved—it takes place now. The prep is intended to lower the chances of infection during delivery and to facilitate the performance of an **episiotomy**. A woman may be given an enema to prevent an involuntary bowel movement during labor. But many women find prepping and enemas degrading and seek obstetricians (physicians who treat women during pregnancy, labor, and recovery from childbirth) who do not perform them routinely.

During the first stage of childbirth, fetal monitoring may be used. One kind of monitor is an electronic device strapped around the woman's abdomen that measures the fetal heart rate as well as the mother's contractions. An abnormal heart rate alerts the medical staff to possible fetal distress so that appropriate steps can be taken, such as speeding up the delivery. When the cervix is nearly fully dilated, the head of the fetus begins to move into the vagina. This process is called **transition**. During transition, which lasts about 30 minutes or less, contractions are usually frequent and strong.

David Castillo Dominici / Alamy Stock Photo

FIG.4.1   STAGES OF CHILDBIRTH

1. Second stage of birth begins

2. Further descent

3. Crowning

4. Anterior shoulder delivered

5. Posterior shoulder

6. Third stage of birth

In the first stage, uterine contractions efface and dilate the cervix. The second stage begins with movement of the baby into the birth canal and ends with birth of the baby. During the third stage, the placenta separates from the uterine wall and is expelled through the birth canal.

The second stage of childbirth begins when the baby appears at the opening of the vagina (now called the *birth canal*). The second stage is briefer than the first, possibly lasting minutes or a few hours and ending with the birth of the baby. The woman may be taken to a delivery room for the second stage.

The contractions of the second stage stretch the skin surrounding the birth canal farther and propel the baby along. The baby's head is said to have crowned when it begins to emerge from the birth canal. Once crowning has occurred, the baby normally emerges completely within minutes.

The physician or nurse may perform an episiotomy once crowning takes place. The purpose of an episiotomy is to prevent random tearing when the area between the birth canal and the anus becomes severely stretched. Women are unlikely to feel the incision of the episiotomy because the pressure of the crowning head tends to numb the region between the vagina and the anus. The episiotomy, like prepping and the enema, is controversial and is not practiced in Europe. The incision may cause itching and discomfort as it heals. The incidence of the use of episiotomy in the United States has been declining, with some studies suggesting that the procedure causes as many problems as it prevents. Some health professionals argue that an episiotomy is warranted when the baby's shoulders are wide or if the baby's heart rate declines for a long period of time. The strongest predictor of whether a practitioner will choose to use episiotomy is not the condition of the mother or the baby, but rather whether the physician normally performs an episiotomy.

To clear the passageway for breathing from any obstructions, mucus is suctioned from the baby's mouth when the head emerges from the birth canal. When the baby is breathing adequately on its own, the umbilical cord is clamped and severed (see Figure 4.2). Mother and infant are now separate beings. The stump of the umbilical cord will dry and fall off on its own in about seven to ten days.

FIG.4.2   CUTTING THE UMBILICAL CORD

BSIP/Science Source

The stump of the cord dries and falls off in about seven to ten days.

Now the baby is frequently whisked away by a nurse, who will perform various procedures, including footprinting the baby, supplying an ID bracelet, putting antibiotic ointment or drops of silver nitrate into the baby's eyes to prevent bacterial infections, and giving the baby a vitamin K injection to help its blood clot properly if it bleeds (newborn babies do not manufacture vitamin K). While these procedures go on, the mother is in the third stage of labor.

The third stage of labor, also called the placental stage, lasts from minutes to an hour or more. During this stage, the placenta separates from the uterine wall and is expelled through the birth canal. Some bleeding is normal. The obstetrician sews the episiotomy, if one has been performed.

4-2 METHODS OF CHILDBIRTH

Childbirth was once a more intimate procedure that usually took place in the woman's home and involved her, perhaps a **midwife**, and family. This pattern is followed in many less-developed nations today, but only rarely in the United States and other developed nations. Contemporary American childbirths usually take place in hospitals, where physicians use sophisticated instruments and anesthetics to protect mother and child from complications and discomfort. Modern medicine has saved lives, but childbearing has also become more impersonal. Some argue that modern methods wrest control from women over their own bodies. They even argue that anesthetics have denied many women the experience of giving

midwife an individual who helps women in childbirth.

anesthetics agents that lessen pain.

general anesthesia elimination of pain by putting a person to sleep.

local anesthetic reduction of pain in an area of the body.

neonate an infant from birth through the first four weeks of life.

natural childbirth childbirth without anesthesia.

FICTION

T (F) After birth, babies are held upside down and slapped on the buttocks to stimulate independent breathing.

It is no longer true that babies are held upside down and slapped on the buttocks to stimulate independent breathing, even though we often see this in old movies. To assist independent breathing, mucus is suctioned from the baby's nose and mouth when the head emerges from the birth canal.

birth, although many or most women admit that they appreciate having the experience "muted."

4-2a ANESTHESIA

Although painful childbirth has historically been seen as the standard for women, today, at least some anesthesia is used in most American deliveries. Two types of **anesthetics** are used to lessen the pain associated with childbirth. **General anesthesia** achieves its anesthetic effect by putting the woman to sleep by means of an injected barbiturate. Tranquilizers and narcotics can be used to reduce anxiety and the perception of pain without causing sleep. General anesthesia reduces the responsiveness of the baby shortly after birth, but there is mixed evidence as to whether there are long-term negative effects (Eger et al., 2014).

Regional or **local anesthetics** deaden pain without putting the mother to sleep. With a *pudendal block*, the mother's external genitals are numbed by local injection. With an *epidural block* and a *spinal block*, anesthesia is injected into the spinal canal or spinal cord, temporarily numbing the body below the waist. Local anesthesia may have minor depressive effects on **neonates** shortly after birth, but the effects have not been shown to linger (Torpy et al., 2011).

In so-called **natural childbirth**, a woman uses no anesthesia. Instead, she is educated about the biological aspects of reproduction and delivery, encouraged to maintain physical fitness, and taught relaxation and breathing exercises.

4-2b HYPNOSIS AND BIOFEEDBACK

Hypnosis has been used to help clients stick to diets, quit smoking, and undergo dental treatments with less discomfort. It has also been used with some success as an alternative to anesthesia during childbirth (Camann, 2014; Landolt & Milling, 2011).

Biofeedback is a method that provides the woman in labor with continuous information as to what is

An epidural anesthesia kit. An *epidural block* permits the woman to stay awake but feel no sensation in the pelvis or below.

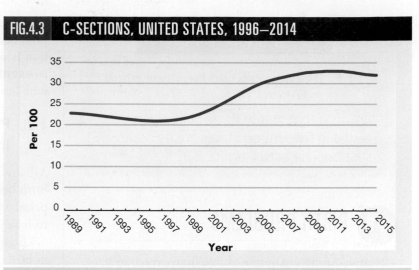

Source: U.S. National Center for Health Statistics (page last updated February 25, 2014). http://www.cdc.gov/nchs/fastats /delivery.htm. (Accessed September 16, 2014).

FIG.4.3   C-SECTIONS, UNITED STATES, 1996–2014

Since 1996, the percentage of American women undergoing C-sections mushroomed from 21% to 33% and appears to have leveled off at 32%–33%.

happening with various bodily functions. Muscle tension and blood pressure are among the functions that can be targeted. Studies suggest that helping women relax muscle tension may have some positive effects early during labor, but greater benefits have not so far been established (Loayza et al., 2011).

4-2c PREPARED CHILDBIRTH

In the **Lamaze method**, or prepared childbirth, women engage in breathing and relaxation exercises that lessen fear and pain and distract them from discomfort. The mother-to-be attends Lamaze classes with a "coach"—most often, her partner—who will aid her in the delivery room by doing things such as massaging her, timing the contractions, offering social support, and coaching her in patterns of breathing and relaxation. Women using the Lamaze method often report less pain and ask for less medication (Camann, 2014; Lothian, 2011).

FICTION

T (F) Women who give birth according to the Lamaze method do not experience pain.

It is not true that women who give birth according to the Lamaze method do not experience pain. However, women using the method often report less pain and ask for less medication.

4-2d CESAREAN SECTION

In a **cesarean section (C-section)**, the physician delivers the baby by surgery. The physician cuts through the mother's abdomen and uterus and physically removes the baby.

Physicians prefer C-sections to vaginal delivery when they believe that normal delivery may threaten the mother or child or may be more difficult than desired. One-third of all births (32.2%) in the United States are currently by C-section (Martin, 2013). To gain some perspective, note that C-sections accounted for only 23% of births in 1989 (see Figure 4.3). Some of the increase is due to medical advances, but some women request C-sections so they can control the time of the delivery, and some physicians perform them to prevent malpractice suits in case something goes wrong during a vaginal delivery.

C-sections are also performed when the physician wants to prevent the circulatory systems of the mother and baby from mixing, as might occur when there is (normal) bleeding during vaginal delivery. C-sections in such cases help prevent transmission of the viruses that cause genital herpes and AIDS. C-sections have been shown to reduce the risk of hypoxia (Roberts et al., 2015).

Lamaze method a childbirth method in which women are educated about childbirth, breathing patterns that lessen pain during birth, and have a coach present.

cesarean section (C-section) delivery of a baby by abdominal surgery.

4-3 BIRTH PROBLEMS

Most deliveries are unremarkable from a medical standpoint (although perhaps every delivery is most remarkable from the parents' point of view). Still, a number of problems can and do occur.

4-3a OXYGEN DEPRIVATION

Researchers use two terms to discuss oxygen deprivation: anoxia and hypoxia. **Anoxia** derives from roots meaning "without oxygen." **Hypoxia** derives from roots meaning "under" and "oxygen," the point again being that the baby does not receive enough oxygen in utero to develop properly. Prenatal oxygen deprivation can impair the development of the fetus's central nervous system, leading to cognitive problems, especially in memory and spatial relations; motor problems; and psychological disorders (Liu et al., 2011; Rennie & Rosenbloom, 2011). Prolonged cutoff of the baby's oxygen supply during delivery can also cause psychological and physical health problems, such as early-onset schizophrenia and cerebral palsy (Kotlicka-Antczak et al., 2014).

Oxygen deprivation can be caused by maternal disorders such as diabetes, by immaturity of the baby's respiratory system, and by accidents, some of which involve pressure against the umbilical cord during birth. Passage through the birth canal is tight, and the umbilical cord is usually squeezed during the process. If the squeezing is temporary, the effect is like holding one's breath for a moment and no problems are likely

anoxia absence of oxygen.

hypoxia less oxygen than required.

breech (bottom-first) presentation buttocks-first childbirth.

preterm born prior to 37 weeks of gestation.

small for gestational age descriptive of neonates who are small for their age.

to ensue. But if constriction of the umbilical cord is prolonged, problems can result. Prolonged constriction is more likely during a **breech (bottom-first) presentation**, when the baby's body may press the umbilical cord against the birth canal.

4-3b PRETERM AND LOW-BIRTH-WEIGHT INFANTS

A baby is considered premature or **preterm** when birth occurs at or before 37 weeks of gestation compared with the normal 40 weeks. A baby is considered to have a low birth weight when it weighs less than 5.5 pounds (about 2,500 grams). When a baby is low in birth weight, even though it is born at full term, it is referred to as being **small for gestational age**. Mothers who smoke, abuse drugs, or are malnourished place their babies at risk of being small for gestational age. Small-for-gestational-age babies tend to remain shorter and lighter than their age-mates and show slight delays in learning and problems in attention when compared with their age-mates (Heinonen et al., 2011). Preterm babies are more likely than small-for-gestational-age babies to achieve normal heights and weights. Prematurity is more common in the case of multiple births—even twins (Kurosawa et al., 2012; Shiozaki et al., 2014).

This newborn shows lanugo and vernix, both characteristics of prematurity.

Tracy Dominey/Science Source

RISKS ASSOCIATED WITH PREMATURITY AND LOW BIRTH WEIGHT Neonates weighing between 3.25 and 5.5 pounds are seven times more likely to die than infants of normal birth weight, whereas those weighing less than 3.3 pounds are nearly 100 times as likely to die (Save the Children, 2013; Strunk et al., 2012). By and large, the lower a child's birth weight, the more poorly he or she fares on measures of neurological development and cognitive functioning throughout the school years (Clark et al., 2013; Edwards et al., 2011).

There are also risks for motor development. One study compared 96 very low birth weight (VLBW) children with normal-term children at 6, 9, 12, and 18 months, correcting for age according to the expected date of delivery (Jeng et al., 2000). The median age at which the full-term infants began to walk was 12 months, compared with 14 months for the VLBW infants. By 18 months of age, all full-term infants were walking, compared to 89% of the VLBW infants.

SIGNS OF PREMATURITY Preterm babies are relatively thin because they have not yet formed the layer of fat that gives full-term children their round, robust appearance. They often have fine, downy hair, referred to as **lanugo**, and an oily white substance on the skin known as **vernix**. If the babies are born six weeks or more before term, their nipples will not have emerged. The testicles of boys born this early will not yet have descended into the scrotum. Boys with undescended testes at birth are at higher risk for testicular cancer later in life.

Preterm babies have immature muscles, so their sucking and breathing reflexes are weak. In addition, the walls of the tiny air sacs in their lungs may tend to stick together because the babies do not yet secrete substances that lubricate the walls of the sacs. As a result, babies born more than a month before full term may breathe irregularly or may suddenly stop breathing, evidence of **respiratory distress syndrome**. Preterm infants with respiratory distress syndrome show poorer development in cognitive, language, and motor skills over the first two years of development than full-term infants. Injecting pregnant women at risk for delivering preterm babies with corticosteroids increases the babies' chances of survival (Murphy et al., 2011).

TREATMENT OF PRETERM BABIES Because of their physical frailty, preterm infants usually remain in the hospital and are placed in **incubators**, which maintain a temperature-controlled environment and afford some protection from disease. The babies may be given oxygen, although excessive oxygen can cause permanent eye injury.

PARENTS AND PRETERM NEONATES Parents often do not treat preterm neonates as well as they treat full-term neonates. For one thing, preterm infants usually do not have the robust, appealing appearance of many full-term babies. Their cries are more high pitched and grating, and they are more irritable (Kaye & Shah, 2015; Gima et al., 2010). The demands of caring for preterm babies can be depressing to parents (Cheng et al., 2016; Welch et al., 2016). Mothers of preterm babies frequently report that they feel alienated from their babies and harbor feelings of failure, guilt, and low self-esteem (Baum et al., 2011; Vigod et al., 2011). Fear of hurting preterm babies can further discourage parents from handling them, but encouraging mothers to massage their preterm infants can help them cope with this fear (Feldman et al., 2014). Once they come home from the hospital, preterm infants remain more passive and less sociable than full-term infants (Korja et al., 2012). Preterm infants fare better when they have responsive and caring parents.

INTERVENTION PROGRAMS Preterm infants profit from early stimulation just as full-term babies do—being cuddled, rocked, talked to, and sung to; being exposed to recordings of their mothers' voices; having mobiles in view; and having live and recorded music in their environment (Nordhov et al., 2012). Other forms of stimulation include massage and "kangaroo care" (Johnston et al., 2011), in which the baby spends time each day lying skin to skin and chest to chest with a parent. By and large, stimulated preterm infants tend to gain weight more rapidly, show fewer respiratory problems, and make greater advances in motor, intellectual, and neurological development than control infants (Fucile & Gisel, 2010; Nordhov et al., 2010).

 4-4 THE POSTPARTUM PERIOD

The **postpartum period** refers to the weeks following delivery, but there is no specific limit. The "parting" from the baby is frequently a happy experience. The family's long wait is over. Concerns about pregnancy and labor are over, fingers and toes have been counted, and despite some local discomfort, the mother finds her "load" to be lightened, most literally. According to the American Psychiatric Association (2014), however, about 70% of new mothers have periods of tearfulness, sadness, and irritability, which the Association refers to as the "baby blues."

lanugo fine, downy hair on premature babies.

vernix oily white substance on the skin of premature babies.

respiratory distress syndrome weak and irregular breathing, typical of preterm babies.

incubator a heated, protective container for premature infants.

postpartum period the period immediately following childbirth.

Maternal and Child Mortality Around the World

Modern medicine has made vast strides in decreasing the rates of maternal and infant mortality, but the advances are not equally spread throughout the world. Save the Children, a nonprofit relief and development organization, tracks the likelihood that a woman will die in childbirth and that an infant will die during its first year. The likelihood of maternal and infant mortality is connected with what Save the Children terms the *Mothers' Index*, which includes factors such as the lifetime risk of maternal death during pregnancy and delivery, the under-five mortality rate for children, the years of formal schooling of mothers, economic status (as measured by national income per person), and participation of women in national government—a measure of the extent to which a society empowers women. Figure 4.4 shows the various

Belinda Images/Superstock

Why are maternal and infant mortality so low in Europe?

reasons why children die, according to a recent edition of *State of the World's Mothers* (Save the Children, 2015).

Number 1 on the *Mothers' Index* is Norway where the chances of the woman dying are about 1 in 14,900 and where only 3 infants in 1,000 die during the first five years (see Table 4.1). Women receive an average of 17 years of formal schooling (the same as in the United States), per capita income is $102,610, and 40% of national government seats are held by women (as compared to only 19% in the United States). In the United States, which ranks number 33 on the list, 1 in 1,800 women stands a lifetime risk of dying during pregnancy or childbirth, and a child has a 6.9 in 1,000 chance of dying under the age of 5. Half the countries in the world have a higher percentage

---

FIG.4.4 | WHY DO YOUNG CHILDREN DIE?

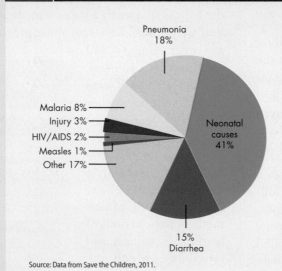

Pneumonia 18%

Malaria 8%
Injury 3%
HIV/AIDS 2%
Measles 1%
Other 17%

Neonatal causes 41%

15% Diarrhea

Source: Data from Save the Children, 2011.

Why do young children die? Estimates show that pneumonia, diarrhea, and malaria remain the leading killers of children under five worldwide. Together they account for 41% of child deaths. More than 40% of all under-five deaths occur in the first month of life. Most of these children could be saved by increasing coverage for known, affordable, and effective interventions. Ensuring proper nutrition is a critical aspect of prevention, since malnutrition contributes to more than a third of all child deaths.

of females in national government than the United States. The performance of the United States in the rankings is related to the large number of "nations within the nation." For example, there is great disparity in wealth, and richer Americans fare better in the rankings than poorer Americans. High-quality medical intervention is more available in some parts of the country than others. Many mobile Americans base their residence, in part, on the availability of good medicine.

| TABLE 4.1 | MATERNAL AND CHILD MORTALITY IN SELECTED COUNTRIES AS RELATED TO INCOME LEVEL AND EMPOWERMENT OF WOMEN |

Readers may wonder why the United States ranks so low on this list. One answer is that states with above-average poverty rates, large rural populations, and less-than-average levels of education have the highest maternal and infant mortality rates. According to a recent report by the Centers for Disease Control's National Center for Health Statistics (http://www.cdc.gov/nchs/linked.htm), African American women have the highest infant mortality rate—13.60 per 1,000 live births as compared to 4.55 per 1,000 births for Cuban American women. European American women had 5.66 infant deaths per 1,000 births, as compared with 8.45 for Native Americans, 7.82 for Puerto Ricans, 5.47 for Mexican Americans, 4.67 for Asian Americans, and 4.65 for Central and South Americans. How do you explain these ethnic differences?

Country	Lifetime risk of maternal mortality (1 in number shown)	Under-five mortality rate (per 1,000 live births)	Average years of formal schooling for women	National income per person (in U.S. dollars)	Participation of women in national government (percentage of seats held by women)	Mothers' Index Rank
Norway	14,900	2.8	17.5	102,610	39.6	1
Ireland	5,500	3.8	18.6	43,110	19.9	22
Italy	17,100	3.6	16.0	35,860	30.1	12
France	4,300	4.2	16.0	43,460	25.7	23
Germany	11,000	3.9	16.5	47,270	36.9	8
Poland	19,800	5.2	15.5	13,240	22.1	28
Japan	12,100	2.9	15.3	46,330	11.6	32
Mexico	900	14.5	13.1	9,940	37.1	53
Sweden	13,600	3.0	15.8	61,760	43.6	5
Canada	5,200	5.2	15.8	52,200	28.2	20
United Kingdom	6,900	4.6	16.2	41,680	23.5	24
United States	1,800	6.9	16.4	53,470	19.5	33
Russia	2,600	10.1	14.7	13,850	14.5	56
China	1,800	12.7	13.1	6,560	23.6	61
Cuba	970	6.2	13.8	5,890	48.9	40
Israel	17,400	4.0	16.0	33,930	22.5	18
Nigeria	31	117.4	9.0	2,710	6.6	166
India	190	52.7	11.7	1,570	12.2	140
Afghanistan	49	97.3	9.7	690	24.8	152

Source: Save the Children (2013, 2014).

4-4a POSSIBLE PSYCHOLOGICAL PROBLEMS THAT MAY AFFECT THE MOTHER

So-called "baby blues" may be considered normal in that they are by experienced by the majority of new mothers (American Psychiatric Association, 2014). Researchers believe that they are often due to hormonal changes that accompany pregnancy and follow delivery (Brummelte & Galea, 2010). They last about ten days and are generally not severe enough to impair the mother's functioning.

About one woman in seven or eight experiences depression or anxiety postpartum. **Major depression with perinatal onset** is a serious mood disorder that begins about a month after delivery and may linger for weeks or months. Major depression with perinatal onset is characterized by serious sadness, feelings of hopelessness, helplessness, and worthlessness,

major depression with perinatal onset serious maternal depression following delivery; characterized by sadness, apathy, and feelings of worthlessness.

difficulty concentrating, mood swings, and major changes in appetite (usually loss of appetite) and sleep patterns (frequently insomnia). Some women show obsessive concern with the well-being of their babies, which is also a sign of anxiety postpartum.

Many researchers suggest that major depression with perinatal onset is caused by a sudden drop in estrogen (O'Hara & McCabe, 2013). The focus is on physiological factors because of the major changes in body chemistry during and after pregnancy and because women around the world seem to experience similar disturbances in mood, even when their life experiences and support systems are radically different from those found in the United States (O'Hara & McCabe, 2013). But it should also be noted that stress can heighten symptoms of major depression with perinatal onset (Hillerer et al., 2012).

According to the American Psychiatric Association (2014), the yet more serious postpartum psychosis affects about 1 woman in 1,000. "Psychosis" may mean a break with reality. Mothers with this disorder may have delusional thoughts about the infant that place the infant at

Have We Found the Daddy Hormones?

Are oxytocin and vasopressin the "Daddy hormones"? Perhaps so, at least in prairie voles, which are a kind of tailless mouse, and sheep. These hormones are connected with the creation of mother–infant bonds in sheep, pair bonds in monogamous voles, and bonds of attachment between vole fathers and their young. Experimental research clearly shows that increasing vasopressin levels transform an indifferent male into a caring, monogamous, and protective mate and father (Keebaugh et al., 2015; Young, 2015).

Oxytocin and vasopressin are secreted by the pituitary gland, which secretes many hormones that are involved in reproduction and the nurturing of young. For example, prolactin regulates maternal behavior in lower mammals and stimulates the production of milk in women. Oxytocin stimulates labor but is also involved in social recognition and bonding. Vasopressin enables the body to conserve water by inhibiting urine production when fluid levels are low; however, it is also connected with paternal behavior patterns in some mammals. For example, male prairie voles form pair-bonds with female prairie voles after mating with them (Keebaugh et al., 2015). Mating stimulates the secretion of vasopressin, and

The hormones oxytocin and vasopressin stimulation formation of the bonds of attachment in voles. Do they play a similar role in humans?

Nature Photographers Ltd/Alamy Stock Photo

vasopressin causes the previously promiscuous male to sing "I only have eyes for you."

After learning about their effects on voles, we may wonder how oxytocin and vasopressin may be connected with the formation of bonds between men and women and between men and children. And will perfume makers soon be lacing new scents with the the hormones?

risk of injury or death. Some women experience delusions that the infant is possessed by the devil. Some women have "command hallucinations" and experience a command to kill the infant as though it is coming from the outside.

Women who experience major depression with perinatal onset usually profit from social support and counseling. Drugs that increase estrogen levels or act as antidepressants may also help.

4-4b BONDING

Bonding—that is, the formation of bonds of attachment between parents and their children—is essential to the survival and well-being of children. Since the publication of controversial research by Marshall Klaus and John Kennell in the 1970s, many have wondered whether extended parent–infant contact is required during the first hours postpartum in order to foster parent–infant bonding (Klaus & Kennell, 1978). In their study, one group

It has been debated whether extended early contact with an infant is needed for mother–infant bonding to take place. The consensus today seems to be that the bonding process is more flexible than Klaus and Kennell's 1970s research suggested.

of mothers was randomly assigned to standard hospital procedure in which their babies were whisked away to the nursery shortly after birth. Throughout the remainder of the hospital stay, the babies visited their mothers only long enough to be fed. The other babies stayed after feeding and spent a total of five hours a day with their mothers. The hospital staff encouraged and reassured the group of mothers who had extended contact. Follow-ups over two years found that mothers with extended contact were more likely than control mothers to cuddle their babies, soothe them when they cried, and interact with them. Critics note that the Klaus and Kennell studies did not separate the benefits of extended contact from benefits attributable to parents' knowledge that they were in a special group and from the extra attention of the hospital staff.

Parent–child bonding has been shown to be a complex process involving desire to have the child; parent–child familiarity with one another's sounds, odors, and tastes; and caring. On the other hand, serious maternal depression can delay bonding with newborns (Klier, 2006), but a Dutch study found that mother–infant attachment appears to be normal by the age of 14 months (Tharner et al., 2012). A history of rejection by parents can interfere with women's bonding with their own children (Brockington, 2011).

Despite the Klaus and Kennell studies, which made a brief splash in the 1970s, it is not necessary that parents have extended early contact with their newborn children for adequate bonding to occur. Many parents, for instance, adopt children at advanced ages and bond closely with them.

bonding formation of parent–infant attachment.

CHARACTERISTICS OF NEONATES

Many neonates come into the world looking a bit fuzzy, but even though they are utterly dependent on others, they are probably more aware of their surroundings than you had imagined. Neonates also make rapid adaptations to the world around them.

4-5a ASSESSING THE HEALTH OF NEONATES

The neonate's overall level of health is usually evaluated at birth according to the **Apgar scale** (see Table 4.2). Apgar scores are based on five signs of health: appearance, pulse, grimace, activity level, and respiratory effort. The neonate can receive a score of 0, 1, or 2 on each sign. The total Apgar score can therefore vary from 0 to 10. A score of 7 or above usually indicates that the baby is not in danger. A score below 4 suggests that the baby is in critical condition and requires medical attention. By one minute after birth, most normal babies attain scores of 8 to 10.

The **Brazelton Neonatal Behavioral Assessment Scale** measures neonates' reflexes and other behavior patterns. This test screens neonates for behavioral and neurological problems by assessing four areas of behavior: motor behavior, response to stress, adaptive behavior, and control over physiological state.

4-5b REFLEXES

Reflexes are simple, automatic, stereotypical responses that are elicited by certain types of stimulation. They occur without thinking. Reflexes are the most complicated motor activities displayed by neonates. Of these reflexes, most are exhibited by neonates very shortly after birth, disappear within a few months, and—if the behaviors still serve a purpose—are replaced by corresponding voluntary actions.

Pediatricians learn about a neonate's neural functioning by testing its reflexes. The absence or weakness of a reflex may indicate immaturity (as in prematurity), slowed responsiveness (which can result from anesthetics used during childbirth), brain injury, or retardation.

The rooting and sucking reflexes are basic to survival. In the **rooting reflex**, the baby turns the head and mouth toward a stimulus that strokes the cheek, chin, or corner of the mouth. The rooting reflex facilitates finding the mother's nipple in preparation for sucking. Babies will suck almost any object that touches their lips. The sucking reflex grows stronger during the first days after birth and can be lost if not stimulated. As the months go on, reflexive sucking becomes replaced by voluntary sucking.

In the startle or **Moro reflex**, the back arches and the legs and arms are flung out and then brought back toward the chest, with the arms in a hugging motion. The Moro reflex occurs when a baby's position is suddenly changed or when support for the head and neck is suddenly lost. It can also be elicited by loud noises, bumping the baby's crib, or jerking the baby's blanket. The Moro reflex is usually lost within six to seven months after birth. Absence of the Moro reflex can indicate immaturity or brain damage.

The Rooting Reflex
Cathy Melloan Resources / PhotoEdit

Apgar scale a measure of a newborn's health that assesses appearance, pulse, grimace, activity level, and respiratory effort.

Brazelton Neonatal Behavioral Assessment Scale a measure of a newborn's motor behavior, response to stress, adaptive behavior, and control over physiological state.

reflex an unlearned, stereotypical response to a stimulus.

rooting reflex turning the mouth and head toward stroking of the cheek or the corner of the mouth.

Moro reflex arching the back, flinging out the arms and legs, and drawing them back to the chest in response to a sudden noise or change in position.

TABLE 4.2 THE APGAR SCALE			
Points	**0**	**1**	**2**
Appearance: Color	Blue, pale	Body pink, extremities blue	Entirely pink
Pulse: Heart rate	Absent (not detectable)	Slow—below 100 beats/minute	Rapid—100–140 beats/minute
Grimace: Reflex irritability	No response	Grimace	Crying, coughing, sneezing
Activity level: Muscle tone	Completely flaccid, limp	Weak, inactive	Flexed arms and legs; resists extension
Respiratory effort: Breathing	Absent (infant is apneic)	Shallow, irregular, slow	Regular breathing; lusty crying

The Moro Reflex

ASTIER / BSIP/ Superstock

The Grasping Reflex

Petit Format/Science Source

The Stepping Reflex

Picture Partners / Science Source

The Tonic-Neck Reflex

Edward Hattersley / Alamy Stock Photo

During the first few weeks following birth, babies show an increasing tendency to reflexively grasp fingers or other objects pressed against the palms of their hands. In this **grasping reflex**, or palmar reflex, they use four fingers only (the thumbs are not included). Absence of the grasping reflex may indicate depressed activity of the nervous system, which can stem from use of anesthetics during childbirth. The grasping reflex is usually lost within three to four months of age, and babies generally show voluntary grasping within five to six months.

Within one or two days after birth, babies show a reflex that mimics walking. When held under the arms and tilted forward so that the feet press against a solid surface, a baby will show a **stepping reflex** in which the feet advance one after the other. A full-term baby "walks" heel to toe, whereas a preterm infant is more likely to remain on tiptoe. The stepping reflex usually disappears by about three or four months of age.

In the **Babinski reflex**, the neonate fans or spreads the toes in response to stroking of the underside of the foot from heel to toes. The Babinski reflex normally disappears toward the end of the first year, to be replaced by curling downward of the toes.

The **tonic-neck reflex** is observed when the baby is lying on its back and turns its head to one side. The arm and leg on that side extend, while the limbs on the opposite side flex.

Some reflexes, such as breathing regularly and blinking the eye in response to a puff of air, remain with us for life. Others, such as the sucking and grasping reflexes, are gradually replaced after a number of months by voluntary sucking and grasping. Still others, such as the Moro and Babinski reflexes, disappear, indicating that the nervous system is maturing on schedule.

4-5c SENSORY CAPABILITIES

In 1890, William James, a founder of modern psychology, wrote that the neonate must sense the world "as one great blooming, buzzing confusion." The neonate emerges from being literally suspended in a temperature-controlled environment to being—again, in James's words—"assailed by eyes, ears, nose, skin, and entrails at once." We now describe the sensory capabilities of neonates, and we see that James, for all his eloquence, exaggerated their disorganization.

VISION Neonates can see, but they are nearsighted. They can best see objects that are about seven to nine inches from their eyes (Braddick & Atkinson, 2011). They also do not have the peripheral vision of older children. Neonates can visually detect movement, and many neonates can visually follow, or track, movement the first day after birth. In fact, they appear to prefer (i.e., they spend more time looking at) moving objects to stationary objects (Arterberry & Kellman, 2016).

Visual accommodation refers to the self-adjustments made by the eye's lens to bring objects into focus. Neonates show little or no visual accommodation; rather; they see as through a

Design Pics/Leah Warkentin

grasping reflex grasping objects that touch the palms.

stepping reflex taking steps when held under the arms and leaned forward so the feet press the ground.

Babinski reflex fanning the toes when the soles of the feet are stroked.

tonic-neck reflex turning the head to one side, extending the arm and leg on that side, and flexing the limbs on the opposite side.

visual accommodation automatic adjustments of the lenses to focus on objects.

fixed-focus camera. As noted above, objects placed about seven to nine inches away are in clearest focus for most neonates, but visual accommodation improves dramatically during a baby's first two months (Arterberry & Kellman, 2016).

Neonates do not have the muscle control to converge their eyes on an object that is close to them. For this reason, one eye may be staring off to the side while the other fixates on an object straight ahead. **Convergence** does not occur until seven or eight weeks of age for nearby objects (Arterberry & Kellman, 2016).

The degree to which neonates perceive color remains an open question. By four months, however, infants can see most of, if not all, the colors of the visible spectrum (Kimura et al., 2010).

Even at birth, babies do not just passively respond to visual stimuli. Babies placed in absolute darkness open their eyes wide and search around (Braddick & Atkinson, 2011).

HEARING Fetuses respond to sound months before they are born. Although the auditory pathways in the brain are not fully developed prior to birth, fetuses' middle and inner ears normally reach their mature shapes and sizes before birth. Normal neonates hear well unless their middle ears are clogged with amniotic fluid (Zhiqi et al., 2010). Most neonates turn their heads toward unusual sounds, such as the shaking of a rattle.

Neonates have the capacity to respond to sounds of different **amplitude** and **pitch**. They are more likely to respond to high-pitched sounds than to low-pitched sounds (Homae et al., 2011). By contrast, speaking or singing to infants softly, in a relatively low-pitched voice, can have a soothing effect (Conrad et al., 2011; Arterberry & Kellman, 2016).

The sense of hearing may play a role in the formation of affectional bonds between neonates and mothers that goes well beyond the soothing potential of the mothers' voices. Neonates prefer their mothers' voices to those of other women, but they do not show similar preferences for the voices of their fathers (DeCasper & Prescott, 1984; Freeman et al., 1993). This preference may reflect prenatal exposure to sounds produced by their mothers.

> Neonates prefer their mothers' voices to those of other women, but they do not show similar preferences for the voices of their fathers.

Neonates are particularly responsive to the sounds and rhythms of speech, although they do not show preferences for specific languages. Neonates can discriminate different speech sounds, and they can discriminate new sounds of speech from those they have heard before (Gervain et al., 2011).

SMELL: THE NOSE KNOWS–EARLY Neonates can discriminate distinct odors, such as those of onions and licorice. They show more rapid breathing patterns and increased bodily movement in response to powerful odors. They also turn away from unpleasant odors, such as ammonia and vinegar, as early as the first day after birth (Werner & Bernstein, 2001). The nasal preferences of neonates are similar to those of older children and adults (Werner & Bernstein, 2001).

The sense of smell, like hearing, may provide a vehicle for mother–infant recognition and attachment (Lee et al., 2011). Neonates may be sensitive to the smell of milk because, when held by the mother, they tend to turn toward her nipple before they have had a chance to see or touch it. In one experiment, Macfarlane (1975, 1977) placed nursing pads above and to the sides of neonates' heads. One pad had absorbed milk from the mother, the other was clean. Neonates less than one week old spent more time turning to look at their mothers' pads than at the new pads.

Breast-fed 15-day-old infants also prefer their mother's underarm odor to odors produced by other milk-producing women and by other women. Bottle-fed infants do not show this preference (Cernoch & Porter, 1985; Porter et al., 1992). Underarm odor, along with odors from breast secretions, might contribute to the early development of recognition and attachment.

TASTE Neonates are sensitive to different tastes, and their preferences, as suggested by their facial expressions in response to various fluids, are like those of adults (Beauchamp & Mennella, 2011). Neonates swallow without showing any facial expression suggestive of a positive or negative response when distilled water is placed on their tongues. Sweet solutions are met with smiles, licking, and eager sucking, as in Figure 4.5a (Rosenstein & Oster, 1988). Neonates discriminate among solutions with salty, sour, and bitter tastes, as suggested by reactions in the lower part of the face (Rosenstein & Oster, 1988). Sour fluids elicit pursing of the lips, nose wrinkling, and eye blinking (see Figure 4.5b). Bitter solutions stimulate spitting, gagging, and sticking out the tongue (see Figure 4.5c).

convergence inward movement of the eyes to focus on an object that is drawing nearer.

amplitude loudness (of sound waves).

pitch highness or lowness (of a sound), as determined by the frequency of sound waves.

Courtesy of Rosenstein, D. S. and Oster, H. (1988)

Neonates are sensitive to different tastes, as shown by their facial expressions when tasting (a) sweet, (b) sour, and (c) bitter solutions.

Sweet solutions have a calming effect on neonates (Fernandes et al., 2011). One study found that sweeter solutions increase the heart rate, suggesting heightened arousal, but also slow down the rate of sucking (Crook & Lipsitt, 1976). Researchers interpret this finding to suggest an effort to savor the sweeter solution, to make the flavor last.

TOUCH The sense of touch is an extremely important avenue of learning and communication for babies. Not only do the skin senses provide information about the external world, but the sensations of skin against skin

Ariel Skelley/Blend Images/Jupiter Images

The sensations of skin against skin appear to provide feelings of comfort and security that contribute to the formation of bonds of attachment between infants and their caregivers.

also appear to provide feelings of comfort and security that may be major factors in the formation of bonds of attachment between infants and their caregivers. Many reflexes—including the rooting, sucking, Babinski, and grasping reflexes, to name a few—are activated by pressure against the skin.

4-5d LEARNING: REALLY EARLY CHILDHOOD "EDUCATION"

The somewhat limited sensory capabilities of neonates suggest that they may not learn as rapidly as older children do. After all, we must sense clearly those things we are to learn about. Neonates do, however, seem capable of conditioning.

CLASSICAL CONDITIONING OF NEONATES
In classical conditioning of neonates, involuntary responses are conditioned to new stimuli. In a typical study (Lipsitt, 2002), neonates were taught to blink in response to a tone. Blinking (the unconditioned response) was elicited by a puff of air directed toward the infant's eye (the unconditioned stimulus). A tone was sounded (the conditioned stimulus) as the puff of air was delivered. After repeated pairings, sounding the tone caused the neonate to blink (the conditioned response).

OPERANT CONDITIONING OF NEONATES
Operant conditioning, like classical conditioning, can take place in neonates. The experiment from Chapter 3 in which neonates learned to suck on a pacifier in such a

way as to activate a recording of their mothers reading *The Cat in the Hat* (DeCasper & Fifer, 1980; DeCasper & Spence, 1991) is a prime example of operant conditioning.

4-5e SLEEPING AND WAKING

As adults, we spend about one-third of our time sleeping. Neonates greatly outdo us, spending two-thirds of their time, or about 16 hours per day, in sleep. And, in one of life's basic challenges to parents, neonates do not sleep their 16 hours consecutively.

A number of different states of sleep and wakefulness have been identified in neonates and infants, as shown in Table 4.3. Although individual babies differ in the amount of time they spend in each of these states, sleep clearly predominates over wakefulness in the early days and weeks of life.

Different infants require different amounts of sleep and follow different patterns of sleep, but virtually all infants distribute their sleeping throughout the day and night through a series of naps. The typical infant has about six cycles of waking and sleeping in a 24-hour period. The longest nap typically approaches four and a half hours, and the neonate is usually awake for a little more than one hour during each cycle.

After a month or so, the infant has fewer but longer sleep periods and will usually take longer naps during the night. By the ages of about six months to one year, many infants begin to sleep through the night. Some infants start sleeping through the night earlier. A number of infants begin to sleep through the night for a week or so and then revert to their wakeful ways again for a while.

REM AND NON-REM SLEEP Sleep can be divided into **rapid-eye-movement (REM) sleep** and **non-rapid-eye-movement (non-REM) sleep** (see Figure 4.6). REM sleep is characterized by rapid eye movements that can be observed beneath closed lids. Adults who are roused during REM sleep

rapid-eye-movement (REM) sleep a sleep period when dreams are likely, as suggested by rapid eye movements.

non-rapid-eye-movement (non-REM) sleep a sleep period when dreams are unlikely.

TABLE 4.3	STATES OF SLEEP AND WAKEFULNESS IN INFANCY
State	**Comments**
Quiet sleep (non-REM)	Regular breathing, eyes closed, no movement
Active sleep (REM)	Irregular breathing, eyes closed, rapid eye movement, muscle twitches
Drowsiness	Regular or irregular breathing, eyes open or closed, little movement
Alert inactivity	Regular breathing, eyes open, looking around, little body movement
Alert activity	Irregular breathing, eyes open, active body movement
Crying	Irregular breathing, eyes open or closed, thrashing of arms and legs, crying

report that they have been dreaming about 80% of the time. Is the same true of neonates?

Note from Figure 4.6 that neonates spend about half their time sleeping in REM sleep. As they develop, the percentage of sleeping time spent in REM sleep declines. By six months or so, REM sleep accounts for only about 30% of the baby's sleep. By two to three years, REM sleep drops off to about 20%–25% (Salzarulo & Ficca, 2002). There is a dramatic falling-off in the total number of hours spent in sleep as we develop (Blumberg & Seelke, 2010).

What is the function of REM sleep in neonates? Research with humans and other animals, including kittens and rat pups, suggests that the brain requires a certain amount of stimulation for the creation of proteins

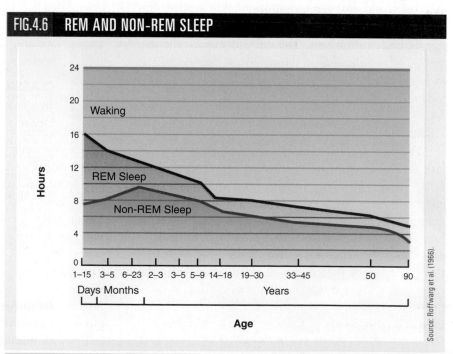

FIG. 4.6 REM AND NON-REM SLEEP

Source: Roffwarg et al. (1966).

The percentage of time spent in REM sleep declines as people age.

that are involved in the development of neurons and synapses (Blumberg & Seelke, 2010). Perhaps neonates create this stimulation by means of REM sleep, which most closely parallels the waking state in terms of brain waves. Preterm babies spend an even greater proportion of their time in REM sleep, perhaps because they need relatively more stimulation of the brain.

CRYING No discussion of the sleeping and waking states of neonates would be complete without mentioning crying, a comment that parents will view as an understatement. The main reason babies cry seems to be simple enough. Studies suggest a one-word answer: pain (Out et al., 2010). Whether crying is healthful remains an open question, but some crying among babies seems to be universal.

Before parenthood, many people wonder whether they will be able to recognize the meaning of their babies' cries, but it usually does not take them long. Parents typically learn to distinguish cries that signify hunger, anger, and pain. The pitch of an infant's cries appears to provide information (Out et al., 2010). Adults perceive high-pitched crying to be more urgent, distressing, and sick sounding than low-pitched crying (Out et al., 2010; Zeifman, 2004). A sudden, loud, insistent cry associated with flexing and kicking of the legs may indicate colic, that is, pain resulting from gas or other sources of distress in the digestive tract. Crying from colic can be severe and persistent; it may last for hours (Barr et al., 2005; Gudmundsson, 2010). Much to the relief of parents, colic tends to disappear by the third to sixth month, as a baby's digestive system matures.

Certain high-pitched cries, when prolonged, may signify health problems. The cries of chronically distressed infants differ from those of nondistressed infants in both rhythm and pitch. Patterns of crying may be indicative of chromosomal abnormalities, infections, fetal malnutrition, and exposure to narcotics (Douglas & Hill, 2011).

Peaks of crying appear to be concentrated in the late afternoon and early evening (McGlaughlin & Grayson, 2001). Although some cries may seem extreme and random at first, they tend to settle into a recognizable pattern. Infants seem to produce about the same number of crying bouts during the first nine months or so, but the duration of the bouts lessens during this period (van Ijzendoorn & Hubbard, 2000). The response of the caregiver influences crying. It turns out that the more frequently mothers ignore their infants' crying bouts in the first nine weeks, the less frequently their infants cry in the following nine-week period (van Ijzendoorn & Hubbard, 2000). This finding should certainly not be interpreted to mean that infant crying is best ignored. At least at first, crying communicates pain and hunger, and these are conditions that it is advisable to correct. Persistent crying can strain the mother–infant relationship (Out et al., 2010).

SOOTHING Sucking seems to be a built-in tranquilizer. Sucking on a **pacifier** decreases crying and agitated movement in hungry neonates (Field, 1999; Shubert et al., 2016). Therefore, the soothing function of sucking need not be learned through experience. Sucking (drinking) a sweet solution also appears to have a soothing effect (Stevens et al., 2005).

Parents soothe infants by picking them up, patting them, caressing and rocking them, swaddling them (wrapping them in a blanket, reminiscent of the womb), and speaking to them in a low voice. Parents then usually try to find the specific cause of the distress by offering a bottle or pacifier or checking the diaper. Parents learn by trial and error what types of embraces and movements are likely to soothe their child, and infants learn quickly that crying is followed by being picked up or other interventions. Parents sometimes worry that if they pick up a crying baby quickly, they are reinforcing the baby for crying. In this way, they believe, the child may become spoiled and find it progressively more difficult to engage in self-soothing to get to sleep.

Fortunately, as infants mature and learn, crying tends to become replaced by less upsetting verbal requests for intervention. Among adults, of course, soothing techniques take very different forms—such as admission that one started the argument.

4-5f SUDDEN INFANT DEATH SYNDROME (SIDS)

It is true that more children die from **sudden infant death syndrome (SIDS)** than die from cancer, heart disease, pneumonia, child abuse, AIDS, cystic fibrosis, and muscular dystrophy combined (Lipsitt, 2003). SIDS—also known as crib death—is a disorder of infancy that apparently strikes while a baby is sleeping. In the typical case, a baby goes to sleep, apparently in perfect health, and is found dead the next morning. There is no sign that the baby struggled or was in pain.

SIDS is more common among the following: babies aged two to five months, babies who are put to sleep on their stomachs or their sides (sleeping prone decreases the oxygen supply to the brain),

pacifier a device such as an artificial nipple or teething ring that soothes babies when sucked.

sudden infant death syndrome (SIDS) the death, while sleeping, of apparently healthy babies who stop breathing.

premature and low-birth-weight infants, male babies, babies in families of lower socioeconomic status, bottle-fed babies, African American babies, babies of teenage mothers, babies whose mothers smoked during or after pregnancy or whose mothers used narcotics during pregnancy, babies of low birth weight, and babies who have respiratory infections.

The incidence of SIDS has been declining, in part because some cases of SIDS have been reattributed to accidental suffocation. Even so, some 2,000–3,000 infants in the United States still die each year of SIDS. It is the most common cause of death during the first year, and most of these deaths occur between two and five months of age (Käll & Lagercrantz, 2012). New parents frequently live in dread of SIDS and check regularly through the night to see if their babies are breathing. It is not abnormal, by the way, for babies occasionally to suspend breathing for a moment.

TRUTH

(T) F   More children in the United States die from sudden infant death syndrome (SIDS) than from cancer, heart disease, pneumonia, child abuse, AIDS, cystic fibrosis, and muscular dystrophy combined.

It is true that in the United States, more children die from sudden infant death syndrome (SIDS) than from all these other causes combined.

THE CHILDREN'S HOSPITAL BOSTON STUDY

Perhaps the most compelling study to date about the causes of SIDS was led by health professionals at the Children's Hospital Boston (Paterson et al., 2006). The study focused on an area in the brain stem called the **medulla**, which is involved in basic functions such as breathing and sleep-wake cycles. The medulla causes us to breathe if we are in need of oxygen. Researchers compared the medullas of babies who had died from SIDS with those of babies who had died at the same ages from other causes. They found that the medullas of the babies who died from SIDS were less sensitive to the brain chemical *serotonin*, a chemical that helps keep the medulla responsive. The problem was particularly striking in the brains of the boys, which could account for the sex difference in the incidence of SIDS.

medulla   a part of the brain stem that regulates vital and automatic functions such as breathing and the sleep-wake cycle.

What should you do about SIDS? Following are some suggestions from the American Academy of Pediatrics (2012):

▶ Place your baby to sleep on her back for every sleep.

▶ Place your baby to sleep on a firm sleep surface. To learn more about crib safety, visit the Consumer Product Safety Commission Web site at www.cpsc.gov.

▶ Keep soft objects, loose bedding, or any objects that could increase the risk of entrapment, suffocation, or strangulation out of the crib.

▶ Place your baby to sleep in the same room where you sleep but not the same bed.

▶ Breast-feed as much and for as long as you can.

▶ Schedule and go to all well-child visits.

▶ Keep your baby away from smokers and places where people smoke.

▶ Do not let your baby get too hot.

▶ Offer a pacifier at nap time and bedtime.

▶ Do not use home cardiorespiratory monitors to help reduce the risk of SIDS.

▶ Do not use products that claim to reduce the risk of SIDS.

Perhaps within a few years we will have a screening test for SIDS and a method for preventing or controlling it. In the next chapter, we continue to follow physical development over the first two years.

STUDY TOOLS 4

READY TO STUDY?

In the book, you can:

☐ Check your understanding of what you've read with the quizzes below.

☐ Rip out the chapter review card at the back of the book to have a summary of the chapter and the key terms handy.

ONLINE AT CENGAGEBRAIN.COM YOU CAN:

☐ View a prenatal assessment and ultrasound in a short video.

☐ Prepare for tests with quizzes.

☐ Review the key terms with Flash Cards.

☐ Play games to master concepts.

SELF-ASSESSMENT

Fill-Ins

Answers can be found in the back of the book.

1. False labor contractions are technically called _____-_____ contractions.

2. In a(n) _____ block, anesthesia is injected into the spinal canal.

3. One sign of prematurity is _____, an oily white substance on the skin.

4. The continent with the lowest risk of maternal mortality is _____.

5. Major depression with perinatal onset is most likely related to changes in _____.

6. Klaus and Kennell argued that extensive early contact is necessary to promote _____.

7. The health of neonates is assessed using the five-point _____ scale.

8. In the _____ reflex, the baby turns the head and mouth toward a stimulus that strokes the cheek, chin, or corner of the mouth.

9. Fifteen-day-old breast-fed infants prefer their mothers' _____ odor to those of other women.

10. The least common kind of maternal depression after delivery is _____ _____.

Multiple Choice

1. **What percentage of American deliveries is by C-section?**
   a. 11%
   c. 32%
   b. 22%
   d. 44%

2. **Injecting pregnant women at risk for delivering premature babies with _____ increases the babies' chances of survival.**
   a. corticosteroids
   c. tetracycline
   b. gamma globulin
   d. saline solution

3. **The risk of maternal mortality during childbirth is highest in**
   a. China.
   c. Cuba.
   b. Egypt.
   d. Afghanistan.

4. **How many new mothers are likely to experience the "baby blues"?**
   a. 2 in 10
   c. 7 in 10
   b. 4 in 10
   d. 9 in 10

5. **In which of the following reflexes does the neonate fan its toes in response to stroking the underside of the foot?**
   a. stepping
   c. Babinski
   b. Moro
   d. tonic neck

6. **Neonates show**
   a. visual accommodation.
   b. nearsightedness.
   c. preference for the color blue.
   d. convergence of the eyes.

7. **Neonates show preference for**
   a. their mothers' voices.
   c. dogs' barks.
   b. their fathers' voices.
   d. music.

8. **According to the text, neonates have a taste preference for _____ solutions.**
   a. sour
   c. sweet
   b. salty
   d. bitter

9. **Neonates spend about _____ hours a day sleeping.**
   a. 6
   c. 12
   b. 8
   d. 16

10. **SIDS is more common among**
   a. female babies.
   b. babies who are put to sleep on their stomachs.
   c. babies of mothers in their 20s.
   d. European American babies.

5 | Infancy: Physical Development

Spencer Rathus

LEARNING OUTCOMES

After studying this chapter, you will be able to…

5-1 Describe trends in the physical development of the infant

5-2 Describe the physical development of the brain and the nervous system

5-3 Describe the key events in the motor development of the infant

5-4 Describe patterns of sensory and perceptual development in infancy

After you finish this chapter, go to **PAGE 90** for **STUDY TOOLS**

What a fascinating creature the newborn is: tiny, delicate, apparently oblivious to its surroundings, yet perfectly formed and fully capable of letting its caregivers know when it is hungry, thirsty, or uncomfortable. And what a fascinating creature is this same child two years later: running, playing, talking, hugging, and kissing.

> It is hard to believe that only two short years—the years of infancy—bring about so many changes.

It is hard to believe that only two short years—the years of infancy—bring about so many changes. It seems that nearly every day brings a new accomplishment. But as we will see, not all infants share equally in the explosion of positive developments. Therefore, we will also enumerate some developmental problems and what can be done about them.

5-1 PHYSICAL GROWTH AND DEVELOPMENT

During the first two years, children make enormous strides in physical growth and development. In this section, we explore sequences of physical development, changes in height and weight, and nutrition. As we see next, development is "head first."

iStockphoto.com/lostinbids

5-1a SEQUENCES OF PHYSICAL DEVELOPMENT

Three key sequences of physical development are cephalocaudal development, proximodistal development, and differentiation.

CEPHALOCAUDAL DEVELOPMENT Development proceeds from the upper part of the head to the lower parts of the body. When we consider the central role of the brain, which is contained within the skull, the cephalocaudal sequence appears quite logical. The brain regulates essential functions, such as heartbeat. Through the secretion of hormones, the brain also regulates the growth and development of the body and influences basic drives, such as hunger and thirst.

The head develops more rapidly than the rest of the body during the embryonic stage. By eight weeks after conception, the head constitutes half the entire length of the embryo. The brain develops more rapidly than the spinal cord. Arm buds form before leg buds. Most newborn babies have a strong, well-defined sucking reflex, although their legs are spindly and their limbs move back and forth only in diffuse excitement or agitation. Infants can hold up their heads before they gain control over their arms, their torsos, and, finally, their legs. They can sit up before they can crawl and walk.

The lower parts of the body, because they get off to a later start, must do more growing to reach adult size. The head doubles in length between birth and maturity, but the torso, arms, and legs increase in length by three, four, and five times, respectively.

PROXIMODISTAL DEVELOPMENT Growth and development also proceed from the trunk outward, from the body's central axis toward the periphery.

TRUTH OR FICTION?

T	F	The head of the newborn child doubles in length by adulthood, but the legs increase in length by about five times.
T	F	Infants triple their birth weight within a year.
T	F	A newborn's brain weights about 25% of its adult weight, but grows to some 70% of its adult weight by the child's first birthday.
T	F	The cerebral cortex—the outer layer of the brain that is vital to human thought and reasoning—is only one-eighth of an inch thick.
T	F	Native American Hopi infants spend the first year of life strapped to a board, yet they begin to walk at about the same time as children who are reared in other cultures.

The proximodistal principle, too, makes sense. The brain and spinal cord follow a central axis down through the body, and it is essential that the nerves be in place before infants can gain control over their arms and legs. Consider also that the life functions of the newborn baby—heartbeat, respiration, digestion, and elimination of wastes—are all carried out by organ systems close to the central axis. These functions must be in operation or ready to operate when the child is born.

1 Head

0.63 in

0.63 in

0.63 in

0.63 in

0.63 in

4 Heads = 1 Leg

3 Heads = 1 Arm

0.63 in   0.63 in   0.63 in   0.63 in

As we develop our body proportions change.

Photolink/Getty Images

5-1b GROWTH PATTERNS IN HEIGHT AND WEIGHT

The most dramatic gains in height and weight occur during prenatal development. Within a span of nine months, children develop from a zygote about 1/175th of an inch long to a neonate about 20 inches in length. Weight increases by billions.

During the first year after birth, gains in height and weight are also dramatic, although not by the standards of prenatal gains. Infants usually double their birth weight in about five months and triple it by the first birthday (World Health Organization, 2010a, 2010b). Their height increases by about 50% in the first year, so that a child whose length at birth was 20 inches is likely to be about 30 inches tall at 12 months.

TRUTH

(T) F   The head of the newborn child doubles in length by adulthood, but the legs increase in length by about five times.

It is true that the head of the newborn child doubles in length by adulthood, and the legs increase in length by about five times. The torso also increases by about three times and the arms by four times.

In terms of motor development, infants gain control over their trunks and their shoulders before they can control their arms, hands, and fingers. Similarly, infants gain control over their hips and upper legs before they can direct their lower legs, feet, and toes.

DIFFERENTIATION As children mature, their behaviors become less loose and global, and more specific and distinct, a tendency called **differentiation**. If a neonate's finger is pricked or burned, he or she may withdraw the finger but also thrash about, cry, and show general signs of distress. Toddlers may also cry, show distress, and withdraw the finger, but they are less likely to thrash about wildly. Thus, the response to pain has become more specific. An older child or adult is also likely to withdraw the finger, but less likely to wail (sometimes) and show general distress.

differentiation the processes by which behaviors and physical structures become specialized.

TRUTH

(T) F   Infants triple their birth weight within a year.

It is true that infants triple their birth weight within a year. They usually double their birth weight in only five months.

Growth in infancy has long been viewed as a slow and steady process. Growth charts in pediatricians' offices resemble the smooth, continuous curves shown in Figure 5.1, but research suggests that infants actually grow in spurts. About 90%–95% of the time, they are not growing at all. One study measured the height of infants throughout their first 21 months (Lampl et al., 1992). The researchers found that the infants would remain the same size for 2 to 63 days and then would shoot up in length from one-fifth of an inch (0.5 centimeter) to a full inch (2.5 centimeters) in less than 24 hours.

Infants grow another four to six inches during the second year and gain another four to seven pounds. Boys generally reach half their adult height by their second birthday. Girls, however, mature more quickly than boys and are likely to reach half their adult height at the age of 18 months (World Health Organization, 2010a, 2010b). The growth rates of taller-than-average infants, as a group, tend to slow down. Those of shorter-than-average infants,

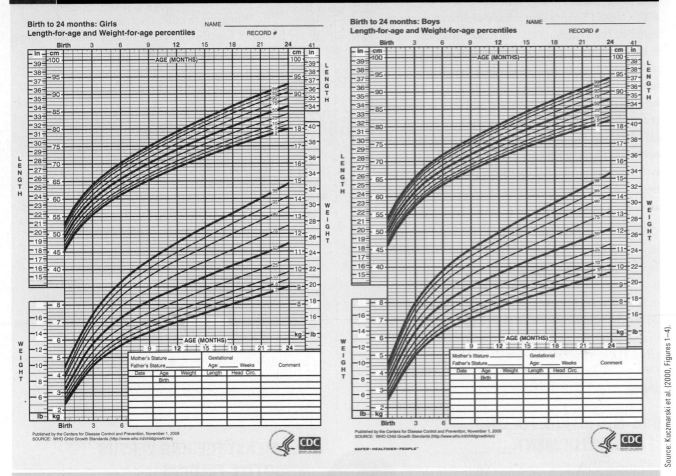

Birth to 24 months: Girls
Length-for-age and Weight-for-age percentiles

Birth to 24 months: Boys
Length-for-age and Weight-for-age percentiles

The curves indicate the percentiles for weight and length at different ages. Lines labeled 97th show the height and weight of children who are taller and heavier than 97% of children of a particular age. Lines marked 50th indicate the height and weight of the average child of a given age.

Source: Kuczmarski et al. (2000, Figures 1–4).

as a group, tend to speed up. I am not suggesting that there is no relationship between infant and adult heights or that we all wind up in an average range. Tall infants, as a group, wind up taller than short infants, but in most cases not by as much as seemed likely during infancy.

CHANGES IN BODY PROPORTIONS As mentioned earlier, development proceeds in a cephalocaudal manner. A few weeks after conception, an embryo is almost all head. At the beginning of the fetal stage, the head is about half the length of the unborn child. In the neonate, it is about one-fourth the length of the body. The head gradually diminishes in proportion to the rest of the body, even though it doubles in size by adulthood.

Typically, an adult's arms are nearly three times the length of the head. The legs are about four times as long. Among neonates, the arms and legs are about equal in length. Each is only about 1½ times the length of the head. By the first birthday, the neck has begun to lengthen, as have the arms and legs. The arms grow more rapidly than the legs at first; by the second birthday, the arms are actually longer than the legs, but soon the legs catch up with and surpass the arms in length.

FAILURE TO THRIVE Haley is four months old. Her mother, as she puts it, is breast-feeding Haley "all the time" because she is not gaining weight. Not gaining weight for a while is normal, but Haley is also irritable and feeds fitfully, sometimes refusing the breast entirely. Her pediatrician is evaluating her for a syndrome called **failure to thrive (FTT)**.

FTT is a serious disorder that impairs growth in infancy and early childhood. Yet FTT is sometimes a fuzzy diagnosis. Historically, researchers have spoken of biologically based (or "organic") FTT versus nonbiologically based

failure to thrive (FTT) a disorder of infancy and early childhood characterized by variable eating and inadequate gains in weight.

("nonorganic") FTT. The idea is that in organic FTT, an underlying health problem accounts for FTT. Nonorganic FTT (NOFTT) apparently has psychological roots, social roots, or both (Jaffe, 2011). In either case, the infant does not make normal gains in weight and size.

Regardless of the cause or causes, feeding problems are central. As in Haley's case, infants are more likely to be described as variable eaters and less often as hungry (Llewellyn, 2011). FTT is linked not only to slow physical growth but also to cognitive, behavioral, and emotional problems (Jaffe, 2011). One study found that children who had been diagnosed with FTT in infancy were smaller, less cognitively advanced, and more emotionally disturbed than normal children at the age of 8½ (Dykman et al., 2001).

CATCH-UP GROWTH A child's growth can be slowed from its genetically predetermined course by many organic factors, including illness and malnutrition. If the problem is alleviated, the child's rate of growth frequently accelerates to approximate its normal course (Parsons et al., 2011). The tendency to return to one's genetically determined pattern of growth is referred to as **canalization**. Once Haley's parents receive counseling and once Haley's FTT is overcome, Haley will put on weight rapidly and almost catch up to the norms for her age.

5-1c NUTRITION: FUELING DEVELOPMENT

The nutritional status of most children in the United States is good compared with that of children in developing countries (Save the Children, 2013). However, infants and young children from low-income families are more likely than other children to display signs of poor nutrition, such as anemia (a reduced number of red blood cells, causing paleness and weakness) and FTT (Save the Children, 2013).

From birth, infants should be fed either breast milk or an iron-fortified infant formula. The introduction of solid foods is not recommended until about four to six months of age, although the American Academy of Pediatrics recommends that infants be fed breast milk throughout the first year and longer if possible

canalization the tendency of growth rates to return to normal after undergoing environmentally induced change.

(Meek, 2011). The first solid food is usually iron-enriched cereal, followed by strained fruits, vegetables, meats, poultry, and fish. Whole cow's milk is normally delayed until the infant is 9 to 12 months old. Finger foods such as teething biscuits are introduced in the latter part of the first year.

Here are some guidelines for infant nutrition (U.S. Department of Agriculture, 2011):

▶ Build up to a variety of foods. Introduce new foods one at a time. The infant may be allergic to a new food, and introducing foods one at a time helps isolate their possible effects.

▶ Pay attention to the infant's appetite to help avoid overfeeding or underfeeding.

▶ Do not restrict fat and cholesterol too much. Infants need calories and some fat.

▶ Do not overdo high-fiber foods.

▶ Generally avoid items with added sugar and salt.

▶ Encourage eating of high-iron foods; infants need more iron, pound for pound, than adults do.

Parents who are on low-fat, high-fiber diets to ward off cardiovascular problems, cancer, and other health problems should not assume that the same diet is healthful for infants.

5-1d BREAST-FEEDING VERSUS BOTTLE-FEEDING

In many developing nations, mothers have to breast-feed. Even in developed nations, where formula is readily available, breast milk is considered by most health professionals to be the "medical gold standard" (Karasahin, K. E., 2016). Over the past few decades, breast-feeding has become more popular, largely because of increased knowledge of its health benefits (U.S. Department of Health and Human Services, 2010). Today, most American mothers—more than 70%—breast-feed their children for at least a while, but only about two women in five continue to breast-feed after six months, and only one in five is still breast-feeding after one year (Centers for Disease Control and Prevention, 2010a).

Many women bottle-feed because they return to work after childbirth and are unavailable to breast-feed. Their partners, extended families, nannies,

Breast-feeding is considered to be the gold standard for mothers in the United States and Canada today. What are the advantages of breast-feeding? Are their circumstances under which women might choose not to breast-feed their children?

RooM the Agency / Alamy Stock Photo

or child-care workers give their children bottles during the day. Some mothers pump their milk and bottle it for use when they are away. Some parents bottle-feed because it permits both parents to share in feeding.

Breast-feeding also has health benefits for the mother: It reduces the risk of early breast cancer and ovarian cancer, and it builds the strength of bones, which can reduce the likelihood of hip fractures that result from osteoporosis following menopause. Breast-feeding also helps shrink the uterus after delivery.

There are downsides to breast-feeding. For example, breast milk is one of the bodily fluids that transmit HIV (Badiou S., et al., 2016). As many as one-third of infants born to mothers who are infected with HIV, the virus that causes AIDS, become infected during pregnancy, childbirth, or breast-feeding (Rose et al., 2014).

Alcohol, many drugs, and environmental hazards such as polychlorinated biphenyls (PCBs) can also be transmitted through breast milk. Moreover, for breast milk to contain the necessary nutrients, mothers must be adequately nourished themselves. The mother also encounters the physical demands of producing and expelling milk, a tendency for soreness in the breasts, and the inconvenience of being continually available to meet the infant's feeding needs.

5-2 DEVELOPMENT OF THE BRAIN AND NERVOUS SYSTEM

The nervous system is a system of **nerves** involved in heartbeat, visual–motor coordination, thought and language, and so on.

5-2a DEVELOPMENT OF NEURONS

The basic units of the nervous system are cells called **neurons**. Neurons receive and transmit messages from one part of the body to another. The messages account for phenomena such as reflexes, the perception of an itch from a mosquito bite, the visual–motor coordination of a skier, the composition of a concerto, and the solution of a math problem.

People are born with about 100 billion neurons, most of which are in the brain. Neurons vary according to their functions and locations in the body. Some neurons in the brain are only a fraction of an inch in length, whereas neurons in the leg can grow several feet long. Each neuron possesses a cell body, dendrites, and an axon (see Figure 5.2 on page 80). **Dendrites** are short fibers that extend from the cell body and receive incoming messages from up to 1,000 adjoining transmitting neurons. The **axon** extends trunklike from the cell body and accounts for much of the difference in length in neurons. An axon can be up to several feet in length if it is carrying messages

Alex Staroseltsev/Shutterstock.com

nerves bundles of axons from many neurons.

neurons cells in the nervous system that transmit messages.

dendrites rootlike parts of neurons that receive impulses from other neurons.

axon a long, thin part of a neuron that transmits impulses to other neurons through branching structures called axon terminals.

FIG.5.2 | ANATOMY OF A NEURON

"Messages" enter neurons through dendrites, are transmitted along the axon, and are sent through axon terminals to muscles, glands, and other neurons. Neurons develop by proliferation of dendrites and axon terminals and through myelination.

current being carried along the axon is minimized, and messages are conducted more efficiently.

The term **myelination** refers to the process by which axons are coated with myelin. Myelination is not complete at birth, but rather is part of the maturation process that leads to the abilities to crawl and walk during the first year after birth. Myelination of the brain's prefrontal matter continues into the second decade of life and is connected with advances in working memory and language ability (Burgaleta, M., et al. 2016). Breakdown of myelin is believed to be associated with Alzheimer's disease, a source of cognitive decline that begins later in life.

In the disease **multiple sclerosis**, myelin is replaced by hard, fibrous tissue that disrupts the timing of neural transmission, interfering with muscle control (Zhang et al., 2016). Phenylketonuria (PKU) causes intellectual disability by inhibiting the formation of myelin in the brain (Velumian & Samoilova, 2014).

from the toes to the spine. Messages are released from axon terminals in the form of chemicals called **neurotransmitters**. These messages are received by the dendrites of adjoining neurons, muscles, or glands. As the child matures, axons lengthen, and dendrites and axon terminals proliferate.

MYELIN Many neurons are tightly wrapped with white, fatty **myelin sheaths** that give them the appearance of a string of white sausages. The high fat content of the myelin sheath insulates the neuron from electrically charged atoms in the fluids that encase the nervous system. In this way, leakage of the electric

neurotransmitter a chemical that transmits a neural impulse across a synapse from one neuron to another.

myelin sheath a fatty, whitish substance that encases and insulates axons.

myelination the coating of axons with myelin.

multiple sclerosis a disorder in which hard fibrous tissue replaces myelin, impeding neural transmission.

5-2b DEVELOPMENT OF THE BRAIN

The brain of the neonate weighs a little less than a pound, or nearly one-fourth its adult weight. In keeping with the principles of cephalocaudal growth, an infant's brain triples in weight, reaching nearly 70% of its adult weight by the age of one year (see Figure 5.3). Let's look at the brain, as shown in Figure 5.4, and discuss the development of the structures within.

TRUTH

(T) F   A newborn's brain weights about 25% of its adult weight, but grows to some 70% of its adult weight by the child's first birthday.

It is true that a newborn's brain weighs about 25% of its adult weight, and that it mushrooms to some 70% of adult weight by the age of one year.

FIG.5.3 GROWTH OF BODY SYSTEMS AS A PERCENTAGE OF TOTAL POSTNATAL GROWTH

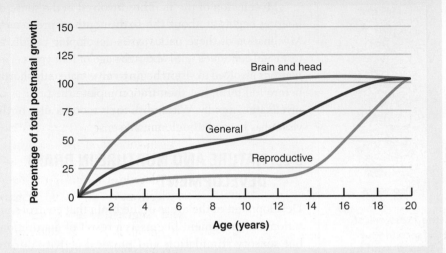

The brain will triple in weight by the infant's first birthday, reaching nearly 70% of its adult weight.

STRUCTURES OF THE BRAIN Many nerves that connect the spinal cord to higher levels of the brain pass through the **medulla**. The medulla, part of an area called the brain stem, is vital in the control of basic functions, such as heartbeat and respiration. Above the medulla lies the **cerebellum**. The cerebellum helps the child maintain balance, control

FIG.5.4 STRUCTURES OF THE BRAIN

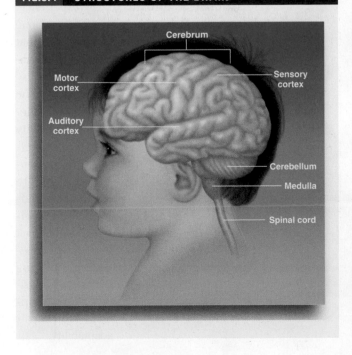

motor behavior, and coordinate eye movements with bodily sensations.

The **cerebrum** is the crowning glory of the brain. It makes possible the breadth and depth of human learning, thought, memory, and language. The surface of the cerebrum consists of two hemispheres that become increasingly wrinkled as the child develops, coming to show ridges and valleys called fissures. This surface is the cerebral cortex. The cerebral cortex is only one-eighth of an inch thick, yet it is the seat of thought and reason. It is here that we receive sensory information from the world outside and command muscles to move.

TRUTH

(T) F The cerebral cortex—the outer layer of the brain that is vital to human thought and reasoning—is only one-eighth of an inch thick.

It is true that the cerebral cortex—the outer layer of the brain that is vital to human thought and reasoning—is only one-eighth of an inch thick. (Look at a ruler and think about that for a while.)

GROWTH SPURTS OF THE BRAIN The first major growth spurt of the brain occurs during the fourth and fifth months of prenatal development, when neurons proliferate. A second growth spurt in the brain occurs between the 25th week of prenatal development and the end of the second year after birth. Whereas the first growth spurt of the brain is due to the formation of neurons, the second growth spurt is due primarily to the proliferation of dendrites and axon terminals (see Figure 5.5).

medulla an area of the lower, back part of the brain involved in heartbeat and respiration.

cerebellum the area of the lower, back part of the brain involved in coordination and balance.

cerebrum the largest, rounded part of the brain, responsible for learning, thought, memory, and language.

FIG.5.5 INCREASE IN NEURAL CONNECTIONS IN THE BRAIN

Image Source/Jupiter Images; Stockbyte/Getty Images

Neonate **Six months** **Two years**

A major growth spurt occurs between the 25th week of prenatal development and the end of the second year after birth, due primarily to the proliferation of dendrites and axon terminals.

BRAIN DEVELOPMENT IN INFANCY There is a link between what infants can do and myelination. At birth, the parts of the brain involved in heartbeat and respiration, sleeping and arousal, and reflex activity are fairly well myelinated and functional. Myelination of motor pathways allows neonates to show stereotyped reflexes, but otherwise neonates' physical activity tends to be random and ill-organized. Myelin develops rapidly along the major motor pathways from the cerebral cortex during the last month of pregnancy and continues to develop after birth) The development of intentional physical activity coincides with myelination as the unorganized movements of the neonate come under increasing control. Myelination of the nerves to muscles is largely developed by the age of two years, although myelination continues to some degree into adolescence.

Although neonates respond to touch and can see and hear quite well, the areas of the cortex that are involved in vision, hearing, and the skin senses are less well myelinated at birth. As myelination progresses and the interconnections

between the various areas of the cortex thicken, children become increasingly capable of complex and integrated sensorimotor activities (Bartzokis et al., 2010).

Myelination of the neurons involved in the sense of hearing begins at about the sixth month of pregnancy. Myelination of these pathways is developing rapidly at term and continues until about the age of four years. The neurons involved in vision begin to myelinate only shortly before full term, but then they complete the process of myelination rapidly. Within five to six months after birth, vision has become the dominant sense.

5-2c NATURE AND NURTURE IN BRAIN DEVELOPMENT

Development of the areas of the brain that control sensation and movement begins as a result of maturation, but sensory stimulation and physical activity during early infancy also spur the development of these areas (Posner et al., 2013; Walker, 2016).

Research with animals shows how sensory stimulation sparks growth of the cortex. Researchers have given rats "amusement parks" with toys such as ladders, platforms, and boxes to demonstrate the effects of enriched environments. In these studies, rats exposed to the more complex environments develop heavier brains than control animals. The weight differences in part reflect more synapses per neuron (Anderson, 2011). On the other hand, animals reared in darkness show shrinkage of the visual cortex, impaired vision, and impaired visual–motor coordination (Anderson, 2011; Talaei & Salami, 2013). If they don't use it, they lose it.

The brain is also affected by experience. Infants actually have more connections among neurons than adults do. Connections that are activated by experience survive; others do not (Awasaki & Ito, 2016).

The great adaptability of the brain appears to be a double-edged sword. Adaptability allows us to develop different patterns of neural connections to meet the demands of different environments, but lack of stimulation—especially during critical early periods of development—can impair adaptability.

BonkersAboutScience/Alamy Stock Photo

Research with animals shows how sensory stimulation sparks growth of the cortex.

5-3 MOTOR DEVELOPMENT

Motor development involves the activity of muscles, leading to changes in posture, movement, and coordination of movement with the infant's developing sensory apparatus. Motor development provides some of the most fascinating changes in infants, because so much happens so fast.

Like physical development, motor development follows cephalocaudal and proximodistal patterns and differentiation. Infants gain control of their heads and upper torsos before they can effectively use their arms. This trend illustrates cephalocaudal development. Infants also can control their trunks and shoulders before they can use their hands and fingers, demonstrating the proximodistal trend.

Grasping is reflexive in newborns. By a year, infants can pick up tiny objects.

5-3a LIFTING AND HOLDING THE TORSO AND HEAD

Neonates can move their heads slightly to the side. They can thus avoid suffocation if they are lying face down and their noses or mouths are obstructed by bedding. At about one month, infants can raise their heads. By about two months, they can also lift their chests while lying on their stomachs.

When neonates are held, their heads must be supported. But by three to six months of age, infants generally manage to hold their heads quite well so supporting the head is no longer necessary. Unfortunately, infants who can normally support their heads cannot do so when they are lifted or moved about in a jerky manner; infants who are handled carelessly can thus develop neck injuries.

5-3b CONTROL OF THE HANDS: GETTING A GRIP

The development of hand skills is an example of proximodistal development. Infants will track slowly moving objects with their eyes shortly after birth, but they will not reach for them. Voluntary reaching and grasping require visual–motor coordination. By about three months, infants will make clumsy swipes at objects. Between four and six months, infants become more successful at grasping objects (Daum et al., 2013). However, they may not know how to let go and may hold an object indefinitely, until their attention is diverted and the hand opens accidentally. Four to six months is a good age for giving children rattles, large plastic spoons, mobiles, and other brightly colored hanging toys that can be grasped but are harmless when they wind up in the mouth.

Grasping is reflexive at first. Voluntary holding replaces reflexive grasping by three to four months. Infants first use an **ulnar grasp**, holding objects clumsily between their fingers and their palm. By four to six months, they can transfer objects back and forth between hands. The oppositional thumb comes into play at about 9 to 12 months, enabling infants to pick up tiny objects in a **pincer grasp**. By about 11 months, infants can hold objects in each hand and inspect them in turn.

Another aspect of visual–motor coordination is stacking blocks. On average, children can stack two blocks at 15 months, three blocks at 18 months, and five blocks at 24 months (Wentworth et al., 2000).

5-3c LOCOMOTION

Locomotion is movement from one place to another. Children gain the capacity to move their bodies through a sequence of activities that includes rolling over, sitting up, crawling, creeping, walking, and running (see Figure 5.6). There is much variation in the ages at which infants first engage in these activities. Although the sequence mostly remains the same, some children will skip a step. For example, an infant may creep without ever having crawled.

Most infants can roll over, from back to stomach and from stomach to back, by about the age of six months. By about seven months, infants usually begin to sit up by themselves. At about eight to nine months, most infants begin to crawl, a motor activity in which they lie on their bellies and use their arms to pull themselves along. Creeping, in which infants move themselves along on their hands and knees, usually appears a month or so after crawling.

ulnar grasp grasping objects between the fingers and the palm.

pincer grasp grasping objects between the fingers and the thumb.

locomotion movement from one place to another.

FIG.5.6 | MOTOR DEVELOPMENT IN INFANCY

Age (weeks)

12

16 — Turns from stomach to side

20 — Turns from stomach to back

24 —

28 — Turns from back to stomach

Sits up

32 — Crawls

36 —

Kneels up

40 —

Creeps

44 —

Stands up

48 —

52 —

56 — Starts walking

60 —

64 —

68 —

72 — Full walking

76 —

80 —

84 —

Motor development proceeds in an orderly sequence, but there is considerable variation in the timing of marker events.

Standing overlaps with crawling and creeping. Most infants can remain in a standing position by holding on to something at the age of eight or nine months. At this age, they may also be able to walk a bit with support. About two months later, they can pull themselves to a standing position by holding on to the sides of their cribs or other objects and can stand briefly without holding on. By 12 to 15 months or so, they walk by themselves, earning them the name **toddler**.

Toddlers soon run about, supporting their relatively heavy heads and torsos by spreading their legs in a bowlegged fashion. Because they are top-heavy and inexperienced, they fall frequently. Many toddlers are skillful at navigating slopes (Adolph & Robinson, 2015). They walk down shallow slopes but prudently choose to slide or crawl down steep ones. Walking lends children new freedom. It allows them to get about rapidly and to grasp objects that were formerly out of reach. Give toddlers a large ball to toss and run after; it is an inexpensive and most enjoyable toy.

As children mature, their muscle strength, bone density, and balance and coordination improve. By the age of two years, they can climb steps one at a time, placing both feet on each step. They can run well, walk backward, kick a large ball, and jump several inches.

Both maturation (nature) and experience (nurture) are involved in motor development. Certain voluntary motor activities are not possible until the brain has matured in terms of myelination and the differentiation of the motor areas of the cortex. Although the neonate shows stepping and swimming reflexes, these behaviors are controlled by more primitive parts of the brain. They disappear when cortical development inhibits some functions of the lower parts of the brain; and, when they reappear, they differ in quality.

Infants also need some opportunity to experiment before they can engage in milestones such as sitting up and walking. Even so, many of these advances can apparently be attributed to maturation. In classic research, Wayne Dennis and Marsena Dennis (1940) reported on the motor development of Native American Hopi children who spent their first year strapped to a cradle board. Although denied a full year of experience in locomotion, the Hopi infants gained the capacity to walk early in their second year, about when other children do.

Can training accelerate the appearance of motor skills? In a classic study with identical twins, Arnold Gesell (1929) gave one twin extensive training in hand coordination, block building, and stair climbing from early infancy. The other twin was allowed to develop on his own. At first, the trained twin had better skills, but as time passed, the untrained twin became just as skilled.

toddler a child who walks with short, uncertain steps.

The development of motor skills can be accelerated by training (Cole et al., 2013; Zelazo & Müller, 2010), but the effect seems slight.

TRUTH

T **F** Native American Hopi infants spend the first year of life strapped to a board, yet they begin to walk at about the same time as children who are reared in other cultures.

It is true that Native American Hopi infants spend the first year of life strapped to a board yet begin to walk at about the same time as children who are reared in other cultures. This finding is strong evidence of a powerful role for maturation.

Although being strapped to a cradle board did not permanently prevent the motor development of Hopi infants, Wayne Dennis (1960) reported that infants in an Iranian orphanage, who were exposed to extreme social and physical deprivation, were significantly set back in their motor development. They grew apathetic, and all aspects of development suffered. By contrast, however, the motor development of similar infants in a Lebanese orphanage accelerated dramatically in

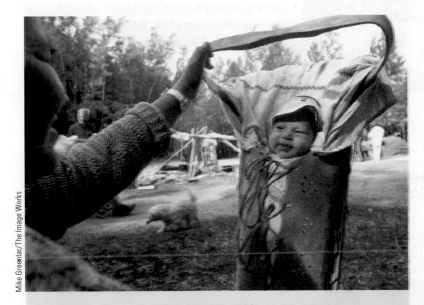

Native American Hopi children are traditionally strapped to a cradle board for the first year of life. Although they are denied the opportunity to experiment with various locomotive tasks, they begin to walk rapidly when they are unstrapped.

response to such minimal intervention as being propped up in their cribs and being given a few colorful toys (Sayegh & Dennis, 1965).

Nature provides the limits—the "reaction range"—for the expression of inherited traits. Nurture determines whether the child will develop skills that reach the upper limits of the range. Even such a fundamental skill as locomotion is determined by a complex interplay of maturational and environmental factors (Adolph & Robinson, 2015). There may be little purpose in trying to train children to enhance motor skills before they are ready. Once they are ready, however, teaching and practice do make a difference. One does not become an Olympic athlete without "good genes," but one also usually does not become an Olympic athlete without solid training.

5-4 SENSORY AND PERCEPTUAL DEVELOPMENT

Many things that are obvious to us are not so obvious to infants. You may know that a coffee cup is the same whether you see it from above or from the side, but make no such assumptions about the infant's knowledge. You may know that an infant's mother is the same size whether she is standing next to the infant or approaching from two blocks away, but do not assume that the infant agrees with you.

5-4a DEVELOPMENT OF VISION

Development of vision involves development of visual acuity or sharpness, development of peripheral vision (seeing things at the sides while looking ahead), visual preferences, depth perception, and perceptual constancies, such as knowing that an object remains the same object even though it may look different when seen from a different angle.

DEVELOPMENT OF VISUAL ACUITY AND PERIPHERAL VISION Newborns are extremely nearsighted, with vision beginning at about 20/600. The most dramatic gains in visual acuity are made between birth and six months of age, with acuity reaching about 20/50 (S. P. Johnson, 2011; Slater et al., 2010). By three to five years, visual acuity generally approximates adult levels (20/20 in the best cases).

Neonates also have poor peripheral vision (Disabato & Daniels, 2013). Adults can perceive objects that are nearly 90 degrees off to the side (i.e., directly to the left or right), although objects at these extremes are unclear. Neonates cannot perceive visual stimuli that are off to the side by an angle of more than 30 degrees, but their peripheral vision expands to an angle of about 45 degrees by the age of seven weeks. By six months, their peripheral vision is about equal to that of an adult.

Let us now consider the development of visual perception. We will see that infants frequently prefer the strange to the familiar and will avoid going off the deep end—sometimes.

VISUAL PREFERENCES Neonates look at stripes longer than at blobs. This finding has been used in much of the research on visual acuity. Classic research found that by the age of 8 to 12 weeks, most infants also show distinct preferences for curved lines over straight ones (Fantz et al., 1975).

Robert Fantz (1961) wondered whether there was something intrinsically interesting about the human face that drew the attention of infants. To investigate this question, he showed two-month-old infants the six disks in Figure 5.7. One disk contained human features, another newsprint, and still another a bull's eye. The remaining three disks were featureless but colored red, white, and yellow. In this study, the infants fixated significantly longer on the human face.

Some studies suggest that the infants in Fantz's (1961) study may have preferred the human face because it had a complex, intriguing pattern of dots (eyes) within an outline, not because it was a face. But de Haan and Groen (2006) assert that "reading" faces (interpreting facial expressions) is important to infants because they do not understand verbal information as communicated through language.

Researchers therefore continue to ask whether humans come into the world "prewired" to prefer human stimuli to other stimuli that are just as complex, and—if so—what it is about human stimuli that draws attention. Some researchers—unlike de Haan and Groen—argue that neonates do not "prefer" faces because they are faces per se but because of the structure of their immature visual systems (Simion et al., 2001). A supportive study of 34 neonates found that the longer fixations on facelike stimuli resulted from a larger number of brief fixations (looks) rather than from a few prolonged fixations (Cassia et al., 2001). The infants' gaze, then, was sort of bouncing around from feature to feature rather than "staring" at the face in general. The researchers interpreted the finding to show that the stimulus properties of the visual object are more important than the fact that it represents a human face. Even so, of course, the "immature visual system" would be providing some "prewired" basis for attending to the face. Is there an evolutionary advantage to neonates' preferring faces? Perhaps. Let us note that among rhesus monkeys, neonatal face-to-face interactions appear to promote subsequent social behavior (Dettmer et al., 2016).

Learning also plays some role. For example, neonates can discriminate their mother's face from a stranger's after eight hours of mother–infant contact spread over four days (Bushnell, 2001).

Neonates appear to direct their attention to the edges of objects. This pattern persists for the first several weeks (S. P. Johnson, 2011). When they are given the opportunity to look at human faces, one-month-old infants tend to pay most attention to the "edges," that is, the chin, an ear, or the hairline. The eye movements of two-month-old infants move in from the edge (see Figure 5.8). The infants focus particularly on the eyes, although they also inspect other features such as the mouth and nose (Aslin, 2012).

Some researchers (e.g., Haith, 1979) explain infants' tendencies to scan from the edges of objects by noting that for the first several weeks, infants seem to be concerned with *where*

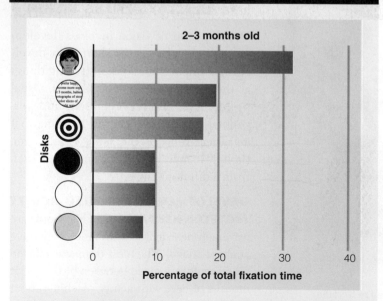

FIG.5.7 | INFANT'S PREFERENCES FOR VISUAL STIMULI

2–3 months old

Disks

Percentage of total fixation time

0   10   20   30   40

Infants appear to prefer complex to simple visual stimuli. By the time they are two months old, they also tend to show a preference for the human face.

FIG.5.8 | EYE MOVEMENTS OF 1- AND 2-MONTH-OLDS

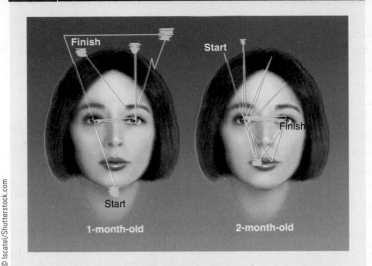

One-month-olds direct their attention to the edges of objects. Two-month-olds move in from the edge.

Psychologists can assess infants' emotional responses to the visual cliff long before infants can crawl. For example, Campos and his colleagues (1970) found that one-month-old infants showed no change in heart rate when placed face down on the "cliff." They apparently did not perceive the depth of the cliff. At two months, infants showed decreases in heart rate when so placed, which psychologists interpret as a sign of interest. But the heart rates of nine-month-olds accelerated on the cliff, which is interpreted as a fear response. The study appears to suggest that infants profit from some experience crawling about (and, perhaps, accumulating some bumps) before they develop fear of heights. The nine-month-olds but not the two-month-olds had had such experience. Other studies support the view that infants usually do not develop fear of heights until they can move around (Dahl et al., 2013).

DEVELOPMENT OF PERCEPTUAL CONSTANCIES

It may not surprise you that a 12-inch ruler is the same length whether it is two feet or six feet away or that a door across the room is a rectangle whether closed or ajar. Awareness of these facts depends not on sensation alone but on the development of perceptual constancies. **Perceptual constancy**

perceptual constancy
perceiving objects as maintaining their identity although sensations from them change as their positions change.

things are. Their attention is captured by movement and sharp contrasts in brightness and shape, such as those found where the edges of objects stand out against their backgrounds. But by about two months, infants tend to focus on the *what* of things, scanning systematically within the boundaries of objects (Aslin, 2012).

DEVELOPMENT OF DEPTH PERCEPTION Many infants respond to cues for depth by the time they are able to crawl (six to eight months of age or so), and most have the good sense to avoid "going off the deep end," that is, crawling off ledges and tabletops into open space (Campos et al., 1978).

In a classic study on depth perception, Gibson and Walk (1960) placed infants of various ages on a fabric-covered runway that ran across the center of a clever device called a visual cliff (see Figure 5.9). The visual cliff is a sheet of Plexiglas that covers a cloth with a checkerboard pattern. On one side, the cloth is placed immediately beneath the Plexiglas; on the other, it is dropped about four feet. In the Gibson and Walk study, eight out of ten infants who had begun to crawl refused to venture onto the seemingly unsupported surface, even when their mothers beckoned encouragingly from the other side.

FIG.5.9 | THE VISUAL CLIFF

This young explorer has the good sense not to crawl out onto an apparently unsupported surface, even when mother beckons from the other side.

is the tendency to perceive an object to be the same, even though the sensations produced by the object may differ under various conditions.

Consider again the example of the ruler. When it is two feet away, its image, as focused on the retina, has a certain "retinal size." From six feet away, the 12-inch ruler is only one-third as long in terms of retinal size, but we perceive it as being the same size because of size constancy. *Size constancy* is the tendency to perceive the same objects as being of the same size even though their retinal sizes vary as a function of their distance. From six feet away, a 36-inch yardstick casts an image equal in retinal size to the 12-inch ruler at two feet, but—if recognized as a yardstick—it is perceived as longer, again because of size constancy.

Bower (1974) conditioned 2½- to 3-month-old infants to turn their heads to the left when shown a 12-inch cube from a distance of three feet. He then presented them with three experimental stimuli: (1) a 12-inch cube nine feet away, whose retinal size was smaller than that of the original cube; (2) a 36-inch cube three feet away, whose retinal size was larger than that of the original cube; and (3) a 36-inch cube nine feet away, whose retinal size was the same as that of the original cube. The infants turned their heads most frequently in response to the first experimental cube, although its retinal image was only one-third the length of that to which they had been conditioned, suggesting that they had achieved size constancy. Later studies have confirmed Bower's finding that size constancy is present in early infancy. Some research suggests that even neonates possess rudimentary size constancy (Slater et al., 2010, Siegler et al., 2016).

Shape constancy is the tendency to perceive an object as having the same shape even though, when perceived from another angle, the shape projected onto the retina may change dramatically. When the top of a cup or a glass is seen from above, the visual sensations are in the shape of a circle. When seen from a slight angle, the sensations are elliptical. However, because of our familiarity with the object, we still perceive the rim of the cup or

habituation becoming used to a stimulus and therefore paying less attention to it.

glass as being a circle. In the first few months after birth, infants see the features of their caregivers, bottles, cribs, and toys from all different angles so that by the time they are four or five months old, a broad grasp of shape constancy seems to be established, at least under certain conditions (Slater et al., 2010).

5-4b DEVELOPMENT OF HEARING

Neonates can crudely orient their heads in the direction of a sound (Burnham & Mattock, 2010). By 18 months of age, the accuracy of sound-localizing ability approaches that of adults. Sensitivity to sounds increases in the first few months of life (Burnham & Mattock, 2010). As infants mature, the range of the pitch of the sounds they can sense gradually expands to include the adult's range of 20 to 20,000 cycles per second. The ability to detect differences in the pitch and loudness of sounds improves considerably throughout the preschool years. Auditory acuity also improves gradually over the first several years (Burnham & Matlock, 2010), although infants' hearing can be so acute that many parents complain their napping infants will awaken at the slightest sound. This is especially true if parents have been overprotective in attempting to keep their rooms as silent as possible. Infants who are normally exposed to a backdrop of moderate noise levels become habituated to them and are not likely to awaken unless there is a sudden, sharp noise.

By the age of one month, infants perceive differences between speech sounds that are highly similar. In a classic study relying on the **habituation** method, infants of this age could activate a recording of "bah" by sucking on a nipple (Eimas et al., 1971). As time went on, habituation occurred, as shown by decreased sucking so as to hear the "bah" sound. Then the researchers switched from "bah" to "pah." If the sounds had seemed the same to the infants, their lethargic sucking patterns would have continued, but they immediately sucked harder, suggesting that they perceived the difference. Other researchers have found that within another month or two, infants reliably discriminate three-syllable words such as *marana* and *malana* (Kuhl et al., 2006).

Our auditory acuity develops gradually over the first few years of life, but we learn to locate sounds rather quickly.

Alloy Photography/Veer

Infants can discriminate the sounds of their parent's voices by 3½ months of age. In classic research, infants of this age were oriented toward their parents as they reclined in infant seats. The experimenters (Spelke & Owsley, 1979) played recordings of the mother's or father's voice while the parents themselves remained inactive. The infants reliably looked at the parent whose voice was being played.

Young infants are capable of perceiving most of the speech sounds present in the world's languages. But after exposure to one's native language, infants gradually lose the capacity to discriminate those sounds that are not found in the native language (Werker & Hensch, 2015), as shown in Figure 5.10 (Werker, 1989).

Infants also learn at an early age to ignore small, meaningless variations in the sounds of their native language, for instance those caused by accents or head colds, as early as six months of age (Kuhl et al., 2006). Kuhl and her colleagues (1997) presented American and Swedish infants with pairs of sounds in either their own language or the other one. The infants were trained to look over their shoulder when they heard a difference in the sounds and to ignore sound pairs that seemed to be the same. The infants routinely ignored variations in sounds that were part of their language, because they apparently perceived them as the same sound. But the infants noticed slight variations in the sounds of the other language.

5-4c DEVELOPMENT OF COORDINATION OF THE SENSES

Young infants can recognize that objects experienced by one sense (e.g., vision) are the same as those experienced through another sense (e.g., touch). This ability has been demonstrated in infants as young as one month of age (Bushnell, 1993). One experiment demonstrating such understanding in five-month-olds showed that infants of this age tend to look longer at novel rather than familiar sources of stimulation. Féron and her colleagues (2006) first allowed five-month-old infants to handle groups of either two or three objects, presented one by one, to their right hand. The infants were then shown visual displays of either two or three objects. The infants looked longer at the group of objects that differed from the one they had handled, showing a transfer of information from the sense of touch to the sense of vision.

5-4d THE ACTIVE–PASSIVE CONTROVERSY IN PERCEPTUAL DEVELOPMENT

Newborn children may have more sophisticated sensory capabilities than you expected. Still, their ways of perceiving the world are largely mechanical, or passive. Neonates seem to be generally at the mercy of external stimuli. When a bright light strikes, they attend to it. If the light moves slowly across the plane of their vision, they track it.

As time passes, broad changes occur in the perceptual processes of children, and the child's role in perception appears to become decidedly more active. Developmental psychologist Eleanor Gibson (1969, 1991) noted a number of these changes:

1. Intentional action replaces "capture" (automatic responses to stimulation). Purposeful scanning and exploration of the environment take the place of mechanical movements and passive responses to stimulation.

2. Systematic search replaces unsystematic search.

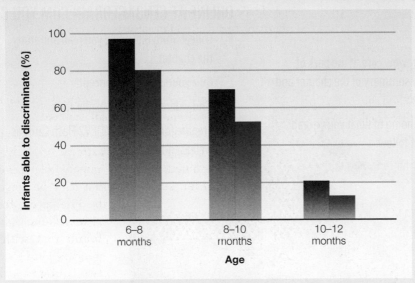

FIG. 5.10 DECLINING ABILITY TO DISCRIMINATE THE SOUNDS OF FOREIGN LANGUAGES

Source: Werker (1989).

Infants show a decline in the ability to discriminate sounds not found in their native language. Before six months of age, infants from English-speaking families could discriminate sounds found in Hindi (red bars) and Salish, a Native American language (blue bars). By 10 to 12 months of age, they could no longer do so.

3. Attention becomes selective. Older children become capable of selecting the information they need from the welter of confusion in the environment.

4. Irrelevant information becomes ignored. That might mean shutting out the noise of cars in the street or radios in the neighborhood so as to focus on a book.

In short, children develop from passive, mechanical reactors to the world about them into active, purposeful seekers and organizers of sensory information.

5-4e NATURE AND NURTURE IN PERCEPTUAL DEVELOPMENT

The nature–nurture issue is found in perceptual development, as in other areas of development.

EVIDENCE FOR THE ROLE OF NATURE Compelling evidence supports the idea that inborn sensory capacities play a crucial role in perceptual development. Neonates arrive in the world with a good number of perceptual skills. They can see nearby objects quite well, and their hearing is usually fine. They are born with tendencies to track moving objects, to systematically scan the horizon, and to prefer certain kinds of stimuli. Preferences for different kinds of visual stimuli appear to unfold on schedule as the first months wear on. Sensory changes, as with motor changes, appear to be linked to maturation of the nervous system.

EVIDENCE FOR THE ROLE OF NURTURE Evidence that experience plays a crucial role in perceptual development is also compelling. Children and lower animals have critical periods in their perceptual development. Failure to receive adequate sensory stimulation during these periods can result in permanent sensory deficits (Cascio, 2010; Lomanowska & Melo, 2016). For example, newborn kittens raised with a patch over one eye wind up with few or no cells in the visual area of the cerebral cortex that would normally be stimulated by light that enters that eye. In effect, that eye becomes blind, even though sensory receptors in the eye itself may fire in response to light. On the other hand, if the eye of an adult cat is patched for the same amount of time, the animal will not lose vision. The critical period will have passed. Similarly, if health problems require that a child's eye must be patched for an extensive period of time during the first year, the child's visual acuity in that eye may be impaired.

Today most investigators would agree that nature and nurture interact to shape perceptual development. In the next chapter, we see how nature and nurture influence the development of thought and language in infants.

SELF-ASSESSMENTS

Fill-Ins

Answers can be found in the back of the book.

1. Failure to receive adequate sensory stimulation during a(n) _____ period can result in permanent sensory deficits.

2. Boys generally reach half their adult height by their _____ birthday.

3. Native American Hopi Indians typically spend the first year strapped to a(n) _____ _____.

4. The tendency to return to one's genetically determined pattern of growth following a period of deprivation is referred to as _____.

5. Breast milk contains the mother's _____ and helps the infant ward off health problems such as ear infections and pneumonia.

6. In the disease _____ _____, myelin is replaced by hard, fibrous tissue that disrupts the timing of neural transmission, interfering with muscle control.

7. The first major growth spurt of the brain occurs during the fourth and fifth months of prenatal development, due to the proliferation of _____.

8. Animals reared in darkness show shrinkage of the _____ _____.

9. By 12 to 15 months or so, infants walk by themselves, earning them the name _____.

10. Fantz shows two-month-old infants disks colored red, white, and yellow, and disks with newsprint, a bull's eye, and a human face. The infants fixated longest on the _____.

Multiple Choice

1. **The American Academy of Pediatrics recommends that infants be fed breast milk for at least**
   - a. four to six months.
   - c. one year.
   - b. six to nine months.
   - d. two years.

2. **Which of the following is untrue about breast-feeding?**
   - a. Breast-feeding cannot transmit HIV.
   - b. Breast-feeding helps shrink the uterus after delivery.
   - c. Breast milk can transmit polychlorinated biphenyls.
   - d. Breast-feeding reduces the risk of ovarian cancer.

3. **How long does it take for a child's brain to reach 70% of its adult weight?**
   - a. one year
   - c. three years
   - b. two years
   - d. five years

4. **Which part of the brain helps the child maintain balance?**
   - a. the medulla
   - c. the auditory cortex
   - b. the amygdala
   - d. the cerebellum

5. **Vision is the infant's dominant sense at**
   - a. birth.
   - c. five–six months.
   - b. one–four months.
   - d. one year.

6. **Myelination of motor pathways allows neonates to engage in**
   - a. reflexes.
   - b. beating of the heart.
   - c. respiration.
   - d. the cycle of waking and sleeping.

7. **Myelination of the neurons involved in the sense of hearing begins**
   - a. in the germinal stage.
   - b. in the embryonic stage.
   - c. in the fetal stage.
   - d. after birth.

8. **At three to four months of age, infants hold objects clumsily between their fingers and their palm. This behavior is known as the**
   - a. reflexive grasp.
   - b. proximodistal grasp.
   - c. pincer grasp.
   - d. ulnar grasp.

9. **Which of the following is true of motor development?**
   - a. Only nature is involved in motor development.
   - b. Only nurture is involved in motor development.
   - c. Nature and nurture are both involved in motor development.
   - d. Neither nature nor nurture is involved in motor development.

10. **At what age does a child's visual acuity first approximate adult levels?**
    - a. at birth
    - b. by one to two years of age
    - c. by three to five years of age
    - d. by six to ten years of age

CDEV
ONLINE

STUDY YOUR WAY
WITH STUDYBITS!

WEAK

Rate and Organize StudyBits

FAIR

STRONG

UNASSIGNED

Collect What's Important

Create Flashcards From Your StudyBits

Track/Monitor Your Progress

85%

CORRECT

INCORRECT

INCORRECT

INCORRECT

Personalize Your Quizzes

4LTR
PRESS

Access **CDEV ONLINE** at www.cengagebrain.com

6 | Infancy: Cognitive Development

O.JO Images Photography/Veer

LEARNING OUTCOMES

After studying this chapter, you will be able to...

6-1 Examine Jean Piaget's studies of cognitive development

6-2 Discuss the information-processing approach to cognitive development

6-3 Identify individual differences in intelligence among infants

6-4 Examine language development in infants

After you finish this chapter, go to **PAGE 112** for **STUDY TOOLS**

Laurent...resumes his experiments of the day before. He grabs in succession a celluloid swan, a box, etc., stretches out his arm and lets them fall. He distinctly varies the position of the fall. Sometimes he stretches out his arm vertically, sometimes he holds it obliquely, in front of or behind his eyes, etc. When the object falls in a new position, he lets it fall two or three times more on the same place, as though to study the spatial relation; then he modifies the situation.

Is this a description of a scientist at work? In a way, it is. Although Swiss psychologist Jean Piaget ([1936] 1963) was describing his 11-month-old son Laurent, children of this age frequently act like scientists, performing what Piaget called "experiments in order to see."

> Cognitive development focuses on the development of children's ways of perceiving and mentally representing the world.

COGNITIVE DEVELOPMENT: JEAN PIAGET

Cognitive development focuses on the development of children's ways of perceiving and mentally representing the world. Piaget labeled children's concepts of the world *schemes*. He hypothesized that children try to use *assimilation* to absorb new events into existing schemes. When assimilation does not allow the child to make sense of novel events, children try to modify existing schemes through *accommodation*.

Piaget ([1936] 1963) hypothesized that cognitive processes develop in an orderly sequence of stages. Some children may advance more quickly than others, but the sequence remains constant (Taber, 2013; Tryphon & Voneche, 2013). Piaget identified four stages of cognitive development: sensorimotor, preoperational, concrete operational, and formal operational. In this chapter, we discuss the sensorimotor stage.

6-1a THE SENSORIMOTOR STAGE

Piaget's **sensorimotor stage** refers to the first two years of cognitive development, a time during which infants progress from responding to events with reflexes, or ready-made schemes, to goal-oriented behavior. Piaget divided the sensorimotor stage into six substages. In each substage, earlier forms of behavior are repeated, varied, and coordinated.

sensorimotor stage Piaget's first stage of cognitive development, which lasts through infancy and is generally characterized by increasingly complex coordination of sensory experiences with motor activity.

1. SIMPLE REFLEXES The first substage covers the first month after birth. It is dominated by the assimilation of sources of stimulation into inborn reflexes such as grasping or visual tracking. At birth, reflexes seem stereotypical and inflexible. But even within the first few hours, neonates begin to modify reflexes as a result of experience. For example, infants will adapt patterns of sucking to the shape of the nipple and the rate of flow of fluid. During the first month or so, however, infants

Steve Allen/Stockbyte/Jupiter Images

TRUTH OR FICTION?

T	F	For two-month-old infants, "out of sight" is truly "out of mind."
T	F	A one-hour-old infant may imitate an adult who sticks out his or her tongue.
T	F	Psychologists can begin to measure intelligence in infancy.
T	F	Infant crying is a primitive form of language.
T	F	You can advance children's development of pronunciation by correcting their errors.
T	F	Children are "prewired" to listen to language in such a way that they come to understand rules of grammar.

apparently make no connection between stimulation perceived through different sensory modalities. They make no effort to grasp objects that they visually track.

2. PRIMARY CIRCULAR REACTIONS The second substage, primary circular reactions, lasts from about one to four months of age and is characterized by the beginnings of the ability to coordinate various sensorimotor schemes. Infants tend to repeat stimulating actions that first occurred by chance. They may lift an arm repeatedly to bring it into view. **Primary circular reactions** focus on the infant's own body rather than on the external environment. Piaget noticed the following primary circular reaction in his son Laurent:

> At 2 months 4 days, Laurent by chance discovers his right index finger and looks at it briefly. At 2 months 11 days, he inspects for a moment his open right hand, perceived by chance. At 2 months 17 days, he follows its spontaneous movement for a moment, then examines it several times while it searches for his nose or rubs his eye.
>
> —Piaget ([1936] 1963, pp. 96–97)

Thus, Laurent, early in the third month, visually tracks the behavior of his hands, but his visual observations do not affect their movement. In terms of assimilation and accommodation, the child is attempting to assimilate the motor scheme (moving the hand) into the sensory scheme (looking at it). But the schemes do not automatically fit. Several days of apparent trial and error pass, during which the infant seems to be trying to make accommodations so that they will fit. By the third month, infants may examine objects repeatedly and intensely. It seems that the infant is no longer simply looking and seeing but is now "looking in order to see."

Because Laurent (and other infants) will repeat actions that allow them to see, cognitive-developmental psychologists consider sensorimotor coordination self-reinforcing. Laurent is acting on his hands to keep them in his field of vision. Piaget considers the desire to prolong stimulation to be as "basic" as the drives of hunger or thirst.

3. SECONDARY CIRCULAR REACTIONS The third substage lasts from about four to eight months and is characterized by **secondary circular reactions**, in which patterns of activity are repeated because of their effect on the environment. In the second substage (primary circular reactions), infants are focused on their own bodies, as in the example given with Laurent. In the third substage (secondary circular reactions), the focus shifts to objects and environmental events. Infants may now learn to pull strings in order to make a plastic face appear or to shake an object in order to hear it rattle.

4. COORDINATION OF SECONDARY SCHEMES In the fourth substage, which lasts from about 8 to 12 months of age, infants no longer act simply to prolong interesting occurrences. Now they can coordinate schemes to attain specific goals. Infants begin to show intentional, goal-directed behavior in which they differentiate between the means of achieving a goal and the goal or end itself. For example, they may lift a piece of cloth to reach a toy that they had seen a parent place under the cloth earlier. In this example, the scheme of picking up the cloth (the means) is coordinated with the scheme of reaching for the toy

primary circular reactions the repetition of actions that first occurred by chance and that focus on the infant's own body.

secondary circular reactions the repetition of actions that produce an effect on the environment.

Picture Partners/Alamy stock Photo

Picture Partners/Alamy Stock Photo

Matt Brasier/Masterfile

1. In the first substage, neonates assimilate sources of stimulation into reflexive responses.

2. In the second substage, infants repeat stimulating actions that first occurred by chance (primary circular reactions).

3. In the third substage, patterns of activity are repeated because of their effect on the environment (secondary circular reactions).

(the goal or end). This example indicates that the infant has mentally represented the toy placed under the cloth.

During the fourth substage, infants also gain the capacity to imitate gestures and sounds that they had previously ignored. The imitation of a facial gesture implies that infants have mentally represented their own faces and can tell what parts of their faces they are moving through feedback from facial muscles.

5. TERTIARY CIRCULAR REACTIONS In the fifth substage, which lasts from about 12 to 18 months of age, Piaget looked on the behavior of infants as characteristic of budding scientists. Infants now engage in **tertiary circular reactions**, or purposeful adaptations of established schemes to specific situations. Behavior takes on a new experimental quality, and infants may vary their actions dozens of times in a deliberate trial-and-error fashion to learn how things work.

Piaget reported an example of tertiary circular reactions by his daughter Jacqueline. The episode was an experiment in which Piaget placed a stick outside Jacqueline's playpen, which had wooden bars (Piaget, 1963 [1936]). At first, Jacqueline grasped the stick and tried to pull it sideways into the playpen. The stick was too long and could not fit through the bars. After days of overt trial and error, however, Jacqueline discovered that she could bring the stick between the bars by turning it upright. In the sixth substage, described next, infants apparently engage in mental trial and error before displaying the correct overt response.

6. INVENTION OF NEW MEANS THROUGH MENTAL COMBINATIONS The sixth substage lasts from about 18 to 24 months of age. It serves as a transition between sensorimotor development and the development of symbolic thought. External exploration is replaced by mental exploration. At about 18 months, children may also use imitation to symbolize or stand for a plan of action.

Piaget presented his other children, Lucienne and Laurent, with the playpen and stick problem at the age of 18 months old. Rather than engage in overt trial and error, the 18-month-old children sat and studied the situation for a few moments. Then they grasped the stick, turned it upright, and brought it into the playpen with little overt effort. Lucienne and Laurent apparently mentally represented the stick and the bars of the playpen and perceived that the stick would not fit through as it was. They must then have rotated the mental image of the stick until they perceived a position that would allow the stick to pass between the bars.

6-1b DEVELOPMENT OF OBJECT PERMANENCE

The appearance of **object permanence** is an important aspect of sensorimotor development. Object permanence is the recognition that an object or person continues to exist when out of sight. For example, your textbook continues to exist when you leave it in the library after studying for the big test, and an infant's mother continues to exist even when she is in another room. The development of object permanence is tied into the development of infants' working memory and reasoning ability (Yermolayeva & Rakison, 2014; Reynolds & Romano, 2016).

tertiary circular reactions the purposeful adaptation of established schemes to new situations.

object permanence recognition that objects continue to exist when they are not in view.

4. In the fourth substage, infants coordinate their behavior to attain specific goals (coordinating secondary schemes).

Myrleen Pearson/PhotoEdit

5. In the fifth substage, infants use overt trial and error to learn how things work (tertiary circular reactions).

David Mendelsohn/Masterfile

6. In the sixth substage, infants use mental trial and error in solving problems.

Stephen Ausmus/Courtesy of the USDA

Neonates show no tendency to respond to objects that are not within their immediate sensory grasp. By the age of two months, infants may show some surprise if an object (such as a toy duck) is placed behind a screen and then taken away so that when the screen is lifted, it is absent. However, they make no effort to search for the missing object. (See Figure 6.1.) Through the first six months or so, when the screen is placed between the object and the infant, the infant behaves as though the object is no longer there. It is true that "out of sight" is "out of mind" for two-month-old infants. Apparently, they do not yet reliably mentally represent objects they see.

There are some interesting advances in the development of the object concept by about the sixth month (Piaget's substage 3). For example, an infant at this age will tend to look for an object that has been dropped, behavior that suggests some form of object permanence. By this age, there is also reason to believe that the infant perceives a mental representation (image) of an object, such as a favorite toy, in response to sensory impressions of part of the object. This perception is shown by the infant's reaching for an object that is partly hidden.

A-not-B error the error made when an infant selects a familiar hiding place (A) for an object rather than a new hiding place, even after the infant has seen it hidden in the new place.

By 8 to 12 months of age (Piaget's substage 4), infants will seek to retrieve objects that have been completely hidden. But in observing his own children, Piaget (1963 [1936]) noted an interesting error known as the **A-not-B error**. Piaget repeatedly hid a toy behind a screen (A), and each time, his infant removed the screen and retrieved the toy. Then, as the infant watched, Piaget

FIG.6.1   DEVELOPMENT OF OBJECT PERMANENCE

Doug Goodman/Science Source

Doug Goodman / Science Source

Doug Goodman / Science Source

Doug Goodman / Science Source

The infant in the top row is in the early part of the sensorimotor stage, in which "out of sight" is literally "out of mind." Once the toy is screened by the piece of paper, the infant loses interest in it. Piaget would have said that the toy is not yet "mentally represented." The older infant in the bottom row has mentally represented an object, and pushes through the towel to reach it after it has been screened from sight.

hid the toy behind another screen (B) in a different place. Still, the infant tried to recover the toy by pushing aside the first screen (A). It is as though the child had learned that a certain motor activity would reinstate the missing toy. The child's concept of the object did not, at this age, extend to recognition that objects usually remain in the place where they have been most recently mentally represented.

Under certain conditions, nine- to ten-month-old infants do not show the A-not-B error. They apparently need a certain degree of maturation of the front lobes of the cerebral cortex, which fosters the development of working memory and attention (Cuevas & Bell, 2010). Also, if infants are allowed to search for the object immediately after seeing it hidden, the error often does not occur. But if they are forced to wait five or more seconds before looking, they are likely to commit the A-not-B error (Wellman et al., 1986).

6-1c EVALUATION OF PIAGET'S THEORY

Piaget's theory remains a comprehensive model of infant cognition. Many of his observations of his own infants have been confirmed by others. The pattern and sequence of events he described have been observed among American, European, African, and Asian infants (Werner, 1988). Still, research has raised questions about the validity of many of Piaget's claims (Reed, 2013).

First, most researchers now agree that cognitive development is not as tied to discrete stages as Piaget suggested (Fuller, 2011; Reed, 2013). Although later developments seem to build on earlier ones, the process appears to be more gradual than discontinuous.

Second, Piaget emphasized the role of maturation, almost to the point of excluding adult and peer influences on cognitive development. However, these interpersonal influences have been shown to play roles in cognitive development (Nisbett, 2016; Reed, 2013).

Third, Piaget appears to have underestimated infants' competence (Reed, 2013). For example, infants display object permanence earlier than he believed (Moore & Meltzoff, 2008). Also consider studies on **deferred imitation** (imitation of an action that may have occurred hours, days, or even weeks earlier). The presence of deferred imitation suggests that children have mentally represented behavior patterns. Piaget believed that deferred imitation appears at about 18 months, but others have found that infants show deferred imitation as early as nine months. In one study, nine-month-old infants watched an adult perform behaviors such as pushing a button to produce a beep (Meltzoff et al., 2013). When given a chance to play with the same objects a day later, many infants imitated the actions they had witnessed.

The **information-processing approach** to cognitive development focuses on how children manipulate or process information coming in from the environment or already stored in the mind. Infants' tools for processing information include their memory and imitation.

6-2a INFANTS' MEMORY

Many of the cognitive capabilities of infants—recognizing the faces of familiar people, developing object permanence, and, in fact, learning in any form—depend on one critical aspect of cognitive development: their memory (Bauer et al., 2010). Even neonates demonstrate memory for stimuli to which they have been exposed previously. For example, neonates adjust their rate of sucking to hear a recording of their mother reading a story she had read aloud during the last weeks of pregnancy, as discussed in Chapter 3 (DeCasper & Fifer, 1980; DeCasper et al., 2011).

Memory improves dramatically between two and six months of age and then again by 12 months (Pelphrey et al., 2004; Rose et al., 2011). The improvement may indicate that older infants are more capable than younger ones of encoding (i.e., storing) information, retrieving information already stored, or both (Patel et al., 2013).

A fascinating series of studies by Carolyn Rovee-Collier and her colleagues (Giles & Rovee-Collier, 2011; Rovee-Collier, 1993) illustrates some of these developmental changes in infant memory. As shown in Figure 6.2, one end of a ribbon was tied to a brightly colored mobile suspended above the infant's crib. The other end was tied to the infant's ankle, so that when the infant kicked, the mobile moved. Infants quickly learned to increase their rate of kicking. To measure memory, the infant's ankle was again fastened to the mobile after a period of one or more days had elapsed. In one study, two-month-olds remembered how to make the mobile move after delays of up to three days, and three-month-olds remembered for more than a week (Greco et al., 1986).

Infant memory can be improved if infants receive a reminder ("priming") before their memory is tested (Imuta et al., 2013).

deferred imitation the imitation of people and events that occurred in the past.

information-processing approach the view of cognitive development that focuses on how children manipulate sensory information and/or information stored in memory.

FIG.6.2 INVESTIGATING INFANT MEMORY

Courtesy of Prof. Carolyn Rovee-Collier

In this technique, developed by Carolyn Rovee-Collier, the infant's ankle is connected to a mobile by a ribbon. Infants quickly learn to kick to make the mobile move. Two- and three-month-olds remember how to perform this feat after a delay of a few days. If they are given a reminder, such as simply viewing the mobile, their memory lasts for two to four weeks.

In one study infants were shown the moving mobile on the day before the memory test, but they were not allowed to activate it. Under these conditions, three-month-olds remembered how to move the mobile after a 28-day delay (Rovee-Collier, 1993).

6-2b IMITATION: INFANT SEE, INFANT DO?

Imitation is the basis for much of human learning. Deferred imitation—that is, the imitation of actions after a time delay—occurs as early as six months of age (Campanella & Rovee-Collier, 2005; Schneider, 2015). To help them remember the imitated act, infants are usually permitted to practice it when they learn it. But in one study, 12-month-old infants were prevented from practicing the behavior they imitated. Yet they were able to demonstrate it four weeks later, suggesting that they had mentally represented the act (Klein & Meltzoff, 1999).

But infants can imitate certain actions at a much earlier age. Neonates only 0.7 to 71 hours old have been found to imitate adults who open

their mouths or stick out their tongues (Meltzoff et al., 2013; Fogassi & Rizzolatti, 2013; see Figure 6.3).

TRUTH

(T) F   A one-hour-old infant may imitate an adult who sticks out his or her tongue.

It is true that a one-hour-old infant may imitate an adult who sticks out his or her tongue. This feat is apparently made possible by mirror neurons.

Some studies have not found imitation in early infancy (Abravanel & DeYong, 1991), and one key factor may be the infants' age. The studies that find imitation generally have been done with very young infants—up to two weeks old—whereas the studies that do not find imitation have tended to use older infants. Therefore, the imitation of neonates is likely to be reflexive—and made possible, as we will see, by "mirror neurons." Thus, imitation might disappear when reflexes are "dropping out" and re-emerge when it has a firmer cognitive footing.

MIRROR NEURONS Many researchers believe that social organization and human culture are made possible by certain kinds of neurons that are present at birth. And

FIG.6.3 IMITATION IN INFANTS

A.N. Meltzoff & M.K. Moore. "Imitation of facial and manual gestures by human neonates." Science, 1977, 198, 75–78.

These two- to three-week-old infants are imitating the facial gestures of an adult experimenter. How are we to interpret these findings? Can we say that the infants "knew" what the experimenter was doing and "chose" to imitate the behavior, or is there another explanation?

these neurons, like so many other important psychological discoveries, were found by accident (Cozolino, 2014; Fogassi & Rizzolatti, 2013).

A research team in Parma, Italy, headed by Vittorio Gallese and including Rizzolatti (Gallese et al., 1996), was recording the activity of individual neurons in monkeys' brains as the animals reached for objects. One of the researchers reached for an object that had been handled by a monkey, and quite to his surprise, a neuron in the monkey's brain fired in the same way it had fired when the animal had picked up the object. The research team followed up the phenomenon and discovered many such neurons in the frontal lobes of their monkeys, just before the motor cortex, which they dubbed *mirror neurons*. These *mirror neurons*, also found in humans, are activated when the individual performs a motor act or observes another individual engaging in the same act (Cattaneo et al., 2010; see Figure 6.4).

Mirror neurons in humans are also connected with emotions. Certain regions of the brain—particularly in the frontal lobe—are active when people experience emotions such as disgust, happiness, pain, and also when they observe another person experiencing an emotion (Rizzolati & Fabbri-Destro, 2011). It thus appears that there is a neural basis for empathy—that is, the identification or vicarious experiencing of feelings in others based on the observation of visual and other cues.

It has also been suggested that mirror neurons are connected with the built-in human capacity to acquire language (Corballis, 2010).

Photobac/Shutterstock.com

Mirror neurons are also apparently connected with gender differences in empathy (females show more of it) and the instinctive human ability to acquire language (Arbib, 2015; Brucker et al., 2015).

6-3 INDIVIDUAL DIFFERENCES IN COGNITIVE FUNCTIONING AMONG INFANTS

Cognitive development does not proceed in the same way or at the same pace for all infants. Efforts to understand the development of infant differences in cognitive development have relied on so-called scales of infant development or infant intelligence.

Measuring cognition or intelligence in infants is quite different from measuring it in adults. Infants cannot, of course, be assessed by asking them to explain the meanings of words, the similarity between concepts, or the rationales for social rules. One of the most important tests of intellectual development among infants—the Bayley Scales of Infant Development, constructed in 1933 by psychologist Nancy Bayley and revised since—contains very different kinds of items.

The Bayley test consists of mental-scale items and motor-scale items. The mental scale assesses verbal communication, perceptual skills, learning and memory, and problem-solving skills. The motor scale assesses gross motor skills, such as standing, walking, and climbing, and fine motor skills, as shown by the ability to manipulate the hands and fingers. A behavior rating scale based on examiner observation of the child during the test is also used. The behavior rating scale assesses attention span, goal directedness, persistence, and aspects of social and emotional development. Table 6.1 contains sample items from the mental and motor scales and shows the ages at which 50% of the infants taking the test passed the items.

FIG.6.4 IMITATION IN INFANT MONKEYS

Gross L (2006) Evolution o' Neonatal Imitation. PLoS Biol 4(9): e311. doi:10.1371/journal.pbio.C040311. © 2006 Public Library of Science

A newborn rhesus monkey imitates protrusion of the tongue, a feat made possible by mirror neurons, not by learning.

TABLE 6.1	ITEMS FROM THE BAYLEY SCALES OF INFANT DEVELOPMENT (BSID—II)	
Age	**Mental-Scale Items**	**Motor-Scale Items**
1 month	The infant quiets when picked up.	The infant makes a postural adjustment when put to examiner's shoulder.
2 months	When examiner presents two objects (bell and rattle) above the infant in a crib, the infant glances back and forth from one to the other.	The infant holds his or her head steady when being carried about in a vertical position.
5 months	The infant is observed to transfer an object from one hand to the other during play.	When seated at a feeding-type table and presented with a sugar pill that is out of reach, the infant attempts to pick it up.
8 months	When an object (toy) in plain view of the infant (i.e., on a table) is covered by a cup, the infant removes the cup to retrieve the object.	The infant raises herself or himself into a sitting position.
12 months	The infant imitates words that are spoken by the examiner	When requested by the examiner, the infant stands up from a position in which she or he had been lying on her or his back on the floor.
14 16 months	The infant builds a tower with two cubes (blocks) after the examiner demonstrates the behavior.	The infant walks alone with good coordination.

Even though psychologists can begin to measure intelligence in infancy, they use items that differ from the kinds of items used with older children and adults. It remains unclear how well results obtained in infancy predict intellectual functioning at later ages.

TRUTH

 T F Psychologists can begin to measure intelligence in infancy.

It is true that psychologists begin to measure intelligence in infancy, but they use items that differ from the kinds of items used with older children and adults. (There is always controversy about what researchers are actually measuring when they set out to measure "intelligence.")

6-3a TESTING INFANTS: WHY AND WITH WHAT?

As you can imagine, it is no easy matter to test an infant. The items must be administered on a one-to-one basis by a patient tester, and it can be difficult to judge whether the infant is showing the targeted response. Why, then, do we test infants?

One reason is to screen infants for handicaps. A tester may be able to detect early signs of sensory or neurological problems, as suggested by development of visual–motor coordination. In addition to the Bayley scales, a number of tests have been developed to screen infants for such difficulties, including the Brazelton

Neonatal Behavioral Assessment Scale (see Chapter 4) and the Denver Developmental Screening Test.

6-3b INSTABILITY OF INTELLIGENCE SCORES ATTAINED IN INFANCY

Researchers have also tried to use infant scales to predict development, but this effort has been less than successful. One study found that scores obtained during the first year of life correlated moderately at best with scores obtained a year later (Harris et al., 2005). Certain items on the Bayley scales appear to predict related intellectual skills later in childhood. For example, Bayley items measuring infant motor skills predict subsequent fine motor and visual–spatial skills at six to eight years of age (Siegel, 1992). Bayley language items also predict language skills at the same age (Siegel, 1992).

Another study found that the Bayley scales and socioeconomic status were able to predict cognitive development among low-birth-weight children from 18 months to 4 years of age (Dezoete et al., 2003). But overall scores on the Bayley and other infant scales apparently do not predict school grades or IQ scores among school children very well (Bornstein & Colombo, 2012). Predictability of teenage and adult intelligence test scores becomes stronger once children reach the ages of six or seven (Bornstein & Colombo, 2012). Perhaps the sensorimotor test items used during infancy are not that strongly related to the verbal and symbolic items used to assess intelligence at later ages.

The overall conclusion seems to be that the Bayley scales can identify gross lags in development and relative strengths and weaknesses. However, they are only moderate predictors of intelligence scores even one year later, and are still poorer predictors of scores taken beyond longer stretches of time.

6-3c USE OF VISUAL RECOGNITION MEMORY

In a continuing effort to find aspects of intelligence and cognition that might remain consistent from infancy through later childhood, a number of researchers have recently focused on visual recognition memory (Reynolds & Romano, 2016). **Visual recognition memory** is the ability to discriminate previously seen objects from novel objects. This procedure is based on *habituation*.

Let us consider longitudinal studies of this type. Susan Rose and her colleagues (Rose et al., 1992) showed seven-month-old infants pictures of two identical faces. After 20 seconds, the pictures were replaced with one picture of a new face and a second picture of the familiar face. The amount of time the infants spent looking at each face in the second set of pictures was recorded. Some infants spent more time looking at the new face than at the older face, suggesting that they had better memory for visual stimulation. The children were given standard IQ tests yearly from ages one through six. It was found that the children with greater visual recognition memory later attained higher IQ scores.

Rose and her colleagues (2001, 2015) also showed that, from age to age, individual differences in capacity for visual recognition memory are stable. This finding is important because intelligence—the quality that many researchers seek to predict from visual recognition memory—is also theorized to be a reasonably stable trait. Similarly, items on intelligence tests are age graded; that is, older children perform better than younger children, even as developing intelligence remains constant. So, too, with visual recognition memory. Capacity for visual recognition memory increases over the first year after birth (Rose et al., 2015).

A number of other studies have examined the relationship between either infant visual recognition memory or preference for novel stimulation (which is a related measure) and later IQ scores. In general, they show good predictive validity for broad cognitive abilities throughout childhood, including measures of intelligence and language ability (Heimann et al., 2006; Rose et al., 2015).

In sum, scales of infant development may provide useful data as screening devices, as research instruments, or simply as a way to describe the things that infants do and do not do, but their predictive power as intelligence tests has been disappointing. Tests of visual recognition hold better promise as predictors of intelligence at older ages.

Now let us turn our attention to a fascinating aspect of cognitive development, the development of language.

> Infant intelligence scores are unstable; that is, a score in infancy cannot be considered to have accurate predictive power for scores obtained later in life.

6-4 LANGUAGE DEVELOPMENT

As children develop language skills, they often begin speaking about the things more closely connected with their environments and their needs. Children enjoy playing with language. In physical development, the most dramatic developments come early—fast and furious—long before the child is born. Language does not come quite as early, and its development may not seem quite so fast and furious. Nevertheless, during the years of infancy, most infants develop from creatures without language to little people who understand nearly all the things that are said to them and who relentlessly sputter words and simple sentences for all the world to hear.

6-4a EARLY VOCALIZATIONS

Children develop language according to an invariant sequence of steps, or stages, as outlined in Table 6.2. We begin with the **prelinguistic** vocalizations. True words are symbols of objects and events. Prelinguistic vocalizations, such as cooing and babbling, do not represent objects or actions, so infant crying is not a primitive form of language.

> **visual recognition memory** the kind of memory shown in an infant's ability to discriminate previously seen objects from novel objects.
>
> **prelinguistic** vocalizations made by the infant before the use of language.

Newborn children, as parents are well aware, have an unlearned but highly effective form of verbal expression: crying and more crying. Crying is about the only sound that infants make during the first month. During the second month, infants begin **cooing**. Infants use their tongues when they coo. For this reason, coos are more articulated than cries. Coos are often vowel-like and may resemble extended "oohs" and "ahs." Cooing appears linked to feelings of pleasure or positive excitement. Infants tend not to coo when they are hungry, tired, or in pain.

Cries and coos are innate but can be modified by experience (Volterra et al., 2004; Waxman & Goswami, 2012). When parents respond positively to cooing by talking to their infants, smiling at them, and imitating them, cooing increases. Early parent–child "conversations," in which parents respond to coos and then pause as the infant coos, may foster infant awareness of taking turns as a way of verbally relating to other people.

By about eight months of age, cooing decreases markedly. Somewhere between six and nine months, children begin to babble. **Babbling** is the first vocalizing that sounds like human speech. In babbling, infants frequently combine consonants and vowels, as in *ba*, *ga*, and, sometimes,

cooing prelinguistic vowel-like sounds that reflect feelings of positive excitement.

babbling the child's first vocalizations that have the sounds of speech.

the much valued *dada* (McCardle et al., 2009). At first, dada is purely coincidental (sorry, you dads), despite the family's jubilation over its appearance.

In verbal interactions between infants and adults, the adults frequently repeat the syllables produced by their infants. They are likely to say "dadada" or "bababa" instead of simply "da" or "ba." Such redundancy apparently helps infants discriminate these sounds from others and further encourages them to imitate their parents (Elkind, 2007; Waxman & Goswami, 2012).

After infants have been babbling for a few months, parents often believe that their children are having conversations with themselves. At 10 to 12 months, infants

TABLE 6.2	MILESTONES IN LANGUAGE DEVELOPMENT IN INFANCY
Approximate Age	**Vocalization and Language**
Birth	• Cries.
12 weeks	• Cries less. • Smiles when talked to and nodded at. • Engages in squealing and gurgling sounds (cooing). • Sustains cooing for 15–20 seconds.
16 weeks	• Responds to human sounds more definitely. • Turns head, searching for the speaker. • Chuckles occasionally.
20 weeks	• Cooing becomes interspersed with consonant-like sounds. • Vocalizations differ from the sounds of mature language.
6 months	• Cooing changes to single-syllable babbling. • Neither vowels nor consonants have fixed pattern of recurrence. • Common utterances sound somewhat like *ma, mu, da,* or *di*.
8 months	• Continuous repetition (reduplication) enters into babbling. • Patterns of intonation become distinct. • Utterances can signal emphasis and emotion.
10 months	• Vocalizations mixed with sound play, such as gurgling, bubble blowing. • Makes effort to imitate sounds made by older people with mixed success.
12 months	• Identical sound sequences replicated more often. • Words (e.g., *mamma* or *dada*) emerge. • Many words and requests understood (e.g., "Show me your eyes").
18 months	• Repertoire of 3–50 words. • Explosive vocabulary growth. • Babbling consists of several syllables with intricate intonation. • Little effort to communicate information. • Little joining of words into spontaneous two-word utterances. • Understands nearly everything spoken.
24 months	• Vocabulary more than 50 words, naming everything in the environment. • Spontaneous creation of two-word sentences. • Clear efforts to communicate.

Source: Table items adapted from Lenneberg (1967, pp. 128–130).
Note: Ages are approximations. Slower development does not necessarily indicate language problems.

tend to repeat syllables, showing what linguists refer to as **echolalia**. Parents overhear them going on and on, repeating consonant–vowel combinations ("ah-bah-bah-bah-bah"), pausing, and then switching to other combinations.

Toward the end of the first year, infants are also using patterns of rising and falling **intonation** that resemble the sounds of adult speech. It may sound as though the infant is trying to speak the parents' language. Parents may think that their children are babbling in English or in whatever tongue is spoken in the home.

6-4b DEVELOPMENT OF VOCABULARY

Vocabulary development refers to the child's learning the meanings of words. In general, children's **receptive vocabulary** development outpaces their **expressive vocabulary** development (Klee & Stokes, 2011). At any given time, they can understand more words than they can use. One study, for example, found that 12-month-olds could speak an average of 13 words but could comprehend the meaning of 84 (Tamis-LeMonda et al., 2006). Infants usually understand much of what others are saying well before they themselves utter any words at all. Their ability to segment speech sounds into meaningful units—or words—before 12 months is a good predictor of their vocabulary at 24 months (Newman et al., 2006).

THE CHILD'S FIRST WORDS Ah, that long-awaited first word! What a milestone! Sad to say, many parents miss it. They are not quite sure when their infants utter their first word, often because the first word is not pronounced clearly or because pronunciation varies from usage to usage.

A child's first word typically is spoken between the ages of 11 and 13 months, but a range of 8 to 18 months is considered normal (Klee & Stokes, 2011). First words tend to be brief, consisting of one or two syllables. Each syllable is likely to consist of a consonant followed by a vowel. Vocabulary acquisition is slow at first. It may take children three or four months to achieve a vocabulary of 10 to 30 words after the first word is spoken.

By about 18 months of age, children may be producing up to 50 words. Many of them are quite familiar, such as *no*, *cookie*, *mama*, *hi*, and *eat*. Others, such as *all gone* and *bye-bye*, may not be found in the dictionary, but they function as words. That is, they are used consistently to symbolize the same meaning.

More than half (65%) of children's first words make up "general nominals" and "specific nominals" (Hoff, 2014; Tamis-LeMonda et al., 2014). General nominals are similar to nouns in that they include the names of classes of objects (*car*, *ball*), animals (*doggy*, *cat*), and people (*boy*, *girl*), but they also include both personal and relative pronouns (*she*, *that*). Specific nominals are proper nouns, such as *Daddy* and *Rover*. Words expressing movement are frequently found in early speech.

At about 18 to 22 months of age, there is a rapid burst in vocabulary (Tamis-LeMonda et al., 2006). The child's vocabulary may increase from 50 to more than 300 words in only a few months. This vocabulary spurt could also be called a naming explosion because almost 75% of the words added during this time are nouns. The rapid pace of vocabulary growth continues through the preschool years, with children acquiring an average of nine new words per day (Hoff, 2006).

OVEREXTENSION Young children try to talk about more objects than they have words for. To accomplish their linguistic feats, children often extend the meaning of one word to refer to things and actions for which they do not have words (E. K. Johnson, 2016). This process is called **overextension**. Eve Clark (1973, 1975) studied diaries of infants' language development and found that overextensions are generally based on perceived similarities in function or form between the original object or action and the new one. She provides the example of the word *mooi*, which one child originally used to designate the moon. The child then overextended *mooi* to designate all round objects, including the letter *o* and cookies and cakes. Overextensions gradually pull back to their proper references as the child's vocabulary and ability to classify objects develop (E. K. Johnson, 2016).

6-4c DEVELOPMENT OF SENTENCES

The infant's first sentences are typically one-word utterances, but they express complete ideas and therefore can be thought of as sentences. Roger Brown (1973) called brief expressions that have the meanings of sentences **telegraphic speech**. Adults who write telegrams (or, today, text messages) often use principles of syntax to cut out unnecessary words. "Home Tuesday" might stand for "I expect to be home on Tuesday." Similarly, only the essential words are used in children's telegraphic speech—in particular, nouns, verbs, and some modifiers.

echolalia the automatic repetition of sounds or words.

intonation the use of pitches of varying levels to help communicate meaning.

receptive vocabulary the number of words one understands.

expressive vocabulary the number of words one can use in the production of language.

overextension use of words in situations in which their meanings become extended.

telegraphic speech type of speech in which only the essential words are used.

Language development in young children may be enhanced when caregivers engage the infant in "conversation."

MEAN LENGTH OF UTTERANCE The **mean length of utterance (MLU)** is the average number of **morphemes** that communicators use in their sentences. Morphemes are the smallest units of meaning in a language. A morpheme may be a whole word or part of a word, such as a prefix or suffix. For example, the word *walked* consists of two morphemes: the verb *walk* and the suffix *ed*, which changes the verb to the past tense. In Figure 6.5, we see the relationship between chronological age and MLU for three children tracked by Roger Brown (1973, 1977): Lin, Victor, and Sarah.

The patterns of growth in MLU are similar for each child, showing swift upward movement, broken by intermittent and brief regressions. Figure 6.5 also shows something about individual differences. Lin was precocious compared with Victor and Sarah, extending her MLU at much

mean length of utterance (MLU) the average number of morphemes used in an utterance.

morpheme the smallest unit of meaning in a language.

holophrase a single word that is used to express complex meanings.

earlier ages. But as suggested earlier, the receptive language of all three children would have exceeded their expressive language at any given time. Also, Lin's earlier extension of MLU does not guarantee that she will show more complex expressive language than Victor and Sarah at maturity.

Let us now consider the features of two types of telegraphic speech: the holophrase and two-word utterances.

HOLOPHRASES Holophrases are single words that are used to express complex meanings. For example, *Mama* may be used by the child to signify meanings as varied as "There goes Mama," "Come here, Mama," and "You are Mama." Most children readily teach their parents what they intend by augmenting their holophrases with gestures, intonations, and reinforcers. That is, they act delighted when parents do as requested and howl when they do not.

TWO-WORD SENTENCES When the child's vocabulary consists of 50 to 100 words (usually somewhere between 18 and 24 months of age), telegraphic two-word sentences begin to appear (Tamis-LeMonda

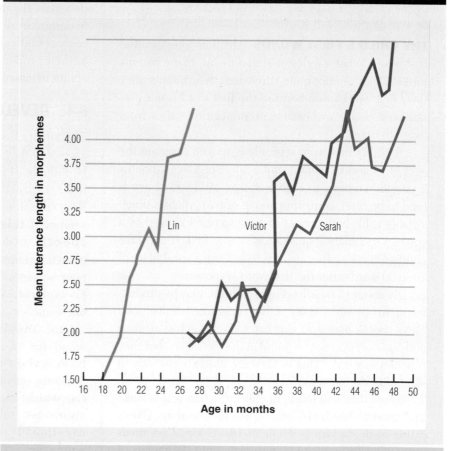

FIG.6.5 MEAN LENGTH OF UTTERANCE FOR THREE CHILDREN

The mean length of utterance (MLU) increases rapidly once speech begins.

Christos Georghiou/Shutterstock.com

et al., 2006). In the sentence "That ball," the words *is* and *a* are implied.

Two-word sentences, although brief and telegraphic, show understanding of **syntax** (Slobin, 2001). The child will say "Sit chair," not "Chair sit," to tell a parent to sit in a chair. The child will say "My shoe," not "Shoe my," to show possession. "Mommy go" means Mommy is leaving, whereas "Go Mommy" expresses the wish for Mommy to go away.

6-4d THEORIES OF LANGUAGE DEVELOPMENT

Billions of children have learned the languages spoken by their parents and have passed them down, with minor changes, from generation to generation. But how do they do so? In discussing this question—and so many others—we refer to the possible roles of nature and nurture. Learning theorists have come down on the side of nurture, and those who point to a basic role for nature are said to hold a nativist view.

6-4e VIEWS THAT EMPHASIZE NURTURE

Learning plays an obvious role in language development. Children who are reared in English-speaking homes learn English, not Japanese or Russian. Learning theorists usually explain language development in terms of imitation and reinforcement.

THE ROLE OF IMITATION From a social cognitive perspective, parents serve as **models**. Children learn language, at least in part, by observation and imitation. Many vocabulary words, especially nouns and verbs, are learned by imitation. But imitative learning does not explain why children spontaneously utter phrases and sentences that they have not observed (Waxman & Goswami, 2012). Parents, for example, are unlikely to model utterances such as "Bye bye sock" and "All gone Daddy" but children say them. And children sometimes steadfastly avoid imitating certain language forms suggested by adults, even when the adults are insistent. Note the following exchange between two-year-old Ben and a (very frustrated) adult (Kuczaj, 1982, p. 48):

Ben: I like these candy. I like they.

Adult: You like them?

Ben: Yes, I like they.

Adult: Say them.

Ben: Them.

Adult: Say "I like them."

Ben: I like them.

Adult: Good.

Ben: I'm good. These candy good too.

Adult: Are they good?

Ben: Yes. I like they. You like they?

Ben is not resisting the adult because of obstinacy. He does repeat "I like them" when asked to do so. But when given the opportunity afterward to construct the object *them*, he reverts to using the subjective form *they*. Ben is likely at this period in his development to use his (erroneous) understanding of syntax spontaneously to actively produce his own language, rather than just imitate a model.

THE ROLE OF REINFORCEMENT B. F. Skinner (1957) allowed that prelinguistic vocalizations such as cooing and babbling may be inborn. But parents reinforce children for babbling that approximates the form of real words, such as *da*, which, in English, resembles *dog* or *daddy*. Children, in fact, do increase their babbling when it results in adults smiling at them, stroking them, and talking back to them. As the first year progresses, children babble the sounds of their native tongues with increasing frequency; foreign sounds tend to drop out. The behaviorist explains this pattern of changing

syntax the rules in a language for placing words in order to form sentences.

models in learning theory, those whose behaviors are imitated by others.

Hurst Photo/Shutterstock.com

frequencies in terms of reinforcement of the sounds of the adults' language and **extinction** of foreign sounds. Another (nonbehavioral) explanation is that children actively attend to the sounds in their linguistic environments and are intrinsically motivated to utter them.

From Skinner's perspective, children acquire their early vocabularies through **shaping**. That is, parents require that children's utterances be progressively closer to actual words before they are reinforced. In support of Skinner's position, research has shown that reinforcement can accelerate the growth of vocabulary in children (Kroeger & Nelson, 2006; Waxman & Goswami, 2012).

But recall Ben's refusal to be shaped into correct syntax. If the reinforcement explanation of language development were sufficient, parents' reinforcement would facilitate children's learning of syntax and pronunciation. However, parents are more likely to reinforce their children for the accuracy, or "truth value," of their utterances than for their grammatical correctness (Brown, 1973). The child who points down and says "The grass is purple" is not likely to be reinforced, despite correct syntax. But the enthusiastic child who shows her empty plate and blurts out "I eated it all up" is likely to be reinforced, despite the grammatical incorrectness of "eated" (Morgenstern et al., 2013).

Selective reinforcement of children's pronunciation can also backfire. Children whose parents reward proper pronunciation but correct poor pronunciation develop vocabulary more slowly than children whose parents are more tolerant about pronunciation (Nelson, 1973).

Learning theory also cannot account for the invariant sequences of language development and for children's spurts in acquisition. The types of questions used, passive versus active sentences and so on, all emerge in the same order.

On the other hand, aspects of the child's language environment do influence the development of language. Studies show that language growth in young children is enhanced when adults (Tamis-LeMonda et al., 2014):

▶ Use "motherese" (technically termed infant-directed speech; see the nearby feature on motherese).

▶ Use questions that engage the child in conversation.

▶ Respond to the child's expressive language efforts in a way that is "attuned"; for example, adults relate their speech to the child's utterance by saying "Yes, your doll is pretty" in response to the child's statement "My doll."

▶ Join the child in paying attention to a particular activity or toy.

▶ Gesture to help the child understand what they are saying.

▶ Describe aspects of the environment occupying the infant's current focus of attention.

▶ Read to the child.

▶ Talk to the child a great deal.

6-4f VIEWS THAT EMPHASIZE NATURE

The nativist view of language development holds that inborn factors cause children to attend to and acquire language in certain ways. From this perspective, children bring an inborn tendency in the form of neurological "prewiring" to language learning. According to Steven Pinker (2007), the structures that enable humans to perceive and produce language evolved in bits and pieces. Those individuals who possessed these "bits" and "pieces" were more likely to reach maturity and transmit their genes from generation to generation because communication ability increased their chances of survival.

extinction decrease in frequency of a response due to absence of reinforcement.

shaping gradual building of complex behavior through reinforcement of successive approximations to the target behavior.

FICTION

T (F) You can advance children's development of pronunciation by correcting their errors.

It is not necessarily true that you can advance children's development of pronunciation by correcting their errors. Their vocabulary may not develop as rapidly if you focus on pronunciation.

"Since all normal humans talk but no house pets or house plants do, no matter how pampered, heredity must be involved in language. But since a child growing up in Japan speaks Japanese whereas the same child brought up in California would speak English, the environment is also crucial. Thus, there is no question about whether heredity or environment is involved in language, or even whether one or the other is "more important." Instead, . . . our best hope [might be] finding out how they interact."

—Steven Pinker

PSYCHOLINGUISTIC THEORY According to **psycholinguistic theory**, language acquisition involves an interaction between environmental influences—such as exposure to parental speech and reinforcement—and an inborn tendency to acquire language. Noam Chomsky (1988, 1990) labeled this innate tendency a **language acquisition device (LAD)**. Evidence for an inborn tendency is found in the universality of human language abilities; in the regularity of the early production of sounds, even among deaf children; and in the invariant sequences of language development among all languages (Pinker, 2007).

The inborn tendency primes the nervous system to learn grammar. On the surface, languages differ much in vocabulary and grammar. Chomsky labels these elements the **surface structure** of language. However, Chomsky believes that the LAD serves children all over the world because languages share a "universal grammar"— an underlying **deep structure** or set of rules for

transforming ideas into sentences. From Chomsky's perspective, children are genetically prewired to attend to language and deduce the rules for constructing sentences from ideas. That is, it appears that children are prewired to listen to language in such a way that they come to understand rules of grammar.

BRAIN STRUCTURES INVOLVED IN LANGUAGE

Many parts of the brain are involved in language development; however, some of the key biological structures that may provide the basis for the functions of the LAD are based in the left hemisphere of the cerebral cortex for nearly all right-handed people and for two out of three left-handed people (Hoff, 2014). In the left hemisphere, the two areas most involved in speech are Broca's area and Wernicke's area (see Figure 6.6 on page 110). Damage to either area is likely to cause an **aphasia**—a disruption in the ability to understand or produce language.

Broca's area is located near the section of the motor cortex that controls the muscles of the tongue and throat and other areas of the face that are used in speech. When Broca's area is damaged, people speak laboriously in a pattern termed **Broca's aphasia**. But they can readily understand speech.

psycholinguistic theory the view that language learning involves an interaction between environmental influences and an inborn tendency to acquire language.

language acquisition device (LAD) neural "prewiring" that eases the child's learning of grammar.

surface structure the superficial grammatical construction of a sentence.

deep structure the underlying meaning of a sentence.

aphasia a disruption in the ability to understand or produce language.

Broca's aphasia an aphasia caused by damage to Broca's area and characterized by difficulty speaking.

TRUTH

 F Children are "prewired" to listen to language in such a way that they come to understand rules of grammar.

It is apparently true that children are "prewired" to listen to language in such a way that they come to understand rules of grammar. There is clearly an inborn biological component to language acquisition.

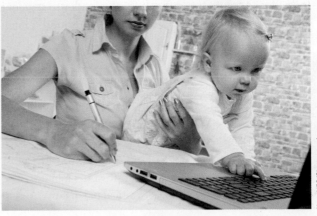

FIG.6.6 BROCA'S AND WERNICKE'S AREAS OF THE CEREBRAL CORTEX

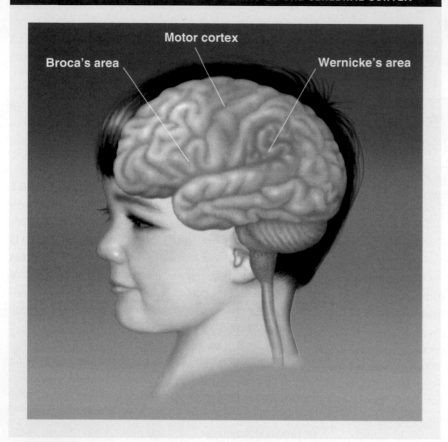

Wernicke's area lies near the auditory cortex and is connected to Broca's area by nerves. People with damage to Wernicke's area may show **Wernicke's aphasia**, in which they speak freely and with proper syntax but have trouble understanding speech and finding the words to express themselves.

A part of the brain called the angular gyrus lies between the visual cortex and Wernicke's area. The angular gyrus "translates" visual information, such as written words, into auditory information (sounds) and sends it on to Wernicke's area. Problems in the angular gyrus can cause problems in reading because it is difficult for the reader to segment words into sounds (Pugh et al., 2013).

wernicke's aphasia an aphasia caused by damage to Wernicke's area and characterized by impaired comprehension of speech and difficulty producing the right word.

critical period the period from about 18 months to puberty when the brain is especially capable of learning language. Also called the *sensitive period*.

THE CRITICAL PERIOD FOR LANGUAGE ACQUISITION Language learning is most efficient during the **critical period**, when children are most sensitive to language. The critical or sensitive period

begins at about 18 to 24 months and lasts until puberty (Bedny et al., 2012; Werker & Hensch, 2015). During this period, neural development provides plasticity of the brain.

Evidence for a critical period is found in recovery from brain injuries in some people. Injuries to the hemisphere that controls language (usually the left hemisphere) can impair or destroy the ability to speak. But before puberty, children suffering left-hemisphere injuries frequently recover a good deal of speaking ability. In young children, left-hemisphere damage may encourage the development of language functions in the right hemisphere. But adaptation ability wanes in adolescence, when brain tissue has reached adult levels of differentiation (Snow, 2006; Garvain, 2015).

The best way to determine whether people are capable of acquiring language once they have passed puberty would be to run an experiment in which one or more children were reared in such severe isolation that they were not exposed to language until puberty. Of course, such an experiment could not be run for ethical reasons. However, the disturbing case history of Genie offers insights into whether there is a critical period for language development (Friedmann & Rusou, 2015).

Genie's father locked her in a small room at the age of 20 months and kept her there until she was 13 years old. Her social contacts during this period were limited to her mother, who entered the room only to feed Genie, and to beatings by her father. When Genie was rescued, she weighed only about 60 pounds, did not speak, was not toilet trained, and could barely stand. She was placed in a foster home, and thereafter her language development followed the normal sequence of much younger children in a number of ways. Five years after her liberation, however, Genie's language remained largely telegraphic. She still showed significant problems with syntax, such as failing to reverse subjects and verbs to phrase questions.

Genie's language development provides support for the critical-period hypothesis, although her language problems might also be partly attributed to her years of malnutrition and abuse. Her efforts to acquire English after puberty were laborious, and the results

"Motherese"—Of "Yummy-Yummy" and "Kitty Cats"

One way that adults attempt to prompt the language development of young children is through the use of baby talk, or "motherese," referred to more technically as *infant-directed speech (IDS)* (Meltzoff et al., 2013; Singh et al., 2009). *Motherese* is a limiting term because grandparents, fathers, siblings, and unrelated people have also been observed using IDS (Braarud & Stormark, 2008). Moreover, women (but usually not men) often talk to their pets as if they were infants (Xu et al., 2013). Infant-directed speech is used in languages as diverse as Arabic, English, Comanche, Italian, French, German, Xhosa (an African tongue), Japanese, Mandarin Chinese, and even a Thai sign language (Lee et al., 2010). Researchers have found that IDS has the following characteristics (McMurray et al., 2013; Meltzoff & Brooks, 2009):

▶ It is spoken more slowly and at a higher pitch than speech addressed to adults. There are distinct pauses between ideas.

▶ Sentences are brief, and adults try to speak in a grammatically correct manner.

▶ Sentences are simple in syntax. The focus is on nouns, verbs, and just a few modifiers.

▶ Key words are placed at the ends of sentences and spoken in a higher and louder voice.

▶ The diminutive morpheme y is frequently added to nouns. *Dad* becomes *Daddy*, and *horse* becomes *horsey*.

▶ Adults repeat sentences several times, sometimes using minor variations, as in "Show me your nose." "Where is your nose?" "Can you touch your nose?" Adults also rephrase children's utterances to expand children's awareness of their expressive opportunities. If the child says, "Baby shoe," the mother may reply, "Yes, that's your shoe. Shall Mommy put the shoe on baby's foot?"

▶ It includes duplication. *Yummy* becomes *yummy-yummy*. *Daddy* may alternate with *Da-da*.

▶ Much IDS focuses on naming objects. Vocabulary is concrete and refers to the child's environment. For example, stuffed lions may be called "kitties."

▶ Objects may be overdescribed with compound labels. Rabbits may become "bunny rabbits," and cats may become "kitty cats." Users of IDS try to ensure that they are using at least one label that the child will recognize.

▶ Parents speak for the children, as in "Is baby tired?" "Oh, we're so tired." "We want to take our nap now, don't we?" Parents seem to be helping children express themselves by offering them models of sentences they can use.

Does IDS encourage communication and foster language development? Research supports its use. Infants as young as two days old prefer IDS to adult talk (N. A. Smith & Trainor, 2008). The short, simple sentences and high pitch are more likely to produce a response from the child and enhance vocabulary development than complex sentences and those spoken in a lower pitch (Singh et al., 2009). Repetition of children's vocalizations appears to encourage vocalizing.

Fubberball

were substandard compared even with the language of many two- and three-year-olds.

In sum, the development of language in infancy represents the interaction of environmental and biological factors. The child brings a built-in readiness to the task of language acquisition, whereas houseplants and other organisms do not. The child must also have the opportunity to hear spoken language and to interact verbally with others. In the next chapter, we see how interaction with others affects social development.

READY TO STUDY?

In the book, you can:

☐ Check your understanding of what you've read with the quizzes below.

☐ Rip out the chapter review card at the back of the book to have a summary of the chapter and the key terms handy.

ONLINE AT CENGAGEBRAIN.COM YOU CAN:

☐ Watch a video showing Piaget's four major stages of cognitive development.

☐ Prepare for tests with quizzes.

☐ Review the key terms with Flash Cards.

☐ Play games to master concepts.

SELF-ASSESSMENTS

Fill-Ins

Answers can be found in the back of the book.

1. According to Piaget, children try to use _____ to absorb new events into existing schemes.

2. In the sensorimotor substage of _____ circular reactions, activity is repeated because of its effect on the environment.

3. By the age of two months, an infant may show some surprise if a toy duck is placed behind a screen and then taken away so that when the screen is lifted, it is absent. But the infant will not look for it because she has not yet developed _____ permanence.

4. The presence of _____ imitation suggests that children have mentally represented behavior patterns.

5. _____ is the first vocalizing that has the sound of human speech.

6. The use of visual _____ memory to assess infants' cognitive development is based on habituation.

7. The ability of the infant to transfer an object from one hand to the other during play is typical of the _____ month of cognitive development.

8. A certain class of neurons, called _____ neurons, makes it possible for newborns to imitate an adult who is sticking out his tongue.

9. At 10 to 12 months, infants tend to repeat syllables, showing what linguists refer to as _____.

10. At first a child uses a word such as *mooi* to refer to the moon. Then she uses the word to refer to round objects in general. This is an example of _____.

Multiple Choice

1. In the fourth substage of the sensorimotor period, infants coordinate schemes to attain goals; that is, they begin to show intentional, goal-directed behavior. This substage lasts approximately from
   a. 4 to 8 months of age.
   b. 8 to 12 months of age.
   c. 12 to 18 months of age.
   d. 18 to 24 months of age.

2. All of the following are prelinguistic vocalizations, with the exception of
   a. holophrases.
   b. crying.
   c. cooing.
   d. babbling.

3. Infants typically say words beginning at about the age of
   a. 6 months.
   b. 12 months.
   c. 18 months.
   d. 24 months.

4. Which of the following is accurate about the Bayley Scales of Infant Development?
   a. Most infants are not yet ready to take them.
   b. Infants can be tested for motor skills but not for mental skills.
   c. The scales predict long-term cognitive development, but are not reliable from testing to testing.
   d. The scales do not predict school grades or IQ scores among school children.

5. Infants do not use their tongues when they
   a. babble.
   b. cry.
   c. coo.
   d. imitate words.

6. What is the relationship between a child's receptive vocabulary development and her expressive vocabulary development?
   a. Receptive vocabulary develops more rapidly than expressive vocabulary.
   b. Expressive vocabulary develops more rapidly than receptive vocabulary.
   c. Receptive vocabulary and expressive vocabulary develop at the same pace.
   d. There is so much individual variation that it is not possible to generalize about the relationship between receptive vocabulary and expressive vocabulary.

7. A child spontaneously creates two-word sentences sometime between the ages of
   a. 4 and 8 months.
   b. 8 and 12 months.
   c. 12 and 18 months.
   d. 18 and 24 months.

8. For the first couple of years, a child's vocabulary is mainly made of
   a. verbs.
   b. adjectives.
   c. adverbs.
   d. nouns.

9. In the study in which two-year-old "Ben" and an adult have a conversation about candy,
   a. Ben extends the meaning of the word *candy* to include animals.
   b. Ben uses his own understanding of syntax to produce his own language.
   c. Ben imitates a model but does not understand why he is doing so.
   d. Ben imitates the model and his language development is accelerated.

10. Infant-directed speech ("motherese") is characterized by all of the following *except*
    a. brief sentences.
    b. the diminutive morpheme y is frequently added to nouns.
    c. speaking slowly and with a higher pitch than normal.
    d. correcting children when their vocabulary or syntax is incorrect.

7 | Infancy: Social and Emotional Development

Lisa Wikstrand/Maskot/Getty Images

LEARNING OUTCOMES

After studying this chapter, you will be able to . . .

7-1 Describe the development of attachment in infancy and theoretical views of how it occurs

7-2 Discuss the relationships between social deprivation, child abuse and neglect, autism spectrum disorders, and attachment

7-3 Discuss the effects of day care on attachment

7-4 Describe the emotional development of the infant

7-5 Describe the personality development of the infant, focusing on the self-concept, temperament, and gender differences

After you finish this chapter, go to **PAGE 132** for **STUDY TOOLS**

When she was two years old, one of my daughters almost succeeded at preventing publication of a book I was writing. When I locked myself into my study, she positioned herself outside the door and called, "Daddy, oh Daddy." At other times she would bang on the door or cry. When I would give in (several times a day) and open the door, she would run in and say, "I want you to pick up me," hold out

> Babies have behavior patterns—crying, smiling, clinging— that stimulate caregiving from adults.

her arms or climb into my lap. How would I finish the book? One solution was to write outside the home, but this solution had the drawback of distancing me from my family. Another solution was to ignore her and let her cry, but I didn't want to discourage her efforts to get to me. **Attachment**, you see, is a two-way street. The third solution was to fit in working when I could, which is how that book got written.

7-1 ATTACHMENT: BONDS THAT ENDURE

Attachment is what most people refer to as affection or love. Mary Ainsworth (1989), a preeminent researcher on attachment, defines attachment as an enduring emotional bond between one animal or person and another. John Bowlby adds that attachment is essential to the survival of the infant (Bowlby, 1988). He notes that babies are born with behaviors—crying, smiling, clinging—that stimulate caregiving from adults.

Infants try to maintain contact with caregivers to whom they are attached. They engage in eye contact, pull and tug at them, and ask to be picked up. When they cannot maintain contact, they show **separation anxiety**—thrash about, fuss, cry, screech, or whine.

7-1a PATTERNS OF ATTACHMENT

Ainsworth and her colleagues (1978) identified various patterns of attachment. Broadly, infants show **secure attachment** or

insecure attachment. Most infants in the United States are securely attached (Beebe et al., 2010; Zeanah et al., 2011).

Ainsworth developed the *Strange Situation method* as a way of measuring the development of attachment (see Figure 7.1 on page 115). In this method, an infant is exposed to a series of separations and reunions with a caregiver (usually the mother) and a stranger who is a confederate of the researchers. In the test, secure infants mildly protest their mother's departure, seek interaction upon reunion, and are readily comforted by her.

There are two major types of insecurity, or "insecure attachment": **avoidant attachment** and **ambivalent/resistant attachment**. Infants who

attachment an affectional bond characterized by seeking closeness with another and distress upon separation.

separation anxiety fear of separation from a target of attachment.

secure attachment a type of attachment characterized by mild distress at leave-takings and being readily soothed by reunion.

insecure attachment attachment behavior characterized by avoiding caregiver, excessive clinging, or inconsistency.

avoidant attachment a type of insecure attachment characterized by apparent indifference to leave-takings by and reunions with an attachment figure.

ambivalent/resistant attachment a type of insecure attachment characterized by severe distress at leave-takings and ambivalent behavior at reunions.

TRUTH OR FICTION?

T	F	Autistic children may respond to people as though they were pieces of furniture.
T	F	Autism can be caused by vaccines.
T	F	Children placed in day care are more aggressive than children who are cared for in the home.
T	F	Fear of strangers is abnormal among infants.
T	F	All children are born with the same temperament. Treatment by caregivers determines whether they are difficult or easygoing.
T	F	Girls may prefer dolls and toy animals, and boys may prefer toy trucks and sports equipment, but these preferences emerge only after they have become aware of the gender roles assigned to them by society.

FIG.7.1   THE STRANGE SITUATION

These historic photos show a 12-month-old child in the Strange Situation. In (a), the child plays with toys, glancing occasionally at mother. In (b), the stranger approaches with a toy. While the child is distracted, mother leaves the room. In (c), mother returns after a brief absence. The child crawls to her quickly and clings to her when picked up. In (d), the child cries when mother again leaves the room.

7-1b ESTABLISHING ATTACHMENT

Attachment is related to the quality of infant care (Oliveira et al., 2015; Sullivan et al., 2011). The parents of secure infants are more affectionate, cooperative, and predictable than parents of insecure infants. They respond more sensitively to their infants' smiles and cries (Bigelow et al., 2010; Xue et al., 2010).

Researchers have found evidence for the "intergenerational transmission of attachment" (Berzenski et al., 2014; Miljkovich et al., 2012). The children of secure mothers show the most secure patterns of attachment themselves (Cicchetti et al., 2006). Siblings may form quite different attachment relationships with their mother (O'Connor et al., 2011). Siblings of the same gender are more likely than girl–boy pairs to form similar attachment relationships with their mother.

Security is also connected with the infant's temperament (Lickenbrock et al., 2013; Solmeyer & Feinberg, 2011). The mothers of "difficult" children are less responsive to them and report feeling more distant from them (Lickenbrock et al., 2013; Wang et al., 2015).

INVOLVEMENT OF FATHERS How involved is the average father with his children? The brief answer, in developed nations, is more so than in the past (Grossmann et al., 2002). But mothers engage in more interactions with their infants. Most fathers are more likely to play with their children than to feed or clean them (Lucassen et al., 2011). Fathers more often than mothers engage in rough-and-tumble play, whereas mothers are more likely to play games involving toys, and patty-cake and peek-a-boo (Lucassen et al., 2011).

How strongly, then, do infants become attached to their fathers? The more sensitive the father is to the infant's needs, the stronger the attachment (Fuertes et al., 2016).

show avoidant attachment are least distressed by their mothers' departure. They play without fuss when alone and ignore their mothers upon reunion. Ambivalent/resistant babies are the most emotional. They show severe signs of distress when their mothers leave and show ambivalence upon reunion by alternately clinging to their mothers and pushing them away. Additional categories of insecure attachment have been proposed, including **disorganized–disoriented attachment**. Babies showing this pattern seem dazed, confused, or disoriented. They may show contradictory behaviors, such as moving toward the mother while looking away from her.

Secure infants and toddlers are happier, more sociable, and more cooperative with caregivers. At ages five and six, they get along better with peers and are better adjusted in school than insecure children (Borelli et al., 2010; George et al., 2010). Insecure attachment in infancy predicts psychological disorders during adolescence (Milan et al., 2013).

disorganized–disoriented attachment a type of insecure attachment characterized by dazed and contradictory behaviors toward an attachment figure.

7-1c STABILITY OF ATTACHMENT

Patterns of attachment tend to persist when care-giving conditions remain constant (Beebe et al., 2010; Stupica et al., 2011). Byron Egeland and Alan Sroufe (1981) followed infants who were severely neglected and others who received high-quality care from 12 to 18 months of age. Attachment patterns remained stable (secure) for infants receiving fine care. But many insecure neglected infants became securely attached over the six-month period, either because of a relationship with a supportive family member or because home life grew less tense. Children can also become less securely attached to caregivers when home life deteriorates (Levendosky et al., 2011). On the positive side, children adopted at various ages can become securely attached to adoptive parents (Niemann & Weiss, 2011; Raby et al., 2013; Schoenmaker et al., 2014).

7-1d STAGES OF ATTACHMENT

Cross-cultural studies have led to a theory of stages of attachment. In one study, Ainsworth tracked the behavior of Ugandan infants. Over a nine-month period, she noted their efforts to maintain contact with the mother, their protests when separated, and their use of the mother as

PHASES OF ATTACHMENT

Mary Ainsworth and her colleagues identified three phases of attachment in infants:

1. **Initial-preattachment**
2. **Attachment-in-the-making**
3. **Clear-cut attachment**

Mary Ainsworth (1913–1999)

a base for exploring the environment. At first, the Ugandan infants showed **indiscriminate attachment**—no particular preferences for a familiar caregiver. Specific attachment to the mother, as evidenced by separation anxiety and other behavior, began to develop at about four months of age and grew intense by about seven months. Fear of strangers developed one or two months later.

In another study, shown in Figure 7.2, Scottish infants showed indiscriminate attachment during the first six months or so after birth (Schaffer & Emerson, 1964). Then, indiscriminate attachment waned. Specific attachments to the mother and other familiar caregivers intensified, as demonstrated by the appearance of separation anxiety, and remained at high levels through the age of 18 months. Fear of strangers occurred a month or so after the intensity of specific attachments began to mushroom. In both this and the Ugandan study, fear of strangers followed separation anxiety and the development of specific attachments by weeks.

From such studies, Ainsworth and her colleagues (1978) identified the following three phases of attachment:

1. The **initial-preattachment phase** lasts from birth to about three months and is characterized by indiscriminate attachment.

2. The **attachment-in-the-making phase** occurs at about three or four months and is characterized by preference for familiar figures.

indiscriminate attachment the display of attachment behaviors toward any person.

initial-preattachment phase the first phase in development of attachment, characterized by indiscriminate attachment.

attachment-in-the-making phase the second phase in development of attachment, characterized by preference for familiar figures.

FIG. 7.2 DEVELOPMENT OF ATTACHMENT

During the first six months, infants tend to show indiscriminate attachment, which wanes as specific attachments intensify.

3. The **clear-cut-attachment phase** occurs at about six or seven months and is characterized by intensified dependence on the primary caregiver, usually the mother.

But most infants have more than one adult caregiver and are likely to form multiple attachments: to the father, day-care providers, grandparents, and other caregivers, as well as the mother.

7-1e THEORIES OF ATTACHMENT

There are several theories of the development of attachment.

COGNITIVE VIEW OF ATTACHMENT The cognitive view suggests that an infant must develop the concept of object permanence before specific attachment becomes possible. If caregivers are to be missed when absent, the infant must perceive that they continue to exist. We have seen that infants tend to develop specific attachments at about the age of six to seven months. Basic object permanence concerning objects develops somewhat earlier (see Chapter 6).

BEHAVIORAL VIEW OF ATTACHMENT Early in the 20th century, behaviorists argued that attachment behaviors are conditioned. Caregivers feed their infants and tend to their other physiological needs. Thus, infants associate their caregivers with gratification and learn to approach them to meet their needs. From this perspective, a caregiver becomes a conditioned reinforcer.

PSYCHOANALYTIC VIEWS OF ATTACHMENT According to psychoanalytic theorists, the caregiver, usually the mother, becomes not just a "reinforcer" but also a love object who forms the basis for all later attachments. Sigmund Freud emphasized the importance of oral activities, such as eating, in the first year. Freud believed that the infant becomes emotionally attached to the mother during this time because she is the primary satisfier of the infant's needs for food and sucking.

Erik Erikson characterized the first year of life as the stage of *trust vs. mistrust*. Erikson believed that the first year is critical for developing a sense of trust in the mother, which fosters attachment. The mother's general sensitivity to the child's needs, not just the need for food, fosters the development of trust and attachment.

THE CAREGIVER AS A SOURCE OF CONTACT COMFORT Harry and Margaret Harlow conducted classic experiments to demonstrate that feeding is not as critical to the attachment process as Freud suggested (Harlow & Harlow, 1966). In one study, the Harlows placed rhesus monkey infants in cages with two surrogate mothers (see Figure 7.3). One "mother" was made from wire mesh from which a baby bottle was extended. The other surrogate mother was made of soft, cuddly terry cloth. Infant monkeys spent most of their time clinging to the cloth mother, even though she did not offer food. The Harlows concluded that monkeys—and presumably humans—have a built-in need for **contact comfort**.

ETHOLOGICAL VIEW OF ATTACHMENT Ethologists note that for many animals, attachment is an inborn or instinctive response to a specific stimulus. Some researchers theorize that a baby's cry stimulates caregiving in women. By two to three months of age, the human

clear-cut-attachment phase the third phase in development of attachment, characterized by intensified dependence on the primary caregiver.

contact comfort the pleasure derived from physical contact with another.

ethologist a scientist who studies the behavior patterns characteristic of various species.

FIG.7.3 CONTACT COMFORT

Time on cloth mother

Time on wire mother

Hours per day

Mean age (days)

Nina Leen/Time Life Pictures/Getty Images

Although this rhesus monkey infant is fed by the "wire-mesh mother," it spends most of its time clinging to a soft, cuddly, "terry-cloth mother."

face begins to elicit a **social smile** in infants, helping to ensure survival by eliciting affection (Ainsworth & Bowlby, 1991; Bowlby, 1988). In circular fashion, the mother's social response to her infant's face can reliably produce infant smiling by eight months of age (Jones & Hong, 2005). The pattern contributes to a mutual attachment.

In many nonhumans, attachment occurs during a **critical period** of life. Waterfowl become attached during this period to the first moving object they encounter. Because the image of the moving object seems to become "imprinted" on the young animal, the process is termed **imprinting**.

Ethologist Konrad Lorenz (1962, 1981) became well known when pictures of his "family" of goslings were made public. Lorenz acquired his "following" by being present when the goslings hatched and allowing them to follow him. The critical period for geese and ducks begins when they first engage in locomotion and ends when they develop fear of strangers. The goslings followed Lorenz persistently, ran to him when frightened, honked with distress at his departure, and tried to overcome barriers placed between them. If you substitute crying for honking, it sounds quite human.

ETHOLOGY, AINSWORTH, AND BOWLBY Let us return to Ainsworth and Bowlby (1991). They wrote that "the distinguishing characteristic of the theory of attachment that we have jointly developed is that it is an ethological approach" (p. 333). But their ethological approach differs from Lorenz's in a number of ways. For example, Ainsworth and Bowlby write that caregiving in humans is largely learned and not inborn. Ainsworth and Bowlby also note that the critical period for attachment in humans (if one exists), as opposed to attachment periods for lower mammals, extends to months or years (Ainsworth & Bowlby, 1991; Takamura et al., 2016). Caregiving itself and infant responsiveness, such as smiling, also promote attachment.

What happens when children are reared with little or no contact with caregivers? When parents neglect or abuse their children? In the case of autism spectrum disorders?

7-2a SOCIAL DEPRIVATION

Studies of children reared in institutions where they receive little social stimulation from caregivers are limited in that they are correlational. In other words, family factors that led to the children's placement in institutions may also have contributed to their developmental problems. Ethical considerations prevent us from conducting experiments in which we randomly assign children to social deprivation. However, experiments of this kind have been undertaken with rhesus monkeys, and the results are consistent with those of the correlational studies of children.

EXPERIMENTS WITH MONKEYS The Harlows and their colleagues conducted studies of rhesus monkeys that were "reared by" wire-mesh and terry-cloth surrogate mothers. In later studies, rhesus monkeys were reared without even this questionable "social" support— without seeing any other animal, monkey or human (Harlow et al., 1971).

The Harlows found that rhesus infants reared in this most solitary confinement later avoided other monkeys. Instead, they cowered in the presence of others. Nor did they try to fend off attacks by other monkeys. Rather, they sat in the corner, clutching themselves, and rocking back and forth. Females who later bore children ignored or abused them.

Can the damage from social deprivation be overcome? When monkeys deprived for six months or

social smile a smile that occurs in response to a human voice or face.

critical period a period during which imprinting can occur.

imprinting the process by which waterfowl become attached to the first moving object they follow.

Konrad Lorenz with his "family" of goslings. This mechanical type of attachment is known as imprinting.

Nina Leen/Time & Life Pictures/Getty Images

more are placed with younger, three- to four-month-old females for a couple of hours a day, the younger monkeys attempt to interact with their deprived elders. Many of the deprived monkeys begin to play with the youngsters after a few weeks, and many eventually expand their social contacts to older monkeys (Suomi et al., 1972). Socially withdrawn children can similarly make gains in their social and emotional development when provided with younger playmates (Kumsta et al., 2010; Rubin & Coplan, 2010).

STUDIES WITH CHILDREN Institutionalized children whose material needs are met but who receive little social stimulation from caregivers encounter problems in all areas of development (Johnson & Gunnar, 2011; Koss et al., 2014). René A. Spitz (1965) found that many institutionalized children show withdrawal and depression. In one institution, infants were maintained in separate cubicles for most of their first year to ward off infectious diseases (Provence & Lipton, 1962).

Adults tended to them only to feed them and change their diapers. As a rule, baby bottles were propped up in their cribs. Attendants rarely responded to their cries; they were rarely played with or spoken to. By the age of four months, the infants showed little interest in adults. A few months later, some of them sat withdrawn in their cribs and rocked back and forth, almost like the Harlows' monkeys. None were speaking at 12 months.

Why do children whose material needs are met show such dramatic deficiencies? The answer may depend, in part, on the age of the child. Classic research by Leon Yarrow and his colleagues (Yarrow et al., 1971; Yarrow & Goodwin, 1973) suggests that deficiencies in sensory stimulation and social interaction may cause more problems than lack of love in infants who are too young to have developed specific attachments. But once infants have developed specific attachments, separation from their primary caregivers can lead to problems.

Sensory stimulation and social interaction may be as important as love in the social development of infants.

Jessica Peterson/Brand X Pictures/Getty Images

THE CAPACITY TO RECOVER FROM SOCIAL DEPRIVATION Infants also have powerful capacities to recover from deprivation. One study showed how many children may be able to recover fully from 13 or 14 months of deprivation (Kagan & Klein, 1973). The natives in an isolated Guatemalan village believe that fresh air and sunshine will sicken children. Children are thus kept in windowless huts until they can walk and are played with infrequently. During their isolation, the infants behave apathetically. They are physically and socially delayed when they start to walk. But by 11 years of age they are as alert and active as their age-mates in the United States.

A classic longitudinal study of orphanage children also offers evidence of the ability of children to recover from social deprivation (Skeels, 1966). In this study, a group of 19-month-old apparently intellectually disabled children were placed in the care of older institutionalized girls. The girls spent a great deal of time playing with and nurturing them. Four years after being placed with the girls, the "disabled" children made dramatic gains in IQ scores, whereas children who did not receive this stimulation showed declines in IQ.

7-2b CHILD ABUSE AND NEGLECT

Consider the following statistics from national surveys (U.S. Department of Health and Human Services [USDHHS], 2013): By the time a child is two years of age, nine in ten parents have engaged in some sort of psychological or emotional abuse; more than half of parents have slapped or spanked their children; and one-third of parents have pushed, grabbed, or shoved their children.

Nearly two-fifths (37.3%) of American children are neglected or abused each year by their parents or caregivers (Finkelhor et al., 2015). About one in ten of these children experiences serious injury. Thousands die. More than 150,000 are sexually abused. But researchers believe that 50% to 60% of cases of child abuse and neglect go unreported, so the actual incidences are likely to be significantly higher (USDHHS, 2013).

The U.S. Department of Health and Human Services recognizes several types of maltreatment of children (USDHHS, 2013):

▶ Physical abuse: actions causing pain and physical injury

▶ Sexual abuse: sexual molestation, exploitation, and intercourse

▶ Emotional abuse: actions that impair the child's emotional, social, or intellectual functioning

▶ Physical neglect: failure to provide adequate food, shelter, clothing, or medical care

▶ Emotional neglect: failure to provide adequate nurturance and emotional support

▶ Educational neglect: for example, permitting or forcing the child to be truant

Although blatant abuse is more horrifying, more injuries, illnesses, and deaths result from neglect (USDHHS, 2013). Table 7.1 shows examples of the three types of neglect.

Why do more than half the cases of abuse and neglect go unreported? One answer is that it can be difficult, especially for abusers, to draw the line between "normal discipline" and abuse. Other reasons include fear of embarrassing a family; fear of legal consequences; and, sometimes, a mother's fear that she will be victimized by the abuser if she reports the crime. In any event, child neglect is responsible for more injuries and deaths than abuse (USDHHS, 2013).

Although most sexually abused children are girls, one-quarter to one-third are boys (USDHHS, 2013). When we sample the population at large rather than rely on cases of abuse that are reported to authorities, it appears that the prevalence of sexual abuse among children is about 2% each year, but the rate for girls aged 14 to 17 is above 10% in a given year (Finkelhor et al., 2015). This chapter is about infants, but many boys in middle childhood and adolescence have been sexually abused by religious leaders and by athletic coaches—as made all too clear in news reports in recent years.

EFFECTS OF CHILD ABUSE Abused children show a high incidence of personal and social problems and psychological disorders (Sousa et al., 2011). In general, abused children are less securely attached to their parents. They are less intimate with peers and more aggressive, angry, and noncompliant than other children (Blow, 2014: Moylan et al., 2010). They have lower self-esteem and perform more poorly in school. Later on, abused children are at greater risk for delinquency, risky sexual behavior, substance abuse, and abusing their own children (Sousa et al., 2011; Sperry & Widom, 2013). When they reach adulthood, they are also more likely to act aggressively toward their intimate partners (Gomez, 2011).

CAUSES OF CHILD ABUSE Various factors contribute to child abuse, including stress, a history of child abuse in at least one parent's family of origin, lack of adequate coping and child-rearing skills, unrealistic expectations of

TABLE 7.1	THE THREE FORMS OF CHILD NEGLECT—EXAMPLES	
Physical Neglect	**Educational Neglect**	**Emotional Neglect**
A 2-year-old who was found wandering in the street late at night, naked and alone	An 11-year-old and a 13-year-old who were chronically truant	Siblings who were subjected to repeated incidents of family violence between their mother and father
An infant who had to be hospitalized for near-drowning after being left alone in a bathtub	A 12-year-old whose parents permitted him to decide whether to go to school, how long to stay there, and in which activities to participate	A 12-year-old whose parents permitted him to drink and use drugs
Children who were living in a home contaminated with animal feces and rotting food	A special education student whose mother refused to believe he needed help in school	A child whose mother helped him shoot out the windows of a neighbor's house

Source: From Mash/Wolfe, Abnormal Child Psychology, 5E. © 2013 Cengage Learning.

children, and substance abuse (Wolfe, 2011). Stress has many sources, including divorce, loss of a job, moving, and birth of a new family member (Wolfe, 2011). Much of the problem is also cultural: The great majority of Americans, male and female, agree with the statement that "It is sometimes necessary to discipline a child with a 'good hard spanking'" (Child Trends Data Bank; see Figure 7.4).

Ironically, infants who are already in pain of some kind and difficult to soothe are more likely to be abused (Stupica et al., 2011). Abusive parents may find the cries of their infants particularly aversive, so infants' crying may precipitate abuse (Schuetze et al., 2003). Children who are irritable, disobedient, inappropriate, or unresponsive are also at greater risk (Wolfe, 2011).

WHAT TO DO Many states require helping professionals such as psychologists and physicians to report any suspicion of child abuse. Some legally require *anyone* who suspects child abuse to report it to authorities.

A number of techniques have been developed to help prevent child abuse. One approach focuses on strengthening parenting skills among the general population (Bugental et al., 2010). Another approach targets groups at high risk for abuse, such as poor, single, teen mothers (Robling et al., 2016). In some programs, home visitors help new parents develop skills in caregiving and home management (Bugental et al., 2010).

A third technique focuses on presenting information about abuse and providing support to families. For instance, many

autism spectrum disorders (ASDs) developmental disorders characterized by impairment in communication and social skills, and by repetitive, stereotyped behavior.

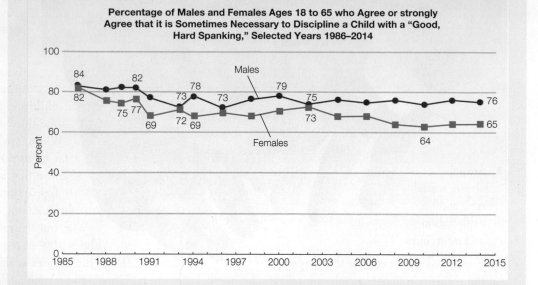

FIG. 7.4 | TRENDS IN ATTITUDE TOWARD SPANKING AMONG U.S. ADULTS

Percentage of Males and Females Ages 18 to 65 who Agree or strongly Agree that it is Sometimes Necessary to Discipline a Child with a "Good, Hard Spanking," Selected Years 1986–2014

Although there have been slight declines in U.S. adults who support "a good, hard spanking" over the last three decades, about three in four males and two in three females continue to agree with the practice.

locales have child abuse hotlines. Readers who suspect child abuse may call for advice. Parents having difficulty controlling aggressive impulses toward their children are also encouraged to call.

7-2c AUTISM SPECTRUM DISORDERS

Autism spectrum disorders (ASDs) are characterized by impairment in communication skills and social interaction, and by repetitive, stereotyped behavior (see Table 7.2). ASDs tend to become evident by the age of three and sometimes before the end of the first year. A Centers for Disease Control and Prevention study of 407,578 children from 14 parts of the United States identified 1 in every 152 children as having an ASD (Rice et al., 2007). Other researchers place the number as high as 1 in 68 children (Bhat et al., 2014; Moyal et al., 2013).

TABLE 7.2 | CHARACTERISTICS OF AUTISM SPECTRUM DISORDERS (ASDS)

Key Indicators	Other Indicators
Does not babble, point, or make meaningful gestures by 1 year of age	Poor eye contact
	Doesn't seem to know how to play with toys
Does not speak one word by 16 months	Excessively lines up toys or other objects
Does not combine two words by 2 years	Is attached to one particular toy or object
Does not respond to being called by his or her name	Doesn't smile
Loses language or social skills	At times seems to be hearing impaired

Source: American Psychiatric Association (2013).

There are several variations of ASDs, but autism is the major type. Other forms of ASDs include:

▶ *Asperger's disorder.* Characterized by social deficits and stereotyped behavior but without the significant cognitive or language delays associated with autism.

▶ *Rett's disorder.* Characterized by a range of physical, behavioral, motor, and cognitive abnormalities that begin after a few months of normal development.

▶ *Childhood disintegrative disorder.* Abnormal functioning and loss of previously acquired skills that begins after about two years of apparently normal development.

AUTISM Autism is four to five times more common among boys than girls. Autistic children do not show interest in social interaction and may avoid eye contact. Attachment to others is weak or absent.

Other features of autism include communication problems, intolerance of change, and ritualistic or stereotypical behavior (Georgiades et al., 2010). Parents of autistic children often say they were "good babies," which usually means they made few demands. But as autistic children develop, they tend to shun affectionate contacts such as hugging, cuddling, and kissing.

Development of speech lags. There is little babbling and communicative gesturing during the first year. Autistic children may show **mutism**, **echolalia**, and pronoun reversal, referring to themselves as "you" or "he." About half use language by middle childhood, but their speech is unusual and troubled.

Autistic children become bound by ritual (Overskeid, 2016). Even slight changes in routines or the environment may cause distress. The teacher of a five-year-old autistic girl would greet her each morning with, "Good morning, Lily, I am very, very glad to see you." Lily would ignore the greeting, but she would shriek if the teacher omitted even one of the *verys*. This feature of autism is termed "preservation of sameness." When familiar objects are moved from their usual places, children with autism may throw tantrums or cry until they are restored. They may insist on eating the same food every day. Autistic children show deficits in peer play, imaginative play, imitation, and emotional expression. Many sleep less than their age-mates (Georgiades et al., 2010).

Some autistic children mutilate themselves, even as they cry out in pain. They may bang their heads, slap their faces, bite their hands and shoulders, or pull out their hair.

TRUTH

(T) F Autistic children may respond to people as though they were pieces of furniture.

It is true that autistic children may respond to people as though they were pieces of furniture. They may ignore other people—for example, walking around them as if they are objects and not persons.

CAUSES OF AUTISM Contrary to what some theorists say or some of the public believe, scientific evidence shows that there is no connection between the development of autism and use of vaccines or deficiencies in child rearing (Archer, 2013; Dixon & Clarke, 2013).

Various lines of evidence suggest a key role for biological factors in autism (Bhat et al., 2014). Possible prenatal factors include exposure to lead, alcohol, mercury, misoprostol, and maternal rubella. Very low birth weight and advanced maternal age may heighten the risk of autism. There is also apparently a role for genetic mechanisms in autism (Vorstman & Burbach, 2014). The concordance (agreement) rates for autism are about 60% among pairs of identical (MZ) twins, who fully share their genetic heritage, compared with about 10% for pairs of fraternal (DZ) twins, whose genetic codes overlap by half (Kendler, 2010; Plomin et al., 1994).

Autistic children tend to shun affectionate contacts, such as hugging, cuddling, and kissing.

BSIP SA/Alamy Stock Photo

autism a disorder characterized by extreme aloneness, communication problems, preservation of sameness, and ritualistic behavior.

mutism refusal to speak.

echolalia automatic repetition of sounds or words.

Biological factors focus on neurological involvement. Many children with autism have abnormal brain wave patterns or seizures (Miyawaki et al., 2016). Other researchers have found that the brains of children with autism have abnormal sensitivities to neurotransmitters such as serotonin, dopamine, acetylcholine, and norepinephrine (Ye et al., 2014). Other researchers note unusual activity in the motor region of the cerebral cortex and less activity in some other areas of the brain (Eilam-Stock et al., 2014.

TREATMENT OF AUTISM Treatment for autism is mainly based on principles of learning, although investigation of biological approaches is also under way (Strock, 2004). Behavior modification has been used to increase the child's ability to attend to others, to play with other children, and to discourage self-mutilation. Brief bursts of physically painful but supposedly nondamaging electric shock rapidly eliminate self-mutilation (Lovaas, 1977). The use of electric shock raises serious moral, ethical, and legal concerns, but O. Ivar Lovaas countered that failure to eliminate self-injurious behavior places the child at yet greater risk.

Because children with autism show behavioral deficits, behavior modification is used to help them develop new behavior. Though autistic children often relate to people as if they were furniture, many can be taught to accept people as reinforcers, rather than objects, by pairing praise with food treats (Chezan & Drasgow, 2010). The most effective treatment programs focus on individualized instruction (Rapin, 1997). In a classic study conducted by Lovaas (Lovaas et al., 1989), autistic children received more than 40 hours of one-to-one behavior modification a week for at least two years. Significant intellectual and educational gains were reported for 9 of 19 children (47%) in the program (Stahmer et al., 2004).

Biological approaches for the treatment of autism are under study. Evidence is mixed as to whether drugs that enhance serotonin activity (selective serotonin reuptake inhibitors, or SSRIs) help prevent self-injury, aggressive outbursts, depression, anxiety, and repetitive behavior (Reiersen & Handen, 2011). Drugs that are usually used to treat schizophrenia—so-called "major tranquilizers"—are helpful with stereotyped behavior, hyperactivity, and self-injury, but not with cognitive and language problems (Moyal et al., 2013; Reiersen & Handen, 2011).

Autistic behavior generally continues into adulthood to one degree or another. Nevertheless, about half of adults who had been diagnosed with autism spectrum disorder in childhood go on to function independently (Eaves & Ho, 2008).

7-3 DAY CARE

Looking for a phrase that can strike fear in the hearts of millions of caregivers? Try *day care*. Most American parents, including mothers with infants, are in the workforce, including 64% of mothers with children under the age of six, and 57% of mothers with infants (O'Brien et al., 2014). As a result, of children under the age of four, 24% are cared for in center-based care, including day care, nursery school, preschool, or Head Start.

Many parents wonder whether day care will affect their children's attachment to them. Some studies have found that the amount of time infants spend in day care is associated with insecure attachment with their parents (Quan et al., 2013). Some researchers suggest that a mother who works full time puts her infant at risk for developing emotional insecurity. Others note that infants whose mothers work may simply become less distressed by her departure and less likely to seek her out when she returns as time goes on, thus providing the appearance of being less attached. However, the likelihood of insecure attachment is not much greater in infants placed in day care than in those cared for in the home. Most infants in both groups are securely attached (O'Brien et al., 2014).

Some studies report that infants with day-care experience are more peer oriented and play at higher developmental levels than do home-reared infants. Children in high-quality day care are more likely to share their toys. They are more independent, self-confident, outgoing, and affectionate as well as more helpful and cooperative with peers and adults (Bekkhus et al., 2011; O'Brien et al., 2014). Participation in day care is also linked with better academic performance in elementary school (Belsky, 2006b).

A study funded by the National Institute on Child Health and Human Development (NICHD) agrees that "high-quality" day care can result in scores on tests of cognitive skills that rival or exceed those of the children

Finding Day Care You (and Your Child) Can Live With

It is normal to be anxious. You are thinking about selecting a day-care center and there are risks. Despite anxiety, you can go about the task with a checklist that can guide your considerations. Above all: Don't be afraid to ask questions. If the day-care provider does not like questions or answer them satisfactorily, you want your child someplace else. Things to think about:

RubberBall /SuperStock

1. Does the day-care center have a license?

2. How many children are cared for at the center? How many caregivers are there? It is important for caregivers not to be overburdened by too many children, especially infants.

3. How were the caregivers hired? How were they trained? Do caregivers engage children in activities and educational experiences, or are they inactive unless a child cries or screams?

4. Is the environment childproof and secure? Can children stick their fingers in electric sockets? Are toys and outdoor equipment in good condition? Are sharp objects within children's reach? Can anybody walk in off the street? What do meals consist of? Will your child find them appetizing or go hungry?

5. Is it possible for you to meet the caregivers who will be taking care of your child? If not, why not?

6. Does the center seem to have an enriching environment? Do you see books, toys, games, and educational objects strewn about?

7. Are there facilities and objects such as swings and tricycles that will enhance your child's physical and motor development? Are children supervised when they play with these things?

8. Does the center's schedule meet your needs?

9. Is the center located conveniently for you?

10. Are parents permitted to visit unannounced?

11. Do you like the overall environment and feel of the center? Listen to your "gut."

---

reared in the home by their mothers (Belsky et al., 2007). The quality of the day care was defined in terms of the richness of the learning environment (availability of toys, books, and other materials), the ratio of caregivers to children (high quality meant more caregivers), the amount of individual attention received by the child, and the extent to which caregivers talked to the children and asked them questions.

However, the researchers also found that children placed in day care may be more aggressive toward peers and adults than children who are reared in the home. The more time spent away from their mothers, the more likely these children were to be rated as defiant, aggressive, and disobedient once they got to kindergarten.

Teacher ratings found that once children who were in day care are in school, they are significantly more likely than children cared for in the home to interrupt in class and tease or bully other children (Belsky et al., 2007). The degree of disturbance generally remained "within normal limits." That is, the children who had been in day care could not be labeled criminals and were not being

expelled. *The quality of the day-care center made no difference.* Children from high-quality day-care centers were also more likely to be disruptive than children cared for in the home. Moreover, the behavioral difference persisted through the sixth grade.

TRUTH

T F Children placed in day care are more aggressive than children who are cared for in the home.

It is true that children placed in day care are more aggressive than children who are cared for in the home. On the other hand, the great majority of the time professional observers place their higher level of aggressive behavior as being "within normal limits."

There are some limitations of the NICHD study. Although the differences in disruptive behavior between children in full-time day care and those cared for in the home are statistically significant—meaning that they are unlikely to be due to chance—they are small. The study implies that day care *causes* the disruptive behavior of concern later on, but there is no control group. Children are *not* assigned at random to day care or care in the home. Therefore, it may be that children placed in day care are those whose caregivers are most stressed by work through their children's primary school years. Also, we do not know whether the so-called disruptive children become less productive and successful adults. Perhaps they actually become "assertive and entrepreneurial," especially since their cognitive skills and other social skills are intact.

In any case, reality intrudes. Millions of parents do not have the option of deciding whether to place their children in day care; their only choice is where. And some parents, given their financial and geographic circumstances, might not even have that choice.

7-4 EMOTIONAL DEVELOPMENT

An emotion is a state of feeling with physiological, situational, and cognitive components. Physiologically, when emotions are strong, our hearts may beat more rapidly and our muscles may tense. Situationally, we may feel anger when frustrated or pleasure or relief when we are being held by a loved one. Cognitively, anger may be triggered by the idea that someone is purposefully withholding something we need.

It is unclear how many emotions babies have, and they cannot tell us what they are feeling. We can only observe how they behave, including their facial expressions. Facial expressions appear to be universal in that they are recognized in different cultures around the world, so they are considered a reliable index of emotion.

Researchers have long debated whether the emotional expression of newborns begins in an undifferentiated state of diffuse excitement or whether several emotions are present (Camras & Shuster, 2013; Soussignan & Schaal, 2005). They have asked whether the newborn baby's crying is nothing more than a reflex in response to discomfort. They have even asked whether the facial expressions of infants, which many researchers claim to express emotions such as anger, joy, fear, and excitement within a few months after birth, actually reflect internal states of feeling. It seems clear enough that as infants develop through the first year, their cognitive appraisal of events, including their interaction with

their caregivers, becomes a key part of their emotional life and their emotional expression (Camras et al., 2007; Soussignan & Schaal, 2005).

Infants' initial emotional expressions appear to comprise two basic states of emotional arousal: a positive attraction to pleasant stimulation, such as the caregiver's voice or being held, and withdrawal from aversive stimulation, such as a sudden loud noise. By the age of two to three months, social smiling has replaced reflexive smiling. Social smiling is usually highly endearing to caregivers. At three to five months, infants laugh at active stimuli, such as repetitively touching their bellies or playing "Ah, boop!"

In sum, researchers agree that infants show only a few emotions during the first few months. They agree that emotional development is linked to cognitive development and social experience. They do not necessarily agree on exactly when specific emotions are first shown or whether discrete emotions are present at birth.

7-4a EMOTIONAL DEVELOPMENT AND PATTERNS OF ATTACHMENT

Emotional development has been linked with various histories of attachment. In a longitudinal study of 112 children at ages 9, 14, 22, and 33 months, Kochanska (2001) studied the development of fear, anger, and joy by using laboratory situations designed to evoke these emotions. Patterns of attachment were assessed using the Strange Situation method. Differences in emotional development could first be related to attachment at the age of 14 months. Resistant children were most fearful and they frequently responded with distress even in episodes designed to evoke joy. When they were assessed repeatedly over time, it became apparent that securely attached children were becoming significantly less angry. By contrast, the negative emotions of insecurely attached children rose: Avoidant children grew more fearful, and resistant children became less joyful. At 33 months of age, securely attached children were less likely to show fear and anger, even when they were exposed to situations designed to elicit these emotions.

7-4b FEAR OF STRANGERS

When another daughter was one year old, her mother and I needed a nanny for a few hours a day so that we could teach, write, breathe, and engage in other life activities. We hired a graduate social work student who had a mild, engaging way about her. She nurtured my daughter and played with her for about four months, during which time my daughter came to somewhat grudgingly accept her, most of the time. Even so, my daughter was never completely comfortable with her and often let out a yowl as if buildings were collapsing around her, although the nanny did nothing except calmly try to soothe her.

Unfortunately, my daughter met the nanny during the period when she had developed fear of strangers. The fear would eventually subside, as these fears do, but during her entire encounter with the nanny, the nanny wondered what she was doing wrong. The answer was simple: She was existing, within sight of my daughter.

Fear of strangers—also called *stranger anxiety*—is normal. Most infants develop it. Stranger anxiety appears at about six to nine months of age (Brooker et al., 2013. By four or five months of age, infants may compare the faces of strangers and their mothers, looking back and forth. Somewhat older infants show distress by crying, whimpering, gazing fearfully, and crawling away. Fear of strangers often peaks at 9 to 12 months and declines in the second year.

FICTION

T (F) Fear of strangers is abnormal among infants.

It is not true that fear of strangers is abnormal among infants. Most infants develop some form of stranger anxiety at around six to nine months of age.

Children with fear of strangers show less anxiety when their mothers are present (Rapee, 2011). Children also are less fearful when they are in familiar surroundings, such as their homes, rather than in the laboratory (Brooker et al., 2013).

Christina Kennedy / Alamy Stock Photo

Stranger anxiety—also called fear of strangers—tends to emerge at about six to nine months of age. It is common but by no means universal.

7-4c SOCIAL REFERENCING: WHAT SHOULD I DO NOW?

Social referencing is the seeking out of another person's perception of a situation to help us form our own view of it. Leslie Carver and Brenda Vaccaro (2007) suggest that social referencing requires three components: (1) looking at another, usually older individual in a novel, ambiguous situation; (2) associating that individual's emotional response with the unfamiliar situation; and (3) regulating their own emotional response in accord with the response of the older individual.

Infants also display social referencing, as early as six months of age. They use caregivers' facial expressions or tone of voice as clues on how to respond (Schmitow & Stenberg, 2013). In one study, eight-month-old infants were friendlier to a stranger when their mothers exhibited a friendly facial expression in the stranger's presence than when she looked worried (Boccia & Campos, 1989).

EMOTIONAL REGULATION: KEEPING ON AN EVEN KEEL Emotional regulation refers to the ways in which young children control their own emotions. Even infants display certain behaviors to control unpleasant emotional states. They may look away from a disturbing event or suck their thumbs (Lewis, 2013; Rothbart & Sheese, 2007). Caregivers help infants learn to regulate their emotions. A two-way communication system develops in which the infant signals the caregiver that help is needed and the caregiver responds. Claire Kopp (1989, p. 347) provides an example of such a system:

> A 13-month-old, playing with a large plastic bottle, attempted to unscrew the cover, but could not. Fretting for a short time, she initiated eye contact with her mother and held out the jar. As her mother took it to unscrew the cover, the infant ceased fretting.

Research evidence suggests that the children of secure mothers are not only likely to be securely attached themselves but also are

social referencing using another person's reaction to a situation to form one's own response.

emotional regulation techniques for controlling one's emotional states.

The infant in the high chair seems to be regulating his emotions better than his parents are regulating theirs.

likely to regulate their own emotions in a positive manner (Lewis, 2013; Thompson & Meyer, 2007). A German longitudinal study (Zimmermann et al., 2001) related emotional regulation in adolescence with patterns of attachment during infancy, as assessed using the Strange Situation method. Forty-one adolescents, aged 16 and 17, were placed in complex problem-solving situations with friends. Those adolescents who were secure as infants were most capable of regulating their emotions to interact cooperatively with their friends.

7-5 PERSONALITY DEVELOPMENT

In this section, we look at the emergence of the self-concept. We then turn to a discussion of temperament. Finally, we consider gender differences in behavior.

7-5a THE SELF-CONCEPT

At birth, we may find the world to be a confusing blur of sights, sounds, and inner sensations—yet the "we" may be missing, at least for a while. When our hands first come into view, there is little evidence we realize that the hands "belong" to us and that we are separate and distinct from the world outside.

The self-concept appears to emerge gradually during infancy. At some point, infants understand that the hands they are moving in and out of sight are "their" hands. At some point, they understand that their own bodies extend only so far and then external objects and the bodies of others begin.

DEVELOPMENT OF THE SELF-CONCEPT Psychologists have devised ingenious methods to assess the development of the self-concept among infants. One of these is the *mirror technique*, which involves the use of a mirror and a dot of rouge. Before the experiment begins, the

researcher observes the infant for baseline data on how frequently the infant touches his or her nose. Then the mother places rouge on the infant's nose, and the infant is placed before a mirror. Not until about the age of 18 months do infants begin to touch their own noses upon looking in the mirror (Keller et al., 2005; Taumoepeau & Reese, 2014).

Nose touching suggests that children recognize themselves and that they perceive that the dot of rouge is an abnormality. Most two-year-olds can point to pictures of themselves, and they begin to use "I" or their own name spontaneously (Smiley & Johnson, 2006).

Self-awareness affects the infant's social and emotional development (Foley, 2006). Knowledge

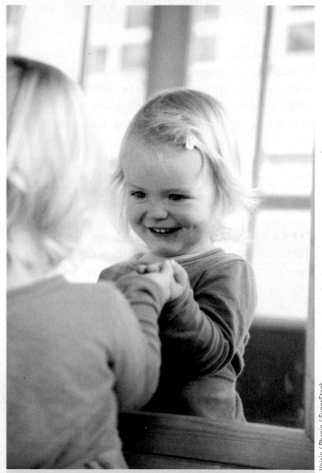

In the middle of the second year, infants begin to develop self-awareness, which has a powerful effect on social and emotional development.

of the self permits the infant and child to develop notions of sharing and cooperation. In one study, two-year-olds with a better developed sense of self were more likely to cooperate with other children (Brownell & Carriger, 1990).

Self-awareness also facilitates the development of "self-conscious" emotions such as embarrassment, envy, empathy, pride, guilt, and shame (Foley, 2006). In another study, Deborah Stipek and her colleagues (1992) found that children older than 21 months often seek their mother's attention and approval when they have successfully completed a task, whereas younger toddlers do not.

7-5b TEMPERAMENT: EASY, DIFFICULT, OR SLOW TO WARM UP?

Each child has a characteristic **temperament**, a stable way of reacting and adapting to the world that is present early in life. Many researchers believe that temperament involves a genetic component (Shiner & DeYoung, 2013; Zuckerman, 2011). The child's temperament includes many aspects of behavior, including activity level, smiling and laughter, regularity in eating and sleep habits, approach or withdrawal, adaptability to new situations, intensity of responsiveness, general cheerfulness or unpleasantness, distractibility or persistence, and soothability (Thomas & Chess, 1989).

TYPES OF TEMPERAMENT Thomas and Chess (1989) found that from the first days of life, many of the children in their study (65%) could be classified into one of three types of temperament: "easy" (40% of their sample), "difficult" (10%), and "slow to warm up" (15%). Some of the differences among these three types of children are shown in Table 7.3. The easy child

---

FICTION

T (F) All children are born with the same temperament. Treatment by caregivers determines whether they are difficult or easygoing.

It is not true that all children are "born" with the same temperament. Tendencies to be easygoing, difficult, or slow to warm up can apparently be inborn, although they can be modified by experience.

---

has regular sleep and feeding schedules, approaches new situations (such as a new food or a new school) with enthusiasm and adapts to them easily, and is generally cheerful. Some children are more inconsistent and show a mixture of temperament traits. For example, a toddler may have a pleasant disposition but be frightened of new situations.

The difficult child, on the other hand, has irregular sleep and feeding schedules, is slow to accept new people and situations, takes a long time to adjust to new routines, and responds to frustrations with tantrums and crying. The slow-to-warm-up child falls between the other two.

STABILITY OF TEMPERAMENT Though not all children are born with the same temperament, as Thomas and Chess found, there is at least moderate consistency in the development of temperament from infancy onward (Shiner et al., 2012; Zuckerman, 2011). The infant who is highly active and cries in novel situations often becomes a fearful toddler. Difficult children in general are at greater risk for developing psychological disorders and adjustment problems later in life (Bales et al., 2013; Sayal et al., 2013). A longitudinal study tracked the progress of infants with a difficult temperament from 1½ through 12 years of age (Guerin et al., 1997). A difficult temperament correlated with parental reports of behavioral problems from ages 3 to 12, and teachers' reports of problems with attention span and aggression.

GOODNESS OF FIT: THE ROLE OF THE ENVIRONMENT

Our daughter was a difficult infant, but we weathered the storm. At the age of 15, she was climbing out the second-story bedroom window at 2 a.m. to be with friends. When we discovered it, she sarcastically asked if we disapproved. "Yes," we said. "Use the front

---

TABLE 7.3   TYPES OF TEMPERAMENT

Temperament Category	Easy	Difficult	Slow to Warm Up
Regularity of biological functioning	Regular	Irregular	Somewhat irregular
Response to new stimuli	Positive approach	Negative withdrawal	Negative withdrawal
Adaptability to new situations	Adapts readily	Adapts slowly or not at all	Adapts slowly
Intensity of reaction	Mild or moderate	Intense	Mild
Quality of mood	Positive	Negative	Initially negative; gradually more positive

Sources: Chess & Thomas (1991) and Thomas & Chess (1989).

---

temperament individual difference in style of reaction that is present early in life.

door; you're less likely to get hurt." She graduated college with honors. She has occasional outbursts, but that's her boyfriend's problem. And they love her on the job. She's a hard worker and the most creative thing they've ever seen.

The environment also affects the development of temperament. An initial biological predisposition to a certain temperament may be strengthened or weakened by the parents' reaction to the child. Parents may react to a difficult child by imposing rigid care-giving schedules, which in turn can cause the child to become even more difficult (Laxman et al., 2013). This example illustrates a poor fit between the child's behavior style and the parents' response.

On the other hand, parents may try to modify a child's initial temperament in a more positive direction to achieve a **goodness of fit** between child and parent. Realization that their youngster's behavior does not mean that the child is weak or deliberately disobedient, or that they

goodness of fit agreement between the parents' expectations of a child and the child's temperament.

are bad parents, helps parents modify their attitudes and behavior toward the child, whose behavior may then improve (Bird et al., 2006; Laxman et al., 2013).

7-5c GENDER DIFFERENCES

All cultures distinguish between females and males and have expectations about how they ought to behave. For this reason, a child's gender is a key factor in society's efforts to shape her or his personality and behavior.

BEHAVIOR OF INFANT GIRLS AND BOYS Girls tend to advance more rapidly in their motor development in infancy: They sit, crawl, and walk earlier than boys (Hines, 2013; Zelazo, 2013). Although a few studies have found that infant boys are more active and irritable than girls, others have not (Hines, 2013; Zelazo, 2013). Girls and boys are similar in their social behaviors. They are equally likely to smile at people's faces, for example, and they do not differ in their dependency on adults (Hines, 2013; Zelazo, 2013). Girls and boys do begin to differ early in their preference for certain toys and play activities. By 12 to 18 months of age, girls prefer to play with dolls, doll furniture, dishes, and toy animals; boys prefer transportation toys (trucks, cars, airplanes, and the like), tools, and sports equipment as early as 9 to 18 months of age (Berenbaum et al., 2008; Leaper & Bigler, 2011). Gender differences that show up later, such as

zhang bo/E+/Getty Images

Do mothers and fathers relate differently to their infants?

differences in spatial relations skills, are not necessarily evident in infancy (Örnkloo & von Hofsten, 2007). By 24 months, both girls and boys appear to be aware of which behaviors are considered appropriate or inappropriate for their gender, according to cultural stereotypes (Hill & Flom, 2007). Thus it appears girls and boys may show a preference for gender stereotypical toys before they have been socialized and possibly before they understand their own sex.

FICTION

T (F) Girls may prefer dolls and toy animals, and boys may prefer toy trucks and sports equipment, but these preferences emerge only after they have become aware of the gender roles assigned to them by society.

It is not true that children prefer stereotypically gender-related toys only *after* they have become aware of the gender roles assigned to them by society. Recent research suggests that children may show a preference for gender stereotypical toys before they have been socialized, and possibly even before they understand which gender they are.

ADULTS' BEHAVIOR TOWARD INFANTS Despite any possible inborn tendencies, research shows that most adults interact differently with girls and boys. Researchers have presented American adults with an unfamiliar infant who is dressed in boy's clothes and has a boy's name or an infant who is dressed in girl's clothing and has a girl's name. (In reality, it is the same baby who simply is given different names and clothing.) When adults believe they are playing with a girl, they are more likely to offer "her" a doll; when they think the child is a boy, they are more likely to offer a football or a hammer. "Boys" also are encouraged to engage in more physical activity than "girls" (Worell & Goodheart, 2006).

Parents, especially fathers, are more likely to encourage rough-and-tumble play in sons than daughters (John et al., 2013; Paquette & Dumont, 2013).

On the other hand, parents talk more to infant daughters than infant sons. They smile more at daughters and are more emotionally expressive toward them (Powlishta et al., 2001).

Infant girls are likely to be decked out in a pink or yellow dress and embellished with ruffles and lace, whereas infant boys wear blue or red (Eccles et al., 2000; Powlishta et al., 2001). Parents provide baby girls and boys with different bedroom decorations and toys. Examination of the contents of rooms of children from five months to six years of age found that boys' rooms were often decorated with animal themes and with blue bedding and curtains. Girls' rooms featured flowers, lace, ruffles, and pastels. Girls owned more dolls; boys had more vehicles, military toys, and sports equipment.

Parents react favorably when their infant daughters play with "girls' toys" and their sons play with "boys' toys." Adults, especially fathers, show more negative reactions when girls play with boys' toys and boys play with girls' toys (Martin et al., 2002; Worell & Goodheart, 2006). Parents thus try to shape their children's behavior during infancy and lay the foundation for development in early childhood. In the following chapter, we examine physical and cognitive developments of early childhood.

Antonio_Diaz/Getty Images

Is it just as easy to imagine the boy's mother in this picture as the father? Why or why not?

READY TO STUDY?

In the book, you can:

☐ Rip out the chapter review card at the back of the book for a handy summary of the chapter and key terms.

☐ Check your understanding of what you've read with the quizzes that follow.

ONLINE AT CENGAGEBRAIN.COM YOU CAN:

☐ Collect StudyBits while you read and study the chapter.

☐ Quiz yourself on key concepts.

☐ Find videos for further exploration.

☐ Prepare for tests with CDEV2 Flash Cards as well as those you create.

SELF-ASSESSMENTS

Fill-Ins

Answers can be found in the back of the book.

1. There are two major types of insecure attachment: avoidant attachment and _____/_____ attachment.

2. The first phase of attachment is the initial-_____ phase.

3. Harry and Margaret _____ conducted classic experiments to demonstrate that contact comfort is critical to the attachment process.

4. According to Lorenz, attachment can occur only during a _____ period.

5. _____ disorder is characterized by social deficits and stereotyped behavior but without significant cognitive or language delays.

6. About _____% of American children under the age of five are cared for in center-based care.

7. Infants display social _____ by using caregivers' facial expressions or tone of voice as clues on how to respond to a situation.

8. Researchers have studied development of the self-concept by placing _____ on the noses of infants.

9. The three basic types of temperament are easy, _____, and slow to warm up.

10. Parents may try to modify a child's initial temperament to achieve a(n) _____ of fit between child and parent.

Multiple Choice

1. **Which kind of attachment is used to describe babies who seem confused and may move toward the mother while looking away from her?**
   a. disorganized–disoriented
   b. secure
   c. avoidant
   d. ambivalent/resistant

2. **Sroufe found that insecure attachment at the age of one year predicts psychological disorders at the age of**
   a. 7.   c. 27.
   b. 17.   d. 37.

3. **According to Ainsworth, the clear-cut attachment phase occurs at about what age?**
   a. 6 to 7 months   c. 16 to 18 months
   b. 10 to 12 months   d. 24 to 36 months

4. **Which of the following views of attachment proposes that there is a critical period for developing attachment?**
   a. behavioral   c. cognitive
   b. psychoanalytic   d. ethological

5. **The natives in one Guatemalan village keep their children in a windowless hut and play with them only rarely until they can walk. By what age do the children act as alert and active as children who have been reared normally?**
   a. Actually, they never show any behavioral delays.
   b. 2
   c. 5
   d. 11

6. **By the time a child is two years of age, nine out of ten parents have**
   a. engaged in some sort of psychological or emotional abuse.
   b. spanked their children.
   c. pushed or shoved their children.
   d. sexually abused their children.

7. **All of the following are symptoms of autism spectrum disorders *except***
   a. losing language or social skills.
   b. failing to respond to being called by name.
   c. developing fear of strangers.
   d. not seeming to know how to play with toys.

8. **What does research evidence show about autism?**
   a. Autism is caused by the vaccine for measles, mumps, and rubella.
   b. Autism is a result of poor child rearing.
   c. Autism runs in families to some degree.
   d. All of the above are true.

9. **If someone asked you whether or not day care were a good idea for her three-year-old, which of the following answers would be based on research evidence?**
   a. Some children in day care learn to be more cooperative than they were.
   b. Some children in day care become somewhat more aggressive than they were.
   c. Children in high-quality day care seem to fare better in some ways than children in poor-quality day care.
   d. All of the above.

10. **Brunhilda's son is eight months old and has suddenly begun to cry hysterically and cling to her when strangers come over in the supermarket to say how cute he is. Knowing you are a psychology student, she asks you what you think. Which of the following would reflect what you learned reading this chapter?**
    a. Brunhilda has probably abused her son.
    b. A stranger has threatened or abused her son.
    c. Her son has an overly reactive nervous system.
    d. Her son is behaving normally.

Spencer Rathus

8 | Early Childhood: Physical Development

LEARNING OUTCOMES

After studying this chapter, you will be able to . . .

8-1 Describe trends in physical development in early childhood

8-2 Describe motor development in early childhood

8-3 Describe trends in health and illness in early childhood

8-4 Describe sleep patterns in early childhood

8-5 Discuss the elimination disorders

After you finish
this chapter, go
to **PAGE 144** for
STUDY TOOLS

The years from two to six are referred to as early childhood or the preschool years. During early childhood, physical growth is slower than in infancy. Children become

> During the preschool years, physical and motor development proceeds, literally, by leaps and bounds.

taller and leaner, and by the end of early childhood they look more like adults than infants. Motor skills develop dramatically. Children become stronger, faster, and better coordinated.

8-1 GROWTH PATTERNS

During the preschool years, physical and motor development proceeds, literally, by leaps and bounds.

8-1a HEIGHT AND WEIGHT

Following the dramatic gains in height in a child's first two years, the growth rate slows during the preschool years (Kuczmarski et al., 2000). Girls and boys tend to gain about two to three inches in height per year, and weight gains remain fairly even at about four to six pounds per year (see Figure 8.1). Children become increasingly slender as they gain in height and shed some "baby fat." Boys as a group become slightly taller and heavier than girls (see Figure 8.1). Noticeable variations in growth occur from child to child. (For a discussion of childhood obesity, see Chapter 11.)

8-1b DEVELOPMENT OF THE BRAIN

The brain develops more quickly than any other organ in early childhood. At two years of age, the brain already has attained 75% of its adult weight. By the age of five, the brain has reached 90% of its adult weight, even though the body weight of the five-year-old is barely one-third of what it will be as an adult.

The increase in brain size is due in part to the continuing myelination of nerve fibers. Completion of myelination of the neural pathways that link the cerebellum to the cerebral cortex facilitates development of fine motor skills, balance, and coordination (Fletcher, 2011; Rilling, 2013).

BRAIN DEVELOPMENT AND VISUAL SKILLS Brain development also improves processing of visual information (Seiler et al., 2011), facilitating learning to read. The parts of the brain that enable the child to sustain attention and screen out distractions become increasingly myelinated between the ages of about four and seven (Otero & Barker, 2014), enabling most children to focus on schoolwork. The speed of processing visual information improves throughout childhood, reaching adult levels at the onset of adolescence (Otero & Barker, 2014; Y. Wang et al., 2016).

RIGHT BRAIN, LEFT BRAIN? We often hear people described as being "right-brained" or "left-brained." The notion is that the hemispheres of the brain are involved in different kinds of intellectual and emotional activities. Research does suggest that in right-handed individuals, the left hemisphere is relatively more involved in intellectual undertakings that require logical analysis and problem-solving, language, and computation (Scull, 2010). The other hemisphere (the right hemisphere) is usually superior in visual–spatial functions (such as piecing puzzles together), aesthetic and emotional responses, and understanding metaphors.

But it is not true that some children are left-brained and others are right-brained. The functions of the left and right hemispheres overlap, and the hemispheres respond simultaneously when we focus on one thing or another

TRUTH OR FICTION?

T	F	Some children are left-brained, and others are right-brained.
T	F	Sedentary parents are more likely to have "couch potatoes" for children.
T	F	Some diseases are normal.
T	F	Infections are the most common cause of death among children in the United States.
T	F	It is dangerous to awaken a sleepwalker.
T	F	Competent parents toilet train their children by their second birthday.

FIG.8.1 GROWTH CURVES FOR HEIGHT AND WEIGHT, AGES TWO TO SIX YEARS

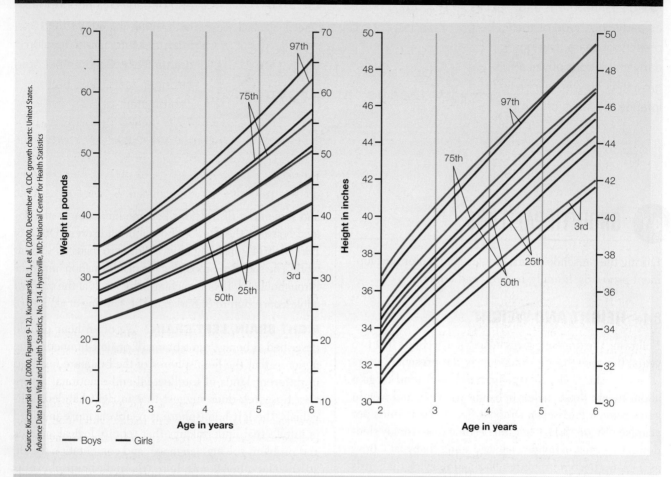

Source: Kuczmarski et al. (2000, Figures 9-12), Kuczmarski, R. J., et al. (2000, December 4). CDC growth charts: United States. Advance Data from Vital and Health Statistics, No. 314. Hyattsville, MD: National Center for Health Statistics

The numbers on the curves indicate the percentiles for height and weight at different ages. The growth rate slows during early childhood. As in infancy, boys are only slightly taller and heavier than girls.

(Franklin, 2013). They are aided in "cooperation" by the myelination of the **corpus callosum**, a thick bundle of nerve fibers that connects the hemispheres (Luders et al., 2010). This process is largely complete by the age of eight, enabling the integration of logical and emotional functioning.

PLASTICITY OF THE BRAIN Many parts of the brain have specialized functions, allowing our behavior to be more complex. But it also means that injuries to certain parts of the brain can result in loss of these functions. However, the brain also shows **plasticity**, or the ability to compensate for injuries to particular areas. Plasticity is greatest at about one to two years of age and then gradually declines

corpus callosum the thick bundle of nerve fibers that connects the left and right hemispheres of the brain.

plasticity the tendency of new parts of the brain to take up the functions of injured parts.

FICTION

T (F) Some children are left-brained, and others are right-brained.

It is not true that some children are left-brained and others are right-brained. The statement is too all-inclusive to be true. The functions of the two brain hemispheres overlap.

(Lohmann & Kessels, 2014; Skoe et al., 2013). When we as adults suffer damage to the areas of the brain that control language, we may lose the ability to speak or understand language. However, other areas of the brain may assume these functions in preschoolers who suffer

8-2 MOTOR DEVELOPMENT

The preschool years witness an explosion of motor skills, as children's nervous systems mature and their movements become more precise and coordinated.

8-2a GROSS MOTOR SKILLS

Gross motor skills involve the large muscles used in locomotion (see Table 8.1). At about the age of three, children can balance on one foot. By age three or four, they can walk up stairs as adults do, by placing a foot on each step. By age four or five, they can skip and pedal a tricycle (Allen et al., 2011). Older preschoolers are better able to coordinate two tasks, such as singing and running at the same time. In general, preschoolers appear to acquire motor skills by teaching themselves and observing other children. Imitating other children seems more important than adult instruction at this age.

Throughout early childhood, girls and boys are similar in motor skills. Girls are somewhat better at balance and precision. Boys show some advantage in throwing and kicking (Haywood & Getchel, 2014; Veldman et al., 2016).

Individual differences are larger than gender differences throughout early and middle childhood. Some children are genetically predisposed to developing better coordination or more strength. Motivation and practice also are important. Motor experiences in infancy may affect the development of motor skills in early childhood. For example, children with early crawling experience perform better than those who do not on tests of motor skills (Haywood & Getchell, 2014).

> **gross motor skills** skills employing the large muscles used in locomotion.

Tom Merton/OJO Images/Jupiter Images

such damage. As a result, they may regain the ability to speak or comprehend language. Neurological factors that enable plasticity include the growth of new dendrites ("sprouting") and the redundancy of neural connections (Lohmann & Kessels, 2014; Skoe et al., 2013).

TABLE 8.1 | DEVELOPMENT OF GROSS MOTOR SKILLS IN EARLY CHILDHOOD

2 Years (24–35 Months)	3 Years (36–47 Months)	4 Years (48–59 Months)	5 Years (60–71 Months)
• Runs well straight ahead	• Goes around obstacles while running	• Turns sharp corners while running	• Runs lightly on toes
• Walks up stairs, two feet to a step	• Walks up stairs, one foot to a step	• Walks down stairs, one foot to a step	• Jumps a distance of 3 feet
• Kicks a large ball	• Kicks a large ball easily	• Jumps from a height of 12 inches	• Catches a small ball, using hands only
• Jumps a distance of 4–14 inches	• Jumps from the bottom step	• Throws a ball overhand	• Hops 2 to 3 yards forward on each foot
• Throws a small ball without falling	• Catches a bounced ball, using torso and arms to form a basket	• Turns sharp corners while pushing and pulling toys	• Stands on one foot for 8–10 seconds
• Pushes and pulls large toys	• Goes around obstacles while pushing and pulling toys	• Hops on one foot, four to six hops	• Climbs actively and skillfully
• Hops on one foot, two or more hops	• Hops on one foot, up to three hops	• Stands on one foot for 3–8 seconds	• Skips on alternate feet
• Tries to stand on one foot	• Stands on one foot	• Climbs ladders	• Rides a bicycle with training wheels
• Climbs on furniture to look out of window	• Climbs nursery-school apparatus	• Skips on one foot	
		• Rides a tricycle well	

Note: The ages are averages; there are individual variations.

8-2b PHYSICAL ACTIVITY

Preschoolers spend an average of more than 25 hours a week in large muscle activity (Haywood & Getchell, 2014). Younger preschoolers are more likely than older preschoolers to engage in physically oriented play, such as grasping, banging, and mouthing objects (Haywood & Getchell, 2014; Hanson, 2013).

Motor activity level begins to decline after two or three years of age. Children become less restless and are able to sit still longer. Between the ages of two and four, children show an increase in sustained, focused attention.

ROUGH-AND-TUMBLE PLAY

Rough-and-tumble play consists of running, chasing, fleeing, wrestling, hitting with an open hand, laughing, and making faces. Rough-and-tumble play, which is more common among boys than among girls, is not the same as aggressive behavior, which involves hitting, pushing, taking, grabbing, and angry looks. Rough-and-tumble play helps develop physical and social skills (Cillessen & Bellmore, 2011; Van Gils, 2014).

INDIVIDUAL DIFFERENCES IN ACTIVITY LEVEL

Physically active parents are likely to have physically active children. In a study of four- to seven-year-olds, children of active mothers were twice as likely to be active as children of inactive mothers (Monroe et al., 1991). Children of active fathers were 3½ times as likely to be active.

Several reasons may explain this relationship. First, active parents may serve as role models for activity. Second, sharing of activities by family members may be responsible. Active parents may also encourage their child's participation

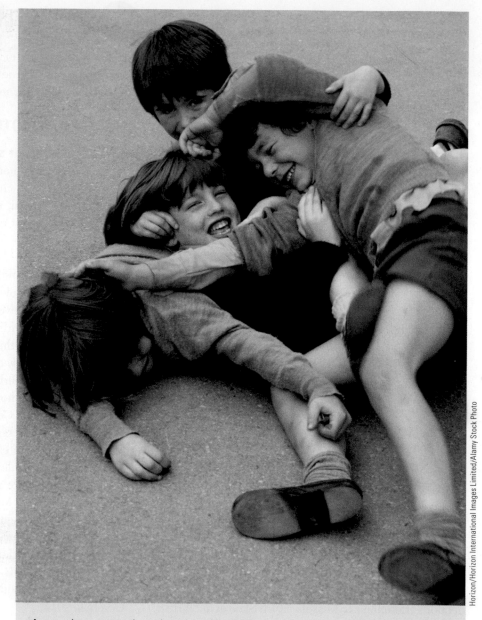

Aggression or normal rough-and-tumble play?

Horizon/Horizon International Images Limited/Alamy Stock Photo

fine motor skills skills employing the small muscles used in manipulation, such as those in the fingers.

TRUTH

(T) F Sedentary parents are more likely to have "couch potatoes" for children.

It is true that sedentary parents are more likely to have couch potatoes for children. Physically active children are more likely to have physically active parents.

TABLE 8.2 DEVELOPMENT OF FINE MOTOR SKILLS IN EARLY CHILDHOOD

2 Years (24–35 Months)	3 Years (36–47 Months)	4 Years (48–59 Months)	5 Years (60–71 Months)
• Builds tower of 6 cubes • Copies vertical and horizontal lines • Imitates folding of paper • Prints on easel with a brush • Places simple shapes in correct holes	• Builds tower of 9 cubes • Copies circle and cross • Copies letters • Holds crayons with fingers, not fist • Strings four beads using a large needle	• Builds tower of 10 or more cubes • Copies square • Prints simple words • Imitates folding paper three times • Uses pencil with correct hand grip • Strings 10 beads	• Builds 3 steps from 6 blocks, using a model • Copies triangle and star • Prints first name and numbers • Imitates folding of piece of square paper into a triangle • Traces around a diamond drawn on paper • Laces shoes

Note: The ages are averages; there are individual variations.

in physical activity. Twin studies also suggest there is a genetic tendency for activity level (Herring et al., 2014; Saudino, 2011).

8-2c FINE MOTOR SKILLS

Fine motor skills involve the small muscles used in manipulation and coordination. These skills develop gradually, a bit more slowly than gross motor skills (Haywood & Getchell, 2014). Control over the wrists and fingers enables children to hold a pencil properly, dress themselves, and stack blocks (see Table 8.2). Preschoolers can labor endlessly in attempting to tie their shoelaces and get their jackets zipped.

8-2d CHILDREN'S ARTISTIC DEVELOPMENT

Children's artistic development is linked to the development of motor and cognitive skills. Children first begin to scribble during the second year of life. Initially, they seem to make marks for the sheer joy of it (Jolley, 2010). Rhoda Kellogg (1959, 1970) found a meaningful pattern in the scribbles. She identified 20 basic scribbles that she considered the building blocks of art (see Figure 8.2).

Children progress through four stages from making scribbles to drawing pictures: the *placement, shape, design,* and *pictorial stages* (see Figure 8.3). Two-year-olds scribble in various locations on the page (e.g., in the middle of the page or near one of the borders). By age three, children are starting to draw basic shapes: circles, squares, triangles, crosses, X's, and odd shapes. As soon as they can draw shapes, children begin to combine them in the design stage. Between ages four and five, children reach the pictorial stage, in which designs begin to resemble recognizable objects.

Children's early drawings tend to be symbolic of broad categories rather than specific. A child might draw the same simple building whether asked to draw a school or a house (Tallandini & Valentini, 1991). Children between three and five usually do not set out to draw a particular thing. They are more likely to see what they have drawn, then name it. As motor and cognitive skills develop beyond the age of five, children become able to draw an object they have in mind. The ability to copy figures also improves (Daglioglu et al., 2010; Rübeling et al., 2011).

FIG.8.2 THE 20 BASIC SCRIBBLES

Ryan McVay/Photodisc/Getty Images
Source: Kellogg (1970).

By the age of two, children can scribble. Rhoda Kellogg has identified these 20 basic scribbles as the building blocks of children's drawings.

8-2e HANDEDNESS

Some infants show no hand preference during infancy (Nelson et al., 2013), but by the age of two to three months, in most cases a rattle placed in an infant's hand is held longer with the right hand than the left (Fitzgerald et al., 1991). By four months of age, most infants show a clear-cut right-hand preference in exploring objects (Streri, 2002). Preferring to grasp with one hand or the other increases markedly between 6 and 14 months (Ferre et al., 2010). Handedness becomes more strongly established during early childhood. Most people are right-handed, although studies vary as to how many are left-handed.

The origins of handedness apparently have a genetic component (Hopkins et al., 2015; Michel, 2013; Willems et al., 2014). If both of your parents are right-handed, your chances of being right-handed are about 92%. If both of your parents are left-handed, your chances of being left-handed are about 50% (Annett, 1999; Clode, 2006). Whether handedness is associated with cognitive or emotional advantages or disadvantages remains an open question.

8-3 HEALTH AND ILLNESS

Good health requires proper nutrition, and we'll provide some guidelines for helping young children obtain what they need. Nevertheless, regardless of how well they eat, nearly all children get ill now and then. Some seem to be ill every other week or so. Most illnesses are minor, and children seem to eventually outgrow many of them. Fortunately, we can prevent or cure many others.

8-3a NUTRITION

Between the ages of two and three, a child needs 1000–1,400 calories of food per day, and between the ages of four and eight, a child requires some 1,200–2,000 calories a day, depending on growth and activity level (Mayo Clinic, 2014). This is a very wide range, so an absolute prescription for a given child is not advisable. The Mayo Clinic advises eating a balanced diet of protein sources (e.g., seafood, lean meats, nuts), fruits, vegetables, grains, and dairy products. During the second and third years, a child's appetite typically becomes erratic, but because the child is growing more slowly than in infancy, he or she needs fewer calories. Children who eat little at one meal may compensate by eating more at another (Cooke et al., 2003).

FIG.8.3 FOUR STAGES IN CHILDREN'S DRAWING

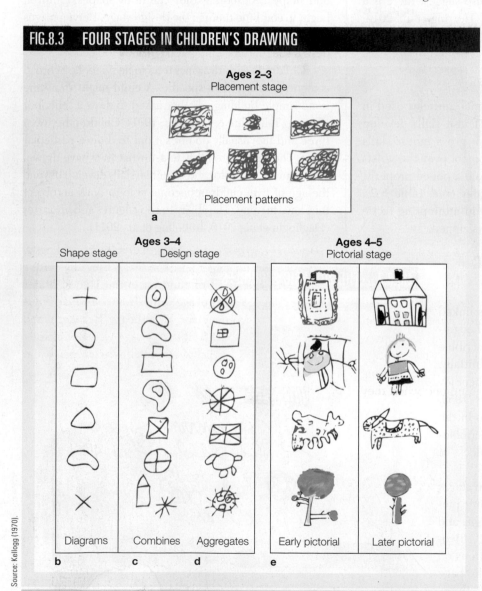

Source: Kellogg (1970).

Children go through four stages in drawing pictures. (a) They first place their scribbles in various locations on the page. They then (b) draw basic shapes and (c, d) combine shapes into designs. Finally, (e) they draw recognizable objects.

Infants seem to be born liking the taste of sugar, although they are fairly indifferent to salt. But preference for sweet and salty foods increases if children are repeatedly exposed to them (Bouhlal et al., 2013). Parents and television advertising also influence the development of food preferences (Bost et al., 2014; Boyland & Halford, 2013).

8-3b MINOR ILLNESSES

Minor illnesses refer to respiratory infections, such as colds, and to gastrointestinal upsets, such as nausea, vomiting, and diarrhea. These diseases are normal in that most children come down with them. They typically last a few days or less and are not life threatening. Although diarrheal illness in the United States is usually mild, it is a leading killer of children in developing countries (Save the Children, 2015).

TRUTH

(T) F   Some diseases are normal.

Respiratory infections, nausea, vomiting, and diarrhea during early childhood are all "normal" in the statistical sense of the word, although they are diseases or unhealthy conditions.

American children between the ages of one and three average eight to nine minor illnesses a year. Between the ages of four and ten, the average drops to four to six. Childhood illnesses can lead to the creation of antibodies that may prevent children from coming down with the same illnesses in adulthood when they can do more harm.

8-3c MAJOR ILLNESSES

Advances in immunization along with the development of antibiotics and other medications have dramatically reduced the incidence and effects of serious childhood diseases. Because most preschoolers and schoolchildren have been inoculated against major childhood illnesses such as rubella (German measles), measles,

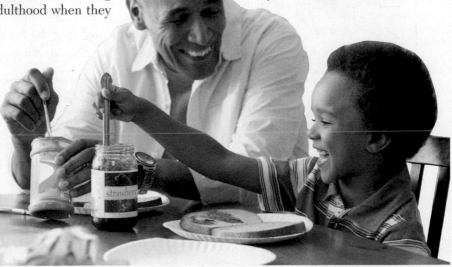

tetanus, mumps, whooping cough, diphtheria, and polio, these diseases no longer pose the threat they once did.

Nearly one-third of children in the United States younger than 18 years of age suffer from a chronic illness (Agency for Healthcare Research and Quality, 2004). These illnesses include arthritis, diabetes, cerebral palsy, and cystic fibrosis.

Although many major childhood diseases have been largely eradicated in the United States and other industrialized nations, they remain fearsome killers of children in developing countries. Around the world, eight to nine million children die each year of just six diseases: pneumonia, diarrhea, measles, tetanus, whooping cough, and tuberculosis (Save the Children, 2015). Air pollution from the combustion of fossil fuels for heating and cooking causes many respiratory infections, which are responsible for nearly one death in five among children who are younger than five years of age (Save the Children, 2015). Diarrhea kills nearly two million children under the age of five each year. Diarrheal diseases are mostly related to unsafe drinking water and poor sanitation and hygiene (Save the Children, 2015).

Many youngsters are exposed to lead in early childhood, often by eating chips of lead paint from their homes or by breathing in dust from the paint. Infants fed formula made with tap water may be at risk of lead poisoning, because water pipes sometimes contain lead (Centers for Disease Control and Prevention, 2013b). Lead causes neurological damage and may result in lowered cognitive functioning and other delays.

8-3d ACCIDENTS

Accidents cause more deaths in early childhood than the next six most frequent causes combined (Johnson et al., 2014; Leading Causes of Death, 2016). The single most common cause of death in early childhood is motor vehicle accidents. Boys are more likely than girls to incur accidental injuries at all ages and in all socioeconomic groups. Poor children are five times as likely to die from fires and more than twice as likely to die in motor vehicle accidents than other children (Leading Causes of Death, 2016). The high accident rate of low-income children may result partly from living in dangerous housing and neighborhoods.

sleep terrors frightening dream-like experiences that occur during the deepest stage of non-REM sleep, shortly after the child has gone to sleep.

FICTION

T (F) Infections are the most common cause of death among children in the United States.

Infections are not the most common cause of death in early childhood in the United States; accidents are.

8-4 SLEEP

Preschoolers do not need as much sleep as infants. The National Sleep Foundation (2015) recommends 11 to 13 hours of sleep in a 24-hour period for preschoolers (see Table 8.3). A common pattern includes nine to ten hours at night and a nap of one to two hours. Many children resist going to bed or going to sleep (Freeman et al., 2012). Getting to sleep late can be a problem, because preschoolers tend not to make up fully for lost sleep (National Sleep Foundation, 2015). Many young children take a so-called "transitional object"—such as a favored blanket or a stuffed animal—to bed with them.

8-4a SLEEP DISORDERS

Not all children get the sleep they need. In this section, we focus on the sleep disorders of sleep terrors, nightmares, and sleepwalking.

SLEEP TERRORS AND NIGHTMARES Sleep terrors are more severe than the anxiety dreams we refer to as nightmares (National Sleep Foundation, 2015). Sleep terrors usually occur during deep sleep. Nightmares take place during lighter rapid-eye-movement (REM) sleep, when about 80% of normal dreams occur.

Sleep terrors usually begin in childhood or early adolescence and are outgrown by late adolescence. They are sometimes associated with stress, as in moving to a new neighborhood, beginning school, adjusting to parental divorce, or being in a war zone. Children with sleep terrors may wake suddenly with a surge in heart and respiration rates, talk incoherently, and thrash about. Children may then fall back into more restful sleep. The incidence of sleep terrors wanes as children develop.

Children who have frequent nightmares or sleep terrors may come to fear going to sleep. They may show distress at bedtime, refuse to get into their pajamas, and insist that the lights be kept on. As a result, they can develop insomnia. Children with frequent nightmares

TABLE 8.3	HOW MUCH SLEEP DO YOU REALLY NEED?
Age	Sleep Needed
Newborns (0–2 months)	12 to 18 hours
Infants (3–11 months)	14 to 15 hours
Toddlers (1–3 years)	12 to 14 hours
Preschoolers (3–5 years)	11 to 13 hours
School-age children (5–10 years)	10 to 11 hours
Teens (10–17 years)	8.5 to 9.25 hours
Adults	7 to 9 hours

Source: National Sleep Foundation (2015).

or sleep terrors need caregivers' understanding and affection. They also profit from a regular routine in which they are expected to get to sleep at the same time each night (Freeman et al., 2012).

SLEEPWALKING Sleepwalking, or **somnambulism**, is more common among children than adults. As with sleep terrors, sleepwalking tends to occur during deep sleep (National Sleep Foundation, 2015). Onset is usually between the ages of three and eight.

When children sleepwalk, they may rearrange toys, go to the bathroom, or go to the refrigerator and have a glass of milk. They then return to their rooms and go back to bed. There are myths about sleepwalking, for instance that sleepwalkers' eyes are closed, that they will avoid harm, and that they will become violently agitated if they are awakened during an episode. All these notions are false.

Denise Hager/Catchlight Visual Services/Alamy Stock Photo

FICTION

T (F) It is dangerous to awaken a sleepwalker.

It is not true that it is dangerous to awaken a sleepwalker. Children may be difficult to rouse when they are sleepwalking, just as during sleep terrors. But if they are awakened, they are more likely to show confusion and disorientation (again, as during sleep terrors) than violence.

Sleepwalking in children is assumed to reflect immaturity of the nervous system. As with sleep terrors, the incidence of sleepwalking drops as children develop. It may help to discuss a child's persistent sleep terrors or sleepwalking with a health professional.

8-5 ELIMINATION DISORDERS

The elimination of waste products occurs reflexively in neonates. As children develop, they learn to inhibit the reflexes that govern urination and bowel movements. The process by which parents teach their children to inhibit these reflexes is referred to as toilet training.

In toilet training, maturation plays a crucial role. During the first year, only an exceptional child can be toilet trained. Most American children are toilet trained between the ages of three and four (American Psychiatric Association, 2013). They may have nighttime "accidents" for another year or so. Children who do not become toilet trained within reasonable time frames may be diagnosed with enuresis, encopresis, or both.

8-5a ENURESIS

Enuresis is failure to control the bladder (urination) once the "normal" age for achieving bladder control has been reached. The American Psychiatric Association (2013) places the cutoff age at five years and does not consider "accidents" to represent enuresis unless they occur at least twice a month for five- and six-year-olds.

FICTION

T (F) Competent parents toilet train their children by their second birthday.

It is not true that competent parents toilet train their children by their second birthday. Most American children are toilet trained between the ages of three and four , although they normally have some "accidents" beyond those ages.

A nighttime "accident" is termed **bed-wetting**. Nighttime control is more difficult to achieve than daytime control. At night, children must first wake up when their bladders are full. Only then can they go to the bathroom. Overall, 8% to 10% of American children wet their beds (Lucas et al., 2015), with the problem about twice as common among boys. Bed-wetting tends to occur during the deepest

somnambulism sleepwalking.

enuresis failure to control the bladder (urination) once the normal age for control has been reached.

bed-wetting failure to control the bladder during the night.

stage of sleep. That is also the stage when sleep terrors and sleepwalking take place.

It is believed that enuresis might have organic causes, most often immaturity of the motor cortex of the brain (Lucas et al., 2015). Just as children outgrow sleep terrors and sleepwalking, they tend to outgrow bed-wetting (Lucas et al., 2015).

8-5b ENCOPRESIS

Soiling, or **encopresis**, is lack of control over the bowels. Soiling, like enuresis, is more common among boys. About 1% to 2% of children at the ages of seven and eight have continuing problems controlling their bowels (Lucas et al., 2015). Soiling, in contrast to enuresis, is more likely to occur during the day. Thus, it can be embarrassing to the child, especially in school.

Encopresis stems from both physical causes, such as chronic constipation, and psychological factors (Mellon, 2012; von Gontard, 2011). Soiling may follow harsh punishment of toileting accidents, especially in children who are already anxious or under stress (Lucas et al., 2015). Punishment may cause the child to tense up on the toilet, when moving one's bowels requires that one

relax the anal sphincter muscles. Soiling, punishment, and anxiety can become a vicious cycle.

> **encopresis** failure to control the bowels once the normal age for bowel control has been reached. Also called soiling.

STUDY TOOLS 8

READY TO STUDY?

In the book, you can:

- ☐ Rip out the chapter review card at the back of the book for a handy summary of the chapter and key terms.
- ☐ Check your understanding of what you've read with the quizzes that follow.

ONLINE AT CENGAGEBRAIN.COM YOU CAN:

- ☐ Collect StudyBits while you read and study the chapter.
- ☐ Quiz yourself on key concepts.
- ☐ Find videos for further exploration.
- ☐ Prepare for tests with CDEV2 Flash Cards as well as those you create.

SELF-ASSESSMENTS

Fill-Ins

Answers can be found in the back of the book.

1. During early childhood, children gain about _____ inches in height each year.

2. In the United States, about one child in _____ suffers from a major chronic illness.

3. Sleep terrors differ from nightmares in that they typically occur during _____ sleep.

4. We would expect a child to be able to catch a small ball, using the hands only, by the age of _____.

5. According the Kellogg, the final stage in children's drawings is the _____ stage.

6. According to the text, if both of a child's parents are left-handed, the child's probability of becoming left-handed is about _____%.

7. During early childhood, completion of myelination of the neurons that connect the _____ to the cerebral cortex facilitates development of balance and coordination.

8. Rough-and-tumble play is more common among (girls or boys?) _____.

9. Although _____ is usually mild in the United States, it is a leading killer of children in less-developed countries.

10. Contamination by _____ in water pipes can cause neurological damage.

Multiple Choice

1. **What happens to the rate of growth between the ages of two and six, when compared to the growth rate during infancy?**
   a. It speeds up.
   b. It slows down.
   c. It remains the same.
   d. There is too much individual variation to make any generalizations.

2. **Plasticity of the brain is greatest**
   a. at about one to two years of age.
   b. during the preschool years of two to five.
   c. during adolescence.
   d. during adulthood.

3. **How many hours of sleep does the National Sleep Foundation recommend that three- to five-year-olds obtain in a 24-hour period?**
   a. 12 to 18   c. 12 to 14
   b. 14 to 15   d. 11 to 13

4. **We would expect a child to first be able to build a tower of six cubes at the age of**
   a. two years.   c. four years.
   b. three years.   d. five years.

5. **Which of the following is true about enuresis?**
   a. Enuresis is a sign that the child is angry or disappointed with his or her parents.
   b. Enuresis is a sign of poor parenting.
   c. Enuresis is more common among girls.
   d. Enuresis is usually outgrown.

6. **Sleepwalking is most common**
   a. during REM sleep.
   b. during deep sleep.
   c. among children being harshly toilet trained.
   d. in developed nations.

7. **American children between the ages of one and three average _____ minor illnesses a year.**
   a. one to two   c. six to seven
   b. three to five   d. eight to nine

8. **Due to immunization, children today are less likely to contract**
   a. diarrhea.   c. whooping cough.
   b. measles.   d. mumps.

9. **Children's activity levels are likely to reflect**
   a. active parental role models.
   b. sharing in family activities.
   c. a genetic tendency.
   d. all of the above.

10. **The left and right hemispheres of the brain "cooperate" due to myelination of the**
    a. corpus callosum.
    b. cerebellum.
    c. hypothalamus.
    d. thalamus.

9 Early Childhood: Cognitive Development

Joakim Leroy/E+/Getty Images

LEARNING OUTCOMES

After studying this chapter, you will be able to . . .

9-1 Describe Piaget's preoperational stage

9-2 Discuss influences on cognitive development in early childhood

9-3 Explain how "theory of mind" affects cognitive development

9-4 Describe memory development in early childhood

9-5 Describe language development in early childhood

After you finish this chapter, go to **PAGE 159** for **STUDY TOOLS**

I was confused when my daughter, Allyn, at the age of 2½, insisted that I continue to play "Billy Joel" on the stereo. Put aside the question of her taste in music. My problem stemmed from the fact that when she asked for Billy Joel, the name of the singer, she could be satisfied only by my playing the song "Moving Out." When "Moving Out" had ended and the next song, "The Stranger," had begun to play, she would insist that I play "Billy Joel" again. "That is Billy Joel," I would protest. "No, no," she would insist, "I want Billy Joel!"

Finally, it dawned on me that for Allyn, the words *Billy Joel* symbolized the song "Moving Out," not the name of the singer. Of course my insistence that the second song was also "Billy Joel" could not satisfy her! She was conceptualizing Billy Joel as a property of a particular song, not as the name of a person who could sing many songs.

Children between the ages of 2 and 4 tend to show confusion between symbols and the objects they represent. They do not yet recognize that words are arbitrary symbols for objects and events and that people can use different words. They tend to think of words as inherent properties of objects and events.

In this chapter, we discuss cognitive development during early childhood. First, we examine Piaget's preoperational stage of cognitive development. Piaget viewed cognitive development largely in terms of maturation; however, in the section on Vygotsky's views on cognitive development, we will see that social and other factors foster cognitive development by placing children in "the zone," as Vygotsky might have put it. Next, we consider other factors in cognitive development, such as how children acquire a "theory of mind" and develop memory. Finally, we continue our exploration of language development.

9-1 JEAN PIAGET'S PREOPERATIONAL STAGE

According to Piaget, the **preoperational stage** of cognitive development lasts from about age two to age seven. Be warned: Any resemblance between the logic of a preschooler and your own may be purely coincidental. *Operations* are mental manipulations of information, and at this stage, young children's logic is at best "under construction."

9-1a SYMBOLIC THOUGHT

Preoperational thought is characterized by the use of symbols to represent objects and relationships among them. Perhaps the most important kind of symbolic activity of young children is language, but children's early use of language leaves something to be desired in the realm of logic. According to Piaget, preschoolers' drawings are symbols of objects, people, and events in children's lives. Symbolism is also expressed as symbolic or pretend play.

TRUTH OR FICTION?

T	F	A preschooler's having imaginary companions is a sign of loneliness or psychological problems.
T	F	Two-year-olds tend to assume that their caregivers are aware of everything that is happening to them, even when their parents are not present.
T	F	"Because Mommy wants me to" may be a perfectly good explanation—for a three-year-old.
T	F	An academic preschool education provides children with advantages in school later on.
T	F	Three-year-olds usually say "Daddy goed away" instead of "Daddy went away" because they don't yet understand rules of grammar.

preoperational stage the second stage in Piaget's scheme, characterized by inflexible and irreversible mental manipulation of symbols.

9-1b SYMBOLIC OR PRETEND PLAY

Children's **symbolic play**—the "let's pretend" type of play—may seem immature to busy adults meeting the realistic demands of the business world, but it requires cognitive sophistication (Hoff, 2013; Taylor, 2013).

Piaget ([1946] 1962) wrote that pretend play usually begins in the second year, when the child begins to symbolize objects. The ability to engage in pretend play is based on the use and recollection of symbols, that is, on mental representations of things children have experienced or heard about.

Children first engage in pretend play at about 12 or 13 months. They make believe that they are performing familiar activities, such as sleeping or feeding themselves. By 15 to 20 months, they can shift their focus from themselves to others. A child may pretend to feed her doll. By 30 months, she or he can make believe that the other object takes an active role. The child may pretend that the doll is feeding itself (Paavola et al., 2006).

The quality of preschoolers' pretend play has implications for subsequent development. For example, preschoolers who engage in violent pretend play are less empathic, less likely to help other children, and more likely to engage in antisocial behavior later on (Dunn & Hughes, 2001). The quality of pretend play is connected with preschoolers' academic performance later on, their creativity, and their social skills (Taylor, 2013).

Imaginary companions—also known as *virtual characters* (Aguiar & Taylor, 2015)—are one example of pretend play. It is estimated that between 10% and 50% of preschoolers have imaginary companions (Davis et al., 2013). Imaginary companions are most commonly found among firstborn and only children (Gleason, 2013; Hoff, 2013). Having an imaginary playmate does not mean that the child has problems with real relationships (Gleason, 2013; Hoff, 2005). In fact, children with imaginary companions are less aggressive, more cooperative, and more creative than other children (Gleason, 2013; Hoff, 2013). They have more real friends, show greater ability to concentrate, and are more advanced in language development (Aguilar & Taylor, 2015).

symbolic play play in which children make believe that objects and toys are other than what they are. Also called pretend play.

egocentrism putting oneself at the center of things such that one is unable to perceive the world from another person's point of view.

FICTION

T (F) A preschooler's having imaginary companions is a sign of loneliness or psychological problems.

It is not true that having imaginary companions is a sign of loneliness or psychological problems. Having imaginary companions is a normal—though not universal—aspect of development.

9-1c EGOCENTRISM: IT'S ALL ABOUT ME

Sometimes the attitude "It's all about me" is a sign of early childhood, not of selfishness. One consequence of one-dimensional thinking is **egocentrism**. Egocentrism, in Piaget's use of the term, means that preoperational children do not understand that other people may have different perspectives on the world. Two-year-olds may, in fact, assume that their parents are aware of everything that is happening to them, even when their parents are not present. When I asked a daughter aged 2½ to tell me about a trip to the store with her mother, she answered, "You tell me." It did not occur to her that I could not see the world through her eyes.

Piaget used the "three-mountains test" (see Figure 9.1) to show that egocentrism prevents young children from taking the viewpoints of others. In this demonstration, the child faces a table before a model of three mountains. One has a house on it, and another has a cross at the summit.

Piaget then placed a doll elsewhere on the table and asked the child what the doll sees. The language

glenda/Shutterstock.com

abilities of very young children do not permit them to provide verbal descriptions of what can be seen from where the doll is situated, so they can answer in one of two ways. They can either select a photograph taken from the proper vantage point, or they can construct another model of the mountains as they would be seen by the doll. The results of a classic experiment with the three-mountains test suggest that five- and

FIG.9.1   THE THREE MOUNTAINS TEST

What does the teddy bear see? You might know the answer, but what might the young boy say? Piaget used the three-mountains test to learn whether children at certain ages are egocentric or can take the viewpoints of others.

six-year-olds usually select photos or build models that correspond to their own viewpoints (Laurendeau & Pinard, 1970).

9-1d CAUSALITY: WHY? BECAUSE.

Preoperational children's responses to questions such as "Why does the sun shine?" show other facets of egocentrism. At the age of two or so, they may answer that they do not know or change the subject. Three-year-olds may report themselves as doing things because they want to do them or "Because Mommy wants me to." In egocentric fashion, this explanation of behavior is extended to inanimate objects. The sun may be thought of as shining because it wants to shine or someone wants it to shine.

Piaget labels this structuring of cause and effect **precausal**. Preoperational children believe that things happen for reasons and not by accident (Sobel & Legare, 2014). Unless preoperational children know the natural causes of an event, their reasons are likely to have an egocentric flavor and not be based on science. Consider the question, "Why does it get dark outside?" The preoperational child usually does not have knowledge of Earth's rotation and is likely to answer something like, "So I can go to sleep."

In **transductive reasoning**, children reason by going from one specific isolated event to another. For example, a three-year-old may argue that she should go on her swings in the backyard *because* it is light outside or that she should go to sleep *because* it is dark outside. That is, separate events, daylight and going on

> **precausal** a type of thought in which natural cause-and-effect relationships are attributed to will and other preoperational concepts.
>
> **transductive reasoning** reasoning from the specific to the specific.

the swings (or being awake), are thought of as having cause-and-effect relationships.

Preoperational children also show **animism** and **artificialism** in their attributions of causality. In animistic thinking, they attribute life and intentions to inanimate objects, such as the sun and the moon. ("Why is the moon gone during the day?" "It is afraid of the sun.") Artificialism assumes that environmental features such as rain and thunder have been designed and made by people.

9-1e CONFUSION OF MENTAL AND PHYSICAL EVENTS

What would you do if someone asked you to pretend you were a galaprock? Chances are, you might inquire what a galaprock is and how it behaves. So might a five-year-old child. But a three-year-old might not think that such information is necessary (Gottfried et al., 2003).

According to Piaget, the preoperational child has difficulty making distinctions between mental and physical events. Children between the ages of two and four show confusion between symbols and the things they represent. Egocentrism contributes to the assumption that their thoughts exactly reflect external reality. They do not recognize that words are arbitrary and that people can use different words to refer to things. In *Play, Dreams, and Imitation in Childhood*, Piaget ([1946] 1962) asked a four-year-old child, "Could you call this table a cup and that cup a table?" "No," the child responded. "Why not?" "Because," explained the child, "you can't drink out of a table!" Another example of the preoperational child's confusion of the mental and the physical is the tendency of many four-year-olds to believe that dreams are real, but begin to understand that they are not real at about the age of seven (Honig & Nealis, 2012). Young boys, by the way, are more likely than girls to dream about fighting, chasing, and power; girls are more likely to dream about family members and joyful experiences (Honig & Nealis, 2012).

9-1f FOCUS ON ONE DIMENSION AT A TIME

To gain further insight into preoperational thinking, consider these two problems. Consider the first problem presented in Figure 9.2. Imagine that you pour the water from one of the low, wide beakers in part (a) into the tall, thin beaker in part (b). Now, as in part (c), consider whether the tall, thin beaker contains more water than, less water than, or the same amount of water as the low, wide beaker. We won't keep you in suspense. If you said the same amount, you were correct.

Next consider the second problem. Imagine taking a ball of clay and flattening it into a pancake. Do you wind up with more, less, or the same amount of clay? If you said the same amount, you were correct once more.

To arrive at the correct answers to these questions, you must understand the law of **conservation**. The law of conservation holds that properties of substances such as volume, mass, and number remain the same—or are conserved—even if you change their shape or arrangement.

Conservation requires the ability to focus on two aspects of a situation at once, such as height and width. A preoperational child focuses or centers on only one dimension at a time, a characteristic of thought that Piaget called **centration**. First, the child is shown two squat glasses or beakers of water and agrees that they have the same amount of water (as in Figure 9.2). Then, as he watches, water is poured from one squat glass into a tall, thin glass. Asked which glass has more water, he points to the tall glass. Why? When he looks at the glasses, he is swayed by the fact that the thinner glass is taller.

animism the attribution of life and intentionality to inanimate objects.

artificialism the belief that environmental features were made by people.

conservation in cognitive psychology, the principle that properties of substances such as weight and mass remain the same (are conserved) when superficial characteristics such as their shapes or arrangement are changed.

centration focusing on an aspect or characteristic of a situation or problem.

Jitloac/Shutterstock.com

Jitloac/Shutterstock.com

FIG.9.2 CONSERVATION

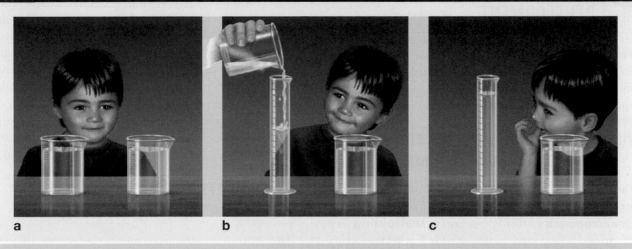

a   b   c

(a) The preoperational boy agrees that the amounts of water in the two containers is the same. (b) He watches as the water from one container is poured into a taller, thinner container. (c) When asked whether the tall and the squat containers now contain the same amount of water, he says no. Why?

The preoperational child's failure to show conservation also comes about because of *irreversibility*. In the case of the water, the child does not realize that pouring water from the wide glass to the tall glass can be reversed, restoring things to their original condition.

After you have tried the experiment with the water, try this experiment on conservation of number. Make two rows with four pennies in each. As a four-year-old child watches, move the pennies in the second row to about an inch apart, as in Figure 9.3. Then ask the child which row has more pennies. What do you think the child will say? Why?

CLASS INCLUSION Class inclusion, as we are using it here, means including new objects or categories in broader mental classes or categories. Class inclusion also requires children to focus on two aspects of a situation at once. In one of Piaget's class-inclusion tasks, the child is shown several pictures from two subclasses of a larger class, for example, four cats and six dogs. She is asked whether there are more dogs or more animals. What do you think she will say? Preoperational children typically answer that there are more dogs than animals (Piaget, [1936] 1963).

Why do preoperational children make this error? According to Piaget, they cannot think about the two subclasses and the larger class at the same time. Therefore, they cannot easily compare them. Children view dogs as dogs, or as animals, but find it difficult to see them as both dogs and animals at once (Muller et al., 2015).

FIG.9.3 CONSERVATION OF NUMBER

Child is shown two rows of pennies.

Experimenter moves pennies in one row.

We begin with two rows of pennies, spread out equally, as on the left. The child agrees that both rows have the same number of pennies. While a four-year-old child watches, we spread out the lower row of pennies so that it becomes wider. We then ask the child, "Do the two rows still have the same number of pennies?" What do you think the child will say? Why

class inclusion
categorizing a new object or concept as belonging to a broader group of objects or concepts.

9-2 FACTORS IN COGNITIVE DEVELOPMENT

Two factors that influence cognitive development in early childhood are Vygotsky's concepts of scaffolding and the zone of proximal development. Others include the home environment, preschool education, and television.

9-2a SCAFFOLDING AND THE ZONE OF PROXIMAL DEVELOPMENT

Parental responsiveness and interaction with children are key ingredients in children's cognitive development. One component of this interaction is **scaffolding** (see Chapter 1). Cognitive scaffolding refers to temporary support provided by a parent or teacher to learning children. The guidance provided by adults decreases as children become capable of carrying out the task on their own (Clark, 2014).

A related concept is Vygotsky's **zone of proximal development (ZPD)**. The zone refers to the area in which children develop new cognitive skills as a function of working with more skilled people. Adults or older children can best guide children through this zone by gearing their assistance to children's capabilities (Clark, 2014). Researchers assert that the key forms of children's cognitive activities develop through interaction with older, more experienced individuals who teach and guide them. In a related study, K. Alison Clarke-Stewart and Robert Beck (1999) had 31 five-year-olds observe a videotaped film segment with their mothers, talk about it with their mothers, and then retell the story to an experimenter. Children whose mothers focused the children's attention on the tape, asked their children to talk about it, and discussed the feelings of the characters told better stories than children whose mothers did not use such scaffolding strategies and children in a control group who did not discuss the story at all.

scaffolding Vygotsky's term for temporary cognitive structures or methods of solving problems that help the child as he or she learns to function independently.

zone of proximal development (ZPD) Vygotsky's term for the situation in which a child carries out tasks with the help of someone who is more skilled, frequently an adult who represents the culture in which the child develops.

9-2b THE "HOME" ENVIRONMENT

Bettye Caldwell and her colleagues (Bradley et al., 2003) developed a measure for evaluating children's home environments labeled, appropriately enough, HOME, an acronym for Home Observation for the Measurement of the Environment. With this method, researchers directly observe parent–child interaction in the home. The HOME inventory contains six subscales, as shown in Table 9.1. The HOME inventory items are better predictors of young children's later IQ scores than social class, mother's IQ, or infant IQ scores (Bradley, 2006). Longitudinal research also shows that a stimulating home environment is connected with occupational success as an adult (Huesmann et al., 2006). On the other hand, harsh home environments have been linked with poor academic outcomes in school (Schwartz et al., 2013).

9-2c EFFECTS OF EARLY CHILDHOOD EDUCATION

How important are academic experiences in early childhood? Do they facilitate cognitive development? Research suggests that preschool education enables children to get an early start on achievement in school.

Children reared in poverty generally perform less well on standardized intelligence tests than children of higher socioeconomic status, and they are at greater risk for school failure (Robbins et al., 2012). As a result, preschool programs were begun in the 1960s to enhance their cognitive

TABLE 9.1 SCALES OF THE HOME INVENTORY

Scale	Sample Items
Parental emotional and verbal responsiveness	The parent spontaneously vocalizes to the child during the visit.
	The parent responds to the child's vocalizations with vocal or other verbal responses.
Avoidance of restriction and punishment	The parent does not shout at the child.
	The parent does not interfere with the child's actions or restrict the child's movements more than three times during the visit.
Organization of the physical environment	The child's play environment seems to be safe and free from hazards.
Provision of appropriate play materials	The child has a push or a pull toy.
	The child has one or more toys or pieces of equipment that promote muscle activity.
	The family provides appropriate equipment to foster learning.
Parental involvement with child	The parent structures the child's play periods.
	The parent tends to keep the child within her or his visual range and looks at the child frequently.
Opportunities for variety in daily stimulation	The child gets out of the house at least four times a week.
	The parent reads stories to the child at least three times a week.

development and readiness for elementary school. Children in these programs typically are exposed to letters and words, numbers, books, exercises in drawing, pegs and pegboards, puzzles, and toy animals and dolls—materials and activities that middle-class children usually take for granted.

Studies of Head Start and other intervention programs show that environmental enrichment can enhance the cognitive development of economically disadvantaged children (Bierman et al., 2014). In the Milwaukee Project, poor children of low-IQ mothers were provided with enriched day care from the age of six months. By the late preschool years, the children's IQ scores averaged about 121, compared with an average of 95 for peers who did not receive day care (Garber, 1988).

TRUTH

(T) F An academic preschool education provides children with advantages in school later on.

Studies of the effects of Head Start and other methods of providing young children with enriched learning environments do show that they can provide children with advantages in school.

9-2d TELEVISION

American children spend more time watching television than they do in school. By the time he or she turns three, the average child already watches two to three hours of television a day (Palmer, 2003). Television has great potential for teaching a variety of cognitive skills, social behaviors, and attitudes.

Sesame Street is the most successful children's educational TV program. The goal of *Sesame Street* is to promote the intellectual growth of preschoolers, particularly those of lower socioeconomic status. Large-scale evaluations of the effects of the program have concluded that regular viewing increases children's learning of numbers, letters, and cognitive skills such as sorting and classification (Mares & Pan, 2013). Preschoolers are often unable to tell the difference between commercials and program content (Chambers et al., 2015; Lillard et al., 2015). Children who are heavy TV viewers are more likely to believe commercial claims.

Then there is the "couch potato" effect. Research in the United States, England, and even China shows that among preschool children, the number of hours watching television is a stronger predictor of being overweight than diet (Borghese et al., 2015; Chen & Wang, 2015)!

9-3 THEORY OF MIND

Adults appear to have a commonsense understanding of how the mind works—that is, a **theory of mind**. We understand that we can gain knowledge through our senses or through hearsay. We know the distinction between actual and mental events and between how things appear and how they really are. We can infer the perceptions, thoughts, and feelings of others. We understand that mental states affect behavior.

Piaget might have predicted that preoperational children are too egocentric and too focused on misleading external appearances to have a theory of mind, but research has shown that even preschoolers can accurately predict and explain human action and emotion in terms of mental states (Wellman et al., 2006).

9-3a FALSE BELIEFS: WHERE ARE THOSE CRAYONS?

One indication of preschoolers' understanding that mental states affect behavior is the ability to understand false beliefs. This concept involves children's ability to separate their beliefs from those of another person who has false knowledge of a situation. It is illustrated in a study of three-year-olds by Louis Moses and John Flavell (1990). The children were shown a videotape in which a girl named Cathy found some crayons in a bag. When Cathy left the room briefly, a clown entered the room. The clown removed the crayons from the bag, hid them in a drawer, and put rocks in the bag instead. When Cathy returned, the children were asked whether Cathy thought there would be rocks or crayons in the bag. Most of the three-year-olds incorrectly answered "rocks," demonstrating their difficulty in understanding that the other person's belief would be different from their own. But by the age of four to five years, children do not have trouble with this concept and correctly answer "crayons" (Flavell, 1993).

9-3b ORIGINS OF KNOWLEDGE

Another aspect of theory of mind is how we acquire knowledge. By age three, most children begin to realize that people gain knowledge about something by looking at it (Lecce et al., 2015). By age four, children understand that particular senses provide information about only certain qualities of an object; for example, we come to know an

theory of mind a commonsense understanding of how the mind works.

object's color through our eyes, but we learn about its weight by feeling it (O'Neill & Chong, 2001). In a study by Daniela O'Neill and Alison Gopnik (1991), three-, four-, and five-year-olds learned about the contents of a toy tunnel in three different ways: They saw the contents, were told about them, or felt them. The children were then asked to state what was in the tunnel and how they knew. Although four- and five-year-olds had no trouble identifying the sources of their knowledge, the three-year-olds did. For example, after feeling but not seeing a ball in the tunnel, a number of three-year-olds told the experimenter that they could tell it was a blue ball. The children did not realize they could not learn the ball's color by feeling it.

9-3c THE APPEARANCE–REALITY DISTINCTION

Children must acquire an understanding of the difference between real events, on the one hand, and mental events, fantasies, and misleading appearances, on the other hand. This understanding is known as the **appearance–reality distinction**.

Piaget's view was that children do not differentiate reality from appearances or mental events until the age of seven or eight. In a study by Marjorie Taylor and Barbara Hort (1990), children age three to five were shown objects that had misleading appearances, such as an eraser that looked like a cookie. The children initially reported that the eraser looked like a cookie. However, once they learned that it was actually an eraser,

they tended to report that it looked like an eraser. Apparently, the children could not mentally represent the eraser as both being an eraser and looking like a cookie.

Three-year-olds also apparently cannot understand changes in their mental states. In one study (Gopnik & Slaughter, 1991), three-year-olds were shown a crayon box with candles inside. Before it was opened, they consistently said they thought crayons were inside. When asked what they had thought was in the box before it was opened, the children now said "candles."

9-4 # DEVELOPMENT OF MEMORY

Children, like adults, often remember what they want to remember (Crisp & Turner, 2011). By the age of four, children can remember events that occurred at least 1½ years earlier (Bauer & Fivush, 2010, 2013). Katherine Nelson (1990, 1993) interviewed children aged two to five to study their memory for recurring events in their lives, such as having dinner, playing with friends, and going to birthday parties. She found that three-year-olds can present coherent, orderly accounts of familiar events. Furthermore, young children seem to form **scripts**, which are abstract, generalized accounts of these repeated events. For example, in describing what happens during a birthday party, a child might say, "You play games, open presents, and eat cake" (Fivush, 2002). However, an unusual experience, such as a hurricane, may be remembered in detail for years (Bauer & Fivush, 2013).

Even though children as young as one and two years of age can remember events, these memories seldom last into adulthood. This memory of specific events—known as **autobiographical memory** or *episodic memory*—is facilitated by children talking about the memories with others (Bauer & Fivush, 2013).

appearance–reality distinction the difference between real events on the one hand and mental events, fantasies, and misleading appearances on the other hand.

scripts abstract, generalized accounts of familiar repeated events.

autobiographical memory the memory of specific episodes or events.

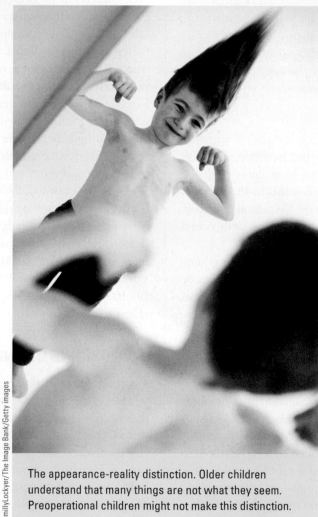

RomillyLockyer/The Image Bank/Getty images

The appearance-reality distinction. Older children understand that many things are not what they seem. Preoperational children might not make this distinction.

9-4a FACTORS INFLUENCING MEMORY

Factors that affect memory include what the child is asked to remember, the interest level of the child, the availability of retrieval cues or reminders, and what memory measure we are using. First, children find it easier to remember events that follow a fixed and logical order than events that do not. For instance, three- and five-year-olds have a better memory for the activities involved in making pretend cookies out of Play-Doh (you put the ingredients in the bowl, then mix the ingredients, then roll out the dough, and so on) than they do for the activities involved in sand play, which can occur in any order (Bauer & Fivush, 2013). Research consistently shows that (most) preschool boys are more interested in playing with toys such as cars and weapons, whereas (most) preschool girls are more interested in playing with dolls, dishes, and teddy bears. Later, the children typically show better recognition and recall for the toys in which they were interested (Goble et al., 2012).

Although young children can remember a great deal, they depend more than older children do on cues provided by others to help them retrieve their memories. Elaborating on the child's experiences and asking questions that encourage the child to contribute information to the narrative generally help children remember an episode (Bauer & Fivush, 2013).

Children's memory can often be measured or assessed by asking them to say what they remember. But verbal reports, especially from preschoolers, appear to underestimate children's memory (Bauer & Fivush, 2013). In one longitudinal study, children's memory for certain events was tested at age two and a half and again at age four. Most of the information recalled at age four had not been mentioned at age two and a half, indicating that when they were younger, the children remembered more than they reported (Fivush & Hammond, 1990). Another study found that when young children were allowed to use dolls to reenact an event, their recall was better than when they gave a verbal report (Schneider, 2010).

9-4b MEMORY STRATEGIES: REMEMBERING TO REMEMBER

Adults and older children use strategies to help them remember things. One strategy is mental repetition, or **rehearsal**. If you are trying to remember a new friend's phone number, for example, you might repeat it several times. Another strategy is to organize things to be remembered into categories. Most preschoolers do not engage in spontaneous rehearsal until about five years of age (Bebko et al., 2014). They also rarely group objects into related categories to help them remember. By about age five, many children have learned to verbalize information silently to themselves by counting mentally, for example, rather than aloud.

Having preschoolers sort objects into categories enhances memory (Howe, 2006; Lange & Pierce, 1992). Even three- and four-year-olds will use rehearsal and labeling if they are asked to try to remember something.

9-5 LANGUAGE DEVELOPMENT: WHY "DADDY GOED AWAY"

Children's language skills mushroom during the preschool years. By the fourth year, children are asking adults and each other questions, taking turns talking, and engaging in lengthy conversations (Hoover et al., 2011).

9-5a DEVELOPMENT OF VOCABULARY

The development of vocabulary proceeds at an extraordinary pace. Preschoolers learn an average of nine new words per day (Tamis-LeMonda et al., 2006, 2014). But how can that be possible when each new word has so many potential meanings? Consider the following example. A toddler observes a small, black dog running through the park. His older sister points to the animal and says, "Doggy." The word *doggy* could mean this particular dog, or all dogs, or all animals. It could refer to one part of the dog (e.g., its tail) or to its behavior (running, barking) or to its characteristics (small, black) (Waxman & Goswami, 2012). Does the child consider all these possibilities before determining what *doggy* actually means?

Word learning, in fact, does not occur gradually but is better characterized as a **fast-mapping** process in which the child quickly attaches a new word to its appropriate concept (Waxman & Goswami, 2012). Children apparently have early cognitive biases or constraints that lead them to prefer certain meanings over others (Waxman & Goswami, 2012).

Children also assume that words refer to whole objects and not to their component parts or their characteristics, such as color, size, or texture (Bloom, 2002). This bias

rehearsal repetition.

fast-mapping a process of quickly determining a word's meaning, which facilitates children's vocabulary development.

is called the **whole-object assumption**. Therefore, the young child would assume that the word *doggy* refers to the dog rather than to its tail, its color, or its barking.

Children also seem to assume that objects have only one label. Therefore, novel terms must refer to unfamiliar objects and not to familiar objects that already have labels. This concept is the **contrast assumption**, which is also known as the mutual exclusivity assumption. Suppose that a child is shown two objects, one of which has a known label ("doggy") and one of which is unknown. Let's further suppose that an adult now says, "Look at the lemur." If the child assumes that "doggy" and "lemur" each can refer to only one object, the child would correctly figure out that "lemur" refers to the other object and is not just another name for "doggy" (Waxman & Goswami, 2012).

9-5b DEVELOPMENT OF GRAMMAR

There is a "grammar explosion" during the third year (Tamis-LeMonda et al., 2014). Children's sentence structure expands to include the words missing in telegraphic speech. Children usually add to their vocabulary an impressive array of articles (*a, an, the*), conjunctions (*and, but, or*), possessive adjectives (*your, her*), pronouns (*she, him, one*), and prepositions (*in, on, over, around, under, through*). Usually between the ages of three and four, children show knowledge of rules for combining phrases and clauses into complex sentences, as in "You goed and Mommy goed, too."

OVERREGULARIZATION The apparent basis of one of the more intriguing language developments— **overregularization**—is that children acquire grammatical rules as they learn language. At young ages they tend to apply these rules rather strictly, even in cases that call for exceptions (Ambridge et al., 2013). Consider the formation of the past tense and plurals in English. We add *d* or *ed* to regular verbs and *s* to regular nouns. Thus, *walk* becomes *walked* and *doggy* becomes *doggies*. But

then there are irregular verbs and irregular nouns. For example, *sit* becomes *sat* and *go* becomes *went*. *Sheep* remains *sheep* (plural) and *child* becomes *children*.

As children become aware of the syntactic rules for forming the past tense and plurals in English, they often misapply them to irregular words. As a result, they tend to make charming errors (Ambridge et al., 2013). Some three- to five-year-olds are more likely to say "Mommy sitted down" than "Mommy sat down" or talk about the "sheeps" they "seed" on the farm and about all the "childs" they ran into at the playground.

Some parents recognize that their children at first were forming the past tense of irregular verbs correctly but that they then began to make errors. Some of these parents become concerned that their children are "slipping" in their language development and attempt to correct them. However, overregularization reflects accurate knowledge of grammar, not faulty language development. In another year or two, *mouses* will be boringly transformed into *mice*, and Mommy will no longer have sitted down. Parents might as well enjoy over-regularization while they can.

Grammar Explosion

ASKING QUESTIONS
Children's first questions are telegraphic and characterized by a rising pitch (which signifies a question mark in English) at the end. Depending on the context, "More milky?" can be translated into "May I have more milk?" "Would you like more milk?" or "Is there more milk?" It is usually toward the latter part of the third year that the *wh* questions appear. Consistent with the child's general cognitive development, certain *wh* questions (*what, who*, and *where*) appear earlier than others (*why, when, which*, and *how*) (Tamis-LeMonda et al., 2006).

whole-object assumption the assumption that words refer to whole objects and not to their component parts or characteristics.

contrast assumption the assumption that objects have only one label.

overregularization the application of regular grammatical rules for forming inflections to irregular verbs and nouns.

Walter Lockwood/Flame/Corbis

Why is usually too philosophical for a two-year-old, and *how* is too involved. Two-year-olds are also likely to be now-oriented, so *when* is of less than immediate concern. By the fourth year, most children are spontaneously producing *why, when,* and *how* questions. These *wh* words are initially tacked on to the beginnings of sentences. "Where Mommy go?" can stand for "Where is Mommy going?" "Where did Mommy go?" or "Where will Mommy go?" and its meaning must be derived from context. Later on, the child will add the auxiliary verbs *is, did,* and *will* to indicate whether the question concerns the present, past, or future.

PASSIVE SENTENCES Passive sentences, such as "The food is eaten by the dog," are difficult for two- and three-year-olds to understand, and so young preschoolers almost never produce them. In a study of children's comprehension (Strohner & Nelson, 1974), two- to five-year-olds used puppets and toys to act out sentences that were read to them. Two- and three-year-olds made errors in acting out passive sentences (e.g., "The car was hit by the truck") 70% of the time. Older children had less difficulty interpreting the meanings of passive sentences correctly. However, most children usually do not produce passive sentences spontaneously even at the ages of five and six.

FICTION

T (F) Three-year-olds usually say "Daddy goed away" instead of "Daddy went away" because they don't yet understand rules of grammar.

Actually, a 3-year-old is likely to say "Daddy goed away" rather than "Daddy went away" because the child does understand rules of grammar. The child is correctly applying a rule for forming the past tense of regular verbs, but applying it to an irregular verb.

9-5c PRAGMATICS

Pragmatics refers to the practical aspects of communication. Children show pragmatism when they adjust their speech to fit the social situation (Nelson, 2006). For example, children show greater formality in their choice of words and syntax when they are role-playing high-status figures, such as teachers or physicians, in their games. They say "please" more often when making requests of high-status people, or when they use "Motherese" in talking to an infant.

pragmatics the practical aspects of communication, such as adaptation of language to fit the social situation.

Serhiy Kobyakov /Alamy Stock Photo

Which Comes First?

Piaget believed that cognitive development precedes language development.

?

Many theorists claim that children create cognitive classes to understand things that are labeled by words.

Preschoolers tend to be egocentric; therefore, a two-year-old telling another child "Gimme my book," without specifying which book, may assume that the other child knows what she herself knows. Once children can perceive the world through the eyes of others, they advance in their abilities to make themselves understood. Now the child recognizes that the other child will require a description of the book or of its location to carry out the request.

9-5d LANGUAGE AND COGNITION

Language and cognitive development are interwoven (Waxman & Goswami, 2012). For example, the child gradually gains the capacity to discriminate between animals on the basis of distinct features, such as size, patterns of movement, and the sounds they make. At the same time, the child also is acquiring words that represent broader categories, such as mammal and animal.

But which comes first? Does the child first develop concepts and then acquire the language to describe them, or does the child's increasing language ability lead to the development of new concepts?

DOES COGNITIVE DEVELOPMENT PRECEDE LANGUAGE DEVELOPMENT? Piaget (1976) believed that cognitive development precedes language development. He argued that children must understand concepts before they use words to describe them. From Piaget's perspective, children learn words to describe classes or categories that they have already created (Nelson, 2005). Children can learn the word *kitty* because they have perceived the characteristics that distinguish cats from other things.

inner speech Vygotsky's concept of the ultimate binding of language and thought. Inner speech originates in vocalizations that may regulate the child's behavior and become internalized by age six or seven.

Some studies support the notion that cognitive concepts may precede language. For example, the vocabulary explosion that occurs at about 18 months of age is related to the child's ability to group a set of objects into two categories, such as "dolls" and "cars" (Gopnik & Meltzoff, 1992). Other research suggests that young children need to experience an action themselves or by observation to learn the meaning of a verb (Pulverman et al., 2006).

DOES LANGUAGE DEVELOPMENT PRECEDE COGNITIVE DEVELOPMENT? Although many theorists argue that cognitive development precedes language development, others reverse the causal relationship and claim that children create cognitive classes to understand things that are labeled by words (Clark, 1983). When children hear the word *dog*, they try to understand it by searching for characteristics that separate dogs from other things.

THE INTERACTIONIST VIEW: OUTER SPEECH AND INNER SPEECH Today, most investigators find something of value in each of these cognitive views (Waxman & Goswami, 2012). In the early stages of language development, concepts often precede words, and many of the infant's words describe classes that have already developed. But later language influences thought.

Vygotsky believed that during most of the first year, vocalizations and thought are separate. But during the second year, thought and speech combine forces. Children discover that objects have labels. Learning labels becomes more self-directed. Children ask what new words mean. Learning new words fosters creation of new categories, and new categories become filled with labels for new things.

Vygotsky's concept of **inner speech** is a key feature of his position. At first children's thoughts are spoken aloud. You can hear the three-year-old instructing herself as she plays with toys. At this age, her vocalizations serve to regulate her behavior, but they gradually become internalized. What was spoken aloud at four and five becomes an internal dialogue by six or seven. Inner speech is the ultimate binding of language and thought. It is involved in the development of planning and self-regulation, and facilitates learning.

In the next chapter, we'll continue our exploration of early childhood, looking at the social and emotional development that take place.

STUDY TOOLS 9

READY TO STUDY?

In the book, you can:

☐ Rip out the chapter review card at the back of the book for a handy summary of the chapter and key terms.

☐ Check your understanding of what you've read with the quizzes that follow.

ONLINE AT CENGAGEBRAIN.COM YOU CAN:

☐ Collect StudyBits while you read and study the chapter.

☐ Quiz yourself on key concepts.

☐ Find videos for further exploration.

☐ Prepare for tests with CDEV2 Flash Cards as well as those you create.

SELF-ASSESSMENTS

Fill-Ins

Answers can be found in the back of the book.

1. There is a debate as to whether language development follows or precedes _____ development.

2. A three-year-old may argue that she should go on the swings because it is light outside. Her logic is an example of _____ reasoning.

3. Piaget believed that children usually begin to engage in pretend play in the second year, when they have developed the ability to _____ objects.

4. According to Piaget, _____ means that preoperational children do not understand that other people may have different perspectives on the world.

5. Organization of the home environment is one of the scales of the _____ inventory.

6. _____ are abstract, generalized accounts of repeated events.

7. Children assume that words or names for things refer to _____ objects and not to characteristics such color, size, or texture.

8. "You goed and Mommy goed too" is an example of a(n) _____ sentence.

9. Children show _____ when they adjust their speech to fit the social situation.

10. By the ages of three and four children realize that people acquire knowledge through the _____.

Multiple Choice

1. **Most preschoolers cannot conserve volume, mass, or number because they**
   a. are lacking in intelligence.
   b. do not understand what the word conservation means.
   c. focus on one dimension of a situation at a time.
   d. have not been taught mathematics in an elementary school setting.

2. **Piaget used the three-mountains test to study _____ in children.**
   a. morality
   b. theory of mind
   c. confusion of mental and physical events
   d. egocentrism

3. **All of the following are scales of the HOME Inventory except**
   a. parental verbal and emotional responsiveness.
   b. parental use of scaffolding and the zone of proximal development.
   c. parental provision of appropriate play materials.
   d. parental avoidance of restriction and punishment.

4. **Studies of Head Start show that it has been effective at**
   a. preventing children from developing major illnesses.
   b. decreasing aggressiveness in the home environment.
   c. helping children understand the appearance–reality distinction.
   d. enhancing the cognitive development of economically deprived children.

5. **Preschoolers' learning of grammatical rules leads to**
   a. vocabulary development.
   b. overregularization.
   c. development of the whole-object assumption.
   d. use of pragmatics.

6. **Which of the following contributes to children's memory of events?**
   a. Sleeping after experiencing the event.
   b. Experiencing the event in a social situation.
   c. Asking children to talk about the events.
   d. Distinguishing appearances from reality.

7. **A four -year-old child is shown two rows of pennies such that each row has 4 pennies that are spread equally far apart. You spread the pennies in one row apart and ask the child which row has more pennies. According to Piaget, the four-year-old is most likely to answer that**
   a. the row that has been spread apart.
   b. the row that has remained the same width.
   c. both rows have the same number of pennies.
   d. "I don't know."

8. **All of the following enhance memory functioning in preschoolers except**
   a. the contrast assumption.
   b. rehearsal.
   c. verbally elaborating children's experiences.
   d. motivation to remember.

9. **A preoperational child is shown 4 cats and 6 dogs. You ask the child whether there are more dogs or more animals, and the child answers more dogs. This error is due to**
   a. fast-mapping.
   b. use of inner speech while attempting to engage in scaffolding.
   c. failure to understand the words in the question.
   d. inability to think about classes and subclasses at the same time.

10. **Of the following, research by Caldwell and her colleagues shows that _____ is the best predictor of a child's IQ score at a later date.**
    a. the IQ of the mother
    b. the HOME environment
    c. the child's social class
    d. the child's infant IQ scores

CDEV
ONLINE

PREPARE FOR TESTS ON
THE STUDYBOARD!

○ CORRECT
○ INCORRECT
○ INCORRECT
○ INCORRECT

**Personalize Quizzes
from Your StudyBits**

**Take Practice
Quizzes by Chapter**

CHAPTER QUIZZES
▶ Chapter 1
Chapter 2
Chapter 3
Chapter 4

4LTR
PRESS

Access CDEV ONLINE at www.cengagebrain.com

10 | Early Childhood: Social and Emotional Development

Steve Murray / Alamy Stock Photo

LEARNING OUTCOMES

After studying this chapter, you will be able to . . .

10-1 Describe the dimensions of child rearing and styles of parenting

10-2 Explain how siblings, birth order, peers, and other factors affect social development during early childhood

10-3 Discuss personality and emotional development during early childhood, focusing on the self, Erikson's views, and fears

10-4 Discuss the development of gender roles and gender differences

After you finish this chapter, go to **PAGE 177** for **STUDY TOOLS**

> Parents decide how restrictive they will be. How will they respond when children make excessive noise, play with dangerous objects, damage property, mess up their rooms, hurt others, or masturbate?

Preschoolers usually spend most of their time with the family. Most parents want preschoolers to develop a sense of responsibility and develop into well-adjusted individuals. They want them to acquire social skills. How do parents try to achieve these goals? What role do siblings play? How do children's peers influence social and emotional development?

10-1 DIMENSIONS OF CHILD REARING

Parents have different approaches to rearing their children. Investigators of parental patterns of child rearing have found it useful to classify them according to two broad dimensions: warmth–coldness and restrictiveness–permissiveness (Baumrind, 1989, 2013).

Warm parents are affectionate toward their children. They tend to hug and kiss them and smile at them frequently. Warm parents are caring and supportive. They communicate their enjoyment in being with their children. Warm parents are less likely than cold parents to use physical discipline (Holden et al., 2011).

Cold parents may not enjoy their children and may have few feelings of affection for them. They are likely to complain about their children's behavior, saying they are naughty or have "minds of their own."

It requires no stretch of the imagination to conclude that it is better to be warm than cold toward children (Laible et al., 2015). The children of parents who are warm and accepting are more likely to develop internal standards of conduct—a moral sense or conscience (Gauvain et al., 2013). Parental warmth also is related to the child's social and emotional well-being.

Where does parental warmth come from? Some of it reflects parental beliefs about how best to rear children, and some reflects parents' tendencies to imitate the behavior of their own parents. But research by Hetherington and her colleagues (Feinberg et al., 2001) suggests that genetic factors may be involved as well.

Parents decide how restrictive they will be. How will they respond when children make excessive noise, play with dangerous objects, damage property, mess up their rooms, hurt others, or masturbate? Parents who are restrictive tend to impose rules and to watch their children closely.

Consistent control and firm enforcement of rules can have positive consequences for the child, particularly when combined with strong support and affection (Grusec & Sherman, 2011). This parenting style is termed the *authoritative style* (Baumrind, 2013). On the other hand, if "restrictiveness" means physical punishment, interference, or intrusiveness, it can give rise to disobedience, rebelliousness, and lower levels of cognitive development (Larzelere et al., 2013).

Permissive parents supervise their children less closely than restrictive parents do. Permissive parents allow their children to do what is "natural," such as make noise, treat toys carelessly, and experiment with their bodies. They may also allow their children to show some aggression, intervening only when another child is in danger.

TRUTH OR FICTION?

T	F	Parents who demand mature behavior wind up with rebellious children, not mature children.
T	F	First-born children are more highly motivated to achieve than later-born children.
T	F	Children who are physically punished are more likely to be aggressive than children who are not.
T	F	There is no scientific evidence that violence in the media contributes to aggression.
T	F	The most common fear among preschoolers is fear of social disapproval.
T	F	A 2½-year-old may know that he is a boy, but still think that he can grow up to be a mommy.

10-1a HOW PARENTS ENFORCE RESTRICTIONS

Regardless of their general approaches to child rearing, most parents are restrictive now and then, even if only when they are teaching their children not to run into the street or to touch a hot stove. Parents tend to use the methods of induction, power assertion, and withdrawal of love.

Inductive methods aim to teach knowledge that will enable children to generate desirable behavior on their own. The main inductive technique is "reasoning," or explaining why one kind of behavior is good and another is not. Reasoning with a one- or two-year-old can be basic. "Don't do that—it hurts!" qualifies as reasoning with toddlers. "It hurts!" is an explanation, though brief. The inductive approach helps the child understand moral behavior and fosters prosocial behavior such as helping and sharing (Grusec, 2014; Grusec & Sherman, 2011).

Power-assertive methods include physical punishment and denial of privileges. Parents often justify physical punishment with sayings such as "Spare the rod, spoil the child." Parents may insist that power assertion is necessary because their children are noncompliant. However, use of power assertion is related to parental authoritarianism as well as children's behavior (Larzelere et al., 2013). Parental power assertion is associated with lower acceptance by peers, poorer grades, and more antisocial behavior in children. The more parents use power-assertive techniques, the less children appear to develop internal standards of conduct. Parental punishment and rejection are often linked with aggression and delinquency.

Some parents control children by threatening withdrawal of love. They isolate or ignore misbehaving children. Because most children need parental approval and contact, loss of love can be more threatening than physical punishment. Withdrawal of love may foster compliance but also instill guilt and anxiety (Grusec, 2014; Grusec & Sherman, 2011).

Preschoolers more readily comply when asked to do something

Consistent enforcement of reasonable rules, combined with warmth and support, usually have positive consequences for children.

Loisjoy Thurstun/Bubbles Photolibrary / Alamy Stock Photo

than when asked to *stop* doing something (Kochanska et al., 2001). One way to manage children who are doing something wrong or bad is to involve them in something else.

10-1b PARENTING STYLES: HOW PARENTS TRANSMIT VALUES AND STANDARDS

Diana Baumrind (2013) focused on the relationship between parenting styles and the development of competent behavior in young children. She used the dimensions of warmth–coldness and restrictiveness–permissiveness to develop a grid of four parenting styles based on whether parents are high or low in each dimension (see Table 10.1).

The parents of the most capable children are rated high in both dimensions (see Table 10.1). They are highly restrictive and make strong demands for maturity. However, they also reason with their children and show strong support and feelings of love. Baumrind (2013) applies the label **authoritative** to these parents; they know what they want their children to do but also respect their children and are warm toward them. Compared with other children, the children of authoritative parents tend to show self-reliance and independence, high self-esteem, high levels of activity and exploratory behavior, and social competence. They are highly motivated to achieve and do well in school (Grusec, 2014; Grusec & Sherman, 2011).

FICTION

T (F) Parents who demand mature behavior wind up with rebellious children, not mature children.

It is not true that parents who are restrictive and demand mature behavior wind up with rebellious, immature children. As long as parents are not severe with the children, consistent control and firm enforcement of rules can have positive consequences for their children.

authoritative a child-rearing style in which parents are restrictive and demanding yet communicative and warm.

TABLE 10.1 BAUMRIND'S PATTERNS OF PARENTING

Parental Style	Parental Behavior Patterns	
	Restrictiveness and Control	Warmth and Responsiveness
Authoritative	High	High
Authoritarian	High	Low
Permissive–Indulgent	Low	High
Rejecting–Neglecting	Low	Low

"Because I say so" could be the motto of parents that Baumrind labels as **authoritarian**. Authoritarians value obedience for its own sake. They have strict guidelines for right and wrong and demand that their children accept them without question. Like authoritative parents, they are controlling. But unlike authoritative parents, their enforcement methods rely on force. Moreover, authoritarian parents do not communicate well with their children or respect their children's viewpoints. Most researchers find them to be generally cold and rejecting (Larzelere et al., 2013).

Baumrind found the sons of authoritarian parents to be relatively hostile and defiant and the daughters to be low in independence and dominance (Baumrind, 2013). Other researchers have found that the children of authoritarian parents are less competent socially and academically than those of authoritative parents. They are anxious, irritable, and restrained in their social interactions. As adolescents, they may be conforming and obedient but have low self-reliance and self-esteem.

Baumrind found two types of parents who are permissive as opposed to restrictive. One is permissive–indulgent and the other rejecting–neglecting. **Permissive-indulgent** parents are low in their attempts to control their children and in their demands for mature behavior. They are easygoing and unconventional. Their brand of permissiveness is accompanied by high nurturance (warmth and support).

Rejecting–neglecting parents are also low in their demands for mature behavior and attempts to control their children. Unlike indulgent parents, they are low in support and responsiveness. The children of neglectful parents are the least competent, responsible, and mature. The children of permissive–indulgent parents, like those of neglectful parents, are

HELLO my name is

Because I say so!

less competent in school and show more misconduct and substance abuse than children of more restrictive, controlling parents. But children from permissive–indulgent homes, unlike those from neglectful homes, are fairly high in social competence and self-confidence (Baumrind, 1991).

10-1c EFFECTS OF THE SITUATION AND THE CHILD ON PARENTING STYLES

Parenting styles are not merely a one-way street, from parent to child. Parenting styles also depend partly on the situation and partly on the characteristics of the child (Grusec, 2014; Grusec & Sherman, 2011). For example, parents are most likely to use power-assertive techniques when dealing with aggressive behavior (Larzalere et al., 2013). Parents prefer power assertion to induction when they believe that children understand the rules they have violated and are capable of acting appropriately. Stress also contributes to use of power.

Baumrind's research suggests that we can make an effort to avoid some of the pitfalls of being authoritarian or overly permissive. Some recommended techniques that parents can use to help control and guide their children's behavior are listed in Table 10.2.

authoritarian a child-rearing style in which parents demand submission and obedience.

permissive–indulgent a child-rearing style in which parents are warm and not restrictive.

rejecting–neglecting a child-rearing style in which parents are neither restrictive and controlling nor supportive and responsive.

TABLE 10.2 ADVICE FOR PARENTS IN GUIDING YOUNG CHILDREN'S BEHAVIOR

Do ...	Don't ...
• Reward good behavior with praise, smiles, and hugs.	• Pay attention only to a child's misbehavior.
• Give clear, simple, realistic rules appropriate to the child's age.	• Issue too many rules or enforce them haphazardly.
• Enforce rules with reasonable consequences.	• Try to control behavior solely in the child's domain, such as thumb sucking, which can lead to frustrating power struggles.
• Ignore annoying behavior such as whining and tantrums.	• Nag, lecture, shame, or induce guilt.
• Childproof the house, putting dangerous and breakable items out of reach.	• Yell or spank.
• Then establish limits.	• Be overly permissive.
• Be consistent.	

C Squared Studios/Photodisc/Getty Images

During early childhood, children make tremendous advances in social skills and behavior (Underwood & Rosen, 2011). Their play increasingly involves other children. They learn how to share, cooperate, and comfort others. But young children, like adults, can be aggressive as well as loving and helpful.

10-2a INFLUENCE OF SIBLINGS

Siblings serve many functions, including giving physical care, providing emotional support and nurturance, offering advice, serving as role models, providing social interaction that helps develop social skills, making demands, and imposing restrictions (Holden et al., 2011).

In early childhood, siblings' interactions have positive aspects (cooperation, teaching, nurturance) and negative aspects (conflict, control, competition) (Parke & Buriel, 2006). Older siblings tend to be more caring but also more dominating than younger siblings. Younger siblings are more likely to imitate older siblings and accept their direction.

In many cultures, older girls care for younger siblings (Clark, 2005). Parents often urge their children to stop fighting among themselves, and there are times when these conflicts look deadly (and occasionally they are). But garden-variety sibling conflict can enhance their social competence, their development of self-identity (who they are and what they stand for), and their ability to rear their own children (Ross et al., 2006).

There is more conflict between siblings when the parents play favorites (Scharf et al., 2005). Conflict between siblings is also greater when the relationships between the parents or between the parents and children are troubled (Kim et al., 2006).

ADJUSTING TO THE BIRTH OF A SIBLING The birth of a sister or brother is often a source of stress for preschoolers because of changes in family relationships. When a new baby comes into the home, the mother pays relatively more attention to that child and spends less time with the older child, and the older child may feel displaced and resentful.

Children show a mixture of negative and positive reactions to the birth of a sibling. They include **regression** to baby-like behaviors, such as increased clinging, crying, and toilet accidents. Anger and naughtiness may increase. But the same children may also show increased independence and

> **regression** a return to behavior characteristic of earlier stages of development.

maturity, insisting on feeding or dressing themselves and helping to care for the baby (Underwood & Rosen, 2011). Parents can help a young child cope with the arrival of a baby by explaining in advance what is to come.

10-2b BIRTH ORDER

Differences in personality and achievement have been linked to birth order. First-born children, as a group, are somewhat more highly motivated to achieve than later-born children (Carette et al., 2011). First-born and only children appear to perform better academically and are more cooperative (Damian & Roberts, 2015). They obtain higher standardized test scores, including IQ and SAT scores (Damian & Roberts, 2015; Sulloway, 2011).

Before discussing differences in personality between first-born and later-born children, let us note that a recent analysis of research in the area charges that most studies have been flawed (Damian & Roberts, 2015). Nevertheless, as a group, several studies have strongly suggested that first-born children are more adult-oriented and less aggressive than later-born children (Beck et al., 2006; Zajonc, 2001). On the negative side, first-born and only children show somewhat greater anxiety levels and are somewhat less self-reliant than later-born children.

TRUTH

T F First-born children are more highly motivated to achieve than later-born children.

Research shows that first-born children are more highly motivated to achieve than later-born children. However, the difference is a group difference and does not apply to all first-born or later-born children.

Later-born children may learn to act aggressively to compete for the attention of their parents and older siblings (Carey, 2007b). Their self-concepts tend to be lower than those of first-born or only children, but the social skills later-born children acquire from dealing with their family position seem to translate into greater popularity with peers (Carey, 2007b). They also tend to be somewhat more rebellious and liberal than first-born children (Beck et al., 2006).

By and large, parents are more relaxed and flexible with later-born children. Many parents see that the first-born child is turning out well and perhaps they assume that later-born children will also turn out well.

The addition of a new baby to the family is often stressful for older siblings.

iloveimages/Veer

10-2c PEER RELATIONSHIPS

Peer interactions foster social skills—sharing, helping, taking turns, and dealing with conflict (Wentzel & Ramani, 2016). Groups teach children how to lead and how to follow. Physical and cognitive skills develop through peer interactions. Peers also provide emotional support (Bukowski et al., 2011).

By about two years of age, children imitate one another's play and engage in social games such as follow the leader (Bukowski et al., 2011). Also by this age, children show preferences for particular playmates—an early sign of friendship (Wentzel & Ramani, 2016). Friendship is characterized by shared positive experiences and feelings of attachment (Grusec & Sherman, 2011). Even early friendships can be fairly stable (Rubin et al., 2006).

When preschoolers are asked what they like about their friends, they typically mention the toys and activities they share (Holder & Coleman, 2015). Primary schoolchildren usually report that their friends are the children with whom they do things and have fun (Holder & Coleman, 2015). Not until late childhood and adolescence do friends' traits and notions of trust, communication, and intimacy become important.

10-2d PLAY—CHILD'S PLAY, THAT IS

Children's play is meaningful, pleasurable, and internally motivated. Play is fun but also serves important functions in the child. Play helps children develop motor skills and coordination (Burghardt, 2015). It contributes to social development because children learn to share play materials, take turns, and try on new roles through **dramatic play**. It supports the development of such cognitive qualities as curiosity, exploration, symbolic thinking, and problem solving (Bergen, 2015; Christie & Roskos, 2015). Play may even help children learn to control impulses (Bergen, 2015).

PLAY AND COGNITIVE DEVELOPMENT Play contributes to and expresses milestones in cognitive development. Jean Piaget ([1946] 1962) identified kinds of play, each characterized by increasing cognitive complexity (De Lisi et al., 2015):

▶ *Functional play.* Beginning in the sensorimotor stage, the first kind of play involves repetitive motor activity, such as rolling a ball or running and laughing.

▶ *Symbolic play.* Also called pretend play, imaginative play, or dramatic play, symbolic play emerges toward the end of the sensorimotor stage and increases during early childhood. In symbolic play, children create settings, characters, and scripts (Mottweiler & Taylor, 2014).

▶ *Constructive play.* Children use objects or materials to draw something or make something, such as a tower of blocks.

▶ *Formal games.* Games with rules include board games, which are sometimes enhanced or invented by children, and games involving motor skills, such as marbles and hopscotch, ball games involving sides or teams, and video games.

PARTEN'S TYPES OF PLAY In classic research on children's play, Mildred Parten observed the development of six types of play among two- to five-year-old nursery schoolchildren: unoccupied play, solitary play, onlooker play, parallel play, associative play, and cooperative play (see Table 10.3) (Dyson, 2015; Henricks, 2015). Solitary play and onlooker play are considered **nonsocial play**, that is, play in which

dramatic play play in which children enact social roles.

nonsocial play solitary forms of play.

TABLE 10.3 PARTEN'S CATEGORIES OF PLAY

Category	Nonsocial or Social?	Description
Unoccupied play	Nonsocial	Children do not appear to be playing. They may engage in random movements that seem to be without a goal. Unoccupied play appears to be the least frequent kind of play in nursery schools.
Solitary play	Nonsocial	Children play with toys by themselves, independently of the children around them. Solitary players do not appear to be influenced by children around them. They make no effort to approach them.
Onlooker play	Nonsocial	Children observe other children who are at play. Onlookers frequently talk to the children they are observing and may make suggestions, but they do not overtly join in.
Parallel play	Social	Children play with toys similar to those of surrounding children. However, they treat the toys as they choose and do not directly interact with other children.
Associative play	Social	Children interact and share toys. However, they do not seem to share group goals. Although they interact, individuals still treat toys as they choose. The association with the other children appears to be more important than the nature of the activity. They seem to enjoy each other's company.
Cooperative play	Social	Children interact to achieve common, group goals. The play of each child is subordinated to the purposes of the group. One or two group members direct the activities of others. There is also a division of labor, with different children taking different roles. Children may pretend to be members of a family, animals, space monsters, and all sorts of creatures.

children do not interact socially. Nonsocial play occurs more often in two- and three-year-olds than in older preschoolers. Parallel play, associative play, and cooperative play are considered **social play**; in each case, children are influenced by other children as they play. Parten found that associative play and cooperative play become common by age five. These types of play are more likely to be found among older and more experienced preschoolers (Bukowski et al., 2011). Girls are somewhat more likely than boys to engage in social play (Underwood & Rosen, 2011).

There are exceptions. Nonsocial play can involve educational activities that foster cognitive development. In fact, many four- and five-year-olds spend a good deal of time in parallel constructive play. For instance, they may work on puzzles or build with blocks near other children. Two-year-olds with older siblings or with group experience may engage in advanced social play (Dunn, 2015).

81A Productions/Corbis

GENDER DIFFERENCES IN PLAY Research shows that infants show visual preferences for gender-stereotyped toys as early as three to eight months of age (Alexander et al., 2009). Although preferences for gender-typed toys are well developed by the ages of 15 to 36 months, girls are more likely to stray from the stereotypes (Underwood & Rosen, 2011). Girls ask for and play with "boys' toys" such as cars and trucks more often than boys choose dolls and other "girls' toys."

Girls and boys differ not only in toy preferences but also in their choice of play environments and activities. During the preschool and early elementary school years, boys prefer vigorous physical outdoor activities such as climbing, playing with large vehicles, and rough-and-tumble play (Underwood & Rosen, 2011). In middle childhood, boys spend more time than girls in play groups of five or more children and in competitive play. Girls are more

social play play in which children interact with and are influenced by others.

likely than boys to engage in arts and crafts and domestic play. Girls' activities are more closely directed and structured by adults (A. Campbell et al., 2002).

Why do children show these early preferences for gender-stereotyped toys and activities? Biological factors may play a role, for example, boys' slightly greater strength and activity levels and girls' slightly greater physical maturity and coordination. But adults treat girls and boys differently. They provide gender-stereotyped toys and room furnishings and encourage gender typing in play and household chores (Leaper, 2011). Children, moreover, tend to seek out information on which kinds of toys and play are "masculine" or "feminine" and then to conform to the label (Martin & Ruble, 2004).

Some studies find that children who "cross the line" by showing interest in toys or activities considered appropriate for the other gender are often teased, ridiculed, rejected, or ignored by their parents, teachers, other adults, and peers. Boys are more likely than girls to be criticized (Zosuls et al., 2011).

Another well-documented finding is that children begin to prefer playmates of the same gender by the age of two. Girls develop this preference somewhat earlier than boys (Hay et al., 2004). The tendency strengthens during middle childhood.

Two factors may be involved in the choice of the gender of playmates in early childhood. One is that boys' play is more oriented toward dominance, aggression, and rough play (Hines, 2011). The second is that boys are not very responsive to girls' polite suggestions. Boys may avoid girls because they see them as inferior (Caplan & Larkin, 1991).

10-2e PROSOCIAL BEHAVIOR

Prosocial behavior, also known as *altruism*, is intended to benefit another without expectation of reward. Prosocial behavior includes sharing, cooperating, and helping and comforting others in distress. It is shown by the preschool and early school years and is linked to the development of empathy and perspective taking (Grusec & Sherman, 2011).

EMPATHY Empathy is sensitivity to the feelings of others and is connected with sharing and cooperation. Infants frequently begin to cry when they hear other children crying, although this early agitated response may be largely reflexive (Roberts et al., 2014). Empathy promotes prosocial behavior and decreases aggressive behavior, and these links are evident by the second year (Hastings et al., 2000). During the second year, many children approach other children and adults who are in distress and try to help them. They may hug a crying child or tell the child not to cry. Toddlers who are rated as emotionally unresponsive to the feelings of others are more likely to behave aggressively throughout the school years (Olson et al., 2000).

Girls show more empathy than boys (Roberts et al., 2014). It is unclear whether this gender difference reflects socialization of girls to be attuned to the emotions of others or genetic factors, although some researchers argue that prenatal exposure to testosterone has a suppressive effect on empathy (Durdiakova et al., 2015; Zilioli et al., 2014).

Brand X Pictures/Jupiterimages

PERSPECTIVE TAKING According to Piaget, preoperational children tend to be egocentric. They tend not to be able to see things from the vantage points of others. It turns out that various cognitive abilities, such as being able to take another person's perspective, are related to knowing when someone is in need or distress. Perspective-taking skills improve with age, and so do prosocial skills. Among children of the same age, those with better developed perspective-taking ability also show more prosocial behavior and less aggressive behavior (Hastings et al., 2000).

INFLUENCES ON PROSOCIAL BEHAVIOR Although altruistic behavior is defined as prosocial behavior that occurs in the absence of rewards or the expectations of rewards, it is influenced by rewards and punishments. The peers of nursery schoolchildren who are cooperative, friendly, and generous respond more positively to them than they do to children whose behavior is self-centered (Grusec &

prosocial behavior behavior that benefits other people, generally without expectation of reward.

Davidov, 2015; Grusec & Hastings, 2015). Children who are rewarded for acting prosocially are likely to continue these behaviors (Grusec & Davidov, 2015).

Parents foster prosocial behavior when they use inductive techniques such as explaining how behavior affects others. ("You made Josh cry. It's not nice to hit.") Parents of prosocial children are more likely to expect mature behavior from their children. They are less likely to use power-assertive techniques of discipline (Roberts et al., 2014).

10-2f DEVELOPMENT OF AGGRESSION

Children, like adults, not only can be loving and altruistic, but they also can be aggressive. Some children, of course, are more aggressive than others. Aggression refers to behavior intended to hurt or injure another person.

Aggressive behavior, as other social behavior, seems to follow developmental patterns. The aggression of preschoolers is frequently instrumental or possession oriented (Persson, 2005). Younger preschoolers tend to use aggression to obtain the toys and situations they want, such as a favored seat at the table or in the car. Older preschoolers are more likely to resolve conflicts over toys by sharing rather than fighting (Underwood, 2011). Anger and aggression in preschoolers usually cause other preschoolers to reject them (Gower et al., 2014; Walter & LaFreniere, 2000).

By age six or seven, aggression becomes hostile and person oriented. Children taunt and criticize one another and call one another names; they also attack one another physically.

Aggressive behavior appears to be generally stable and predictive of social and emotional problems later on, especially among boys (Nagin & Tremblay, 2001; Tapper & Boulton, 2004). Toddlers who are perceived as difficult and defiant are more likely to behave aggressively throughout the school years (Olson et al., 2000). A longitudinal study of more than 600 children found that aggressive eight-year-olds tended to remain more aggressive than their peers 22 years later, at age 30 (Kokko et al., 2014). Aggressive children of both genders are more likely to have criminal convictions as adults, to abuse their spouses, and to drive while drunk.

10-2g THEORIES OF AGGRESSION

What causes some children to be more aggressive than others? Aggression in childhood appears to result from a complex interplay of biological factors and environmental factors such as reinforcement and modeling.

Evidence suggests that genetic factors may be involved in aggressive behavior, including criminal and antisocial behavior (Bezdjian et al., 2011). There is a greater concordance (agreement) rate for criminal behavior between monozygotic (MZ) twins, who fully share their genetic code, than dizygotic (DZ) twins, who, like other brothers and sisters, share only half of their genetic code (Tehrani & Mednick, 2000). If genetics is involved in aggression, genes may do their work at least in part through the male sex hormone testosterone. Testosterone is apparently connected with feelings of self-confidence, high activity levels, and—the negative side—aggressiveness (Carre & Olmstead, 2015; Platje et al., 2015).

Cognitive research with primary schoolchildren finds that children who believe in the legitimacy of aggression are more likely to behave aggressively when they are presented with social provocations (Yaros et al., 2014). Aggressive children are also often found to be lacking in empathy and the ability to see things from the perspective of other people (Gini et al., 2014; Underwood & Rosen, 2011). They fail to conceptualize the experiences of their victims and are thus less likely to inhibit aggressive impulses.

Social cognitive explanations of aggression focus on environmental factors such as reinforcement and observational learning. When children repeatedly push, shove, and hit to grab toys or break into line, other children usually let them have their way (Kempes et al., 2005). Children who are thus rewarded for acting aggressively are likely to continue to use aggressive means, especially if they do not have alternative means to achieve their ends. Aggressive children may also associate with peers who value and encourage aggression (Stauffacher & DeHart, 2006).

Children who are physically punished are more likely to be aggressive themselves than children who are not physically punished (Patterson, 2005). Physically aggressive parents serve as models for aggression and also stoke their children's anger.

TRUTH

(T) F Children who are physically punished are more likely to be aggressive than children who are not.

It is true that children who are physically punished are more likely to be aggressive than children who are not. Perhaps punitive parents model punitive behavior and instill hostility in their children.

MEDIA INFLUENCES A classic experiment by Bandura, Ross, and Ross (1963) suggests the powerful influence of televised models on children's aggressive behavior. One group of preschool children observed a film of an adult model hitting and kicking an inflated Bobo doll, while a control group saw an aggression-free film. The experimental and control children were then left alone in a room with the same doll as hidden observers recorded their behavior. The children who had observed the aggressive model showed significantly more aggressive behavior toward the doll themselves (see Figure 10.1). Many children imitated bizarre attack behaviors devised for the model in this experiment—behaviors that they would not have thought up themselves.

Television is a fertile source of aggressive models, and most organizations of health professionals agree that media violence contributes to aggression in children (Huesmann et al., 2003; 2013). This relationship has

Photodisc/Getty Images

Do we fully understand the effects of television on young children?

been found for girls and boys of different ages, social classes, ethnic groups, and cultures (Huesmann et al., 2013). Consider a number of ways that depictions of violence make their contribution (Anderson et al., 2015; Huesmann et al., 2013):

▸ *Observational learning.* Children learn from observation. TV violence supplies models of aggressive "skills," which children may acquire.

▸ *Disinhibition.* Punishment inhibits behavior. Conversely, media violence may **disinhibit** aggressive behavior, especially when characters "get away" with it.

disinhibit to encourage a response that has been previously suppressed.

FIG.10.1 BANDURA'S STUDY OF THE IMITATION OF AGGRESSION

© Albert Bandura/Dept. of Psychology, Stanford University

The top row of photos shows an adult striking a Bobo doll. The second and third rows show a boy and a girl who observed the adult imitating the aggressive behavior.

- *Increased arousal.* Media violence and aggressive video games increase viewers' level of arousal. We are more likely to be aggressive under high levels of arousal.

- *Priming of aggressive thoughts and memories.* Media violence "primes" or arouses aggressive ideas and memories.

- *Habituation.* We become used to repeated stimuli. Children exposed to violence are more likely to assume that violence is acceptable or normal and become desensitized to it.

FICTION

T (F) There is no scientific evidence that violence in the media contributes to aggression.

It is not true that scientific evidence is lacking on whether media violence contributes to aggression. Studies going back half a century show that children imitate violence they observe in the media.

Violent video games may create the greatest risk of violence because they require audience participation (DeLisi et al., 2013; Lin, 2013). Players don't just watch; they participate (Dubow et al., 2010). Playing violent video games increases aggressive thoughts and behavior in the laboratory (Anderson et al., 2015). Males are relatively more likely than females to act aggressively after playing violent video games and are more likely to see the world as a hostile place. However, students of both genders who obtain higher grades are less likely than students of lower achievement to behave aggressively following exposure to violent video games. Thus, cultural stereotyping of males and females, possible biological gender differences, and moderating variables like academic achievement also figure into the effects of media violence. There is no simple one-to-one connection between media violence and violence in real life. There seems to be a circular relationship between exposure to media violence and aggressive behavior (Anderson et al., 2015). Yes, TV violence and violent video games contribute to aggressive behavior, but aggressive youngsters are also more likely to seek out this kind of "entertainment." Figure 10.2 explores the possible connections between TV violence and aggressive behavior among viewers.

self-concept one's self-description and self-evaluation according to various categories, such as child, adolescent, or adult, one's gender, and one's skills.

categorical self definitions of the self that refer to external traits.

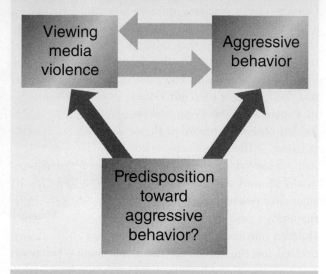

FIG. 10.2 WHAT ARE THE CONNECTIONS BETWEEN MEDIA VIOLENCE AND AGGRESSIVE BEHAVIOR?

Does media violence cause aggressive behavior? Do aggressive children prefer to view violent TV shows or play violent video games? Or do other factors, such as personality traits, create a predisposition toward both seeking media violence and behaving aggressively?

10-3 PERSONALITY AND EMOTIONAL DEVELOPMENT

In early childhood, children's sense of self—who they are and how they feel about themselves—develops and grows more complex. They begin to acquire a sense of their own abilities and their increasing mastery of the environment. As they move out into the world, they also face new experiences that may cause them to feel fearful and anxious.

10-3a THE SELF

The sense of self, or the **self-concept**, emerges gradually during infancy. Infants and toddlers visually begin to recognize themselves and differentiate themselves from other individuals such as their parents.

In the preschool years, children continue to develop their sense of self. Almost as soon as they begin to speak, they describe themselves in terms of certain categories, such as age groupings (baby, child, adult) and gender (girl, boy). Self-definitions that refer to concrete external traits have been called the **categorical self**.

Children as young as three years are able to describe themselves in terms of behaviors and internal states that occur often and are fairly stable over time (Rosen & Patterson, 2011). For example, in response to the question "How do you feel when you're scared?" young children frequently respond, "Usually like running away" (Eder, 1989). In answer to the question "How do you usually act around grown-ups?" a typical response might be, "I mostly been good with grown-ups."

One aspect of the self-concept is self-esteem. Children with high self-esteem are more likely to be securely attached and have parents who are attentive to their needs (Roisman & Groh, 2011). They also are more likely to show prosocial behavior (Grusec & Davidov, 2015).

Preschool children begin to make evaluative judgments about two different aspects of themselves by the age of four (Underwood & Rosen, 2011). One is their cognitive and physical competence (e.g., being good at puzzles, counting, swinging, tying shoes), and the second is their social acceptance by peers and parents (e.g., having lots of friends, being read to by Mom). But preschoolers do not yet clearly distinguish between different areas of competence. A preschooler is not likely to report being good in school but poor in physical skills. One is either "good at doing things" or one is not (MacDonald & Leary, 2011; Piek et al., 2006).

Children also become increasingly capable of self-regulation in early childhood. They become more and more capable of controlling their eliminatory processes, of controlling aggressive behavior, of engaging in play with other children, and of focusing on cognitive tasks such as learning to count and to sound out letters. Self-regulatory abilities are connected with maturation of the brain and the rearing practices of caregivers.

10-3b INITIATIVE VERSUS GUILT

As preschoolers continue to develop a separate sense of themselves, they increasingly move out into the world and take the initiative in learning new skills. Erik Erikson (1963) refers to these early childhood years as the stage of *initiative versus guilt*.

Children in this stage strive to achieve independence from their parents and master adult behaviors. They are curious, try new things, and test themselves. Children learn that not all their plans, dreams, and fantasies can be realized. Adults prohibit children from doing certain things, and children begin to internalize adult rules. Fear of violating the rules may cause the child to feel guilty and may curtail efforts to master new skills. Parents can help children develop and maintain a healthy sense of initiative by encouraging their attempts to learn and explore and by not being unduly critical and punitive.

10-3c FEARS: THE HORRORS OF EARLY CHILDHOOD

In Erikson's view, fear of violating parental prohibitions can be a powerful force in the life of a young child. Children's fears change as they move from infancy into the preschool years. The number of fears seems to peak between two and a half and four years and then taper off (Muris & Field, 2011). The preschool period is marked by a decline in fears of loud noises, falling, sudden movement, and strangers. Fear of social disapproval is not the most common fear among preschoolers. Preschoolers are most likely to fear animals, imaginary creatures, the dark, and personal danger (Muris & Field, 2011). The fantasies of young children frequently involve stories they are told and media imagery (Pearce & Field, 2016). Frightening images of imaginary creatures can persist. Many preschoolers are reluctant to have the lights turned off at night for fear that such creatures may assault them. Real objects and situations also cause many preschoolers to fear for their personal safety—lightning, thunder and other loud noises, high places, sharp objects and being cut, blood, unfamiliar people, strange people, and stinging and crawling insects.

Michael Blann/Stone/Getty Images

FICTION

T (F) The most common fear among preschoolers is fear of social disapproval.

Actually, preschoolers are more likely to fear animals, imaginary creatures, the dark, and personal danger than social disapproval.

During middle childhood, children become less fearful of imaginary creatures, but fears of bodily harm and injury remain common. Children grow more fearful of failure and criticism in school and in social relationships (Underwood & Rosen, 2011). Girls report more fears and higher levels of anxiety than boys.

10-4 DEVELOPMENT OF GENDER ROLES AND GENDER DIFFERENCES

These lyrics are from the song "I Am Woman" by Helen Reddy and Ray Burton. They caught attention because they counter the **stereotype** of a vulnerable woman who needs the protection of a man. The stereotype of the vulnerable woman is a fixed, oversimplified, and conventional idea. So is the stereotype of the chivalrous, protective man. Unfortunately, these stereotypes create demands and limit opportunities for both genders.

Cultural stereotypes of males and females are broad expectations of behavior that we call **gender roles** (Leaper & Farkas, 2015). Researchers who investigate perceptions of gender differences in personality have found that people in our culture agree on certain groups of "masculine" and "feminine" traits, such as those in Table 10.4.

Gender-role stereotypes develop in stages. First, children learn to label the genders. At about 2 to 2½ years of age, they can identify pictures of girls and boys (Alexander et al., 2009). By age three, they display knowledge of gender stereotypes for toys, clothing, work, and activities (Campbell et al., 2004). Children of this age generally agree that boys play with cars and trucks, help their fathers, and tend to hit others. They agree that girls play with dolls, help their mothers, and do not hit others (Cherney et al., 2006). One study found that preschool boys but not girls were rejected by their peers when they showed distress (Walter & LaFreniere, 2000).

Children become increasingly traditional in their stereotyping of activities, jobs, and personality traits between the ages of three and nine or ten (Hilliard & Liben, 2010). For example, traits such as "cruel" and "repairs broken things" are viewed as masculine, and traits such as "often is afraid" and "cooks and bakes" are seen as feminine.

Children and adolescents perceive their own gender in a somewhat better light. For example, girls perceive other girls as nicer, more hardworking, and less selfish than

stereotype a fixed, conventional idea about a group.

gender role a cluster of traits and behaviors that are considered stereotypical of females and males.

TABLE 10.4 CULTURAL STEREOTYPES OF "MASCULINE" AND "FEMININE" TRAITS. ARE THEY ACCURATE?	
Masculine	**Feminine**
Adventurous	Affectionate
Aggressive	Agreeable
Assertive	Appreciative
Capable	Artistic
Coarse	Cautious
Confident	Dependent
Courageous	Emotional
Determined	Fearful
Disorderly	Fickle
Enterprising	Gentle
Hardheaded	Kind
Independent	Nurturing
Intelligent	Patient
Pleasure-seeking	Prudish
Quick	Sensitive
Rational	Sentimental
Realistic	Shy
Reckless	Softhearted
Scientific	Submissive
Sensation-seeking	Suggestible
Stern	Talkative
Tough	Unambitious

boys. Boys, on the other hand, think that they are nicer, more hardworking, and less selfish than girls (Hilliard & Liben, 2010; Martin & Dinella, 2011).

10-4a GENDER DIFFERENCES

Clearly, females and males are anatomically different. And according to gender-role stereotypes, people believe that females and males also differ in their behaviors, personality characteristics, and abilities (Maccoby, 2015). Gender differences in infancy are small and rather inconsistent. Preschoolers display some differences in their choices of toys and play activities. Boys engage in more rough-and-tumble play and are more aggressive. Girls tend to show more empathy and to report more fears. Girls show somewhat greater verbal ability than boys, whereas boys show somewhat greater visual–spatial ability than girls.

10-4b THEORIES OF THE DEVELOPMENT OF GENDER DIFFERENCES

Why is it that little girls (often) grow up to behave according to the cultural stereotypes of what it means to be female? Why is it that little boys (often) grow up to behave like male stereotypes?

THE ROLES OF EVOLUTION AND HEREDITY

According to evolutionary psychologists, gender differences were fashioned by natural selection in response to problems in adaptation that were repeatedly encountered by humans over thousands of generations (Buss & Hawley, 2011; Bugental et al., 2015). Men, who have generally been the hunters, breadwinners, and warriors, are more likely to be seen as adventurous, aggressive, and assertive (see Table 10.4). Women, who have more often been the homemakers and caretakers, are more likely to be seen as affectionate, agreeable, and emotional. The story of the survival of our ancient ancestors is etched in our genes. Genes that bestow attributes that increase an organism's chances of surviving to produce viable offspring are most likely to be transmitted to future generations. We thus possess the genetic codes for traits that helped our ancestors survive and reproduce. These traits include structural gender differences, such as those found in the brain, and differences in body chemistry, such as hormones. The question is whether evolution has also etched social and psychological gender differences into our genes.

ORGANIZATION OF THE BRAIN The organization of the brain is largely genetically determined. The hemispheres of the brain are specialized to perform certain functions, as noted in Chapter 7. Both males and females have a left hemisphere and a right hemisphere, but the question is whether they use them in quite the same way. Consider the hippocampus, a brain structure that is involved in the formation of memories and the relay of incoming sensory information to other parts of the brain. Matthias Riepe and his colleagues (Grön et al., 2000) have studied the ways in which humans and rats use the hippocampus when they are navigating mazes. Males use the hippocampus in both hemispheres when they are navigating (Grön et al., 2000). Women, however, rely on the hippocampus in the right hemisphere along with the right prefrontal cortex, an area

Does this woman's dress and behavior fit the traditional feminine gender-role stereotype? Why or why not?

PhotoStock-Israel / Alamy Stock Photo

of the brain that evaluates information and makes plans. Riepe and his colleagues wonder whether different patterns of brain activities might contribute to preference for using landmarks or maps.

SEX HORMONES Researchers suggest that the development of gender differences in personality, along with the development of anatomical gender differences, may be related to prenatal levels of sex hormones (Avinum & Knafo-Noam, 2015). Although the results of many studies attempting to correlate prenatal sex hormone levels with subsequent gender-typed play have been mixed, a study of 212 pregnant women conducted by Bonnie Auyeung and her colleagues (2009) found that higher-than-normal levels of testosterone in the fetal environment, due to maternal stress, were related to more masculine-typed play among girls at the age of eight and a half years. Emily Barrett and her colleagues (2014) found that exposure to the prenatal environments of stressed mothers can boost masculine-typed play in girls and decrease it in boys. Other studies have shown that children display gender-typed preferences—with boys preferring transportation toys and girls preferring dolls—as early as the age of 13 months (Knickmeyer et al., 2005). Another study investigated the gender-typed visual preferences of 30 human infants at the early ages of three to eight months (Alexander et al., 2009). The researchers assessed interest in a toy truck and a doll by using eye-tracking technology to indicate the direction of visual attention. Girls showed a visual preference for the doll over the truck (i.e., they made a greater number of visual fixations on the doll), and boys showed a visual preference for the truck.

Heide Benser/Corbis

Are there such things as "boys' toys"? As "girls' toys"? Where do such ideas come from?

SOCIAL COGNITIVE THEORY Social cognitive theorists consider both the roles of rewards and punishments (reinforcement) in gender typing and the ways in which children learn from observing others and decide which behaviors are appropriate for them. Children learn much about what society considers "masculine" or "feminine" by observing and imitating models of the same gender. These models may be their parents, other adults, other children, even characters in electronic media such as TV and video games.

Socialization also plays a role (Maccoby, 2015). Parents, teachers, other adults—even other children—provide children with information about the gender-typed behaviors expected of them (Leaper & Farkas, 2015). Children are rewarded with smiles and respect and companionship when they display "gender-appropriate" behavior. Children are punished with frowns and loss of friends when they display "inappropriate" behavior.

Boys are encouraged to be independent, whereas girls are more likely to be restricted. Boys are allowed to roam farther from home at an earlier age and are more likely to be left unsupervised after school (Miller et al., 2006).

Primary schoolchildren show less stereotyping if their mothers frequently engage in traditionally "masculine" tasks such as washing the car, taking children to ball games, or assembling toys (Leaper & Farkas, 2015). Maternal employment is associated with less polarized gender-role concepts for girls and boys (Leaper & Farkas, 2015).

COGNITIVE-DEVELOPMENTAL THEORY

Lawrence Kohlberg (1966) proposed a cognitive-developmental view of gender typing. According to this perspective, children form concepts about gender and then fit their behavior to the concepts (Zosuls et al., 2011). These developments occur in stages and are entwined with general cognitive development.

According to Kohlberg, gender typing involves the emergence of three concepts: gender identity, gender stability, and gender constancy. The first step in gender typing is attaining **gender identity**. Gender identity is the knowledge that one is male or female. At two years, most children can say whether they are boys or girls. By the age of three, many children can discriminate anatomic gender differences (Campbell et al., 2004; Zosuls et al., 2011).

At around age four or five, most children develop the concept of **gender stability**, according to Kohlberg. They recognize that people retain their gender for a lifetime. Girls no longer believe that they can grow up to be daddies, and boys no longer think that they can become mommies.

TRUTH

T F   A 2½-year-old may know that he is a boy, but still think that he can grow up to be a mommy.

Yes, a 2½-year-old will likely have developed gender identity but not yet gender stability.

By the age of five to seven years, Kohlberg believes that most children develop the more sophisticated concept of **gender constancy** and recognize that people's gender does not change, even if they change their dress or behavior. A woman who cuts her hair short remains a woman. A man who dons an apron and cooks remains a man. Once children have established concepts of gender stability and constancy, they seek to behave in ways that are consistent with their gender (Liben et al., 2014; Zosuls et al., 2011).

Sylvie Villeger/Science Source

gender identity knowledge that one is female or male.

gender stability the concept that one's gender is unchanging.

gender constancy the concept that one's gender remains the same despite changes in appearance or behavior.

Cross-cultural studies in the United States, Samoa, Nepal, Belize, and Kenya have found that the concepts of gender identity, gender stability, and gender constancy emerge in the order predicted by Kohlberg (Leonard & Archer, 1989; Munroe et al., 1984). But research shows that gender-typed play emerges earlier than gender identity. Girls show preferences for dolls and soft toys and boys for hard transportation toys under the age of a year, but they are not fitting it to their concept of gender identity, which is yet to emerge (Alexander et al., 2009).

GENDER-SCHEMA THEORY

Gender-schema theory proposes that children use gender as one way of organizing their perceptions of the world (Leaper, 2013; Martin & Ruble, 2004). A gender schema is a cluster of concepts about male and female physical traits, personality traits, and behaviors. According to gender-schema theory, once children come to see themselves as female or male, they begin to seek information concerning gender-typed traits and try to live up to them (Liben et al., 2014; Tenenbaum et al. 2010). Jack will retaliate when provoked because boys are expected to do so. Jill will be "sugary and sweet" if such is expected of little girls.

Today, most scholars would agree that both biology and social cognition interact to affect most areas of behavior and mental processes—including the complex processes involved in gender typing.

Rob Marmion/Shutterstock.com

gender-schema theory the view that one's knowledge of the gender schema in one's society guides one's assumption of gender-typed preferences and behavior patterns.

STUDY TOOLS 10

READY TO STUDY?

In the book, you can:

☐ Rip out the chapter review card at the back of the book for a handy summary of the chapter and key terms.

☐ Check your understanding of what you've read with the quizzes that follow.

ONLINE AT CENGAGEBRAIN.COM YOU CAN:

☐ Collect StudyBits while you read and study the chapter.

☐ Quiz yourself on key concepts.

☐ Find videos for further exploration.

☐ Prepare for tests with CDEV2 Flash Cards as well as those you create.

SELF-ASSESSMENTS

Fill-Ins

Answers can be found in the back of the book.

1. Research shows that children tend to distort their _____ to conform to their gender schemas.

2. According to Erikson, early childhood is the stage of _____ versus guilt.

3. Self-definitions that refer to concrete external traits have been called the _____ self.

4. Research shows that the hormone _____ is connected with feelings of self-confidence, high activity levels, and aggressiveness.

5. The children of _____ parents tend to show self-reliance and independence, high self-esteem, high levels of activity and exploratory behavior, and social competence.

6. According to Piaget, the first type of play is _____ play.

7. _____ behavior is also known as altruism.

8. Anger and aggression in preschoolers usually cause other preschoolers to _____ them.

9. Children try on new roles through _____ play.

10. The classic study of aggression by _____ and his colleagues (1963) showed people attacking Bobo doll.

Multiple Choice

1. **Which of the following is part of the feminine gender-role stereotype?**

   a. patient

   b. independent

   c. realistic

   d. disorderly

2. **Which of the following are children in early childhood least likely to fear?**

   a. lightning

   b. stinging and crawling insects

   c. strange people

   d. social disapproval

3. **All of the following are listed as reasons that viewing violent media can contribute to aggressive behavior, *except***

   a. disinhibition of aggressive impulses.

   b. explaining that media violence is not real.

   c. priming of aggressive thoughts and memories.

   d. observational learning.

4. **Which of the following statements best describes the relationship between empathy and gender?**

   a. Girls show more empathy than boys do.

   b. Boys show more empathy than girls do.

   c. Girls and boys show equal amounts of empathy.

   d. The research literature on the subject is inconclusive.

5. **Children first show visual preferences for stereotypical "boys' toys" or "girls' toys"**

   a. before the first birthday.

   b. between the ages of one to two years.

   c. between the ages of two to five years.

   d. between the ages of five to eight years.

6. **Which of the following, according to Parten's types, is a form of nonsocial play?**

   a. cooperative play

   b. associative play

   c. onlooker play

   d. parallel play

7. **When preschoolers are asked what they like about friends, they are most likely to report that**

   a. they and their friends can share their innermost thoughts.

   b. their friends are the people they can trust.

   c. they and their friends share toys and activities.

   d. their friends are of the same gender and ethnic background.

8. **Compared to later-born children, first-born children are**

   a. less anxious.

   b. more self-reliant.

   c. more adult-oriented.

   d. more aggressive.

9. **Baumrind found the sons of _____ parents to be hostile and defiant and the daughters to be low in independence and social dominance.**

   a. authoritative

   b. authoritarian

   c. permissive–indulgent

   d. rejecting–neglecting

10. **Children who are physically punished**

    a. are more likely to be motivated to succeed.

    b. are less intelligent than other children.

    c. do not understand why they are being disciplined.

    d. are more likely to be aggressive than other children.

Middle Childhood: Physical Development

Steve Skjold/Alamy Stock Photo

LEARNING OUTCOMES

After studying this chapter, you will be able to...

11-1 Describe trends in physical development in middle childhood

11-2 Discuss the origins of the problem of being overweight in middle childhood, and suggest solutions

11-3 Discuss the origins and treatment of childhood asthma

11-4 Describe gross and fine motor development in middle childhood

11-5 Discuss the diagnosis, origins, and treatment of attention-deficit/hyperactivity disorder

11-6 Describe learning disorders, and discuss their origins and treatment

After you finish this chapter, go to **PAGE 187** for **STUDY TOOLS**

> Boys are slightly heavier and taller than girls through the age of nine or ten. Girls then begin their adolescent growth spurt and surpass boys in height and weight at about 13 or 14.

11-1 GROWTH PATTERNS

Middle childhood is typically defined as the ages from 6 to 12, beginning with the school years and bound at the upper end by the beginning of the adolescent **growth spurt** at about the age of 12. Following the growth trends of early childhood, boys and girls continue to gain a little over two inches in height per year until the spurt begins (see Figure 11.1). The average gain in weight during middle childhood is five to seven pounds a year, but children grow less stocky and more slender (Kuczmarski et al., 2000).

11-1a NUTRITION AND GROWTH

In middle childhood, the average child's body weight doubles. Children also spend a good deal of energy in physical activity and play. To fuel this growth and activity, schoolchildren eat more than preschoolers. The average four- to six-year-old needs 1,400 to 1,800 calories per day, but the average seven- to ten-year-old requires 2,000 calories.

Nutrition involves more than calories. It is healthful to eat fruits and vegetables, fish, poultry (without skin), and whole grains, and to limit intake of fats, sugar, and starches. However, most foods in school cafeterias and elsewhere are heavy in sugar, animal fats, and salt (Bray & Bouchard, 2014).

GENDER SIMILARITIES AND DIFFERENCES IN PHYSICAL GROWTH Boys are slightly heavier and taller than girls through the age of nine or ten (see Figure 11.1). Girls then begin their adolescent growth spurt and surpass boys in height and weight at about 13 or 14. Then boys spurt and grow taller and heavier than girls. The steady gains in height and weight in middle childhood are paralleled by increased muscle strength in both genders. Beginning at about age 11, boys develop relatively more muscle, and girls develop relatively more fat.

growth spurt a period during which growth advances at a dramatically rapid rate compared with other periods.

11-2 WEIGHT

Between 16% and 25% of children and adolescents in the United States are overweight or obese (see Figure 11.2). Consider some facts about childhood overweight and obesity (Bray & Bouchard, 2014; Ogden et al., 2014):

▸ Over the past 20 to 30 years the prevalence of obesity among children has doubled.

▸ Latin American boys are significantly more likely than European American boys to be overweight.

▸ African American girls are significantly more likely than European American girls to be overweight.

▸ Children who are obese are more likely to develop high blood pressure and high cholesterol—as children!

▸ Children who are obese are more likely to develop diabetes.

TRUTH OR FICTION?

T	F	Children outgrow " baby fat."
T	F	The typical American child is exposed to about 10,000 food commercials each year.
T	F	Most American children are physically fit.
T	F	Hyperactivity is caused by chemical food additives.
T	F	Stimulants are often used to treat children who are already hyperactive.

FIG.11.1 GROWTH CURVES FOR WEIGHT AND HEIGHT

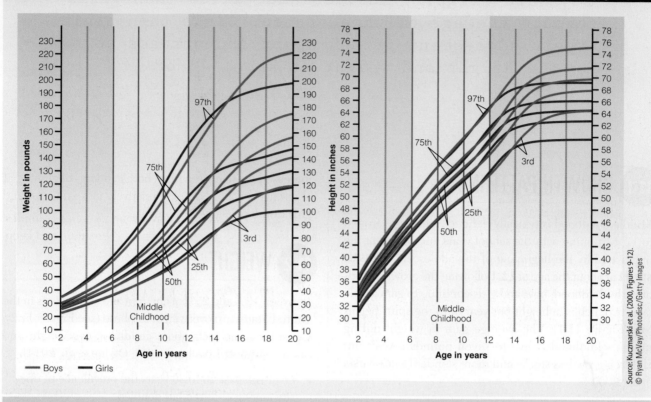

Gains in height and weight are fairly steady during middle childhood.

Source: Kuczmarski et al. (2000, Figures 9-12).
© Ryan McVay/Photodisc/Getty Images

▶ Obese children are more likely to develop breathing problems and asthma, joint problems, fatty liver disease, gallstones, and acid reflux—all in childhood.

▶ Although parents often assume that heavy children will outgrow their baby fat, most overweight children become overweight adults.

There's more: Overweight children are often rejected by peers or are a source of derision (Bray & Bouchard, 2014; Williams et al., 2013). They are usually poor at sports and less likely to be considered attractive in adolescence. Overweight children are also at greater risk of health problems throughout life—including heart disease, diabetes, and some types of cancer.

Mike Kemp/Rubberball/Getty Images

FICTION

T (F) Children outgrow "baby fat."

Although parents often assume that heavy children will "outgrow" their "baby fat," most overweight children actually become overweight adults. But biology isn't necessarily destiny; we will see that caregivers can help children manage their weight.

11-2a CAUSES OF BEING OVERWEIGHT

Evidence from kinship studies, including twin studies, and adoption studies shows that heredity plays a role in being overweight (den Hoed & Loos, 2014; Perusse et al., 2014). Some people inherit a tendency

FIG.11.2 OVERWEIGHT CHILDREN IN THE UNITED STATES

Source of data: Ogden et al., etc.

Latin American: 61.7, 22.4, 15.9
African American: 64.8, 20.2, 15
European American: 71.5, 14.1, 14.4

Normal/Under Weight | Overweight | Obese

Percentage of children (ages 6–11) and adolescents (ages 12–19) who are overweight, according to the American Heart Association (AHA).

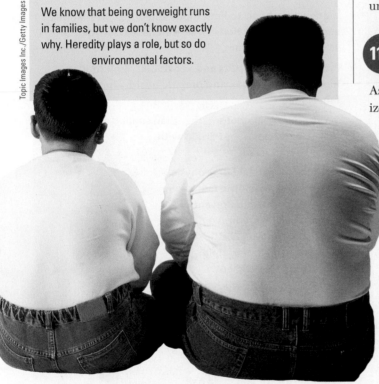

We know that being overweight runs in families, but we don't know exactly why. Heredity plays a role, but so do environmental factors.

Topic Images Inc./Getty Images

to burn up extra calories, whereas others inherit a tendency to turn extra calories into fat.

Except in rare cases of gene therapy, there is nothing one can do about one's heredity. Other factors that contribute to child overweight and obesity include consumption of sugary drinks and less healthful food at schools and child-care centers, the advertising of fattening foods, lack of regular physical activity (and for low-income children, lack of community places in which to play or exercise), limited access to healthful affordable foods, availability of "high energy" (translation: high sugar) drinks, large portion sizes (supersizing), lack of breast-feeding, and TV and other media

(couch-potato syndrome) (Leech et al., 2014; Berge et al., 2015). Overweight parents may serve as examples of poor exercise habits, encourage overeating, and keep unhealthful foods in the home (Berge et al., 2015).

11-3 CHILDHOOD ASTHMA

Asthma is an allergy-type respiratory disorder characterized by spasms in the lungs, difficulty breathing, wheezing, often coughing (dry hacking), and a feeling of tightness in the chest that prevents the sufferer from getting enough air. The wheezing can be severe enough to disturb sleep and speech.

Childhood asthma is more prevalent in developed nations, but it is more severe in undeveloped nations. Some children die from severe attacks of asthma, as do some adults. Just as asthma tends to be more severe in poor nations, it is more likely to be lethal among poorer Americans. Children with previous respiratory infections and skin irritations (dermatitis) are at higher risk of developing asthma. Other risk factors for asthma include male gender, administration of oxygen after birth, prescription of antibiotics during the first six months, and asthma in the family.

The National Institutes of Health lists medicines for treating asthma (NHLBI, 2011). Nasal corticosteroids block reaction to allergens and reduce airway constriction. Other medicines include cromolyn sodium and nedocromil, immunomodulators, leukotriene modifiers, and long-acting beta-agonist (LABA) bronchodilators (NHLBI, 2011). Parents are also typically advised to try to remove dust, dander, mites, and other sources of respiratory irritation from the home as much as possible. Some children "outgrow" asthma, meaning that symptoms tend to improve in some children when they reach adolescence and young adulthood (Sozener et al., 2015). For some, the symptoms do not return; for others, they may return after some years have passed.

11-4 MOTOR DEVELOPMENT

The school years are marked by increases in the child's speed, strength, agility, and balance. These developments lead to more skillful motor activities.

11-4a GROSS MOTOR SKILLS

Throughout middle childhood, children show steady improvement in their ability to perform gross motor skills. Children are hopping, jumping, and climbing by age six or so; by age six or seven, they are usually capable of pedaling and balancing on a bicycle. By the ages of eight to ten, children are showing the balance, coordination, and strength that allow them to engage in gymnastics and team sports.

During these years, muscles grow stronger, and neural pathways that connect the cerebellum to the cortex become more myelinated. Experience refines sensorimotor abilities, but there are also inborn differences. Some people have better visual acuity, depth perception, or coordination than others.

Reaction time is basic to the child's timing a swing of the bat or hitting a tennis ball. It gradually improves (decreases) from early childhood to about age 18, but there are individual differences (Swartz et al., 2014). Reaction time increases again in adulthood.

reaction time the amount of time required to respond to a stimulus.

11-4b FINE MOTOR SKILLS

By the age of six to seven, children can usually tie their shoelaces and hold pencils as adults do. Their abilities to fasten buttons, zip zippers, brush their teeth, wash themselves, coordinate a knife and fork,

How Can Parents Prevent or Reverse Childhood Overweight and Obesity?

Parents can't give their children new genes, but they can take measures including the following (Bray & Bouchard, 2014; Conrad, 2016):

▸ Follow the advice of the American Academy of Pediatrics and limit media time for kids to no more than one to two hours of playing handheld video games or watching television per day whether at home, school, or child care.

▸ Visit the child-care centers to see if they serve healthy foods and drinks, and limit TV and video time.

▸ Work with schools to limit foods and drinks with added sugar, fat, and salt that can be purchased outside the school lunch program.

▸ Provide plenty of fruits and vegetables, limit foods high in fat and sugar, and prepare healthy foods at family meals.

▸ Serve your family water rather than sugar drinks. (Ask your doctor about drinks with sugar substitutes.)

▸ Make sure your child gets physical activity every day. (The Centers for Disease Control and Prevention recommend 60 minutes a day. It doesn't all have to be brisk activity or weight training! Fast walking is excellent. Jump-rope and sit-ups and push-ups, with pauses in-between, are all good. Or simply encourage being on the playground for an hour a day. If an hour a day is unrealistic for you, try a half hour. Some is better than none.)

and use chopsticks all develop during the early school years and improve during childhood (Beilei et al., 2002; Gaul & Issartel, 2016).

11-4c GENDER DIFFERENCES

Throughout middle childhood, boys and girls perform similarly in most motor activities. Boys show slightly greater strength, especially more forearm strength, which aids them in swinging a bat or throwing a ball (Hay et al., 2011). Girls show somewhat greater limb

Cultura Creative/Alamy Stock Photo

Rubberball/Mike Kemp/Getty Images

coordination and overall flexibility, which is valuable in dancing, balancing, and gymnastics (Bruton et al., 2013).

At puberty, gender differences favoring boys increase. But prior to that, boys are more likely than girls to receive encouragement and opportunities in sports (White, 2016). Between middle childhood and adolescence, physical activities become increasingly stereotyped by children as being masculine (e.g., football) or feminine (e.g., dance) (Boiche et al., 2014).

11-4d EXERCISE AND FITNESS

Exercise reduces the risk of heart disease, stroke, diabetes, and certain forms of cancer (Trost et al., 2014). Physically active children also have a better self-image and coping skills than those who are inactive (Noordstar et al., 2016). Yet most children in the United States are not physically fit (Pate et al., 2013).

Cardiac and muscular fitness is developed by participation in aerobic exercises such as running, walking quickly, swimming laps, bicycling, or jumping rope for several minutes at a time. However, schools and parents tend to focus on sports such as baseball and football, which are less apt to promote fitness.

FICTION

T (F) Most American children are physically fit.

Actually, most children in the United States are not physically fit. How can we reverse that trend?

11-5 ATTENTION-DEFICIT/ HYPERACTIVITY DISORDER (ADHD)

Certain developmental problems are most apt to be noticed in the middle childhood years, when the child enters school. The school setting requires that a child sit still, pay attention, and master certain academic skills. But some children have difficulty with these demands:

Nine-year-old Eddie is a problem in class. His teacher complains that he is so restless and fidgety that the rest of the class cannot concentrate on their work. He . . . is in constant motion, roaming the classroom, talking to other children while they

are working. He has been suspended repeatedly for outrageous behavior, most recently swinging from a fluorescent light fixture. . . . He has never needed much sleep and always awakened before anyone else in the family, . . . wrecking things in the living room and kitchen. Once, at the age of four, he unlocked the front door and wandered into traffic, but was rescued by a passerby.

Psychological testing shows Eddie to be average in academic ability but to have a "virtually nonexistent" attention span. He shows no interest in television or in games or toys that require some concentration.

—Adapted from Spitzer et al. (2002)

In **attention-deficit hyperactivity disorder (ADHD)**, the child shows excessive inattention, impulsivity, and **hyperactivity**. The degree of hyperactive behavior is crucial, because many normal children are overactive and fidgety from time to time.

ADHD typically occurs by age seven. The hyperactivity and restlessness impair children's ability to function in school. They cannot sit still. They have difficulty getting along with others. ADHD is diagnosed in about 11% of school-age children and about twice as often in boys than girls (Schwartz & Cohen, 2013).

ADHD is frequently overdiagnosed (Gordon et al., 2016; Schwartz & Cohen, 2013). Some children who misbehave in school are diagnosed with ADHD and medicated to encourage more acceptable behavior.

11-5a CAUSES OF ADHD

Because ADHD is characterized in part by excessive motor activity, many theorists focus on possible physical causes. For one thing, ADHD tends to run in families for both girls and boys with the disorder (Martel et al., 2011). Some researchers suggest that there may be a genetic component to the disorder (Martel et al., 2011). If so, at least one genetic component might involve the manner in which children process the brain messengers dopamine and serotonin (Groenman et al., 2015; Tong et al., 2015).

In the 1970s, it was widely believed that food coloring and preservatives caused ADHD, but research has shown that this view is incorrect (Nigg & Holton, 2014); Rytter, et al. 2015). Researchers suggest that ADHD reflects lack of executive control of the brain over motor and more primitive functions (Hale et al., 2011).

attention-deficit hyperactivity disorder (ADHD) a disorder characterized by excessive inattention, impulsiveness, and hyperactivity.

hyperactivity excessive restlessness and overactivity; a characteristic of ADHD.

11.5b TREATMENT AND OUTCOME

Stimulants such as Ritalin are the most widespread treatment for ADHD, promoting the activity of the brain chemicals dopamine and noradrenaline, which stimulate the "executive center" of the brain to control more primitive areas of the brain. Stimulants increase children's attention spans and improve their academic performance (Pearson & Crowley, 2012). Many children with ADHD continue to have problems in attention, conduct, or learning in adolescence and adulthood (Martel et al., 2012).

11-6 LEARNING DISORDERS

stimulants drugs that increase the activity of the nervous system.

dyslexia a reading disorder characterized by letter reversals, mirror reading, slow reading, and reduced comprehension.

learning disorders disorders characterized by inadequate development of specific academic, language, and speech skills.

Some children who are intelligent and provided with enriched home environments cannot learn how to read (**dyslexia**) or do simple math problems (Armstrong et al., 2013). Many such children have **learning disorders**. Learning-disordered children may show problems in math,

FIG.11.3 WRITING SAMPLE OF A DYSLEXIC CHILD

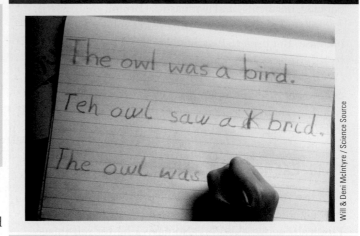

Will & Deni McIntyre / Science Source

Dyslexic children may perceive letters as upside down (confusing *w* with *m*) or reversed (confusing *b* with *d*), leading to rotations or reversals in writing, as shown here.

writing, or reading. Some have difficulties in articulating the sounds of speech or in understanding spoken language. Others have problems in motor coordination. Children are usually diagnosed with a learning disorder when they are performing below the level expected for their age and intelligence, and when there is no evidence of other handicaps such as vision or hearing problems, intellectual disability, or socioeconomic disadvantage (Ferrer et al., 2010). Learning disorders may persist through life, but with early recognition and remediation, many children can learn to compensate for their disorder.

11-6a DYSLEXIA

It has been estimated that dyslexia affects anywhere from 5% to 17.5% of American children (Shaywitz & Shaywitz, 2013). Most studies show that dyslexia is much more common in boys than in girls. Figure 11.3 shows a writing sample from a dyslexic child.

Theories of dyslexia focus on the ways in which sensory and neurological problems may contribute to the reading problems we find in dyslexic individuals. Genetic factors appear to be involved; from 25% to 65% of children who have one dyslexic parent are dyslexic themselves (Plomin et al., 2013a). About 40% of the siblings of children with dyslexia are dyslexic.

Genetic factors may give rise to neurological problems or circulation problems in the left hemisphere of the brain (Shaywitz & Shaywitz, 2013). The circulation problems would result in oxygen deficiency. The part of the brain called the angular gyrus "translates" visual information, such as written words, into auditory information (sounds). Problems in the angular gyrus may give rise to reading problems by making it difficult for the reader to associate letters with sounds (Shaywitz & Shaywitz, 2013).

Most researchers also focus on *phonological processing*. That is, dyslexic children may not discriminate sounds as accurately as other children do (Tanaka et al., 2011). As a result, *b*'s and *d*'s and *p*'s may be hard to tell apart, creating confusion that impairs reading ability (Shaywitz & Shaywitz, 2013).

In childhood, treatment of dyslexia focuses on remediation (Bakker, 2006). Children are given highly structured exercises to help them become aware of how to blend sounds to form words, such as identifying word pairs that rhyme and do not rhyme. Later in life, the focus tends to be on accommodation rather than on remediation. For example, college students with dyslexia may be given extra time to do the reading involved in taking tests.

Evidence is mixed on whether placing disabled children in separate classes can also stigmatize them and segregate them from other children. In **mainstreaming**, disabled children are placed in regular classrooms that have been adapted to their needs. Most students with mild learning disabilities spend most of the school day in regular classrooms (Fergusson, 2007).

mainstreaming placing disabled children in classrooms with nondisabled children.

STUDY TOOLS 11

READY TO STUDY?

In the book, you can:

☐ Rip out the chapter review card at the back of the book for a handy summary of the chapter and key terms.

☐ Check your understanding of what you've read with the quizzes that follow.

ONLINE AT CENGAGEBRAIN.COM YOU CAN:

☐ Collect StudyBits while you read and study the chapter.

☐ Quiz yourself on key concepts.

☐ Find videos for further exploration.

☐ Prepare for tests with CDEV2 Flash Cards as well as those you create.

SELF-ASSESSMENTS

Fill-Ins

Answers can be found in the back of the book.

1. Children with difficulty sitting still in school and paying attention are often diagnosed with attention-deficit/_____ disorder.

2. _____ are slightly heavier and taller than _____ through the age of nine or ten.

3. Children who are obese are more likely to have high _____ pressure and high cholesterol.

4. Evidence from kinship studies shows that _____ plays a role in being overweight.

5. Childhood _____ is characterized by wheezing.

6. During these years, muscles grow stronger, and neural pathways that connect the cerebellum to the cortex become more _____.

7. The drugs that are usually used to treat ADHD belong to the class of drugs called _____.

8. The learning disorder in which a child has great difficulty learning to read is called _____.

9. _____ are less likely than _____ to receive encouragement and opportunities in sports.

10. Recent research suggests that _____ may be overdiagnosed because about 11% of children are diagnosed with the problem.

Multiple Choice

1. According to the text, over the past 20 to 30 years, the prevalence of obesity among children has
   a. decreased.
   b. remained about the same.
   c. shown a slight increase.
   d. doubled.

2. All of the following have contributed to childhood obesity except
   a. breast-feeding.
   b. lack of regular exercise.
   c. overweight parents.
   d. consumption of high-energy drinks.

3. Which of the following activities is least likely to foster physical fitness?
   a. running
   c. football
   b. fast walking
   d. bicycling

4. ADHD is characterized by all of the following except
   a. hyperactivity.
   c. impulsivity.
   b. inattention.
   d. aggression.

5. ADHD is most often treated medically by use of
   a. depressants.
   b. stimulants.
   c. antidepressant drugs.
   d. antipsychotic drugs.

6. All of the following are risk factors for asthma except
   a. a history of respiratory infections.
   b. use of nasal corticosteroids.
   c. a family history of asthma.
   d. male gender.

7. Researchers theorize that dyslexia may involve problems with
   a. the voice box.
   b. the motor cortex of the brain.
   c. the reticular activating system.
   d. the angular gyrus.

8. In terms of motor behavior and skills, boys tend to have greater _____ than girls in middle childhood.
   a. flexibility
   c. strength
   b. determination
   d. determination

9. Asthma is characterized by all of the following except
   a. fever.
   b. spasms in the lungs.
   c. wheezing.
   d. feelings of tightness in the chest.

10. Which of the following statements about ADHD is not supported by scientific research?
   a. ADHD is caused by chemical food additives.
   b. There may be a genetic component to the development of ADHD.
   c. ADHD appears to be connected with the brain chemical dopamine.
   d. ADHD involves lack of executive control over motor and more primitive functions.

12 | Middle Childhood: Cognitive Development

LEARNING OUTCOMES

After studying this chapter, you will be able to...

12-1 Describe Piaget's concrete-operational stage

12-2 Discuss Piaget's and Kohlberg's theories of moral development

12-3 Describe developments in information processing in middle childhood

12-4 Describe intellectual development in middle childhood, focusing on theories of intelligence

12-5 Describe language development in middle childhood, including reading and bilingualism

After you finish this chapter, go to **PAGE 210** for **STUDY TOOLS**

Did you hear the one about the judge who pounded her gavel and yelled, "Order! Order in the court!"? "A hamburger and french fries, Your Honor," responded the defendant. Or how about this one? "I saw a man-eating lion at the zoo." "Big deal! I saw a man eating snails at a restaurant." Or how about, "Make me a glass of chocolate milk!"? "Poof! You're a glass of chocolate milk." Such children's jokes are based on ambiguities in the

> In middle childhood, children show the beginnings of adult logic.

meanings of words and phrases. Most seven-year-olds will find the joke about order in the court funny because they recognize that the word *order* has more than one meaning. At about the age of 11, children can understand ambiguities in grammatical structure. Children make enormous strides in their cognitive development during middle childhood as their thought processes and language become more logical and complex.

12-1 PIAGET: THE CONCRETE-OPERATIONAL STAGE

According to Jean Piaget, the typical child is entering the stage of **concrete operations** by the age of seven. In this stage, which lasts until about 12, children show the beginnings of adult logic but generally focus on tangible objects rather than abstract ideas, which is why they are "concrete."

Concrete-operational thought is reversible and flexible. Adding the numbers two and three to get five is an operation. Subtracting two from five to get three reverses the operation. Subtracting three from five to get two demonstrates flexibility.

Concrete-operational children are less egocentric than preoperational children. They recognize that people see things in different ways because of different situations and values. Concrete-operational children also engage in **decentration**. They can focus on multiple parts of a problem at once.

> **concrete operations** the third stage in Piaget's scheme, characterized by flexible, reversible thought concerning tangible objects and events.
>
> **decentration** simultaneous focusing on more than one aspect or dimension of a problem or situation.

If A > B, and B > C, then A > C.

An example of transitivity.

Studio Araminta/Shutterstock.com

TRUTH OR FICTION?

T	F	You can't use the "Yes, but" defense with a five-year-old. If you did it, you're guilty, even if it was an accident.
T	F	"IQ" is another term for "intelligence."
T	F	Two children can answer exactly the same items on an intelligence test correctly, yet one can be above average in intelligence and the other below average.
T	F	Highly intelligent children are creative
T	F	Adopted children are more similar in intelligence test scores to their adoptive parents than to their biological parents.
T	F	Bilingual children have more academic problems than children who speak only one language.

12-1a CONSERVATION

Concrete-operational children show understanding of the laws of conservation. A seven-year-old child would say that the flattened ball of clay from the example in Chapter 9 still has the same amount of clay as the round one "because you can roll it up again." The concrete-operational child knows that objects can have several properties or dimensions. By attending to both the height and the width of the clay, the child recognizes that the loss in height compensates for the gain in width.

12-1b TRANSITIVITY

If your parents are older than you are and you are older than your children, are your parents older than your children? The answer, of course, is yes. But how did you arrive at this answer? If you said yes simply on the basis of knowing that your parents are older than your children (e.g., 58 and 56 compared with 5 and 3), your answer did not require concrete-operational thought. One aspect of such thought is the principle of **transitivity**: If A exceeds B in some property (say, age or height) and if B exceeds C, then A must also exceed C.

Researchers can assess whether children understand the principle of transitivity by asking them to place objects in a series, or order, according to some property, such as lining up one's family members according to age, height, or weight. Placing objects in a series is termed **seriation**. Consider some examples with preoperational and concrete-operational children.

Piaget assessed children's abilities at seriation by asking them to place ten sticks in order of size. Children who are four to five usually place the sticks in a random sequence, or in small groups, as in small, medium, or large. But consider the approach of seven- and eight-year-olds who are capable of concrete operations.

FIG. 12.1 A DEMONSTRATION OF SERIATION

Small, dark → Darkest to lightest → Small, light

Smallest to largest

Large, dark   Large, light

To classify these leaves, children must focus on two dimensions at once: size and lightness. They must also understand the principle of transitivity—that if A > B and B > C, then A > C.

They look over the array, then select either the longest or shortest and place it at the point from which they will begin. Then they select the next longest (or shortest) and continue until the task is complete.

Concrete-operational children also have the decentration capacity to allow them to seriate in two dimensions at once, unlike preoperational children. Consider a seriation task used by Piaget and his longtime colleague, Barbel Inhelder (Inhelder & Piaget, 1959). In this test, children are given 49 leaves and asked to classify them according to size and brightness (from small to large and from dark to light) (see Figure 12.1). As the grid is completed from left to right, the leaves become lighter. As it is filled in from top to bottom, the leaves become larger.

12-1c CLASS INCLUSION

Imagine a four-year-old being shown pictures of four cats and six dogs. When asked whether there are more dogs or more animals, she replies more dogs. The preoperational child apparently cannot focus on the two subclasses (dogs, cats) and the larger subclass (animals) at the same time. But concrete-operational children can do so. Therefore, they are more likely to answer the question about the dogs and the animals correctly.

transitivity the principle that if A > B and B > C, then A > C.
seriation placing objects in an order or series according to a property or trait.

12-1d APPLICATIONS OF PIAGET'S THEORY TO EDUCATION

Piaget believed that learning involves active discovery. Also, instruction should be geared to the child's level of development. When teaching a concrete-operational child about fractions, for example, the teacher should not only lecture but should also allow the child to divide concrete objects into parts. Third, Piaget believed that learning to take into account the perspectives of others is a key ingredient in the development of both cognition and morality.

12-2 MORAL DEVELOPMENT: THE CHILD AS JUDGE

On a cognitive level, moral development concerns the basis on which children make judgments that an act is right or wrong. Jean Piaget and Lawrence Kohlberg believed that moral reasoning undergoes the same cognitive-developmental pattern around the world. The moral considerations that children weigh at a given age may be influenced by the values of the cultural settings in which they are reared, but also reflect the unfolding of cognitive processes (Nucci et al., 2014). Moral reasoning is related to the child's overall cognitive development.

12-2a PIAGET'S THEORY OF MORAL DEVELOPMENT

Piaget observed children playing games such as marbles and making judgments on the seriousness of the wrongdoing of characters in stories. On the basis of these observations, he concluded that children's moral judgments develop in two overlapping stages: moral realism and autonomous morality (Piaget, 1932).

The first stage is usually referred to as the stage of **moral realism**, or **objective morality**. During this stage, which emerges at about the age of five, children consider behavior correct when it conforms to authority or to the rules of the game. When asked why something should be done in a certain way, the five-year-old may answer "Because that's the way to do it" or "Because my Mommy

Early in the preoperational stage, children believe that the rules of the game are somehow embedded in reality.

UpperCut Images Photography/Jupiter Images

It is true that you are guilty for having done something "wrong" in the eyes of a five-year-old, even when your behavior was an accident. Preoperational children tend to focus on only one dimension at a time. Therefore, they tend to judge the wrongness of an act in terms of the amount of damage done, rather than considering both the damage done and the intentions of the wrongdoer.

says so." Five-year-olds perceive rules as embedded in the structure of things. Rules, to them, reflect ultimate reality, hence the term *moral realism*. Rules and right and wrong are seen as absolute, not as deriving from people to meet social needs. Early in the preoperational stage, children believe that the rules of the game are somehow embedded in reality.

Another consequence of viewing rules as embedded in the fabric of the world is **immanent justice**, or automatic retribution. This involves thinking that negative experiences are punishment for prior misdeeds, even when realistic causal links are absent.

Preoperational children tend to focus on only one dimension at a time. Therefore, they judge the wrongness of an act only in terms of the amount of damage done, not in terms of the intentions of the wrongdoer. Consider children's response to Piaget's story about the broken cups. Piaget told children a story in which one child breaks 15 cups accidentally and another child breaks one cup deliberately. Children in the

moral realism the judgment of acts as moral when they conform to authority or to the rules of the game.

objective morality the perception of morality as objective, that is, as existing outside the cognitive functioning of people.

immanent justice the view that retribution for wrongdoing is a direct consequence of the wrongdoing.

stage of moral realism typically say that the child who did the most damage is the naughtiest and should be punished most (Piaget, 1932).

Piaget found that when children reach the ages of 9 to 11, they begin to show **autonomous morality**. Their moral judgments tend to become more self-governed, as children come to view social rules as social agreements that can be changed. Children realize that circumstances can warrant breaking rules. Children who show autonomous morality can focus simultaneously on multiple dimensions, so they consider social rules and the motives of the wrongdoer.

Children in this stage also show a greater capacity to take the point of view of others, to empathize with them. Decentration and increased empathy prompt children to weigh the intentions of the wrongdoer more heavily than the amount of damage done. The child who broke one cup deliberately may be seen as deserving of more punishment than the child who broke 15 cups accidentally. Accidents are less likely to be considered crimes.

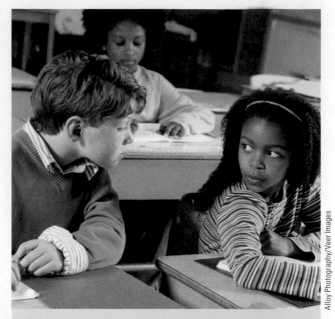

Why do some children cheat while others do their own work?

12-2b KOHLBERG'S THEORY OF MORAL DEVELOPMENT

Kohlberg (1981, 1985) advanced the cognitive-developmental theory of moral development by elaborating on the kinds of information children use and on the complexities of moral reasoning. Before we discuss Kohlberg's views, read the tale that Kohlberg used in his research and answer the questions that follow.

In Europe, a woman was near death from a special kind of cancer. There was one drug that the doctors thought might save her. It was a form of radium that a druggist in the same town had recently discovered. The drug was expensive to make, but the druggist was charging 10 times what the drug cost him to make. He paid $200 for the radium and charged $2,000 for a small dose of the drug. The sick woman's husband, Heinz, went to everyone he knew to borrow the money, but he could only get together about $1,000, which was half of what it cost. He told the druggist that his wife was dying and asked him to sell it cheaper or let him pay later. But the druggist said: "No, I discovered the drug and I'm going to make money from it." So Heinz got desperate and broke into the man's store to steal the drug for his wife.

—Kohlberg (1969)

autonomous morality the second stage in Piaget's cognitive-developmental theory of moral development, in which children base moral judgments on the intentions of the wrongdoer and on the amount of damage done.

preconventional level according to Kohlberg, a period during which moral judgments are based largely on expectations of rewards or punishments.

Kohlberg emphasized the importance of being able to view the moral world from the perspective of another person. Look at the situation from Heinz's perspective. What do you think? Should Heinz have tried to steal the drug? Was he right or wrong? As you can see from Table 12.1, the issue is more complicated than a simple yes or no. Heinz is caught in a moral dilemma in which legal or social rules (in this case, laws against stealing) are pitted against a strong human need (Heinz's desire to save his wife). According to Kohlberg's theory, children and adults arrive at yes or no answers for different reasons. These reasons can be classified according to the level of moral development they reflect.

Children (and adults) are faced with many moral dilemmas. Consider cheating in school. When children fear failing a test, they may be tempted to cheat. Different children may decide not to cheat for different reasons. One child may fear getting caught. Another may decide that it is more important to live up to her moral principles than to get the highest possible grade. In each case, the child's decision is not to cheat. However, the decisions reflect different levels of reasoning.

Kohlberg argued that the developmental stages of moral reasoning follow the same sequence in all children. Children progress at different rates—not everyone reaches the highest stage. But children must experience Stage 1 before Stage 2, and so on. Kohlberg theorizes three levels of moral development and two stages within each level.

THE PRECONVENTIONAL LEVEL At the **preconventional level**, children base their moral judgments on

TABLE 12.1 KOHLBERG'S LEVELS AND STAGES OF MORAL DEVELOPMENT

Stage of Development	Examples of Moral Reasoning That Support Heinz's Stealing the Drug	Examples of Moral Reasoning That Oppose Heinz's Stealing the Drug
Level I: Preconventional—Typically Begins in Early Childhood[a]		
Stage 1: Judgments guided by obedience and the prospect of punishment (the consequences of the behavior)	It is not wrong to take the drug. Heinz did try to pay the druggist for it, and it is only worth $200, not $2,000.	Taking things without paying is wrong because it is against the law. Heinz will get caught and go to jail.
Stage 2: Naively egoistic, instrumental orientation (things are right when they satisfy people's needs)	Heinz ought to take the drug because his wife really needs it. He can always pay the druggist back.	Heinz should not take the drug. If he gets caught and winds up in jail, it won't do his wife any good.
Level II: Conventional—Typically Begins in Middle Childhood		
Stage 3: Good-boy/good-girl orientation (moral behavior helps others and is socially approved)	Stealing is a crime, so it is bad, but Heinz should take the drug to save his wife or else people would blame him for letting her die.	Stealing is a crime. Heinz should not just take the drug because his family will be dishonored and they will blame him.
Stage 4: Law-and-order orientation (moral behavior is doing one's duty and showing respect for authority)	Heinz must take the drug to do his duty to save his wife. Eventually, he has to pay the druggist for it, however.	If we all took the law into our own hands, civilization would fall apart, so Heinz should not steal the drug.
Level III: Postconventional—Typically Begins in Adolescence[b]		
Stage 5: Contractual, legalistic orientation (one must weigh pressing human needs against society's need to maintain social order)	This thing is complicated because society has a right to maintain law and order, but Heinz has to take the drug to save his wife.	I can see why Heinz feels he has to take the drug, but laws exist for the benefit of society as a whole and cannot simply be cast aside.
Stage 6: Universal ethical principles orientation (people must follow universal ethical principles and their own consciences, even if it means breaking the law)	In this case, the law comes into conflict with the principle of the sanctity of human life. Heinz must take the drug because his wife's life is more important than the law.	If Heinz truly believes that stealing the drug is worse than letting his wife die, he should not take it. People have to make sacrifices to do what they think is right.

[a]Tends to be used less often in middle childhood
[b]May not develop at all

the consequences of their behavior. Stage 1 is oriented toward obedience and punishment. Good behavior means being obedient so one can avoid punishment. In Stage 2, good behavior allows people to satisfy their own needs and, perhaps, the needs of others. In a study of U.S. children aged 7 through 16, Kohlberg (1963) found that Stage 1 and 2 types of moral judgments were offered most frequently by seven- to ten-year-olds. Stage 1 and 2 judgments fell off steeply after age ten.

THE CONVENTIONAL LEVEL At the **conventional level** of moral reasoning, right and wrong are judged by conformity to conventional (family, religious, societal) standards of right and wrong. According to the Stage 3 "good-boy/good-girl orientation," it is good to meet the needs and expectations of others. Moral behavior is what is "normal," what the majority does. In Stage 4, moral judgments are based on rules that maintain the social order. Showing respect for authority and duty is valued highly. Many people do not develop beyond the conventional level. Kohlberg (1963) found that Stage 3 and 4 types of judgments emerge during middle childhood. They are all but absent among seven-year-olds. However, they are reported by about 20% of ten-year-olds and by higher percentages of adolescents.

THE POSTCONVENTIONAL LEVEL At the **post-conventional level**, moral reasoning is based on the person's own moral standards (Snarey & Samuelson, 2014). If this level of reasoning develops at all, it is found among adolescents and adults.

12-3 INFORMATION PROCESSING: LEARNING, REMEMBERING, PROBLEM SOLVING

Key elements in children's information processing include the following:

▶ Development of selective attention

▶ Development of the capacity of memory and of children's understanding of the processes of memory

▶ Development of the ability to solve problems as, for example, by finding the correct formula and applying it

conventional level according to Kohlberg, a period during which moral judgments largely reflect social rules and conventions.

postconventional level according to Kohlberg, a period during which moral judgments are derived from moral principles, and people look to themselves to set moral standards.

12-3a DEVELOPMENT OF SELECTIVE ATTENTION

The ability to focus one's attention and screen out distractions advances steadily through middle childhood (Lim et al., 2015). Preoperational children engaged in problem solving tend to focus (or center) their attention on one element of the problem at a time, which is a major reason they lack conservation. Concrete-operational children can attend to multiple aspects of the problem at once, permitting them to conserve number and volume.

A classic experiment illustrates how selective attention and the ability to ignore distraction develop during middle childhood. The researchers (Strutt et al., 1975) asked children between 6 and 12 years of age to sort a deck of cards as quickly as possible on the basis of the figures depicted on each card (e.g., circle versus square). In one condition, only the relevant dimension (i.e., form) was shown on each card. In another condition, a dimension not relevant to the sorting also was present (e.g., a horizontal or vertical line in the figure). In a third condition, two irrelevant dimensions were present (e.g., a star above or below the figure, in addition to a horizontal or vertical line in the figure). As seen in Figure 12.2, the irrelevant information interfered with sorting ability for all age groups, but older children were much less affected than younger children.

12-3b DEVELOPMENTS IN THE STORAGE AND RETRIEVAL OF INFORMATION

Psychologists use the term *memory* to refer to the processes of storing and retrieving

sensory memory the structure of memory first encountered by sensory input. Information is maintained in sensory memory for only a fraction of a second.

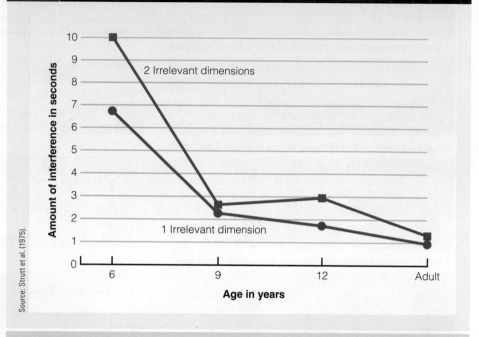

FIG.12.2 DEVELOPMENT OF THE ABILITY TO IGNORE DISTRACTIONS

Source: Strutt et al. (1975).

2 Irrelevant dimensions

1 Irrelevant dimension

Amount of interference in seconds

Age in years

In this study, irrelevant information interfered with sorting ability for all age groups, but older children were less affected than younger ones.

information. Many psychologists divide memory functioning into three major processes or structures: sensory memory, working memory, and long-term memory (see Figure 12.3).

SENSORY MEMORY When we look at an object and then blink our eyes, the visual impression of the object lasts for a fraction of a second in what is called **sensory memory**, or the

During middle childhood, children's ability to focus their attention increases.

Jack Kurt/The Image Works

FIG.12.3   THE STRUCTURE OF MEMORY

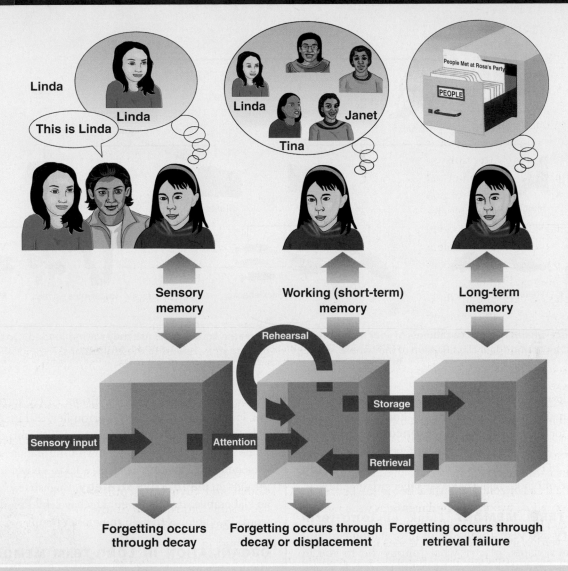

Sensory
memory

Working (short-term)
memory

Long-term
memory

Rehearsal

Storage

Sensory input   Attention

Retrieval

Forgetting occurs
through decay

Forgetting occurs through
decay or displacement

Forgetting occurs through
retrieval failure

Many psychologists divide memory into three processes or "structures." Sensory information enters (1) sensory memory, where memory traces are held briefly before decaying. If we attend to the information, much of it is transferred to (2) working memory (also called *short-term memory*), where it may decay or be displaced if it is not transferred to long-term memory. We may use rehearsal (repetition) or elaborative strategies to transfer memories to (3) long-term memory, from which memories can be retrieved with the correct cues.

sensory register. Then the "trace" of the stimulus decays. The concept of sensory memory applies to all the senses. For example, when we are introduced to somebody, the trace of the sound of the name also decays, but we can remember the name by focusing on it.

WORKING MEMORY (SHORT-TERM MEMORY)

When children focus on a stimulus in the sensory register, it tends to be retained in **working memory** (also called *short-term memory*) for up to 30 seconds after the

trace of the stimulus decays. Ability to maintain information in short-term memory depends on cognitive strategies and on capacity to continue to perceive a vanished stimulus. Memory function in middle childhood seems largely adult-like in organization and strategies and shows only quantitative improvement through early adolescence (Alloway & Alloway, 2013).

sensory register another term for sensory memory.

working memory the structure of memory that can hold a sensory stimulus for up to 30 seconds after the trace decays.

FIG.12.4 THE CATEGORICAL STRUCTURE OF LONG-TERM MEMORY

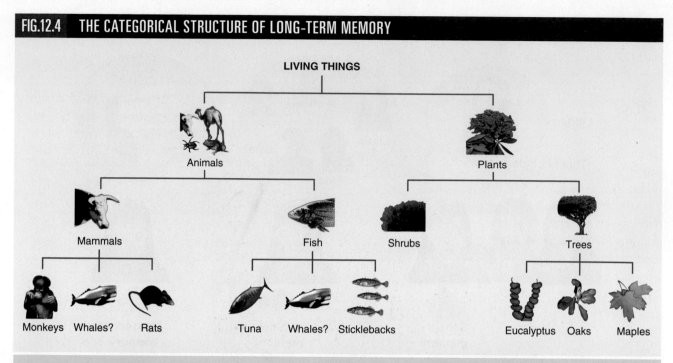

Where are whales filed in the cabinets of your memory? Do whales breathe underwater? Are they warm-blooded? Do they nurse their young? Your classification of the "whale" concept will provide your answers to these questions.

Auditory stimuli can be maintained longer in short-term memory than can visual stimuli. For this reason, one strategy for promoting memory is to **encode** visual stimuli as sounds. Then the sounds can be repeated out loud or mentally. In Figure 12.3, mentally repeating or **rehearsing** the sound of Linda's name helps the other girl remember it.

LONG-TERM MEMORY Think of **long-term memory** as a vast storehouse of information containing names, dates, places, what Johnny did to you in second grade, what Alyssa said about you when you were 12. Long-term memories may last days, years, or, for practical purposes, a lifetime.

There is no known limit to the amount of information that can be stored in long-term memory. From time to time, it may seem that we have forgotten, or lost, a long-term memory, such as the names of elementary or high school classmates. But it is more likely that we cannot find the right cues to retrieve it. It is "lost" in the same way we misplace an object but know it is still in the house.

Older children are more likely than younger children to use rote rehearsal, or repetition, to try to remember information (Camos & Barrouillet, 2011). A more effective method than rote rehearsal is to purposefully relate new material to well-known information, making it meaningful. Relating new material to known material is called an **elaborative strategy**. English teachers use an elaborative strategy when they have children use new words in sentences to help remember them.

ORGANIZATION IN LONG-TERM MEMORY As children's knowledge of concepts advances, the storehouse of their long-term memory becomes organized according to categories. Preschoolers tend to organize their memories by grouping objects that share the same function (Towse, 2003). "Toast" may be grouped with "peanut butter sandwich," because both are edible. In middle childhood toast and peanut butter are likely to be joined as foods.

When items are correctly categorized in long-term memory, children are more likely to recall accurate information about them (see Figure 12.4). For instance, do you "remember" whether whales breathe underwater? If you did not know that whales are mammals or if you knew nothing about mammals, a correct answer might depend on an instance of rote learning. If children have incorrectly classified whales as fish, they might search their "memories" and construct the wrong answer.

encode to transform sensory input into a form that is more readily processed.

rehearsing repeat—in this case, mentally.

long-term memory the memory structure capable of relatively permanent storage of information.

elaborative strategy a method for increasing retention of new information by relating it to well-known information.

Children's Eyewitness Testimony

Jean Piaget distinctly "remembered" an attempt to kidnap him from his baby carriage as he was being wheeled along the Champs-Élysées. He recalled the excited throng, the abrasions on the face of the nurse who rescued him, the police officer's white baton, and the flight of the assailant. Although they were graphic, Piaget's memories were false. Years later, the nurse admitted that she had made up the tale.

The child witness is typically asked questions to prompt information. But such questions may be "leading," that is, they may suggest an answer. For example, "What happened at school?" is not a leading question, but "Did your teacher touch you?" is. Can children's

Rob Crandall/SCPhotos/Alamy Stock Photo

testimony be distorted by leading questions? It appears that by the age of 10 or 11, children are no more suggestible than adults, but younger children are more likely to be misled (Goodman et al., 2011). Research also indicates that repeated questioning may lead children to make up events that never happened to them (Klemfuss & Ceci, 2012).

What, then, are investigators to do when the only witnesses to criminal events are children? Maggie Bruck and her colleagues (2006) recommend that interviewers avoid leading or suggestive questions to minimize influencing the child's response.

Knowledge in a particular area increases the capacity to store and retrieve related information. Chess experts are superior to amateurs at remembering where chess pieces have been placed on the board (Gobet & Simon, 2000). In these studies, the experts were 8- to 12-year-old children and the amateurs were adults!

12-3c DEVELOPMENT OF RECALL MEMORY

Children's memory is a good overall indicator of their cognitive ability (Alloway & Alloway, 2013; Gignac & Weisse, 2015). In an experiment on categorization and memory, researchers placed objects that fell into four categories (furniture, clothing, tools, fruit) on a table before second- and fourth-graders (Hasselhorn, 1992). The children were allowed three minutes to arrange the pictures as they wished and to remember as many as they could. Fourth-graders were more likely to categorize and recall the pictures than second-graders.

12-3d DEVELOPMENT OF METACOGNITION AND METAMEMORY

Children's knowledge and control of their cognitive abilities is termed **metacognition**. The development of metacognition is shown by the ability to formulate problems, awareness of the processes required to solve a problem, activation of cognitive strategies, maintaining focus on the problem, and checking answers.

As a sixth-grader decides which homework assignments to do first, memorizes the state capitals for tomorrow's test, and then tests herself to see which she needs to study more, she is displaying metacognition. **Metamemory** is an aspect of metacognition that refers to children's awareness of the functioning memory. Older students are more likely to accurately assess their knowledge. So, older children store and retrieve information more effectively (Daugherty & Ofen, 2015).

Older children also show more knowledge of strategies that can be used to facilitate memory. Preschoolers will usually use rehearsal if someone suggests they do, but not until about the age of six or seven do children use it on their own (Camos & Barrouillet, 2011). As children develop, they are more likely to use selective rehearsal to remember important information.

metacognition awareness of and control of one's cognitive abilities.

metamemory knowledge of the functions and processes involved in one's storage and retrieval of information.

12-4 INTELLECTUAL DEVELOPMENT, CREATIVITY, AND ACHIEVEMENT

At an early age, we gain impressions of how intelligent we are compared with other family members and schoolmates. We associate **intelligence** with academic success, advancement on the job, and appropriate social behavior (Mayer, 2011). Despite our sense of familiarity with the concept of intelligence, intelligence cannot be seen, touched, or measured physically. For this reason, intelligence is subject to various interpretations.

Intelligence is usually perceived as a child's underlying competence or *learning ability*, whereas **achievement** involves a child's acquired competencies or *performance*. Most psychologists also would agree that many of the competencies underlying intelligence are seen during middle childhood, when most children are first exposed to formal schooling.

What is intelligence? How does it develop?

Marnie Burkhart/Fancy/Jupiterimages

12-4a THEORIES OF INTELLIGENCE

Let's consider some theoretical approaches to intelligence. Then we will see how researchers and practitioners assess intellectual functioning.

FACTOR THEORIES Many investigators view intelligence as consisting of one or more major mental abilities, or factors (Willis et al., 2011). In 1904, Charles Spearman suggested that the behaviors we consider intelligent have a common underlying g factor, or general intelligence, which represents broad reasoning and problem-solving abilities, and that specific capacities, or s factors, account for certain individual abilities, like music or poetry.

Psychologist Louis Thurstone (1938) believed that intelligence consists of several specific factors, or *primary mental abilities*, such as the ability to learn the meaning of words and visual–spatial abilities. Thurstone's research suggested that these factors were somewhat independent.

STERNBERG'S THEORY OF INTELLIGENCE Psychologist Robert Sternberg (Sternberg, 2015) constructed a three-part, or "triarchic," theory of intelligence. The parts are *analytical intelligence, creative intelligence*, and *practical intelligence* (see Figure 12.5). Analytical intelligence is academic ability. Creative intelligence is defined by the abilities to invent solutions to problems and cope with novel situations. Practical intelligence, or "street smarts," enables people to adapt to the demands of their environment, including the social environment.

GARDNER'S THEORY OF MULTIPLE INTELLIGENCES Psychologist Howard Gardner (1983; Sternberg, 2015), like Sternberg, believes that intelligence—or intelligences—reflect more than academic ability. Gardner

intelligence a general mental capability that involves the ability to reason, plan, solve problems, think abstractly, comprehend complex ideas, learn quickly, and learn from experience

achievement that which is attained by one's efforts and presumed to be made possible by one's abilities.

FIG.12.5 STERNBERG'S TRIARCHIC THEORY OF INTELLIGENCE

Analytical intelligence
(academic ability)
Abilities to solve problems, compare and contrast, judge, evaluate, and criticize

Creative intelligence
(creativity and insight)
Abilities to invent, discover, suppose, and theorize

Practical intelligence
("street smarts")
Abilities to adapt to the demands of one's environment and apply knowledge in practical situations

Robert Sternberg views intelligence as having three parts: academic ability, creativity, and "street smarts."

refs to each kind of intelligence in his theory as "an intelligence" because each differs in quality (see Figure 12.6).

Three of Gardner's intelligences are verbal (linguistic) ability, logical–mathematical reasoning, and spatial intelligence (visual–spatial skills). Others include bodily–kinesthetic intelligence (as shown by dancers and gymnasts), musical intelligence, interpersonal intelligence (as shown by empathy and ability to relate to others), and personal knowledge (self-insight). Individuals may show great "intelligence" in one area without notable abilities in others. Critics agree that many people have special talents, as in music, but they question whether such talents are "intelligences" (Neisser et al., 1996).

12-4b MEASUREMENT OF INTELLECTUAL DEVELOPMENT

There may be disagreements about the nature of intelligence, but thousands of intelligence tests are administered by psychologists and educators every day (Urbina, 2011).

The Stanford–Binet Intelligence Scale (SBIS) and the Wechsler scales for children and adults are the most widely used and well respected intelligence tests. The SBIS and Wechsler scales yield scores called **intelligence quotients (IQs)**. The concept of intelligence per se is more difficult to define. The SBIS and Wechsler scales have been carefully developed and revised over the years. Each of them has been used to make vital educational decisions about children. In many cases, children whose test scores fall below or above certain scores are placed in special classes for intellectually disabled or gifted children.

THE STANFORD–BINET INTELLIGENCE SCALE

The SBIS originated in the work of Frenchmen Alfred Binet and Theodore Simon about a century ago for the

FIG.12.6 GARDNER'S THEORY OF MULTIPLE INTELLIGENCES

Linguistic

Logical–mathematical

Naturalist

Spatial

Bodily–kinesthetic

Musical

Intrapersonal

Interpersonal

Existential

Gardner asserts that there are many "intelligences," not just one, and that each is based in different areas of the brain.

intelligence quotient (IQ)
(1) a ratio obtained by dividing a child's mental age on an intelligence test by his or her chronological age; (2) a score on an intelligence test.

In 1905 Alfred Binet and Theodore Simon in France introduced the idea of measuring intelligence. This version of the test was produced in 1937 by Lewis Terman and Maude Merrill in the United States and was specifically designed for younger children.

French public school system. Binet assumed that intelligence increased with age. Therefore, older children should get more items right. Thus, Binet arranged a series of questions in order of difficulty, from easier to harder. It has since undergone revision and refinement.

The Binet–Simon scale yielded a score called a **mental age (MA)**. The MA shows the intellectual level at which a child is functioning. A child with an MA of 6 is functioning, intellectually, like the average six-year-old child.

mental age (MA) the intellectual level at which a child functions, based on the typical performance of a child of a certain age.

chronological age (CA) a person's age.

Louis Terman adapted the Binet–Simon scale for use with American children in 1916. Because Terman carried out his work at Stanford University, it is now named the Stanford–Binet Intelligence Scale. The SBIS yielded an intelligence quotient, or IQ, rather than an MA. The SBIS today can be used with children from the age of two up to adults. Table 12.2 shows the kinds of items given at various ages.

The IQ states the relationship between a child's mental age and his or her actual or **chronological age (CA)**. An MA of 8 is an above-average score for a six-year-old but a below-average score for a ten-year-old.

The IQ is computed by the following formula:

$$IQ = \frac{Mental\,Age\,(MA)}{Chronological\,Age\,(CA)} \times 100$$

According to this formula, a child with an MA of 6 and a CA of 6 would have an IQ of 100. Furthermore, because of the factor of chronological age in the formula,

TRUTH

 F Two children can answer exactly the same items on an intelligence test correctly, yet one can be above average in intelligence and the other below average.

It is true that two children can answer exactly the same items on an intelligence test correctly, yet one can be above average in intelligence and the other below average. The younger child would have the higher IQ score, because his or her performance is compared to those of others in his or her age group.

Age	Item
TABLE 12.2	**ITEMS SIMILAR TO THOSE ON THE STANFORD–BINET INTELLIGENCE SCALE**
2 years	1. Children show knowledge of basic vocabulary words by identifying parts of a doll, such as the mouth, ears, and hair. 2. Children show counting and spatial skills along with visual–motor coordination by building a tower of four blocks to match a model.
4 years	1. Children show word fluency and categorical thinking by filling in the missing words when they are asked questions such as "Father is a man; mother is a _____?" and "Hamburgers are hot; ice cream is _____?" 2. Children show comprehension by answering correctly when they are asked questions such as "Why do people have automobiles?" and "Why do people have medicine?"
9 years	1. Children can point out verbal absurdities, as in this question: "In an old cemetery, scientists unearthed a skull which they think was that of George Washington when he was only 5 years of age. What is silly about that?" 2. Children display fluency with words, as shown by answering questions such as "Can you tell me a number that rhymes with snore?" and "Can you tell me a color that rhymes with glue?"
Adult	1. Adults show knowledge of the meanings of words and conceptual thinking by correctly explaining the differences between word pairs such as "sickness and misery," "house and home," and "integrity and prestige." 2. Adults show spatial skills by correctly answering questions such as "If a car turned to the right to head north, in what direction was it heading before it turned?"

TABLE 12.3 KINDS OF ITEMS FOUND ON WECHSLER'S INTELLIGENCE SCALES

Verbal Items	Nonverbal-Performance Items
• Information: "What is the capital of the United States?" "Who was Shakespeare?" • Comprehension: "Why do we have ZIP codes?" "What does 'A stitch in time saves 9' mean?" • Arithmetic: "If 3 candy bars cost 25 cents, how much will 18 candy bars cost?" • Similarities: "How are good and bad alike?" "How are peanut butter and jelly alike?" • Vocabulary: "What does canal mean?" • Digit span: Repeating a series of numbers, presented by the examiner, forward and backward.	• Picture completion: Pointing to the missing part of a picture. • Picture arrangement: Arranging cartoon pictures in sequence so that they tell a meaningful story. • Block design: Copying pictures of geometric designs using multicolored blocks. • Object assembly: Putting pieces of a puzzle together so that they form a meaningful object. • Coding: Rapid scanning and drawing of symbols that are associated with numbers. • Mazes: Using a pencil to trace the correct route from a starting point to home.

children of different ages might answer the same items on a test the same but end up receiving different IQ scores.

Today, IQ scores on the SBIS are derived by comparing children's and adults' performances with those of other people of the same age. People who get more items correct than average attain IQ scores above 100, and people who answer fewer items correctly attain scores below 100.

THE WECHSLER SCALES David Wechsler (1975) developed a series of scales for use with school-age children (Wechsler Intelligence Scale for Children; WISC), younger children (Wechsler Preschool and Primary Scale of Intelligence; WPPSI), and adults (Wechsler Adult Intelligence Scale; WAIS).

The Wechsler scales group test questions into subtests (such as those shown in Table 12.3) that measure different intellectual tasks. For this reason, subtests compare a person's performance on one type of task (such as defining words) with another (such as using blocks to construct geometric designs). The Wechsler scales thus suggest children's strengths and weaknesses as well as provide overall measures of intellectual functioning.

Wechsler described some subtests as measuring verbal tasks and others as assessing performance tasks. In general, verbal subtests require knowledge of verbal concepts, whereas performance subtests (see Figure 12.7 on page 203) require familiarity with spatial-relations concepts. Wechsler's scales permit the computation of verbal and performance IQs.

Figure 12.8 on page 204 indicates the labels that Wechsler assigned to various IQ scores and the approximate percentages of the population who attain IQ scores at those levels. Most children's IQ scores cluster around the average. Only about 5% of the population have IQ scores above 130 or below 70.

FIG.12.7 PERFORMANCE ITEMS ON AN INTELLIGENCE TEST

Picture arrangement

These pictures tell a story, but they are in the wrong order. Put them in the right order so that they tell a story.

Picture completion

What part is missing from this picture?

Block design

Put the blocks together to make this picture.

Object assembly

Put the pieces together as quickly as you can.

This figure shows items that resemble those found on the performance subtest of the Wechsler Intelligence Scale for Children (WISC).

FIG.12.8 IDEALIZED DISTRIBUTION OF IQ SCORES

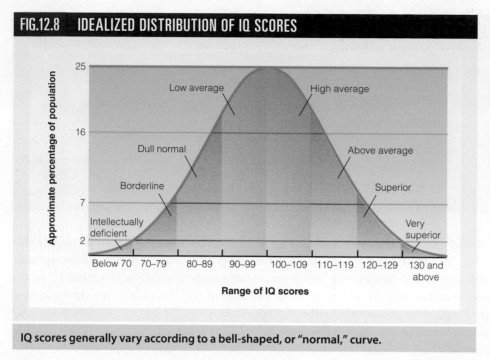

IQ scores generally vary according to a bell-shaped, or "normal," curve.

THE TESTING CONTROVERSY Most psychologists and educational specialists consider intelligence tests to be at least somewhat biased against African Americans and members of lower social classes (Daley & Onwuegbuzie, 2011; Saklofske et al., 2015). If scoring well on intelligence tests requires a certain type of cultural experience, the tests are said to have a **cultural bias**. For this reason, psychologists have tried to construct **culture-free** or culture-fair intelligence tests.

Some tests do not rely on expressive language at all. For example, Raymond Cattell's (1949) Culture-Fair Intelligence Test

cultural bias a factor hypothesized to be present in intelligence tests that provides an advantage for test takers from certain cultural backgrounds.

culture-free descriptive of a test in which cultural biases have been removed.

evaluates reasoning ability through the child's comprehension of the rules that govern a progression of geometric designs, as shown in Figure 12.9.

But culture-free tests have not lived up to their promise. First, middle-class children still outperform lower-class children on them (Daley & Onwuegbuzie, 2011; Saklofske et al., 2015). Middle-class children, for example, are more likely to have basic familiarity with materials used in the testing such as blocks and pencils and paper. They are more likely to have played with blocks (a practice relevant to the Cattell test). Second, culture-free tests do not predict academic success as well as other intelligence tests, and scholastic aptitude remains the central concern of educators (Daley & Onwuegbuzie, 2011; Saklofske et al., 2015).

12-4c PATTERNS OF INTELLECTUAL DEVELOPMENT

Intellectual growth seems to occur in at least two major spurts. The first occurs at about the age of six. It coincides with entry into school and also with the shift from preoperational to concrete- operational thought (Rose & Fischer, 2011). School may help crystallize intellectual functioning at this time. The second spurt occurs at about age 10 or 11.

But once they reach middle childhood, children appear to undergo relatively more stable patterns of gains in intellectual functioning, although there are still spurts (Rose & Fischer, 2011). As a result, intelligence tests gain greater predictive power. In a classic study by Marjorie Honzik and her colleagues (1948), intelligence test scores taken at the age of nine correlated strongly (+0.90) with scores at the age of ten and more moderately (+0.76) with scores at the age of 18.

FIG.12.9 SAMPLE ITEMS FROM CATTELL'S CULTURE-FAIR INTELLIGENCE TEST

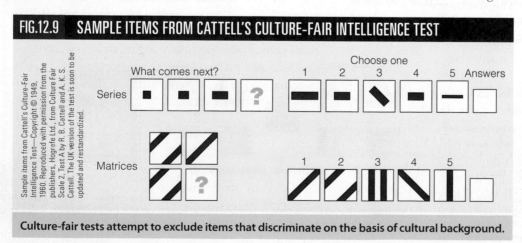

Sample items from Cattell's Culture-Fair Intelligence Test—Copyright © 1949, 1960. Reproduced with permission from the publishers, Hogrefe Ltd., from Culture Fair Scale 2, Test A by R. B. Cattell and A. K. S. Cattell. The UK version of the test is soon to be updated and restandardized.

Culture-fair tests attempt to exclude items that discriminate on the basis of cultural background.

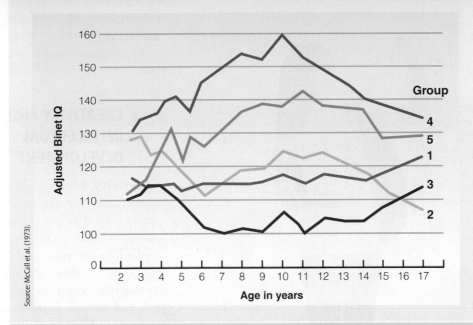

Source: McCall et al. (1973).

In the study, IQ scores remained stable between the ages of 2½ and 17 for only one of five groups, Group 1.

Testing at age 11 even shows a moderate to high relationship with scores at the age of 77 (Deary et al., 2004).

Despite the increased predictive power of intelligence tests during middle childhood, individual differences exist. In the classic Fels Longitudinal Study (see Figure 12.10), two groups of children (Groups 1 and 3) made reasonably consistent gains in intelligence test scores between the ages of 10 and 17, whereas three groups declined. Group 4, children who had shown the most intellectual promise at age ten, went on to show the most precipitous decline, although they still wound up in the highest 2% to 3% of the population (McCall et al., 1973). Many factors influence changes in IQ scores, including changes in the home, socioeconomic circumstances, and education (Rose & Fischer, 2011).

12-4d DIFFERENCES IN INTELLECTUAL DEVELOPMENT

The average IQ score in the United States is close to 100. About half the children in the United States attain IQ scores in the broad average range from 90 to 110. Nearly 95% attain scores between 70 and 130. Children who attain IQ scores below 70 are generally labeled "intellectually disabled." Children who attain scores of 130 or above are usually labeled "gifted."

INTELLECTUAL DISABILITY According to the American Association on Intellectual and Developmental Disabilities (AAIDD, 2016), "Intellectual disability is . . . characterized by significant limitations both in intellectual functioning and in adaptive behavior, which covers many everyday social and practical skills. This disability originates before the age of 18." Intellectual disability involves an IQ score of no more than 70 to 75.

Most of the children (more than 80%) who are intellectually disabled are mildly disabled. Mildly disabled children are the most capable of adjusting to the demands of educational institutions and to society at large (Hodapp et al., 2011). Many mildly disabled children are mainstreamed in regular classrooms rather than placed in special-needs classes.

Children with Down's syndrome are most likely to be moderately intellectually disabled. They can learn to speak; to dress, feed, and clean themselves; and to engage in useful work under supportive conditions, as in a sheltered workshop, but they usually do not acquire skills in reading and math. Severely and profoundly disabled children may not acquire speech and self-help skills and may remain dependent on others for survival.

Some causes of intellectual disability are biological (Carlier & Roubertoux, 2014). Intellectual disability can stem from chromosomal abnormalities, such as Down's syndrome; genetic disorders such as phenylketonuria (PKU); and brain damage (Haier, 2011; Hodapp et al., 2011). Brain damage can have many origins, including childhood accidents and problems during pregnancy. For example, maternal alcohol abuse, malnutrition, or diseases can damage the fetus. In **cultural–familial disability**, children are biologically normal but do not develop age-appropriate behavior at the normal pace because of an impoverished home environment (Carlier & Roubertoux, 2014). They may have little opportunity to interact with adults or play with stimulating toys.

> **cultural–familial disability**
> substandard intellectual performance stemming from lack of opportunity to acquire knowledge and skills.

GIFTEDNESS Giftedness involves more than excellence on the tasks provided by standard intelligence tests. In determining who is gifted, most educators include children who have outstanding abilities; are capable of high performance in a specific academic area, such as language or mathematics; or who show creativity, leadership, distinction in the visual or performing arts, or bodily talents, as in gymnastics and dancing (Reis & Renzulli, 2011).

SOCIOECONOMIC AND ETHNIC DIFFERENCES IN IQ

Research has found differences in IQ scores between socioeconomic and ethnic groups. Lower-class American children obtain IQ scores some 10 to 15 points lower than those obtained by middle- and upper-class children. African American, Latin American, and Native American children all tend to score below the norms for European Americans (Nisbett, 2013). However, as noted by Robinson (2011), "a gap has opened up between an educated middle-class Black America and a poor, undereducated Black America." In other words, we cannot lump all African Americans together. Youth of Asian descent frequently outscore youth of European backgrounds on achievement tests in math and science, including the math portion of the SAT (Suzuki et al., 2011). In addition, people of Asian Indian, Korean, Japanese, Filipino, and Chinese descent are more likely than European Americans, African Americans, and Latin Americans to graduate from high school and complete college (Kurtz-Costes et al., 2014).

Most psychologists believe that such ethnic differences reflect cultural attitudes toward education rather than inborn racial differences (Nisbett, 2009). Asian students and their mothers tend to attribute academic success to hard work, whereas American mothers are more likely to attribute academic success to natural ability (Sternberg & Kaufman, 2011). Thus Asian students may work harder.

12-4e CREATIVITY AND INTELLECTUAL DEVELOPMENT

Creativity is the ability to do things that are novel and useful (Plucker et al., 2015). Creative children and adults can solve problems to which there are no preexisting solutions, no tried and tested formulas ((Kaufman & Plucker, 2011). Creative children take chances, refuse to accept limitations, appreciate art and music, challenge social norms, and examine ideas that other people accept at face value.

Some scientists argue that creativity and innovation require high levels of general intelligence, but the tests we use to measure intelligence and creativity tend to show only a moderate relationship between IQ scores and measures of creativity (Sternberg et al., 2012). Some children who obtain average IQ scores excel in creative areas such as music or art.

creativity a trait characterized by flexibility, ingenuity, and originality.

wong yu liang/Shutterstock.com

FICTION

T (F) Highly intelligent children are creative.

It is not necessarily true that highly intelligent children are creative—unless, of course, one considers creativity to be an aspect of intelligence, as in Robert Sternberg's triarchic theory of intelligence.

Children mainly use convergent thinking to arrive at the correct answers on intelligence tests. In **convergent thinking**, thought is limited to present facts; the problem solver narrows his or her thinking to find the best solution. A child uses convergent thinking to arrive at the right answer to a multiple-choice question or to a question on an intelligence test.

Creative thinking tends to be divergent rather than convergent (Plucker et al., 2015). In **divergent thinking**, the child associates freely to the elements of the problem. (We use divergent thinking when we are trying to generate ideas to answer an essay question or to find keywords to search on the Internet.) Tests of creativity determine how flexible, fluent, and original a person's thinking is. A measure of creativity might ask you how many ways you can classify the following group of names:

Martha   Paul   Jeffry   Sally   Pablo   Joan

Other measures of creativity include suggesting improvements or unusual uses for a familiar toy or object,

naming things that belong in the same class, producing words similar in meaning, and writing different endings for a story.

12-4f DETERMINANTS OF INTELLECTUAL DEVELOPMENT

If heredity is involved in human intelligence, closely related people ought to have more similar IQs than distantly related or unrelated people, even when they are reared separately (Bouchard, 2013). Figure 12.11 on page 207 shows the averaged results of more than 100 studies of IQ and heredity (McGue et al., 1993; Plomin et al., 2013b). The IQ scores of identical (monozygotic; MZ) twins are more alike than the scores for any other pairs, even when the twins have

convergent thinking a thought process that attempts to focus on the single best solution to a problem.

divergent thinking free and fluent association to the elements of a problem.

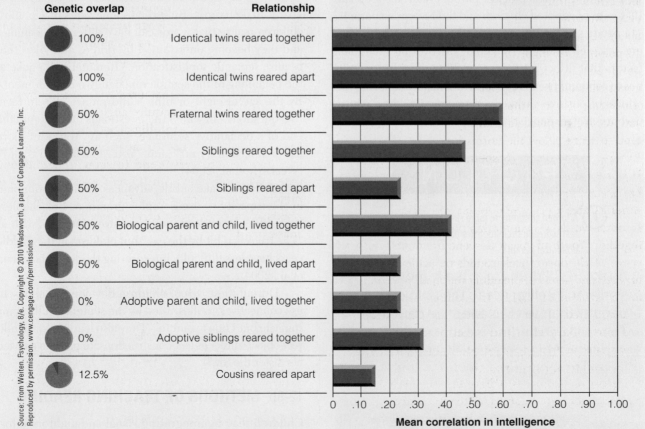

FIG.12.11 FINDINGS OF STUDIES OF THE RELATIONSHIP BETWEEN IQ SCORES AND HEREDITY

Genetic overlap	Relationship
100%	Identical twins reared together
100%	Identical twins reared apart
50%	Fraternal twins reared together
50%	Siblings reared together
50%	Siblings reared apart
50%	Biological parent and child, lived together
50%	Biological parent and child, lived apart
0%	Adoptive parent and child, lived together
0%	Adoptive siblings reared together
12.5%	Cousins reared apart

Source: From Weiten. Psychology, 8/e. Copyright © 2010 Wadsworth, a part of Cengage Learning, Inc. Reproduced by permission. www.cengage.com/permissions

Mean correlation in intelligence

Correlations are stronger for persons who are more closely related and for persons who are reared together or living together, thus supporting both genetic and environmental hypotheses of the origins of intelligence.

been reared apart. The average correlation for MZ twins reared together is +0.85; for those reared apart, it is +0.67. Correlations between the IQ scores of fraternal (dizygotic; DZ) twins, siblings, and parents and children are generally comparable, as is their degree of genetic relationship. The correlations tend to vary from about +0.40 to +0.59.

Overall, studies suggest that the **heritability** of intelligence is between 40% and 60% (Plomin et al., 2013b; Wadsworth et al., 2014). About half of the difference between your IQ score and those of other people can be explained in terms of genetic factors.

Let's return to Figure 12.11. Genetic pairs (such as MZ twins) reared together show higher correlations between IQ scores than similar genetic pairs (such as other MZ twins) who were reared apart. This finding holds for MZ twins, siblings, parents, children, and unrelated people. For this reason, the same group of studies that suggests that heredity plays a role in determining IQ scores also suggests that the environment plays a role.

Classic projects involving adopted children in Colorado, Texas, and Minnesota (Plomin et al., 2013a; Scarr, 1993; Sternberg & Kaufman, 2011) have found a stronger relationship between the IQ scores of adopted children and their biological parents than between the IQ scores of adopted children and their adoptive parents.

Studies of environmental influences on IQ use several research strategies, including discovering situational factors that affect IQ scores, exploring children's abilities to rebound from early deprivation, and exploring the effects of positive early environments. Children whose parents are responsive and provide appropriate play

FICTION

T (F) Adopted children are more similar in intelligence test scores to their adoptive parents than to their biological parents.

Adopted children are actually more similar in intelligence to their biological parents than to their adoptive parents. This research finding is suggestive of an important role for genetic factors in intellectual functioning.

heritability the degree to which the variations in a trait from one person to another can be attributed to genetic factors.

word-recognition method a method for learning to read in which children come to recognize words through repeated exposure to them.

materials and varied experiences during the early years attain higher IQ and achievement test scores (Bradley, 2006). Graduates of Head Start and other preschool programs also show significant gains in IQ and other test scores (Bierman et al., 2014).

Many psychologists believe that heredity and environment interact to influence intelligence (Daley & Onwuegbuzie, 2011; Haier, 2011). An impoverished environment may prevent some children from living up to their potential. An enriched environment may encourage others to realize their potential.

12-5 LANGUAGE DEVELOPMENT AND LITERACY

Children's language ability grows more sophisticated in middle childhood. Children learn to read as well. Many children are exposed to a variety of linguistic experiences, and these experiences affect cognitive development.

12-5a VOCABULARY AND GRAMMAR

By the age of six, the child's vocabulary has expanded to nearly 10,000 words. By seven to nine years of age, most children realize that words can have different meanings, and they become entertained by riddles and jokes that require semantic sophistication. (Remember the joke at the beginning of the section on cognitive development.) By the age of eight or nine, children are able to form "tag questions," in which the question is tagged on to the end of a declarative sentence, such as "You want more ice cream, don't you?" and "You're sick, aren't you?" (Weckerly et al., 2004).

Children make subtle advances in articulation and in the capacity to use complex grammar. Preschoolers have difficulty understanding passive sentences such as "The truck was hit by the car," but children in the middle years have less difficulty interpreting them (Aschermann et al., 2004).

During these years, children develop the ability to use connectives, as illustrated by the sentence "I'll eat my spinach, but I don't want to." They also learn to form indirect object–direct object constructions. (e.g., "She showed her sister the toy.")

12-5b METHODS OF TEACHING READING

Children read by integrating visual and auditory information (they associate what they see with sounds), whether they use the word-recognition method or the phonetic method. The **word-recognition method** associates visual stimuli such as *cat* and *Robert* with the sound combinations that produce the spoken words. This capacity is usually acquired by rote learning, or extensive repetition.

In the **phonetic method**, children learn to associate written letters and letter combinations (such as *ph* or *sh*) with the sounds they indicate. Then they sound out words. The phonetic method provides skills children can use to decode new words, but some children learn more rapidly at early ages through the word-recognition method. The phonetic method can slow them down with familiar words. Most children and adults read familiar words by word recognition and make some effort to sound out new words.

Some English words can be read only by recognition, as with *one* and *two*. This method is useful when it comes to words such as *danger*, *stop*, *poison*, and a child's name, because it provides children with a basic **sight vocabulary**. But decoding skills help children read new words on their own.

12-5c BILINGUALISM: LINGUISTIC PERSPECTIVES ON THE WORLD

In 2015, 50 to 60 million Americans spoke a language other than English at home (U.S. Census Bureau, 2015). Thirty-five to forty million people speak Spanish, and more than a million each speak Chinese, French, Vietnamese, German, and Korean. Figure 12.12 estimates the number of languages spoken in major metropolitan areas of the United States.

A century ago it was widely believed that children reared in **bilingual** homes were delayed in their cognitive development. The theory was that mental capacity is limited, so people who store two linguistic systems are crowding their mental abilities (Barac & Bialystok, 2011). Bilingual children do show some differences with monolingual children, but this may largely be because the vocabularies used at home and in the school are not identical (Bialystok et al., 2010). Bilingual children do not generally encounter more academic problems than children who speak only one language (Barac & Bialystok, 2011). There is some "mixing" of languages by bilingual children (Gonzalez, 2005), but they can generally separate the two languages from an early age. At least half the children in the United States who speak

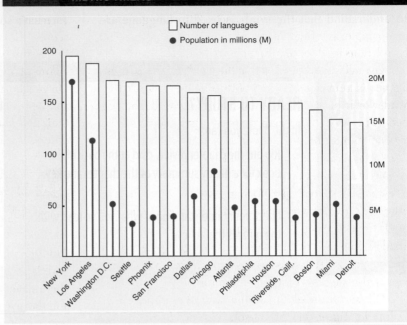

FIG.12.12 NUMBER OF LANGUAGES SPOKEN IN THE 15 LARGEST METRO AREAS

☐ Number of languages
● Population in millions (M)

U.S. Census Bureau, https://www.census.gov/content/dam/Census/newsroom/releases/2015/cb15-185_graphic.jpg

Spanish in the home are proficient in both languages (Shin & Bruno, 2003).

Today most linguists consider it advantageous for children to be bilingual because knowledge of more

FICTION

T (F) Bilingual children have more academic problems than children who speak only one language.

It is not true that **bilingual** children have more academic problems than children who speak only one language. There is some "mixing" of languages by bilingual children, but they can generally separate the two languages from an early age.

phonetic method a method for learning to read in which children decode the sounds of words based on their knowledge of the sounds of letters and letter combinations.

sight vocabulary words that are immediately recognized on the basis of familiarity with their overall shapes, rather than decoded.

bilingual using or capable of using two languages with nearly equal or equal facility.

than one language contributes to the complexity of the child's cognitive processes (Barac & Bialystok, 2011). For example, bilingual children are more likely to understand that the symbols used in language are arbitrary. Monolingual children are more likely to think erroneously that the word *dog* is somehow intertwined with the nature of the beast. Bilingual children therefore have somewhat more cognitive flexibility.

STUDY TOOLS 12

READY TO STUDY?

In the book, you can:

☐ Rip out the chapter review card at the back of the book for a handy summary of the chapter and key terms.

☐ Check your understanding of what you've read with the quizzes that follow.

ONLINE AT CENGAGEBRAIN.COM YOU CAN:

☐ Collect StudyBits while you read and study the chapter.

☐ Quiz yourself on key concepts.

☐ Find videos for further exploration.

☐ Prepare for tests with CDEV2 Flash Cards as well as those you create.

SELF-ASSESSMENTS

Fill-Ins

Answers can be found in the back of the book.

1. The good-boy/good-girl orientation is characteristic of the _____ level of moral development.

2. In _____ memory, forgetting occurs through decay.

3. The Binet–Simon IQ score is computed by dividing _____ age by chronological age and then multiplying the result by 100.

4. The Wechsler Intelligence Scales have both verbal items and _____ items.

5. In the United States, the language other than English most likely to be spoken in the home is _____.

6. In the _____ method of teaching reading, teachers associate visual stimuli such as *dog* and *John* with the sound combinations that produce the spoken word.

7. Spearman suggested that the behaviors we consider intelligent have a common underlying factor, which he labeled _____.

8. Children who realize that if A exceeds B and B exceeds C, then A exceeds C, are showing understanding of the principle of _____.

9. An IQ is a _____ on an intelligence test.

10. According to Piaget, children who judge right and wrong only in terms of the amount of harm done are said to be in the stage of _____ morality.

Multiple Choice

1. The ability to ignore distractions increases most dramatically between
   a. 6 and 9 years of age.
   b. 9 and 12 years of age.
   c. 12 and 16 years of age.
   d. early adulthood and late adulthood.

2. Children are said to be intellectually disabled when they obtain IQ scores of no more than
   a. 70–75.   c. 90–95.
   b. 80–85.   d. 100.

3. The group most likely to show similarity in IQ scores is
   a. children and their adoptive parents.
   b. children and their biological parents.
   c. fraternal twins reared together.
   d. identical twins reared apart.

4. Which of the following theorists considers bodily–kinesthetic ability to be an intelligence?
   a. Sternberg.   c. Gardner.
   b. Wechsler.   d. Terman.

5. The best way to keep information in working memory is by
   a. sensory input.
   b. rehearsal.
   c. hierarchical organization.
   d. decay.

6. At the preconventional level of moral development, children judge what is right and wrong on the basis of
   a. universal abstract principles.
   b. weighing human needs against social needs.
   c. obedience and the prospect of punishment.
   d. one's duty to others, as set down in the law.

7. Each of the following is a kind of intelligence according to the triarchic theory, except
   a. creativity.
   b. academic ability.
   c. street smarts.
   d. regulation of emotions.

8. A judge demands "Order! Order in the court!"? Th defendant yells out "A hamburger and french fries, Your Honor." Children at about the age of 11 "get" the joke because they
   a. can understand ambiguities in the grammatical structure of language.
   b. have advanced academic ability.
   c. can engage in transitivity.
   d. have above-average intelligence.

9. At about the ages of 9 to 11, children can focus on the amount of wrongdoing done by a person and also on the intentions of the wrongdoer. According to Piaget, the child is demonstrating
   a. moral realism.
   b. conventional moral reasoning.
   c. autonomous morality.
   d. postconventional moral reasoning.

10. Remembering new information by relating it to what is already known is an example of
    a. rote rehearsal.
    b. an elaborative strategy.
    c. analytical intelligence.
    d. comprehension.

13 | Middle Childhood: Social and Emotional Development

Mat Hayward/Shutterstock.com

LEARNING OUTCOMES

After studying this chapter, you will be able to . . .

13-1 Explain theories of social and emotional development in middle childhood

13-2 Discuss the influences of the family on social development in middle childhood

13-3 Discuss the influences of peers on social development in middle childhood

13-4 Describe the influence of the school on social development in middle childhood

13-5 Discuss social and emotional problems that tend to develop in middle childhood

After you finish this chapter, go to **PAGE 229** for **STUDY TOOLS**

People are social creatures, and social relationships, which begin in infancy between the infant and one or two central caregivers, widen to emphasize the role of peers. Entry into school exposes the child to the influence of teachers. Relationships with parents change as children develop greater independence.

13-1 THEORIES OF SOCIAL AND EMOTIONAL DEVELOPMENT IN MIDDLE CHILDHOOD

The major theories of personality have had less to say about this age group than about the other periods of childhood and adolescence. Nevertheless, some common threads emerge.

13-1a PSYCHOANALYTIC THEORY

According to Freud, children in the middle years are in the **latency stage**. Freud believed that sexual feelings remain repressed (unconscious) during this period. Children use this period to focus on developing intellectual, social, and other culturally valued skills.

Erik Erikson, like Freud, saw the major developmental task of middle childhood as the acquisition of cognitive and social skills. Erikson labeled this stage **industry versus inferiority**. Children who are able to master the challenges of the middle years develop a sense of industry or competence. Children who have difficulties in school or with peer relationships may develop a sense of inferiority.

latency stage in psychoanalytic theory, the fourth stage of psychosexual development, characterized by repression of sexual impulses and development of skills.

industry versus inferiority a stage of psychosocial development in Erikson's theory occurring in middle childhood. Mastery of tasks leads to a sense of industry, whereas failure produces feelings of inferiority.

social cognition development of children's understanding of the relationship between the self and others.

13-1b SOCIAL COGNITIVE THEORY

Social cognitive theory focuses on the importance of rewards and modeling in middle childhood. During these years, children depend less on external rewards and punishments and increasingly regulate their own behavior. Children are exposed to an increasing variety of models. Not only parents but also teachers, other adults, peers, and symbolic models (such as TV characters or the heroine in a story) serve as influential models (Grusec, 2015; Richert et al., 2011).

13-1c COGNITIVE-DEVELOPMENTAL THEORY AND SOCIAL COGNITION

According to Piaget, middle childhood coincides with the stage of concrete operations and is partly characterized by a decline in egocentrism and an expansion of the capacity to view the world and oneself from other people's perspectives. This cognitive advance affects the child's social relationships (Slaughter, 2011).

Social cognition refers to perception of the social world, and our concern is the development of children's perspective-taking skills (Bengtsson & Arvidsson, 2011). Robert Selman and his colleagues (Kwok & Selman, 2013) studied the development of these skills by presenting children with a social dilemma such as the following:

Holly is an eight-year-old girl who likes to climb trees. She is the best tree climber in the neighborhood. One day while climbing down from a tall

TRUTH OR FICTION?

T	F	Children's self-esteem tends to rise in middle childhood.
T	F	The daughters of employed women are more achievement-oriented and set higher career goals for themselves than the daughters of unemployed women.
T	F	In middle childhood, popular children tend to be attractive and relatively mature for their age.
T	F	Some children blame themselves for all the problems in their lives, whether they deserve the blame or not.
T	F	It is better for children with school phobia to remain at home until the origins of the problem are uncovered and resolved.

tree, she falls off the bottom branch but does not hurt herself. Her father sees her fall. He is upset and asks her to promise not to climb trees any more. Holly promises. Later that day, Holly and her friends meet Sean. Sean's kitten is caught up in a tree and can't get down. Something has to be done right away, or the kitten may fall. Holly is the only one who climbs trees well enough to reach the kitten and get it down, but she remembers her promise to her father.

—Selman, (1980, p. 36)

The children then were asked questions such as "How will Holly's father feel if he finds out she climbed the tree?" Based on the children's responses, Selman (1976) described five levels of perspective-taking skills in childhood (see Table 13.1). Children with better perspective-taking skills tend to have better peer relationships (Abrams et al., 2014; Smith & Rose, 2011).

13-1d DEVELOPMENT OF THE SELF-CONCEPT IN MIDDLE CHILDHOOD

In early childhood, children's self-concepts focus on concrete external traits, such as appearance, activities, and living situations. But as children undergo the cognitive developments of middle childhood, more abstract internal traits, or personality traits, begin to play a role. Social relationships and group memberships take on significance (Bukowski & Veronneau, 2014; Rosen & Patterson, 2011).

An investigative method called the Twenty Statements Test bears out this progression. Children are given a sheet of paper with the question "Who am I?" and 20 spaces in which to write answers. Consider the answers of a 9-year-old boy and an 11-year-old girl:

The nine-year-old boy: My name is Bruce C. I have brown eyes. I have brown hair. I have brown eyebrows. I'm nine years old. I LOVE? sports. I have seven people in my family. I have great? eye site. I have lots! of friends. I live on 1923 Pinecrest Drive. I'm going on ten in September. I'm a boy. I have a uncle that is almost seven feet tall. My school is Pinecrest. My teacher is Mrs. V. I play hockey! I'm also the smartest boy in the class. I LOVE! food. I love fresh air. I LOVE school.

The 11-year-old girl: My name is A. I'm a human being. I'm a girl. I'm a truthful person. I'm not pretty. I do so-so in my studies. I'm a very good

Level	Approximate Age (Years)	What Happens
0	3–6	Children are egocentric and do not realize that other people have perspectives different from their own. A child of this age will typically say that Holly will save the kitten because she likes kittens and that her father will be happy because he likes kittens too. The child assumes that everyone feels as she does.
1	5–9*	Children understand that people in different situations may have different perspectives. The child still assumes that only one perspective is "right." A child might say that Holly's father would be angry if he did not know why she climbed the tree. But if she told him why, he would understand. The child recognizes that the father's perspective may differ from Holly's because of lack of information. But once he has the information, he will assume the "right" (i.e., Holly's) perspective.
2	7–12*	The child understands that people may think or feel differently because they have different values or ideas. The child also recognizes that others are capable of understanding the child's own perspective. Therefore, the child is better able to anticipate reactions of others. The typical child of this age might say that Holly knows that her father will understand why she climbed the tree and that he therefore will not punish her.
3	10–15*	The child finally realizes that both she and another person can consider each other's point of view at the same time. The child may say something similar to this reasoning: Holly's father will think that Holly shouldn't have climbed the tree. But now that he has heard her side of the story, he would feel that she was doing what she thought was right. Holly realizes that her father will consider how she felt.
4	12 and above*	The child realizes that mutual perspective taking does not always lead to agreement. The perspectives of the larger social group also must be considered. A child of this age might say that society expects children to obey their parents and therefore that Holly should realize why her father might punish her.

*Ages may overlap.
Source: Selman (1976).

Radius Images/Getty Images

cellist. I'm a very good pianist. I'm a little bit tall for my age. I like several boys. I like several girls. . . . I play tennis. I am a very good musician. . . . I'm always ready to be friends with anybody. Mostly I'm good, but I lose my temper. I'm not well liked by some girls and boys. I don't know if boys like me or not. Montemayor, R., & Eisen, M. (1977).

Only the nine-year-old lists his age and address, discusses his family, and focuses on physical traits, such as eye color, in his self-definition. The nine-year-old mentions his likes, which can be considered rudimentary psychological traits, but they are tied to the concrete, as would be expected of a concrete-operational child. The 9- and 11-year-olds list their competencies. The 11-year-old's struggle to bolster her self-esteem—her insistence on her musical abilities despite her qualms about her attractiveness—shows a greater concern with psychological traits and social relationships.

SELF-ESTEEM As children enter middle childhood, they evaluate their self-worth in many different areas (Rosen & Patterson, 2011). Preschoolers tend to see themselves as generally "good at doing things" or not. But by five to seven years of age, children are able to judge their performance in seven different areas: physical ability, physical appearance, peer relationships, parent relationships, reading, math, and general school performance. They also report a general self-concept (Harter, 2012).

Children's self-esteem declines throughout middle childhood, reaching a low ebb at 12 or 13. Then it increases during adolescence (Harter, 2012). What accounts for the decline? Because preschoolers are egocentric, their self-concepts may be unrealistic. By middle childhood, children can compare themselves with other children and arrive at a more honest and critical self-appraisal. Girls tend to have more positive self-concepts regarding reading, general academics, and helping others than boys. Boys tend to have more positive self-concepts

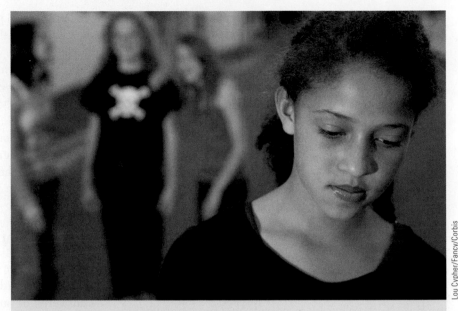

Children's self-esteem tends to decline during middle childhood, in part because they come to evaluate their physical appearance and their performance in academic and social domains more realistically.

in math, physical ability, and physical appearance (Tobin et al., 2010; Underwood & Rosen, 2011).

FICTION

T **(F)** Children's self-esteem tends to rise in middle childhood.

It is not true that children's self-esteem rises during middle childhood. In fact, it tends to decline, reaching a low ebb at 12 or 13, as children confront more realistic evaluations of their strengths and shortcomings.

Authoritative parenting apparently contributes to children's self-esteem (Chan & Koo, 2011; Scales, 2014). Children with a favorable self-image tend to have parents who are restrictive, involved, and loving. Children with low self-esteem are more likely to have authoritarian or rejecting–neglecting parents.

Social acceptance by peers is related to self-perceived competence in academic, social, and athletic domains (Cillessen & Bellmore, 2011). Parents and classmates have an equally strong effect on children's self-esteem in middle childhood. Friends and teachers have relatively less influence but also matter (Harter, 2012).

Lou Cypher/Fancy/Corbis

LEARNED HELPLESSNESS One outcome of low self-esteem in academics is known as **learned helplessness**. Learned helplessness is the acquired belief that one is unable to obtain the rewards that one seeks. "Helpless" children tend to quit following failure, whereas children who believe in their own ability tend to persist or change their strategies (Steca et al., 2014). One reason for this difference is that "helpless" children believe that success is due more to ability than effort and that they have little ability in a particular area. Consequently, persistence seems futile. Helpless children typically obtain lower grades and lower scores on IQ and achievement tests (Burnette et al., 2013; Dweck, 2015).

A gender difference emerges in mathematics (Else-Quest et al., 2013; Hyde, 2014). Researchers have found that even when girls are performing as well as boys in math and science, they have less confidence in their ability (Hall, 2012). Why? Many parents hold the stereotype that girls have less math ability than boys despite their daughters' demonstrated skills.

13-2 THE FAMILY

In middle childhood, the family continues to play a key role in socializing the child, although peers, teachers, and other outsiders begin to play a greater role (Dunn, 2015; Grusec & Davidov, 2015).

13-2a PARENT–CHILD RELATIONSHIPS

Parent–child interactions focus on some new concerns during middle childhood. They include school-related matters, assignment of chores, and peer activities (Grusec & Davidov, 2015). Parents do less monitoring of children's activities and provide less direct feedback than they did in the preschool years. Control is gradually transferred from parent to child in a process known as **coregulation** (Maughan, 2011). Children begin to internalize the standards of their parents.

Children and parents spend less time together in middle childhood than in the preschool years. Children spend more time with their mothers than with their fathers. Mothers' interactions with school-age children continue to revolve around caregiving; fathers are relatively more involved in recreation (Keown & Palmer, 2014; Demby et al., 2015).

Because of their developing cognitive ability, 10- to 12-year-olds evaluate their parents more harshly than they did in early childhood (Grusec & Davidov, 2015). But throughout middle childhood, children rate their parents as their best source of emotional support (Grusec, 2015).

13-2b LESBIAN AND GAY PARENTS

"Where did you get that beautiful necklace?" I asked the little girl in the pediatrician's office. "From my Moms," she answered. It turned out that her family consisted of two women, each of whom had a biological child, one girl and one boy.

Research on lesbian and gay parenting has fallen into two general categories: the general adjustment of children and whether the children of lesbian and gay parents are more likely than other children to be lesbian or gay themselves. Research by Charlotte Patterson and her colleagues (e.g., Farr & Patterson, 2013) has generally found that the psychological adjustment of children of lesbian and gay parents is comparable to that of children of heterosexual parents. Despite the stigma attached to homosexuality, lesbians and gay men are as likely to sustain positive family relationships (Tasker & Granville, 2011).

Mahdees Mahjoob / Alamy Stock Photo

Being reared by lesbian or gay parents has not been shown to influence children's adjustment or their sexual orientation. But LGBT families, as lesbian, gay, or transgender individuals, fare better in supportive communities.

learned helplessness an acquired (hence, learned) belief that one is unable to control one's environment.

coregulation a gradual transferring of control from parent to child, beginning in middle childhood.

However, we must also note that the psychological adjustment of lesbian and gay couples and their children is superior in communities in which there is social support for lesbian and gay families in the area (Lick et al., 2012; Oswald et al., 2013). Locales in which there is greater density of lesbian and gay populations—such as major metropolitan areas—generally offer more support.

What of the sexual orientation of the children of lesbian and gay parents? Green (1978) observed 37 children and young adults, age 3 to 20, who were being reared—or had been reared—by lesbian or **transgender** parents. All but one of the children reported or recalled preferences for toys, clothing, and friends (male or female) that were typical for their gender and age. All the 13 older children who reported sexual fantasies or sexual behavior were heterosexually oriented.

13-2c GENERATION X OR GENERATION EX? WHAT HAPPENS TO CHILDREN WHOSE PARENTS GET DIVORCED?

Is this the time of "Generation Ex"—a generation characterized by ex-wives and ex-husbands? More than one million American children each year experience the divorce of their parents. Nearly 40% of European American children and 75% of African American children in the United States who are born to married parents will spend at least part of their childhoods in single-parent families as a result of divorce (U.S. Bureau of the Census, 2015).

Superstock / Alamy Stock Photo

Divorce may be tough on parents; it can be even tougher on children (Kim, 2011; Moon, 2011). No longer do children eat with both parents. No longer do they go to ball games, movies, or Disneyland with both of them. The parents are now often supporting two households, resulting in fewer resources for the children. Many children who live with their mothers scrape by—or fail to scrape by—in poverty. The mother who was once available may become an occasional visitor, spending more time at work and placing the kids in day care for extended periods.

Most children live with their mothers after a divorce. Some fathers remain devoted to their children despite the split, but others tend to spend less time with their children as time goes on. Not only does the drop-off in paternal attention deprive children of activities and social interactions, but it also saps their self-esteem: "Why doesn't Daddy love me anymore? What's wrong with me?"

The children of divorce are more likely to have conduct disorders, to abuse drugs, and to have poor grades in school (Amato & Anthony, 2014; Hicks et al., 2013). Their physical health may decline (Brockmann, 2013). By and large, the fallout for children is worst during the first year after the breakup. Children tend to rebound after a couple of years (Malone et al., 2004).

LIFE IN STEPFAMILIES: HIS, HERS, THEIRS, AND . . . Most divorced people remarry, usually while the children are young. More than one in three American children will spend part of his or her childhood in a stepfamily (U.S. Bureau of the Census, 2015).

The rule of thumb about the effects of living in stepfamilies is that there is no rule of thumb (Harvey & Fine, 2011). Many stepparents treat stepchildren as though they were biologically their own (Marsiglio, 2004), but there are also some risks to living in stepfamilies, such as the greater risk of being physically abused by stepparents than by biological parents (Adler-Baeder, 2006). There is also a significantly higher incidence—by a factor of eight—of sexual abuse by stepparents than natural parents.

Why do we find these risks in stepfamilies? According to evolutionary psychologists, people often behave as though they want their genes to flourish in the next generation. Thus, it could be that stepparents are less devoted to rearing other people's children.

SHOULD WE REMAIN MARRIED "FOR THE SAKE OF THE CHILDREN"? Many people believe—for moral reasons—that marriage and family life must be permanent, no matter what. People must consider the moral aspects of divorce in the light of their own value systems. But—from a purely psychological perspective— what should bickering parents do? The answer

> **transgender** referring to people who feel as though they are persons of the other sex who are 'trapped' in the body of the wrong sex. Some transgender individuals (also called 'trans') are content to adopt the clothing and cosmetic appearance of people of the other sex; others undergo hormone treatments and surgery to achieve the body shape and external physical traits of persons of the other sex.

Talking to Children About Divorce

Talking to children about a divorce is difficult. The following tips can help both the child and parents with the challenge and stress of these conversations:

▶ **Do not keep it a secret or wait until the last minute.**

▶ **Tell your children together with your spouse.**

▶ **Keep things simple and straightforward.**

▶ **Tell them the divorce is not their fault.**

▶ **Admit that this will be sad and upsetting for everyone.**

▶ **Reassure your children that you both still love them and will always be their parents.**

▶ **Do not discuss each other's faults or problems with the children.**

Source: American Academy of Child & Adolescent Psychiatry (2008).

seems to depend largely on how they behave in front of the children. Research shows that severe parental bickering is linked to the same kinds of problems that children experience when their parents get separated or divorced (Troxel & Holt-Lunstad, 2013). When children are exposed to adult or marital conflict, they display a biological "alarm reaction": their heart rate, blood pressure, and sweating rise sharply (El-Sheikh, 2007). Therefore, a number of researchers acknowledge that some children tend to fare better after parents who fight continually get divorced (Amato & Anthony, 2014)

13-2e THE EFFECTS OF MATERNAL EMPLOYMENT

Why is this section labeled "The Effects of Maternal Employment"? Why not "Parental Employment" or "Paternal Employment"? Perhaps because of the traditional role of women as homemakers. A half-century ago, most women remained in the home, but today, nearly three out of four married mothers of children under age 18 are employed, as are four out of five divorced, separated, or widowed mothers (O'Brien et al., 2014).

Many commentators have been concerned about the effects of maternal employment on children. In part, this has been based on more traditional values that argue that the mother ought to remain in the home. Research results are mixed. Some studies suggest that maternal employment can have negative effects on children (Belsky, 2006b). Other studies suggest that

employed mothers provide greater learning opportunities for their children (Buehler et al., 2014).

One common belief is that Mom's being in the workforce rather than in the home leads to delinquency. Researchers using data on 707 adolescents, ages 12 to 14, from the National Longitudinal Survey of Youth examined whether the occupational status of a mother was connected with delinquent behavior (Vander Ven & Cullen, 2004). They found that maternal employment per se made no difference, but delinquency was connected with lack of supervision. Similar results have been found in the European Union (Cabrera et al., 2014).

There are benefits for maternal employment. Daughters of employed women are more achievement-oriented and set higher career goals for themselves than daughters of nonworking women (Greene et al., 2013). Children of working mothers tend to be more prosocial, less anxious, and flexible in their gender role stereotypes (Goldberg et al., 2012; Greene et al., 2013).

TRUTH

(T) F The daughters of employed women are more achievement-oriented and set higher career goals for themselves than the daughters of unemployed women.

It is true that the daughters of employed women are more achievement-oriented and set higher career goals for themselves than the daughters of unemployed women. One possible explanation is that the mothers serve as role models for their daughters.

13-3 PEER RELATIONSHIPS

Families exert the most powerful influence on a child during his or her first few years (Carr, 2011; Grusec, 2015). But as children move into middle childhood, peers take on more importance (Wentzel & Muenks, 2016).

13-3a PEERS AS SOCIALIZATION INFLUENCES

Parents can provide children only with experience relating to adults. Children profit from experience with peers because peers have interests and skills that reflect the child's generation (Eivers et al., 2012; Gauvain, 2016).

Peers afford practice in cooperating, relating to leaders, and coping with aggressive impulses, including their own. Peers can be important confidants (Dunn, 2015; Wentzel, 2014). Peers, like parents, help children learn what types of impulses—affectionate, aggressive, and so on—they can safely express. Children who are at odds with their parents can turn to peers as sounding boards. They can compare feelings and experiences. When children share troubling ideas and experiences with peers, they realize they are normal and not alone (Wentzel, 2014).

13-3b PEER ACCEPTANCE AND REJECTION

Acceptance or rejection by peers is important in childhood because problems with peers affect adjustment later on (Dunn, 2015; Wentzel, 2014). Popular children tend to be attractive, mature for their age, and successful in sports or academics, although attractiveness seems to be more important for girls than boys (Rennels & Langlois, 2014). Socially speaking, popular children are friendly, nurturant, cooperative, helpful, and socially skillful (Rodkin et al., 2013; Xie et al., 2006). They also have high self-esteem.

TRUTH

 T F In middle childhood, popular children tend to be attractive and relatively mature for their age.

It is true that popular children tend to be attractive and relatively mature for their age—although, in the case of attractiveness, the statement applies more to girls than to boys.

Children who are aggressive and disrupt group activities are sometimes rejected by peers (Boivin et al., 2005). However, some aggressive children are popular; there is apparently no general rule (Ojanen & Findley-Van Nostrand, 2014; Troop-Gordon & Ranney, 2014).

13-3c DEVELOPMENT OF FRIENDSHIPS

In the preschool years and early years of middle childhood, friendships are based on geographic closeness or proximity. Friendships are superficial; quickly formed, easily broken. What matters are shared activities and who has the swing set or sandbox (Berndt, 2004; MacEvoy et al., 2016).

Between ages 8 and 11, children recognize the importance of friends meeting each other's needs and possessing desirable traits (Lansford et al., 2014). They are more likely to say that friends are nice and share their interests. They increasingly pick friends who are similar in behavior and personality. Trustworthiness, mutual understanding, and a willingness to disclose personal information characterize friendships in middle childhood and beyond (Lansford et al., 2014). Girls tend to develop closer friendships than boys, to seek confidants (Zarbatany et al., 2000).

Robert Selman (1980) described five stages in children's changing concepts of friendship (see Table 13.2). The stages correspond to the levels of perspective-taking skills discussed earlier.

Friends behave differently with each other than with other children. School-age friends are more verbal, attentive, relaxed, and responsive to each other during play than are mere acquaintances (Saldarriage et al. (2015)). Conflicts can occur among friends, but when they do, they tend to be less intense and get resolved in positive ways (Bowker et al., 2011).

TABLE 13.2	STAGES IN CHILDREN'S CONCEPTS OF FRIENDSHIP		
Stage	Name	Approximate Age (Years)	What Happens
0	Momentary physical interaction	3–6	Children remain egocentric. Their concept of a friend is one who likes to play with the same things and lives nearby.
1	One-way assistance	5–9*	Children are less egocentric but view a friend as someone who does what they want.
2	Fair-weather cooperation	7–12*	Friends are viewed as doing things for one another, but the focus remains on self-interest.
3	Intimate and mutual sharing	10–15*	The focus is on the relationship rather than on the individuals separately. Friendship is viewed as providing mutual support over a long period of time.
4	Autonomous interdependence	12 and above*	Children (adolescents, and adults) understand that friendships grow and change as people change and that they may need different friends to satisfy different needs.

*Ages can overlap
Source: Selman (1980).

Bullying: An Epidemic of Pain

I was called really horrible, profane names very loudly in front of huge crowds of people, and my schoolwork suffered at one point. . . . I didn't want to go to class. And I was a straight-A student, so there was a certain point in my high school years where I just couldn't even focus on class because I was so embarrassed all the time. I was so ashamed of who I was.

—Lady Gaga[1]

Eleven-year-old Michael Wilson committed suicide in 2011. His family found him with a plastic bag tied around his head (Nurwisah, 2011). Michael had had muscular dystrophy. He used a walker to get by in school. At school, a 12-year-old mugged him for his iPhone. A few months before his death, Michael said, "If I have to go back to that school, I'll kill myself." And he did.

Twelve-year-old Rebecca killed herself by climbing a platform at an abandoned cement plant and jumping off. She had received a continuous stream of threatening and taunting text messages and cellphone photo-sharing—aspects of all too common **cyberbullying** (Alvarez, 2013).

Bullying has devastating effects on the school atmosphere. It transforms the perception of school from a safe place into a violent place (Lorenzo-Blanco et al., 2016). Nine-year-old Stephanie had gotten into a disagreement with Susan, and Susan had told her she would beat her mercilessly if she showed up at school again. To highlight her warning, Susan had shoved Stephanie across the hall. Stephanie did not know it, but, ironically, Susan was also bullied from time to time by a couple of other girls at school. Stephanie's response was to refuse to go to school, not suicide.

Was there something unusual about Michael, Rebecca, and Stephanie's situations? Sadly, no. Bullying is everywhere and there are all too many suicides from victims who are bullied on Facebook and in other ways on the Internet (Kowalski et al., 2014). Suicide is especially common among middle schoolers who have not yet developed a strong sense of who they are and where they are going in life (Henry et al., 2014).

cyberbullying the use of electronic devices such as cellphones, computers, and tablets to transmit threatening and taunting messages.

Lady Gaga may be a superstar now, but bullying led her to have serious self-doubts in school.

Boys are more likely than girls to be bullies, but many girls engage in bullying (Juvonen & Graham, 2014). All in all, at least half of middle school students in the United States have been exposed to bullying (Baly et al., 2014).

Many bullies have things in common. Their achievement tends to be lower than average, such that peer approval or deference might be more important to them than academics (Espelage & Colbert, 2016; Leiner et al., 2104). Bullies are more likely to come from homes of lower socioeconomic status with parental violence (Perren & Alsaker, 2006). Bullying is also associated with more frequent diagnoses of conduct disorder, oppositional defiant disorder, and attention deficit hyperactivity disorder (ADHD) (Leiner et al., 2014). Victims of bullies, like Michael, Rebecca, and Stephanie, are commonly anxious and depressed, and they often find other peers avoiding them, so that the others can avoid getting involved (Howard et al., 2014).

[1] In Nicholas D. Kristof. (2012, March 1). Born to not get bullied. *The New York Times*, p. A31.

Children in middle childhood will typically say they have more than one "best" friend (Berndt et al., 1989; Bowker et al., 2011). Nine-year-olds report an average of four best friends. Best friends tend to be more alike than other friends. In middle childhood, boys tend to play in larger groups than girls. Children's friendships are almost exclusively with others of the same gender, continuing the trend of gender segregation.

13-4 THE SCHOOL

The school exerts a powerful influence on many aspects of the child's development. Schools, like parents, set limits on behavior, make demands for mature behavior, attempt to communicate, and are oriented toward nurturing positive physical, social, and cognitive development. Schools influence children's IQ scores, achievement motivation, and career aspirations (Kaplan & Owings, 2015; Woolfolk, 2013). Schools also influence social and moral development (Kaplan & Owings, 2015).

Schools are also competitive environments, and children who do too well—as well as students who do not do well enough—may incur the resentment or ridicule of others.

13-4a ENTRY INTO SCHOOL

Children must master many new tasks when they start school—new academic challenges, new school and teacher expectations, fitting into a new peer group, coping with extended separation from parents, and developing increased self-control and self-help skills.

How well prepared are children to enter school? School readiness involves at least three critical factors:

1. The diversity and inequity of children's early life experiences

2. Individual differences in young children's development and learning

3. The degree to which schools establish reasonable and appropriate expectations of children's capabilities when they enter school

Some children enter school less well prepared than others. Kindergarten teachers report that many students begin school unprepared to learn (Kaplan & Owings, 2015; Woolfolk, 2013). Most teachers say that children often lack the language skills needed to succeed. Poor health care and nutrition, and lack of adequate parental stimulation and support, place many children at risk for academic failure before they enter school.

13-4b THE SCHOOL ENVIRONMENT: SETTING THE STAGE FOR SUCCESS OR . . .

Research summaries (Kaplan & Owings, 2015; Patrick et al., 2016) indicate that an effective school has the following characteristics:

▶ An active, energetic principal

▶ An orderly but not oppressive atmosphere

▶ Empowerment of teachers; that is, teachers participating in decision making

▶ Teachers with high expectations that children will learn

▶ A curriculum that emphasizes academics

▶ Frequent assessment of student performance

▶ Empowerment of students; that is, students participating in setting goals, making decisions, and engaging in cooperative learning activities

Certain aspects of the school environment are important as well. One key factor is class size. Smaller classes permit students to receive more individual attention and are particularly useful in teaching the "basics"—reading, writing, and arithmetic—to students at risk for academic failure (Kaplan & Owings, 2015; Wentzel & Ramani, 2016).

13-4b TEACHERS

Teachers, like parents, set limits, make demands, communicate values, and foster development. They are powerful role models and dispensers of reinforcement. After all, children spend several hours each weekday with teachers.

TEACHER INFLUENCES ON STUDENT PERFORMANCE Achievement is enhanced when teachers expect students to master the curriculum, allocate most of the available time to academic activities, and manage the classroom effectively. Students learn more in classes when they are actively instructed or supervised by teachers than when they are working on their own. The most effective teachers ask questions, give personalized feedback, and provide opportunities for drill and practice (Kaplan & Owings, 2015; Fox & Dinsmore, 2016).

Student achievement also is linked to the emotional climate of the classroom (Meyer, 2016; Woolfolk, 2013). Students do not do as well when teachers rely heavily on criticism, ridicule, threats, or punishment. Achievement is high in classrooms with a pleasant, friendly—but not overly warm—atmosphere.

The Value of Good Teaching

Is it possible to determine what makes a good teacher? Is it possible to measure "good teaching" objectively? A team of economists—not educators—tried to do precisely that, and they did it in terms of money—what students earned over the years. Raj Chetty and his colleagues (2012) tracked elementary and high school students over a period of 20 years and found that "good teachers"—defined for the sake of the study as teachers who raise students' scores on standardized achievement texts—contribute to lasting academic and financial gains for the students. The research team labeled such teaching "value added" teaching, and, as you see in Figure 13.1, there is a strong correlation between value-added teaching and financial outcome at age 28. (The relatively low dollar amounts reflect the times during which data was gathered.) Value-added teaching even lowered the risk of unwanted teenage pregnancy. One commentator summarized the data as showing that "having a good fourth-grade teacher" increases the likelihood that a student will go on to college by 25%, lowers the risk of teen pregnancy by 25%, and boosts the student's lifetime income by an average of $25,000 (Kristof, 2012).

FIG.13.1   THE LONG-TERM IMPACT OF GOOD TEACHING

Source: Chetty, Friedman, & Rockoff (2012).

Teaching that raises students' standardized achievement test scores also raises their income potential and lowers the risk of teenage pregnancy.

TEACHER EXPECTATIONS There is a saying that "You find what you're looking for." Consider the so-called **Pygmalion effect** in education. In Greek mythology, the amorous sculptor Pygmalion breathed life into a beautiful statue he had carved. Teachers also try to bring out positive traits they believe dwell within their students. A classic experiment by Robert Rosenthal and Lenore Jacobson (1968) suggested that teacher expectations can become **self-fulfilling prophecies**. Rosenthal and Jacobson (1968) first gave students a battery of psychological tests. Then they informed teachers that a handful of the students, although average in performance to date, were about to blossom forth intellectually in the current school year.

In fact, the tests indicated nothing about the chosen children. These children had been selected at random. The purpose of the experiment was to determine whether enhancing teacher expectations could affect student performance. It did; the identified children made significant gains in IQ scores.

In subsequent research, however, results have been mixed. Some studies have found support for the Pygmalion effect (Madon et al., 2001; Sarrazin et al., 2005a, 2005b). Others have not. But these findings have serious implications for children from ethnic minority and low-income families because there is some indication that teachers expect less from children in these groups (Kaplan & Owings, 2015; Woolfolk, 2013). Teachers who expect less may spend less time encouraging and working with children.

Pygmalion effect a positive self-fulfilling prophecy in which an individual comes to display improved performance because of the positive expectation of the people with whom he or she interacts.

self-fulfilling prophecy an event that occurs because of the behavior of those who expect it to occur.

What are some of the ways that teachers can help motivate all students to do their best? Here are some suggestions (Gehlbach & Robinson, 2016; Wubbels et al., 2016):

▶ Make the classroom and the lesson interesting and inviting.

▶ Ensure that students can profit from social interaction.

▶ Make the classroom a safe and pleasant place.

▶ Recognize that students' backgrounds can give rise to diverse patterns of needs.

▶ Help students take appropriate responsibility for their successes and failures.

▶ Encourage students to perceive the links between their own efforts and their achievements.

▶ Help students set attainable short-term goals.

SEXISM IN THE CLASSROOM Although girls were systematically excluded from formal education for centuries, today we might not expect to find **sexism** among teachers. Teachers, after all, are generally well educated. They are also trained to be fair minded and sensitive to the needs of their young charges in today's changing society.

However, we may not have heard the last of sexism in our schools. According to a classic review of more than 1,000 research publications about girls and education, girls are treated unequally by their teachers, their male peers, and the school curriculum (Sadker & Silber, 2007). The reviewers concluded:

▶ Many teachers pay less attention to girls than boys, especially in math, science, and technology classes.

▶ Many girls are subjected to **sexual harassment**—unwelcome verbal or physical conduct of a sexual nature—from male classmates, and many teachers ignore it.

▶ Some textbooks still stereotype or ignore women, portraying males as the movers and shakers in the world.

In a widely cited study, Myra Sadker and David Sadker (Sadker & Silber, 2007) observed students in fourth-, sixth-, and eighth-grade classes in four states and in the District of Columbia. Teachers and students were European American and African American, urban, suburban, and rural. In almost all cases, the findings were depressingly similar. Boys generally dominated classroom communication, whether the subject was math (a traditionally "masculine" area) or language arts (a traditionally "feminine" area). Despite the stereotype that girls are more likely to talk or even chatter, boys were eight times more likely than girls to call out answers without raising their hands. So far, it could be said, we have evidence of a gender difference, but not of sexism. However, teachers were less than impartial in responding to boys and girls when they called out. Teachers, male and female, were more likely to accept calling out from boys. Girls were more likely to be reminded that they should raise their hands and wait to be called on. Boys, it appears, are expected to be impetuous, but girls are reprimanded for "unladylike behavior." Until they saw videotapes of themselves, the teachers were largely unaware they were treating girls and boys differently.

sexism discrimination or bias against people based on their gender.

sexual harassment unwelcome verbal or physical conduct of a sexual nature.

Cheryl Casey/Shutterstock.com

13-5 SOCIAL AND EMOTIONAL PROBLEMS

Millions of children in the United States suffer from emotional or behavioral problems and could profit from professional treatment, but most of them are unlikely to receive it (Cicchetti, 2013). Here, we focus on conduct disorders, depression, and anxiety.

13-5a CONDUCT DISORDERS

David is a 16-year-old high school dropout. He has just been arrested for the third time in two years for stealing video equipment and computers from people's homes. Acting alone, David was caught in each case when he tried to sell the stolen items. In describing his actions in each crime, David expressed defiance and showed a lack of remorse. In fact, he bragged about how often he had gotten away with similar crimes.

—Adapted from Halgin & Whitbourne (1993, p. 335)

David has a **conduct disorder**. Children with conduct disorders persistently break rules or violate the rights of others. They exhibit behaviors such as lying, stealing, fire setting, truancy, cruelty to animals, and fighting (American Psychiatric Association, 2013). Conduct disorders typically emerge by eight years of age and are much more common in boys than girls (American Psychiatric Association, 2013; Seguin & Tremblay, 2013).

Children with conduct disorders are often involved in sexual activity before puberty and smoke, drink, and abuse other substances. They have a low tolerance for frustration and may have temper flare-ups. They tend to blame other people for their scrapes. Academic achievement is usually below grade level, but intelligence is usually at least average. Many children with conduct disorders also are diagnosed with ADHD (American Psychiatric Association, 2013).

ORIGINS OF CONDUCT DISORDERS Conduct disorders may have a genetic component (Kendler et al., 2013). Other contributors include antisocial family members, deviant peers, inconsistent discipline, parental insensitivity to the child's behavior, physical punishment, and family stress (Wu et al., 2015).

conduct disorder disorder marked by persistent breaking of the rules and violations of the rights of others.

TREATMENT OF CONDUCT DISORDERS The treatment of conduct disorders is challenging, but it seems that cognitive-behavioral techniques involving parent training hold promise (Graham & Reynolds, 2013). Children profit from interventions in which there are consequences (such as time-outs) for unacceptable behavior and positive social behavior is rewarded.

One method teaches children social skills and problem-solving skills to manage interpersonal conflicts (Burke & Loeber, 2016). Social skills include asking other children to stop annoying behavior rather than hitting them. Children are also taught to "stop and think" before engaging in aggressive behavior.

13-5b CHILDHOOD DEPRESSION

Kristin, age 11, feels "nothing is working out for me." For the past year, she has been failing in school, although she previously had been a B student. She has trouble sleeping, feels tired all the time, and has started refusing to go to school. She cries easily and thinks her peers are making fun of her because she is "ugly and stupid." Her mother recently found a note written by Kristin that said she wanted to jump in front of a car "to end my misery."

—Adapted from Weller & Weller (1991, p. 655)

Many children, like Kristin, are depressed. Depressed children may feel sad, blue, down in the dumps. They may show poor appetite, insomnia, lack of energy and inactivity,

Childhood depression can have many origins, including feelings of failure and helplessness, losses, self-blame for problems that are not of one's own making—and, possibly, genetic factors.

Ocean Photography/Veer Images

loss of self-esteem, difficulty concentrating, loss of interest in people and activities they usually enjoy, crying, feelings of hopelessness and helplessness, and thoughts of suicide (American Psychiatric Association, 2013).

But many children do not recognize depression in themselves until the age of seven or so. When children cannot report their feelings, depression is inferred from behavior, such as withdrawal from social activity. In some cases, childhood depression is "masked" by conduct disorders, physical complaints, academic problems, and anxiety.

It has been estimated that between 5% and 9% of children are seriously depressed in any given year. Childhood depression occurs equally often in girls and boys.

ORIGINS OF DEPRESSION The origins of depression are complex and varied. Psychological and biological explanations have been proposed.

Some social cognitive theorists explain depression in terms of relationships between competencies (knowledge and skills) and feelings of self-esteem. Children who gain academic, social, and other competencies usually have high self-esteem. Perceived low levels of competence are linked to helplessness, low self-esteem, and depression. Longitudinal studies have found that problems in academics, socializing, physical appearance, and sports can predict feelings of depression (Peterson, 2013). Some competent children might not credit themselves because of excessive parental expectations. Or children may be perfectionistic themselves. Perfectionistic children may be depressed because they cannot meet their own standards.

A tendency to blame oneself (an internal attribution) or others (an external attribution) is called a child's **attributional style**. Certain attributional styles can contribute to helplessness and hopelessness and hence to depression (Cohen et al., 2011). Research shows that children who are depressed are more likely to attribute the causes of their failures to internal, stable, and global factors, factors they are relatively helpless to change (Cohen et al., 2011; Schleider et al., 2014). Helplessness triggers depression. Consider the case of two children who do poorly on a math test. John thinks, "I'm a jerk! I'm just no good in math! I'll never learn." Jim thinks, "That test was tougher than I thought it would be. I'll have to work harder next time." John is perceiving the problem as global (he's "a jerk") and stable (he'll "never learn"). Jim perceives the problem as specific rather than global (related to the type of math test the teacher makes up) and as unstable rather than stable (he can change the results by working harder). In effect, John thinks, "It's me" (an internal attribution). By contrast, Jim thinks, "It's the test" (an external attribution).

There is also evidence of genetic factors in depression (Kendler et al., 2011). A Norwegian study of 2,794 twins estimated that the heritability of depression in females was 49% and 25% in males (Orstavik et al., 2007). On a neurological level, evidence suggests that depressed children (and adults) "underutilize" the neurotransmitter **serotonin** (Rice, 2014; Hankin, 2015).

TREATMENT OF DEPRESSION Parents and teachers can do a good deal to alleviate relatively mild feelings of depression among children—involve them in enjoyable activities, encourage them to develop skills, praise them when appropriate, and point out when they are being too hard on themselves. But if feelings of depression persist, treatment is called for.

Psychotherapy for depression tends to be cognitive-behavioral today. Children (and adolescents) are encouraged to do enjoyable things and build social skills. They are made aware of their tendencies to minimize their accomplishments, exaggerate their problems, and overly blame themselves for shortcomings.

Because depressed children may underutilize serotonin, drugs that increase the action of serotonin in the brain (selective serotonin reuptake inhibitors, or SSRIs, such as Luvox, Prozac, and Zoloft) are sometimes used to treat childhood depression. Although SSRIs are often effective, the Food and Drug Administration has warned that there may be a link between their use and suicidal thinking in children (Gupta et al., 2015).

attributional style the way in which one is disposed toward interpreting outcomes (successes or failures), as in tending to place blame or responsibility on oneself or on external factors.

serotonin a neurotransmitter that is involved in mood disorders such as depression.

13-5c CHILDHOOD ANXIETY

Children show many kinds of anxiety disorders, and they are accompanied by depression in 50% to 60% of children (Cummings et al., 2014; Rice, 2014). Yet many children show anxiety disorders, such as **generalized anxiety disorder (GAD)**, in the absence of depression (Vallance & Garralda, 2011). Other anxiety disorders shown by children include **phobias**, such as **separation anxiety disorder (SAD)**, and stage fright.

SEPARATION ANXIETY DISORDER It is normal for children to show anxiety when they are separated from their caregivers. Separation anxiety is normal and begins during the first year. But the sense of security that is usually provided by bonds of attachment encourages children to explore their environment and become progressively independent.

Separation anxiety disorder affects an estimated 4% to 5% of children and young adolescents (American Psychiatric Association, 2013). It occurs more often in girls and is often associated with school refusal (Vallance & Garralda, 2011). The disorder may persist into adulthood, leading to an exaggerated concern about the wellbeing of one's children and spouse and difficulty tolerating separation from them.

SAD is diagnosed when separation anxiety is persistent and excessive, when it is inappropriate for the child's developmental level, and when it interferes with activities or development tasks, such as attending school. Six-year-olds ought to be able to enter first grade without nausea and vomiting and without dread that they or their parents will come to harm. Children with SAD tend to cling to their parents and follow them around the house. They may voice concerns about death and dying and insist that someone stay with them at bedtime. They may complain of nightmares and have stomachaches on school days. They may throw tantrums or plead with their parents not to leave the house.

SAD may occur before middle childhood, preventing adjustment to day care or nursery school. SAD usually becomes a significant problem in middle childhood because that is when children are expected to adjust to school.

SEPARATION ANXIETY DISORDER, SCHOOL PHOBIA, AND SCHOOL REFUSAL SAD is an extreme form of separation anxiety. It is characterized by anxiety about separating from parents and may be expressed as **school phobia**—fear of school—or of refusal to go to school (which can be based on fear or other factors). Separation anxiety is not behind all instances of school refusal. Some children refuse school because they perceive it as unpleasant, unsatisfying, or hostile, and it may be—as in the case of bullying. Some children are concerned about doing poorly in school or being asked questions in class (in which case, they may have stage fright). High parental expectations may heighten concern, as may problems with classmates.

TREATMENT OF SCHOOL PHOBIA OR SCHOOL REFUSAL Except for extreme cases, such as the threatening and taunting of severe bullying, it is usually not better for children with school phobia to remain at home. In cases of bullying and other forms of harsh treatment, the parents should work with the school to resolve the issue

Jake Wyman/Photolibrary/Getty Images

generalized anxiety disorder (GAD) an anxiety disorder in which anxiety appears to be present continuously and is unrelated to the situation.

phobia an irrational, excessive fear that interferes with one's functioning.

separation anxiety disorder (SAD) an extreme form of otherwise normal separation anxiety that is characterized by anxiety about separating from parents; SAD often takes the form of refusal to go to school.

school phobia fear of attending school, marked by extreme anxiety at leaving parents.

Alison—A Case of Separation Anxiety Disorder

SAD frequently develops after a stressful life event, such as illness, the death of a relative or pet, or a change of schools or homes. Alison's problems followed the death of her grandmother:

Alison's grandmother died when Alison was seven years old. Her parents decided to permit her request to view her grandmother in the open coffin. Alison took a tentative glance from her father's arms across the room, then asked to be taken out of the room. Her five-year-old sister took a leisurely close-up look, with no apparent distress.

Alison had been concerned about death for two or three years by this time, but her grandmother's passing brought on a new flurry of questions: "Will I die?" "Does everybody die?" and so on. Her parents tried to reassure her by saying, "Grandma was very, very old, and she also had a heart condition. You are very young and in perfect health. You have many, many years before you have to start thinking about death."

Alison also could not be alone in any room in her house. She pulled one of her parents or her sister along with her everywhere she went. She also reported nightmares about her grandmother and, within a couple of days, insisted on sleeping in the same room with her parents. Fortunately, Alison's fears did not extend to school. Her teacher reported that Alison spent some time talking about her grandmother, but her academic performance was apparently unimpaired.

Alison's parents decided to allow Alison time to "get over" the loss. Alison gradually talked less and less about death, and by the time three months had passed, she was able to go into any room in her house by herself. She wanted to continue to sleep in her parents' bedroom, however. So her parents "made a deal" with her. They would put off the return to her own bedroom until the school year had ended (a month away), if Alison would agree to return to her own bed at that time. As a further incentive, a parent would remain with her until she fell asleep for the first month. Alison overcame the anxiety problem in this fashion with no additional delays.

Author's files

---

before the child returns. But if there is no actual threat to the child, most professionals agree that the first rule in the treatment of most cases of school phobia is: Get the child back into school. The second rule is: Get the child back into school. And the third rule . . . you get the idea. The disorder often disappears once the child is back in school on a regular basis.

FICTION

T (F) It is better for children with school phobia to remain at home until the origins of the problem are uncovered and resolved.

When a child is in danger at school, as in being threatened by bullies, it may be better to keep the child at home until the problem is resolved. But in most cases it is better to get the child back in school.

There is nothing wrong with trying to understand why a child refuses to attend school. Knowledge of the reasons for refusal can help parents and educators devise strategies for assisting the child. But perhaps such understanding—again with certain exceptions—need not always precede insistence that the child return to school.

Antidepressant medication has been used with school phobia with some success (Mohatt et al., 2013; Warnke, 2014). However, drugs do not teach children how to cope. Many psychologists and educators suggest that drugs are best used only when psychological treatments, such as challenging irrational ideas as to why the child should be remaining out of school, have proven to be ineffective (Maric et al., 2013; Walter et al., 2014).

It seems unfortunate to depart middle childhood following a discussion of social and emotional problems. Most children in developed nations come through middle childhood quite well, in good shape for the challenges and dramas of adolescence.

Getting a Phobic Child Back into School

There is nothing wrong with trying to understand why a child refuses to attend school. Knowledge of the reasons for refusal can help parents and educators devise strategies for helping the child adjust. But should such understanding precede insistence that the child return to school? Again, depending on the apparent causes of school refusal, insisting on an early return to school might be the best course of action. Here are some things parents can do to get a child back into school:

▶ **Do not give in to the child's demands to stay home. If the child complains of being tired or ill, tell the child that he or she may feel better at school and can rest there if necessary.**

▶ **Discuss the problem with the child's teacher, principal, and school nurse. (Gain the cooperation of school professionals.)**

▶ **If there is a specific school-related problem, such as an overly strict teacher, help the child find ways to handle the situation. (Finding ways to handle such problems can be accomplished while the child is in school. Not all such problems need to be ironed out before the child returns to school.)**

▶ **Reward the child for attending school. (Yes, parents shouldn't "have to" reward children for "normal" behavior, but do you want the child in school or not?)**

What if these measures don't work? Can professionals help? A variety of therapeutic approaches have been tried, and it appears that cognitive-behavioral approaches are the most effective (Chu et al., 2014; James et al., 2015). One cognitive-behavioral method involves gradually requiring the child to spend more and more time in school to reduce his or her fear step by step. In this gradual method, the child may also attend some after-school activities with friends or work individually with teachers for a while. In systematic desensitization,

the child might be shown photos or videos of the school while remaining in supportive surroundings. In cognitive restructuring, the child might be encouraged to talk about why school is "awful," and parents or therapists can counter the child's arguments in constructive ways. In the technique of "flooding," which needs to be handled very carefully, the child is simply thrust back into the school and presumably learns, as terrible things do not happen, that the school is not as awful as anticipated. But keep in mind that other students are likely to notice and react to a child who has been absent for a while and is now trembling at his or her desk.

Antidepressant medication has been used—often in conjunction with cognitive-behavioral methods—with a good deal of success (Mohatt et al., 2013; Warnke, 2014). Antidepressants can have side effects, however, such as abdominal discomfort. Moreover, some health professionals fear that antidepressants can trigger suicidal thoughts in children. However, drugs in themselves do not teach children how to cope with situations. Many health professionals suggest that the drugs—in this case, antidepressants—are best used only when psychological treatments, such as challenging irrational ideas as to why the child should remain out of school, have proven to be ineffective (Maric et al., 2013; Walter et al., 2014).

Cultura RM / Alamy Stock Photo

SELF-ASSESSMENTS

Fill-Ins

Answers can be found in the back of the book.

1. According to psychoanalytic theory, children in middle childhood are in the _____ stage of psychosexual development.

2. Erik Erikson labeled the life crisis of middle childhood as _____ versus inferiority.

3. Selman described five levels of _____-taking in childhood.

4. During middle childhood, control is gradually transferred from parent to child in a process known as _____.

5. Selective serotonin reuptake inhibitors are most likely to be prescribed for childhood _____.

6. Teachers who expect more from students often get more. This is an example of a(n) _____ prophecy.

7. Children with _____ disorders persistently break rules or violate the rights of others.

8. Children who are depressed are more likely than other children to attribute their failures and shortcomings to internal, stable, and _____ factors.

9. In middle childhood, mothers' interactions with children continue to revolve around _____, whereas fathers' interactions are relatively more involved in recreational activities.

10. In their self-concepts, children in middle childhood are more likely to focus on _____ traits than are children in early childhood.

Multiple Choice

1. **What happens to children's self-esteem in middle childhood?**
   a. It rises.
   b. It declines.
   c. It remains the same.
   d. It rises, then declines.

2. **What kind of parenting contributes to high self-esteem in a child?**
   a. authoritarian
   b. authoritative
   c. rejecting–neglecting
   d. permissive

3. **How do 10- to 12-year-olds evaluate their parents in middle childhood as compared to how they evaluated them in early childhood?**
   a. The same
   b. Less harshly
   c. More harshly
   d. There is no evidence on this matter.

4. **What is the likelihood that the children of lesbian or gay parents will have a lesbian or gay sexual orientation?**
   a. About 50-50 (half)
   b. Somewhat more than children raised by heterosexual parents
   c. About the same as children raised by heterosexual parents
   d. Less than that of children raised by heterosexual parents

5. **According to the text, the research about whether parents in conflict should remain together for the sake of the children shows that**
   a. they should stay together if their religion forbids divorce.
   b. even fighting parents provide a better environment for children than do single parents or stepfamilies.
   c. they should get a divorce.
   d. it depends on how the parents behave in front of and toward their children.

6. **According to evolutionary theory, stepparents may be less devoted to rearing stepchildren because**
   a. they do not have enough resources.
   b. they have not had the experience of how to get along with stepchildren for the same amount of time as with their own children.
   c. the stepchildren do not care for them as much as they care for their biological parents.
   d. people often behave as if they want their own genes to flourish in the next generation.

7. **All of the following are helpful ideas about talking to children about a divorce *except***
   a. reassuring the children that you both love them and will always be their parents.
   b. waiting until the last minute.
   c. admitting that the divorce will be sad and upsetting for everyone.
   d. telling the children that the divorce is not their fault.

8. **Does maternal employment increase the likelihood that children will become delinquent?**
   a. No
   b. Yes—almost always
   c. Yes, but only if maternal employment is connected with lack of supervision
   d. Yes, for girls but not for boys

9. **Between the ages of 7 and 12, children see friends as**
   a. doing things for one another, with a focus on self-interest.
   b. doing what they want.
   c. providing mutual support over a long period of time.
   d. changing as people change and develop new goals for friendships.

10. **Which of the following is accurate about bullies?**
    a. They are less likely than other children to have attention-deficit/hyperactivity disorder.
    b. They are likely to come from homes with higher socioeconomic status.
    c. Their school achievement is the same as other children's.
    d. They are more likely to have conduct disorders.

CDEV
ONLINE

REVIEW FLASHCARDS ANYTIME, ANYWHERE!

Create Flashcards from Your StudyBits

Review Key Term Flashcards Already Loaded on the StudyBoard

4LTR
PRESS

14 | Adolescence: Physical Development

rubberball/Getty Images

LEARNING OUTCOMES

After studying this chapter, you will be able to . . .

14-1 Discuss growth in adolescence, focusing on the growth spurt and asynchronous growth

14-2 Describe the biological events of puberty and discuss gender differences in the effects of maturing early or late

14-3 Discuss health in adolescence, focusing on causes of death and nutritional needs

14-4 Discuss the eating disorders anorexia nervosa and bulimia nervosa, including their origins

14-5 Discuss adolescent substance use and abuse

After you finish this chapter, go to **PAGE 245** for **STUDY TOOLS**

Perhaps no other period of life is as exciting—and bewildering—as adolescence, bounded at the lower end by the ages of 11 or 12 and at the upper end by the ages of 18 or 19. Except for infancy, more changes occur during adolescence than any other time of life. In our society, adolescents are "neither fish nor fowl," as the saying goes, neither children nor adults. Adolescents may be old enough to reproduce and be as large as their parents, yet they may not be allowed to get drivers' licenses until they are 16 or 17, and they cannot attend R-rated films unless accompanied by an adult. Given the restrictions placed on them, their growing yearning for independence, and a sex drive heightened by high levels of sex hormones, it is not surprising that adolescents are occasionally in conflict with their parents.

> The reasonably stable patterns of growth and development that occurred in early and middle adulthood end abruptly in adolescence. What are the psychological effects of dramatic physical change?

The idea that adolescence is an important and separate developmental stage was proposed by G. Stanley Hall (1904). Hall believed that adolescence is marked by turmoil and used the German phrase *Sturm und Drang* ("storm and stress") to refer to the conflicts of adolescence.

Contemporary theorists no longer see adolescent storm and stress as inevitable (Hollenstein & Lougheed, 2013; Smetana, 2011). Instead, they see adolescence as a period when biological changes drive certain kinds of behavior but are shaped by environmental influences and adolescents' ability to regulate their emotions and behavior (Hollenstein & Lougheed, 2013). In any case, adolescents need to adapt to biological changes and social expectations.

14-1 PUBERTY: THE BIOLOGICAL ERUPTION

Puberty is a stage of development characterized by reaching sexual maturity and the ability to reproduce. The onset of adolescence coincides with the advent of puberty. Puberty is controlled by a **feedback loop** involving the hypothalamus, pituitary gland, the gonads—the ovaries in females and the testes in males—and hormones. The hypothalamus signals the pituitary gland, which, in turn, releases hormones that control physical growth and the gonads. The gonads respond to pituitary hormones by increasing their production of sex hormones (androgens and estrogens). The sex hormones further stimulate the hypothalamus, perpetuating the feedback loop.

The sex hormones also trigger the development of primary and secondary sex characteristics. The **primary sex characteristics** are the structures that make reproduction possible. In girls, these are the ovaries, vagina, uterus, and fallopian tubes. In boys, they are the penis, testes, prostate gland, and seminal vesicles. The **secondary sex characteristics** are physical indicators

puberty the biological stage of development characterized by changes that lead to reproductive capacity.

feedback loop a system in which glands regulate each other's functioning through a series of hormonal messages.

primary sex characteristics the structures that make reproduction possible.

secondary sex characteristics physical indicators of sexual maturation—such as changes to the voice and growth of bodily hair—that do not directly involve reproductive structures.

TRUTH OR FICTION?

T	F	American adolescents are growing taller than their parents.
T	F	Girls are fertile immediately after their first menstrual period.
T	F	Girls who mature early have higher self-esteem than those who mature late.
T	F	Most adolescents in the United States are unaware of the risks of HIV/AIDS.
T	F	Substance abuse is the leading cause of death among male adolescents in the United States.

of sexual maturation that are not directly involved in reproduction. They include breast development, deepening of the voice, and the appearance of facial, pubic, and underarm hair.

14-1a THE ADOLESCENT GROWTH SPURT

The stable growth patterns in height and weight that characterize early and middle childhood end abruptly with the adolescent growth spurt. Girls start to spurt in height sooner than boys, at an average age of a little more than ten. Boys start to spurt about two years later. Girls and boys reach their peak growth in height about two years after the growth spurt begins, at about 12 and 14 years, respectively (see Figure 14.1). The spurt in height for both girls and boys continues for about another two years at a gradually declining pace. Boys add nearly four inches per year during the fastest year of the spurt compared with slightly more than three inches per year for girls. Overall, boys add an average of 14½ inches during the spurt and girls add a little more than 13 inches (Hills & Byrne, 2011; Tanner et al., 1991a).

Adolescents begin to spurt in weight about half a year after they begin to spurt in height. The period of peak growth in weight occurs about a year and a half after the onset of the spurt. As with height, the growth spurt in weight then continues for a little more than two years (see Figure 14.2). Because the spurt in weight lags the spurt in height, many adolescents are relatively slender compared with their

Is adolescence a period of *Sturm und Drang* (storm and stress)?

preadolescent stature. However, adolescents tend to eat enormous quantities of food to fuel their growth spurts. Active 14- and 15-year-old boys may consume 3,000 to 4,000 calories a day without becoming obese.

Girls' and boys' body shapes begin to differ in adolescence. Girls develop relatively broader hips compared with their shoulders, whereas the opposite is true for boys. A girl's body shape is more rounded than a boy's because girls gain almost twice as much fatty tissue as boys. Boys gain twice as much muscle tissue as girls.

ASYNCHRONOUS GROWTH Adolescents may be awkward and gawky due to **asynchronous growth**; different parts of the body grow at different rates. The hands and feet mature before the arms and legs do. As a consequence, adolescent girls and boys may complain of big hands or feet. Legs reach their peak growth before

asynchronous growth
unbalanced growth, such as the growth that occurs during the early part of adolescence and causes many adolescents to appear gawky.

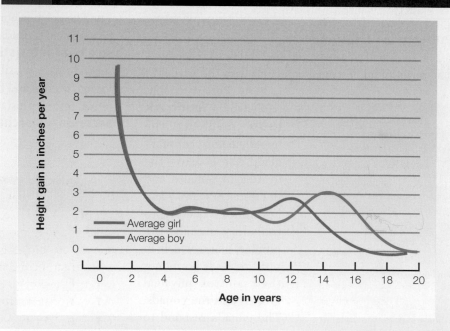

FIG.14.1 SPURTS IN GROWTH

Girls begin the adolescent growth spurt about two years earlier than boys. Girls and boys reach their periods of peak growth about two years after the spurt begins.

FIG.14.2   GROWTH CURVES FOR WEIGHT AND HEIGHT

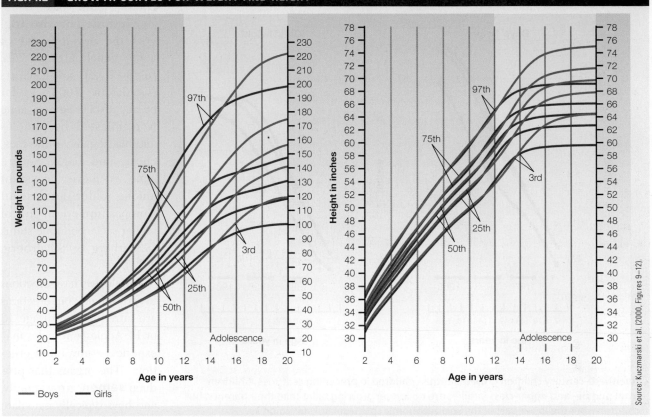

Source: Kuczmarski et al. (2000. Figures 9–12).

Girls are taller and heavier than boys from about age 9 or 10 until about age 13 because their growth spurt occurs earlier. Once boys begin their spurt, they catch up with girls and eventually become taller and heavier.

the shoulders and chest. Boys stop growing out of their pants about a year before they stop growing out of their jackets (Tanner, 1989).

THE SECULAR TREND During the 20th century, children in the Western world grew dramatically more rapidly and wound up taller than children from earlier times (Johnson et al., 2013; Ulijaszek, 2010). This historical trend toward increasing adult height was also accompanied by an earlier onset of puberty, and is known as the **secular trend**. Figure 14.3 shows that Swedish boys and girls grew more rapidly in 1938 and 1968 than they did in 1883 and ended up several inches taller. At the age of 15, boys were more than six inches taller and girls were more than three inches taller, on average, than their counterparts from the previous century (Tanner, 1989). The occurrence of a secular trend in height and weight has been documented in nearly all European countries and the United States.

However, children from middle- and upper-class families in developed nations, including the United States, no longer grow taller, whereas their poorer counterparts continue to gain in height from generation to generation. Although it is clear that heredity is the major contributor to adult height, nutrition and general health also play key roles (NCD-RisC, 2016).

FICTION

T (F) American adolescents are growing taller than their parents.

The statement that adolescents are growing taller than their parents is too general to be considered true. The average height for adults is greater than it was 100 years ago, but the upward trend seems to have stopped for middle- and upper-class children. It does seem to remain true for children of lower socioeconomic status.

secular trend a historical trend toward increasing adult height and earlier puberty.

FIG.14.3   ARE WE STILL GROWING TALLER THAN OUR PARENTS?

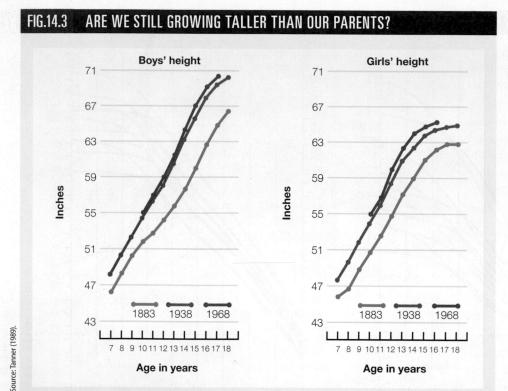

Boys' height — Girls' height — 1883, 1938, 1968 — Age in years — Inches

Source: Tanner (1989).

Twentieth-century children grew taller than children in preceding centuries. Children from middle- and upper-class families are no longer growing taller than their parents, but children from the lower part of the socioeconomic spectrum are still doing so.

14-1b CHANGES IN BOYS

At puberty, the pituitary gland stimulates the testes to increase their output of testosterone, leading to further development of the male genitals. The first visible sign of puberty is accelerated growth of the testes, which begins at an average age of about 11½ plus or minus 2 years. Testicular growth further accelerates testosterone production and other pubertal changes.

The penis growth spurt begins about a year later, and still later, pubic hair develops.

Underarm and facial hair appears at about age 15. Only half of American boys shave (of necessity) by 17. At 14 or 15, the voice deepens because of growth of the "voice box," or larynx, and the lengthening of the vocal cords. The process is gradual, and adolescent boys sometimes encounter an embarrassing cracking of the voice.

Testosterone also triggers the development of acne, which afflicts 75% to 90% of adolescents (Goldstein, 2004; Taylor et al., 2011). Severe acne is manifested by pimples and blackheads on the face, chest, and back. Severe acne is more prevalent among older adolescent European American girls of higher socioeconomic status (Silverberg & Silverberg, 2014).

Males can have erections in early infancy, but erections are infrequent until age 13 or 14. Adolescent males may experience unwanted erections. The organs that produce **semen** grow rapidly, and boys typically ejaculate seminal fluid by age 13 or 14. About a year later they begin to have **nocturnal emissions**, also called "wet dreams" because of the false myth that emissions necessarily accompany erotic dreams. Mature sperm are found in ejaculatory emissions by about the age of 15.

Nearly half of all boys experience enlargement of the breasts, or **gynecomastia**, which usually declines in a year or two. Gynecomastia stems from the small amount of female sex hormones secreted by the testes.

At age 20 or 21, men stop growing taller because testosterone causes **epiphyseal closure**, which prevents the long bones from making further gains in length. Puberty for males draws to a close.

14-1c CHANGES IN GIRLS

In girls, the pituitary gland signals the ovaries to boost estrogen production at puberty. Estrogen may stimulate the growth of breast tissue ("breast buds") as early as the age of eight or nine, but the breasts usually begin to enlarge during the tenth year. The development of fatty tissue and ducts elevates the areas of the breasts surrounding the nipples and causes the nipples to protrude. The breasts typically reach full size in about three years, but the *mammary glands* do not mature fully until a woman has a baby. Estrogen also promotes the growth

semen the fluid that contains sperm and substances that nourish and help transport sperm.

nocturnal emission emission of seminal fluid while asleep.

gynecomastia enlargement of breast tissue in males.

epiphyseal closure the process by which the cartilage that separates the long end of a bone from the main part of the bone turns to bone.

menarche the onset of menstruation.

of the fatty and supporting tissue in the hips and buttocks, which, along with the widening of the pelvis, causes the hips to round. Beginning at about age 11, girls develop pubic and underarm hair.

Estrogen causes the *labia*, vagina, and uterus to develop during puberty, and androgens cause the *clitoris* to develop. The vaginal lining varies in thickness according to the amount of estrogen in the bloodstream. Estrogen typically brakes the female growth spurt some years before testosterone brakes that of males.

MENARCHE The current mean age for **menarche** (first menstruation) in the United States is the thirteenth year (with, for example, 12.8 years the average for European Americans and 12.2 years the average for African Americans) (Cabrera et al., 2014). During the past 150 years, menarche has occurred at progressively earlier ages in Western nations, another example of the secular trend (see Figure 14.4).

What accounts for the earlier age of puberty? One hypothesis is that girls must reach a certain body weight to trigger pubertal changes such as menarche. Body fat could trigger the changes because fat cells secrete a protein that signals the brain to secrete hormones that raise estrogen levels. Menarche comes later to girls who have a

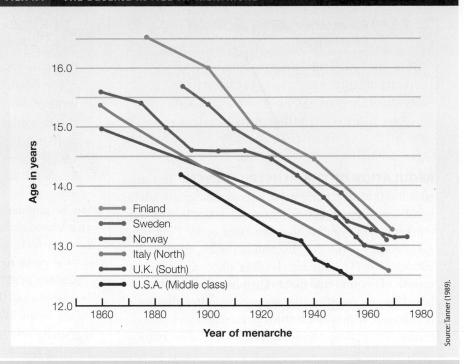

FIG.14.4 THE DECLINE IN AGE AT MENARCHE

Age in years (y-axis), Year of menarche (x-axis)

- Finland
- Sweden
- Norway
- Italy (North)
- U.K. (South)
- U.S.A. (Middle class)

Source: Tanner (1989).

The age at menarche has been declining since the mid-1800s among girls in Western nations, apparently because of improved nutrition and health care.

lower percentage of body fat, such as those with eating disorders or athletes (Crocker et al., 2014; Terasawa et al., 2012). The average body weight for triggering menarche depends on the girl's height (Novotny et al., 2011). Today's girls are larger than those of the early 20th century because of improved nutrition and health care.

In girls, estrogen stimulates the growth of breast tissue and the development of the female genital organs.

Purestock/Jupiterimages

REGULATION OF THE MENSTRUAL CYCLE Testosterone levels remain fairly stable in boys throughout adulthood, but estrogen and progesterone levels in girls vary markedly and regulate the menstrual cycle. Following menstruation—the sloughing off of the endometrium—estrogen levels increase, leading once more to the growth of endometrial tissue. Girls usually begin to ovulate 12 to 18 months after menarche. After the ovum is released, if it is not fertilized, estrogen and progesterone levels drop suddenly, triggering menstruation once again.

The average menstrual cycle is 28 days, but variations are common. Girls' cycles are often irregular for a few years after menarche but later become more regular. Most cycles during the first 12 to 18 months after menarche occur without ovulation.

14-1d EARLY VERSUS LATE MATURERS

Early-maturing boys tend to be more popular than their late-maturing peers and more likely to be leaders in school (Teunissen et al., 2011). They are more poised, relaxed, and good-natured. Their edge in sports and the admiration of their peers heighten their sense of worth. On the negative side, early maturation is associated with greater risks of aggression and delinquency (Dimler & Natsuaki, 2015) and abuse of alcohol and other drugs (Modecki et al., 2014). Coaches may expect too much of them in sports, and peers may want them to fight their battles. Sexual opportunities may create demands before they know how to respond (James et al., 2012).

Late maturers have the "advantage" of not being rushed into maturity. On the other hand, late-maturing boys often feel dominated by early-maturing boys. They have been found to be more dependent and insecure and may be more likely to get involved in substance abuse (Vroman, 2010).

Although boys who mature early usually have higher self-esteem than those who mature late, the research evidence is somewhat mixed for girls. Early-maturing girls may be popular in that boys like them and they "have" what late-maturing girls would like to develop. However, they may feel awkward, because they are among the first of their peers to begin the physical changes of puberty (Teunissen et al., 2011). They become conspicuous with their height and their developing breasts. Tall girls of dating age frequently find that shorter boys are reluctant to approach them or be seen with them. All in all, early-maturing girls are at greater risk for psychological problems and substance abuse than girls who mature later on (Graber, 2013; Mrug et al., 2014). Many girls who mature early obtain lower grades in school and initiate sexual activity earlier (Mrug et al., 2014). For reasons such as these, the parents of early-maturing girls may increase their vigilance and restrictiveness, leading to new child–parent conflicts.

BODY IMAGE Adolescents are quite concerned about their physical appearance, particularly in early adolescence during the rapid physical changes of puberty (Bucchianeri et al., 2013). By age 18, girls and boys are more satisfied with their bodies (Bucchianeri et al., 2013). Adolescent females in our society tend to be more preoccupied with body weight and slimness than adolescent males (Tiggeman, 2014; Tiggeman, & Slater, 2013). Many adolescent males want to gain weight to build their muscle mass (Field et al., 2014).

14-2 EMERGING SEXUALITY AND THE RISKS OF SEXUALLY TRANSMITTED INFECTIONS

In an episode of the TV series *Growing Pains*, an adolescent was referred to as a "hormone with feet." Many or most adolescents are preoccupied with sex to some degree—a preoccupation fueled by a powerful sex drive. And many or most adolescents are not quite sure what

TABLE 14.1 U. S. ADOLESCENTS AND ADULTS WITH AIDS—NUMBER OF CASES BY EXPOSURE CATEGORY

| | ESTIMATED NUMBER OF AIDS CASES, THROUGH 2006 | | |
TRANSMISSION CATEGORY	ADULT AND ADOLESCENT MALES	ADULT AND ADOLESCENT FEMALES	TOTAL
Male-to-male sexual contact	465,965	—	465,965
Injection drug use	170,171	74,718	244,889
Male-to-male sexual contact and injection drug use	68,516	—	68,516
Male–female sexual contact	65,241	108,252	173,493
Other*	13,893	6,596	20,489

* Includes hemophilia, blood transfusion, perinatal exposure, and risk not reported or not identifi ed.

Source: Centers for Disease Control and Prevention. (2008, August 3). AIDS cases by transmission category. Retrieved January 7, 2009, from http://www.cdc.gov/hiv/topics/surveillance/basic.htm

to do about these pressing urges. Should they masturbate? Should they pet? Should they engage in sexual intercourse? Parents and sex educators often say "No," or "Wait." Yet it can seem that "Everyone's doing it." In Chapter 16, we discuss various sexual outlets. Here, we focus on sexually transmitted infections (STIs).

Given a body that is suddenly sexually mature, a high sex drive, vulnerability to peer pressure, and limited experience in handling temptation, teenagers are at particular risk for STIs. Sexually active adolescents have higher rates of STIs than any other age group. Each year, an estimated one of every six American adolescents contracts an STI (Centers for Disease Control and Prevention [CDC], 2006b). Chlamydia (a bacterial infection of the vagina or urinary tract that can result in sterility) is the most commonly occurring STI in adolescents, followed by gonorrhea, genital warts, genital herpes, syphilis, and **HIV/AIDS**. Because of its lethality, HIV/AIDS tends to capture most of the headlines. However, other STIs are more widespread, and some of them can also be deadly.

The incidence of chlamydia is especially high among teenagers and college students (CDC, 2006). Chlamydia is a major cause of pelvic inflammatory disease (PID), which can lead to infertility.

Infections with the human papilloma virus (HPV) cause genital warts and are associated with cervical cancer. A vaccine prevents most young women from being infected and is best administered before they become sexually active (Pichichero, 2006). It is estimated that more than half of the sexually active adolescent women in some cities in the United States are infected with HPV. Genital warts may appear in visible areas of the skin, but most appear in unseen areas, such as on the cervix in women or in the urethra in men. Women who initiate sexual intercourse before the age of 18 and who have many sex partners are particularly susceptible to infection. Fortunately, most healthy young women clear HPV infections on their own.

14-2a HIV/AIDS

HIV/AIDS is the most devastating of STIs; if left untreated, it is lethal. And the long-term prospects of those who do receive treatment remain unknown. HIV—the virus that causes AIDS—is spreading rapidly around the world, and, by the end of the 20th century, it had infected nearly 39 million people worldwide (Joint United Nations Programme on HIV/AIDS [UNAIDS], 2006). About 1,100,000 people in the United States are now living with HIV/AIDS (CDC, 2008a; Hall et al., 2008). Young gay males and homeless and runaway youths have elevated risk for HIV/AIDS. Anal intercourse is a likely route of transmission of HIV and is often practiced by gay males (see Table 14.1). Injecting drugs is another risk factor, because sharing infected needles can transmit HIV.

Women account for a minority of cases of HIV/AIDS in the United States but a United Nations study in Europe, Africa, and Southeast Asia found that sexually active teenage girls have higher rates of HIV infection than older women or young men (UNAIDS, 2006). It is erroneous to think that worldwide HIV/AIDS is primarily a disease of gay men and people who inject drugs. The primary mode of transmission worldwide is male–female intercourse. More than half of U.S. women with HIV/AIDS are infected by male–female intercourse (CDC, 2008a; see Table 14.1).

Nearly all high school students know that HIV/AIDS is transmitted by sexual intercourse, but about half do not modify their sexual practices as a result of fear of the disease (Santelli et al., 2000). Adolescents often deny that HIV/AIDS could be a threat to them. As one

HIV/AIDS Human immunodefi ciency virus (HIV) is the cause of acquired immunodefi ciency syndrome (AIDS), a condition that cripples the immune system.

Age	15	16	17	18	19	20–21	22–24
TABLE 14.2 PERCENTAGE OF ADOLESCENTS WHO HAVE ENGAGED IN SEXUAL INTERCOURSE, ACCORDING TO THE NATIONAL SURVEY OF FAMILY GROWTH							
Male	25	37	46	62	69	85	89
Female	25	40	49	70	77	81	92

Source: Mosher et al. (2005, figures 2 and 3).

FICTION

T (F) Most adolescents in the United States are unaware of the risks of HIV/AIDS.

False; studies regarding knowledge, attitudes, and beliefs about HIV/AIDS find that even children in the early school years are aware of HIV/AIDS.

high school girl said, "I can't believe that anyone I would have sex with would be infected." Some are, of course.

14-2b RISK FACTORS

Adolescents often take risks, with harmful consequences for their health and well-being. The most obvious risk factor for STIs is sexual activity itself. A U.S. government survey found that the percentage of adolescents who engage in sexual intercourse increases dramatically between the ages of 15 and 18 (Table 14.2). At the age of 15, about one adolescent in four has engaged in sexual intercourse, but the number surges to about two out of three by the age of 18.

A second risk factor for contracting STIs is sex with multiple partners. About 15% of high school students have had four or more sex partners (CDC, 2008b).

A third factor is failure to use condoms. In a recent survey by the Centers for Disease Control and Prevention, only about 62% of high school students used a condom the last time they had sexual intercourse (CDC, 2008b).

A fourth factor is drug abuse (UNAIDS, 2006). Adolescents who abuse drugs are also more likely to engage in other risky behaviors, such as sex without condoms (Abbey et al., 2006; Appel et al., 2006; Parkes et al., 2007).

The causes, methods of transmission, symptoms, and treatments for STIs are described in Table 14.3.

14-2c PREVENTION OF STIS

Prevention and education are the basic weapons against STIs (UNAIDS, 2006). Adolescents need to know about the transmission, symptoms, and consequences of STIs

and about safer sex techniques, including abstinence and the use of condoms. Educating young people to use condoms lowers levels of infection (Wingood et al., 2006).

But knowledge alone may not change behavior. For example, many female adolescents lack power in their relationships. Males are likely to pressure them into unwanted or unprotected sex (Wingood et al., 2006).

14-3 HEALTH IN ADOLESCENCE

Around five of six U.S. adolescents are in very good or excellent health (Adolescent Health, 2014). Few are chronically ill or miss school. Injuries tend to heal quickly. Only 1% to 2% are in fair or poor health (Adolescent Health, 2014).

14-3a CAUSES OF DEATH

Death rates are low in adolescence, but they are nearly twice as great for male adolescents as female adolescents. A major reason for this discrepancy is that males take more risks that end in death as a result of accidents, homicide, or suicide (see Figure 14.5). These three causes of death account for most adolescent deaths (Heron, 2016). Nearly 80% of adolescent deaths are due to injuries, and motor vehicle and firearm injuries account for more than half of them. Firearms account for 80% of homicides and nearly 50% of suicides.

14-3b NUTRITION

Physical growth occurs more rapidly in the adolescent years than at any other time after birth, with the exception of the first year of infancy. To fuel the adolescent growth spurt, the average girl needs 1,800 to 2,400 calories per day, and the average boy needs 2,200 to 3,200 calories (Nutrition Facts, 2013). The nutritional needs of adolescents vary according to their activity level and stage of pubertal development. At the peak of the growth spurt, adolescents use twice as much calcium, iron, zinc, magnesium, and nitrogen as during other years of adolescence (Nutrition Facts, 2013). Calcium intake is particularly important for females to build bone density and

FIG.14.5 LEADING CAUSES OF DEATH AMONG 15- TO 19-YEAR-OLDS IN THE UNITED STATES

MALES:

Accidents

Suicide

Homicide

Cancer

Heart disease

Congenital health problems

Influenza and pneumonia

Chronic respiratory diseases

Diabetes

Stroke

Golden Pixels LLC/Alamy Stock Photo

FEMALE:

Accidents

Suicide

Cancer

Homicide

Heart disease

Congenital health problems

Problems related to pregnancy and childbirth

Influenza and pneumonia

Stroke

Chronic respiratory diseases

Sources: Minino, Xu, & Kochanek (2010); National Center for Health Statistics, Health (2009), United States, 2008 with Chartbook, Hyattsville, MD, Table 31.

The great majority of U.S. 15- to 19-year-olds are in good or excellent health, which is why the leading causes of death for this age group are accidents and suicide.

help prevent **osteoporosis** later in life, but most teenagers do not consume enough calcium. Adolescents are also likely to obtain less vitamin A, thiamine, and iron but more fat, sugar, and sodium than recommended (Nutrition Facts, 2013).

One reason for adolescents' nutritional deficits is irregular eating patterns. Breakfast is often skipped, especially by dieters (Wennberg et al., 2014). Teenagers may rely on fast food and junk food, which is high in fat and calories. Junk food is connected with being overweight, and being overweight in adolescence can lead to chronic illness and premature death in adulthood (Wennberg et al., 2014).

14-4 EATING DISORDERS

The American ideal has slimmed down to where most American females of normal weight are dissatisfied with the size and shape of their bodies (Tiggeman, 2014;

FICTION

T (F) Substance abuse is the leading cause of death among male adolescents in the United States.

It is not true that substance abuse is the leading cause of death among male adolescents in the United States. Accidents, homicide, and suicide all account for larger numbers of deaths.

Prendergast et al., 2015). In the section on cognitive development, we will see that adolescents also tend to think that others are paying a great deal of attention to their appearance. Because of cultural emphasis on slimness and the psychology of the adolescent, they are highly vulnerable to eating disorders, which are characterized by gross disturbances in patterns of eating.

ANOREXIA NERVOSA **Anorexia nervosa** is a life-threatening eating disorder characterized by extreme fear of being heavy, dramatic weight loss, a distorted body image, and resistance to eating enough to maintain a healthful weight. Anorexia nervosa afflicts males as well as females, but most studies put the female-to-male ratio at ten to one or greater (Stice et al., 2013a). By and large, anorexia nervosa afflicts females during adolescence and young adulthood (Stice et al., 2013a). The typical person with anorexia is a young European American female of higher socioeconomic status (Striegel-Moore et al., 2003). Affluent females are more likely to read the magazines that idealize slender bodies and shop in the boutiques that cater to females with svelte figures (Tiggeman, 2014). Female athletes are also at risk. The *female athlete triad* describes women who have low availability of energy (as from eating poorly), menstrual problems, and lessened bone density, which usually afflicts people in late adulthood (House et al., 2013; Mountjoy & Goolsby, 2015).

osteoporosis a condition involving progressive loss of bone tissue.

anorexia nervosa an eating disorder characterized by irrational fear of weight gain, distorted body image, and severe weight loss.

Females with anorexia nervosa can drop 25% or more of their weight within a year. Severe weight loss triggers abnormalities in the endocrine system (i.e., with hormones) that prevent ovulation (Mehler & Brown, 2015). General health declines. Problems arise in the respiratory system and the cardiovascular system (Mehler & Brown, 2015). The mortality rate for anorexic females is about 4% to 5%.

Girls often develop anorexia nervosa to lose weight after gains from menarche (Shroff et al., 2006). Dieting and exercise continue well after the weight has been lost, and even after others say things are going too far. Denial is a major factor of anorexia nervosa. Distortion of the body image is also a major feature of the disorder (Harrison, 2013).

BULIMIA NERVOSA Bulimia nervosa is characterized by recurrent cycles of binge eating and purging. Binge eating often follows on the heels of dieting (Martire et al., 2015). There are various methods of purging. Vomiting is common. Other avenues include strict dieting or fasting, laxatives, and demanding exercise regimes. Individuals with eating disorders will not settle for less than their idealized body shape and weight (Chang et al., 2013; Wade et al., 2015). Bulimia, like anorexia, is connected with irregular menstrual cycles (Mendelsohn & Warren, 2010) and tends to afflict females during adolescence and young adulthood (Bravender et al., 2010). Eating disorders are upsetting and dangerous in themselves, but are also connected with depression (Erikson et al., 2014; Stice et al., 2013b).

PERSPECTIVES ON EATING DISORDERS Psychoanalytic theory suggests that anorexia nervosa may help young women cope with sexual fears, especially fear of pregnancy. Their breasts and hips flatten, and perhaps, in adolescents' fantasies, they remain asexual children. Anorexia prevents some

James Worrell/Photodisc/Getty Images

bulimia nervosa an eating disorder characterized by cycles of binge eating and purging as a means of controlling weight gain.

adolescents from separating from their families and assuming adult responsibilities.

A particularly disturbing risk factor for eating disorders in adolescent females is a history of child abuse, particularly sexual abuse, although the numbers of eating disorders that are reported as attributable to abuse and neglect are variable (Dworkin et al., 2014; Mitchell & Bulik, 2013). Certainly young women have a very slender social ideal set before them in women such as runway models. As the cultural ideal slenderizes, women with normal body weight, according to health charts, feel fat, and heavy women feel huge (Harrison, 2013; Tiggeman, 2014). Eating disorders tend to run in families, which raises the possibility of genetic involvement. Genetic factors would not directly cause eating disorders, but might involve obsessionistic and perfectionistic personality traits (Dodge & Simic, 2015; Halmi et al., 2014).

14-5 SUBSTANCE USE AND SUBSTANCE USE DISORDERS

The United States is flooded with drugs that can distort your perceptions and change your mood—drugs that can pull you up, let you down, and move you across town. Some of these drugs are legal, others illegal. Some are used recreationally, others medically. Some are safe if used correctly and dangerous if they are not. Some adolescents use drugs because their friends do or because their parents tell them not to. Some are seeking pleasure; others are seeking escape.

Do these catwalk models have the ideal figure of the 2010's? Unfortunately, too many teenage U.S. girls attempt to emulate them.

Karl Prouse/Catwalking /Catwalking/Getty Images

Bulimia Nervosa: The Case of Nicole

Nicole awakens in her cold dark room and already wishes it was time to go back to bed. She dreads the thought of going through this day, which will be like so many others in her recent past. She asks herself the question every morning, "Will I be able to make it through the day without being totally obsessed by thoughts of food, or will I blow it again and spend the day [binge eating]?" She tells herself that today she will begin a new life, today she will start to live like a normal human being. However, she is not at all convinced that the choice is hers.

—Boskind-White & White (1983, p. 29)

David J. Green - Lifestyle / Alamy Stock Photo

Adolescents often become involved with drugs that impair their ability to learn at school and are connected with reckless behavior (Pani et al., 2010). Alcohol is the most popular drug on high school (and college) campuses (see Table 14.3; Johnston et al., 2016). Nearly half of high school 12th graders have smoked marijuana (Johnston et al., 2016). Two in five have tried cigarettes. Some use amphetamines or other stimulants, and of these, some use stimulants to help them focus on their studying. Cocaine was once a toy of the well-to-do, but price breaks have brought it into the lockers of high school students.

Alcohol and cigarettes are the most widely used substances by adolescents. Likelihood of use increases from 8th grade through 12th grade (see Table 14.1). Why? One reason is simply that 12th graders have had more years of opportunity to use drugs. But note that the researchers asked whether students had ever used the drug. Therefore, many yes answers reflect an incident or two of experimentation, and not regular use. Other drugs, like heroin, may be in the news, but they have been used by only about 1% of high schoolers. Johnston and his colleagues (2016) note that parental and societal warnings may be getting through to adolescents because their substance use declined steadily over the past generation. Marijuana is one of the few drugs that has seen an increase in popularity.

Where does substance use end and a **substance use disorder** begin? Most psychologists use the

Diagnostic and Statistical Manual of Mental Disorders of the American Psychiatric Association (5th edition, 2013) in defining substance use disorders. Substance use disorders may develop with repeated use of a substance, according to the manual, leading to changes in "brain circuitry" that are connected with impaired control over use of the substance, social problems, risky behavior (such as reckless driving or "unprotected" sex), and biological factors suggestive of addiction. Some substances can lead to physical addiction, so that when the dosage is lowered, withdrawal symptoms, also known as **abstinence syndrome**, occur. When addicted individuals lower their intake of alcohol, for example, they may experience symptoms such as tremors (shakes), high blood pressure, rapid heart and pulse rate, anxiety, restlessness, and weakness. Three of the most common types of abused substances are depressants, stimulants, and hallucinogens.

TABLE 14.3	HAVE YOU USED _____ IN YOUR _____?		
Percent saying "Yes"			
	Lifetime	**Last year**	**Last 30 days**
Alcohol	45.2	39.9	21.8
Amphetamines	9.1	6.2	2.7
Cigarettes	21.1	N/A	7.0
E-cigarettes	N/A	N/A	13.2
Cocaine	2.7	1.7	0.8
Ecstasy	3.5	2.2	0.8
Heroin	0.7	0.4	0.2
LSD	2.8	1.9	0.7
Marijuana	30.0	23.7	14.0

Source: Johnston, L. D., O'Malley, P. M., Miech, R. A., Bachman, J. G., & Schulenberg, J. E. (2016). Monitoring the Future national survey results on drug use, 1975–2015: Overview, key findings on adolescent drug use. Ann Arbor: Institute for Social Research, The University of Michigan.

Notes: Drug use increases from the 8th grade through the 12th grade. Use of e-cigarettes has surpassed use of tobacco cigarettes among adolescents. Finally, results reflect usage only among adolescents in school; dropouts are not included.

substance use disorder a persistent pattern of use of a substance characterized by frequent intoxication; impairment of physical, social, or emotional well-being; and possible physical addiction.

abstinence syndrome a characteristic cluster of symptoms that results from a sudden decrease in the level of usage of a substance.

14-5a DEPRESSANTS

Depressants slow the activity of the nervous system. Depressants include alcohol, narcotics derived from the opium poppy (such as heroin, morphine, and codeine), and sedatives (such as barbiturates and methaqualone).

Alcohol lessens inhibitions so that drinkers may do things when drinking that they might otherwise resist (Winograd & Sher, 2015). Alcohol is also an intoxicant: It distorts perceptions, impairs concentration, hinders coordination, and slurs the speech. Alcohol use is most prevalent among 21- to 34-year-olds. More than one million students between the ages of 18 and 24 are accidentally injured each year while under the influence, assaulted by other students who have been drinking, or raped by college men who have been drinking.

The major medical use of heroin, morphine, and other opioids is relief from pain. But they also can provide a euphoric "rush." Heroin is addictive, and regular users develop tolerance. *Barbiturates* are depressants with various legitimate medical uses, such as relief from pain, anxiety, and tension, but people can become rapidly dependent on them.

14-5b STIMULANTS

Stimulants speed up the heartbeat and other bodily functions. Nicotine, cocaine, and amphetamines are the most common stimulants. Nicotine is the addictive chemical in tobacco (Brody, 2014). Nearly 450,000 Americans die from smoking-related problems each year (American Lung Association, 2014). Cigarette smoke contains carbon monoxide, which causes shortness of breath, and hydrocarbons ("tars"). Smoking is responsible for most respiratory diseases and lung cancer. E-cigarettes contain nicotine, but not the hydrocarbons (Brody, 2014).

Cocaine accelerates the heart rate, spikes the blood pressure, constricts the arteries of the heart, and thickens the blood, a combination that can cause cardiovascular and respiratory collapse (Liaudet et al., 2014). Overdoses can cause restlessness, insomnia, tremors, and even death. Amphetamines can keep users awake for long periods and reduce their appetites. Tolerance for amphetamines develops rapidly. The powerful amphetamine called methamphetamine is apparently physically addictive (Shoptaw, 2014). Methamphetamine abuse can cause brain damage, leading to problems in learning and memory.

Do You Have a Problem with Alcohol?

How can you tell whether you may have a drinking problem? Answering the following four questions can help you find out (NIAAA, 2005):

Yes No Have you ever felt you should cut down on your drinking?

Yes No Have people annoyed you by criticizing your drinking?

Yes No Have you ever felt bad or guilty about your drinking?

Yes No Have you ever had a drink first thing in the morning (as an "eye opener") to steady your nerves or get rid of a hangover?

Just one "yes" answer suggests a possible alcohol problem. Two or more yeses make it highly likely that a problem exists. In either case, it is advisable to discuss your answers with your doctor or another health care provider.

F1online digitale Bildagentur GmbH/Alamy Stock Photo

14-5c HALLUCINOGENICS

Hallucinogenics give rise to perceptual distortions called hallucinations, which sometimes can be so strong as to be confused with reality. Marijuana, Ecstasy, LSD, and PCP are hallucinogenic drugs. Marijuana, which is typically smoked, helps users relax, elevates their mood, increases sensory awareness, and can induce visual hallucinations, for example, time seeming to slow down. Marijuana carries health risks such as impairing the perceptual–motor coordination and short-term memory (Ratzan, 2014). Regular users may experience withdrawal, which is a sign of addiction (American Psychiatric Association, 2013).

Ecstasy, a popular "party" drug, provides the boost of a stimulant and mild hallucinogenic effects. The combination appears to free users from inhibitions and awareness of the consequences of risky behavior, such as unprotected sex. Ecstasy can also impair working memory, increase anxiety, and lead to depression (Lamers et al., 2006). LSD is the acronym for lysergic acid diethylamide, another hallucinogenic drug. High doses of hallucinogenics can impair coordination and judgment (driving while using hallucinogenic drugs poses grave risks), change the mood, and cause paranoid delusions.

hallucinogenics drugs that give rise to hallucinations.

STUDY TOOLS 14

READY TO STUDY?

In the book, you can:

- ☐ Rip out the chapter review card at the back of the book for a handy summary of the chapter and key terms.
- ☐ Check your understanding of what you've read with the quizzes that follow.

ONLINE AT CENGAGEBRAIN.COM YOU CAN:

- ☐ Collect StudyBits while you read and study the chapter.
- ☐ Quiz yourself on key concepts.
- ☐ Find videos for further exploration.
- ☐ Prepare for tests with CDEV2 Flash Cards as well as those you create.

SELF-ASSESSMENTS

Fill-Ins

Answers can be found in the back of the book.

1. _____ triggers the development of acne, which afflicts 75% to 90% of adolescents.

2. Menstruation is the sloughing off of the _____.

3. The major cause of death for adolescents is _____.

4. A disturbing risk factor for eating disorders in adolescent females is a history of _____ abuse.

5. Adolescents may be awkward and gawky due to _____ growth.

6. _____ emissions are also known as "wet dreams."

7. The historical trend toward increasing adult height was accompanied by an earlier onset of puberty, and is known as the _____ trend.

8. The advent of menstruation is termed _____.

9. Alcohol lessens _____ so that drinkers might do risky things that they might otherwise resist.

10. The three most widely used substances by adolescents are alcohol, cigarettes, and _____

Multiple Choice

1. Government statistics show that firearms account for about _____% of adolescent suicides.
   - a. 10
   - b. 25
   - c. 50
   - d. 75

2. According to the text, perfectionistic and obsessionistic personality traits play a role in
   - a. dropping out of school.
   - b. committing suicide.
   - c. achieving Stage 6 of Kohlberg's levels and stages of moral development.
   - d. eating disorders.

3. Gynecomastia stems from the small amount of female sex hormones secreted by the
   - a. testes.
   - b. endometrium.
   - c. epiphyses.
   - d. uterus.

4. Of the following, the least likely cause of death for an adolescent is
   - a. homicide.
   - b. pneumonia.
   - c. cancer.
   - d. suicide.

5. Which of the following is true about early- and late-maturing adolescents?
   - a. Early-maturing boys are more likely to be agitated and ill-natured.
   - b. Early-maturing boys are often dominated by late-maturing boys.
   - c. Early-maturing girls become conspicuous with their height and development of their breasts.
   - d. Early-maturing girls are at less risk for psychological problems and substance abuse.

6. Which of the following is not part of the female athletic triad?
   - a. muscle growth
   - b. lack of energy
   - c. loss of bone density
   - d. menstrual problems

7. Which of the following traits is associated with anorexia nervosa?
   - a. intelligence
   - b. openness to experience
   - c. perfectionism
   - d. conscientiousness

8. Which of the following substances increases blood pressure and constricts arteries?
   - a. alcohol
   - b. LSD
   - c. marijuana
   - d. cocaine

9. Heroin is classified as a _____
   - a. stimulant.
   - b. depressant.
   - c. hallucinogenic.
   - d. none of the above.

10. Which of the following brakes the adolescent growth spurt in females?
    - a. substance abuse
    - b. testosterone
    - c. estrogen
    - d. development of secondary sex characteristics

15 | Adolescence: Cognitive Development

Moodboard/Alamy Stock Photo

LEARNING OUTCOMES

After studying this chapter, you will be able to . . .

15-1 Discuss adolescent cognitive development and the key events of Piaget's stage of formal operations

15-2 Describe gender differences in cognitive abilities

15-3 Discuss Kohlberg's theory of moral development in adolescence

15-4 Discuss the roles of the school in adolescence, focusing on dropping out

15-5 Discuss adolescent work experiences and career choices

After you finish this chapter, go to **PAGE 258** for **STUDY TOOLS**

I am a college student of extremely modest means. Some crazy psychologist interested in something called "formal operational thought" has just promised to pay me $20 if I can make a coherent logical argument for the proposition that the federal government should under no circumstances ever give or lend more to needy college students. Now what could people who believe that possibly say by way of supporting that argument? Well, I suppose they could offer this line of reasoning ...

> Adolescents can follow and formulate arguments from premise to conclusion and back once more, even if they do not believe in them

This "college student of extremely modest means" is thinking like an adolescent. Concrete-operational children are bound by the facts as they are, but the adolescent, as the adult, can ponder abstract ideas and see the world as it could be. Our college student recognizes that a person can find arguments for causes in which he or she does not believe.

—Flavell et al. (2002)

15-1 PIAGET'S STAGE OF FORMAL OPERATIONS

The stage of **formal operations** is the top level in Jean Piaget's theory. Adolescents in this stage have reached cognitive maturity, even if rough edges remain. For many children in developed nations, the stage of formal operations can begin at about the time of puberty, 11 or 12 years old. But some reach this stage somewhat later, and some not at all. Piaget describes the accomplishments of the stage of formal operations in terms of the individual's increased ability to classify objects and ideas, engage in logical thought, and

In the formal-operational stage, adolescents are capable of sophisticated use of symbols, such as those found in geometry.

hypothesize, just as researchers make hypotheses in their investigations. The adolescent can group and classify symbols, statements, and even theories. Adolescents can follow and formulate arguments from premise to conclusion and back once more, even if they do not believe in them. Hypothetical thinking, the use of symbols to represent other symbols, and deductive reasoning allow the adolescent to more fully comprehend the real world and to play with the world that dwells within the mind alone.

formal operations the fourth stage in Piaget's cognitive-developmental theory, characterized by the capacity for flexible, reversible operations concerning abstract ideas and concepts, such as symbols, statements, and theories.

TRUTH OR FICTION?

T	F	Many adolescents see themselves as being on stage.
T	F	It is normal for male adolescents to think of themselves as action heroes and to act as though they are made of steel.
T	F	Adolescent boys outperform adolescent girls in mathematics.
T	F	Most adolescents make moral decisions based on their own ethical principles and may choose to disobey the laws of the land if these laws conflict with their principles.
T	F	Adolescents who work after school get lower grades.

15-1a HYPOTHETICAL THINKING

In formal-operational thought, adolescents discover the concept of "what might be." Adolescents can project themselves into situations that transcend their immediate experience and become wrapped up in fantasies. Adolescents can think ahead, systematically trying out various possibilities in their minds. They "conduct research" to see whether their hypotheses about themselves and their friends and teachers are correct, for example, "trying on" different clothes and attitudes to see which work best for them.

In terms of career decisions, the wealth of possible directions leads some adolescents to experience anxiety about whether they will pick the career that is the best fit for them and to experience a sense of loss because they may be able to choose only one.

15-1b SOPHISTICATED USE OF SYMBOLS

Children in elementary school can understand what is meant by abstract symbols such as 1 and 2. They can also perform operations in which numbers are added, subtracted, and so on. But consider x, the primary algebraic symbol for variables. Children up to the age of 11 or 12 or so usually cannot fully understand the symbolic meaning of this concept, even if they can be taught the mechanics of solving for x in simple equations. But formal-operational children can grasp intuitively what is meant by x. Formal-operational children, or adolescents, can perform mental operations with symbols that stand for nothing in their own experience.

These symbols include those used in geometry. Adolescents work with points that have no dimensions, lines that have no width and are infinite in length, and circles that are perfectly round, even though such things are not found in nature. The ability to manipulate these symbols will permit them to work in theoretical physics or math or to obtain jobs in engineering or architecture.

Formal-operational individuals can understand, appreciate, and sometimes produce metaphors—figures of speech in which words or phrases that ordinarily signify one thing are applied to another. We find metaphors in literature, but consider how everyday figures of speech enhance our experience: *squeezing* out a living, *basking in the sunshine* of fame or glory, *hanging by a thread*, or *jumping* to conclusions.

imaginary audience the belief that others around us are as concerned with our thoughts and behaviors as we are; one aspect of adolescent egocentrism.

personal fable the belief that our feelings and ideas are special and unique and that we are invulnerable; one aspect of adolescent egocentrism.

Enhanced cognitive abilities can backfire when adolescents adamantly advance their religious, political, and social ideas without recognition of the subtleties and practical issues that might give pause to adults. For example, let's begin with the premise, "Industries should not be allowed to pollute the environment." If Industry A pollutes the environment, an adolescent may argue to shut down Industry A, at least until it stops polluting. The logic is reasonable and the goal is noble, but Industry A may be indispensable to the nation, or many thousands of people may be put out of work if it is shut down. More experienced people might prefer to seek a compromise.

15-1c ADOLESCENT EGOCENTRISM

Adolescents show a new egocentrism in which they comprehend the ideas of other people, but have difficulty sorting out those things that concern other people from the things that concern themselves.

THE IMAGINARY AUDIENCE Many adolescents fantasize about becoming rock stars or movie stars adored by millions. The concept of the **imaginary audience** achieves part of that fantasy, in a way. It places the adolescent on stage, but surrounded by critics more than by admirers. Adolescents assume that other people are concerned with their appearance and behavior, more so than they really are (Martin & Soko, 2011). The self-perception of adolescents as being on stage may account for their intense desire for privacy and their preoccupation with their appearance.

FICTION

T (F) Many adolescents see themselves as being on stage.

It is true that adolescents generally see themselves as being on stage—with countless eyes peering in on them. This self-perception may account for the common adolescent intense desire for privacy.

THE PERSONAL FABLE Spider-Man and Batman, stand aside! Because of the **personal fable**, many adolescents become action heroes, at least in their own minds. In the personal fable, one believes that one's thoughts and emotions are special and unique (Hill et al., 2011). It also refers to the common adolescent belief that one is invulnerable.

(T) F It is normal for male adolescents to think of themselves as action heroes and to act as though they are made of steel.

It is true that it is normal for male adolescents to think of themselves as action heroes and to act as though they are made of steel. These are examples of the "personal fable" at work. The fable in males is grounded in high levels of testosterone and immaturity of the part of the brain involved in judgment.

The personal fable is connected with such behaviors as showing off and risk taking (Smith et al., 2014). Many adolescents assume that they can smoke with impunity (Morrell et al., 2015). Cancer? "It can't happen to me," or, "I've got years and years to think about that." They may drive recklessly. They often engage in spontaneous, unprotected sexual activity, allowing the biological drive to rule them and possibly assuming that sexually transmitted infections (STIs) and unwanted pregnancies happen to other people, not to them.

Many adolescents believe that their parents and other adults—even their peers—could never feel what they are feeling or know the depth of

Adolescents may spend a great deal of time seeking imperfections—or admiring themselves—in the mirror. The concept of the imaginary audience places them on stage, but surrounded more by critics than admirers.

Thomas Northcut/Stone/Getty Images

their passions. "You just don't understand me!" claims the adolescent. But, at least often enough, we do.

15-2 GENDER DIFFERENCES IN COGNITIVE ABILITIES

Although females and males do not differ noticeably in overall intelligence, beginning in childhood (Miller & Halpern, 2014), gender differences appear in certain cognitive abilities. Females are somewhat superior to males in verbal ability. Males seem somewhat superior in visual–spatial skills. The picture for mathematics is more complex, with females excelling in some areas and males in others.

15-2a VERBAL ABILITY

Verbal abilities include reading, spelling, grammar, oral comprehension, and word fluency. As a group, females surpass males in verbal ability throughout their lives (Halpern, 2012). These differences show up early. Girls seem to acquire language faster than boys. They make more prelinguistic vocalizations, utter their first word sooner, and develop larger vocabularies. Boys in the United States are more likely than girls to have reading problems (Brun et al., 2009).

Why do females excel in verbal abilities? Biological factors such as the organization of the brain may play a role, but do not discount cultural factors—whether a culture stamps a skill as gender-neutral, masculine, or feminine (Goldstein, 2005). In Nigeria and England, reading is looked on as a masculine activity, and boys traditionally surpass girls in reading ability. But in the United States and Canada, reading tends to be stereotyped as feminine, and girls tend to excel.

FIG.15.1 EXAMPLES OF TESTS USED TO MEASURE VISUAL–SPATIAL ABILITY

Mental-rotation test. If you mentally rotate the figure on the left, which of the five figures on the right would you obtain?

1.   a   b   c   d   e

2.   a   b   c   d   e

No gender differences are found on the spatial visualization tasks. The gender difference is greatest on the mental rotation tasks. What are some possible reasons for these differences?

15-2b VISUAL–SPATIAL ABILITY

Visual–spatial ability refers to the ability to visualize objects or shapes and to mentally manipulate and rotate them. This ability is important in such fields as art, architecture, and engineering. Boys begin to outperform girls on many types of visual–spatial tasks starting at age eight or nine, and the difference persists into adulthood (Halpern, 2012; Sneider et al., 2015). The gender difference is particularly notable on tasks that require imagining how objects will look if they are rotated in space (see Figure 15.1).

Some researchers link visual–spatial performance to evolutionary theory and sex hormones. It may be related to a genetic tendency to create and defend a territory (Lawton, 2010). An environmental theory is that gender stereotypes influence the spatial experiences of children. Gender-stereotyped "boys' toys," such as blocks, Legos, and Erector sets, provide more practice with spatial skills than gender-stereotyped "girls' toys." Boys are also more likely to engage in sports, which involve moving balls and other objects through space (Hoffman et al., 2011).

Image Source /Jupiter Images

15-2c MATHEMATICAL ABILITY

For half a century or more, it has been believed that male adolescents generally outperform females in mathematics, and research has tended to support that belief (Else-Quest et al., 2013; Miller & Halpern, 2014). But a study by Hyde and her colleagues (2008) of some 7 million second-through eleventh-graders found no mean gender differences for performance in mathematics on standardized tests, although boys were somewhat more represented at the extremes—extreme high and low scores. The complexity of the test items apparently made no difference. Although girls may be generally as capable as boys in math, most Americans have different expectations for them, and these expectations may

FICTION

T (F) Adolescent boys outperform adolescent girls in mathematics.

A study by Janet Shibley Hyde and her colleagues (2008) of some seven million second-through eleventh-graders found no gender differences for performance in mathematics on standardized tests. The complexity of the test items apparently made no difference.

still discourage girls from entering "STEM fields" (i.e., fields in science, technology, engineering, and math) (Else-Quest et al., 2013).

15-3 MORAL DEVELOPMENT

Children in early childhood tend to view right and wrong in terms of rewards and punishments. Lawrence Kohlberg referred to such judgments as *preconventional*. In middle childhood, *conventional* thought tends to

TABLE 15.1 KOHLBERG'S POSTCONVENTIONAL LEVEL OF MORAL DEVELOPMENT

Stage	Examples of Moral Reasoning That Support Heinz's Stealing the Drug	Examples of Moral Reasoning That Oppose Heinz's Stealing the Drug
Stage 5: Contractual, legalistic orientation: One must weigh pressing human needs against society's need to maintain social order.	This thing is complicated because society has a right to maintain law and order, but Heinz has to take the drug to save his wife.	I can see why Heinz feels he has to take the drug, but laws exist for the benefit of society as a whole and cannot simply be cast aside.
Stage 6: Universal ethical principles orientation: People must follow universal ethical principles and their own consciences, even if it means breaking the law.	In this case, the law comes into conflict with the principle of the sanctity of human life. Heinz must take the drug because his wife's life is more important than the law.	If Heinz truly believes that stealing the drug is worse than letting his wife die, he should not take it. People have to make sacrifices to do what they think is right.

emerge, and children usually begin to judge right and wrong in terms of social conventions, rules, and laws (see Table 9.1 on page 152). In adolescence, many—not all—individuals become capable of formal-operational thinking, which allows them to derive conclusions about what they should do in various situations by reasoning from ethical principles. And many of these individuals engage in *postconventional* moral reasoning. They *deduce* proper behavior.

15-3a THE POSTCONVENTIONAL LEVEL

In the **postconventional level**, moral reasoning is based on the person's own moral standards. Consider once more the case of Heinz that was introduced in Chapter 9. Moral judgments are derived from personal values, not from conventional standards or authority figures. In the contractual, legalistic orientation of Stage 5, it is recognized that laws stem from agreed-on procedures and that many rights have great value and should not be violated (see Table 15.1). But under exceptional circumstances, such as in the case of Heinz, laws cannot bind the individual. A Stage 5 reason for stealing the drug might be that it is the right thing to do, even though it is illegal. Conversely, it could be argued that if everyone in need broke the law, the legal system and the social contract would be destroyed.

Stage 6 thinking relies on supposed universal ethical principles, such as those of human life, individual dignity, justice, and *reciprocity*. Behavior that is consistent with these principles is considered right. If a law is seen as unjust or contradicts the right of the individual, it is wrong to obey it.

In the case of Heinz, it could be argued from the perspective of Stage 6 that the principle of preserving life takes precedence over laws prohibiting stealing. Therefore, it is morally necessary for Heinz to steal the drug, even if he must go to jail. It could also be asserted, from the principled orientation, that if Heinz finds the social contract or the law to be the highest principle, he must remain within the law, despite the consequences.

Stage 5 and 6 moral judgments were virtually absent among the seven-and ten-year-olds in Kohlberg's (1963) sample of American children. They increased in frequency during the early and middle teens. By age 16, Stage 5 reasoning was shown by about 20% of adolescents and Stage 6 reasoning was demonstrated by about 5% of adolescents. However, Stage 3 and 4 judgments were made more frequently at all ages—7 through 16—studied by Kohlberg and other investigators (Commons et al., 2006; Rest, 1983) (see Figure 15.2).

15-3b MORAL BEHAVIOR AND MORAL REASONING

Are individuals whose moral judgments are more mature more likely to engage in moral behavior? The answer seems to be yes (Bazerman & Tenbrunsel, 2011; Cheng, 2014).

FICTION

T (F) Most adolescents make moral decisions based on their own ethical principles and may choose to disobey the laws of the land if these laws conflict with their principles.

It is not true that most adolescents make moral decisions based on their own ethical principles. Although research suggests that post conventional moral reasoning, if it occurs at all, appears no earlier than in adolescence, the research also shows that most adolescents (and most adults!) actually reason at lower levels.

postconventional level according to Kohlberg, a period during which moral judgments are derived from moral principles and people look to themselves to set moral standards.

FIG.15.2 AGE AND TYPE OF MORAL JUDGMENT

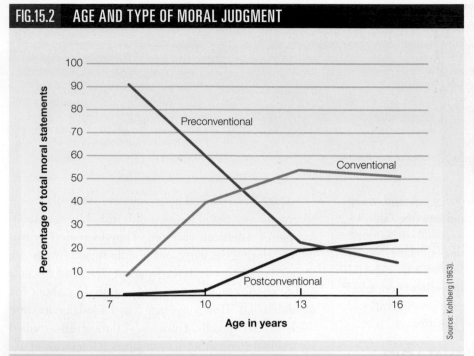

Source: Kohlberg (1963).

The incidence of preconventional reasoning declines from more than 90% of moral statements at age 7 to less than 20% of statements at age 16. Conventional moral statements increase with age between the ages of 7 and 13 but then level off to account for 50% to 60% of statements at ages 13 and 16. Postconventional moral statements are all but absent at ages 7 and 10 but account for about 20% to 25% of statements at ages 13 and 16.

reasoning reflects Kohlberg's personal ideals and not a natural, universal stage of development (Gibbs, 2014). In his later years, Kohlberg (1985) dropped Stage 6 reasoning from his theory in recognition of this possibility.

15-4 THE ADOLESCENT IN SCHOOL

How can we emphasize the importance of the school to the development of the adolescent? Adolescents are highly influenced by the opinions of their peers and their teachers. Their self-esteem rises or falls with the pillars of their skills.

The transition to middle, junior high, or high school generally involves a shift from a smaller neighborhood elementary school to a larger, more impersonal setting with more students and different teach-

Adolescents with higher levels of moral reasoning are more likely to exhibit moral behavior. Studies have also found that group discussion of moral dilemmas elevates delinquents' levels of moral reasoning (Walker & Frimer, 2011).

15-3c EVALUATION OF KOHLBERG'S THEORY

Evidence supports Kohlberg's view that the moral judgments of children develop in an upward sequence (Boom et al., 2007), even though most children do not reach postconventional thought. Postconventional thought, when found, first occurs during adolescence, apparently because formal-operational thinking is a prerequisite for it (Patenaude et al., 2003).

Kohlberg believed that the stages of moral development follow the unfolding of innate sequences and are therefore universal. But he may have underestimated the influence of social, cultural, and educational institutions (Dawson, 2002).

Postconventional thinking is all but absent in developing societies (Snarey, 1994). Perhaps postconventional

ers for different classes. These changes may not fit the developmental needs of early adolescents. For example, adolescents express a desire for increased autonomy, yet teachers in junior high typically allow less student input and exert more control than teachers in elementary school (Tobbell, 2003).

The transition to the new school setting is often accompanied by a decline in grades and participation in school activities. Students may also experience a drop in self-esteem and an increase in stress (Rudolph & Flynn, 2007).

The transition from elementary school appears to be more difficult for girls than boys. Girls are more likely to be undergoing puberty and to earn the attention of boys in higher grades, whereas younger boys are not likely to be of interest to older girls. Girls experience major life changes, and children who experience many life changes at once find it more difficult to adjust (Tobbell, 2003).

But the transition need not be that stressful (Rudolph et al., 2001). Elementary and middle schools can help ease the transition. Some middle schools create a more intimate, caring atmosphere by establishing

Gender Differences in Moral Development

Do males reason at higher levels of moral development than females? Kohlberg and Kramer (1969) reported that the average stage of moral development for men was Stage 4, which emphasizes justice, law, and order. The average stage for women was reported to be Stage 3, which emphasizes caring and concern for others.

Carol Gilligan (Gilligan, 1982) argues that this gender difference reflects patterns of socialization: 11-year-old Jake views Heinz's dilemma as a math problem. He sets up an equation showing that life has greater value than property. Heinz should thus steal the drug. But 11-year-old Amy notes that stealing the drug and letting Heinz's wife die are both wrong. She searches for alternatives, such as getting a loan, saying that it wouldn't be wise for Heinz to go to jail and no longer be around to help his wife.

Although Gilligan sees Amy's reasoning as being as sophisticated as Jake's, it could be said to show a lower level of moral development according to Kohlberg's system. Yet Gilligan and other researchers note that Amy, like other girls, has been socialized into being sensitive to the needs of others and foregoing simplistic judgments of right and wrong (You et al., 2011). They consider girls therefore to be more morally sensitive, that is, to be more likely to base their moral judgments and behavior on empathy (Loewenthal, 2016). To Jake, clear-cut conclusions are to be derived from a set of premises, but it is questionable whether his methodology suggests a higher level of moral development.

Rubberball/Getty Images

smaller schools within the school building. Others have "bridge programs" during the summer that introduce students to the new school culture and strengthen their academic skills.

15-4a DROPPING OUT

Completing high school is a critical developmental task. The consequences of dropping out can be grim. Dropouts are more likely to be unemployed or have low incomes (Catterall, 2011). Dropouts are more likely to develop delinquency, criminal behavior, and substance abuse (Catterall, 2011).

Excessive school absence and reading below grade level are two predictors of school dropout (Lever et al., 2004). Other risk factors include low grades, low self-esteem, problems with teachers, substance abuse, being old for one's grade level, and being male (Chapman et al., 2012). Adolescents who adopt adult roles early, especially marrying at a young age or becoming a parent, are also more likely to drop out (Chapman et al., 2012). Students from low-income households or large urban areas are also at greater risk (Chapman et al., 2012).

PREVENTING DROPPING OUT Many programs have been developed to prevent dropping out of school. Successful programs have some common characteristics (Bost & Riccomini, 2006; Reschly & Christenson, 2006): early preschool interventions (such as Head Start); identification and monitoring of high-risk students; small class size, individualized instruction, and counseling; vocational components that link learning and community work experiences; involvement of families or community organizations; and clear and reasonable educational goals.

Unfortunately, most intervention efforts are usually not introduced until students are on the verge of dropping out—when it is usually too late.

15-5 ADOLESCENTS IN THE WORKFORCE

Life experiences help shape vocational development. One life experience that is common among American teenagers is holding a job.

15-5a PREVALENCE OF ADOLESCENT EMPLOYMENT

About half of all high school sophomores, two-thirds of juniors, and almost three-fourths of seniors have a job during the school year (Bachman et al., 2013). European Americans are more likely than minority students to work (Bachman et al., 2013). Girls and boys are equally likely to be employed, but boys work more hours (Staff et al., 2004).

Although millions of adolescents between the ages of 14 and 18 are legally employed, another two to three million work illegally (Holloway, 2004). Others work too many hours, work late hours on school nights, or hold hazardous jobs. Middle-class teenagers are twice as likely to be employed as lower-income teenagers, but employed lower-income adolescents work longer hours (Bachman et al., 2003).

15-5b PROS AND CONS OF ADOLESCENT EMPLOYMENT

The potential benefits of adolescent employment include developing a sense of responsibility, self-reliance, and discipline; learning to appreciate the value of money and education; acquiring positive work habits and values; and enhancing occupational aspirations (Rosenbaum et al., 2014). Disadvantaged adolescent female African Americans are more likely to graduate from high school and avoid coercive romantic relationships, yet they are more likely to use illicit substances and alcohol (Rosenbaum et al., 2014). Working apparently provides more of an opportunity to access various substances. Other researchers not that students who work lengthy hours—more than 11 to 13 hours per week—report lower grades, higher rates of drug and alcohol use, more delinquent behavior, lower self-esteem, and higher levels of psychological problems than students who do not work or who work only a few hours (Brandstätter & Farthofer, 2003). Ironically, adolescents whose grade point averages are most negatively affected by school-year employment are European Americans and Asian Americans with the most highly educated parents (Bachman et al., 2013).

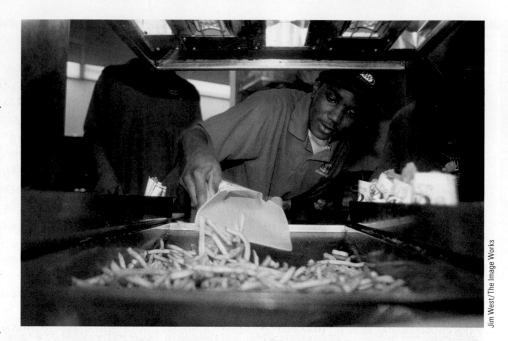

Jim West/The Image Works

Parents and educators apparently need to consider the number of hours adolescents should be working during the school year.

FICTION

T (F) Adolescents who work after school get lower grades.

Adolescents who work after school, as a group, do appear to get lower grades. Students who work more than 11–13 hours per week also report higher rates of drug and alcohol use, more delinquent behavior, and lower self-esteem than students who do not work or work only a few hours a week.

15-5c CAREER CHOICES

When I was a child, I wanted to be an astronaut or an explorer. I became a psychologist and author. My daughter Allyn wanted to be a rock star. Now she is a drama teacher.

Children's career aspirations may not be practical at first. They become increasingly realistic—and often more conventional—as children mature and gain experience. In adolescence, ideas about the kind of work one wants to do tend to become more firmly established, or crystallized, but some people do not choose a particular occupation until the college years or even afterward (Creed & Wamelink, 2015; Rogers & Creed, 2011).

Sometimes we plan our careers on the basis of our perceived abilities and personality traits (Garcia et al., 2015; Rottinghaus & Van Esbroeck, 2011). Sometimes our early work experiences point us in certain directions (Creed & Wamelink, 2015).

JOHN HOLLAND'S CAREER TYPOLOGY Psychologists have devised approaches to matching personality traits with careers to predict adjustment in a given career. Holland's (1997) RIASEC method, as used in his Vocational Preference Inventory, matches six personality types to various kinds of careers: realistic, investigative, artistic, social, enterprising, and conventional (see Figure 15.3). Within each "type" of career, some options are more sophisticated than others and require more education and training.

▶ Realistic people, according to Holland, are concrete in thinking. They are mechanically oriented. They tend to be best adjusted in occupations that involve motor activity. Examples of such occupations are unskilled labor, such as attending gas stations; farming; and the skilled trades, such as auto repair, electrical work, plumbing, and construction work.

▶ Investigative people are abstract in their thinking. They are creative and tend to be introverted but open to new experience. They tend to do well in college and university teaching and in research positions.

FIG.15.3 ASSESSING AN ADOLESCENT'S CAREER TYPE BY ATTENDING A "JOB FAIR"

Conventional
These people have clerical or numerical skills. They like to work with data, to carry out other people's directions, or to carry things out in detail.

Realistic
These people have mechanical or athletic abilities. They like to work with machines and tools, to be outdoors, or to work with animals or plants.

Investigative
These people like to learn new things. They enjoy investigating and solving problems and advancing knowledge.

Enterprising
These people like to work with people. They like to lead and influence others for economic or organizational gains.

Social
This group enjoys working with people. They like to help others, including the sick. They enjoy informing and enlightening people.

Artistic
This group is highly imaginative and creative. They enjoy working in unstructured situations. They are artistic and innovative.

Adolescents can gain insight into where they might fit in the career world by picturing themselves at a job fair such as the one illustrated here. Students and employers have a chat. As time passes, they discover mutual interests and begin to collect in groups accordingly. Adolescents can consider the types of people in the six groups by reading the descriptions for each. Then they can ask themselves, "Which group would I most like to join?" What does their answer suggest about the career choices that might be of greatest interest to them?

- Artistic people also tend to be creative and open to new experience. As a group, they are emotional, interested in the emotional life, and intuitive. They tend to be happiest in the visual and the performing arts.

- Socially oriented people tend to be outgoing (extraverted) and concerned about social welfare. They often are agreeable and have a need for affiliation. They gravitate toward occupations in teaching (kindergarten through high school), counseling, and social work.

- Enterprising people tend to be adventurous. They tend to be outgoing and dominant. They gravitate toward industrial roles that involve leadership and planning. They climb the ladder in government and social organizations.

- Conventional people thrive on routine. They are not particularly imaginative. They have needs for order, self-control, and social approval. They gravitate toward occupations in banking, accounting, clerical work, and the military.

Many people combine vocational types. A copywriter in an advertising agency might be both artistic and enterprising. Clinical and counseling psychologists tend to be investigative, artistic, and socially oriented. Military people and beauticians tend to be realistic and conventional, but military leaders who plan major operations and form governments are also enterprising, and individuals who create new hairstyles and fashions are also artistic. Holland's Vocational Preference Inventory assesses these personality types, as do various vocational tests that are used in high schools and colleges.

All in all, more than 20,000 occupations are found in the *Dictionary of Occupational Titles*, which is compiled by the U.S. Department of Labor. But most young people choose from a relatively small range of occupations on the basis of their personalities, experiences, and opportunities (Sawitri & Creed, 2015). Many sort of fall into jobs that are offered to them or follow career paths that are blazed by parents or role models in the community (Kaziboni & Uys, 2015; Sawitri & Creed, 2015).

STUDY TOOLS 15

READY TO STUDY?

In the book, you can:

- ☐ Rip out the chapter review card at the back of the book for a handy summary of the chapter and key terms.

- ☐ Check your understanding of what you've read with the quizzes that follow.

ONLINE AT CENGAGEBRAIN.COM YOU CAN:

- ☐ Collect StudyBits while you read and study the chapter.

- ☐ Quiz yourself on key concepts.

- ☐ Find videos for further exploration.

- ☐ Prepare for tests with CDEV2 Flash Cards as well as those you create.

SELF-ASSESSMENTS

Fill-Ins

Answers can be found in the back of the book.

1. The stage of _____ operations is the top level in Jean Piaget's theory.

2. On a cognitive level, research evidence shows that adolescent males tend to outperform adolescent females on tasks requiring _____ ability.

3. Two predictors of school dropout are reading below grade level and excessive school _____.

4. Holland's Vocational Preference Inventory matches six _____ types with possible careers.

5. Carol Gilligan argued that Kohlberg's methods of gathering data underestimated girls' _____ reasoning.

6. Adolescents can understand _____ such as "hanging by a thread" or "squeezing out a living."

7. The self-perception of adolescents as being on _____ may account for their intense desire for privacy and their preoccupation with their appearance.

8. As opposed to their performance in the United States, boys in Nigeria and England traditionally surpass girls in _____ ability.

9. Test questions involving mental rotation are used to measure _____ ability.

10. The transition from elementary school to high schools tends to be more difficult for (girls or boys).

Multiple Choice

1. **All of the following are risk factors for adolescents dropping out of school** *except*

   a. living in a rural area.

   b. excessive school absence.

   c. reading below grade level.

   d. becoming a parent as a teenager.

2. **Adolescents who have reached Piaget's stage of formal operations differ from children who are still at Piaget's stage of concrete operations in that they are capable of**

   a. seriating a distribution of numbers.

   b. conserving volume.

   c. object permanence.

   d. hypothetical thinking.

3. **In terms of Kohlberg's theory of moral development, Stage 6 moral reasoning is least likely to be based on**

   a. the concept of reciprocity.

   b. seeking revenge for insults.

   c. universal ethical principles.

   d. belief in human dignity.

4. **We would probably find that, as a group, adolescent females tend to be somewhat better than boys in**

   a. studying maps.

   b. imagining how objects will look if they are rotated in space.

   c. learning algebra.

   d. reading.

5. **Many adolescents believe that their parents and other adults—even other adolescents—could never understand what they are feeling or the depth of their passions. This way of thinking reflects**

   a. the imaginary audience.

   b. the personal fable.

   c. sophisticated use of symbols.

   d. hypothetical thinking.

6. **According to Kohlberg's research, 16-year-old adolescents are most likely to show _____ moral reasoning.**

   a. preconventional.   c. postconventional.

   b. unconventional.   d. conventional.

7. **The benefits of adolescent employment after school include all of the following except:**

   a. obtaining higher grades.

   b. developing a sense of responsibility.

   c. learning to appreciate the value of money.

   d. acquiring positive work habits.

8. **Kohlberg and Kramer reported that the average stage of moral development for men was stage:**

   a. 2.   c. 4.

   b. 3.   d. 6.

9. **Hyde and her colleagues studied the math scores of seven million 2nd through 11th graders on standardized tests and conclude that**

   a. boys were superior in math to girls.

   b. girls were superior in math to boys.

   c. there were no gender differences in scores.

   d. boys were more likely to obtain extreme high and low scores.

10. **The personal fable is a result of**

    a. the imaginary audience.

    b. hypothetical thinking.

    c. egocentrism.

    d. ability in math.

16 | Adolescence: Social and Emotional Development

Blend Images / Alamy Stock Photo

LEARNING OUTCOMES

After studying this chapter, you will be able to . . .

16-1 Discuss the formation of identity in adolescence

16-2 Describe relationships with parents and peers during adolescence

16-3 Discuss sexuality during adolescence, focusing on sexual orientation, sexual behavior, and teenage pregnancy

16-4 Discuss the characteristics of juvenile delinquents

16-5 Discuss risk factors in adolescent suicide

After you finish this chapter, go to **PAGE 277** for **STUDY TOOLS**

What am I like as a person? Complicated! I'm sensitive, friendly and outgoing, though I can also be shy, self-conscious, and even obnoxious. . . . I'm responsible, even studious every now and then, but on the other hand I'm a goof-off too, because if you're too studious, you won't be popular. . . . Sometimes I feel phony, especially around boys. . . . I'll be flirtatious and fun-loving. And then everybody else is looking at me . . . Then I get self-conscious and embarrassed and become radically introverted, and I don't know who I really am! I can be my true self with my close friends. I can't be my real self with my parents. They don't understand me. They treat me like I'm still a kid. That gets confusing, though. I mean, which am I, a kid or an adult?[1]

These thoughts of a 15-year-old girl illustrate a key aspect of adolescence: the search for an answer to the question "Who am I?" She is struggling to reconcile contradictory traits and behaviors to determine the "real me." Adolescents are preoccupied not only with their present selves but also with what they want to become.

16-1 DEVELOPMENT OF IDENTITY: "WHO AM I?"

In this chapter, we explore social and emotional development in adolescence. We begin with the formation of identity.

16-1a ERIKSON AND IDENTITY DEVELOPMENT

ego identity vs. role diffusion Erikson's fifth life crisis, during which adolescents develop a firm sense of who they are and what they stand for (ego identity), or they do not develop a sense of who they are and tend to be subject to the whims of others.

psychological moratorium a period when adolescents experiment with different roles, values, beliefs, and relationships.

Erik Erikson's fifth stage of psychosocial development is called **ego identity versus role diffusion**. The primary task is for adolescents to develop ego identity: a sense of who they are and what they stand for. They are faced with choices about their future occupations, political and religious beliefs, gender roles, and more. Because of formal-operational thinking, adolescents can weigh options they have not experienced (Moshman, 2013).

One aspect of identity development is a **psychological moratorium** during which adolescents experiment with different roles, values, beliefs, and relationships (Erikson, 1968). During this time, adolescents

TRUTH OR FICTION?

T	F	U.S. adolescent males are more concerned than U.S. adolescent females about occupational choices.
T	F	Adolescents are in a constant state of rebellion against their parents.
T	F	Most adolescents' friends are "bad influences."
T	F	About three-quarters of a million U.S. teenagers become pregnant each year.
T	F	Suicide is the leading cause of death among U.S. adolescents.

[1]Adapted from Harter (1990, pp. 352–353).

undergo an **identity crisis** in which they examine their values and make decisions about their life roles. Should they attend college? What career should they pursue? Should they become sexually active? With whom?

In their search for identity, many—not all—adolescents join "in" groups, slavishly imitating their peers' clothing, speech, hairstyles, and ideals (Erikson, 1963). Those who successfully resolve their identity crises develop a strong sense of who they are and what they stand for. Those who do not may be intolerant of people who are different and blindly follow people who adhere to convention.

16-1b IDENTITY STATUSES

Building on Erikson's approach, James Marcia (2010) theorized four *identity statuses* that represent the four possible combinations of the dimensions of exploration and commitment that Erikson believed were critical to the development of identity (Kroger & Marcia, 2011; Marcia, 2010) (see Table 16.1). *Exploration* involves active questioning and searching among alternatives to establish goals, values, or beliefs. *Commitment* is a stable investment in one's goals, values, or beliefs.

Identity diffusion is the least advanced status and includes adolescents who neither have commitments nor are trying to form them. This stage is characteristic of younger adolescents and of older adolescents who drift through life or become alienated and rebellious.

In the **foreclosure** status, individuals make commitments without considering alternatives. These commitments are usually established early in life and are often based on identification with parents, teachers, or religious leaders who have made a strong impression.

The **moratorium** status refers to a person who is actively exploring alternatives in an attempt to make choices. Such individuals are often anxious and intense.

Identity achievement refers to those who have explored alternatives and developed relatively firm commitments. They generally have high self-esteem and self-acceptance.

DEVELOPMENT OF IDENTITY STATUSES Before high school, children show little interest in questions of identity. Most are either in identity diffusion or foreclosure statuses. During the high school and college years, adolescents increasingly move from the diffusion and foreclosure statuses to the moratorium and achievement statuses (Marcia, 2014; Moshman, 2013). The greatest gains in identity formation occur in college (Bartoszuk & Pittman, 2010; Berzonsky, 2011). College students are exposed to a variety of lifestyles, beliefs, and career choices, which spur consideration of identity issues. Are you a student who has changed majors once or twice (or more)? If so, you have most likely experienced the moratorium identity status, which is common among college students. College seniors have a stronger sense of identity than first-year students as a result of resolving identity crises (Meeus, 2011), and a sense of identity is associated with higher self-esteem and grades (Perez et al., 2014; Ryeng et al., 2013).

16-1c ETHNICITY AND DEVELOPMENT OF IDENTITY

The development of self-identity is a key task for all adolescents (Kunnen & Metz, 2015). The task is more complex for adolescents who are members of ethnic minority groups (Azmitia, 2015; Worrell, 2015; Umana-Taylor, 2016). Adolescents who belong to the

identity crisis a turning point in development during which one examines one's values and makes decisions about life roles.

identity diffusion an identity status that characterizes those who have no commitments and who are not in the process of exploring alternatives.

foreclosure an identity status that characterizes those who have made commitments without considering alternatives.

moratorium an identity status that characterizes those who are actively exploring alternatives in an attempt to form an identity.

identity achievement an identity status that characterizes those who have explored alternatives and have developed commitments.

TABLE 16.1	THE FOUR IDENTITY STATUSES OF JAMES MARCIA		
		Exploration	
		Yes	No
Commitment	Yes	**Identity Achievement** • Most developed in terms of identity • Has experienced a period of exploration • Has developed commitments • Has a sense of personal well-being, high self-esteem, and self-acceptance • Cognitively flexible • Sets goals and works toward achieving them	**Foreclosure** • Makes commitments without considering alternatives • Commitments based on identification with parents, teachers, or other authority figures • Often authoritarian and inflexible
	No	**Moratorium** • Actively exploring alternatives • Attempting to make choices with regard to occupation, ideological beliefs, and so on • Often anxious and intense • Ambivalent feelings toward parents and authority figures	**Identity Diffusion** • Least developed in terms of identity • Lacks commitments • Not trying to form commitments • May be carefree and uninvolved or unhappy and lonely • May be angry, alienated, rebellious

dominant culture—in this country, European Americans of Christian, especially Protestant, heritage—are usually faced with assimilating one set of cultural values into their identities. However, adolescents who belong to ethnic minority groups, such as African Americans and Islamic Americans, confront two sets of cultural values: the values of the dominant culture and those of their particular ethnic group. If the cultural values conflict, the adolescent needs to sort out the values that are most meaningful to him or her and incorporate them into his or her identity (Cooper et al., 2015). Some adolescents do it cafeteria style; they take a little bit of this and a little bit of that. For example, a young Catholic woman may decide to use artificial means of birth control even though doing so conflicts with her religion's teachings.

Adolescents from ethnic minority groups also often experience prejudice and discrimination. Their cultural heroes may be ignored. A relative scarcity of successful role models can be a problem, particularly for youth who live in poverty. Identifying too strongly with the dominant culture may also lead to rejection by the minority group. On the other hand, rejecting the dominant culture's values for those of the minority group may limit opportunities for advancement in the larger society.

Some researchers hypothesize three stages in the development of **ethnic identity** (Phinney & Baldelomar, 2011). The first is **unexamined ethnic identity**. It is similar to Marcia's identity statuses of diffusion or foreclosure. In the second stage, the adolescent embarks on an **ethnic identity search**. This second

Who do I want to become?

Adolescents who belong to ethnic minority groups may need to sort out two sets of cultural values.

Geri Lavrow/Photographer's Choice/Getty Images

Alejandro Rivera/E+/Getty Images

stage, similar to Marcia's moratorium, may be based on some incident that makes the adolescent aware of his or her ethnicity. During this stage, the adolescent may explore his or her ethnic culture, participating in cultural events, reading, and discussion. In the third stage, individuals have an **achieved ethnic identity** that involves self-acceptance as a member of one's ethnic group and helps individuals withstand the stress that comes from societal discrimination (Romero et al., 2014).

16-1d GENDER AND DEVELOPMENT OF IDENTITY

Erikson believed that there were gender differences in the development of identity, and his views reflected the times in which he wrote. Identity development relates to relationships and occupational choice, among other matters. Erikson (1968, 1975) assumed that relationships were more important to women's development of identity, while occupational and ideological matters were relatively more important to men's. He believed that a young woman's identity was intimately bound up with her roles as wife and mother. Studies today show that both adolescent females and males are concerned about occupational choices, even though females are more likely to expect that they will have to balance the demands of a career and a

ethnic identity a sense of belonging to an ethnic group.

unexamined ethnic identity the first stage of ethnic identity development; similar to the diffusion or foreclosure identity statuses.

ethnic identity search the second stage of ethnic identity development; similar to the moratorium identity status.

achieved ethnic identity the final stage of ethnic identity development; similar to the identity achievement status.

family (Cinamon & Rich, 2014; Skorikov & Vondracek, 2011). Despite cultural lip service to gender equality, this gender difference has persisted because females continue to assume primary responsibility for child rearing, even though most women are employed outside the home.

16-1e DEVELOPMENT OF THE SELF-CONCEPT

Before adolescence, children describe themselves primarily in terms of their physical characteristics and their actions. As they approach adolescence, children begin to incorporate psychological characteristics and social relationships into their self-descriptions (Arnett, 2015).

Adolescents' self-perceptions become more complex than those of younger children (Arnett, 2015). According to Susan Harter's Self-Perception Profile of academically talented adolescents (see Table 16.2), many factors come into play. Adolescents may describe themselves as anxious or sarcastic with parents but as talkative and cheerful with friends. Such contradictions and conflicts in self-description reach their peak at about age 14 and then decline (Schwartz et al., 2011). The advanced formal-operational skills of older adolescents allow them to integrate contradictory aspects of the self. The older adolescent might say: "I'm very adaptable. When I'm around my friends, who think that what I say is important, I'm very talkative; but around my family, I'm quiet because they're not interested enough to really listen to me" (Damon, 1991, p. 988).

16-1f SELF-ESTEEM

Self-esteem tends to decline as the child progresses from middle childhood to about the age of 12 or 13 (Harter & Whitesell, 2003). The growing cognitive maturity of young adolescents makes them increasingly aware of the disparity between their ideal selves and their real selves, especially in terms of physical appearance (Fourchard & Courtinat-Camps, 2013; Stieger et al., 2014). Boys might fantasize they would like to have the physiques of the warriors they see in video games or in the media. Most American girls want to be thin, thin, thin (Daniels & Gillen, 2015).

After hitting a low point at about age 12 or 13, self-esteem gradually improves (Harter & Whitesell, 2003). Perhaps adolescents adjust their ideal selves to better reflect reality. Also, as adolescents develop academic, physical, and social skills, they may grow less self-critical (Schwartz et al., 2011).

For most adolescents, low self-esteem produces temporary discomfort (Harter & Whitesell, 2003). For others, low self-esteem has serious consequences. For example, low self-esteem is often found in teenagers and adults who are depressed or suicidal (Stieger at al., 2014).

Emotional support from parents and peers is important in self-esteem. Adolescents who feel highly regarded by family and friends are more likely to feel positive about themselves (Boudreault-Bouchard et al., 2013; Smetana, 2011).

16-2 RELATIONSHIPS WITH PARENTS AND PEERS

Adolescents coping with the task of establishing a sense of identity and direction in their lives are heavily influenced both by parents and peers.

16-2a RELATIONSHIPS WITH PARENTS

Although most adolescents get along well with their parents, they spend less time with their parents than they did in childhood (Smetana, 2011). Adolescents continue to interact more with their mothers than their fathers.

TABLE 16.2	FACTORS IN SUSAN HARTER'S SELF-PERCEPTION PROFILE FOR ADOLESCENTS
Harter's test contains items similar to these:	
1. I'm good-looking. (factor: general attractiveness)	
2. I get good grades. (scholastic competence)	
3. I have a lot of friends. (peer support)	
4. I do well at sports. (athletic competence)	
5. I'm ready to do well in a job. (job competence)	
6. I don't get into trouble. (conduct)	
7. I date the people I'm attracted to. (romantic appeal)	

Source: Worrell (1997).

Teenagers have more conflicts with their mothers, but they also view their mothers as being more supportive and knowing them better (Rote & Smetana, 2015; Smetana et al., 2013). Adverse relationships with fathers are often associated with depression in adolescents, but good relations with fathers contribute to psychological well-being (Rote & Smetana, 2015).

The decrease in time spent with family may reflect the adolescents' striving for independence (Smetana, 2011). A certain degree of distancing from parents may be adaptive as adolescents form relationships outside the family. However, adolescents continue to maintain love, loyalty, and respect for their parents (Collins & Laursen, 2006). And adolescents who feel close to their parents have more self-reliance and self-esteem, better school performance, and fewer adjustment problems (Costigan et al., 2007; Rote & Smetana, 2015).

The relationship between parents and teens is not always rosy, of course. Early adolescence, in particular, is characterized by increased bickering and a decrease in shared activities and expressions of affection (Smetana, 2011; van den Akker et al., 2010). Conflicts typically center on the everyday details of family life, such as chores, homework, curfews, personal appearance, finances, and dating—often because adolescents believe that they should manage matters that were previously controlled by parents (Costigan et al., 2007). But parents, especially mothers, continue to believe that they should retain control in most areas, for example, encouraging adolescents to do their homework and clean their rooms. As adolescents get older,

they and their parents are more likely to compromise (Smetana, 2011, 2013). On the other hand, parents and adolescents are usually quite similar in their values and beliefs regarding social, political, religious, and economic issues (Collins & Laursen, 2006). Even though the notion of a generation gap between adolescents and their parents may persist as a stereotype, there is little evidence of one.

FICTION

T (F) Adolescents are in a constant state of rebellion against their parents.

It is not true that adolescents are in a constant state of rebellion against their parents. Parents and adolescents are usually quite similar in their values and beliefs regarding social, political, religious, and economic issues.

As adolescents grow older, parents are more likely to relax controls and less likely to use punishment (Smetana, 2011, 2013). Although parent–child relationships change, most adolescents feel that they are close to and get along with their parents, even though they may develop a less idealized view of them (Collins & Laursen, 2006).

PARENTING STYLES Differences in parenting styles continue to influence the development of adolescents (Kenney et al., 2015; Vermeulen-Smit et al., 2015). Adolescents from authoritative homes—whose parents are willing to exert control and explain the reasons for doing so—show the most competent behavior. They are more self-reliant, do better in school, have better mental health, and show the lowest incidence of psychological problems and misconduct, including drug use.

16-2b RELATIONSHIPS WITH PEERS

The transition from childhood to adolescence is accompanied by a shift in the relative importance of parents and peers. Although relationships with parents generally remain positive, the role of peers as a source of activities, influence, and support increases. Parents are perceived as the most frequent

Adolescents are often in conflict with their parents over the desire for autonomy, but most adolescents and parents agree on political, religious, and economic issues.

providers of social and emotional support by fourth-graders—by seventh grade, friends of the same gender are seen to be as supportive as parents. By tenth grade, same-gender friends are viewed as providing more support than parents (Furman & Winkles, 2010; Laursen et al., 2010).

FRIENDSHIPS IN ADOLESCENCE Adolescents have more friends than younger children do (Laursen et al., 2010). Most adolescents have one or two "best friends" and several good friends. Teenagers see, text, or spend time with their friends on the phone or the Internet frequently, usually several hours a day. According to the Pew Research Center (A. Smith, 2014), Facebook is used by more than half (57%) of U.S. adults, and almost three out of four (73%) of U.S. adolescents aged 12–17. The four top dislikes of Facebook users (A. Smith, 2014) are:

▶ People share too much information about themselves (36%)

▶ Other people post information—including photos—about you without your permission (36%)

▶ Other people see comments or posts that you meant to keep private (27%)

▶ There is pressure to disclose too much information about yourself (24%)

Many adolescent Facebook users reported that they were concerned that more and more adults were using Facebook, that it was crucial that they manage their self-presentation carefully, the burden of "drama" (negative social interactions), and friends sharing too much information (Madden, 2013). An overwhelming percentage (94%!) of teenagers who are social media users have Facebook profiles, as compared with 26% who report having Twitter profiles or the 11% who report having Instagram profiles.

Adolescents and young adults report having more Facebook friends than all adults combined: whereas 15% of all adults report having more than 500 friends, nearly twice that amount (27%) of users aged 18–29 report having more than 500 friends. Sixty-five-year-olds also use Facebook, but nearly three in four of them (72%) have 100 friends or fewer. This finding is consistent with research that finds that older people have fewer (actual) friends than younger people have, but that their friends have more in common with them and are more deeply committed to them at advanced ages.

Friendships in adolescence differ from the friendships of childhood. Adolescents are more likely to stress acceptance, intimate self-disclosure, and mutual understanding (Hall, 2011). There are some gender differences. Adolescent girls are more likely to stress the importance of loyalty, intimacy, and companionship, but status—having friends on one's level of social dominance—was more important for males (Hall, 2011). One eighth-grade girl described her best friend this way: "I can tell her things and she helps me talk. And she doesn't laugh at me if I do something weird—she accepts me for who I am" (Berndt & Perry, 1990, p. 269).

Adolescents and their friends are similar in many respects. They typically are the same age and race. They almost always are the same gender. Even though romantic attachments increase during the teen years, most adolescents still choose members of their own gender as best friends (Field et al., 2014; Hartl et al., 2015). Friends are often alike in school attitudes, educational aspirations, and grades. Friends also tend to have similar attitudes about drinking, drug use, and sexual activity.

Friendship contributes to psychological adjustment. Adolescents who have a close friend have higher self-esteem than adolescents who do not (Brendgen et al., 2010).

Intimacy and closeness appear to be more central to the friendships of girls than of boys (Leaper, 2013). Adolescent and adult females also are generally more likely than males to disclose secrets, personal problems, thoughts, and feelings to their friends (Hall, 2011).

Friendship networks among girls are smaller and more exclusive than networks among boys (Leaper, 2013). Girls tend to have one or two close friends, whereas boys tend to congregate in larger, less intimate groups. The activities of girls' and boys' friendship networks differ as well. Girls are more likely to engage in unstructured activities such as talking and listening to music. Boys are more likely to engage in organized group activities, games, and sports.

PEER GROUPS Most adolescents belong to one or more peer groups: *cliques* and *crowds* (Brown, 2013). **Cliques** consist of five to ten individuals who hang around together, sharing activities and confidences. **Crowds** are larger groups who may or may not spend much time together and are identified by their activities or attitudes. Crowds are usually given labels by other adolescents— "jocks," "brains," "druggies," or "nerds." The most negatively labeled groups ("druggies," "rejects") show higher levels of alcohol and drug abuse, delinquency, and depression.

Adolescent peer groups function with less adult guidance or control than childhood peer groups (Staff et al., 2004). Adolescent peer groups may include members of the other gender, sharply contrasting with the gender

clique a group of five to ten individuals who hang around together and who share activities and confidences.

crowd a large, loosely organized group of people who may or may not spend much time together and who are identified by the activities of the group.

segregation of childhood peer groups. Such associations may lead to dating and romantic relationships.

DATING AND ROMANTIC RELATIONSHIPS Romantic relationships usually begin during early and middle adolescence, and most adolescents start dating or going out by the time they graduate from high school (Florsheim, 2003). For heterosexuals, the development of dating typically takes the following sequence: putting oneself in situations where peers of the other gender probably will be present (e.g., hanging out at the mall), group activities including peers of the other gender (e.g., school dances or parties), group dating (e.g., joining a mixed-gender group at the movies), and then traditional two-person dating (Connolly et al., 2004; Kreager et al., 2015).

Dating serves a number of functions. First and foremost, people date to have fun. Dating, especially in early adolescence, also serves to enhance prestige with peers. Dating gives adolescents additional experiences in learning to relate to people. Finally, dating prepares adolescents for adult courtship (Florsheim, 2003).

Dating relationships tend to be casual and short-lived in early adolescence. In late adolescence, relationships tend to become more stable and committed (Connolly et al., 2000). Eighteen-year-olds are more likely than 15-year-olds to mention love, trust, and commitment when describing romantic relationships (Furman & Winkles, 2010; Hall, 2011).

PEER INFLUENCE Peer pressure is fairly weak in early adolescence. It peaks during mid-adolescence and declines after about age 17 (Reis & Youniss, 2004). Peer influence may increase during adolescence because peers provide a standard by which adolescents measure their own behavior as they develop independence from the family (Smetana, 2011). Peers also provide support in times of trouble (Smetana, 2011).

Parents often worry that their teenage children will fall in with the wrong crowd and be persuaded to engage in self-destructive behavior. Despite the widespread assumption that peer and parental influences will be in conflict, with peers exerting pressure on adolescents to engage in negative behaviors such as alcohol and drug abuse, research paints a more complex picture. Parents and peers are usually complementary rather than competing influences (Smetana et al., 2013).

Parents and peers also seem to exert influence in different domains. Adolescents are more likely to conform to peer standards in matters pertaining to style and taste, such as clothing, hairstyles, speech patterns, and music (Smetana, 2011). They are more likely to agree with their parents on moral principles and future educational and career goals (Smetana, 2011).

Adolescents influence each other positively and negatively. In many cases, peer pressure to finish high school and achieve academically can be stronger than pressures to engage in misconduct (Smetana et al., 2013). Yet many times adolescents discourage one another from doing well or from doing too well in school. Adolescents who smoke, drink, use drugs, and engage in sexual activity also often have friends who engage in these behaviors, but adolescents tend to choose friends and peers who are like them to begin with.

FICTION

T (F) Most adolescents' friends are "bad influences."

It is certainly not true that most adolescents' friends are "bad influences." Parents and peers are usually complementary rather than competing influences.

16-3 SEXUALITY

My first sexual experience occurred in a car after the high school junior prom. We were both virgins, very uncertain but very much in love. We had been going together since eighth grade. The experience was somewhat painful. I remember wondering if I would look different to my mother the next day. I guess I didn't because nothing was said.

Because of the flood of sex hormones, adolescents tend to experience a powerful sex drive. In addition, they are bombarded with sexual messages in the media, including scantily clad, hip-grinding, crotch-grabbing pop stars; print ads for barely there underwear; and countless articles on "How to tell if your boyfriend has been [whatever]" and "The 10 things that will drive your girlfriend wild." Teenagers are strongly motivated to follow the crowd, yet they are also influenced by the views of their parents and teachers. So what is a teen to do?

What teens do takes various directions. In this section we first consider adolescent sexual behavior, including masturbation and male–female sexual behavior. As noted in Chapter 15, adolescents often take risks that adults might avoid—in this case, sex without adequate precautions. For that reason we next consider the issues of teenage pregnancy and sexually transmitted infections (STIs). More than half a million American adolescent girls become pregnant each year, and STIs are contracted by millions of adolescents each year.

We also examine the issues involving the fact that not all adolescents desire members of the other sex as partners; some prefer members of their own sex. They are said to have a homosexual (gay male or lesbian) orientation. Although gay males and lesbians prefer members of the own sex for sexual activity, sexual orientation is not simply a matter of "preference" or choice. As we'll see, the sexual orientation of gay males and lesbians—just like the sexual orientation of those who prefer to have sex with members of the other sex—is biologically built in *before* birth.

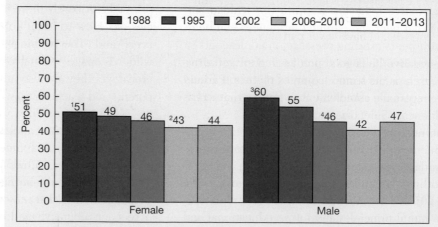

Ammentorp Photography / Alamy Stock Photo

16-3a ADOLESCENT SEXUAL BEHAVIOR

MASTURBATION **Masturbation**, or sexual self-stimulation, is the most common sexual outlet in adolescence. Surveys indicate that most adolescents masturbate at some time and most educated adolescents and early adults see masturbation as beneficial. Although it has not been shown to be physically harmful, beliefs that masturbation is harmful and guilt about masturbating lessen the incidence of masturbation (Robbins et al., 2011).

About three-quarters of adolescent males and half of adolescent females masturbate (Robbins et al., 2011). Males who masturbate do so more often than females who masturbate. It is unclear whether this gender difference reflects a stronger sex drive in

masturbation sexual self-stimulation.

petting kissing and touching the breasts and genitals.

males, greater social constraints on females, or both, but young women are more likely than young men to struggle in coming to terms with the contradiction between social stigma and pleasure (Robbins et al., 2011; Hakim, 2015).

MALE–FEMALE SEXUAL BEHAVIOR

Adolescents today start dating and going out earlier than in past generations. Teens who date earlier are more likely to engage in sexual activity during high school (Temple et al., 2014). Teens who initiate sexual activity earlier are also less likely to use contraception and more likely to become pregnant. But early dating does not always lead to early sex, and early sex does not always lead to unwanted pregnancies.

Petting is practically universal among U.S. adolescents and has been for many generations. Adolescents use petting to express affection, satisfy their curiosities, heighten their sexual arousal, and reach orgasm while avoiding pregnancy and maintaining virginity. Many adolescents do not see themselves as having sex if they stop short of vaginal intercourse (De Rosa et al., 2010). Girls are more likely than boys to be pushed into petting and to feel guilty about it (Slotboom et al., 2011).

Since the early 1990s, the percentage of high school students who have engaged in sexual intercourse has been gradually declining. The incidences of kissing, "making out," oral sex, and sexual intercourse all increase with age. Figure 16.1 summarizes some findings about teenage male–female sexual behavior with results from the National Survey of Family Growth (Martinez & Abma, 2015). There was a gradual decline in the incidence of

FIG.16.1   NEVER-MARRIED TEENAGERS, AGED 15–19, WHO HAVE HAD SEXUAL INTERCOURSE

Legend: 1988 | 1995 | 2002 | 2006–2010 | 2011–2013

Female: [1]51, 49, 46, [2]43, 44
Male: [3]60, 55, [4]46, 42, 47

(Percent, y-axis 0–100)

Source: Martinez, G., & Abma, J. C. (2015). Sexual activity, contraceptive use, and childbearing of teenagers aged 15–19 in the United States. U.S. Department of Health and Human Services, National Center for Health Statistics. NCHS Data Brief, No. 209, Figure 1.

sexual intercourse between 1988 and the first decade of the 21st century, but the incidence of never-married teenagers between the ages of 15 and 19 who have had sex has leveled off at about 44% for females and 47% for males. It should not be surprising that the probability of having had sex rises dramatically between the ages of 15 and 19. More than 90% of the girls aged 15–19 who have had sex have used a condom at one time or another, and majorities have used the withdrawal method of birth control (which is all but useless) or the birth-control pill.

EFFECTS OF PUBERTY The hormonal changes of puberty probably are partly responsible for the onset of sexual activity. In boys, levels of testosterone are associated with sexual behavior. In girls, however, testosterone levels are linked to sexual interests but not to sexual behavior. Social factors may therefore play a greater role in regulating sexual behavior in girls than boys (De Rosa et al., 2010).

The physical changes associated with puberty also may trigger the onset of sexual activity. For example, the development of secondary sex characteristics such as breasts in girls and muscles and deep voices in boys may make them more sexually attractive. Early-maturing girls are more likely to have older friends, who may draw them into sexual relationships.

PARENTAL INFLUENCES Teenagers who have close relationships with their parents are less likely to initiate sexual activity at an early age (Bynum, 2007). Adolescents who communicate well with their parents also delay the onset of sexual activity (Aspy et al., 2007). If these youngsters do have sexual intercourse, they are more likely to use birth control and have fewer partners.

PEER INFLUENCES A good predictor of sexual activity for adolescents is the sexual activity of their best friends. When teenagers are asked why they do not wait to have sex until they are older, the main reason reported is usually peer pressure (Ali & Dwyer, 2011). Peers, especially those of the same gender, also serve as a key source of sex education for adolescents. Adolescents report that they are somewhat more likely to receive information about sex from friends and media sources—TV shows, films, magazines, and the Internet—than from sex education classes or their parents (Kaiser Family Foundation et al., 2003).

SEXTING Sexting is short for *sex texting*, and refers to sending or receiving text messages with sexual content. Sexting can be used to titillate the recipient, to highlight the intimacy of one's relationship, to humiliate someone—or to ask or arrange for a sexual encounter (Walrave et al., 2015).

A survey of Texas high school students found that 28% said they had transmitted a nude photo of themselves in a text message or an email (Temple & Choi, 2014). Three in ten (31%) had requested a "sext" message, and more than half (57%) had asked someone else to send them a sexual text or email. Girls who had sexted were more likely to begin dating early and to engage in risky sexual behavior.

Baron Bratby / Alamy Stock Photo

What about you? Before pressing "send," consider:

▸ *Don't believe that what you sext will remain private.* Many teens say they have received a sext that was meant to be private.

▸ *Whatever you sext may never go away.* Potential employers, college recruiters, teachers and coaches, parents, friends, and total strangers may be able to access your posts, even if you delete them.

▸ *Resist pressure to sext.* Many adolescent girls say that "pressure from guys" is a reason they sext.

▸ *Consider the recipient's reaction before you press send.* A girl may send sexually suggestive content for a "joke," but guys may think that the girl will hook up in real life.

▸ *Nothing you post or send will necessarily remain anonymous.* People you meet online can often track you down on the basis of your screen name and other information you have provided.

16-3b TEENAGE PREGNANCY

In the United States today, the great majority of single adolescents who become pregnant do so accidentally and without committed partners (America's Children, 2013). Most young women in developed nations defer pregnancy until after they have completed some or all of their education. Many do so until they are well into their careers and in their late 20s, their 30s, even their 40s.

Why do single U.S. adolescents get pregnant? For one thing, adolescent girls typically get little advice in school or at home about how to deal with boys' sexual advances. Another reason is failure to use contraception. Some initiate sex at very early ages, when they are least likely to use contraception (Martin et al., 2015; Martinez & Abma, 2015). Many adolescent girls, especially younger adolescents, do not have access to contraceptive devices. Among those who do, fewer than half use them reliably.

Some teenage girls purposefully get pregnant to try to force their partners to make a commitment to them. Some are rebelling against their parents or the moral standards of their communities. But most girls are impregnated because they and their partners miscalculate the odds of getting pregnant (Guttmacher Institute, 2013).

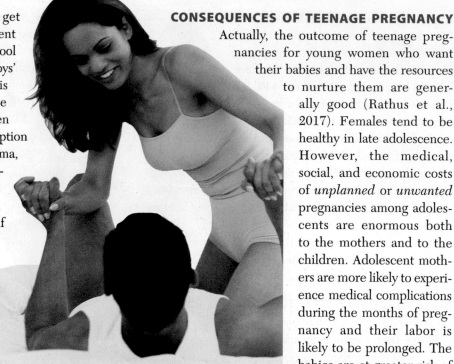

Fuse/Getty Images

About 700,000 U.S. teenagers become pregnant each year. Most of them do so accidentally, and without a committed partner.

For all these reasons, about 700,000 teenage girls in the United States are impregnated each year. The pregnancies result in about 400,000 births. However, large this number may sound, 10 to 20 years ago, about one million girls were getting pregnant each year. Researchers at the Centers for Disease Control and Prevention attribute the drop-off in careless sex to educational efforts by schools, the media, religious institutions, and communities (America's Children, 2013).

Nearly half of pregnant teenagers will have an abortion (Guttmacher Institute, 2016). Most others will become single mothers.

TRUTH

 F About three-quarters of a million U.S. teenagers become pregnant each year.

It is true that about three-quarters of a million single U.S. teenagers become pregnant each year, mostly because of miscalculation of the odds of getting pregnant.

CONSEQUENCES OF TEENAGE PREGNANCY

Actually, the outcome of teenage pregnancies for young women who want their babies and have the resources to nurture them are generally good (Rathus et al., 2017). Females tend to be healthy in late adolescence. However, the medical, social, and economic costs of *unplanned* or *unwanted* pregnancies among adolescents are enormous both to the mothers and to the children. Adolescent mothers are more likely to experience medical complications during the months of pregnancy and their labor is likely to be prolonged. The babies are at greater risk of being premature and of low birth weight (Mathews & MacDorman, 2007). These medical problems are not necessarily because of the age of the mother, but rather because single teenage mothers—especially poor single teenage mothers—are less likely to have access to prenatal care or to obtain adequate nutrition.

The teenage mother is less likely than her peers to graduate from high school or move on the postsecondary education. Therefore, she will earn less and be in greater need of public assistance. Few teenage mothers obtain assistance from the babies' fathers. The fathers typically cannot support themselves, much less a family.

PREVENTING TEENAGE PREGNANCY The past several decades have seen a dramatic increase in programs to help prevent teenage pregnancies. Prevention efforts include educating teenagers about sexuality and contraception and providing family planning services. A majority of U.S. parents want their children to have sex education in the schools.

How successful are sex education programs? The better programs increase students' knowledge about sexuality. Despite fears that sex education will increase sexual activity in teenagers, some programs seem to delay the onset of sexual activity (Bennett & Assefi, 2005; Kirby, 2011). Among teenagers who already are sexually active, sex education is associated with the increased use of effective contraception.

16-3c SEXUALLY TRANSMITTED INFECTIONS (STIs)

Each year an estimated 2 1/2 million adolescents contract a sexually transmitted infection (STI), including about six million new infections caused by the human papilloma virus (HPV) (Genital HPV Infection—CDC Fact Sheet, 2014), which causes genital warts and is associated with cervical cancer. At least 50% of sexually active women and men contract HPV at some time in their lives. A vaccine is available that prevents most young women from being infected with HPV and is best administered before they become sexually active.

Chlamydia, a bacterial infection of the vagina or urinary tract that can result in sterility, is the next most commonly occurring STI in young adults, followed by gonorrhea, HPV/genital warts, genital herpes, syphilis, and HIV/AIDS. Because of its lethality, HIV/AIDS tends to capture most of the headlines. However, other STIs are more widespread, and some of them can also be deadly.

Nearly 2.8 million new chlamydia infections occur each year (Chlamydia—CDC Fact Sheet, 2014). The incidence of chlamydia is especially high among college students. Chlamydia is a major cause of pelvic inflammatory disease (PID), which can lead to infertility.

HIV/AIDS HIV/AIDS is the most devastating STI. If left untreated, it is lethal, and the long-term prospects of those who do receive treatment remain unknown. HIV—the virus that causes AIDS—has spread rapidly around the world and some 37 million people are living with HIV/AIDS, of which 2.5 million are children under the age of 15 (World Health Organization, 2015). More than 1.1 million Americans are living with HIV/AIDS, and about one in six people are unaware of it (HIV in the United States, 2015). The primary mode of HIV transmission worldwide is male–female intercourse, but anal

TABLE 16.3 | OVERVIEW OF SEXUALLY TRANSMITTED INFECTIONS (STIs)

Sti and Cause	Transmission	Symptoms	Diagnosis	Treatment
Chlamydia and nongonococcal urethritis: caused by *Chlamydia trachomatis* bacterium in women	Vaginal, oral, or anal sex. To newborns passing through the birth canal of an infected mother.	Women and men may be symptom-free or experience frequent and painful urination and a discharge.	Analysis of cervical smear in women. Analysis of penile fluid in men.	Antibiotics.
Genital herpes: caused by Herpes simplex virus-type 2 (HSV-2)	Vaginal, oral, or anal sex.	Painful, reddish bumps around the genitals, thighs, or buttocks. Bumps become blisters that fill with pus and break, shedding viral particles. Fever, aches, and pains possible.	Clinical inspection of sores. Culture and examination of fluid drawn from sore.	Antiviral drugs may provide relief and help with healing but are not cures.
Gonorrhea ("clap," "drip"): Gonococcus bacterium (*Neisseria gonorrhoeae*)	Vaginal, oral, or anal sex. To newborns passing through the birth canal of an infected mother.	In men, yellowish, thick discharge, burning urination. Women may be symptom-free or have vaginal discharge, burning urination, or irregular menstruation.	Clinical inspection. Culture of discharge.	Antibiotics.
HIV/AIDS: Acronym for human immunodeficiency virus, the cause of acquired immunodeficiency syndrome	Vaginal or anal sex. Infusion of contaminated blood by needle sharing or from mother to baby during childbirth or breast-feeding.	Usually symptom-free for many years. Swollen lymph nodes, fever, weight loss, fatigue, diarrhea. Deadly "opportunistic infections."	Blood, saliva, or urine tests detect HIV antibodies. Other tests confirm the presence of HIV itself.	There is no cure for HIV/AIDS. A "cocktail" of highly active antiviral therapy (HAART) prolongs life in many people living with the condition.
HPV/Genital warts: caused by human papillomavirus (HPV)	Sexual contact. Contact with infected towels or clothing.	Painless warts resembling cauliflowers on the genitals or anus or in the rectum. Associated with cervical cancer.	Clinical inspection.	A vaccine can prevent infection in most young people. Warts may be removed by freezing, topical drugs, burning, and surgery.
Pubic lice ("crabs"): *Pthirus pubis* (an insect, not a crab)	Sexual contact. Contact with an infested towel, sheet, or toilet seat.	Intense itching in pubic area and other hairy regions to which lice can attach.	Clinical inspection.	Topical drugs containing pyrethrins or piperonal butoxide.
Syphilis: *Treponema pallidum*	Vaginal, oral, or anal sex. Touching an infectious chancre.	Hard, painless chancre appears at site of infection within two to four weeks. May progress through additional stages if untreated.	Clinical inspection or examination of fluid from a chancre. Blood test.	Antibiotics.

intercourse is the primary mode of HIV transmission in the United States (HIV/AIDS—CDC Fact Sheet, 2014). Injecting drugs is another way in which HIV is spread because sharing needles with infected individuals can transmit HIV. Other major risk factors include having sex with multiple partners, failing to use condoms, and abusing drugs and alcohol (HIV in the United States, 2015).

The causes, methods of transmission, symptoms, and treatment—where it exists—of HIV/AIDS and other STIs are described in Table 16.3.

16-3d SEXUAL ORIENTATION AND SEXUAL IDENTITY

Most people, including a majority of adolescents, have a heterosexual sexual orientation. They are sexually attracted to and interested in forming romantic relationships with people of the other gender. However, some people have a **homosexual** orientation. They are attracted to and interested in forming romantic relationships with people of their own gender. Males with a homosexual orientation are referred to as *gay males*. Females with a homosexual orientation are referred to as *lesbians*. However, males and females with a homosexual orientation are sometimes categorized together as "gay people," or "gays." **Bisexual** people are attracted to both females and males. **Transgender** individuals feel that they are actually members of the other gender, "trapped" in the body of the wrong gender. Collectively, lesbian, gay, bisexual, and transgender individuals are frequently referred to as **LGBT** people.

A person's **sexual identity** is the label that he or she adopts to inform others as to who they are as a sexual being, especially concerning sexual orientation. Most people's sexual identity is consistent with their sexual orientation. That is, most people who are attracted to members of the other gender identify themselves as "heterosexual" or "straight." Most people who are attracted to people of the same gender see themselves as being "lesbian" or "gay." However, some people's sexual orientation does not correspond to their sexual identity.

About 7% of U.S. women and men define themselves as being "other than heterosexual," but the behavior of the other 93% doesn't exactly match up with the way in which people label themselves. For example, nearly twice as many people—about 14%—say they have had oral sex with a person of the same gender (Herbenick et al., 2010a, 2010b, 2010c; Reece et al., 2010).

DEVELOPMENT OF SEXUAL ORIENTATION Theories of the origins of sexual orientation look both at nature and nurture—the biological makeup of the individual and environmental factors. Some theories bridge the two.

Social cognitive theorists look for the roles of factors such as reinforcement and observational learning. From this perspective, reinforcement of sexual behavior with members of one's own gender—as in reaching orgasm with them when members of the other gender are unavailable—might affect one's sexual orientation. Similarly, childhood sexual abuse by someone of the same gender could lead to a pattern of sexual activity with people of one's own gender and affect sexual orientation. Observation of others engaged in enjoyable male–male or female–female sexual encounters could also affect the development of sexual orientation. But critics point out that most individuals become aware of their sexual orientation before they experience sexual contacts with other people of either gender (Calzo et al., 2011; Savin-Williams, 2011). Moreover, in a society where many still frown upon the LGBT community, young people are unlikely to believe that an other-than-heterosexual orientation or identity will have positive effects for them.

There is evidence for genetic factors in sexual orientation or identity (Brakefield et al., 2014). About 52% of identical (MZ) twin pairs are concordant (in agreement) for a gay male sexual orientation compared with 22% for fraternal (DZ) twins and 11% for adoptive brothers (Dawood et al., 2009). Monozygotic (MZ) twins fully share their genetic heritage, whereas dizygotic (DZ) twins, like other pairs of siblings, overlap 50%.

It has been demonstrated repeatedly that sex hormones predispose lower animals toward stereotypical masculine or feminine mating patterns (Hines et al., 2015; Pradhan et al., 2015). But can sex hormones influence the developing human embryo and fetus (Garcia-Falgueras & Swaab, 2010)? Swedish neuroscientists Ivanka Savic and her colleagues (2011) report evidence that one's gender identity as being male or being female and one's sexual orientation (heterosexual, homosexual, bisexual, or transgender) can develop during the intra-uterine period. They point out that sexual differentiation of the sex organs occurs during the first two months of pregnancy, whereas sexual differentiation of the

homosexual referring to an erotic orientation toward members of one's own gender.

bisexual attracted to individuals of both genders.

transgendered psychologically belonging to the other gender—that is, the gender that is inconsistent with one's sexual anatomy.

LGBT acronym for *lesbian*, *gay*, *bisexual*, and *transgender*.

sexual identity the label a person uses to signal who she or he is as a sexual being, especially concerning her or his sexual orientation.

brain begins later, during the second half of pregnancy. Sexual differentiation of the genitals and the brain both depend on surges of testosterone, but because they happen at different times, they can occur independently. Therefore, it is possible that an individual's sex organs can develop in one direction while the biological factors that may underlie one's sexual orientation develop in another direction.

According to Ritch Savin-Williams (2011), the development of sexual orientation in gay males and lesbians involves several steps: attraction to members of the same gender, self-labeling as gay or lesbian, sexual contact with members of the same gender, and eventual disclosure of one's sexual orientation to other people. There is generally a gap of about ten years between initial attraction to members of the same gender, which tends to occur at about the age of eight or nine, and disclosure of one's orientation to other people, which usually occurs at about age 18. But some gay males and lesbians never disclose their sexual orientations to anyone or to certain people, such as their parents.

The process of "coming out"—that is, accepting one's sexual minority identity and declaring it to others—can be a long and painful struggle (Mustanski et al., 2014). Gay adolescents may be ostracized and rejected by family and friends. Depression and suicide rates are higher among gay youth than among heterosexual adolescents (Stone et al., 2014). About one in three LGBT adolescents has attempted suicide or engaged in self-harm (Liu & Mustanski, 2012). LGBT adolescents often engage in substance abuse, run away from home, and do poorly in school (Moskowitz et al., 2013; Dermody et al., 2016).

"Coming out to others" sometimes means an open declaration to the world. More often, an adolescent feels more comfortable telling a couple of close friends. Before they inform family members, gay adolescents often anticipate their family's negative reactions, including denial, anger, and rejection (Mustanski et al., 2014). Yet some families are more accepting.

16-4 JUVENILE DELINQUENCY

The term **juvenile delinquency** refers to children or adolescents who engage in illegal activities and come into contact with the criminal justice system. At the most extreme end, juvenile delinquency includes serious behaviors such as homicide, rape, and robbery. Less serious offenses, such as truancy, underage drinking, running away from home, and sexual promiscuity, are considered illegal only when performed by minors. Hence, these activities are termed *status offenses*.

Antisocial and criminal behaviors show a dramatic increase in many societies during adolescence and then taper off during adulthood. For example, about four in ten serious crimes in the United States are committed by individuals under the age of 21, and about three in ten are committed by adolescents under 18 (Snyder & Sickmund, 2006).

Many delinquent acts do not result in arrest or conviction. And when adolescents are arrested, their cases may be disposed of informally, as by referral to a mental health agency (Snyder & Sickmund, 2006).

Boys are much more likely than girls to engage in delinquent behavior, especially crimes of violence. On the other hand, girls are more likely to commit status offenses such as truancy or running away (Snyder & Sickmund, 2006).

16-5 SUICIDE: WHEN THE ADOLESCENT HAS NOTHING—EXCEPT EVERYTHING—TO LOSE

Adolescence is such an exciting time of life. For many, the future is filled with promise. Many count the days until they

juvenile delinquency
conduct in a child or adolescent characterized by illegal activities.

graduate high school, until they enter college. Many enjoy thrilling fantasies of what might be. And then there are those who take their own lives. Suicide is the second leading cause of death among adolescents (Heron, 2016). Since 1960, the suicide rate has more than tripled for young people aged 15 to 24. About 1 to 2 U.S. adolescents in 10,000 commit suicide each year. About 1 in 10 has attempted suicide at least once.

16-5a RISK FACTORS IN SUICIDE

Most suicides among adolescents and adults are linked to feelings of depression and hopelessness (Miranda & Shaffer, 2013). Suicidal adolescents experience four areas of psychological problems: (1) confusion about the self, (2) impulsiveness, (3) emotional instability, and (4) interpersonal problems (Rathus & Miller, 2002). Some suicidal teenagers are highly achieving, rigid perfectionists who have set impossibly high expectations for themselves. Many teenagers throw themselves into feelings of depression and hopelessness by comparing themselves negatively with others, even when the comparisons are inappropriate. ("Yes, you didn't get into Harvard, but you did get into the University of California at Irvine, and it's a great school.")

Adolescent suicide attempts are more common after stressful life events, especially events that entail loss of social support, as in the death of a parent or friend, breaking up with a boyfriend or girlfriend, or a family member's leaving home (Nock et al., 2013). Other contributors to suicidal behavior include concerns over sexuality, school grades, problems at home, and substance abuse (Nock et al., 2013). It is not always a stressful event itself that precipitates suicide, but the adolescent's anxiety or fear of being "found out" for something, such as failing a course or getting arrested.

Suicide tends to run in families (Centers for Disease Control and Prevention, 2013, 2014). Do genetic factors play a role, possibly leading to psychological problems, such as depression, that are connected with suicide?

Researchers have found the following warning signs of suicide among adolescents (May & Klonsky, 2011):

▶ Belief that it is acceptable to kill oneself

▶ Drug abuse and other kinds of delinquency

▶ Victimization by bullying

▶ Extensive body piercing

▶ Stress

▶ Hostility

▶ Depression and other psychological disorders

▶ Heavy smoking

▶ Low self-esteem

▶ Increasing age from 11 to 21

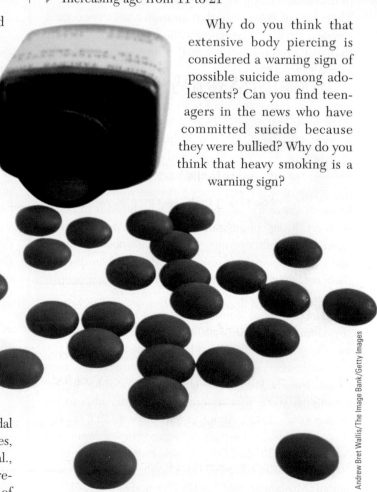

Andrew Bret Wallis/The Image Bank/Getty Images

Why do you think that extensive body piercing is considered a warning sign of possible suicide among adolescents? Can you find teenagers in the news who have committed suicide because they were bullied? Why do you think that heavy smoking is a warning sign?

16-5b ETHNICITY, GENDER, AND SUICIDE

Rates of suicide and suicide attempts vary among different ethnic groups. Native American and Latin American teenagers have the highest suicide rates, in part because of the stresses to which they are exposed, in part because of their lack of access to health care (Centers for Disease Control and Prevention, 2014). European Americans are next. African American teens are least likely to attempt suicide or to think about it (Heron, 2016).

About three times as many adolescent females as males attempt suicide, but about four times as many males complete a suicide (Heron, 2016).

STUDY TOOLS 16

READY TO STUDY?

In the book, you can:

☐ Rip out the chapter review card at the back of the book for a handy summary of the chapter and key terms.

☐ Check your understanding of what you've read with the quizzes that follow.

ONLINE AT CENGAGEBRAIN.COM YOU CAN:

☐ Collect StudyBits while you read and study the chapter.

☐ Quiz yourself on key concepts.

☐ Find videos for further exploration.

☐ Prepare for tests with CDEV2 Flash Cards as well as those you create.

SELF-ASSESSMENTS

Fill Ins

Answers can be found in the back of the book.

1. In terms of parenting styles, adolescents with _____ parents show the most competent behavior.

2. _____ appears to be more central to the friendships of girls than of boys.

3. Eighteen-year-olds are more likely than 15-year-olds to mention _____ when describing romantic relationships.

4. Peer influence declines after about age _____.

5. Because of the flood of sex hormones, adolescents tend to experience a powerful _____ drive.

6. Most adolescents have a(n) _____ sexual orientation.

7. About _____ of identical (MZ) twins are concordant (in agreement) for a gay male sexual orientation.

8. According to Savin-Williams and Diamond, the first step in the development of sexual orientation in gay males and lesbians involves _____.

9. When teenagers are asked why they do not wait to have sex until they are older, the main reason reported is usually _____.

10. Most adolescent suicides are linked to feelings of _____.

Multiple Choice

1. **Which of the following has not been shown to be a risk factor for adolescent suicide?**
   a. belief that it is unacceptable to kill oneself.
   b. extensive body piercing.
   c. depression.
   d. increasing from age 11 to age 21.

2. **About _____ % of serious crimes in the United States are committed by individuals under the age of 21.**
   a. 10.
   b. 20.
   c. 40.
   d. 60.

3. **Which of the following is true of sexual orientation?**
   a. Sexual orientation is a preference.
   b. The majority of people in the United States are lesbian, gay, or bisexual.
   c. Diet affects sexual orientation.
   d. More people engage in sexual behavior with people of the same gender than report that they are gay or lesbian.

4. **Which of the following is accurate about the incidences of kissing, petting, oral sex, and sexual intercourse?**
   a. There is no way of estimating the incidence of these behaviors.
   b. The incidence of these behaviors increases with age.
   c. The incidence of these behaviors among teenagers has been declining rapidly.
   d. Adolescents who engage in petting or oral sex are no longer virgins.

5. **Adolescents are likely to have attitudes similar to their parents concerning all of the following except**
   a. career goals.
   b. religious preference.
   c. belief in the value of education.
   d. clothing and hair styles.

6. **Of teenagers who use social media, approximately _____% report having Facebook profiles or accounts.**
   a. 34.
   b. 54.
   c. 74.
   d. 94.

7. **Which of the following is the most accurate statement about U.S. adolescents' relationships with their fathers?**
   a. The majority of adolescents live in a home without a father.
   b. Most adolescents are involved in constant bickering with their fathers.
   c. Male adolescents interact more with their fathers than their mothers.
   d. Good relations with fathers contribute to adolescents' well-being.

8. **Self-esteem tends to hit a low point at the age of**
   a. 10 or 11.
   b. 12 or 13.
   c. 14 or 15.
   d. 16 or 17.

9. **In terms of Marcia's identity statuses, the adolescent who is most developed in terms of identity has the status of**
   a. identity achievement.
   b. foreclosure.
   c. moratorium.
   d. identity diffusion.

10. **Which of the following statements about adolescents and their friends is *not* true?**
    a. Friends tend to be of the same race.
    b. Girls tend to have one or two close friends.
    c. Adolescents prefer friends of the other gender.
    d. Friendship contributes to psychological adjustment.

ANSWERS TO STUDY TOOLS QUESTIONS

Chapter 1

FILL-INS

1. Locke
2. superego
3. psychosocial
4. bladder
5. assimilation
6. species
7. exosystem
8. Terman
9. positive
10. sequential

MULTIPLE CHOICE

1. b
2. d
3. a
4. d
5. b
6. a
7. a
8. c
9. d
10. c

Chapter 2

FILL-INS

1. Genes
2. zygote
3. meiosis
4. autosomes
5. allele
6. 50
7. 25
8. XYY
9. Sickle
10. genetics (or heredity)

MULTIPLE CHOICE

1. d
2. c
3. d
4. c
5. b
6. d
7. c
8. a
9. d
10. b

Chapter 3

FILL-INS

1. calcium
2. endometriosis
3. trophoblast
4. placenta
5. Preeclampsia
6. oxygen
7. 7
8. neural
9. placenta
10. hormones

MULTIPLE CHOICE

1. b
2. a
3. a
4. b
5. a
6. b
7. d
8. a
9. c
10. b

Chapter 4

FILL-INS

1. Braxton-Hicks
2. epidural
3. vernix
4. Europe
5. hormones
6. bonding
7. Apgar
8. rooting
9. underarm
10. postpartum psychosis

MULTIPLE CHOICE

1. c
2. a
3. d
4. c
5. c
6. b
7. a
8. c
9. d
10. b

Chapter 5

FILL-INS

1. critical
2. second
3. cradle board
4. canalization
5. antibodies
6. multiple sclerosis
7. neurons
8. visual cortex
9. toddler
10. face

MULTIPLE CHOICE

1. c
2. a
3. a
4. d
5. c
6. a
7. c
8. d
9. c
10. c

Chapter 6

FILL-INS

1. assimilation
2. secondary
3. object
4. deferred
5. Babbling
6. recognition
7. fifth
8. mirror
9. echolalia
10. overextension

MULTIPLE CHOICE

1. b
2. a
3. b
4. d
5. b
6. a
7. d
8. d
9. b
10. d

Chapter 7

FILL-INS

1. ambivalent/resistant
2. preattachment
3. Harlow
4. critical
5. Asperger's
6. 24
7. referencing
8. rouge
9. difficult
10. goodness

MULTIPLE CHOICE

1. a
2. b
3. a
4. d
5. d
6. a
7. c
8. c
9. d
10. d

Chapter 8

FILL-INS

1. 2, or 3, or 2–3
2. three
3. deep
4. 5 years, or any answer between 60–71 months
5. pictoral
6. 50
7. cerebellum
8. boys
9. diarrhea
10. lead

MULTIPLE CHOICE

1. b
2. a
3. d
4. a
5. d
6. b
7. d
8. a
9. c
10. a

Chapter 9

FILL-INS

1. cognitive
2. transductive
3. Symbolize
4. egocentrism
5. HOME
6. Scripts
7. whole
8. complex
9. pragmatism
10. senses

MULTIPLE CHOICE

1. c
2. d
3. b
4. d
5. b
6. c
7. a
8. a
9. d
10. b

Chapter 10

FILL-INS

1. memories
2. initiative
3. categorical
4. testosterone
5. authoritative
6. functional
7. Prosocial
8. reject
9. dramatic
10. Bandura

MULTIPLE CHOICE

1. a
2. d
3. b
4. a
5. a
6. c
7. c
8. c
9. b
10. d

Chapter 11

FILL-INS

1. hyperactivity
2. boys, girls
3. blood
4. heredity or genetics
5. asthma
6. myelinated
7. stimulatns
8. dyslexia
9. girls, boys
10. ADHD

MULTIPLE CHOICE

1. d
2. a
3. c
4. d
5. b
6. b
7. d
8. c
9. a
10. a

Chapter 12

FILL-INS

1. conventional
2. sensory
3. mental
4. performance
5. Spanish
6. word-recognition
7. g factor or general intelligence
8. transitivity
9. score
10. objective

MULTIPLE CHOICE

1. a
2. a
3. d
4. c
5. b
6. c
7. d
8. a
9. c
10. b

Chapter 13

FILL-INS

1. latency
2. industry
3. perspective
4. coregulation
5. depression
6. self-fulfilling
7. conduct
8. global
9. caregiving
10. inner, personality, psychological

MULTIPLE CHOICE

1. b
2. b
3. c
4. c
5. d
6. d
7. b
8. c
9. a
10. d

Chapter 14

FILL-INS

1. Testosterone
2. endometrium
3. accidents, injuries
4. child, sexual
5. asynchronous
6. Nocturnal
7. secular
8. menarche
9. inhibitions
10. marijuana

MULTIPLE CHOICE

1. c
2. d
3. a
4. b
5. c
6. a
7. c
8. d
9. b
10. c

Chapter 15

FILL-INS

1. formal
2. visual–spatial
3. absence
4. personality
5. moral
6. metaphors
7. stage
8. reading
9. visual-spatial
10. girls

MULTIPLE CHOICE

1. a
2. d
3. b
4. d
5. b
6. d
7. a
8. c
9. d
10. c

Chapter 16

FILL-INS

1. authoritative
2. Intimacy, Closeness, Self-disclosure
3. love, trust, commitment
4. 17
5. sex
6. heterosexual
7. half, 50%, 52%
8. attraction to members of the same gender
9. peer pressure
10. depression, hopelessness, low self-esteem

MULTIPLE CHOICE

1. a
2. c
3. d
4. b
5. d
6. d
7. d
8. b
9. a
10. c

REFERENCES

A

Abravanel, E., & DeYong, N. G. (1991). Does object modeling elicit imitative-like gestures from young infants? *Journal of Experimental Child Psychology*, 52, 22–40.

Adler-Baeder, F. (2006). What do we know about the physical abuse of stepchildren? A review of the literature. *Journal of Divorce & Remarriage*, 44(3–4), 67–81.

Adolescent Health. (2014). Summary health statistics: National Health Interview Survey, 2014. Table C-5a. Centers for Disease Control and Prevention. http://ftp.cdc.gov/pub/Health_Statistics/NCHS/NHIS/SHS/2014_SHS_Table_C-5.pdf.

Adolph, K. E., & Robinson, S. R. (2015). Motor development, vol. 2: Cognitive processes. *Handbook of Child Psychology and Developmental Sciences*, DOI: 10.1002/9781118963418.childpsy204

Agency for Healthcare Research and Quality. (2004, April). Chronic illnesses. In *Child Health Research Findings*. (Program Brief, AHRQ Publication 04-P011). Rockville, MD: Author. Retrieved from http://www.ahrq.gov/research/childfind/chfchrn.htm

Aguiar, N. R., & Taylor, M. (2015). Children's concepts of the social affordances of a virtual dog and a stuffed dog. *Cognitive Development*, 34, 16–27.

Ainsworth, M. D. S. (1989). Attachments beyond infancy. *American Psychologist*, 44, 709–716.

Ainsworth, M. D. S., & Bowlby, J. (1991). An ethological approach to personality development. *American Psychologist*, 46(4), 333–341.

Ainsworth, M. D. S., Blehar, M. C., Waters, E., & Wall, S. (1978). *Patterns of attachment: A psychological study of the Strange Situation*. Hillsdale, NJ: Erlbaum.

Alexander, G. M., Wilcox, T., & Woods, R. (2009). Sex differences in infants' visual interest in toys. *Archives of Sexual Behavior*, 38(3), 427–433.

Ali, M. M., & Dwyer, D. S. (2011). Estimating peer effects in sexual behavior among adolescents. *Journal of Adolescence*, 34(1), 183–190.

Allen, G., et al. (2011). Functional neuroanatomy of the cerebellum. In A. S. Davis (Ed.), *Handbook of pediatric neuropsychology* (pp. 147–160). New York, NY: Springer.

Alloway, R. G., & Alloway, T. P. (2013). Working memory in development. In T. P. Alloway, & R. G. Alloway (Eds.). *Working memory: The connected intelligence* (pp. 63–82). New York: Psychology Press.

Amato, P. R., & Anthony, C. J. (2014). Estimating the effects of parental divorce and death with fixed effects models. *Journal of Marriage and Family*, 76(2), 370–386.

Anderson, B. J. (2011). Plasticity of gray matter volume: The cellular and synaptic plasticity that underlies volumetric change. *Developmental Psychobiology*, 53(5), 456–465.

Annett, M. (1999). Left-handedness as a function of sex, maternal versus paternal inheritance, and report bias. *Behavior Genetics*, 29(2), 103–114.

Arbib, M. A. (2015). Language evolution: An emergentist perspective. In B. MacWinney, & W. O'Grady (Eds.). *The handbook of language emergence* (pp. 600–623). West Sussex, UK: Wiley.

Arterberry, M. E., & Kellman, P. J. (2016). *Development of perception in infancy*. New York: Oxford University Press.

Aschermann, E., Gülzow, I., & Wendt, D. (2004). Differences in the comprehension of passive voice in German-and English-speaking children. *Swiss Journal of Psychology*, 63(4), 235–245.

Aslin, R. N. (2012). Infant eyes: A window on cognitive development. *Infancy: Special Issue: Advances in Eye Tracking in Infancy Research*, 17(1), 126–140.

Aspy, C. B., et al. (2007). Parental communication and youth sexual behaviour. *Journal of Adolescence*, 30(3), 449–466.

Auyeung, B., et al. (2009). Fetal testosterone predicts sexually differentiated childhood behavior in girls and in boys. *Psychological Science*, 20(2), 144–148.

Avinum, R., & Knafo-Noam, A. (2015). Socialization, genetics, and their interplay in development. In J. E. Grusec & P. D. Hastings (Eds.). *Handbook of socialization: Theory and Research* (pp. 347–371). New York. Guilford.

Awasaki, T., & Ito, K. (2016). Neurodevelopment: Regeneration is a gas. *Nature*, 531, 182–183.

Azmitia, M. (2015). Reflections on the cultural lenses of identity development. In K. C. McLean, & M. Syed (Eds.). *The Oxford handbook of identity development* (pp. 286–298). New York: Oxford University Press.

B

Bachman, J. G., Safron, D. J., Sy, S. R., & Schulenberg, J. E. (2003). Wishing to work: New perspectives on how adolescents' part-time work intensity is linked to educational disengagement, substance use, and other problem behaviours. *International Journal of Behavioral Development*, 27(4), 301–315.

Badious, S., et al. (2016). Association between breast milk and HIV-1 transmission through breastfeeding. Prostaglandins, Leukotrienes, and *Essential Fatty Acids (PLEFA)*, 105, 35–42.

Bakker, D. J. (2006). Treatment of developmental dyslexia: A review. *Pediatric Rehabilitation*, 9(1), 3–13.

Bakker, R., et al. (2010). Maternal caffeine intake from coffee and tea, fetal growth, and the risks of adverse birth outcomes: The Generation R Study. *The American Journal of Clinical Nutrition*, 91(6), 1691–1698.

Bandura, A. (1986). *Social foundations of thought and action: A social-cognitive theory*. Englewood Cliffs, NJ: Prentice Hall.

Bandura, A. (2011). The social and policy impact of social cognitive theory. In M. M. Mark, S. I. Donaldson, & B. Campbell (Eds.), *Social psychology and evaluation* (pp. 33–71). New York, NY: Guilford.

Bandura, A., Ross, S. A., & Ross, D. (1963). Imitation of film-mediated aggressive models. *Journal of Abnormal and Social Psychology*, 66, 3–11.

Bangal, V. B., Giri, P. A., & Mahajan, A. S. (2012). Maternal and foetal outcome in pregnancy induced hypertension: A study from rural tertiary care teaching hospital in India. *International Journal of Biomedical Research*, 2(12), 595–599.

Barac, R., & Bialystok, E. (2011). Cognitive development in bilingual children. *Language Teaching*, 44, 36–54.

Barr, R. G., Paterson, J. A., MacMartin, L. M., Lehtonen, L., & Young, S. N. (2005). Prolonged and unsoothable crying bouts in infants with and without colic. *Journal of Developmental & Behavioral Pediatrics, 26*(1), 14–23.

Bartoszuk, K., & Pittman, J. F. (2010). Profiles of identity exploration and commitment across domains. *Journal of Child and Family Studies, 19*(4), 444–450.

Bartzokis, G., et al. (2010). Lifespan trajectory of myelin integrity and maximum motor speed. *Neurobiology of Aging, 31*(9), 1554–1562.

Bauer, P. J., & Fivush, R. (2010). Context and consequences of autobiographical memory development. *Cognitive Development, 25*(4), 303–308.

Bauer, P., San Souci, P., & Pathman, T. (2010). Infant memory. *Wiley Interdisciplinary Reviews: Cognitive Science, 1*, 267–277.

Baum, N., Weidberg, Z., Osher, Y., & Kohelet, D. (2011). No longer pregnant, not yet a mother: Giving birth prematurely to a very low birth weight baby. *Qualitative Health Research, 22*(6). doi:10.1177/1049732311422899

Baumrind, D. (1989). Rearing competent children. In W. Damon (Ed.), *Child development today and tomorrow.* San Francisco, CA: Jossey-Bass.

Baumrind, D. (1991a). The influence of parenting style on adolescent competence and substance use. *Journal of Early Adolescence, 11*, 56–95.

Bazerman, M. H., & Tenbrunsel, A. A. (2011). *Blind spots: Why we fail to do what's right and what to do about it.* Princeton, NJ: Princeton University Press.

Beauchamp, G. K., & Mennella, J. A. (2011). Flavor perception in human infants: Development and functional significance. *Digestion, 83*(Suppl. 1), 1–6.

Bebko, J. M., McMorris, C. A., Metcalfe, A., Ricciuti, C., & Goldstein, G. (2014). Language proficiency and metacognition as predictors of spontaneous rehearsal in children. *Canadian Journal of Experimental Psychology, 68*(1), 46–58.

Beck, E., Burnet, K. L., & Vosper, J. (2006). Birth-order effects on facets of extraversion. *Personality and Individual Differences, 40*(5), 953–959.

Beebe, B., et al. (2010). The origins of 12-month attachment: A microanalysis of 4-month mother-infant interaction. *Attachment & Human Development, 12*(1–2), 3–141.

Beilei, L., Lei, L., Qi, D., & von Hofsten, C. (2002). The development of fine motor skills and their relations to children's academic achievement. *Acta Psychologica Sinica, 34*(5), 494–499.

Bekkhus, M., Rutter, M., Maughan, B., & Borge, A. I. H. (2011). The effects of group daycare in the context of paid maternal leave and high-quality provision. *European Journal of Developmental Psychology, 8*(6), 681–696.

Belmonte, M. K., & Carper, R. A. (2006). Monozygotic twins with Asperger syndrome: Differences in behaviour reflect variations in brain structure and function. *Brain and Cognition, 61*(1), 110–121.

Belsky, J. (2006b). Early child care and early child development: Major findings of the NICHD Study of Early Child Care. *European Journal of Developmental Psychology, 3*(1), 95–110.

Belsky, J., et al. (2007). Are there long-term effects of early child care? *Child Development, 78*(2), 681–701.

Bengtsson, H., & Arvidsson, A. (2011). The impact of developing social perspective-taking skills on emotionality in middle and late childhood. *Social Development, 20*(2), 353–375.

Bennett, S. E., & Assefi, N. P. (2005). School-based teenage pregnancy prevention programs: A systematic review of randomized controlled trials. *Journal of Adolescent Health, 36*(1), 72–81.

Berenbaum, S. A., Martin, C. L., Hanish, L. D., Briggs, P. T., & Fabes, R. A. (2008). Sex differences in children's play. In J. B. Becker et al. (Eds.), *Sex differences in the brain* (pp. 275–290). New York, NY: Oxford University Press.

Berge, J. M., et al. (2015). All in the family: Correlations between parents' and adolescent siblings' weight and weight-related behaviors. *Obesity, 23*(4), 833–839.

Bergen, D. (2015). Psychological approaches to the study of play. In J. E. Johnson et al. (Eds.). *The handbook of the study of play, Vol. 2* (pp. 51–70). Lanham, MD: Rowman & Littlefield.

Berndt, T. J. (2004). Friendship and three A's (aggression, adjustment, and attachment). *Journal of Experimental Child Psychology, 88*(1), 1–4.

Berndt, T. J., & Perry, T. B. (1990). Distinctive features and effects of early adolescent friendships. In R. Montemayor, G. R. Adams, & T. P. Gullotta (Eds.), *From childhood to adolescence: A transitional period?* Newbury Park, CA: Sage.

Berndt, T. J., Miller, K. E., & Park, K. E. (1989). Adolescents' perceptions of friends and parents' influence on aspects of their school adjustment. *Journal of Early Adolescence, 9*, 419–435.

Berzonsky, M. D. (2011). A social-cognitive perspective on identity construction. In S. J. Schwartz et al. (Eds.), *Handbook of identity theory and research* (Part 1, pp. 55–76). New York, NY: Springer.

Bezdjian, S., Tuvblad, C., Raine, A., & Baker, L. A. (2011). The genetic and environmental covariation among psychopathic personality traits, and reactive and proactive aggression in children. *Child Development, 82*(4), 1267–1281.

Bialystok, E., Luk, G., Peets, K. F., & Yang, S. (2010). Receptive vocabulary differences in monolingual and bilingual children. *Bilingualism: Language and Cognition, 13*, 525–531.

Bierman, K. L., et al. (2014). Effects of Head Start REDI on children's outcomes 1 year later in different kindergarten contexts. *Child Development, 85*(1), 140–159.

Bigelow, A. E., et al. (2010). Maternal sensitivity throughout infancy: Continuity and relation to attachment security. *Infant Behavior and Development, 33*(1), 50–60.

Bird, A., Reese, E., & Tripp, G. (2006). Parent–child talk about past emotional events: Associations with child temperament and goodness-of-fit. *Journal of Cognition and Development, 7*(2), 189–210.

Bloom, P. (2002). Mind reading, communication, and the learning of names for things. *Mind and Language, 17*(1–2), 37–54.

Blum, K., et al. (2009). *Genes and happiness. Gene Therapy and Molecular Biology, 13*, 91–129.

Blumberg, M. S., & Seelke, A. M. H. (2010). The form and function of infant sleep: From muscle to neocortex. In M. S. Blumberg, J. H. Freeman, & S. R. Robinson (Eds.), *Oxford Handbook of Developmental Behavioral Neuroscience* (pp. 391–423). New York, NY: Oxford University Press.

Boccia, M., & Campos, J. J. (1989). Maternal emotional signals, social referencing, and infants' reactions to strangers. In N. Eisenberg (Ed.), *New directions for child development* (No. 44): *Empathy and related emotional responses*. San Francisco, CA: Jossey-Bass.

Boivin, M., Vitaro, F., & Poulin, F. (2005). Peer relationships and the development of aggressive behavior in early childhood. In R. E. Tremblay, W. W. Hartup, & J. Archer (Eds.), *Developmental origins of aggression* (pp. 376–397). New York, NY: Guilford.

Boom, J., Wouters, H., & Keller, M. (2007). A cross-cultural validation of stage development: A Rasch re-analysis of longitudinal socio-moral reasoning data. *Cognitive Development, 22*(2), 213–229.

Borelli, J., et al. (2010). Attachment and emotion in school-aged children. *Emotion, 10*(4), 475–485.

Borghese, M. M., et al. (2015). Television viewing and food intake during television viewing in normal-weight, overweight and obese 9- to 11-year-old Canadian children: a cross-sectional analysis. *Journal of Nutritional Science, 4*, DOI: http://dx.doi.org/10.1017/jns.2014.72.

Bost, L. W., & Riccomini, P. J (2006). Effective instruction: An inconspicuous strategy for dropout prevention. *Remedial and Special Education, 27*(5), 301–311.

Bouchard, T. J., Jr., & Loehlin, J. C. (2001). Genes, evolution, and personality. *Behavior Genetics, 31*(3), 243–273.

Bowker, J. C., Thomas, K. K., Norman, K. E., & Spencer, S. V. (2011). Mutual best friend involvement. *Journal of Youth and Adolescence, 40*(5), 545–555.

Bowlby, J. (1988). *A secure base*. New York, NY: Basic Books.

Braarud, H. C., & Stormark, K. M. (2008). EJ814142—Prosodic modification and vocal adjustments in mothers' speech during face-to-face interaction with their two- to four-month-old infants: A double video study. *Social Development, 17*(4), 1074–1084.

Braddick, O., & Atkinson, J. (2011). Development of human visual function. *Vision Research, 51*(13), 1588–1609.

Bradley, R. H. (2006). The home environment. In N. F. Watt et al. (Eds.), *The crisis in youth mental health: Critical issues and effective programs* (Vol. 4): *Early intervention programs and policies, Child psychology and mental health* (pp. 89–120). Westport, CT: Praeger/Greenwood.

Bradley, R. H., Caldwell, B. M., & Corwyn, R. F. (2003). The child care HOME inventories: Assessing the quality of family child care homes. *Early Childhood Research Quarterly, 18*(3), 294–309.

Brandstätter, H., & Farthofer, A. (2003). Influence of part-time work on university students' academic performance. *Zeitschrift für Arbeits-und Organisationspsychologie, 47*(3), 134–145s.

Bravender, T., et al. (2010). Classification of eating disturbance in children and adolescents: Proposed changes for the *DSM-V. European Eating Disorders Review, 18*(2), 79–89.

Bray, G., & Bouchard, C. (2014). *Handbook of obesity: Epidemiology, etiology, and physiopathology* (4th ed.). CRC Press.

Brendgen, M., et al. (2010). Link between friendship relations and early adolescents' trajectories of depressed mood. *Developmental Psychology, 46*(2), 491–501.

Brigham, N. B., Yoder, P. J., Jarzynka, M. A., & Tapp, J. (2011). The sequential relationship between parent attentional cues and attention to objects in young children with autism. *Journal of Autism and Developmental Disorders, 40*(2), 200–208.

Brockington, I. (2011). Maternal rejection of the young child: Present status of the clinical syndrome. *Psychopathology, 44*(5), 329–336.

Bronfenbrenner, U., & Morris, P. A. (2006). The bioecological model of human development. In R. M. Lerner & W. Damon (Eds.), *Handbook of child psychology* (6th ed., Vol. 1), *Theoretical models of human development* (pp. 793–828). Hoboken, NJ: Wiley.

Brown, R. (1973). *A first language: The early stages*. Cambridge, MA: Harvard University Press.

Brown, R. (1977). Introduction. In C. A. Snow & C. Ferguson (Eds.), *Talking to children*. New York, NY: Cambridge University Press.

Brown, S. D., & Lent, R. W. (2016). Vocational psychology: Agency, equity, and well-being. *Annual Review of Psychology, 67*, 541–565.

Brownell, C. A., & Carriger, M. S. (1990). Changes in cooperation and self-other differentiation during the second year. *Child Development, 61*, 1164–1174.

Bruck, M., Ceci, S. J., & Principe, G. F. (2006). The child and the law. In K. Renninger, I. E. Sigel, W. Damon, & R. M. Lerner (Eds.), *Handbook of child psychology* (6th ed., Vol. 4), *Child psychology in practice* (pp. 776–816). Hoboken, NJ: Wiley.

Brucker, B., et al. (2015). Watching corresponding gestures facilitates learning with animations by activating human mirror-neurons: An fNIRS study. *Learning and Instruction, 36001*), 27–37.

Brummelte, S., & Galea, L. A. M. (2010). Depression during pregnancy and postpartum: Contribution of stress and ovarian hormones. *Progress in Neuro-Psychopharmacology and Biological Psychiatry, 34*(5), 766–776.

Brun, C. C., et al. (2009). Sex differences in brain structure in auditory and cingulate regions. *NeuroReport: For Rapid Communication of Neuroscience Research, 20*(10), 930.

Buehler, C., O'Brien, M., Swartout, K. M., & Zhou, N. (2014). Maternal employment and parenting through middle childhood: Contextualizing factors. *Journal of Marriage and Family, 76*(5), 1025–1046.

Bugental, D. B., et al. (2010). A cognitive approach to child abuse prevention. *Psychology of Violence, 1*(Suppl.), 84–106.

Bugental, D. B., Corpuz, R., & Beaulieu, D. A. (2015). An evolutionary approach to socialization. In J. E. Grusec & P. D. Hastings (Eds.). *Handbook of socialization: Theory and Research* (pp. 325–346). New York. Guilford.

Bukowski, W. M., Buhrmeister, D., & Underwood, M. K. (2011). Peer relations as a developmental context. In M. K. Underwood & L. H. Rosen (Eds.), *Social development: Relationships in infancy, childhood, and adolescence* (pp. 153–179). New York, NY: Guilford.

Buratovic, S., et al. (2016). Developmental effects of fractionated low-dose exposure to gamma radiation on behaviour and susceptibility of the cholinergic system in mice. *International Journal of Radiation Biology, 92*(7), DOI: 10.3109/09553002.2016.1164911.

Burgaleta, M., et al. (2016). Bilingualism at the core of the brain. Structural differences between bilinguals and monolinguals revealed by subcortical shape analysis. *NeuroImage, 125*, 437–445.

Burghardt, G. M. (2015). Integrative approaches to the biological study of play. In J. E. Johnson et al. (Eds.). *The handbook of the study of play, Vol. 2* (pp. 21–40). Lanham, MD: Rowman & Littlefield.

Burke, J. D., & Loeber, R. (2016). Mechanisms of behavioral and affective treatment outcomes in a cognitive behavioral intervention for boys. *Journal of Abnormal Child Psychology, 44*(1), 179–189.

Burnham, D., & Matlock, K. (2010). Auditory development. In J. G. Bremner & T. D. Wachs (Eds.), *The Wiley-Blackwell handbook of infant development* (2nd ed., Vol. 1, pp. 81–119). Oxford, UK: Wiley-Blackwell. doi:10.1002/9781444327564.ch3

Bushnell, E. W. (1993, June). *A dualprocessing approach to cross-modal matching: Implications for development*. Paper presented at the Society for Research in Child Development, New Orleans, LA.

Bynum, M. S. (2007). African American mother–daughter communication about sex and daughters' sexual behavior: Does college racial composition make a difference? *Cultural Diversity & Ethnic Minority Psychology, 13*(2), 151–160.

C

Callahan, R., et al. (2015). Pregnancy and contraceptive use among women participating in the FEM-PrEP Trial. *Journal of Acquired Immune Deficiency Syndrome, 68*(2), 196–203.

Campanella, J., & Rovee-Collier, C. (2005). Latent learning and deferred imitation at 3 months. *Infancy, 7*(3), 243–262.

Campbell, A., Shirley, L., & Caygill, L. (2002). Sex-typed preferences in three domains: Do two-year-olds need cognitive variables? *British Journal of Psychology, 93*(2), 203–217.

Campbell, S. B., et al. (2004). The course of maternal depressive symptoms and maternal sensitivity as predictors of attachment security at 36 months. *Development and Psychopathology, 16*(2), 231–252.

Campos, J. J., Hiatt, S., Ramsey, D., Henderson, C., & Svejda, M. (1978). The emergence of fear on the visual cliff. In M. Lewis & L. Rosenblum (Eds.), *The origins of affect.* New York, NY: Plenum.

Campos, J. J., Langer, A., & Krowitz, A. (1970). Cardiac responses on the visual cliff in prelocomotor human infants. *Science, 170,* 196–197.

Camras, L. A., et al. (2007). Do infants show distinct negative facial expressions for fear and anger? Emotional expression in 11-month-old European American, Chinese, and Japanese Infants. *Infancy, 11*(2), 131–155.

Caplan, P. J., & Larkin, J. (1991). The anatomy of dominance and self-protection. *American Psychologist, 46,* 536.

Carey, B. (2007b, June 22). Research finds firstborns gain the higher I.Q. *The New York Times online.*

Carr, A. (2011). Social and emotional development in middle childhood. In D. Skuse, H. Bruce, L. Dowdney, & D. Mrazek (Eds.), *Child psychology and psychiatry: Frameworks for practice* (2nd ed., pp. 56–61). Hoboken, NJ: Wiley.

Carre, J. M., & Olmstead, N. A. (2015). Social neuroendocrinology of human aggression: Examining the role of competition-induced testosterone dynamics. *Neuroscience, 286,* 171–186.

Carver, L. J., & Vaccaro, B. G. (2007). 12-month-old infants allocate increased neural resources to stimuli associated with negative adult emotion. *Developmental Psychology, 43*(1), 54–69.

Cascio, C. J. (2010). Somatosensory processing in neurodevelopmental disorders. *Journal of Neurodevelopmental Disorders, 2*(2), 62–69.

Cassia, V. M., Simion, F., & Umilta, C. (2001). Face preference at birth: The role of an orienting mechanism. *Developmental Science, 4*(1), 101–108.

Cattaneo, L., Sandrini, M., & Schwarzbach, J. (2010). State-dependent TMS reveals a hierarchical representation of observed acts in the temporal, parietal, and premotor cortices. *Cerebral Cortex, 20*(9), 2252–2258.

Cattell, R. B. (1949). *The culture-fair intelligence test.* Champaign, IL: Institute for Personality and Ability Testing.

Centers for Disease Control and Prevention. (2006). *HIV/AIDS surveillance report, 2005, Vol. 17.* Atlanta, GA: U.S. Department of Health and Human Services, Centers for Disease Control and Prevention. Retrieved from http://www.cdc.gov/hiv/topics/surveillance/resources/reports

Centers for Disease Control and Prevention. (2010a). *Breastfeeding FAQs.* Retrieved from http://www.cdc.gov/breastfeeding/faq

Centers for Disease Control and Prevention. National Center for Health Statistics. (2009). Early release of selected estimates based on data from the 2008 National Health Interview Survey. Retrieved from http://www.cdc.gov/nchs/nhis/released200906.htm

Cernoch, J., & Porter, R. (1985). Recognition of maternal axillary odors by infants. *Child Development, 56,* 1593–1598.

Chan, T. W., & Koo, A. (2011). Parenting style and youth outcomes in the UK. *European Sociological Review, 27*(3), 385–399.

Chambers, S. A., Freeman, R., Anderson, A. S., & MacGillivray, S. (2015). Reducing the volume, exposure and negative impacts of advertising for foods high in fat, sugar and salt to children: A systematic review of the evidence from statutory and self-regulatory actions and educational measures. *Preventive Medicine.* http://www.sciencedirect.com/science/article/pii/S0091743515000626; and Lillard, A. S., Li, H., & Boguszewski, K. (2015). Chapter 7–Television and children's executive function. *Advances in Child Development and Behavior, 48,* 219–248.

Chen, H., & Wang, Y. (2015). Do weight status and television viewing influence children's subsequent dietary changes? A National Longitudinal Study in the United States. *International Journal of Obesity,* DOI: 10.1038/ijo.2015.16.

Cheng, E. R., et al. (2016). Postnatal depressive symptoms among mothers and fathers of infants born preterm: Prevalence and impacts on children's early cognitive function. *Journal of Developmental and Behavioral Pediatrics, 37*(1), 33–42.

Cherney, I. D., Harper, H. J., & Winter, J. A. (2006). Nouveaux jouets: Ce que les enfants identifient comme "jouets de garcons" et "jouets de filles." *Enfance, 58*(3), 266–282.

Chetty, R., Friedman, J. N., & Rockoff, J. E. (2012). *The long-term impacts of teachers: Teacher value-added and student outcomes in adulthood.* Retrieved from http://obs.rc.fas.harvard.edu/chetty/value_added.pdf

Chezan, L. C., & Drasgow, E. (2010). Pairing vocalizations with preferred edibles and toys may produce a modest increase in the frequency of vocalizations in three young children with autism. *Evidence-Based Communication Assessment and Intervention, 4*(2), 101–104.

Chomsky, N. (1988). *Language and problems of knowledge.* Cambridge, MA: MIT Press.

Chomsky, N. (1990). On the nature, use, and acquisition of language. In W. G. Lycan (Ed.), *Mind and cognition.* (pp. 627–646.) Oxford, UK: Blackwell.

Christie, J. F., & Roskos, K. A. (2015). How does play contribute to literacy? In J. E. Johnson et al. (Eds.). *The handbook of the study of play, Vol. 2* (pp. 417–424). Lanham, MD: Rowman & Littlefield.

Cicchetti, D., Rogosch, F. A., & Toth, S. L. (2006). Fostering secure attachment in infants in maltreating families through preventive interventions. *Development and Psychopathology, 18*(3), 623–649.

Cillessen, A. H. N., & Bellmore, A. D. (2011). Social skills and social competence in interactions with peers. In P. K. Smith & C. H. Hart (Eds.), *The Wiley-Blackwell handbook of childhood social development* (2nd ed.) (pp. 393–412). Oxford, UK: Wiley-Blackwell. doi:10.1002/9781444390933.ch21

Clark, E. V. (1973). What's in a word? On the child's acquisition of semantics in his first language. In E. Moore (Ed.), *Cognitive development and the acquisition of language.* (pp. 65–110.) New York, NY: Academic Press.

Clark, E. V. (1975). Knowledge, context, and strategy in the acquisition of meaning. In D. P. Date (Ed.), *Georgetown University roundtable on language and linguistics.* (pp. 77–98.) Washington, DC: Georgetown University Press.

Clark, J. (2005). Sibling relationships: Theory and issues for practice. *Child & Family Social Work, 10*(1), 90–91.

Clark, J. C. (2014). Towards a cultural historical theory of knowledge mapping: Collaboration and activity in the zone of proximal development. In D. Ifenthaler, & R. Hanewld (Eds.). *Digital knowledge maps in education* (pp. 161–174). New York: Springer Science + Business Media

Clark, R. (1983). *Family life and school achievement: Why poor black children succeed or fail.* Chicago, IL: University of Chicago Press.

Clarke-Stewart, K. A., & Beck, R. J. (1999). Maternal scaffolding and children's narrative retelling of a movie story. *Early Childhood Research Quarterly, 14*(3), 409–434.

Clode, D. (2006). Review of A left-hand turn around the world: Chasing the mystery and meaning of all things southpaw. *Laterality: Asymmetries of Body, Brain and Cognition, 11*(6) 580–581.

Cohen, J. R., Young, J. F., & Abela, J. R. Z. (2011). Cognitive vulnerability to depression in children. *Cognitive Therapy and Research.* doi:10.1007/s10608-011-9431-6

Commons, M. L., Galaz-Fontes, J. F., & Morse, S. J. (2006). Leadership, crosscultural contact, socio-economic status, and formal operational reasoning about moral dilemmas among Mexican nonliterate adults and high school students. *Journal of Moral Education, 35*(2), 247–267.

Conniff, J., & Evensen, A. (2016). Preexposure prophylaxis (PrEP) for HIV prevention: The primary care perspective. *Journal of the American Board of Family Medicine, 29*(1), 143–151.

Connolly, J., Craig, W., Goldberg, A., & Pepler, D. (2004). Mixed-gender groups, dating, and romantic relationships in early adolescence. *Journal of Research on Adolescence, 14*(2), 185–207.

Connolly, J., Furman, W., & Konarski, R. (2000). The role of peers in the emergence of heterosexual romantic relationships in adolescence. *Child Development, 71*(5), 1395–1408.

Conrad, N. J., Walsh, J. A., Allen, J. M., & Tsang, C. D. (2011). Examining infants' preferences for tempo in lullabies and playsongs. *Canadian Journal of Experimental Psychology/Revue canadienne de psychologie expérimentale, 65*(3), 168–172.

Cooke, B. M., Breedlove, S. M., & Jordan, C. L. (2003). Both estrogen receptors and androgen receptors contribute to testosterone-induced changes in the morphology of the medial amygdala and sexual arousal in male rats. *Hormones & Behavior, 43*(2), 336–346.

Corballis, M. C. (2010). Mirror neurons and the evolution of language. *Brain and Language, 112*(1), 25–35.

Costigan, C. L., Cauce, A. M., & Etchison, K. (2007). Changes in African American mother–daughter relationships during adolescence: Conflict, autonomy, and warmth. In B. J. R. Leadbeater & N. Way (Eds.), *Urban girls revisited: Building strengths* (pp. 177–201). New York, NY: New York University Press.

Cozolino, L. (2014). *The neuroscience of human relationships* (2nd Ed.). New York: W. W. Norton.

Creed, P. A., & Wamelink, S. H. (2015). Antecedents and consequences to perceived career goal-progress discrepancies. *Journal of Vocational Behavior, 87,* 43–53.

Crisp, R. J., & Turner, R. N. (2011). Cognitive adaptation to the experience of social and cultural diversity. *Psychological Bulletin, 137*(2), 242–266.

Crook, C. K., & Lipsitt, L. P. (1976). Neonatal nutritive sucking: Effects of taste stimulation upon sucking rhythm and heart rate. *Child Development, 47,* 518–522.

Cuevas, K., & Bell, M. A. (2010). Developmental progression of looking and reaching performance on the A-not-B task. *Developmental Psychology, 46*(5), 1363–1371.

Cummings, C. M., Caporino, N. E., & Kendall, P. C. (2014). Comorbidity of anxiety and depression in children and adolescents: 20 years after. *Psychological Bulletin, 140*(3), 816–845.

D

Daglioglu, H. E., Calisandemir, F., Alemdar, M., & Bencik Kangal, S. (2010). Examination of human figure drawings by gifted and normally developed children at preschool period. *Elementary Education Online, 9*(1), 31–43.

Daley, C. E., & Onwuegbuzie, A. J. (2011). Race and intelligence. In R. J. Sternberg & S. J. Kaufman (Eds.), *The Cambridge handbook of intelligence* (pp. 293–308). New York, NY: Cambridge University Press.

Damian, R. I., & Roberts, B. W. (2015). Settling the debate on birth order and personality. *Proceedings of the National Academy of Sciences of the United States of America, 112*(46), 14119–14120.

Damon, W. (1991). Adolescent self-concept. In R. M. Lerner, A. C. Petersen, & J. Brooks-Gunn (Eds.), *Encyclopedia of adolescence.* New York, NY: Garland.

Daniels, E. A.,& Gillen, M. M. (2015). Body image and identity: A call for new research. In S. J. Schwatrz, K. Luyckx, & V. L. Vignoles (Eds.). *Handbook of identity theory and research* (pp. 406–422). New York: Springer Science + Business Media.

Daryanani, I., Hamilton, J. L., Abramson, L. Y., & Alloy, L. B. (2016). Single mother parenting and adolescent psychopathology. *Journal of Abnormal Child Psychology,* 1–13. DOI: 10.1007/s10802–016-0128-x

Daugherty, A. M., & Ofen, N. (2015). That's a good one! Belief in efficacy of mnemonic strategies contributes to age-related increase in associative memory. *Journal of Experimental Child Psychology, 136,* 17–29.

Dawood, K., Bailey, J. M., & Martin, N. G. (2009). Genetic and environmental influences on sexual orientation. In Y.-K. Kim (Ed.), *Handbook of behavior genetics* (pp. 269–279). New York, NY: Springer.

Dawson, C., et al. (2011). Dietary treatment of phenylketonuria: The effect of phenylalanine on reaction time. *Journal of Inherited Metabolic Disease, 34*(2), 449–454.

Dawson, T. L. (2002). New tools, new insights: Kohlberg's moral judgement stages revisited. *International Journal of Behavioral Development, 26*(2), 154–166.

De Haan, M., & Groen, M. (2006). Neural bases of infants' processing of social information in faces. In P. J. Marshall & N. A. Fox (Eds.), *The development of social engagement: Neurobiological perspectives. Series in affective science* (pp. 46–80). New York, NY: Oxford University Press.

De Rosa, C. J., et al. (2010). Sexual intercourse and oral sex among public middle school students: Prevalence and correlates. *Perspectives on Sexual and Reproductive Health, 42*(3), 197–205.

De Lisi, R. (2015). Piaget's sympathetic but unromantic account of children's play. In J. E. Johnson et al. (Eds.). *The handbook of the study of play, Vol. 2* (pp. 227–238). Lanham, MD: Rowman & Littlefield.

de Souza, A. S., Fernandes, F. S., & do Carmo, M. (2011). Effects of maternal malnutrition and postnatal nutritional rehabilitation on brain fatty acids,learning, and memory. *Nutrition Reviews, 69*(3), 132–144.

Deary, I. J., Whiteman, M. C., Starr, J. M., Whalley, L. J., & Fox, H. C. (2004). The impact of childhood intelligence on later life: Following up the Scottish mental surveys of 1932 and 1947. *Journal of Personality and Social Psychology, 86*(1), 130–147.

DeCasper, A. J., & Fifer, W. P. (1980). Of human bonding: Newborns prefer their mothers' voices. *Science, 208,* 1174–1176.

DeCasper, A. J., & Prescott, P. A. (1984). Human newborns' perception of male voices: Preference, discrimination, and reinforcing value. *Developmental Psychobiology, 17,* 481–491.

DeCasper, A. J., & Spence, M. J. (1991). Auditorially mediated behavior during the perinatal period: A cognitive view. In M. J. Weiss & P. R. Zelazo (Eds.), *Infant attention* (pp. 142–176). Norwood, NJ: Ablex.

Demby, K. P., Riggs, S. A., & Kaminski, P. L. (2015). Attachment and family processes in children's psychological adjustment in middle childhood. *Family Process,* DOI: 10.1111/famp.12145.

Dennis, W. (1960). Causes of retardation among institutional children: Iran. *Journal of Genetic Psychology, 96,* 47–59.

Dennis, W., & Dennis, M. G. (1940). The effect of cradling practices upon the onset of walking in Hopi children. *Journal of Genetic Psychology, 56,* 77–86.

Dermody, S. S., Marchal, M. P., Burton, C. M., & Chisolm, D. J. (2016). Risk of heavy drinking among sexual minority adolescents: Indirect pathways through sexual orientation-related victimization and affiliation with substance-using peers. *Addiction,* DOI: 10.1111/add.13409.

Dettmer, A. M., et al. (2016). Neonatal face-to-face interactions promote social behaviour in infant rhesus monkeys. *Nature Communications,* DOI: 10.1038/ncomms11940.

Dezoete, J. A., MacArthur, B. A., & Tuck, B. (2003). Prediction of Bayley and Stanford–Binet scores with a group of very low birth-weight children. *Child: Care, Health and Development, 29*(5), 367–372.

DiPietro, J. A. (2010). Psychological and psychophysiological considerations regarding the maternal–fetal relationship. *Infant and Child Development, 19*(1), 27–38.

Dimler, L. M., & Natsuaki, M. N. (2015). The effects of pubertal timing on externalizing behaviors in adolescence and early adulthood. *Journal of Adolescence, 45,* 160–170.

Dodge, E., & Simic, M. (2015). Anorexia runs in families: does this make the families responsible? A commentary on "Anorexia runs in families: is this due to genes or the family environment?" (Dring, 2014). *Journal of Family Therapy, 37*(1), 93–102

Douglas, P. S., & Hill, P. S. (2011). The crying baby: What approach? *Current Opinion in Pediatrics, 23*(5), 523–529.

Dubow, E. F., et al. (2010). Exposure to conflict and violence across contexts: Relations to adjustment among Palestinian children. *Journal of Clinical Child and Adolescent Psychology, 39*(1), 103–116.

Dunn, J., & Hughes, C. (2001). "I got some swords and you're dead!": Violent fantasy, antisocial behavior, friendship, and moral sensibility in young children. *Child Development, 72*(2), 491–505.

Dunn, J., (2015). Siblings. In J. E. Grusec & P. D. Hastings (Eds.). *Handbook of socialization: Theory and Research* (pp. 182–201). New York: Guilford.

Durdiakova, J., et al. (2015). Differences in salivary testosterone, digit ratio and empathy between intellectually gifted and control boys. *Intelligence, 48,* 76–84.

Dweck, C. S. (2015). The secret to raising smart kids. *Scientific American, 23,* 76–83.

Dworkin, E., Javdani, S., Verona, E., & Campbell, R. (2014). Child sexual abuse and disordered eating: The mediating role of impulsive and compulsive tendencies. *Psychology of Violence, 4*(1), 21–36.

Dykman, R. A., Casey, P. H., Ackerman, P. T., & McPherson, W. B. (2001). Behavioral and cognitive status in school-aged children with a history of failure to thrive during early childhood. *Clinical Pediatrics, 40*(2), 63–70.

Dyson, J. C. (2015). Play in America: A historical overview. In J. E. Johnson et al. (Eds.). *The handbook of the study of play, Vol. 2* (pp. 41–50). Lanham, MD: Rowman & Littlefield.

E

Eaves, L. C., & Ho, H. H. (2008). Young adult outcome of autism spectrum disorder. *Journal of Autism and Developmental Disorders, 38*(4), 739–747.

Ebstein, R., Israel, S., Chew, S., Zhong, S., & Knafo, A. (2010). Genetics of human social behavior. *Neuron, 65*(6), 831–844.

Eccles, J. S., et al. (2000). Gender-role socialization in the family: A longitudinal approach. In T. Eckes & H. M. Trautner (Eds.), *The developmental social psychology of gender* (pp. 333–360). Mahwah, NJ: Erlbaum.

Edwards, J., et al. (2011). Developmental coordination disorder in school-aged children born very preterm and/or at very low birth weight: A systematic review. *Journal of Developmental Behavioral Pediatrics, 32*(9), 678–687.

Egeland, B., & Sroufe, L. A. (1981). Attachment and early maltreatment. *Child Development, 52,* 44–52.

Eimas, P. D., Sigueland, E. R., Juscyk, P., & Vigorito, J. (1971). Speech perception in infants. *Science, 171,* 303–306.

Eivers, A. R., Brendgen, M., Vitaro, F., & Borge, A. I. H. (2012). Concurrent and longitudinal links between children's and their friends' antisocial and prosocial behavior in preschool. *Early Childhood Research Quarterly, 27*(1), 137–146.

Elkind, D. (2007). *The power of play: How spontaneous imaginative activities lead to happier, healthier children.* Cambridge, MA: Da Capo Press.

El-Sheikh, M. (2007). Children's skin conductance level and reactivity: Are these measures stable over time and across tasks? *Developmental Psychobiology, 49*(2), 180–186.

Erikson, E. H. (1963). *Childhood and society.* New York, NY: Norton.

Erikson, E. H. (1968). *Identity: Youth and crisis.* New York, NY: Norton.

Erikson, E. H. (1975). *Life history and the historical moment.* New York, NY: Norton.

Espelage, D. L., & Colbert, C. L. (2016). In K. R. Wentzel, & G. B. Ramani (Eds.). *Handbook of social influences in school contexts: Social-emotional, motivation, and cognitive outcomes* (pp. 405–422). New York: Routledge.

F

Fantz, R. L. (1961). The origin of form perception. *Scientific American, 204,* 66–72.

Fantz, R. L., Fagan, J. F., III, & Miranda, S. B. (1975). Early visual selectivity. In L. B. Cohen & P. Salapatek (Eds.), *Infant perception: From sensation to cognition* (Vol. 1). New York, NY: Academic Press.

Farr, R. H., & Patterson, C. J. (2013). Lesbian and gay adoptive parents and their children. In A. E Goldberg, & K. R. Allen (Eds.). *LGBT-parent families: Innovations in research and implications for practice* (pp. 39–55). New York: Springer Science + Business Media.

Feinberg, M. E., Neiderhiser, J. M., Howe, G., & Hetherington, E. M. (2001). Adolescent, parent, and observer perceptions of parenting: Genetic and environmental influences on shared and distinct perceptions. *Child Development, 72*(4), 1266–1284.

Feldman, R., Rosenthal, Z., & Eidelman, A. I. (2014). Maternal-preterm skin-to-skin contact enhances child physiologic organization and cognitive control across the first 10 years of life. *Biological Psychiatry, 75*(1), 56–64.

Fergusson, A. (2007). What successful teachers do in inclusive classrooms: Research-based teaching strategies that help special learners succeed. *European Journal of Special Needs Education, 22*(1), 108–110.

Fernandes, A., Campbell-Yeo, M., & Johnston, C. C. (2011). Procedural pain management for neonates using nonpharmacological strategies: Part 1: Sensorial interventions. *Advances in Neonatal Care, 11*(4), 235–241s.

Féron, J., Gentaz, E., & Streri, A. (2006). Evidence of amodal representation of small numbers across visuo-tactile modalities in 5-month-old infants. *Cognitive Development, 21*(2), 81–92.

Ferre, C. L., Babik, I., & Michel, G. F. (2010). Development of infant prehension handedness: A longitudinal analysis during the 6- to 14-month age period. *Infant Behavior and Development, 33*(4), 492–502.

Ferrer, E., et al. (2010). Uncoupling of reading and IQ over time. *Psychological Science, 21*(1), 93–101.

Field, T. (1999). Sucking and massage therapy reduce stress during infancy. In M. Lewis & D. Ramsay (Eds.), *Soothing and stress* (pp. 157–169). Hillsdale, NJ: Erlbaum.

Field, T., Orozco, A., Corbin, J., Dominguez, G., & Frost, P. (2014). Face-to-face interaction behaviors of preadolescent same-sex and opposite-sex friends and acquaintances. *Journal of Child and Adolescent Behavior*, DOI: 10.4172/jcalb.1000134

Finkelhor, D., Turner, H. A., Shattuck, A., & Hamby, S. L. (2015). Prevalence of childhood exposure to violence, crime, and abuse: Results from the National Survey of Children's Exposure to Violence. *JAMA Pediatrics, 169*(8), 746–754.

Fitzgerald, H. E., et al. (1991). The organization of lateralized behavior during infancy. In H. E. Fitzgerald, B. M. Lester, & M. W. Yogman (Eds.), *Theory and research in behavioral pediatrics*. New York, NY: Plenum.

Fivush, R. (2002). Scripts, schemas, and memory of trauma. In N. L. Stein et al. (Eds.), *Representation, memory, and development: Essays in honor of Jean Mandler* (pp. 53–74). Mahwah, NJ: Erlbaum.

Fivush, R., & Hammond, N. R. (1990). Autobiographical memory across the preschool years: Toward reconceptualizing childhood amnesia. In R. Fivush & J. A. Hudson (Eds.), *Knowing and remembering in young children*. Cambridge, UK: Cambridge University Press.

Flavell, J. H. (1993). Young children's understanding of thinking and consciousness. *Current Directions in Psychological Science, 2*, 40–43.

Flavell, J. H., Miller, P. H., & Miller, S. A. (2002). *Cognitive development* (4th ed.). Upper Saddle River, NJ: Prentice Hall.

Fletcher, K. L. (2011). Neuropsychology of early childhood (3 to 5 years old). In A. S. Davis (Ed.), *Handbook of pediatric neuropsychology*. New York, NY: Springer.

Florsheim, P. (Ed.). (2003). *Adolescent romantic relations and sexual behavior: Theory, research, and practical implications*. Mahwah, NJ: Erlbaum.

Foley, G. M. (2006). Self and social–emotional development in infancy: A descriptive synthesis. In G. M. Foley & J. D. Hochman (Eds.), Mental health in early intervention: Achieving unity in principles and practice (pp. 139–173). Baltimore: Paul H. Brookes.

Fogassi, L., & Rizzolatti, G. (2013). The mirror mechanism as neurophysiological basis for action and intention understanding. In A. Suarez, & P. Adams (Eds.). *Is science compatible with free will?* (pp. 117–134). New York: Springer.

Fox, E., & Dinsmore, D. L. (2016). Teacher influences on the development of students' personal interest in academic domains. In K. R. Wentzel, & G. B. Ramani (Eds.). *Handbook of social influences in school contexts: Social-emotional, motivation, and cognitive outcomes* (pp. 143–157). New York: Routledge.

Freeman, M. S., Spence, M. J., and Oliphant, C. M. (1993, June). *Newborns prefer their mothers' low-pass filtered voices over other female filtered voices*. Paper presented at the meeting of the American Psychological Society, Chicago.

Friedmann, N., & Rusou, D. (2015). Critical period for first language: The crucial role of language input during the first year of life. *Current Opinion in Neurobiology, 35*, 27–34.

Fucile, S., & Gisel, E. G. (2010). Sensorimotor interventions improve growth and motor function in preterm infants. Neonatal Network: *The Journal of Neonatal Nursing, 29*(6), 359–366.

Fuertes, M., Faria, A., Beeghly, M., & Lopes-dos-Santos, P. (2016). The effects of parental sensitivity and involvement in caregiving on mother-infant and father-infant attachment in a Portuguese sample. *Journal of Family Psychology, 30*(1), 147–156.

Fuller, T. (2011). Is scientific theory change similar to early cognitive development? Gopnik on science and childhood. *Philosophical Psychology*. doi:10.1080/09515089.2011.625114

Furman, W., & Winkles, J. K. (2010). Predicting romantic involvement, relationship cognitions, and relationship qualities from physical appearance, perceived norms, and relational styles regarding friends and parents. *Journal of Adolescence, 33*(6), 827–836.

G

Gallese, V., Fadiga, L., Fogassi, L., & Rizzolatti, G. (1996). Action recognition in the premotor cortex. *Brain, 119*(2), 593–609.

Garber, H. L. (1988). *The Milwaukee Project: Preventing mental retardation in children at risk*. Washington, DC: American Association on Mental Retardation.

Garcia, P. R. J. M., et al. (2015). Career optimism: The roles of contextual support and career decision-making self-efficacy. *Journal of Vocational Behavior, 88*, 10–18.

Garcia-Falgueras, A., & Swaab, D. F. (2010). Sex hormones and the brain: An essential alliance for sexual identity and sexual orientation. In S. Loche et al. (Eds.), *Pediatric neuroendocrinology* (Vol. 17, pp. 22–35). Basel, Switzerland: Karger.

Gardner, H. (1983). *Frames of mind: The theory of multiple intelligences*. New York, NY: Basic Books.

Garvain, J. (2015). Plasticity in early language acquisition: The effects of prenatal and early childhood experience. *Current Opinion in Neurobiology, 35*, 13–20.

Gaul, D., & Issartel, J. (2016). Fine motor skill proficiency in typically developing children: On or off the maturation track? *Human Movement Science, 46*, 78–85.

Gauvain, M. (2016). Peer contributions to cognitive development. In K. R. Wentzel, & G. B. Ramani (Eds.). *Handbook of social influences in school contexts: Social-emotional, motivation, and cognitive outcomes* (pp. 80–95). New York: Routledge.

Gee, R. E., Wood, S. F., & Schubert, K. G. (2014). Women's health, pregnancy, and the U.S. Food and Drug Administration. *Obstetrics & Gynecology, 123*(1), 161–165.

Gehlbach, H., & Robinson, C. D. (2016). Commentary: The foundational role of teacher-student relationships. In K. R. Wentzel, & G. B. Ramani (Eds.). *Handbook of social influences in school contexts: Social-emotional, motivation, and cognitive outcomes* (pp. 230–238). New York: Routledge.

George, M. R. W., Koss, K. J., McCoy, K. P., Cummings, E. M., & Davies, P. T. (2010). Examining the family context and relations with attitudes to school and scholastic competence. *Advances in School Mental Health Promotion, 3*(4), 51–62.

Georgiades, S., et al. (2010). Phenotypic overlap between core diagnostic features and emotional/behavioral problems in preschool children with autism spectrum disorder. *Journal of Autism and Developmental Disorders, 41*(10), 1321–1329.

Gervain, J., Berent, I., & Werker, J. F. (2011). Binding at birth: The newborn brain detects identity relations and sequential position in speech. *Journal of Cognitive Neuroscience, 24*(3), 564–574.

Gesell, A. (1928). *Infancy and human growth.* New York, NY: Macmillan.

Gesell, A. (1929). Maturation and infant behavior patterns. *Psychological Review, 36*, 307–319.

Gibson, E. J. (1969). *Principles of perceptual learning and development.* New York, NY: Appleton-Century-Crofts.

Gibson, E. J. (1991). *An odyssey in learning and perception.* Cambridge, MA: MIT Press.

Gibson, E. J., & Walk, R. D. (1960). The visual cliff. *Scientific American, 202*, 64–71.

Gignac, G. E., & Weisse, L. G. (2015). Digit span is (mostly) related linearly to general intelligence: Every extra bit of span counts. *Psychological Assessment, 27*(4), 1312–1323.

Giles, A., & Rovee-Collier, C. (2011). Infant long-term memory for associations formed during mere exposure. *Infant Behavior and Development, 34*(2), 327–338.

Gilligan, C. (1982). *In a different voice.* Cambridge, MA: Harvard University Press.

Gima, H., Ohgi, S., Fujiwara, T., & Abe, K. (2010). Stress behavior in premature infants with periventricular leukomalacia. *Journal of Physical Therapy Science, 22*(2), 109–115.

Gobet, F., & Simon, H. A. (2000). Five seconds or sixty? Presentation time in expert memory. *Cognitive Science, 24*(4), 651–682.

Goble, P., Martin, C. L., Hanish, L. D., & Fabes, R. A. (2012). Children's gender-typed activity choices across preschool social contexts. *Sex Roles, 67*(7-8), 435–451.

Goldberg, W. A., et al. (2012). The more things change, the more they stay the same: Gender, culture, and college students' views about work and family. *Journal of Social Issues, 68*(4), 814–837.

Goldschmidt, L., Day, N. L., & Richardson, G. A. (2000). Effects of prenatal marijuana exposure on child behavior problems at age 10. *Neurotoxicology and Teratology, 22*(3), 325–336.

Goldstein, E. B. (2005). *Cognitive psychology: Connecting mind, research, and everyday experience.* Belmont, CA: Wadsworth.

Goldstein, H. (2004). International comparisons of student attainment. *Assessment in Education: Principles, Policy & Practice, 11*(3), 319–330.

Gomez, A. M. (2011). Testing the cycle of violence hypothesis: Child abuse and adolescent dating violence as predictors of intimate partner violence in young adulthood. *Youth & Society, 43*(1), 171–192.

Goodman, G. S., Pipe, M-E., & McWilliams, K. (2011). Children's eyewitness testimony: Methodological issues. In B. Rosenfeld & S. D. Penrod (Eds.), *Research methods on forensic psychology* (pp. 257–282). Hoboken, NJ: Wiley.

Gopnik, A., & Meltzoff, A. N. (1992). Categorization and naming: Basic-level sorting in eighteen-month-olds and its relation to language. *Child Development, 63*, 1091–1103.

Gopnik, A., & Slaughter, V. (1991). Young children's understanding of changes in their mental states. *Child Development, 62*, 98–110.

Gordon, M. K., et al. (2016). Comparison of performance on ADHD quality of care indicators. *Journal of Attention Disorders*, DOI: 10.1177/1087054715624227.

Gottfried, G. M., Hickling, A. K., Totten, L. R., Mkroyan, A., & Reisz, A. (2003). To be or not to be a galaprock: Preschoolers' intuitions about the importance of knowledge and action for pretending. *British Journal of Developmental Psychology, 21*(3), 397–414.

Graber, J. A. (2013). Pubertal timing and the development of psychopathology in adolescence and beyond. *Hormones and Behavior, 64*(2), 262–269.

Greco, C., Rovee-Collier, C., Hayne, H., Griesler, P., & Early, L. (1986). Ontogeny of early event memory: II. Encoding and retrieval by 2- and 3-month-olds. *Infant Behavior and Development, 9*, 461–472.

Greene, F. J., Han, L., & Marlow, S. (2013). Like mother, like daughter? Analyzing maternal influences upon women's entrepreneurial propensity. *Entrepreneurship: Theory and Practice, 37*(4), 687–711.

Green, R. (1978). Sexual identity of 37 children raised by homosexual or transsexual parents. *American Journal of Psychiatry, 135*, 692–697.

Grön, G., Wunderlich, A. P., Spitzer, M., Tomczak, R., & Riepe, M. W. (2000). Brain activation during human navigation: Gender-different neural networks as substrate of performance. *Nature Neuroscience, 3*(4), 404–408.

Groenman, A. P. et al. (2015). Dopamine and serotonin genetic risk scores predicting substance and nicotine use in attention deficit/hyperactivity disorder. *Addiction Biology*, DOI: 10.1111/adb.12230.

Grossmann, K., et al. (2002). The uniqueness of the child–father attachment relationship: Fathers' sensitive and challenging play as a pivotal variable in a 16-year longitudinal study. *Social Development, 11*(3), 307–331.

Grusec, J. E., & Sherman, A. (2011). Prosocial behavior. In M. K. Underwood & L. H. Rosen (Eds.), *Social development: Relationships in infancy, childhood, and adolescence* (pp. 263–288). New York, NY: Guilford.

Grusec, J. E., & Davidov, M. (2015). Analyzing socialization from a domain-specific perspective. In J. E. Grusec, & P. D. Hastings (Eds.). *Handbook of socialization: Theory and research*, 2nd ed. (pp. 158–181). New York. Guilford.

Grusec, J. E. (2015). Family relationships and development. *Emerging Trends in the Social and Behavioral Sciences*, DOI: 10.1002/9781118900772.etrds0130.

Gudmundsson, G. (2010). Infantile colic: Is a pain syndrome. *Medical Hypotheses, 75*(6), 528–529.

Guerin, D. W., Gottfried, A. W., & Thomas, C. W. (1997). Difficult temperament and behaviour problems: A longitudinal study from 1.5 to 12 years. *International Journal of Behavioral Development, 21*(1), 71–90.

Gupta, S., Gersing, K. R., Erkanli, A., & Burt, T. (2015). Antidepressant regulatory warnings, prescription patterns, suicidality and other aggressive behavirs in major depressive disorder and anxiety disorder. *Psychiatric Quarterly*, 1–14, DOI: 10.1007/s11126–015-9389–8.

Guttmacher Institute. (2016). *Teen pregnancy*. https://www.guttmacher .org/united-states/teens/teen-pregnancy (Accessed April 3, 2016).

H

Haier, R. J. (2011). Biological basis of intelligence. In R. J. Sternberg & S. J. Kaufman (Eds.), *The Cambridge handbook of intelligence* (pp. 351–370). New York, NY: Cambridge University Press.

Haith, M. M. (1979). Visual cognition in early infancy. In R. B. Kearsly & I. E. Sigel (Eds.), *Infants at risk: Assessment of cognitive functioning*. Hillsdale, NJ: Erlbaum.

Hakim, C. (2015). The male sexual deficit: A social fact of the 21st century. *International Sociology, 30*(3), 314–335.

Hale, J. B., et al. (2011). Executive impairment determines ADHD medication response. *Journal of Learning Disabilities, 44*(2), 196–212.

Halgin, R. P., & Whitbourne, S. K. (1993). *Abnormal psychology*. Fort Worth, TX: Harcourt Brace Jovanovich.

Hall, G. S. (1904). *Adolescence: Its psychology and its relations to physiology, anthropology, sociology sex, crime, religion and education* (Vol. II). New York: D Appleton & Company.

Hall, J. (2012). Gender issues in mathematics. *Journal of Teaching and Learning, 8*(1), 59–72.

Hall, J. A. (2011). Sex differences in friendship expectations: A meta-analysis. *Journal of Social and Personal Relationships, 28*(6), 723–747.

Halmi, K. A., et al. (2014). Perfectionism in anorexia nervosa: Variation by clinical subtype, obsessionality, and pathological eating behavior. *The American Journal of Psychiatry, 157*(11), 1799–1805.

Hankin, B. L. (2015). Depression from childhood through adolescence: Risk mechanisms across multiple systems and levels of analysis. *Current Opinion in Psychology, 4*, 13–20.

Harlow, H. F., & Harlow, M. K. (1966). Learning to love. *American Scientist, 54*, 244–272.

Harlow, H. F., Harlow, M. K., & Suomi, S. J. (1971). From thought to therapy: Lessons from a primate laboratory. *American Scientist, 59*, 538–549.

Harris, S. R., Megens, A. M., Backman, C. L., & Hayes, V. E. (2005). Stability of the Bayley II Scales of Infant Development in a sample of low-risk and high-risk infants. *Developmental Medicine & Child Neurology, 47*(12), 820–823.

Harter, S. (1990). Self and identity development. In S. S. Feldman & G. R. Elliott (Eds.), *At the threshold: The developing adolescent*. Cambridge, MA: Harvard University Press.

Harter, S., & Whitesell, N. R. (2003). Beyond the debate: Why some adolescents report stable self-worth over time and situation, whereas others report changes in self-worth. *Journal of Personality, 71*(6), 1027–1058.

Harter, S. (2012). *The construction of the self: Developmental and Sociocultural Foundations*, 2nd ed. New York: Guilford.

Hartl, A. C., Laursen, B., & Cillessen, A. H. N. (2015). A survival analysis of adolescent friendships: The downside of dissimilarity. *Psychological Science, 26*(8), 1304–1315.

Harvey, J. H., & Fine, M. A. (2011). *Children of divorce*. New York, NY: Routledge, Taylor & Francis Group.

Hasselhorn, M. (1992). Task dependency and the role of typicality and metamemory in the development of an organizational strategy. *Child Development, 63*, 202–214.

Hastings, P. D., Zahn-Waxler, C., Robinson, J., Usher, B., & Bridges, D. (2000). The development of concern for others in children with behavior problems. *Developmental Psychology, 36*(5), 531–546.

Hay, D. F., Payne, A., & Chadwick, A. (2004). Peer relations in childhood. *Journal of Child Psychology and Psychiatry. 45*(1), 84–108.

Haywood, K. M., & Getchell, N. (2014). *Life span motor development* (6th ed.). Champaign, IL: Human Kinetics.

Heimann, M., et al. (2006). Exploring the relation between memory, gestural communication, and the emergence of language in infancy: A longitudinal study. *Infant and Child Development, 15*(3), 233–249.

Heinonen, K., et al. (2011). Trajectories of growth and symptoms of attention-deficit/hyperactivity disorder in children: A longitudinal study. *BMC Pediatrics, 11*(84). doi:10.1186/1471-2431-11-84

Henricks, T. S. (2015). Classic theories of play. In J. E. Johnson et al. (Eds.). *The handbook of the study of play, Vol. 2* (pp. 163–180). Lanham, MD: Rowman & Littlefield.

Herbenick, D., et al. (2010a). Sexual behavior in the United States: Results from a national probability sample of males and females ages 14 to 94. *Journal of Sexual Medicine, 7*(Suppl. 5), 255–265.

Herbenick, D., et al. (2010b). Sexual behaviors, relationships, and perceived health among adult women in the United States: Results from a national probability sample. *Journal of Sexual Medicine, 7*(Suppl. 5), 277–290.

Herbenick, D., et al. (2010c). An event-level analysis of the sexual characteristics and composition among adults ages 18 to 59: Results from a national probability sample in the United States. *Journal of Sexual Medicine, 7*(Suppl. 5), 346–361.

Hergenhahn, B. R., & Henley, T. (2014). *An introduction to the history of psychology* (7th ed.). San Francisco: Cengage Learning.

Heron, M. (2016). Deaths: Leading causes for 2013. *National Vital Statistics Reports, 65*(2).

Hetherington, E. M. (2006). The effects of marital discord, divorce, and parental psychopathology. *New Directions for Child and Adolescent Development, 1984*(24), 6–33.

Hill, P. L., Duggan, P. M., & Lapsley, D. K. (2011). Subjective invulnerability, risk behavior, and adjustment in early adolescence. *The Journal of Early Adolescence*. doi:10.1177/0272431611400304

Hill, S. E., & Flom, R. (2007). 18- and 24-month-olds' discrimination of gender-consistent and inconsistent activities. *Infant Behavior & Development, 30*(1) 168–173.

Hilliard, L. J., & Liben, L. S. (2010). Differing levels of gender salience in preschool classrooms: Effects on children's gender attitudes and intergroup bias. *Child Development, 81*(6), 1787–1798.

Hills, A. P., & Byrne, N. M. (2011). An overview of physical growth and maturation. In J. Jurimae, A. P. Hills, & T. Jurimae (Eds.), *Cytokines, growth mediators and physical activity in children during puberty* (pp. 1–13). Basel, Switzerland: S. Karger.

Hines, M. (2011). Gender development and the human brain. *Annual Review of Neuroscience, 34*, 69–88.

Hines, M., Constantinescu, M., & Spencer, D. (2015). Early androgen exposure and human gender development. *Biology of Sex Differences, 6*(3), DOI: 10.1186/s13293-015-0022-1.

Hodapp, R. M., Griffin, M. M., Burke, M. M., & Fisher, M. H. (2011). Intellectual disabilities. In R. J. Sternberg & S. J. Kaufman (Eds.), *The Cambridge handbook of intelligence* (pp. 193–209). New York, NY: Cambridge University Press.

Hoff, E. (2006). Language experience and language milestones during early childhood. In K. McCartney & D. Phillips (Eds.), *Blackwell handbook of early childhood development., Blackwell handbooks of developmental psychology* (pp. 233–251). Malden, MA: Blackwell.

Hoff, E. (2014). *Language development* (5th Ed.). San Francisco: Cengage Learning. Tamis-LeMonda, C. S., et al. (2014). Children's vocabulary growth in English and Spanish across early development and associations with school readiness skills. *Developmental Neuropsychology, 39*(2), 69–87.

Hoff, E. V. (2005). A friend living inside me—The forms and functions of imaginary companions. *Imagination, Cognition and Personality, 24*(2), 151–189.

Hoffman, M., Gneezy, U., & List, J. A. (2011). Nurture affects gender differences in spatial abilities. *Proceedings of the National Academy of Sciences, 108*(36), 14786–14788.

Holden, G. W., Vittrup, B., & Rosen, L. H. (2011). Families, parenting and discipline. In M. K. Underwood & L. H. Rosen (Eds.), *Social development: Relationships in infancy, childhood, and adolescence* (pp. 127–152). New York, NY Guilford.

Holder, M. D., & Coleman, B. (2015). Children's friendships and positive well-being. In M. Demir (Ed.) *Friendship and happiness* (pp. 81–97). Dordrecht, Netherlands: Springer Science + Business Media.

Holland, J. L. (1997). *Making vocational choices: A theory of vocational personalities and work environments* (3rd ed.). Odessa, FL: Psychological Assessment Resources.

Holloway, J. H. (2004). *Part-time work and student achievement.* Alexandria VA: Association for Supervision and Curriculum Development. Retrieved from http://www.ascd.org/publications/ed_lead/200104/holloway.html

Honig, A. S., & Nealis, A. L. (2012). What do young children dream about? *Early Child Development and Care, 182*(6), 771–795.

Honzik, M. P., Macfarlane, J. W., & Allen, L. (1948). The stability of mental test performance between two and eighteen years. *Journal of Experimental Education, 17*, 309–324.

Hoover, J. R., Sterling, A. M., & Storkel, H. L. (2011). Speech and language development. In A. S. Davis (Ed.), *Handbook of pediatric neuropsychology*. New York, NY: Springer.

Hopkins, W. D., Reamer, L., Mareno, M. C., & Schapiro, S. J. (2015). Genetic basis in motor skill and hand preference for tool use in chimpanzees (Pan troglodytes). *Proceedings of the Royal Society B, 282*(1800), DOI: 10.1098/rspb.2014.1223.

Hossain, M., Chetana, M., & Devi, P. U. (2005). Late effect of prenatal irradiation on the hippocampal histology and brain weight in adult mice. *International Journal of Developmental Neuroscience, 23*(4), 307–313.

Howe, M. L. (2006). Developmentally invariant dissociations in children's true and false memories: Not all relatedness is created equal. *Child Development, 77*(4), 1112–1123.

Huesmann, L. R., Dubow, E. F., Eron, L. D., & Boxer, P. (2006). Middle childhood family contextual factors as predictors of adult outcomes. In A. C. Huston & M. N. Ripke (Eds.), *Middle Childhood: Contexts of Development*. Cambridge, UK: Cambridge University Press.

Huesmann, L. R., Moise-Titus, J., Podolski, C., & Eron, L. D. (2003). Longitudinal relations between children's exposure to TV violence and their aggressive and violent behavior in young adulthood: 1977–1992. *Developmental Psychology, 39*(2), 201–221.

Hur, Y. (2005). Genetic and environmental influences on self-concept in female preadolescent twins: Comparison of Minnesota and Seoul data. *Twin Research and Human Genetics, 8*(4), 291–299.

Hyde, J. S., Lindberg, S. M., Linn, M. C., Ellis, A. B., & Williams, C. C. (2008). Gender similarities characterize math performance. *Science, 321*, 494–495.

I

Inhelder, B., & Piaget, J. (1959). *The early growth of logic in the child: Classification and seriation*. New York: Harper & Row.

J

Jacobson, J. L., Jacobson, S. W., Padgett, R. J., Brumitt, G. A., & Billings, R. L. (1992). Effects of prenatal PCB exposure on cognitive processing efficiency and sustained attention. *Developmental Psychology, 28*, 297–306.

Jaffe, A. C. (2011). Failure to thrive: Current clinical concepts. *Pediatrics in Review, 32*(3), 100–108.

James, D. K. (2010). Fetal learning: A critical review. *Infant and Child Development, 19*(1), 45–54.

Jeng, S.-F., Yau, K.-I. T., Liao, H.-F., Chen, L.-C., & Chen, P.-S. (2000). Prognostic factors for walking attainment in very low-birthweight preterm infants. *Early Human Development, 59*(3), 159–173.

Jenkins, L. N., Floress, M. T., & Reinke, W. (2015). Rates and types of teacher praise: A review and future directions. *Psychology in the Schools, 52*(5), 463–476.

Johnson, D. A., & Gunnar, M. R. (2011). Growth failure in institutionalized children. *Monographs of the Society for Research in Child Development, 76*(4), 92–126.

Johnson, E. K. (2016). Constructing a proto-lexicon: An integrative view of infant language development. *Annual Review of Linguistics, 2*, 391–412.

Johnson, S. P. (2011). Development of visual perception. *WIREs Cognitive Science, 2*, 515–528. doi:10.1002/wcs.128

Johnson, N. B., et al. (2014). CDC National Health Report: Leading causes of morbidity and mortality and associated risk and protective factors–United States, 2005 – 2013. *Centers for Disease Control and Prevention*, http://www.cdc.gov/mmwr/preview/mmwrhtml/su6304a2.htm; Leading Causes of Death. (2016, February 26). Centers for Disease Control and Prevention. http://www.cdc.gov/nchs/fastats/leading-causes-of-death.htm

Johnston, C. C., Campbell-Yeo, M., & Fillon, F. (2011). Paternal vs maternal kangaroo care for procedural pain in preterm neonates: A randomized crossover trial. *Archives of Pediatrics and Adolescent Medicine, 165*(9), 792–796.

Johnston, L. D., O'Malley, P. M., Miech, R. A., Bachman, J. G., & Schulenberg, J. E. (2016). Monitoring the Future national survey results on drug use, 1975–2015: Overview, key findings on adolescent drug use. Ann Arbor: Institute for Social Research, The University of Michigan.

Jolley, R. P. (2010). Children and pictures: Drawing and understanding. Chichester, West Sussex, UK: Wiley-Blackwell.

Jones, S. S., & Hong, H.-W. (2005). How some infant smiles get made. *Infant Behavior & Development*, 28(2), 194–205.

K

Kagan, J., & Klein, R. E. (1973). Cross-cultural perspectives on early development. *American Psychologist*, 28, 947–961.

Kaiser Family Foundation, Holt, T., Greene, L., & Davis, J. (2003). National Survey of Adolescents and Young Adults: Sexual health knowledge, attitudes, and experiences. Menlo Park, CA: Author.

Käll, A., & Lagercrantz, H. (2012). Highlights in this issue. *Acta Paediatrica*, 101(1), 1. doi:10.1111/j.1651-2227.2011.02524.x

Kaminski, R. A., & Stormshak, E. A. (2007). Project STAR: Early intervention with preschool children and families for the prevention of substance abuse. In P. Tolan, J. Szapocznik, & S. Sambrano (Eds.), *Preventing youth substance abuse: Science-based programs for children and adolescents* (pp. 89–109). Washington, DC: American Psychological Association.

Karasahin, K. E. (2016). The emotional storms of breast feeding and points to remember. *Midwifery*, 35, 1–2.

Kaufman, J. C., & Plucker, J. A. (2011). Intelligence and creativity. In R. J. Sternberg & S. J. Kaufman (Eds.), *The Cambridge Handbook of Intelligence* (pp. 771–783). New York, NY: Cambridge University Press.

Kaye, D. A., & Shah, R. V. (2015). *Case studies in pain management*. Cambridge, UK: Cambridge University Press.

Keller, H., Kärtner, J., Borke, J., Yovsi, R., & Kleis, A. (2005). Parenting styles and the development of the categorical self: A longitudinal study on mirror self-recognition in Cameroonian Nso and German families. *International Journal of Behavioral Development*, 29(6), 496–504.

Kellogg, R. (1959). *What children scribble and why*. Oxford, UK: National Press.

Kellogg, R. (1970). Understanding children's art. In P. Cramer (Ed.), *Readings in developmental psychology today*. Del Mar, CA: CRM.

Kempes, M., Matthys, W., de Vries, H., & van Engeland, H. (2005). Reactive and proactive aggression in children: A review of theory, findings and the relevance for child and adolescent psychiatry. *European Child & Adolescent Psychiatry*, 14(1), 11–19.

Kendler, K. S. (2010). Advances in our understanding of genetic risk factors for autism spectrum disorders. *American Journal of Psychiatry*, 167(11), 1291–1293.

Kendler, K. S., et al. (2011). The impact of environmental experiences on symptoms of anxiety and depression across the life span. *Psychological Science*, 22(1), 1343–1352.

Kenney, S. R., et al. (2015). Pathways of parenting style on adolescents' college adjustment, academic achievement, and alcohol risk. *Journal of College Student Retention: Research, Theory & Practice*, 17(2), 186–203.

Kim, H. S. (2011). Consequences of parental divorce for child development. *American Sociological Review*, 76(3), 487–511.

Kim, J.-Y., McHale, S. M., Osgood, D. W., & Crouter, A. C. (2006). Longitudinal course and family correlates of sibling relationships from childhood through adolescence. *Child Development*, 77(6), 1746–1761.

Kimura, et al. (2010). Infants' recognition of objects using canonical color. *Journal of Experimental Child Psychology*, 105(3), 256–263.

Klaus, M. H., & Kennell, J. H. (1978). Parent-to-infant attachment. In J. H. Stevens Jr. & M. Mathews (Eds.), *Mother/child, father/child relationships*. Washington, DC: National Association for the Education of Young Children.

Klee, T., & Stokes, S. F. (2011). Language development. In D. Skuse et al. (Eds.), *Child psychology and psychiatry: frameworks for practice* (2nd ed.) (pp. 45–50). Chichester, UK: John Wiley & Sons. doi:10.1002/9781119993971.ch8

Klein, P. J., & Meltzoff, A. N. (1999). Long-term memory, forgetting and deferred imitation in 12-month-old infants. *Developmental Science*, 2(1), 102–113.

Klier, C. M. (2006). Mother–infant bonding disorders in patients with postnatal depression: The Postpartum Bonding Questionnaire in clinical practice. *Archives of Women's Mental Health*, 9(5), 289–291.

Knickmeyer, R., et al. (2005). Gender-typed play and amniotic testosterone. *Developmental Psychology*, 41, 517–528.

Kochanska, G. (2001). Emotional development in children with different attachment histories: The first three years. *Child Development*, 72(2), 474–490.

Kohlberg, L. (1963). Moral development and identification. In H. W. Stevenson (Ed.), *Child psychology: 62nd yearbook of the National Society for the Study of Education* (pp. 277–332). Chicago, IL: University of Chicago Press.

Kohlberg, L. (1966). Cognitive stages and preschool education. *Human Development*, 9, 5–17.

Kohlberg, L. (1969). Stage and sequence: The cognitive-developmental approach to socialization. In D. A. Goslin (Ed.), *Handbook of socialization theory and research* (pp. 347–480). Chicago, IL: Rand McNally.

Kohlberg, L. (1981). *The meaning and measurement of moral development*. Worcester, MA: Clark University Press.

Kohlberg, L. (1985). *The psychology of moral development*. San Francisco, CA Harper & Row.

Kohlberg, L., & Kramer, R. (1969). Continuities and discontinuities in childhood and adult moral development. *Human Development*, 12, 93–120.

Kokko, K., et al. (2014). Country, sex, and parent occupational status: Moderators of the continuity of aggression from childhood to adulthood. *Aggressive Behavior*, 40(6), 552–567.

Kooistra, L., Crawford, S., Gibbard, B., Ramage, B., & Kaplan, B. (2010). Differentiating attention deficit in child with fetal alcohol spectrum disorder or attention-deficit-hyperactivity disorder. *Developmental Medicine & Child Neurology*, 52(2), 205–211.

Kopp, C. B. (1989). Regulation of distress and negative emotions: A developmental view. *Developmental Psychology*, 25, 343–354.

Kreager, D. A., Molloy, L. E., Moody, J., & Feinberg, M. E. (2015). Friends first? The peer network origins of adolescent dating. *Journal of Research on Adolescence*, DOI: 10.1111/jora.12189.

Kristof, N. D. (2012, January 11). The value of teachers. *The New York Times*, p. A7.

Kroeger, K. A., & Nelson, W. M., III. (2006). A language programme to increase the verbal production of a child dually diagnosed with Down syndrome and autism. *Journal of Intellectual Disability Research*, 50(2), 101–108.

Kroger, J., & Marcia, J. E. (2011). The identity statuses: Origins, meanings, and interpretations. In S. J. Schwartz et al. (Eds.), *Handbook of identity theory and research* (Part 1, pp. 31–53). New York, NY Springer.

Kuczaj, S. A., II. (1982). On the nature of syntactic development. In S. A. Kuczaj II (Ed.), *Language development, Vol. 1: Syntax and semantics*. Hillsdale, NJ: Erlbaum.

Kuczmarski, R. J., et al. (2000, December 4). CDC growth charts: United States. *Advance Data from Vital and Health Statistics, No. 314*. Hyattsville, MD: National Center for Health Statistics.

Kuhl, P. K., et al. (1997). Cross-language analysis of phonetic units in language addressed to infants. *Science, 277*(5326), 684–686.

Kuhl, P. K., et al. (2006). Infants show a facilitation effect for native language phonetic perception between 6 and 12 months. *Developmental Science, 9*(2) F13–F21.

Kurosawa, K., Masuno, M., & Kuroki, Y. (2012). Trends in occurrence of twin births in Japan. *American Journal of Medical Genetics, 158A*(1), 75–77.

L

Laible, D., Thompson, R. A., & Froimson, J. (2015). Early socialization: The influence of close relationships. In J. E. Grusec & P. D. Hastings (Eds.). *Handbook of socialization: Theory and Research* (pp. 35–59). New York: Guilford.

Lampl, M., Veldhuis, J. D., & Johnson, M. L. (1992). Saltation and stasis: A model of human growth. *Science, 258*, 801–803.

Landolt, A. S., & Milling, L. S. (2011). The efficacy of hypnosis as an intervention for labor and delivery pain: A comprehensive methodological review. *Clinical Psychology Review, 31*(6), 1022–1031.

Lange, G., & Pierce, S. H. (1992). Memory-strategy learning and maintenance in preschool children. *Developmental Psychology, 28*, 453–462.

Laurendeau, M., & Pinard, A. (1970). *The development of the concept of space in the child*. New York, NY: International Universities Press.

Laursen, B., DeLay, D., & Adams, R. E. (2010). Trajectories of perceived support in mother–adolescent relationships. *Developmental Psychology, 46*(6), 1792–1798.

Leaper, C. (2011). More similarities than differences in contemporary theories of social development? A plea for theory bridging. *Advances in Child Development and Behavior, 40*, 337–378.

Leaper, C., & Bigler, R. S. (2011). Gender. In M. K. Underwood & L. H. Rosen (Eds.), *Social development: Relationships in infancy, childhood, and adolescence* (pp. 289–315). New York, NY: Guilford.

Leaper, C., & Farkas, T. (2015). The socialization of gender during childhood and adolescence. In J. E. Grusec & P. D. Hastings (Eds.). *Handbook of socialization: Theory and Research* (pp. 541–565). New York: Guilford.

Lecanuet, J. P., Graniere-Deferre, C., Jacquet, A.-Y., & DeCasper, A. J. (2000). Fetal discrimination of low-pitched musical notes. *Developmental Psychobiology, 36*(1), 29–39.

Lecce, S., Demicheli, P., Zocchi, A., & Palladino, P. (2015). The origins of children's metamemory: The role of theory of mind. *Journal of Experimental Child Psychology, 131*, 56–72.

Lee, A. C., He, J., & Ma, M. (2011). Olfactory marker protein is crucial for functional maturation of olfactory sensory neurons and development of mother preference. *The Journal of Neuroscience, 31*(8), 2974–2982.

Lenneberg, E. H. (1967). *Biological foundations of language*. New York, NY: Wiley.

Leonard, S. P., & Archer, J. (1989). A naturalistic investigation of gender constancy in three- to four-year-old children. *British Journal of Developmental Psychology, 7*, 341–346.

Leonardo, E. D., & Hen, R. (2006). Genetics of affective and anxiety disorders. *Annual Review of Psychology. 57*, 117–137.

Levendosky, A. A., Bogat, G. A., Huth-Bocks, A. C., Rosenblum, K., & von Eye, A. (2011). *Journal of Clinical Child & Adolescent Psychology, 40*(3), 398–410.

Lever, N., et al. (2004). A drop-out prevention program for high-risk inner-city youth. *Behavior Modification, 28*(4), 513–527.

Lewis, B. A., et al. (2004). Four-year language outcomes of children exposed to cocaine in utero. *Neurotoxicology and Teratology, 26*(5), 617–627.

Lick, D. J., Tornello, S. L., Riskind, R. G., Schmidt, K. M., & Patterson, C. J. (2012). Social climate for sexual minorities predicts well-being among heterosexual offspring of lesbian and gay parents. *Sexuality Research and Social Policy, 9*(2), 99–112.

Lim, L., et al. (2015). Disorder-specific grey matter deficits in attention deficit hyperactivity disorder relative to autism spectrum disorder. *Psychological Medicine, 45*(5), 965–976.

Lipsitt, L. P. (2002). Early experience and behavior in the baby of the twenty-first century. In J. Gomes-Pedro et al. (Eds.), *The infant and family in the twentyfirst century* (pp. 55–78). London: Brunner-Routledge.

Liu, W., et al. (2011). Protective effects of hydrogen on fetal brain injury during maternal hypoxia. *Intracerebral Hemorrhage Research, 111*(3), 307–311.

Loayza, I. M., Sola, I., & Prats, C. J. (2011). *Biofeedback for pain management during labor*. John Wiley & Sons: The Cochrane Library. doi:10.1002/14651858.CD006168.pub2.

Loewenthal, K. M. (2016). Psychological views of conscience. In D. A. Leeming (Ed.). *Encyclopedia of psychology and religion* (pp. 1–4). Berlin Heidelberg: Springer-Verlag Berlin Heidelberg.

Lomanowska, A. M., & Melo, A. I. (2016). Deconstructing the function of maternal stimulation in offspring development: Insights from the artificial rearing model in rats. *Hormones and Behavior, 77*, 224–236.

Lorenz, K. (1962). *King Solomon's ring*. London: Methuen.

Lorenz, K. (1981). *The foundations of ethology*. New York, NY: Springer-Verlag.

Lorenzo-Blanco, E. I., et al. (2016). Profiles of bullying victimization, discrimination, social support, and school safety: Links with Latino/a youth acculturation, gender, depressive symptoms, and cigarette use. *American Journal of Orthopsychiatry, 86*(1), 37–48.

Lothian, J. A. (2011). Lamaze breathing. *The Journal of Perinatal Education, 20*(2), 118–120.

Lovaas, O. I. (1977). *The autistic child: Language development through behavior modification*. New York, NY: Halstead Press.

Lovaas, O. I., Smith, T., & McEachin, J. J. (1989). Clarifying comments on the young autism study: Reply to Schapler, Short, and Mesibov. *Journal of Consulting and Clinical Psychology, 57*, 165–167.

Lucas, C. P., Hazen, E. P., & Shaffer, D. (2015). Childhood elimination disorders. In A. Tasman et al. (Eds.). *Psychiatry*, 4th ed. (pp. 1250ff). Hoboken, NJ: Wiley.

Lucassen, N., et al. (2011). The association between paternal sensitivity and infant– father attachment security: A meta-analysis of three decades of research. *Journal of Family Psychology, 25*(6), 986–992.

Luciano, M., Kirk, K. M., Heath, A. C., & Martin, N. G. (2005). The genetics of tea and coffee drinking and preference for source of caffeine in a large community sample of Australian twins. *Addiction, 100*(10), 1510–1517.

Luders, E., Thompson, P. M., & Toga, A. W. (2010). The development of the corpus callosum in the healthy human brain. *The Journal of Neuroscience, 30*(33), 10985–10990.

M

Maccoby, E. E. (2015). Historical overview of socialization research and theory. In J. E. Grusec & P. D. Hastings (Eds.). *Handbook of socialization: Theory and Research* (pp. 3–34). New York: Guilford.

MacDonald, G., & Leary, M. R. (2011). Individual differences in self-esteem. In M. R. Leary, & J. P. Tangney (Eds.). *Handbook of Self and Identity*, second edition (pp. 354–377). New York: Guilford Press.

MacEvoy, J. P., Papadakis, A. A., Fedigan, S. K., & Ash, S. E. (2016). Friendship expectations and children's friendship-related behavior and adjustment. *Merrill-Palmer Quarterly*, *62*(1), 74–104.

Macfarlane, A. (1975). Olfaction in the development of social preferences in the human neonate. In M. A. Hofer (Ed.), *Parent–infant interaction* (pp. 103–117). Amsterdam: Elsevier.

Macfarlane, A. (1977). *The psychology of childbirth*. Cambridge, MA: Harvard University Press.

Madon, S., et al. (2001). Am I as you see me or do you see me as I am? Self-fulfilling prophecies and self-verification. *Personality and Social Psychology Bulletin*, *27*(9), 1214–1224.

Malone, P. S., et al. (2004). Divorce and child behavior problems: Applying latent change score models to life event data. *Structural Equation Modeling*, *11*(3), 401–423.

Marcia, J. E. (2010). Life transitions and stress in the context of psychosocial development. In T. W. Miller (Ed.), *Handbook of stressful transitions across the lifespan* (Part 1, pp. 19–34). New York, NY: Springer Science + Business Media.

Marcia, J. E. (2014). From industry to integrity. *Identity: An International Journal of Theory and Research*, *14*(3), 165–176.

Markus, H. R. (2016). What moves people to action? Culture and motivation. *Current Opinion in Psychology*, *8*, 161–166.

Marsiglio, W. (2004). When stepfathers claim stepchildren: A conceptual analysis. *Journal of Marriage and Family*, *66*(1), 22–39.

Martel, M. M., et al. (2011). The dopamine receptor D4 gene (DRD4) moderates family environmental effects on ADHD. (2011). *Journal of Abnormal Child Psychology*, *39*(1), 1–10.

Martel, M. M., von Eye, A., & Nigg, J. (2012). Developmental differences in structure of attention-deficit/hyperactivity disorder (ADHD) between childhood and adulthood. *International Journal of Behavioral Development*, *36*(4), 279–292.

Martin, C. L., & Dinella, L. M. (2011). Congruence between gender stereotypes and activity preference in self-identified tomboys and non-tomboys. *Archives of Sexual Behavior*. doi: 10.1007/s10508–011–9786–5

Martin, C. L., & Ruble, D. (2004). Children's search for gender cues: Cognitive perspectives on gender development. *Current Directions in Psychological Science*, *13*(2), 67–70.

Martin, C. L., Ruble, D. N., & Szkrybalo, J. (2002). Cognitive theories of early gender development. *Psychological Bulletin*, *128*(6), 903–933.

Martin, J., & Soko, B. (2011). Generalized others and imaginary audiences: A neo-Meadian approach to adolescent egocentrism. *New Ideas in Psychology*, *29*(3), 364–375.

Martin, J. A., Hamilton, B. E., Osterman, M. J. K., Curtin, S. C., & Mathews, T. J. (2015). Births: Final data for 2013. National Vital Statistics Reports. *64*(1).

Martinez, G. M., & Abma, J. C. (2015). Sexual activity, contraceptive use, and childbearing of teenagers aged 15–19 in the United States. NCHS data brief, no 209. Hyattsville, MD: National Center for Health Statistics.

Martire, S. I., Westbrook, R. F., & Morris, M. J. (2015). Effects of long-term cycling between palatable cafeteria diet and regular chow on intake, eating patterns, and response to saccharin and sucrose. *Physiology & Behavior*, *139*, 80–88.

Mathews, T. J., & MacDorman, M. F. (2007). Infant mortality statistics from the 2004 period linked birth/infant death data set. *National Vital Statistics Reports*, *55* (14). Hyattsville, MD: National Center for Health Statistics.

Maughan, B. (2011). Family and systemic influences. In D. Skuse, H. Bruce, L. Dowdney, & D. Mrazek (Eds.), *Child psychology and psychiatry: Frameworks for practice* (2nd ed., pp. 1–7). Hoboken, NJ: Wiley.

May, A., & Klonsky, E. D. (2011). Validity of suicidality items from the Youth Risk Behavior Survey in a high school sample. *Assessment*, *18*(3), 379–381.

Mayer, R. E. (2011). Intelligence and achievement. In R. J. Sternberg & S. J. Kaufman (Eds.), *The Cambridge handbook of intelligence* (pp. 738–747). New York, NY: Cambridge University Press.

McCall, R. B., Applebaum, M. I., & Hogarty, P. S. (1973). *Developmental changes in mental performance. Monographs of the Society for Research in Child Development*, *38*(3, ser. 150).

McCardle, P., Colombo, J., & Freud, L. (2009). Measuring language in infancy. In J. Colombo, P. McCardle, & L. Freud (Eds.), *Infant pathways to language: Methods, models, and research disorders* (pp. 1–12). New York, NY: Psychology Press.

McCrae, R. R., et al. (2000). Nature over nurture: Temperament, personality, and life span development. *Journal of Personality and Social Psychology*, *78*(1), 173–186.

McGlaughlin, A., & Grayson, A. (2001). Crying in the first year of infancy: Patterns and prevalence. *Journal of Reproductive and Infant Psychology*, *19*(1), 47–59.

McGue, M., Bouchard, T. J., Jr., Iacono, W. G., & Lykken, D. T. (1993). Behavioral genetics of cognitive ability: A life-span perspective. In R. Plomin & G. E. McClearn (Eds.), *Nature, nurture & psychology* (pp. 59–76). Washington, DC: American Psychological Association.

Meek, J. Y. (Ed.). (2011). *American Academy of Pediatrics new mother's guide to breastfeeding* (2nd ed.). New York, NY: Bantam Books.

Meeus, W. (2011). The study of adolescent identity formation 2000–2010: A review of longitudinal research. *Journal of Research on Adolescence*, *21*(1), 75–94.

Mehler, P. S., & Brown, C. (2015). Anorexia nervosa—Medical complications. *Journal of Eating Disorders*, *3*(11). DOI 10.1186/s40337–015–0040–8.

Meltzoff, A. N., & Brooks, R. (2009). Social cognition and language: The role of gaze following in early word learning. In J. Colombo, P. McCardle, & L. Freund (Eds.), *Infant pathways to language: Methods, models, and research disorders* (pp. 169–194). New York, NY: Psychology Press.

Mendelsohn, F., & Warren, M. (2010). Anorexia, bulimia, and the female athlete triad: Evaluation and management. *Endocrinology and Metabolism Clinics of North America*, *39*(1), 155–167.

Meyer, D. K. (2016). Emotion regulation in K-12 classrooms. In K. R. Wentzel, & G. B. Ramani (Eds.). *Handbook of social influences in school contexts: Social-emotional, motivation, and cognitive outcomes* (pp. 192–207). New York: Routledge.

Miller, C. F., Trautner, H. M., & Ruble, D. N. (2006). The role of gender stereotypes in children's preferences and behavior. In L. Balter & C. S. Tamis-LeMonda (Eds.), *Child psychology: A handbook of contemporary issues* (2nd ed., pp. 293–323). New York, NY: Psychology Press.

Minino, A. M., Xu, J., & Kochanek, K. D. (2010). *Deaths: National Vital Statistics Reports, 59*(2).

Minnes, S., Lang, A., & Singer, L. (2011). Prenatal tobacco, marijuana, stimulant, and opiate exposure: Outcomes and practice implications. *Addiction Science & Clinical Practice, 6*(1), 57–70.

Miscarriage. (2016). Mayo Clinic. http://www.mayoclinic.org/diseases-conditions/pregnancy-loss-miscarriage/home/ovc-20213664 (Accessed August 1, 2016).

Misra, D. P., Caldwell, C., Young, A. A., & Abelson, S. (2010). Do fathers matter? Paternal contributions to birth outcomes and racial disparities. *American Journal of Obstetrics & Gynecology, 202*(2), 99–100.

Miyawaki, D., et al. (2016). Psychogenic nonepileptic seizures as a manifestation of psychological distress associated with undiagnosed autism spectrum disorder. *Neuropyschiatric Disease and Treatment, 12*, 185–189.

Montemayor, R., & Eisen, M. (1977). The development of self-conceptions from childhood to adolescence. *Developmental Psychology, 13*, 314–319.

Moon, M. (2011). The effects of divorce on children: Married and divorced parents' perspectives. *Journal of Divorce & Remarriage, 52*(5), 344–349.

Moore, M. K., & Meltzoff, A. N. (2008). Factors affecting infants' manual search for occluded objects and the genesis of object permanence. *Infant Behavior and Development, 31*(2), 168–180.

Morgenstern, A., Leroy-Collombel, M., & Caet, S. (2013). Self- and other-repairs in child-adult interaction at the intersection of pragmatic abilities and language acquisition. *Journal of Pragmatics, 56*, 151–167.

Morrell, H. E. R., Lapsley, D. K., & Halpern-Felsher, B. L. (2015). Subjective invulnerability and perceptions of tobacco-related benefits predict adolescent smoking behavior. *The Journal of Early Adolescence*, DOI: 10.1177/0272431615578274.

Moses, L. J., & Flavell, J. H. (1990). Inferring false beliefs from actions and reactions. *Child Development, 61*, 929–945.

Mosher, W. D., Chandra, A., & Jones, J. (2005). *Sexual behavior and selected health measures: men and women 15–44 years of age, United States, 2002. Advance data from vital and health statistics.* Centers for Disease Control and Prevention. National Center for Health Statistics, Number 362, Figures 2 and 3.

Moshman, D. (2013). Epistemic cognition and development. In P. Barrouillet, & C. Gauffroy (Eds.). *The development of thinking and reasoning* (pp. 13–33). New York: Psychology Press.

Mountjoy, M. L., & Goolsby, M. (2015). Female athlete triad. *Handbook of sports medicine and science: The female athlete.* Hoboken, NJ: Wiley.

Moylan, C. A., et al. (2010). The effects of child abuse and exposure to domestic violence on adolescent internalizing and externalizing behavior problems. *Journal of Family Violence, 25*(1), 53–63.

Muller, U., Ten Eycke, K., & Baker, L. (2015). Piaget's theory of intelligence. In S. Goldstein, D. Princiotta, & J. A. Naglieri (Eds.). *Handbook of intelligence* (pp. 137–151). New York: Springer Science + Business Media.

Munroe, R. H., Shimmin, H. S., & Munroe, R. L. (1984). Gender role understanding and sex role preference in four cultures. *Developmental Psychology, 20*, 673–682.

Muris, P., & Field, A. P. (2011). The "normal" development of fear. In W. K. Silverman, & A. P. Field (Eds.), *Anxiety disorders in children and adolescents* (pp. 76–89). New York: Cambridge University Press.

Murphy, K. E., et al. (2011). Maternal side-effects after multiple courses of antenatal corticosteroids (MACS): The three-month follow-up of women in the Randomized Controlled Trial of MACS for Preterm Birth Study. *Journal of Obstetrics and Gynecology, Canada, 33*(9), 909–921.

N

Nagin, D. S., & Tremblay, R. E. (2001). Parental and early childhood predictors of persistent physical aggression in boys from kindergarten to high school. *Archives of General Psychiatry, 58*(4), 389–394.

National Sleep Foundation. (2015). Children and sleep. http://sleepfoundation.org/sleep-topics/children-and-sleep

NCD Risk Factor Collaboration (NCD-RisC). eLife 2016;5:e13410. DOI: 10.7554/eLife.13410

Neisser, U., et al. (1996). Intelligence: Knowns and unknowns. *American Psychologist, 51*, 77–101.

Nelson, K. (1973). Structure and strategy in learning to talk. *Monographs for the Society for Research in Child Development, 38*(1–2, ser. 149).

Nelson, K. (1990). Remembering, forgetting, and childhood amnesia. In R. Fivush & J. A. Hudson (Eds.), *Knowing and remembering in young children.* Cambridge, UK: Cambridge University Press.

Nelson, K. (1993). Events, narratives, memory: What develops? In C. A. Nelson (Ed.), *Minnesota symposia on child psychology, Vol. 26: Memory and affect in development.* Hillsdale, NJ: Erlbaum.

Nelson, K. (2005). Cognitive functions of language in early childhood. In B. D. Homer & C. S. Tamis-LeMonda (Eds.), *The development of social cognition and communication* (pp. 7–28). Mahwah, NJ: Erlbaum.

Nelson, K. (2006). Advances in pragmatic developmental theory: The case of language acquisition. *Human Development, 49*(3), 184–188.

Newman, R., Ratner, N. B., Jusczyk, A. M., Jusczyk, P. W., & Dow, K. A. (2006). Infants' early ability to segment the conversational speech signal predicts later language development: A retrospective analysis. *Developmental Psychology, 42*(4), 643–655.

Nguyen, T., et al. A testosterone-related structural brain phenotype predicts aggressive behavior from childhood to adulthood. *Psychoneuroendocrinology, 63*, 109–118.

NHLBI (National Heart, Lung, and Blood Institute). 2011. Asthma guidelines. https://www.nhlbi.nih.gov/health-pro/resources/lung/naci/asthma-info/asthma-guidelines.htm (Accessed May 7, 2016)

Niemann, S., & Weiss, S. (2011). Attachment behavior and children adopted internationally at six months post adoption. *Adoption Quarterly, 14*(4), 246–267.

Nigg, J. T. & Holton, K. (2014). Restriction and elimination diets in ADHD treatment. *Child and Adolescent Psychiatric Clinics of North America, 23*(4), 937–953.

Nisbett, R. E. (2009). *Intelligence and how to get it: Why schools and cultures count*. New York, NY: W. W. Norton.

Nisbett, R. E. (2013, Spring). Schooling makes you smarter. *American Educator*, 10–39.

Nisbett, R. E. (2016). Think big, bigger . . . and smaller. In M. Scherer (Ed.). *On poverty and learning: Readings from educational leadership* (pp. 94–103). Alexandria, VA: ASCD.

Noordstar, J. J., et al. (2016). Global self-esteem, perceived athletic competence, and physical activity in children: A longitudinal cohort study. *Psychology of Sport and Exercise*, 22, 83–90.

Nordhov, S. M., et al. (2010). Early intervention improves cognitive outcomes for preterm infants: Randomized controlled trial. *Pediatrics*, 126(5), e1088–e1094.

Nordhov, S. M., et al. (2012). Early intervention improves behavioral outcomes for preterm infants: Randomized controlled trial. *Pediatrics*, 129(1), e9–e16.

Novotny, R., et al. (2011). Puberty, body fat, and breast density in girls of several ethnic groups. *American Journal of Human Biology*, 23(3), 359–365.

Nurwisah, R. (2011, September 29). Mitchell Wilson suicide: Disabled boy's death raises bullying concerns. *The Huffington Post Canada*.

O

O'Connor, K. A., et al. (2011). The puzzle of sibling attachment non-concordance. *Psychology Presentations*, Paper 32. Retrieved from http://ir.lib.uwo.ca/psychologypres/32

Ogden, C. L., et al. (2014). Prevalence of childhood and adult obesity in the United States, 2011–2012. *Journal of the American Medical Association*, 311(8), 806–814.

Ojanen, T., & Findley-Van Nostrand, D. (2014). Social, goals, aggression, peer preference, and popularity: Longitudinal links during middle school. *Developmental Psychology*, 50(8), 2134–2143.

O'Leary, C. M., et al. (2010). Prenatal alcohol exposure and risk of birth defects. *Pediatrics*, 126(4), e843-e850.

O'Neill, D. K., & Chong, S. C. F. (2001). Preschool children's difficulty understanding the types of information obtained through the five senses. *Child Development*, 72(3), 803–815.

O'Neill, D. K., & Gopnik, A. (1991). Young children's ability to identify the sources of their beliefs. *Developmental Psychology*, 27, 390–397.

Oliveira, P. S., Fearon, R. M. P., Belsky, J., Fachada, I., & Soares, I. (2015). Quality of institutional care and early childhood development. *International Journal of Behavioral Development*, 39(2), 161–170.

Olson, S. D., Fauci, L. J., & Suarez, S. S. (2011). Mathematical modeling of calcium signaling during sperm hyperactivation. *Molecular Human Reproduction*, 17(8), 500–510.

Olson, S. L., Bates, J. E., Sandy, J. M., & Lanthier, R. (2000). Early developmental precursors of externalizing behavior in middle childhood and adolescence. *Journal of Abnormal Child Psychology*, 28(2), 119–133.

Örnkloo, H., & von Hofsten, C. (2007). Fitting objects into holes: On the development of spatial cognition skills. *Developmental Psychology*, 43(2), 404–416.

Orstavik, R. E., Kendler, K. S., Czajkowski, N., Tambs, K., & Reichborn-Kjennerud, T. (2007). Genetic and environmental contributions to depressive personality disorder in a population-based sample of Norwegian twins. *Journal of Affective Disorders*, 99(1–3), 181–189.

Oswald, R. F., et al. (2013). LGB families in community context. In A. E Goldberg, & K. R. Allen (Eds.). *LGBT-parent families: Innovations in research and implications for practice* (pp. 193–208). New York: Springer Science + Business Media.

Out, D., Pieper, S., Bakermans-Kranenburg, M., Zeskind, P., van Ijzendoorn, M. (2010). Intended sensitive and harsh caregiving responses to infant crying: The role of cry pitch and perceived urgency in an adult twin sample. *Child Abuse & Neglect*, 34(11), 863–873.

P

Paavola, L., Kemppinen, K., Kumpulainen, K., Moilanen, I., & Ebeling, H. (2006). Maternal sensitivity, infant co-operation and early linguistic development: Some predictive relations. *European Journal of Developmental Psychology*, 3(1), 13–30.

Palmer, E. L. (2003). Realities and challenges in the rapidly changing televisual media landscape. In E. L. Palmer & B. M. Young (Eds.), *The faces of televisual media: Teaching, violence, selling to children* (2nd ed., pp. 361–377). Mahwah, NJ: Erlbaum.

Parke, R. D., & Buriel, R. (2006). Socialization in the family: Ethnic and ecological perspectives. In N. Eisenberg, W. Damon, & R. M. Lerner (Eds.), *Handbook of child psychology, Vol. 3: Social, emotional, and personality development* (6th ed., pp. 429–504). Hoboken, NJ: Wiley.

Parsons, H. G., George, M. A., & Innis, S. M. (2011). Growth assessment in clinical practice: Whose growth curve? *Current Gastroenterology Reports*, 13(3), 286–292.

Patenaude, J., Niyonsenga, T., & Fafard, D. (2003). Changes in students' moral development during medical school: A cohort study. *Canadian Medical Association Journal*, 168(7), 840–844.

Paterson, D. S., et al. (2006). Multiple serotonergic brainstem abnormalities in sudden infant death syndrome. *Journal of the American Medical Association*, 296, 2124–2132.

Patrick, H., Turner, J. C., & Strati, A. D. (2016). Classroom and school influences on student motivation. In K. R. Wentzel, & G. B. Ramani (Eds.). *Handbook of social influences in school contexts: Social-emotional, motivation, and cognitive outcomes* (pp. 241–257). New York: Routledge.

Patterson, G. R. (2005). The next generation of PMTO models. *The Behavior Therapist*, 28(2), 27–33.

Pearce, L. J., & Field, A. P. (2016). The impact of "scary" TV and film on children's internalizing emotions: A meta-analysis. *Human Communication Research*, 42(1), 98–121.

Pearson, G. S., & Crowley, A. A. (2012). Attention deficit hyperactivity disorder. In E. L. Yearwood, G. S. Pearson, & J. A. Newland (Eds.), *Child and adolescent behavioral health* (pp. 139–152). Chichester, West Sussex, UK: Wiley-Blackwell.

Pelphrey, K. A., et al. (2004). Development of visuospatial short-term memory in the second half of the first year. *Developmental Psychology*, 40(5), 836–851.

Persson, G. E. B. (2005). Developmental perspectives on prosocial and aggressive motives in preschoolers' peer interactions. *International Journal of Behavioral Development*, 29(1), 80–91.

Phinney, J. S., & Baldelomar, O. A. (2011). Identity development in multiple cultural contexts. In L. A. Jensen (Ed.), *Bridging cultural and developmental approaches to psychology* (pp. 161–186). New York, NY: Oxford University Press.

Piaget, J. (1932). *The moral judgment of the child*. London: Kegan Paul.

Piaget, J. (1962). *Play, dreams, and imitation in childhood*. New York, NY: Norton. (Originally published in 1946.)

Piaget, J. (1963). *The origins of intelligence in children*. New York, NY: Norton. (Originally published in 1936.)

Piaget, J. (1976). *The grasp of consciousness: Action and concept in the young child*. Cambridge, MA: Harvard University Press.

Piek, J. P., Baynam, G. B., & Barrett, N. C. (2006). The relationship between fine and gross motor ability, self-perceptions and self-worth in children and adolescents. *Human Movement Science*, 25(1), 65–75.

Pinker, S. (2007). *The stuff of thought: Language as a window into human nature*. New York, NY: Penguin Books.

Platje, E., et al. (2015). Testosterone and cortisol in relation to a nonclinical sample of boys and girls. *Aggressive Behavior*, DOI: 10.1002/ab.21585.

Plomin, R., & Asbury, K. (2005). Nature and nurture: Genetic and environmental influences on behavior. *The Annals of the American Academy of Political and Social Science*, 600(1), 86–98.

Plomin, R., & Haworth, C. M. A. (2009). Genetics of high cognitive abilities. *Behavior Genetics*, 39(4), 347–349.

Plomin, R., Owen, M. J., & McGuffin, P. (1994). The genetic basis of complex human behaviors. *Science*, 264, 1733–1739.

Plucker, J. A., Esping, A., Kaufman, J. C., & Avitia, M. J. (2015). Creativity and intelligence. In S. Goldstein, D. Princiotta, & J. A. Naglieri (Eds.). *Handbook of intelligence: Evolutionary theory, historical perspective, and current concepts* (pp. 283–291). New York: Springer Science + Business Media.

Plunkett, J., et al. (2011). An evolutionary genomic approach to identify genes involved in human birth timing. *PLoS Genetics*, 7(4): e1001365. doi:10.1371/journal.pgen.1001365

Porter, R. H., Makin, J. W., Davis, L. B., & Christensen, K. M. (1992). Breast-fed infants respond to olfactory cues from their own mother and unfamiliar lactating females. *Infant Behavior and Development*, 15, 85–93.

Powlishta, K. K., Sen, M. G., Serbin, L. A., Poulin-Dubois, D., & Eichstedt, J. A. (2001). From infancy through middle childhood: The role of cognitive and social factors in becoming gendered. In R. K. Unger (Ed.), *Handbook of the psychology of women and gender* (pp. 116–132). New York, NY: Wiley.

Pradhan, D. S., Solomon-Lane, T. K., & Grober, M. S. (2015). Contextual modulation of social and endocrine correlates of fitness: Insights from the life history of a sex changing fish. *Frontiers in Neuroscience*, 9(8), DOI: 10.3389/fnins.2015.00008.

Prendergast, G., West, D. C., & Yan, L. K. (2015). Eating disorders: The role of advertising and editorial. In H. E. Spotts (Ed.). *Developments in marketing science: Proceedings of the Academy of Marketing Science* (pp. 175–178). New York: Springer International Publishing.

Provence, S., & Lipton, R. C. (1962). *Infants in institutions*. New York, NY: International Universities Press.

Pulverman, R., Hirsh-Pasek, K., Golinkoff, R. M., Pruden, S., & Salkind, S. J. (2006). Conceptual foundations for verb learning: Celebrating the event. In K. Hirsh-Pasek & R. M. Golinkoff (Eds.), *Action meets word: How children learn verbs* (pp. 134–159). New York, NY: Oxford University Press.

R

Ramey, C. T., Campbell, F. A., & Ramey, S. L. (1999). Early intervention: Successful pathways to improving intellectual development. *Developmental Neuropsychology*, 16(3) 385–392.

Rapee, R. M. (2011). Family factors in the development and management of anxiety disorders. *Clinical Child and Family Psychology Review*. doi:10.1007/s10567-011-0106-3

Rapin, I. (1997). Autism. *New England Journal of Medicine*, 337, 97–104.

Rathus, J. H., & Miller, A. L. (2002). Dialectical Behavior Therapy adapted for suicidal adolescents. *Suicide and Life-Threatening Behavior*, 32(2), 146–157.

Rathus, S. A. et al. (2017). *Human sexuality in a changing world*. Hoboken, NJ: Pearson.

Raynes-Greenough, C. H., Gordon, A., Li, Q., & Hyett, J. A. (2013). A cross-sectional study of maternal perception of fetal movements and antenatal advice in a general pregnant population, using a qualitative framework. *BMC Pregnancy and Childbirth*, 13, 32.

Reece, M., et al. (2010). Sexual behaviors, relationships, and perceived health among adult men in the United States: Results from a national probability sample. *Journal of Sexual Medicine*, 7(Suppl. 5), 291–304.

Reiersen, A. M., & Handen, B. (2011). Commentary on "Selective serotonin reuptake inhibitors (SSRIs) for autism spectrum disorders (ASD)." *Evidence-Based Child Health: A Cochrane Review Journal*, 6, 1082–1085.

Reis, O., & Youniss, J. (2004). Patterns in identity change and development in relationships with mothers and friends. *Journal of Adolescent Research*, 19(1), 31–44.

Reis, S. M., & Renzulli, J. S. (2011). Intellectual giftedness. In R. J. Sternberg & S. J. Kaufman (Eds.), *The Cambridge handbook of intelligence* (pp. 235–252). New York, NY: Cambridge University Press.

Rennie, J., & Rosenbloom, L. (2011). How long have we got to get the baby out? A review of the effects of acute and profound intrapartum hypoxia and ischaemia. *The Obstetrician and Gynecologist*, 13(3), 169–174.

Reschly, A., & Christenson, S. L. (2006). School completion. In G. G. Bear & K. M. Minke (Eds.), *Children's needs III: Development, prevention, and intervention* (pp. 103–113). Washington, DC: National Association of School Psychologists.

Rest, J. R. (1983). Morality. In P. H. Mussen (Ed.), *Handbook of child psychology, Vol. 3: Cognitive development* (pp. 556–629). New York, NY: Wiley.

Reynolds, G. D., & Romano, A. C. (2016). The development of attention systems and working memory in infancy. *Frontiers in Systems Neuroscience*, 10, DOI: 10.3389/fnsys.2016.00015

Rice, C. E., et al. (2007). A public health collaboration for the surveillance of autism spectrum disorders. *Paediatric and Perinatal Epidemiology*, 21(2), 179–190.

Richert, R. A., Robb, M. B., & Smith, E. I. (2011). Media as social partners: The social nature of young children's learning from screen media. *Child Development*, 82(1), 82–95.

Rizzolati, G., & Fabbri-Destro, M. (2011). Mirror neurons: From discovery to autism. *Experimental Brain Research*, 200(3–4), 223–237.

Roberts, C. L., et al. (2015). Association of prelabor cesarean delivery with reduced mortality in twins born near term. *Obstetrics & Gynecology*, 125(1), 103–110.

Robling, M., et al. (2016). Effectiveness of a nurse-led intensive home-visitation programme for first-time teenage mothers (Building Blocks). *The Lancet, 387*(10014), 146–155.

Rogers, M. A., & Creed, P. A. (2011). A longitudinal investigation of adolescent career planning and exploration using a social cognitive career theory framework. *Journal of Adolescence, 34*(1), 163–172.

Roisman, G. I., & Groh, A. M. (2011). Attachment theory and research in developmental psychology: An overview and appreciative critique. In M. K. Underwood & L. H. Rosen (Eds.), *Social development: Relationships in infancy, childhood, and adolescence* (pp. 101–126). New York, NY: Guilford.

Ronald, A., et al. (2006). Genetic heterogeneity between the three components of the autism spectrum: A twin study. *Journal of the American Academy of Child & Adolescent Psychiatry, 45*(6), 691–699.

Rose, L. Y., & Fischer, K. W. (2011). Intelligence in childhood. In R. J. Sternberg & S. J. Kaufman (Eds.), *The Cambridge handbook of intelligence* (pp. 144–173). New York, NY: Cambridge University Press.

Rose, S. A., Feldman, J. F., & Jankowski, J. J. (2001). Visual short-term memory in the first year of life: Capacity and recency effects. *Developmental Psychology, 37*(4), 539–549.

Rose, S. A., Feldman, J. F., & Wallace, I. F. (1992). Infant information processing in relation to six-year cognitive outcomes. *Child Development, 63*, 1126–1141.

Rose, S. A., Feldman, J. F., Jankowski, J. J., & van Rossem, R. (2011). The structure of memory in infants and toddlers: An SEM study with full-terms and preterms. *Developmental Science, 14*(1), 83–91.

Rose, S. A., Feldman, J. F., & Jankowski, J. J. (2015). Pathways from toddler information processing to adolescent lexical proficiency. *Child Development, 86*(6), 1935–1947.

Rosen, L. H., & Patterson, M. M. (2011). The self and identity. In M. K. Underwood & L. H. Rosen (Eds.), *Social development: Relationships in infancy, childhood, and adolescence* (pp. 73–100). New York, NY: Guilford.

Rosenstein, D., & Oster, H. (1988). Differential facial responses to four basic tastes. *Child Development, 59*, 1555–1568.

Rosenthal, R., & Jacobson, L. (1968). *Pygmalion in the classroom.* New York, NY: Holt, Rinehart & Winston.

Ross, H., Ross, M., Stein, N., & Trabasso, T. (2006). How siblings resolve their conflicts: The importance of first offers, planning, and limited opposition. *Child Development. 77*(6) 1730–1745.

Rote, W. M., & Smetana, J. G. (2015). Parenting, adolescent-parent relationships, and social domain theory: Implications for identity development. In S. J. Schwatrz, K. Luyckx, & V. L. Vignoles (Eds.). *Handbook of identity theory and research* (pp. 437–453). New York: Springer Science + Business Media.

Rothbart, M. K., & Sheese, B. E. (2007). Temperament and emotion regulation. In J. J. Gross (Ed.), *Handbook of emotion regulation* (pp. 331–350). New York, NY: Guilford.

Rottinghaus, P. J., & Van Esbroeck, R. (2011). Improving person–environment fit and self-knowledge. In P. J. Hartung & L. M. Subich (Eds.), *Developing self in work and career: Concepts, cases, and contexts* (pp. 35–52). Washington, DC: American Psychological Association.

Rovee-Collier, C. (1993). The capacity for long-term memory in infancy. *Current Directions in Psychological Science, 2*, 130–135.

Rübeling, H., Schwarzer, S., Keller, H., & Lenk, M. (2011). Young children's nonfigurative drawings of themselves and their families in two different cultures. *Journal of Cognitive Education and Psychology, 10*(1), 63–76.

Rubin, K. H., & Coplan, R. J. (Eds.). (2010). *The development of shyness and social withdrawal.* New York, NY: Guilford.

Rubin, K. H., Bukowski, W. M., & Parker, J. G. (2006). Peer interactions, relationships, and groups. In N. Eisenberg, W. Damon, & R. M. Lerner (Eds.), *Handbook of child psychology* (6th ed.), *Vol. 3: Social, emotional, and personality development* (pp. 571–645). Hoboken, NJ: Wiley.

Rudolph, K. D., & Flynn, M. (2007). Childhood adversity and youth depression: Influence of gender and pubertal status. *Development and Psychopathology, 19*(2), 497–521.

Rudolph, K. D., Lambert, S. F., Clark, A. G., & Kurlakowsky, K. D. (2001). Negotiating the transition to middle school: The role of self-regulatory processes. *Child Development, 72*(3), 929–946.

Russo, N. F., Pirlott, A. G., & Cohen, A. B. (2012). The psychology of women and gender in international perspective: Issues and challenges. In F. T. L. Leong, W. E. Pickren, M. M. Leach, & A. J. Marsella (Eds.), *Internationalizing the psychology curriculum in the United States* (pp. 157–178). New York, NY: Springer.

Rytter,m M. J. H., et al. (2015). Diet in the treatment of ADHD in children—A systematic review of the literature. *Nordic Journal of Psychiatry, 69*(1), 1–18.

S

Sadker, D. M., & Silber, E. S. (Eds.) (2007). *Gender in the classroom: Foundations, skills, methods, and strategies across the curriculum.* Mahwah, NJ: Erlbaum.

Sadler, T. W. (Ed.). (2005). Abstracts of papers presented at the thirty-fifth annual meeting the Japanese Teratology Society, Tokyo, Japan. *Teratology, 52*(4), b1–b51.

Saklofske, D. H., van de Vijver, F. J. R., Oakland, T., Mpofu, E., & Suzuki, L. A. (2015). Intelligence and culture: History and assessment. In S. Goldstein, D. Princiotta, & J. A. Naglieri (Eds.). *Handbook of intelligence: Evolutionary theory, historical perspective, and current concepts* (pp. 341–365). New York: Springer Science + Business Media.

Saldarriage, L. M., Bukowski, W. M., & Greco, C. (2015). Friendship and happiness: A bidirectional dynamic process. In Demir, M. *Friendship and happiness: Across the life-span and cultures* (pp. 59–78). Netherlands: Springer Science + Media.

Salzarulo, P., & Ficca, G. (Eds.). (2002). *Awakening and sleep–wake cycle across development.* Amsterdam: John Benjamins.

Sarrazin, P., Trouilloud, D., & Bois, J. (2005a). Attentes du superviseur et performance sportive du pratiquant. Amplitude et fonctionnement de l'effet Pygmalion en contexte sportif. *Bulletin de Psychologie, 58*(1), 63–68.

Sarrazin, P., Trouilloud, D., Tessier, D., Chanal, J., & Bois, J. (2005b). Attentes de motivation et comportements différenciés de l'enseignant d'éducation physique et sportive à l'égard de ses élèves: une étude en contexte naturel d'enseignement. *Revue Européenne de Psychologie Appliquée, 55*(2), 111–120.

Saudino, K. J. (2011). Sources of continuity and change in activity level in early childhood. *Child Development. 82*(6), 2138–2143.

Save the Children. (2015). *State of the World's Mothers.* Fairfield, CT: Save the Children.

Save the Children. (2011). *State of the world's mothers* 2011. Westport, CT: Author. Retrieved from http://www.savethechildren.org

Savic, I., Garcia-Falgueras, A., & Swaab, D. F. (2011). Sexual differentiation of the human brain in relation to gender identity and sexual orientation. In I. Savic (Ed.). *Sex differences in the human brain, Their underpinnings and implications: Progress in brain research, 186* (pp. 41–64). New York: Elsevier.

Sayegh, Y., & Dennis, W. (1965). The effect of supplementary experiences upon the behavioral development of infants in institutions. *Child Development, 36*(1), 81–90.

Scarr, S. (1993, March). *IQ correlations among members of transracial adoptive families.* Paper presented at the meeting of the Society for Research in Child Development, New Orleans, LA.

Schaffer, H. R., & Emerson, P. E. (1964). The development of social attachments in infancy. *Monographs of the Society for Research in Child Development, 29*(94).

Scharf, M., Shulman, S., & Avigad-Spitz, L. (2005). Sibling relationships in emerging adulthood and in adolescence. *Journal of Adolescent Research, 20*(1), 64–90.

Schneider, W. (2010). Memory development in childhood. In U. Goswami (Ed.), *The Wiley-Blackwell handbook of childhood cognitive development.* (2nd ed.) (pp. 347–376). Chichester, West Sussex, UK: Wiley-Blackwell.

Schneider, W. (2015). Memory development during the infant and toddler years. *Motor development from early childhood through emerging adulthood* (pp. 39–74). Switzerland: Springer International Publishing.

Schuetze, P., Zeskind, P. S., & Eiden, R. D. (2003). The perceptions of infant distress signals varying in pitch by cocaine-using mothers. *Infancy, 4*(1), 65–83.

Schwartz, D., Lansford, J. E., Dodge, K. E., Pettit, G. S., & Bates, J. E. (2013). The link between harsh home environments and negative academic trajectories is exacerbated by victimization in the elementary school peer group. *Developmental Psychology, 49*(2), 305–316.

Shubert, T. R., Sitaram, S., & Jadcherla, S. R. (2016). Effects of pacifier and taste on swallowing, esophageal motility, transit, and respiratory rhythm in human neonates. *Neurogastroenterology & Motility, 28*(4), 532–542.

Schwartz, S. J., et al. (2011). Daily dynamics of personal identity and self-concept clarity. *European Journal of Personality, 25*(5), 373–385.

Schwartz, A., & Cohen, S. (2013, March 31). ADHD seen in 11% of U.S. children as diagnoses rise. *The New York Times.* http://www.nytimes.com/2013/04/01/health/more-diagnoses-of-hyperactivity-causing-concern.html?pagewanted=all&_r=0.

Scull, A. (2010). Left brain, right brain: One brain, two brains. *Brain, 133*(10), 3153–3156.

Seiler, C. B., Jones, K. E., Shera, D., & Armstrong, C. L. (2011). Brain region white matter associations with visual selective attention. *Brain Imaging and Behavior, 5*(4), 262–273.

Selman, R. L. (1976). Social-cognitive understanding. In T. Lickona (Ed.), *Moral development and behavior: Theory, research, and social issues.* New York, NY: Holt, Rinehart & Winston.

Selman, R. L. (1980). *The growth of interpersonal understanding: Developmental and clinical analysis.* New York, NY: Academic Press.

Shin, H. B., & Bruno, R. (2003, October). *Language use and English speaking ability: 2000.* Washington, DC: U.S. Bureau of the Census.

Shroff, H., et al. (2006) Features associated with excessive exercise in women with eating disorders. *International Journal of Eating Disorders, 39*(6), 454–461.

Siegel, L. S. (1992). Infant motor, cognitive, and language behaviors as predictors of achievement at school age. In C. Rovee-Collier & L. P. Lipsitt (Eds.), *Advances in infancy research* (Vol. 7) (pp. 227–237). Norwood, NJ: Ablex.

Siegler, R., et al. (2016). Die fruhe kindheit–Sehen, denken und tun. In S. Pauen (Ed.). *Entwicklungspsychologie im kindes-und jugendalter* (pp. 155–196). Berlin Heidelberg: Springer-Verlag Berlin Heidelberg.

Signorello, L. B., & McLaughlin, J. K. (2004). Maternal caffeine consumption and spontaneous abortion: A review of the epidemiologic evidence. *Epidemiology, 15*(2), 229–239.

Silverberg, J. I., & Silverberg, N. B. (2014). Epidemiology and extracutaneous comorbidities of severe acne in adolescence: A U.S. population-based study. *British Journal of Dermatology, 170*(5), 1136–1142.

Simion, F., Cassia, V. M., Turati, C., & Valenza, E. (2001). The origins of face perception: Specific versus nonspecific mechanisms. *Infant and Child Development, 10*(1–2), 59–65.

Simpson, J. L., Bailey, L. B., Pietrzik, K., Shane, B., & Holzgreve. (2011). Micronutrients and women of reproductive potential: Required dietary intake and consequences of dietary deficiency or excess. Part II—Vitamin D, Vitamin A, iron, zinc, iodine, essential fatty acids. *Journal of Maternal–Fetal and Neonatal Medicine, 24*(1), 1–24.

Singh, L., Nestor, S., Parikh, C., & Yull, A. (2009). Influences of infant-directed speech on early word recognition. *Infancy, 14*(6), 654–666.

Skeels, H. M. (1966). *Adult status of children with contrasting early life experiences: A follow-up study.* Monographs of the Society for Research in Child Development, 31 (3, ser. 105).

Skinner, B. F. (1957). *Verbal behavior.* New York, NY: Appleton.

Skorikov, V. B., & Vondracek, F. W. (2011). Occupational identity. In S. J. Schwartz et al. (Eds.), *Handbook of identity theory and research* (Part 1, pp. 693–714). New York, NY: Springer.

Slater, A., et al. (2010). Visual perception. In J. G. Bremner & T. D. Wachs (Eds.), *The Wiley-Blackwell handbook of infant development* (2nd ed., Vol. 1, pp. 40–80). Oxford, UK: Wiley-Blackwell. doi:10.1002/9781444327564.ch2

Slaughter, V. (2011). Development of social cognition. In D. Skuse, H. Bruce, L. Dowdney, & D. Mrazek (Eds.), *Child psychology and psychiatry: Frameworks for practice* (2nd ed., pp. 51–55). Hoboken, NJ: Wiley.

Slobin, D. I. (2001). Form/function relations: How do children find out what they are? In M. Tomasello & E. Bates (Eds.), *Language development: The essential readings* (pp. 267–290). Malden, MA: Blackwell.

Smetana, J. G. (2011). *Adolescents, families, and social development.* Chichester, West Sussex, UK: Wiley-Blackwell.

Smetana, J. G., Jambon, M., & Ball, C. (2013). The social domain approach to children's moral and social judgments. In M. Killen, & J. G. Smetana (Eds.). *Handbook of moral development,* 2nd ed. (pp. 23–45). New York: Psychology Press.

Smiley, P. A., & Johnson, R. S. (2006). Self-referring terms, event transitivity and development of self. *Cognitive Development, 21*(3), 266–284.

Smith, N. A., & Trainor, L. J. (2008). Infant-directed speech is modulated by infant feedback. *Infancy, 13*(4), 410–420.

Smith, R. L., & Rose, A. J. (2011). The "cost of caring" in youths' friendships: Considering associations among social perspective taking, co-rumination, and empathetic distress. *Developmental Psychology, 47*(6), 1792–1803.

Smith, A. R., Chein, J., & Steinberg, L. (2014). Peers increase adolescent risk taking even when the probabilities of negative outcomes are known. *Developmental Psychology, 50*(5), 1564–1568.

Snarey, J. R. (1994). Cross-cultural universality of social-moral development: A critical review of Kohlbergian research. In B. Puka (Ed.), *New research in moral development* (pp. 268–298). New York, NY: Garland.

Snarey, J., & Samuelson, P. L. (2014). Lawrence Kohlberg's revolutionary ideas: Moral education in the cognitive-developmental tradition. In L. Nucci, T. Krettenauer, & D. Narvaez. *Handbook of moral and character education* (pp. 61–83). New York: Routledge.

Sneider, J. T., et al. (2015). Sex differences in spatial navigation and perception in human adolescents and emerging adults. *Behavioural Processes, 111*, 42–50.

Snow, C. (2006). Cross-cutting themes and future research directions. In D. August & T. Shanahan (Eds.), *Developing literacy in second-language learners: Report of the National Literacy Panel on Language-Minority Children and Youth* (pp. 631–651). Mahwah, NJ: Erlbaum.

Snyder, H. M., & Sickmund, M. (2006). *Juvenile offenders and victims: 2006 national report.* Washington, DC: U.S. Department of Justice, Office of Justice Programs, Office of Juvenile Justice and Delinquency Prevention.

Sobel, D. M., & Legare, C. H. (2014). Causal learning in children. *Wiley Interdisciplinary Reviews: Cognitive Science, 5*(4), 423–427.

Solmeyer, A. R., & Feinberg, M. E. (2011). Mother and father adjustment during early parenthood: The roles of infant temperament and coparenting relationship quality. *Infant Behavior and Development, 34*(4), 504–514.

Sontag, L. W., & Richards, T. W. (1938). *Studies in fetal behavior: Fetal heart rate as a behavioral indicator. Child Development Monographs, 3*(4).

Sousa, C., et al. (2011). Longitudinal study of the effects of child abuse and children's exposure to domestic violence, parent-child attachments, and antisocial behavior in adolescence. *Journal of Interpersonal Violence, 26*(1), 111–136.

Soussignan, R., & Schaal, B. (2005). Emotional processes in human newborns: a functionalist perspective. In J. Nadel & D. Muir (Eds.), *Emotional development: Recent research advances* (pp. 127–159). New York, NY: Oxford University Press.

Sozener, Z. C., et al. (2015). Prognosis of adult asthma: A 7-year follow-up study. *Annals of Allergy, Asthma and Immunology,* HYPERLINK "http://dx.doi.org/10.1016/j.anai.2015.02.010" \t "doilink" doi:10.1016/j.anai.2015.02.010 (Accessed May 7, 2016).

Spelke, E. S., & Owsley, C. (1979). Intermodal exploration and knowledge in infancy. *Infant Behavior and Development, 2*, 13–27.

Spitz, R. A. (1965). *The first year of life: A psychoanalytic study of normal and deviant object relations.* New York, NY: International Universities Press.

Spitzer, R. L., Gibbon, M., Skodol, A. E., Williams, J. B. W., & First, M. B. (2002). *DSM–IV–TR casebook.* Washington, D.C.: American Psychiatric Press.

Staff, J., Mortimer, J. T., & Uggen, C. (2004). Work and leisure in adolescence. In Lerner, R. M., & Steinberg, L. (Eds.), *Handbook of adolescent psychology* (2nd ed., pp. 429–450). Hoboken, NJ: Wiley.

Stahmer, A. C., Ingersoll, B., & Koegel, R. L. (2004). Inclusive programming for toddlers autism spectrum disorders: Outcomes from the Children's Toddler School. *Journal of Positive Behavior Interventions, 6*(2), 67–82.

Stauffacher, K., & DeHart, G. B. (2006). Crossing social contexts: Relational aggression between siblings and friends during early and middle childhood. *Journal of Applied Developmental Psychology, 27*(3), 228–240.

Sternberg, R. J. (2015). Multiple intelligences in the new age of thinking. In S. Goldstein, D. Princiotta, & J. A. Naglieri (Eds.). *Handbook of intelligence: Evolutionary theory, historical perspective, and current concepts* (pp. 229–241). New York: Springer Science + Business Media.

Sternberg, R. J., & Kaufman, S. J. (Eds.). (2011). *The Cambridge handbook of intelligence.* New York, NY: Cambridge University Press.

Stevens, B., et al. (2005). Consistent management of repeated procedural pain with sucrose in preterm neonates: Is it effective and safe for repeated use over time? *Clinical Journal of Pain, 21*(6), 543–548.

Stillbirth Collaborative Research Network Writing Group. (2011). *The Journal of the American Medical Association, 306*(22), 2469–2479.

Stipek, D., Recchia, S., & McClintic, S. (1992). *Self-evaluation in young children.* Monographs of the Society for Research in Child Development, 57(1, ser. 226).

Streri, A. (2002). Hand preference in 4-month-old infants: Global or local processing of objects in the haptic mode. *Current Psychology Letters: Behaviour, Brain and Cognition, 7*, 39–50.

Striegel-Moore, R. H., et al. (2003). Eating disorders in White and Black women. *American Journal of Psychiatry, 160*(7), 1326–1331.

Strock, M. (2004). *Autism spectrum disorders (pervasive developmental disorders).* NIH Publication NIH-04-5511. Bethesda, MD: National Institute of Mental Health, National Institutes of Health, U.S. Department of Health and Human Services. Retrieved from http://www.nimh.nih.gov/publicat/autism.cfm

Strohner, H., & Nelson, K. E. (1974). The young child's development of sentence comprehension: Influence of event probability, nonverbal context, syntactic form, and strategies. *Child Development, 45*, 567–576.

Strunk, T., Simmer, K., & Burgner, D. (2012). Prematurity and mortality in childhood and early adulthood. *Journal of the American Medical Association, 307*(1). doi:10.1001/jama.2011.1952

Strutt, G. F., Anderson, D. R., & Well, A. D. (1975). A developmental study of the effects of irrelevant information on speeded classification. *Journal of Experimental Child Psychology, 20*, 127–135.

Stupica, B., Sherman, L. J., & Cassidy, J. (2011). Newborn irritability moderates the association between infant attachment security and toddler exploration and sociability. *Child Development, 82*(5), 1381–1389.

Sullivan, R., et al. (2011). Infant bonding and attachment to the caregiver: Insights from basic and clinical science. *Clinics in Perinatology, 38*(4), 643–655.

Suomi, S. J., Harlow, H. F., & McKinney, W. T. (1972). Monkey psychiatrists. *American Journal of Psychiatry, 128*, 927–932.

Suzuki, L. A., Short, E. L., & Lee, C. S. (2011). Racial and ethnic group differences in intelligence in the United States. In R. J. Sternberg & S. J. Kaufman (Eds.), *The Cambridge handbook of intelligence* (pp. 273–292). New York, NY: Cambridge University Press.

Swaggart, K. A., Pavlicev, M., & Muglia, L. J. (2015). Genomics of preterm birth. *Coldspring Harbor Perspectives in Medicine*, DOI:10.1101/cshperspect.a023127

T

Takamura, T., Nishitani, S., Doi, Hirokazu, & Shinohara, K. (2016). Possible neural correlates of young child attachment to mother in 4 to 5 year olds. *Acta Medica Nagasakiensia*, 60(2), 45–51.

Tallandini, M. A., & Valentini, P. (1991). Symbolic prototypes in children's drawings of schools. *Journal of Genetic Psychology*, 152, 179–190.

Tamis-LeMonda, C. S., Cristofaro, T. N., Rodriguez, E. T., & Bornstein, M. H. (2006). Early language development: Social influences in the first years of life. In L. Balter & C. S. Tamis-LeMonda (Eds.), *Child psychology: A handbook of contemporary issues* (2nd ed., pp. 79–108). New York, NY: Psychology Press.

Tanaka, H., et al. (2011). The brain basis of the phonological deficit in dyslexia is independent of IQ. *Psychological Science*, 22(11), 1442–1451.

Tanner, J. M. (1989). *Fetus into man: Physical growth from conception to maturity*. Cambridge, MA: Harvard University Press.

Tanner, J. M. (1991a). Adolescent growth spurt, I. In R. M. Lerner, A. C. Petersen, & J. Brooks-Gunn (Eds.), *Encyclopedia of adolescence*. New York, NY: Garland.

Tapper, K., & Boulton, M. J. (2004). Sex differences in levels of physical, verbal, and indirect aggression amongst primary school children and their associations with beliefs about aggression. *Aggressive Behavior*, 30(2), 123–145.

Tasker, F., & Granville, J. (2011). Children's views of family relationships in lesbian-led families. *Journal of GLBT Studies*, 7(1–2), 182–199.

Taylor, M., & Hort, B. (1990). Can children be trained in making the distinction between appearance and reality? *Cognitive Devlopment 5*, 89–99.

Taylor, M., Gonzalez, M., & Porter, R. (2011). Pathways to inflammation: Acne pathophysiology. *European Journal of Dermatology*, 21(3), 323–333.

Tehrani, J. A., & Mednick, S. A. (2000). Genetic factors and criminal behavior. *Federal Probation*, 64(2), 24–27.

Tenenbaum, H. R., et al. (2010). "It's a boy because he's painting a picture." Age differences in children's conventional and unconventional gender schemas. *British Journal of Psychology*, 101(1), 137–154.

Teunissen, H. A., et al. (2011). The interaction between pubertal timing and peer popularity for boys and girls. *Journal of Abnormal Child Psychology*, 39(3), 413–423.

Tharner, A., et al. (2012). Maternal lifetime history of depression and depressive symptoms in the prenatal and early postnatal period do not predict infant–mother attachment quality in a large, population-based Dutch cohort study. *Attachment & Human Development*, 14(1), 63–81.

Thomas, A., & Chess, S. (1989). Temperament and personality. In G. A. Kohnstamm, J. E. Bates, & M. K. Rothbart (Eds.), *Temperament in childhood* (pp. 249–261). Chichester, UK: Wiley.

Thompson, R. A., & Meyer, S. (2007). Socialization of emotion regulation in the family. In J. J. Gross (Ed.), *Handbook of emotion regulation* (pp. 249–268). New York, NY: Guilford.

Thompson, R. B., Foster, B. J., & Kapinos, J. R. (2016). Poverty, affluence, and the Socratic method: Parents' questions versus statements within collaborative problem-solving. *Language & Communication*, 47, 23–29.

Thurstone, L. L. (1938). *Primary mental abilities*. Psychometric Monographs, 1.

Tobbell, J. (2003). Students' experiences of the transition from primary to secondary school. *Educational and Child Psychology*, 20(4), 4–14.

Tobin, D. D., et al. (2010). The intrapsychics of gender: A model of self-socialization. *Psychological Review*, 117(2), 601–622.

Tong, J. H. S., et al. (2015). An association between a dopamine transporter gene (SLC6A3) haplotype and ADHD symptom measures in nonclinical adults. *American Journal of Medical Genetics: Neuropsychiatric genetics*, 168(2), 89–96.

Torpy, J. M., Lynm, C., & Golub, R. M. (2011). Local anesthesia. *Journal of the American Medical Association*, 306(12), 1395.

Towse, J. (2003). Lifespan development of human memory. *Quarterly Journal of Experimental Psychology: Human Experimental Psychology*, 56A(7), 1244–1246.

Troop-Gordon, W., & Ranney, J. D. (2014). Popularity among same-sex and cross-sex peers: A process-oriented examination of links to aggressive behaviors and depressive affect. *Developmental Psychology*, 50(6), 1721–1733.

U

U.S. Bureau of the Census. (2015). America's families and living arrangements: 2015. http://www.census.gov/hhes/families/.

U.S. Bureau of Census. (2015). QuickFacts, United States. http://www.census.gov/quickfacts/table/PST045215/00

U.S. Department of Health and Human Services. (2010). *Child maltreatment 2010*. Administration for Children and Families—Administration on Children, Youth and Families, Children's Bureau. Retrieved from http://www.acf.hhs.gov/programs/cb/stats_research/index.htm#can

Ulijaszek, S. J. (2010). Variation in human growth patterns due to environmental factors. In M. P. Muehlenbein (Ed.), *Human evolutionary biology* (pp. 396–404). New York, NY: Cambridge University Press.

Umana-Taylor, A. J. (2016). Ethnic-racial identity: Conceptualization, development, and youth adjustment. (pp. 305–328). In L. Balter & C. S. Tamis-LeMonda (Eds.). *Child psychology: A handbook of contemporary issues*, 3rd ed. New York: Routledge.

Underwood, M. K. (2011). Aggression. In M. K. Underwood & L. H. Rosen (Eds.), *Social development: Relationships in infancy, childhood, and adolescence* (pp. 207–234). New York, NY: Guilford.

Underwood, M. K., & Rosen, L. H. (Eds.). (2011). *Social development: Relationships in infancy, childhood, and adolescence* (pp. 289–315). New York, NY: Guilford.

Urbina, S. (2011). Tests of intelligence. In R. J. Sternberg & S. J. Kaufman (Eds.), *The Cambridge handbook of intelligence* (pp. 20–38). New York, NY: Cambridge University Press.

V

Vallance, A., & Garralda, E. (2011). Anxiety disorders in children and adolescents. In D. Skuse, H. Bruce, L. Dowdney, & D. Mrazek (Eds.), *Child psychology and psychiatry: Frameworks for practice* (2nd ed., pp. 169–174). Hoboken, NJ: Wiley.

van den Akker, A. L., Dekovic, M., & Prinzie, P. (2010). Transitioning to adolescence: How changes in child personality and overreactive parenting predict adolescent adjustment problems. *Development and Psychopathology, 22,* 151–163.

van Ijzendoorn, M. H., & Hubbard, F. O. A. (2000). Are infant crying and maternal responsiveness during the first year related to infant–mother attachment at 15 months? *Attachment and Human Development, 2*(3), 371–391.

Vander Ven, T., & Cullen, F. T. (2004). The impact of maternal employment on serious youth crime: Does the quality of working conditions matter? *Crime & Delinquency, 50*(2), 272–291.

Veldman, S. L. C., Palmer, K. K., Okely, A. D., & Robinson, L. E. (2016). Promoting ball skills in preschool-age girls. *Journal of Science and Medicine in Sport,* DOI:10.1016/j.jsams.2016.04.009

Vélez, C. E., Wolchik, S. A., Tein, J-Y., & Sandler, I. (2011). Protecting children from the consequences of divorce: A longitudinal study of the effects of parenting on children's coping processes. *Child Development, 82*(1), 244–257.

Verlohren, S., Stepan, H., & Dechend, R. (2012). Angiogenic growth factors in the diagnosis and prediction of pre-eclampsia. *Clinical Science, 122,* 43–52.

Verloop, J., van Leeuwen, F., Helmerhorst, T., van Boven, H., & Rookus, M. (2010). Cancer risk in DES daughters. *Cancer Causes Control, 21*(7), 999–1007.

Vermeulen-Smit, E., Verdurmen, J. E. E., Engels, R. C. M. E., & Vollebergh, W. A. M. (2015). The role of general parenting and cannabis-specific practices in adolescent cannabis and other illicit drug use. *Drug and Alcohol Dependence, 147,* 222–228.

Volterra, M. C., Caselli, O., Capirci, E., & Pizzuto, E. (2004). Gesture and the emergence and development of language. In M. Tomasello & D. I. Slobin (Eds.), *Beyond nature–nurture* (pp. 3–40). Mahwah, NJ. Erlbaum.

Von Gontard, A., et al. (2011). Psychological and psychiatric issues in urinary and fecal incontinence. *The Journal of Urology, 185*(4), 1432–1437.

Vygotsky, L. S. (1962). *Thought and language.* Cambridge, MA: MIT Press.

W

Wade, T. D., Wilksch, S. M., Paxton, S. J., Byrne, S. M., & Austin, S. B. (2015). How perfectionism and ineffectiveness influence growth of eating disorder risk in young adolescent girls. *Behaviour Research and Therapy, 66,* 56–63.

Walker, D. W. (Ed.). (2016). *Prenatal and postnatal determinants of development. Neuromethods, Vol. 109.* New York: Springer Science + Business Media.

Walker, L. J., & Frimer, J. A. (2011). The science of moral development. In M. K. Underwood & L. H. Rosen (Eds.), *Social development* (pp. 235–263). New York, NY: Guilford.

Walter, J. L., & LaFreniere, P. J. (2000). A naturalistic study of affective expression, social competence, and sociometric status in preschoolers. *Early Education and Development, 11*(1), 109–122.

Wang, F., Cox, M. J., Mills-Koonce, R., & Snyder, P. (2015). Parental behaviors and beliefs, child temperament, and attachment disorganization. *Family Relations, 64*(2), 191–204.

Wang, Y. et al. (2016). Development of tract-specific white matter pathways during early reading development in at-risk children and typical controls. *Cerebral Cortex,* DOI: 10.1093/cercor/bhw095

Weckerly, J., Wulfeck, B., & Reilly, J. (2004). The development of morphosyntactic ability in atypical populations: The acquisition of tag questions in children with early focal lesions and children with specific-language impairment. *Brain and Language, 88*(2), 190–201.

Welch, M. G., et al. (2016). Depression and anxiety symptoms of mothers of preterm infants are decreased at 4 months corrected age with Family Nurture Intervention in the NICU. *Archive of Women's Mental Health, 19*(1), 51–61.

Weller, E. B., & Weller, R. A. (1991). Mood disorders. In M. Lewis (Ed.), *Child and adolescent psychiatry: A comprehensive textbook* (pp. 646–664). Baltimore, MD: Williams & Wilkins.

Wellman, H. M., Cross, D., & Bartsch, K. (1986). *Infant search and object permanence: A meta-analysis of the A-not-B error.* Monographs of the Society for Research in Child Development, 5(3, ser. 214).

Wellman, H. M., Fang, F., Liu, D., Zhu, L., & Liu, G. (2006). Scaling of theory-of-mind understandings in Chinese children. *Psychological Science, 17*(12), 1075–1081.

Wentworth, N., Benson, J. B., & Haith, M. M. (2000). The development of infants' reaches for stationary and moving targets. *Child Development, 71*(3), 576–611.

Wentzel, K. R. (2014). Prosocial behavior and peer relations in adolescence. In L. M. Padilla-Walker, & G. Carlo (Eds.). *Prosocial development: A multidimensional approach* (pp. 178–200). New York: Oxford University Press.

Wentzel, K. R., & Muenks, K. (2016). Peer influence on students' motivation, academic achievement, and social behavior. In K. R. Wentzel, & G. B. Ramani (Eds.). *Handbook of social influences in school contexts: Social-emotional, motivation, and cognitive outcomes* (pp. 13–30). New York: Routledge.

Wentzel, K. R., & Ramani, G. B. (2016). *Handbook of social influences in school contexts.* New York: Routledge.

Werker, J. F. (1989). Becoming a native listener. *American Scientist, 77,* 54–59.

Werker, J. F., & Hensch, T. K. (2015). Critical periods in speech perception: New directions. *Annual Review of Psychology, 66,* 173–196.

Werner, E. E. (1988). A cross-cultural perspective on infancy. *Journal of Cross-Cultural Psychology, 19,* 96–113.

Werner, L. A., & Bernstein, I. L. (2001). Development of the auditory, gustatory, olfactory, and somatosensory systems. In E. B. Goldstein (Ed.), Blackwell handbook of perception., *Handbook of experimental psychology series* (pp. 669–708). Boston, MA: Blackwell.

White, A. (2016). Public health in sporting settings: A gender perspective. In D. Conrad, & A. White. (Eds.). *Sports-based health interventions* (pp. 61–76). New York: Springer Science + Business Media.

Williams, M., El-Sheikh, A., Mallick, A., & Gardosi, J. (2011). Maternal age and risk of stillbirth. *Archives of Disease in Childhood Fetal & Neonatal Edition*, 96(Suppl. 1). doi:10.1136/adc.2011.300160.6.

Willis, J. O., Dumont, R., & Kaufman, A. S. (2011). Factor-analytic models of intelligence. In R. J. Sternberg & S. J. Kaufman (Eds.), *The Cambridge handbook of intelligence* (pp. 39–57). New York, NY: Cambridge University Press.

Winograd, R. P., & Sher, K. J. (2015). *Binge drinking and alcohol misuse: Advances in psychotherapy*. Boston: The Hogrefe Group Publishing.

Wolfe, D. A. (2011). Violence against women and children. In J. W. White, M. P. Koss, & A. E. Kazdin (Eds.), *Violence against women and children, Vol. 1: Mapping the terrain* (pp. 31–53). Washington, DC: American Psychological Association.

Woolfolk, A. (2013). *Educational psychology* (12th ed.). Upper Saddle River, NJ: Pearson.

Worell, J., & Goodheart, C. D. (Eds.). (2006). *Handbook of girls' and women's psychological health: Gender and well-being across the lifespan*. New York, NY: Oxford University Press.

World Health Organization. (2015). HIV/AIDS. http://www.who.int/features/qa/71/en/.

Worrell, F. C. (2015) Culture as race/ethnicity. In K. C. McLean, & M. Syed (Eds.). *The Oxford handbook of identity development* (pp. 249–268). New York: Oxford University Press.

Wubbels, T., et al. (2016). Teacher-student relationships and student achievement. In K. R. Wentzel, & G. B. Ramani (Eds.). *Handbook of social influences in school contexts: Social-emotional, motivation, and cognitive outcomes* (pp. 127–142). New York: Routledge.

Wu, T., et al. (2015). Conduct disorder. In G. M. Kapalka (Ed.). *Treating disruptive disorders*. New York: Routledge.

X

Xie, H. L., Yan, B., Signe M., Hutchins, B. C., & Cairns, B. D. (2006). What makes a girl (or a boy) popular (or unpopular)? African American Children's perceptions and developmental differences. *Developmental Psychology*, 42(4), 599–612.

Xue, Y. F., Moran, G., Pederson, D. R., & Bento, S. (2010, March). *The continuity of attachment development from infancy to toddlerhood: The role of maternal sensitivity*. International Conference on Infant Studies, Baltimore, MD.

Y

Yaros, A., Lochman, J. E., Rosenbaum, J., & Jimenez-Camargo, L. A. (2014). Real-time hostile attribution measurement and aggression in children. *Aggressive Behavior*, 40(5), 409–420.

Yarrow, L. J., & Goodwin, M. S. (1973). The immediate impact of separation: Reactions of infants to a change in mother figures. In L. J. Stone, H. T. Smith, & L. B. Murphy (Eds.), *The competent infant: Research and commentary*. New York, NY: Basic Books.

Yarrow, L. J., Goodwin, M. S., Manheimer, H., & Milowe, I. D. (1971, March). *Infant experiences and cognitive and personality development at ten years*. Paper presented at the meeting of the American Orthopsychiatric Association, Washington, DC.

Yermolayeva, Y., & Rakison, D. H. (2014). Connectionist modeling of developmental changes in Infancy: Approaches, challenges, and contributions. *Psychological Bulletin*, 140(1), 224–255.

You, D., Maeda, Y., & Bebeau, M. J. (2011). Gender differences in moral sensitivity: A meta-analysis. *Ethics & Behavior*, 21(4), 263–282.

Z

Zajonc, R. B. (2001). The family dynamics of intellectual development. *American Psychologist*, 56(6/7), 490–496.

Zarbatany, L., McDougall, P., & Hymel, S. (2000). Gender-differentiated experience in the peer culture: Links to intimacy in preadolescence. *Social Development*, 9(1), 62–79.

Zeanah, C. H., Berlin, L. J. & Boris, N. W. (2011). Practitioner review: Clinical applications of attachment theory and research for infants and young children. *The Journal of Child Psychology & Psychiatry*, 52(8), 819–833.

Zeifman, D. M. (2004). Acoustic features of infant crying related to intended caregiving intervention. *Infant and Child Development*, 13(2), 111–122.

Zelazo, P. D., & Müller, U. (2010) Executive function in typical and atypical development. In U. Goswami (Ed.), *The Wiley-Blackwell handbook of childhood cognitive development* (2nd ed., pp. 574–603). Oxford, UK: Wiley-Blackwell. doi:10.1002/9781444325485.ch22

Zhang, Y., et al. (2016). Quantitative susceptibility mapping and R2 measured changes during white matter lesion development in multiple sclerosis: Myelin breakdown, myelin debris degradation and removal, and iron accumulation. *American Journal of Neuroradiology*, DOI:10.3174/ajnr.A4825.

Zhiqi, L., Kun, Y., & Zhiwu, H. (2010). Tympanometry in infants with middle ear effusion having been identified using spiral computerized tomography. *American Journal of Otolaryngology*, 31(2), 96–103.

Zilioli, S., Ponzi, D., Henry, A., & Maestripieri, D. (2014). Testosterone, cortisol, and empathy: Evidence for the dual-hormone hypothesis. *Adaptive Human Behavior and Physiology*, DOI:10.1007/s40750-014-0017-x.

Zimmermann, P., Maier, M. A., Winter, M., & Grossmann, K. E. (2001). Attachment and adolescents' emotion regulation during a joint problem-solving task with a friend. *International Journal of Behavioral Development*, 25(4), 331–343.

Zosuls, K.M., et al. (2011). "It's not that we hate you": Understanding children's gender attitudes and expectancies about peer relationships. *British Journal of Developmental Psychology*, 29, 288–304.

Zuckerman, M. (2011). Personality science: Three approaches and their applications to the causes and treatment of depression. In M. Zuckerman (Ed.), *Three approaches and their applications to the causes and treatment of depression* (pp. 47–77). Washington, DC: American Psychological Association.

NAME INDEX

A

Abma, J. C., 270, 272
Abrams, 214
Abravanel, E., 100
Adhikari, 37
Adler-Baeder, E., 217
Adolph, K. E., 84, 85
Aguilar, N. R., 148
Ainsworth, D. S., 115–117, 119
Akolekar, 32
Alexander, G. M., 138, 174, 175, 177
Ali, M. M., 271
Alison, 227
Allen, G., 137
Alloway, R. G., 197, 199
Alloway, T. P., 197, 199
Alvarez, 220
Amato, P. R., 217, 218
Ambridge, B., 156
Anderson, B. J., 82
Anderson, C. A., 171, 172
Annett, M., 140
Anthony, C. J., 217, 218
Arbib, M. A., 101
Archer, J., 123, 177
Armstrong, C. L., 186
Arnett, J. J., 266
Arterberry, M. E., 67, 68
Arvidsson, A., 213
Asbury, K., 25
Aschermann, E., 208
Aslin, R. N., 86, 87
Aspy, C. B., 271
Atkinson, J., 67, 68
Auyeung, B., 175
Avinum, R., 175
Awasaki, T., 82
Azmitia, M., 264

B

Bachman, J. G., 256
Badiou, S., 79
Bakker, D. J., 49, 187
Baldelomar, O. A., 265
Bales, 129
Baly, 220
Bandura, A., 9, 171
Bangal, V. B., 47
Barac, R., 209, 210
Barker, 135

Barr, R. G., 71
Barrett, E., 175
Barrouillet, P., 198, 199
Bartoszuk, K., 264
Bartzokis, G., 82
Baum, N., 61
Baumrind, D., 163–165
Bayley, N., 101
Bazerman, M. H., 253
Beauchamp, G. K., 68
Bebko, J. M., 155
Beck, R., 152, 166
Bedny, M., 110
Beebe, B., 115, 117
Beilei, L., 184
Bekkhus, M., 124
Bell, M. A., 99
Bellmore, A. D., 138, 215
Belmonte, M. K., 33
Belsky, J., 124, 125
Bengtsson, H., 213
Bennett, S. E., 272
Berenbaum, S. A., 130
Berge, J. M., 183
Bergen, D., 167
Berndt, T. J., 219, 221, 268
Bernstein, I. L., 68
Berzenski, 116
Berzonsky, 264
Bezdjian, S., 170
Bhat, 122, 123
Bialystok, E., 209, 210
Bierman, K. L., 153, 208
Bigelow, A. E., 116
Bigler, R. S., 130
Bloom, P., 155
Blow, 121
Blum, K., 25
Blumberg, M. S., 70, 71
Boiche, 185
Boivin, M., 219
Boom, J., 254
Borelli, J., 116
Borghese, M. M., 153
Bornstein, M. H., 102
Bost, L. W., 141, 255
Bouchard, C., 181, 182, 184, 207, 266
Bouchard, T. J., 33
Boudreault-Bouchard, 266
Bouhlal, 141
Boulton, M. J., 170
Bower, 88

Bowker, J. C., 219, 221
Bowlby, J., 115, 119
Boyland, 141
Braddick, O., 67, 68
Bradley, R. H., 152
Brakefield, 274
Brandstätter, H., 256
Bravender, T., 242
Bray, G., 181, 182, 184
Brendgen, M., 268
Brigham, N. B., 11
Brockington, I., 65
Brockmann, 217
Brody, 244
Bronfenbrenner, U., 12, 13
Brooker, R. J., 127
Brooks, R. B., 111
Brown, 268
Brown, C., 242
Brown, R., 105, 106
Brownell, C. A., 129
Bruck, M., 199
Brucker, B., 101
Brummelte, S., 64
Brun, C. C., 251
Bruno, R., 209
Bruton, 185
Bucchianeri, 238
Bugental, D. B., 122, 175
Bukowski, W. M., 167, 168, 214
Bulik, 242
Buratovic, S., 49
Burbach, 123
Burgaleta, M., 80
Burghardt, G. M., 167
Buriel, R., 166
Burke, J. D., 224
Burnette, 216
Burnham, D., 88
Bushnell, E. W., 86, 89
Buss, D. M., 175
Bynum, M. S., 271
Byrne, N. M., 234

C

Cabrera, 218, 237
Caldwell, B., 152
Callahan, J. J., 46
Calvete, 11
Calzo, 274
Camann, 58, 59

Camos, 198
Camos Barrouillet, 199
Campanella, J., 100
Campbell, A., 169
Campbell, D. A., 174, 176
Campos, J. J., 87
Camras, L. A., 126
Caplan, P. J., 169
Carette, 166
Carey, B., 166
Carlier, 205
Carper, R. A., 33
Carr, A., 218
Carre, J. M., 170
Carriger, M. S., 129
Carver, L., 127
Cascio, C. J., 90
Casey, D. A., 30
Cassia, V. M., 86
Cattaneo, L., 101
Cattell, R., 204
Catterall, 255
Cernoch, J., 68
Chambers, S. A., 153
Chan, T. W., 215
Chang, 242
Chapman, 255
Chen, H., 49, 153
Cheng, E. R., 61
Cheng, S.-T., 253
Cherney, I. D., 174
Chess, S., 129
Chetty, R., 222
Chezan, L. C., 124
Choi, 271
Chomsky, N., 109
Chong, S. C. E., 154
Christenson, S. L., 33, 255
Christie, J. F., 167
Chu, 228
Cicchetti, D., 116, 224
Cillessen, A. H. N., 138, 215
Cinamon, 266
Clark, E., 105
Clark, J., 166
Clark, J. C., 60
Clark, R., 158
Clarke, 123
Clarke-Stewart, K. A., 152
Clode, D., 140
Cohen, J. R., 225
Cohen, S., 185
Colbert, C. L., 220

SUBJECT INDEX

cognitive-developmental theory
  cognitive perspective, 10–11
  gender differences, 176–177
  social cognition and, 213–214
cognitive perspective, 10–11
cohort effect, 20
conception, 37
concrete operations stage,
    191–193, 213
conduct disorders
  bullying and, 220
  origins of, 224
  overview of, 224
  treatment of, 224
congenital, 45
conservation, 150, 151, 192
contact comfort, 118, 118
continuity-discontinuity
    controversy, 15–16
control group, 19
conventional level, 195
convergence, 68
cooing, 104
coregulation, 216
corpus callosum, 136
correlation, 18
correlation coefficient, 18
creativity, and intellectual
    development in middle
    childhood, 206–207
critical periods, 45, 46, 110–111,
    119
cross-sectional research, 19, 20,
    20–21
crying, 71
C-section. See cesarean section
cultural bias, 204
cultural-familial disability, 205
culture-fair intelligence
    test, 204, 204
culture-free intelligence test,
    204
CVS. See chorionic villus
    sampling
cyberbullying, 220
cystic fibrosis, 31

D

dating, 269
day care, 124–126
death and dying, adolescent,
    240, 241
decentration, 191
deferred imitation, 99
dendrites, 79
deoxyribonucleic acid (DNA),
    25, 26
dependent variable, 19
depressants, 244
depression
  bullying and, 220
  eating disorders and, 241–242
  origins of, 225
  treatment of, 225
depth perception, 87
DES. See diethylstilbestrol
development
  biological perspective, 11–12
  cognitive perspective, 10–11
  contexts of human, 13
  controversies in, 15–16

ecological perspective, 12–13
learning perspective, 7–10
process of study, 17–21
psychoanalytic perspective,
    5–7
sociocultural perspective, 14
study of, 3–4
theories of, 4–15
diarrhea, 141, 142
diethylstilbestrol (DES), 48
differentiation, 76
dilate, 56
disabilities
  intellectual, 205–206
  learning, 186–187
disinhibit, 171
disorders
  educating children with, 187
  learning, 186–187
disorganized-disoriented
    attachment, 116
divergent thinking, 207
diversity, 14–15
divorce, in middle childhood,
    217–218
dizygotic (DZ) twins, 27, 33, 170
DNA. See deoxyribonucleic acid
dominant trait, 27, 28
donor IVF, 40
Down's syndrome, 29, 205
dramatic play, 167
drawing, stages in, 140
dyslexia, 186–187
DZ twins. See dizygotic twins

E

early childhood
  accidents, 142
  artistic development, 139
  brain development, 135
  cognitive development,
      152–153
  development of gender roles
      and gender differences,
      174–177
  dimensions of child rearing in,
      163–165
  effects of education, 153
  elimination disorders, 143–144
  emotional development,
      172–174
  fear in, 173–174
  fine motor skills in, 139, 139
  gross motor skills in, 137, 137
  growth curves for height and
      weight, 136
  growth patterns, 135–137
  handedness, 140
  height in, 135, 136
  illness, 140–142
  initiative vs. guilt stage, 173
  language development,
      155–158
  memory development,
      154–155
  motor development, 137–140
  nutrition, 140–141
  personality development,
      172–174
  physical activity, 138
  play, 148

role of television in, 153
sleep, 142–143
sleep disorders, 142–143
social behaviors, 166–172
weight in, 135, 136
eating disorders and, 241–242
  anorexia nervosa, 241–242
  bulimia nervosa, 242
  perspectives on, 242
echolalia, 105, 123
ecological perspective, 12–13
ecological systems theory, 12
ecology, 12
ectoderm, 42
education
  applications of Piaget's theory,
      193
  educating children with
      disabilities, 187
  effects of early childhood, 153
efface, 56
egocentrism
  adolescent, 250–251
  in early childhood, 148–149
ego identity vs. role diffusion, 263
elaborative strategy, 198
elimination disorders, early
    childhood, 143–144
embryonic disk, 42
embryonic stage, 42–43
emotional development
  in adolescence, 263–277
  in early childhood, 172–174
  in infancy, 126–128
  middle childhood, 213–216
emotional regulation, 127–128
empathy, 169
employment
  adolescence, 256
  effects of maternal, 218
encode, 198
encopresis, 144
endoderm, 42
endometriosis, 39
endometrium, 37
enuresis, 143–144
epiphyseal closure, 236
episiotomy, 56
episodic memory, 154
equilibration, 11
estrogen, 30, 236, 237
ethical considerations, 21
ethnic identity, 265
ethnic identity search, 265
ethnicity, 277
ethologist, 118
ethology, 11
European Americans, IQ scores
    of, 206
evolutionary psychology, 12
exosystem, 13
experimental group, 19
experiments, 18–19
extinction, 8–9, 108

F

failure to thrive (FTT), 77–78
false beliefs, 153
families
  in middle childhood, 216–218
  stepfamilies, 217

FAP. See fixed action pattern
FAS. See fetal alcohol syndrome
fast-mapping, 155
fathers, 116
fear, 173–174
fear of strangers, 126–127
feedback loop, 233
fetal alcohol syndrome (FAS),
    48, 49
fetal movements, 44
fetal perception, 44
fine motor skills
  in early childhood, 139, 139
  in middle childhood, 184
first words, 105
fitness, 185
fixed action pattern (FAP), 12
food preferences, 141
foreclosure, 264
formal operations stage,
    249–251
fraternal twins, 26–27
friendships
  development of, 219–221
  stages in children's concepts
      of, 219
FTT. See failure to thrive

G

GAD. See generalized anxiety
    disorder
Gardner's theory of multiple,
    intelligences, 200, 200–201
gays
  development of sexual
      orientation and, 274–275
  HIV/AIDS and, 239
  as parents, 216–217
gender
  as aspect of human
      diversity, 15
  identity development and,
      265–266
gender constancy, 176
gender development of identity,
    265–266
gender differences
  in adolescent cognitive
      abilities, 251–252
  development of gender roles
      and, 174–177
  gender-schema theory, 177
  in infancy, 130–131
  in middle childhood, 184–185
  in moral development, 255
  organization of the brain
      and, 175
  and physical growth in middle
      childhood, 181
  in play, 168–169
  roles of evolution and
      heredity, 175
  sex hormones, 175
  social cognitive theory, 176
  stereotypes, 174
  theories of development,
      174–177
gender identity, 176
gender roles, 174
gender-schema theory, 177
gender stability, 176

general anesthesia, 58
generalized anxiety disorder
    (GAD), 226
genes, 25, *26*
genetic abnormalities, 30–31
genetic counseling, prenatal
    testing and, 31–32
genetic counselors, 31
genetics, 25
genotypes, 33
germinal stage, 41
giftedness, 206
goodness of fit, 130
grammar development, in early
    childhood, 156–157
grasping, 83
grasping reflex, 67, *67*
gross motor skills
    in early childhood, 137, *137*
    in middle childhood, 184
growth spurts
    adolescent, *234,* 234–236
    of brain, 81, *82*
    in middle childhood, 181
gynecomastia, 236

H

habituation, 88
hallucinogenics, 245
handedness, 140
Head Start, 153
health
    in adolescence, 240–241
    assessing health of
        newborns, 66
hearing
    ability to discriminate
        sounds, 89
    infancy, 88–89
    newborns, 68
heavy metals, 49
height
    in adolescence, 234–236,
        235, 236
    in early childhood, 135, *135*
    in middle childhood, 181, *182*
hemophilia, 31
heredity
    basics of, 25–32
    determinants of intellectual
        development and, 207–208
    environment and, 33–34
    prenatal development and,
        41–50
    role of conception, 37–41
heritability, 208
heroin, 48
heterozygous, 27
HID. *See* Huntington's disease
hippocampus, 175
HIV/AIDS, 45–46
holophrase, 106
HOME inventory, 152, *152*
homosexual orientation, 274
homozygous, 27
hormones, 175
hormones, prenatal
    development and, 48
Huntington's disease (HD), 30
hyperactivity, 185
hypnosis, 58–59

hypothesis, 18
hypothetical thinking, 250
hypoxia, 60

I

identical twins, 26–27
identity achievement, 264
identity crisis, 7, 264
identity development, Erikson
    and, 263–264
identity diffusion, 264
IDS. *See* infant-directed speech
imaginary audience, 250
imitation, 100–101, 107–108
immanent justice, 193
imprinting, 119
incubators, 61
independent variable, 19
indiscriminate attachment, 117
inductive methods, 164
industry *vs.* inferiority, 213
infancy
    brain and nervous system
        development, 79–82
    breast-feeding *vs.* bottle-
        feeding, 78–79
    cognitive development, 95–111
    emotional development,
        126–128
    gender differences, 130–131
    imitation in, 100–101
    individual differences in
        intelligence, 101–103
    information processing,
        99–101
    language development in, *104*
    memory, 99–100
    memory development in
        middle childhood, 196–199
    motor development, 83–85, *84*
    nutrition, 78
    patterns in height and weight,
        76–78, *77*
    perceptual development,
        85–90
    personality development,
        128–130
    physical growth and
        development, 75–79
    sensory development, 85–90
    sequences of physical
        development, 75–76
    social development, 115–126
    testing, 102
infant-directed speech (IDS), 111
infant mortality, 62, *63*
infertility, 39–41
information processing
    approach, 99
    in infancy, 99–101
    metacognition development,
        199
    metamemory development,
        199
    in middle childhood, 195–199
    recall memory development
        in middle childhood, 199
    selective attention
        development, 196
information-processing
    theory, 11, 99

initial-preattachment phase, 117
initiative *vs.* guilt stage, 173
inner speech, 158
insecure attachment, 115
intellectual development
    differences in, 205–206
    giftedness, 206
    measurement of, 201–204
    in middle childhood, 200–208
    socioeconomic and ethnic
        differences, IQ, 206
intellectual disability, 205
intelligence
    factor theories, 200
    individual differences in
        infants, 101–103
    multiple intelligences,
        200–201, *201*
    scores in infancy, 102
    Sternberg's theory of,
        200, *200*
    testing, 102
    theories of, 200–201
intelligence quotient (IQ)
    factors influencing changes in
        scores, 205
    idealized distribution of
        scores, *204*
    items similar to those on
        SBIS, *202*
    measurement of intellectual
        development, 201–204
    performance items on
        intelligence test, *203*
    relationship between IQ
        scores and heredity, *207*
    socioeconomic and ethnic
        differences, IQ, 206
    Stanford-Binet Intelligence
        Scale and, 201–202
    teacher expectations and gains
        in scores, 222–223
    testing controversy, 204
    Wechsler intelligence scales,
        203, *203*
intervention programs, 61
intonation, 105
in vitro fertilization (IVF), 40
IQ. *See* intelligence quotient
IVF. *See* in vitro fertilization

J

juvenile delinquency, 275

K

kinship studies, 33
Klinefelter syndrome, 29
knowledge acquisition, 153–154
Kohlberg's theory of moral
    development, 194–195,
    255, *255*

L

Lamaze method, 59
language development
    early childhood, 155–158
    early vocalizations, 103–105
    in infancy, 103–111, *104*

middle childhood, 208–209
    theories of, 107
    views that emphasize nature,
        108–111
    views that emphasize nurture,
        107–108
lanugo, 61
latency stage, 213
lead, 142
learned helplessness, 216
learning disorders, 186–187
learning perspective, 7–10
left-brained, 135–136
lesbians, as parents, 216–217
life crisis, 7
life-span perspective, study of
    human development and, 4
local anesthetics, 58
locomotion, 83–85
longitudinal research, 19–21
long-term memory, 198
low-birth-weight infants
    and preterm infants, 60–61
    risks associated with, 60–61
Luvox, 225

M

MA. *See* mental age
macrosystem, 13
mainstreaming, 187
major depression with perinatal
    onset, 64
malnutrition, 205
marijuana (cannabis), 48
marriage, divorce and, 217
masturbation, 270
maternal alcohol abuse, 205
maternal employment, 218
maternal mortality, *62, 63*
mathematical ability, in
    adolescence, 252
maturation, 5
mean length of utterance
    (MLU), 106
measles, 142
media, 171–172
medulla, 72, 81
memory
    development in middle
        childhood, 196–199
    development of metacogni-
        tion and metamemory, 199
    development of recall, 199
    early childhood, 155
    factors influencing, 155
    infant, 99–100, *100*
    long-term, 198
    organization in long-term,
        198–199
    sensory, 196–197
    strategies, 155
    structures of, 196, *197*
    working, 197–198
menarche
    decline in age at, *237*
    overview of, 237
    regulation of menstrual
        cycle, 238
menstrual cycle, regulation
    of, 238
mental age (MA), 202

1-1 Relate the history of the study of child development. In centuries past, children often were viewed as innately evil, and discipline was harsh. The philosopher John Locke focused on the role of experience in development. Jean-Jacques Rousseau argued that children are good by nature, and if allowed to express their natural impulses, will develop into moral people. G. Stanley Hall founded child development as an academic discipline and brought scientific attention to focus on the period of adolescence. Alfred Binet developed the first standardized intelligence test. By the start of the 20th century, child development had emerged as a scientific field of study. Soon major theories about the developing child were proposed by theorists such as Arnold Gesell, Sigmund Freud, John B. Watson, and Jean Piaget.

Developmental psychology is the discipline that studies the physical, cognitive, social, and emotional development of humans. It focuses on the many influences on behavior, including the effects of the person's physical, social, and cultural environment and how these factors interact to influence the developments that occur over time. William Perry and Gisella Labouvie-Vief have studied the development of cognitive complexity from adolescence to late adulthood. K. Warner Schaie and others have studied trends in crystallized and fluid mental abilities throughout adulthood.

developmental psychology the discipline that studies the physical, cognitive, social, and emotional development of humans

1-2 Compare and contrast theories of child development. Psychoanalytic theory focuses on the roles of internal conflict. Sigmund Freud believed that children undergo five stages of psychosexual development. Erik Erikson focused on social relationships and included adulthood by extending Freud's five developmental stages to eight.

Learning theorists focus on how learning influences behavior. Behaviorists such as John B. Watson and B. F. Skinner stressed classical and operant conditioning. Social cognitive theorists, such as Albert Bandura, argue that much learning occurs by observation and that we choose whether to engage in learned behavior.

Jean Piaget's cognitive developmental theory hypothesizes that children's cognitive processes develop in an invariant series of stages, culminating with *formal operational* reasoning. Other cognitive theorists suggest that adults can experience *postformal* reasoning. Information-processing theory deals with the ways in which we encode information, manipulate it, place it in memory, and retrieve it.

The biological perspective refers to genetics and developments such as conception, health, gains in height and weight, puberty, and peak performance and decline in adulthood. Ethology involves instinctive behavior patterns. *Evolutionary psychology* is the branch of psychology that deals with the ways in which the history of human adaptation to the environment influences behavior and mental processes, with special focus on aggressive behavior and mating strategies.

Urie Bronfenbrenner's ecological theory explains development in terms of the *reciprocal interaction* between children and the settings in which development occurs. Lev Semenovich Vygotsky's sociocultural perspective has the key concepts of the *zone of proximal development (ZPD)* and *scaffolding*. The sociocultural perspective more broadly addresses the richness of diversity, as in the influences of ethnicity, gender, and socioeconomic status on development.

behaviorism Watson's view that science must study observable behavior only and investigate relationships between stimuli and responses

maturation the unfolding of genetically determined traits, structures, and functions

psychosexual development the process by which libidinal energy is expressed through different erogenous zones during different stages of development

stage theory a theory of development characterized by distinct periods of life

psychosocial development Erikson's theory, which emphasizes the importance of social relationships and conscious choice throughout eight stages of development

life crisis an internal conflict that attends each stage of psychosocial development

identity crisis according to Erikson, a period of inner conflict during which one examines one's values and makes decisions about one's life roles

classical conditioning a simple form of learning in which one stimulus comes to bring forth the response usually brought forth by a second stimulus by being paired repeatedly with the second stimulus

operant conditioning a simple form of learning in which an organism learns to engage in behavior that is reinforced

reinforcement the process of providing stimuli following responses that increase the frequency of the responses

positive reinforcer a reinforcer that, when applied, increases the frequency of a response

negative reinforcer a reinforcer that, when removed, increases the frequency of a response

extinction the cessation of a response that is performed in the absence of reinforcement

social cognitive theory a cognitively oriented learning theory that emphasizes observational learning

cognitive-developmental theory the stage theory that holds that the child's abilities to mentally represent the world and solve problems unfold as a result of the interaction of experience and the maturation of neurological structures

scheme an action pattern or mental structure that is involved in the acquisition and organization of knowledge

adaptation the interaction between the organism and the environment, consisting of assimilation and accommodation

assimilation the incorporation of new events or knowledge into existing schemes

accommodation the modification of existing schemes to permit the incorporation of new events or knowledge

equilibration the creation of an equilibrium, or balance, between assimilation and accommodation

ethology the study of behaviors that are specific to a species

(continues)

(continued)

evolutionary psychology the branch of psychology that deals with the ways in which humans' historical adaptations to the environment influence behavior and mental processes, with special focus on aggressive behavior and mating strategies

fixed action pattern (FAP) a stereotyped pattern of behavior that is evoked by a "releasing stimulus"; an instinct

ecology the branch of biology that deals with the relationships between living organisms and their environment

ecological systems theory the view that explains child development in terms of the reciprocal influences between children and environmental settings

microsystem the immediate settings with which the child interacts, such as the home, the school, and peers

mesosystem the interlocking settings that influence the child, such as the interaction of the school and the larger community

exosystem community institutions and settings that indirectly influence the child, such as the school board and the parents' workplaces

macrosystem the basic institutions and ideologies that influence the child

chronosystem the environmental changes that occur over time and have an effect on the child

zone of proximal development (ZPD) Vygotsky's term for the situation in which a child carries out tasks with the help of someone who is more skilled

scaffolding Vygotsky's term for temporary cognitive structures or methods of solving problems that help the child as he or she learns to function independently

---

1-3 **Enumerate key controversies in child development.** The discussion about theories of development reveals that developmentalists can see things in very different ways. There are three major debates in the field.

nature the processes within an organism that guide it to develop according to its genetic code

nurture environmental factors that influence development

empirical based on observation and experimentation

1-4 **Describe ways in which researchers study child development.** Development is studied through gathering sound information and conducting research. Naturalistic observation is conducted in "the field"—the settings in which people develop. The case study is a carefully drawn account or biography of behavior. Correlational studies reveal relationships between variables but not cause and effect, as demonstrated in Figure 1.5. Experiments seek to determine cause and effect by exposing research participants to treatments and observing the results.

Researchers have devised different strategies for comparing children of one age with children or adults of other ages. Longitudinal research studies the same people repeatedly over time. Cross-sectional research observes and compares people of different ages. A drawback to cross-sectional research is the cohort effect. Cross-sequential research combines the longitudinal and cross-sectional methods by breaking the span of the ideal longitudinal study down into convenient segments. Ethical standards require that researchers not use treatments that harm participants.

naturalistic-observation a scientific method in which organisms are observed in their natural environments

case study a carefully drawn biography of the life of an individual

standardized test a test in which an individual's score is compared to the scores of a group of similar individuals

correlation coefficient a number ranging from +1.00 to –1.00 that expresses the direction (positive or negative) and strength of the relationship between two variables

positive correlation a relationship between two variables in which one variable increases as the other increases

negative correlation a relationship between two variables in which one variable increases as the other decreases

experiment a method of scientific investigation that seeks to discover cause-and-effect relationships by introducing independent variables and observing their effects on dependent variables

hypothesis a proposition to be tested

independent variable a condition in a scientific study that is manipulated so that its effects can be observed

dependent variable a measure of an assumed effect of an independent variable

experimental group a group made up of subjects who receive a treatment in an experiment

control group a group made up of subjects in an experiment who do not receive the treatment but for whom all other conditions are comparable to those of subjects in the experimental group

longitudinal research the study of developmental processes by taking repeated measures of the same group of participants at various stages of development

cross-sectional research the study of developmental processes by taking measures of participants of different age groups at the same time

cohort effect similarities in behavior among a group of peers that stem from the fact that group members were born at the same time in history

cross-sequential research an approach that combines the longitudinal and cross-sectional methods by following individuals of different ages for abbreviated periods of time .

time-lag the study of developmental processes by taking measures of participants of the same age group at different times

CHAPTER 2 LEARNING OUTCOMES / KEY TERMS

CHAPTER REVIEW

2-1 Describe the influences of heredity on development. Heredity is the biological transmission of traits from one generation to another. People normally have 46 strands of DNA called chromosomes, which are organized into 23 pairs (see Figure 2.3). Genes, which regulate the development of traits, are segments of chromosomes.

Sperm and ova are produced by meiosis and have 23 rather than 46 chromosomes. Monozygotic (MZ) or identical twins develop from a single fertilized ovum that splits in two. Dizygotic (DZ) or fraternal twins develop from two fertilized ova. Traits are determined by pairs of genes, either from "averaging" the genetic instructions, or by dominant genes. Carriers of a trait bear one dominant gene and one recessive gene for it.

FIG.2.3 THE 23 PAIRS OF HUMAN CHROMOSOMES

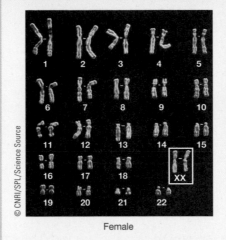

© CNRI/SPL/Science Source

Female

Male

People normally have 23 pairs of chromosomes. Females have two X chromosomes, whereas males have an X and a Y sex chromosome.

genetics the branch of biology that studies heredity

chromosomes rod-shaped structures composed of genes that are found within the nuclei of cells

gene the basic unit of heredity. Genes are composed of deoxyribonucleic acid (DNA)

polygenic resulting from many genes

deoxyribonucleic acid (DNA) genetic material that takes the form of a double helix composed of phosphates, sugars, and bases

mitosis the form of cell division in which each chromosome splits lengthwise to double in number. Half of each chromosome combines with chemicals to retake its original form and then moves to the new cell

mutation a sudden variation in a heritable characteristic, as by an accident that affects the composition of genes

meiosis the form of cell division in which each pair of chromosomes splits so that one member of each pair moves to the new cell. As a result, each new cell has 23 chromosomes

autosome a member of a pair of chromosomes (with the exception of sex chromosomes)

sex chromosome a chromosome in the shape of a Y (male) or X (female) that determines the anatomic sex of the child

monozygotic (MZ) twins twins that derive from a single zygote that has split into two; identical twins. Each MZ twin carries the same genetic code

dizygotic (DZ) twins twins that derive from two zygotes; fraternal twins

ovulation the releasing of an ovum from an ovary

allele a member of a pair of genes

homozygous having two identical alleles

heterozygous having two different alleles

dominant trait a trait that is expressed

recessive trait a trait that is not expressed when the gene or genes involved have been paired with dominant genes

carrier a person who carries and transmits characteristics but does not exhibit them

2-2 Discuss chromosomal and genetic abnormalities. Chromosomal abnormalities are more likely as parents age. Down syndrome is caused by an extra chromosome on the 21st pair. Sex-linked disorders include XYY males and single-X girls. Genetic disorders include phenylketonuria (PKU), Huntington's disease, sickle-cell anemia, Tay-Sachs disease, cystic fibrosis, and hemophilia.

multifactorial problems problems that stem from the interaction of heredity and environmental factors

Down's syndrome a chromosomal abnormality characterized by intellectual disabilities and caused by an extra chromosome in the 21st pair

sex-linked chromosomal abnormalities abnormalities that are transmitted

from generation to generation and carried by a sex chromosome

Klinefelter syndrome a chromosomal disorder found among males that is caused by an extra X sex chromosome and that is characterized by infertility and mild intellectual disabilities

testosterone a male sex hormone produced mainly by the testes

Turner syndrome a chromosomal disorder found among females that is caused by having a single X sex chromosome and is characterized by infertility

estrogen a female sex hormone produced mainly by the ovaries

phenylketonuria (PKU) a genetic abnormality in which phenylalanine builds up and causes intellectual disabilities

(continues)

(continued)

Huntington's disease (HD) a fatal genetic neurological disorder whose onset is in middle age

sickle-cell anemia a genetic disorder that decreases the blood's capacity to carry oxygen

Tay-Sachs disease a fatal genetic neurological disorder

cystic fibrosis a fatal genetic disorder in which mucus obstructs the lungs and pancreas

hemophilia a genetic disorder in which blood does not clot properly

sex-linked genetic abnormalities abnormalities resulting from genes that are found on the X sex chromosome. They are more likely to be shown by male offspring (who do not have an opposing gene from a second X chromosome) than by female offspring

muscular dystrophy a chronic disease characterized by a progressive wasting away of the muscles

2-3 **Discuss methods of prenatal testing for chromosomal and genetic abnormalities.** Prenatal blood tests, ultrasound, and amniocentesis can determine the presence of various genetic and chromosomal abnormalities.

genetic counselors health workers who compile information about a couple's genetic heritage to advise them as to whether their children might develop genetic abnormalities

prenatal before birth

amniocentesis a procedure for drawing and examining fetal cells sloughed off into amniotic fluid to determine the presence of various disorders

miscarriage the expulsion of an embryo or fetus before it can sustain life on its own, most often due to defective development

chorionic villus sampling (CVS) a method for the prenatal detection of genetic abnormalities that samples the membrane enveloping the amniotic sac and fetus

uterus the hollow organ within females in which the embryo and fetus develop

ultrasound sound waves too high in pitch to be sensed by the human ear

sonogram a procedure for using ultrasonic sound waves to create a picture of an embryo or fetus

alpha-fetoprotein (AFP) assay a blood test that assesses the mother's blood level of alpha-fetoprotein, a substance that is linked with fetal neural tube defects

FIG.2.4 TRANSMISSION OF DOMINANT AND RECESSIVE TRAITS

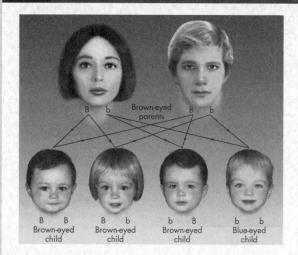

2-4 **Explain ways in which researchers sort out the effects of heredity and the environment in development.** Our genotypes are the sets of traits that we inherit. But environmental conditions can vary their expression, resulting in our phenotypes. Researchers can study the heritability of a trait by observing its expression among relatives who differ in genetic closeness. Parents and children have a 50% overlap in genes, as do siblings, with the exception of monozygotic (MZ) twins, who have 100% overlap. MZ twins resemble each other more closely than dizygotic (DZ) twins on physical and psychological traits, even when reared apart. Expressed traits in adopted children that more closely resemble those of the natural parents are more likely to have a genetic basis.

genotype the genetic form or constitution of a person as determined by heredity

phenotype the actual form or constitution of a person as determined by heredity and environmental factors

autism a developmental disorder characterized by failure to relate to others, communication problems, intolerance of change, and ritualistic behavior

Did you know that you can have brown eyes but be carrying a gene for blue or green eyes? The genes for brown eyes are dominant—meaning that they are the ones that will be shown, and the genes for blue eyes are recessive. Here each of the two parents carries a gene for brown eyes (so they both have brown eyes) and a gene for blue eyes (which remain recessive, or hidden). Their children inherit the genes for brown or blue eyes by chance. Therefore, three out of four of their children will have brown eyes. Of the three, two will have a recessive gene for blue eyes as well as the gene for brown eyes. Only the fourth child, who inherits two genes for blue eyes, will actually have blue eyes.

CHAPTER 3 LEARNING OUTCOMES / KEY TERMS

3-1 **Describe the process of conception.** Conception is the union of an ovum and a sperm cell and usually occurs in a fallopian tube (see Figure 3.1). More boys are conceived than girls, but they have a higher rate of miscarriage. Once a sperm cell has entered the ova, the chromosomes from the sperm cell line up across from the corresponding chromosomes in the egg cell. They form 23 new pairs with a unique set of genetic instructions.

conception the union of a sperm cell and an ovum that occurs when the chromosomes of each of these cells combine to form 23 new pairs

endometrium the inner lining of the uterus

FIG.3.1 FEMALE REPRODUCTIVE ORGANS

The ovaries release egg cells (ova), which find their ways into fallopian tubes—exactly how is not fully known. Fertilization normally takes place in a fallopian tube. The fertilized ovum begins to divide while it travels through the tube into the uterus, where it becomes implanted in the wall and grows to term.

3-2 **Discuss the causes of infertility and alternate ways of becoming parents.** The diagnosis of infertility usually is not applied until the couple has failed to conceive on their own for one year. A low sperm count—or lack of sperm—is the most common infertility problem in men. The most common problem in women is irregular ovulation or lack of ovulation; others include infections such as PID, endometriosis, and obstructions. Fertility drugs regulate ovulation. Other ways of conceiving include artificial insemination and in vitro fertilization (IVF). Preimplantation genetic diagnosis permits prenatal sex selection.

motility self-propulsion

pelvic inflammatory disease (PID) an infection of the abdominal region that may have various causes and that may impair fertility

endometriosis inflammation of endometrial tissue sloughed off into the abdominal cavity rather than out of the body during menstruation; the condition is characterized by abdominal pain and sometimes infertility

artificial insemination injection of sperm into the uterus to fertilize an ovum

in vitro fertilization (IVF) fertilization of an ovum in a laboratory dish

donor IVF the transfer of a donor's ovum, fertilized in a laboratory dish, to the uterus of another woman

3-3 **Describe what happens during the three stages of prenatal development.** During the germinal stage, the zygote divides repeatedly and travels through a fallopian tube to the uterus, where it implants. Before implantation, it is nourished by the yolk of the original egg cell. Once implanted in the uterine wall, it is nourished by the mother. The embryonic stage lasts from implantation until the eighth week of development, during which the major organ systems differentiate. Development follows cephalocaudal and proximodistal trends. The heart begins to beat during the fourth week. By the end of the second month, facial features are becoming distinct, teeth buds have formed, the kidneys are working, and the liver is producing red blood cells. Male sex hormones spur development of the male reproductive system. The embryo and fetus exchange nutrients and wastes with the mother through the placenta. Some disease organisms, such as those that cause syphilis and rubella, can pass through the placenta. Some drugs also pass through, including aspirin, narcotics, and alcohol.

The fetal stage is characterized by maturation of organs and gains in size. It lasts from the end of the embryonic stage until birth. The fetus begins to turn at the ninth or tenth week. It responds to sound waves by the 13th week of pregnancy. By the end of the second trimester, the fetus opens and shuts its eyes, sucks its thumb, and alternates between wakefulness and sleep. During the third trimester, it becomes increasingly capable of sustaining independent life.

FIG.3.3 A HUMAN EMBRYO AT 7 WEEKS

Petit Format/Nestle/Science source

By the time this photo was taken, the embryo's heart had already been beating for about a month. By another week, all the major organs systems will have formed, and the embryo will enter the fetal stage.

germinal stage the period of development between conception and the implantation of the embryo

blastocyst a stage within the germinal period of prenatal development in which the zygote has the form of a sphere of cells surrounding a cavity of fluid

embryonic disk the platelike inner part of the blastocyst that differentiates into the ectoderm, mesoderm, and endoderm of the embryo

trophoblast the outer part of the blastocyst from which the amniotic sac, placenta, and umbilical cord develop

umbilical cord a tube that connects the fetus to the placenta

placenta an organ connected to the uterine wall and to the fetus by the umbilical cord. The placenta serves as a relay station between mother and fetus for the exchange of nutrients and wastes

(continues)

(continued)

embryonic stage the stage of prenatal development that lasts from implantation through the eighth week of pregnancy; it is characterized by the development of the major organ systems

cephalocaudal from head to tail

proximodistal from the inner part (or axis) of the body outward

ectoderm the outermost cell layer of the newly formed embryo from which the skin and nervous system develop

neural tube a hollowed-out area in the blastocyst from which the nervous system develops

endoderm the inner layer of the embryo from which the lungs and digestive system develop

mesoderm the central layer of the embryo from which the bones and muscles develop

androgens male sex hormones

amniotic sac the sac containing the fetus

amniotic fluid fluid within the amniotic sac that suspends and protects the fetus

placenta the organ formed in the lining of the uterus that provides nourishment for the fetus and elimination of its waste products

fetal stage the stage that begins with the third month of pregnancy and ends with childbirth, during which organ systems mature and there are gains in size

---

3-4 **Discuss various environmental influences on prenatal development, including critical periods of vulnerability.** Maternal malnutrition is linked to low birth weight, prematurity, and cognitive and behavioral problems. Teratogens are most harmful during critical periods, when certain organs are developing. Women who contract rubella can bear children who suffer from deafness, mental retardation, heart disease, or cataracts. Syphilis can cause miscarriage or stillbirth. Toxemia is characterized by high blood pressure and is connected with preterm or small babies. In Rh incompatibility, the mother's antibodies cause brain damage or death. Environmental agents that can harm the embryo and fetus include thalidomide, tetracycline, DES, high doses of vitamins A and D, narcotics, marijuana, cocaine, alcohol (see Figure 3.5), cigarette smoke, heavy metals, PCBs, and radiation.

Teenage mothers have a higher incidence of infant mortality and children with low birth weight. Older parents run an increasing risk of chromosomal abnormalities and stillborn or preterm babies.

stillbirth the birth of a dead fetus

teratogens environmental influences or agents that can damage the embryo or fetus

critical period in this usage, a period during which an embryo is particularly vulnerable to a certain teratogen

syphilis a sexually transmitted infection that, in advanced stages, can attack major organ systems

congenital present at birth and resulting from genetic or chromosomal abnormalities or from exposure to the prenatal environment

HIV/AIDS HIV stands for human immunodeficiency virus, which cripples the body's immune system. AIDS stands for acquired immuno-deficiency syndrome, a condition in which the immune system is weakened such that it is vulnerable to diseases it would otherwise fight off

rubella a viral infection that can cause retardation and heart disease in the embryo. Also called German measles

preeclampsia (or **toxemia**) a life-threatening disease that can afflict pregnant women; it is characterized by high blood pressure

premature born before the full term of gestation. Also referred to as preterm

Rh incompatibility a condition in which antibodies produced by the mother are transmitted to the child, possibly causing brain damage or death

thalidomide a sedative used in the 1960s that has been linked to birth defects, especially deformed or absent limbs

Progestin a synthetic hormone used to maintain pregnancy that can cause masculinization of the fetus

DES diethylstilbestrol, an estrogen that has been linked to cancer in the reproductive organs of children of women who used the hormone when pregnant

fetal alcohol syndrome (FAS) a cluster of symptoms shown by children of women who drank heavily during pregnancy, including characteristic facial features and intellectual disabilities

FIG.3.5 **FETAL ALCOHOL SYNDROME (FAS)**

Small head
Flat face

Small eye openings
Short nose
Low nasal bridge
Underdeveloped jaw

Thin upper lip

Fetal Alcohol Syndrome

Gwen Shockey/Science Source

The children of many mothers who drank alcohol during pregnancy exhibit FAS. This syndrome is characterized by developmental lags and such facial features as an underdeveloped upper jaw, a flattened nose, and widely spaced eyes.

FIG.3.6 **AUTISM RISK INCREASES WITH PATERNAL AGE**

Chance of autism spectrum disorder among 132,271 subjects, by paternal age:

6 in 10,000

15- to 29-year-old fathers

9 in 10,000

30- to 39-year-old fathers

32 in 10,000

40- to 49-year-old fathers

52 in 10,000

50- year-old fathers and older

CHAPTER 4 LEARNING OUTCOMES / KEY TERMS

4-1 **Identify the stages of childbirth.** The first uterine contractions are called Braxton-Hicks contractions, or "false labor" contractions. A day or so before labor begins, women might spot blood. About 1 woman in 10 has a rush of amniotic fluid. Maternal hormones stimulate contractions strong enough to expel the baby.

Childbirth begins with the onset of regular contractions of the uterus, which efface and dilate the cervix. The first stage may last from hours to more than a day. During transition, the head of the fetus moves into the vagina. The second stage begins when the baby appears at the opening of the birth canal and ends with birth of the baby. Mucus is suctioned from the baby's mouth so that breathing is not obstructed. The umbilical cord is severed. During the third stage, the placenta is expelled.

term the typical nine-month period from conception to childbirth

Braxton-Hicks contractions the first, usually painless, contractions of childbirth

cervix the narrow lower end of the uterus, through which a baby passes to reach the vagina

prostaglandins hormones that stimulate uterine contractions

oxytocin a hormone that stimulates labor contractions

efface to become thin

dilate to widen

episiotomy a surgical incision between the birth canal and anus that widens the vaginal opening

transition movement of the head of the fetus into the vagina

4-2 **Examine different methods of childbirth.** General anesthesia renders the woman unconscious, but it decreases the strength of uterine contractions and lowers the responsiveness of the neonate. Local anesthetics deaden pain in parts of the body. The Lamaze method teaches women to dissociate uterine contractions from pain and fear by associating responses such as relaxation with contractions. A coach aids the mother. A Cesarean section (C-section) delivers a baby surgically through the abdomen. C-sections are most likely when the baby is large or in distress. Herpes and HIV infections can be bypassed by C-section.

midwife an individual who helps women in childbirth

anesthetics agents that lessen pain

general anesthesia elimination of pain by putting a person to sleep

local anesthetic reduction of pain in an area of the body

neonate an infant from birth through the first four weeks of life

natural childbirth childbirth without anesthesia

Lamaze method a childbirth method in which women are educated about childbirth, breathe in patterns that lessen pain during birth, and have a coach present

cesarean section (C-section) delivery of a baby by abdominal surgery

4-3 **Discuss potential problems with childbirth.** Prenatal oxygen deprivation can be fatal or impair development of the nervous system. A baby when birth occurs at or before 37 weeks of gestation. A baby has a low birth weight when it weighs less than 5.5 pounds (about 2,500 grams). Risks of prematurity include infant mortality and delayed neurological and motor development. Preterm babies are relatively thin. Sucking may be weak, and they can show respiratory distress. Preterm babies usually remain in the hospital in incubators, but they profit from early stimulation.

anoxia absence of oxygen

hypoxia less oxygen than required

breech (bottom-first) presentation buttocks-first childbirth

preterm born prior to 37 weeks of gestation

small for gestational age descriptive of neonates who are small for their age

lanugo fine, downy hair on premature babies

vernix oily white substance on the skin of premature babies

respiratory distress syndrome weak and irregular breathing, typical of preterm babies

incubator a heated, protective container for premature infants

4-4 **Describe the postpartum period.** Women may encounter the "baby blues," postpartum depression, and postpartum psychosis (see Table 4-2). These problems probably reflect hormonal changes following birth, although stress can play a role.
Postpartum depression symptoms include:

- serious sadness
- feelings of hopelessness, helplessness, and worthlessness
- difficulty concentrating
- mood swings
- major changes in appetite (usually loss of appetite)
- abnormal sleep patterns (frequently insomnia)

Early infant bonding has not been shown to be critical, despite oft-cited research suggesting that the first few hours after birth present a maternal-sensitive period during which hormone levels dispose the mother to bonding.

postpartum period the period immediately following childbirth

major depression with perinatal onset serious maternal depression following delivery; characterized by sadness, apathy, and feelings of worthlessness

bonding formation of parent–infant attachment

4-5 **Examine the characteristics of a neonate.** The neonate's health is usually evaluated by the Apgar scale, displayed below. The Brazelton Neonatal Behavioral Assessment Scale also screens for behavioral and neurological problems. The neonate's rooting and sucking reflexes are basic to survival. Other key reflexes include the startle reflex, the grasping reflex, the stepping reflex, the Babinski reflex, and the tonic-neck reflex. Most reflexes disappear or are replaced by voluntary behavior within months. Neonates are nearsighted. They visually detect movement, and many track movement. Neonates are particularly responsive to the sounds and rhythms of speech. The nasal and taste preferences of neonates are similar to those of older children and adults. The sensations of skin against skin can contribute to attachment.

Neonates are capable of classical and operant conditioning. Neonates spend two-thirds of their time in sleep, distributing sleep through naps. Neonates spend about half their time sleeping in REM sleep, but as time goes on, REM sleep accounts for less of their sleep. REM sleep might be connected with brain development. Babies cry mainly because of pain and discomfort. Crying communicates hunger, anger, pain, and the presence of health problems.

SIDS is the most common cause of death in infants between the ages of one month and one year. SIDS is more common among babies who are put to sleep in the prone position, preterm and low-birth-weight infants, male infants, and infants whose mothers smoked during or after pregnancy.

TABLE 4.2   THE APGAR SCALE

Points	0	1	2
Appearance: Color	Blue, pale	Body pink, extremities blue	Entirely pink
Pulse: Heart rate	Absent (not detectable)	Slow—below 100 beats/minute	Rapid—100–140 beats/minute
Grimace: Reflex irritability	No response	Grimace	Crying, coughing, sneezing
Activity level: Muscle tone	Completely flaccid, limp	Weak, inactive	Flexed arms and legs; resists extension
Respiratory effort: Breathing	Absent (infant is apneic)	Shallow, irregular, slow	Regular breathing; lusty crying

Apgar scale a measure of a newborn's health that assesses appearance, pulse, grimace, activity level, and respiratory effort

Brazelton Neonatal Behavioral Assessment Scale a measure of a newborn's motor behavior, response to stress, adaptive behavior, and control over physiological state

reflexe an unlearned, stereotypical response to a stimulus

rooting reflex turning the mouth and head toward stroking of the cheek or the corner of the mouth

Moro reflex arching the back, flinging out the arms and legs, and drawing them back to the chest in response to a sudden noise or change in position

grasping reflex grasping objects that touch the palms

stepping reflex taking steps when held under the arms and leaned forward so the feet press the ground

Babinski reflex fanning the toes when the soles of the feet are stroked

tonic-neck reflex turning the head to one side, extending the arm and leg on that side, and flexing the limbs on the opposite side

visual accommodation automatic adjustments of the lenses to focus on objects

convergence inward movement of the eyes to focus on an object that is drawing nearer

amplitude loudness (of sound waves)

pitch highness or lowness (of a sound), as determined by the frequency of sound waves

rapid-eye-movement (REM) sleep a sleep period when dreams are likely, as suggested by rapid eye movements

non-rapid-eye-movement (non-REM) sleep a sleep period when dreams are unlikely

pacifier a device such as an artificial nipple or teething ring that soothes babies when sucked

sudden infant death syndrome (SIDS) the death, while sleeping, of apparently healthy babies who stop breathing

medulla a part of the brain stem that regulates vital and automatic functions such as breathing and the sleep–wake cycle

5-1 **Describe trends in the physical development of the infant.** Three key sequences of physical development are cephalocaudal development, proximodistal development, and differentiation. Infants usually double their birth weight in five months and triple it by their first birthday. Height increases by about half in the first year. Infants grow another 4 to 6 inches and gain another 4 to 7 pounds in the second year. The head diminishes in proportion to the rest of the body. Failure to thrive (FTT) impairs growth in infancy and early childhood. FTT can have organic causes or inorganic causes, possibly including deficiencies in caregiver-child interaction.

Infants require breast milk or an iron-fortified formula. Introduction of solid foods is recommended at four to six months. Breast-feeding is connected with the mother's availability, knowledge of the advantages of breast-feeding, and availability of alternatives. Breast milk is tailored to human digestion, contains essential nutrients, contains the mothers' antibodies, helps protect against infant diarrhea, and is less likely than formula to cause allergies.

differentiation the processes by which behaviors and physical structures become specialized

failure to thrive (FTT) a disorder of infancy and early childhood characterized by variable eating and inadequate gains in weight

canalization the tendency of growth rates to return to normal after undergoing environmentally induced change

5-2 **Describe the physical development of the brain and the nervous system.** Neurons receive and transmit messages in the form of neurotransmitters. As the child matures, axons grow in length, dendrites and axon terminals proliferate, and many neurons become wrapped in myelin, making them more efficient. The brain triples in weight by the first birthday, reaching nearly 70% of its adult weight. There are two major prenatal growth spurts: Neurons proliferate during the first, and the second spurt is mainly from the proliferation of dendrites and axon terminals. Sensory and motor areas of the brain begin to develop because of maturation, but sensory stimulation and motor activity spur development. Malnutrition is connected with a smaller brain, fewer neurons, and less myelination.

FIG.5.4 STRUCTURES OF THE BRAIN

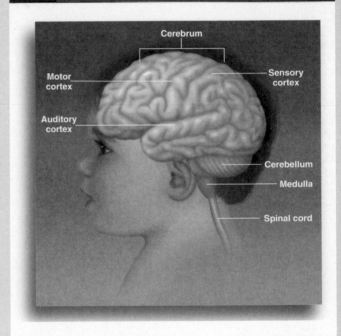

Cerebrum

Motor cortex

Sensory cortex

Auditory cortex

Cerebellum

Medulla

Spinal cord

nerves bundles of axons from many neurons

neurons cells in the nervous system that transmit messages

dendrites rootlike parts of neurons that receive impulses from other neurons

axon a long, thin part of a neuron that transmits impulses to other neurons through branching structures called axon terminals

neurotransmitter a chemical that transmits a neural impulse across a synapse from one neuron to another

myelin sheath a fatty, whitish substance that encases and insulates axons

myelination the coating of axons with myelin

multiple sclerosis a disorder in which hard fibrous tissue replaces myelin, impeding neural transmission

medulla an area of the lower, back part of the brain involved in heartbeat and respiration

cerebellum the area of the lower, back part of the brain involved in coordination and balance

cerebrum the largest, rounded part of the brain, responsible for learning, thought, memory, and language

5-3 **Describe the key events in the motor development of the infant.** Motor development is connected with changes in posture, movement, and coordination. Children gain the ability to move their bodies through a sequence of activities that includes rolling over, sitting up, crawling, creeping, walking, and running. Although the sequence remains stable, some children skip a step. Both maturation (nature) and experience (nurture) play roles in motor development. Development of motor skills can be accelerated by training, but the effect is generally slight.

CHAPTER **REVIEW**

CHAPTER 5 LEARNING OUTCOMES / KEY TERMS

ulnar grasp grasping objects between the fingers and the palm

pincer grasp grasping objects between the fingers and the thumb

locomotion movement from one place to another

toddler a child who walks with short, uncertain steps

5-4 **Describe patterns of sensory and perceptual development in infancy.** Neonates are nearsighted and have poor peripheral vision. Acuity and peripheral vision approximate adult levels by the age of six months. Neonates attend longer to stripes than blobs, and by 8–12 weeks of age they prefer curved lines to straight ones. Two-month-old infants fixate longer on the human face than on other stimuli. Infants can discriminate the mother's face from a stranger's after about 8 hours of contact. Neonates direct their attention to the edges of objects, but two-month-olds scan objects from the edges inward.

Researchers use the visual cliff apparatus to study depth perception. Most infants refuse to venture out over the cliff by the time they can crawl. Perhaps infants need some experience crawling before they develop fear of heights. Size constancy appears to be present by 2½ to 3 months of age; shape constancy develops by age four to five months. Neonates reflexively orient their heads toward a sound.

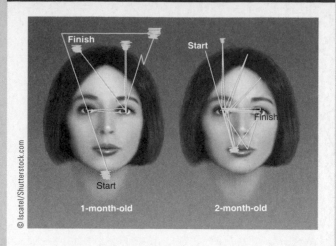

FIG.5.8 EYE MOVEMENTS OF 1- AND 2-MONTH-OLDS

Finish

Start

Start

Finish

Start

1-month-old

2-month-old

© Iscate/Shutterstock.com

One-month-olds direct their attention to the edges of objects. Two-month-olds move in from the edge.

Infants discriminate caregivers' voices by 3½ months of age. Early infants can perceive most of the speech sounds used in the world's languages, but by 10–12 months of age, this ability lessens.

Neonates seem to be at the mercy of external stimuli but, later, intentional action replaces "capture." Systematic search replaces unsystematic search, attention becomes selective, and irrelevant information gets ignored. Sensory changes are linked to maturation of the nervous system (nature), but experience (nurture) also plays a crucial role. There are critical periods in the perceptual development of children and lower animals during which sensory experience is required to optimize—or maintain— sensory capacities.

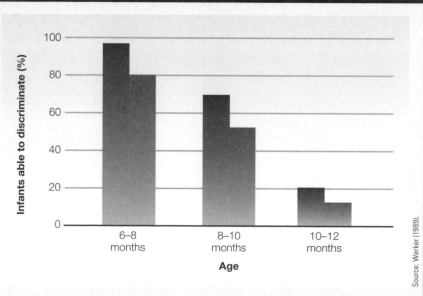

FIG.5.10 DECLINING ABILITY TO DISCRIMINATE THE SOUNDS OF FOREIGN LANGUAGES

Infants able to discriminate (%)

100

80

60

40

20

0

6–8 months

8–10 months

10–12 months

Age

Source: Werker (1989).

Infants show a decline in the ability to discriminate sounds not found in their native language. Before six months of age, infants from English-speaking families could discriminate sounds found in Hindi (red bars) and Salish, a Native American language (blue bars). By 10 to 12 months of age, they could no longer do so.

perceptual constancy perceiving objects as maintaining their identity although sensations from them change as their positions change

habituation becoming used to a stimulus and therefore paying less attention to it

6-1

Examine Jean Piaget's studies of cognitive development. Piaget hypothesized that cognitive processes develop in an orderly sequence of stages: sensorimotor, preoperational, concrete operational, and formal operational. The sensorimotor stage refers to the first two years of cognitive development and involves the progression from responding to events with reflexes to displaying goal-oriented behavior.

A critical milestone in the sensorimotor stage is the appearance of early signs of object permanence, or the ability of an infant to appreciate that an object continues to exist physically even when out of view.

Researchers who question the validity of Piaget's claims argue that

- development is not tied to discrete stages
- adult and peer influences play a role in cognitive development
- infants are more competent than Piaget estimated

sensorimotor stage Piaget's first stage of cognitive development, which lasts through infancy and is generally characterized by increasingly complex coordination of sensory experiences with motor activity

primary circular reactions the repetition of actions that first occurred by chance and that focus on the infant's own body

secondary circular reactions the repetition of actions that produce an effect on the environment

tertiary circular reactions the purposeful adaptation of established schemes to new situations

object permanence recognition that objects continue to exist when they are not in view

A-not-B error the error made when an infant selects a familiar hiding place (A) for an object rather than a new hiding place, even after the infant has seen it hidden in the new place

deferred imitation the imitation of people and events that occurred in the past

6-2

Discuss the information-processing approach to cognitive development. The information-processing approach focuses on how children manipulate or process information coming from the environment or already stored in the mind. Two primary tools used in this processing are memory and imitation. Even neonates demonstrate memory to stimuli, and between two and six months of age, infants' memory develops dramatically. Infant memory can be improved if infants receive a reminder before given a memory test. Researchers disagree about how early nonreflexive imitation is exhibited in infants. Deferred imitation occurs as early as six months of age.

information-processing approach the view of cognitive development that focuses on how children manipulate sensory information and/or information stored in memory

6-3

Identify individual differences in intelligence among infants. The Bayley Scales of Infant Development are one of the most important tests of intellectual development among infants. A total of 287 scale items tests for mental skills (verbal communication, perceptual skills, learning and memory, and problem-solving skills) and motor skills (gross and fine). Infant intelligence is tested to determine the presence of handicaps, and although the Bayley scales can identify gross lags in development and relative strengths and weaknesses, infant intelligence scores are generally poor predictors of intelligence scores taken more than a year later.

Assessing visual recognition memory is another way of studying infant intelligence. Longitudinal studies by Susan Rose and her colleagues showed that the capacity for visual recognition memory is stable and the trait shows predictive validity for broad cognitive abilities throughout childhood, including intelligence and language ability.

visual recognition memory the kind of memory shown in an infant's ability to discriminate previously seen objects from novel objects

6-4

Examine language development in infants. Children develop language according to an invariant sequence of steps or stages. The first stage involves prelinguistic vocalizations such as cooing, babbling, and echolalia. Once children can express themselves with words, they try to talk about more objects than they have words for. Just as first words are simple syllabic combinations, first sentences are often single words that on their own express simple but complete ideas. Developing language skills are marked by changes in the mean length of utterance (MLU). In early language acquisition, children use telegraphic speech to communicate full ideas.

Theories about language development are divided into those emphasizing nurture and those emphasizing nature. Proponents of nurture theories build on the work of B. F. Skinner and cite the roles of imitation and reinforcement in language development. Proponents of the nativist view, like Noam Chomsky, argue that the ability to acquire language is innate and therefore biological. The work of Steven Pinker, among others, shows, however, that language acquisition results from an interaction of environmental and biological factors (or, is a combination of nature and nurture).

FIG.6.5 MEAN LENGTH OF UTTERANCE FOR THREE CHILDREN

The mean length of utterance (MLU) increases rapidly once speech begins.

FIG.6.6 BROCA'S AND WERNICKE'S AREAS OF THE CEREBRAL CORTEX

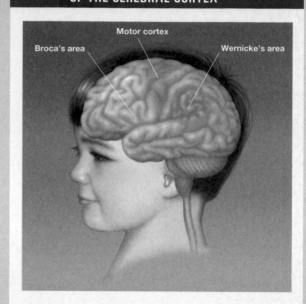

prelinguistic vocalizations made by the infant before the use of language

cooing prelinguistic vowel-like sounds that reflect feelings of positive excitement

babbling the child's first vocalizations that have the sounds of speech

echolalia the automatic repetition of sounds or words

intonation the use of pitches of varying levels to help communicate meaning

receptive vocabulary the number of words one understands

expressive vocabulary the number of words one can use in the production of language

overextension use of words in situations in which their meanings become extended

telegraphic speech type of speech in which only the essential words are used

mean length of utterance (MLU) the average number of morphemes used in an utterance

morpheme the smallest unit of meaning in a language

holophrase a single word that is used to express complex meanings

syntax the rules in a language for placing words in order to form sentences

models in learning theory, those whose behaviors are imitated by others

extinction decrease in frequency of a response due to absence of reinforcement

shaping gradual building of complex behavior through reinforcement of successive approximations to the target behavior

psycholinguistic theory the view that language learning involves an interaction between environmental influences and an inborn tendency to acquire language

language acquisition device (LAD) neural "prewiring" that eases the child's learning of grammar

surface structure the superficial grammatical construction of a sentence

deep structure the underlying meaning of a sentence

aphasia a disruption in the ability to understand or produce language

Broca's aphasia an aphasia caused by damage to Broca's area and characterized by difficulty speaking

Wernicke's aphasia an aphasia caused by damage to Wernicke's area and characterized by impaired comprehension of speech and difficulty producing the right word

critical period the period from about 18 months to puberty when the brain is especially capable of learning language. Also called the *sensitive period*

CHAPTER 7 LEARNING OUTCOMES / KEY TERMS

7-1 **Describe the development of attachment in infancy and theoretical views of how it occurs.** Most infants in the United States are securely attached. In the Strange Situation, secure infants mildly protest mother's departure and are readily comforted by her. The two major types of insecure attachment are avoidant attachment and ambivalent/resistant attachment. Secure infants are happier, more sociable, and more competent. They use the mother as a secure base from which to explore the environment. Parents of securely attached infants are more likely to be affectionate and sensitive to their needs.

According to Ainsworth's studies of the development of attachment, the initial-preattachment phase lasts from birth by about three months and is characterized by indiscriminate attachment. The attachment-in-the-making phase occurs by about three or four months and is characterized by preference for familiar figures. The clear-cut-attachment phase occurs at six or seven months and involves dependence on the primary caregiver.

Cognitive theorists suggest that an infant must develop object permanence before specific attachment is possible. Behaviorists suggest that infants become attached to caregivers because caregivers meet their physical needs. Psychoanalysts suggest that the primary caregiver becomes a love object. The Harlows' experiments with monkeys suggest that contact comfort is a key to attachment. Ethologists view attachment as an instinct (fixed action pattern) that occurs during a critical period.

attachment an affectional bond characterized by seeking closeness with another and distress upon separation

separation anxiety fear of separation from a target of attachment

secure attachment a type of attachment characterized by mild distress at leave-takings and being readily soothed by reunion

insecure attachment attachment behavior characterized by avoiding caregiver, excessive clinging, or inconsistency

avoidant attachment a type of insecure attachment characterized by apparent indifference to leave-takings by and reunions with an attachment figure

ambivalent/resistant attachment a type of insecure attachment characterized by severe distress at leave-takings and ambivalent behavior at reunions

disorganized–disoriented attachment a type of insecure attachment characterized by dazed and contradictory behaviors toward an attachment figure

indiscriminate attachment the display of attachment behaviors toward any person

initial-preattachment phase the first phase in development of attachment, characterized by indiscriminate attachment

FIG.7.2 **DEVELOPMENT OF ATTACHMENT**

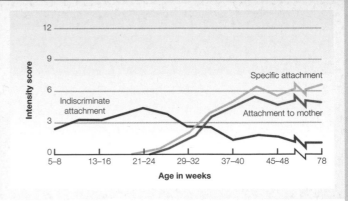

During the first six months, infants tend to show indiscriminate attachment, which wanes as specific attachments intensify.

FIG.7.3 **CONTACT COMFORT**

Nina Leen/Time Life Pictures/Getty Images

Although this rhesus monkey infant is fed by the "wire-mesh mother," it spends most of its time clinging to a soft, cuddly, "terry-cloth mother."

attachment-in-the-making phase the second phase in development of attachment, characterized by preference for familiar figures

clear-cut-attachment phase the third phase in development of attachment, characterized by intensified dependence on the primary caregiver

contact comfort the pleasure derived from physical contact with another

ethologist a scientist who studies the behavior patterns characteristic of various species

social smile a smile that occurs in response to a human voice or face

critical period a period during which imprinting can occur

imprinting the process by which waterfowl become attached to the first moving object they follow

7-2 **Discuss the relationships between social deprivation, child abuse and neglect, autism spectrum disorders and attachment.** The Harlows found that rhesus infants reared in isolation later avoided contact with other monkeys. Females who later had offspring tended to neglect or abuse them. Many institutionalized children who receive little social stimulation develop withdrawal and depression. Mistreated children are less intimate with peers and are more aggressive, angry, and noncompliant than other children. Child abuse tends to run in families, perhaps because abusive parents serve as role models. Some parents rationalize that they are hurting their children "for their own good" to discourage bad behavior.

Autism spectrum disorders (ASDs) are characterized by impairment in communication skills and social interactions, and repetitive, stereotyped behavior. The most striking feature of autism is the child's aloneness. Other features include communication problems, intolerance of change,

and self-mutilation. Twin studies suggest that autism involves heredity, and neurological impairment is also suspected. Behavior modification has been used to increase the child's attention to others and social play and to decrease self-mutilation. Researchers are studying the use of SSRIs and major tranquilizers.

autism spectrum disorders (ASDs) developmental disorders characterized by impairment in communication and social skills, and by repetitive, stereotyped behavior

autism a disorder characterized by extreme aloneness, communication problems, preservation of sameness, and ritualistic behavior

mutism refusal to speak

echolalia automatic repetition of sounds or words

7-3 **Discuss the effects of day care on attachment** Infants with day-care experience are more independent, self-confident, outgoing, affectionate, and more cooperative with peers and adults than infants who are not in day care. Children in high-quality day care outperform children who remain in the home in terms of cognitive development. Children in day care are more aggressive than other children, but some aggression may indicate independence, not maladjustment.

7-4 **Describe the emotional development of the infant.** Researchers debate whether the emotional expression of newborns begins in an undifferentiated state of diffuse excitement or whether several emotions are present. Infants' initial emotional expressions appear to comprise either a positive attraction to pleasant stimulation or withdrawal from aversive stimulation. By the age of two to three months, social smiling has replaced reflexive smiling. Most infants develop fear of strangers by about six to nine months.

Infants display social referencing as early as six months of age, when they use caregivers' facial expressions or

tones of voice for information about how to respond in novel situations. Emotional regulation is emotional self-control. The children of secure mothers are more likely to regulate their emotions well.

social referencing using another person's reaction to a situation to form one's own response

emotional regulation techniques for controlling one's emotional states

7-5 **Describe the personality development of the infant, focusing on the self-concept, temperament, and gender differences.** Research using the mirror technique finds that the self-concept develops by about 18 months of age. Self-awareness enables the child to develop concepts of sharing and cooperation and emotions such as embarrassment, envy, empathy, pride, guilt, and shame.

An infant's temperament (see Table 7.3) involves activity level, regularity, approach or withdrawal, adaptability, response threshold, response intensity, quality of mood, distractibility, attention span, and persistence. Thomas and Chess found that most infants can be classified as having easy, difficult,

or slow-to-warm-up temperaments. Temperament remains moderately consistent from infancy through young adulthood.

Female infants sit, crawl, and walk earlier than boys do. By 12 to 18 months of age, girls prefer to play with dolls and similar toys, whereas boys prefer sports equipment and transportation toys.

temperament individual difference in style of reaction that is present early in life

goodness of fit agreement between the parents' expectations of a child and the child's temperament

TABLE 7.3 TYPES OF TEMPERAMENT

Temperament Category	Easy	Difficult	Slow to Warm Up
Regularity of biological functioning	Regular	Irregular	Somewhat irregular
Response to new stimuli	Positive approach	Negative withdrawal	Negative withdrawal
Adaptability to new situations	Adapts readily	Adapts slowly or not at all	Adapts slowly
Intensity of reaction	Mild or moderate	Intense	Mild
Quality of mood	Positive	Negative	Initially negative; gradually more positive

Sources: Chess & Thomas (1991) and Thomas & Chess (1989).

8-1 **Describe trends in physical development in early childhood.** Children gain about 2 to 3 inches in height and 4 to 6 pounds in weight per year in early childhood. Boys are slightly larger than girls. The brain develops more quickly than any other organ in early childhood, in part because of myelination. The left hemisphere is relatively more involved in logical analysis, language, and computation. The right hemisphere is usually superior in visual–spatial functions, emotional responses, and creative mathematical reasoning. But the hemispheres work together. The brain shows plasticity in early childhood. Two factors involved in the brain's plasticity are the growth of new dendrites and the redundancy of neural connections.

FIG.8.1 GROWTH CURVES FOR HEIGHT AND WEIGHT, AGES TWO TO SIX YEARS

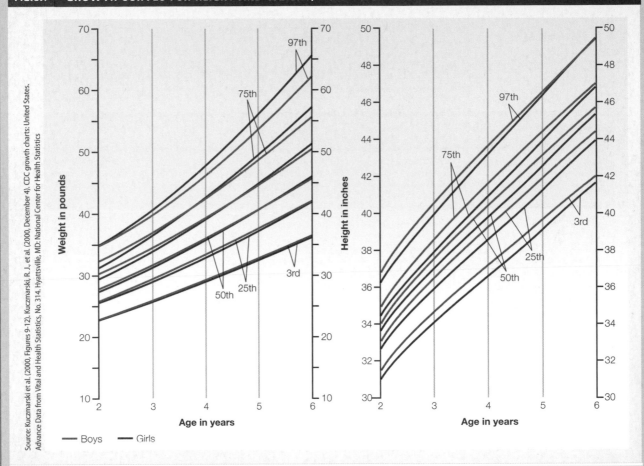

Source: Kuczmarski et al. (2000, Figures 9-12). Kuczmarski, R. J., et al. (2000, December 4). CDC growth charts: United States. Advance Data from Vital and Health Statistics, No. 314. Hyattsville, MD: National Center for Health Statistics

The numbers on the curves indicate the percentiles for height and weight at different ages. The growth rate slows during early childhood. As in infancy, boys are only slightly taller and heavier than girls.

corpus callosum the thick bundle of nerve fibers that connects the left and right hemispheres of the brain

plasticity the tendency of new parts of the brain to take up the functions of injured parts

8-2 **Describe motor development in early childhood.** Preschoolers make great strides in the development of gross motor skills. Girls are somewhat better in balance and precision; boys have some advantage in throwing and kicking. Physically active parents are likely to have physically active children. Fine motor skills develop gradually. Kellogg identified 20 scribbles that she considers the building blocks of art. Handedness emerges by six months. Left-handedness may be connected with some language and health problems, yet a disproportionately large number of artists, musicians, and mathematicians are left-handed.

gross motor skills skills employing the large muscles used in locomotion

fine motor skills skills employing the small muscles used in manipulation, such as those in the fingers

TABLE 8.1 DEVELOPMENT OF GROSS MOTOR SKILLS IN EARLY CHILDHOOD

2 Years (24–35 Months)	3 Years (36–47 Months)	4 Years (48–59 Months)	5 Years (60–71 Months)
• Runs well straight ahead	• Goes around obstacles while running	• Turns sharp corners while running	• Runs lightly on toes
• Walks up stairs, two feet to a step	• Walks up stairs, one foot to a step	• Walks down stairs, one foot to a step	• Jumps a distance of 3 feet
• Kicks a large ball	• Kicks a large ball easily	• Jumps from a height of 12 inches	• Catches a small ball, using hands only
• Jumps a distance of 4–14 inches	• Jumps from the bottom step	• Throws a ball overhand	• Hops 2 to 3 yards forward on each foot
• Throws a small ball without falling	• Catches a bounced ball, using torso and arms to form a basket	• Turns sharp corners while pushing and pulling toys	• Stands on one foot for 8–10 seconds
• Pushes and pulls large toys	• Goes around obstacles while pushing and pulling toys	• Hops on one foot, four to six hops	• Climbs actively and skillfully
• Hops on one foot, two or more hops	• Hops on one foot, up to three hops	• Stands on one foot for 3–8 seconds	• Skips on alternate feet
• Tries to stand on one foot	• Stands on one foot	• Climbs ladders	• Rides a bicycle with training wheels
• Climbs on furniture to look out of window	• Climbs nursery-school apparatus	• Skips on one foot	
		• Rides a tricycle well	

Note: The ages are averages; there are individual variations.

TABLE 8.2 DEVELOPMENT OF FINE MOTOR SKILLS IN EARLY CHILDHOOD

2 Years (24–35 Months)	3 Years (36–47 Months)	4 Years (48–59 Months)	5 Years (60–71 Months)
• Builds tower of 6 cubes	• Builds tower of 9 cubes	• Builds tower of 10 or more cubes	• Builds 3 steps from 6 blocks, using a model
• Copies vertical and horizontal lines	• Copies circle and cross	• Copies square	• Copies triangle and star
• Imitates folding of paper	• Copies letters	• Prints simple words	• Prints first name and numbers
• Prints on easel with a brush	• Holds crayons with fingers, not fist	• Imitates folding paper three times	• Imitates folding of piece of square paper into a triangle
• Places simple shapes in correct holes	• Strings four beads using a large needle	• B Uses pencil with correct hand grip	• Traces around a diamond drawn on paper
		• Strings 10 beads	• Laces shoes

Note: The ages are averages; there are individual variations.

8-3 Describe trends in health and illness in early childhood. The incidence of minor illnesses, such as colds, nausea and vomiting, and diarrhea, is high. Diarrheal diseases are almost completely related to unsafe drinking water and lack of sanitation in developing countries and are a leading cause of death there. Immunization and antibiotics reduce the incidence of disease. Air pollution contributes to respiratory infections. Lead poisoning causes neurological damage. Accidents cause more deaths in early childhood than the next six most frequent causes combined.

8-4 Describe sleep patterns in early childhood. Most two- and three-year-olds sleep about 10 hours at night and nap during the day. Sleep terrors are more severe than nightmares. Sleep terrors and sleepwalking usually occur during deep sleep. Sleepwalkers' eyes are usually open; if awakened, they may show confusion but are unlikely to be violent.

> **sleep terrors** frightening dreamlike experiences that occur during the deepest stage of non-REM sleep, shortly after the child has gone to sleep
>
> **somnambulism** sleepwalking

TABLE 8.3 HOW MUCH SLEEP DO YOU REALLY NEED?

Age	Sleep Needed
Newborns (0–2 months)	12 to 18 hours
Infants (3–11 months)	14 to 15 hours
Toddlers (1–3 years)	12 to 14 hours
Preschoolers (3–5 years)	11 to 13 hours
School-age children (5–10 years)	10 to 11 hours
Teens (10–17 years)	8.5 to 9.25 hours
Adults	7 to 9 hours

Source: National Sleep Foundation (2015).

8-5 Discuss the elimination disorders. Most U.S. children are toilet trained by 3 or 4 but continue to have "accidents." Enuresis is apparently connected with physical immaturity and stress. Encopresis can stem from constipation and stress.

enuresis failure to control the bladder (urination) once the normal age for control has been reached

bed-wetting failure to control the bladder during the night

encopresis failure to control the bowels once the normal age for bowel control has been reached. Also called soiling

CHAPTER 9 LEARNING OUTCOMES / KEY TERMS

9-1 **Describe Piaget's preoperational stage.** Piaget's preoperational stage lasts from about 2 to 7 and is characterized by the use of symbols. Preoperational thinking is characterized by pretend play, egocentrism, precausal thinking, confusion between mental and physical events, and ability to focus on only one dimension at a time. Conservation is lacking because it requires focusing on two aspects of a situation at once.

FIG.9.2 CONSERVATION

a   b   c

(a) The preoperational boy agrees that the amounts of water in the two containers is the same. (b) He watches as the water from one container is poured into a taller, thinner container. (c) When asked whether the tall and the squat containers now contain the same amount of water, he says no. Why?

preoperational stage the second stage in Piaget's scheme, characterized by inflexible and irreversible mental manipulation of symbols

symbolic play play in which children make believe that objects and toys are other than what they are. Also called pretend play

egocentrism putting oneself at the center of things such that one is unable to perceive the world from another person's point of view

precausal a type of thought in which natural cause-and-effect relationships are attributed to will and other preoperational concepts

transductive reasoning reasoning from the specific to the specific

animism the attribution of life and intentionality to inanimate objects

artificialism the belief that environmental features were made by people

conservation in cognitive psychology, the principle that properties of substances such as weight and mass remain the same (are conserved) when superficial characteristics such as their shapes or arrangement are changed

centration focusing on an aspect or characteristic of a situation or problem

class inclusion categorizing a new object or concept as belonging to a broader group of objects or concepts

9-2 **Discuss influences on cognitive development in early childhood.** Vygotsky envisions scaffolding and the zone of proximal development as two factors in cognitive development. The HOME scale was developed to evaluate children's home environments. The scale includes six factors that influence child development, including parental emotional and verbal responsiveness, avoidance of restriction and punishment, organization of the physical environment, provision of appropriate play materials, parental involvement with the child, and opportunities for variety in daily stimulation. The children of parents who provide appropriate play materials and stimulating experiences show gains in social and language development. Head Start programs enhance economically disadvantaged children's academic readiness and skills.

scaffolding Vygotsky's term for temporary cognitive structures or methods of solving problems that help the child as he or she learns to function independently

zone of proximal development (ZPD) Vygotsky's term for the situation in which a child carries out tasks with the help of someone who is more skilled, frequently an adult who represents the culture in which the child develops

9-3 **Explain how "theory of mind" affects cognitive development.** Children come to understand that there are distinctions between external and mental events and between appearances and realities. By age three, most children begin to realize that people gain knowledge through the senses, and by age four, they understand which senses provide certain kinds of information.

theory of mind a commonsense understanding of how the mind works

appearance–reality distinction the difference between real events on the one hand and mental events, fantasies, and misleading appearances on the other hand

9-4 **Describe memory development in early childhood.** Preschoolers recognize more items than they can recall. Autobiographical memory is linked to language skills. Factors affecting memory include what the child is asked to remember, interest level and motivation, the availability of retrieval cues, and the memory measure being used. Preschoolers engage in behavior such as looking, pointing, and touching when trying to remember. Preschoolers can be taught to use memory strategies such as rehearsal and grouping of items.

scripts abstract, generalized accounts of familiar repeated events

autobiographical memory the memory of specific episodes or events

rehearsal repetition

9-5 **Describe language development in early childhood.** Preschoolers acquire about nine new words per day, some of which occur because of fast mapping. During the third year, children usually add articles, conjunctions, possessive adjectives, pronouns, and prepositions. Between the ages of three and four, children combine phrases and clauses into complex sentences. Preschoolers overregularize irregular verbs and nouns as they learn grammar. Piaget believed that children learn words to describe classes they have created. Other theorists argue that children create classes to understand words. To Vygotsky, inner speech is the ultimate binding of language and thought.

fast mapping a process of quickly determining a word's meaning, which facilitates children's vocabulary development

whole-object assumption the assumption that words refer to whole objects and not to their component parts or characteristics

contrast assumption the assumption that objects have only one label

overregularization the application of regular grammatical rules for forming inflections to irregular verbs and nouns

pragmatics the practical aspects of communication, such as adaptation of language to fit the social situation

inner speech Vygotsky's concept of the ultimate binding of language and thought. Inner speech originates in vocalizations that may regulate the child's behavior and become internalized by age six or seven

CHAPTER 10 LEARNING OUTCOMES / KEY TERMS

10-1 **Describe the dimensions of child rearing and styles of parenting.** Approaches to child rearing can be classified according to two broad dimensions: warmth–coldness and restrictiveness–permissiveness. Consistent control and firm enforcement of rules can have positive consequences for the child. Parents tend to use inductive methods, power assertion, and withdrawal of love to enforce rules. Inductive methods use "reasoning," or explaining why one sort of behavior is good and another is not. Authoritative parents are restrictive but warm and tend to have the most competent and achievement-oriented children. Authoritarian parents are restrictive and cold. The sons of authoritarian parents tend to be hostile and defiant; daughters are low in independence. Children of neglectful parents show the least competence and maturity.

TABLE 10.1 BAUMRIND'S PATTERNS OF PARENTING

Parental Style	Parental Behavior Patterns	
	Restrictiveness and Control	Warmth and Responsiveness
Authoritative	High	High
Authoritarian	High	Low
Permissive–Indulgent	Low	High
Rejecting–Neglecting	Low	Low

authoritative a child-rearing style in which parents are restrictive and demanding yet communicative and warm

authoritarian a child-rearing style in which parents demand submission and obedience

permissive–indulgent a child-rearing style in which parents are warm and not restrictive

rejecting–neglecting a child-rearing style in which parents are neither restrictive and controlling nor supportive and responsive

10-2 **Explain how siblings, birth order, peers, and other factors affect social development during early childhood.** Siblings provide caregiving, emotional support, advice, role models, social interaction, restrictions, and cognitive stimulation. However, they are also sources of conflict, control, and competition. Younger siblings usually imitate older siblings. First-born and only children are generally more highly motivated to achieve, more cooperative, more helpful, more adult-oriented, and less aggressive, but later-born children tend to have greater social skills with peers. Children learn social skills—such as sharing, taking turns, and coping with conflict—from peers. Peers also provide emotional support. Preschoolers' friendships are characterized by shared activities and feelings of attachment.

FIG.10.1 BANDURA'S STUDY OF THE IMITATION OF AGGRESSION

© Albert Bandura/Dept. of Psychology, Stanford University

The top row of photos shows an adult striking a Bobo doll. The second and third rows show a boy and a girl who observed the adult imitating the aggressive behavior.

Play develops motor, social, and cognitive skills. Parten followed the development of six types of play among two- to five-year-olds: unoccupied play, solitary play, onlooker play, parallel play, associative play, and cooperative play. Children show preferences for gender-stereotyped toys by 15 to 30 months of age. Boys' toys commonly include transportation toys (cars and trucks) and weapons; girls' toys more often include dolls. Boys prefer vigorous outdoor activities and rough-and-tumble play. Girls are more likely to prefer arts and crafts. Preschool children generally prefer playmates of their own gender partly because of shared interest in activities. Boys' play is more oriented toward dominance, aggression, and rough play.

Prosocial behavior begins to develop in the first year, when children begin to share. Development of prosocial behavior is linked to the development of empathy and perspective taking. Girls show more empathy than boys do.

Preschool aggression is often instrumental. By age six or seven, aggression becomes hostile. Aggressive behavior appears to be stable and to predict problems in adulthood. Genetic factors may be involved in aggressive behavior, partly because of testosterone. Social cognitive theory suggests that children become aggressive as a result of frustration and observational learning. Aggressive children are often rejected by less aggressive peers. Children who are physically punished are more likely to behave aggressively. Observing aggressive behavior teaches aggressive skills, disinhibits the child, and habituates children to violence.

regression a return to behavior characteristic of earlier stages of development

dramatic play play in which children enact social roles

nonsocial play solitary form of play

social play play in which children interact with and are influenced by others

prosocial behavior behavior that benefits other people, generally without expectation of reward

disinhibit to encourage a response that has been previously suppressed

---

10-3 **Discuss personality and emotional development during early childhood, focusing on the self, Erikson's views, and fears.** Children as young as 3 can describe themselves in terms of behavior and internal states.

Secure attachment and competence contribute to self-esteem. Preschoolers are most likely to fear animals, imaginary creatures, and the dark. Girls report more fears than boys do.

self-concept one's self-description and self-evaluation according to various categories, such as child, adolescent, or adult, one's gender, and one's skills

categorical self definitions of the self that refer to external traits

---

10-4 **Discuss the development of gender roles and gender differences.** Females are stereotyped as dependent, gentle, and home-oriented. Males are stereotyped as aggressive, self-confident, and independent. Cultural expectations of females and males are called gender roles. Males tend to excel in math and spatial-relations skills, whereas girls tend to excel in verbal skills. Stereotypical gender preferences for toys and play activities are in evidence at an early age. Males are more aggressive and more interested in sex than females. Testosterone may specialize the hemispheres of the brain more in males than females, explaining why females excel in verbal skills that require some spatial organization, such as reading. Social cognitive theorists explain the development of gender-typed behavior in terms of observational learning and socialization. According to Kohlberg's cognitive-developmental theory, gender-typing involves the emergence of gender identity, gender stability, and gender constancy. According to gender-schema theory, preschoolers attempt to conform to the cultural gender schema. Theorists differ as to whether it is beneficial to promote psychological androgyny.

stereotype a fixed, conventional idea about a group

gender role a cluster of traits and behaviors that are considered stereotypical of females and males

gender identity knowledge that one is female or male

gender stability the concept that one's gender is unchanging

gender constancy the concept that one's gender remains the same despite changes in appearance or behavior

gender-schema theory the view that one's knowledge of the gender schema in one's society guides one's assumption of gender-typed preferences and behavior patterns.

11-1 Describe trends in physical development in middle childhood. Children tend to gain a little more than 2 inches in height and 5 to 7 pounds in weight per year during middle childhood. Boys are slightly heavier and taller than girls through age 9 or 10, until girls begin their adolescent growth spurt.

growth spurt a period during which growth advances at a dramatically rapid rate compared with other periods

FIG.11.1 GROWTH CURVES FOR WEIGHT AND HEIGHT

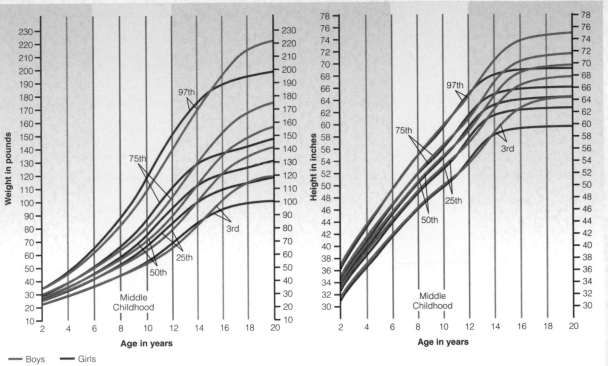

Source: Kuczmarski et al. (2000, Figures 9-12).
© Ryan McVay/Photodisc/Getty Images

— Boys — Girls

Gains in height and weight are fairly steady during middle childhood.

11-2 Discuss the origins of the problem of being overweight in middle childhood, and suggest solutions. Overweight children usually do not outgrow baby fat. Heredity plays a role in weight. Sedentary habits also foster weight gain.

11-3 Discuss the origins and treatment of childhood asthma. Asthma is an allergy-type respiratory disorder. Attacks prevent the sufferer from getting enough air. Severe attacks can result in death. Childhood asthma is more prevalent in developed nations, but is more severe in undeveloped nations. Risk factors include previous respiratory infections and skin irritations, male gender, administration of oxygen after birth, prescription of antibiotics during the first six months, and asthma in the family. Some children "outgrow" asthma.

FIG.11.2 OVERWEIGHT CHILDREN IN THE UNITED STATES

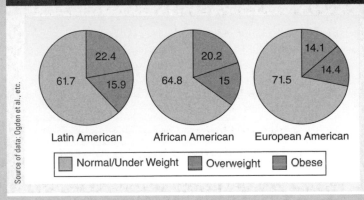

Source of data: Ogden et al., etc.

Latin American — 61.7 / 22.4 / 15.9
African American — 64.8 / 20.2 / 15
European American — 71.5 / 14.1 / 14.4

☐ Normal/Under Weight ☐ Overweight ☐ Obese

Percentage of children (ages 6–11) and adolescents (ages 12–19) who are overweight, according to the American Heart Association (AHA).

11-4 **Describe gross and fine motor development in middle childhood.** Middle childhood is marked by increases in speed, strength, agility, and balance. Children improve in gross and fine motor skills as pathways that connect the cerebellum to the cortex become more myelinated. Reaction time decreases. Boys have slightly greater overall strength, whereas girls have better coordination and flexibility. Most U.S. children are not physically fit, in part because of the amount of time spent watching TV.

Cultura Creative/Alamy Stock Photo

reaction time the amount of time required to respond to a stimulus

11-5 **Discuss the diagnosis, origins, and treatment of attention-deficit/hyperactivity disorder.** Attention-deficit/hyperactivity disorder (ADHD) runs in families, and brain damage might be involved. Children with ADHD are often treated with stimulants because they stimulate the cerebral cortex to inhibit more primitive areas of the brain.

attention deficit hyperactivity disorder (ADHD) a disorder characterized by excessive inattention, impulsiveness, and hyperactivity

hyperactivity excessive restlessness and overactivity; a characteristic of ADHD

stimulants drugs that increase the activity of the nervous system

11-6 **Describe learning disorders, and discuss their origins and treatment.** Dyslexia also runs in families. The double-deficit hypothesis suggests that dyslexic children have problems in phonological processing and naming speed. Some learning-disabled children profit from mainstream classrooms; others find them overwhelming.

dyslexia a reading disorder characterized by letter reversals, mirror reading, slow reading, and reduced comprehension

learning disabilities disorders characterized by inadequate development of specific academic, language, and speech skills

mainstreaming placing disabled children in classrooms with nondisabled children

FIG.11.3 WRITING SAMPLE OF A DYSLEXIC CHILD

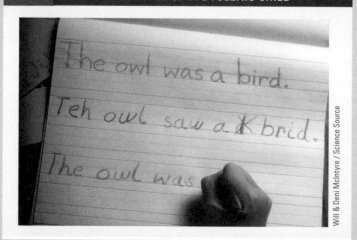

Will & Deni McIntyre / Science Source

Dyslexic children may perceive letters as upside down (confusing *w* with *m*) or reversed (confusing *b* with *d*), leading to rotations or reversals in writing, as shown here.

12-1 **Describe Piaget's concrete-operational stage.** By the age of 11, many children begin to recognize ambiguities in grammar and their thought processes become more logical and complex. Piaget characterized children during this period as entering the concrete-operational stage, in which children begin to think in logical terms but focus on tangible objects rather than abstract ideas. Concrete-operational children are less egocentric, engage in decentration, and understand concepts such as conservation, transitivity, seriation, and class inclusion.

concrete operations the third stage in Piaget's scheme, characterized by flexible, reversible thought concerning tangible objects and events

decentration simultaneous focusing on more than one aspect or dimension of a problem or situation

transitivity the principle that if A > B and B > C, then A > C

seriation placing objects in an order or series according to a property or trait

12-2 **Discuss Piaget's and Kohlberg's theories of moral development.** Piaget and Kohlberg both presumed that moral reasoning in children was related to overall cognitive development. Piaget proposed that children's moral judgments develop in two overlapping stages, which he termed moral realism and autonomous morality. Kohlberg's theory emphasized the importance of being able to view a situation from multiple perspectives, and the reasons on which people base their judgments reflect their level of moral development. At a preconventional level, moral judgments are based on the positive or negative consequences of one's actions. At the conventional level, moral judgments are based on conformity to conventional standards. At a postconventional level, moral judgments are based on personal moral standards.

moral realism the judgment of acts as moral when they conform to authority or to the rules of the game

objective morality the perception of morality as objective, that is, as existing outside the cognitive functioning of people

immanent justice the view that retribution for wrongdoing is a direct consequence of the wrongdoing

autonomous morality the second stage in Piaget's cognitive-developmental theory of moral development, in which children base moral judgments on the intentions of the wrongdoer and on the amount of damage done

preconventional level according to Kohlberg, a period during which moral judgments are based largely on expectations of rewards or punishments

conventional level according to Kohlberg, a period during which moral judgments largely reflect social rules and conventions

postconventional level according to Kohlberg, a period during which moral judgments are derived from moral principles, and people look to themselves to set moral standards

12-3 **Describe developments in information processing in middle childhood.** Key elements in children's information processing capabilities include development in selective attention; development in the storage and retrieval of sensory, short-term, and long-term memory; development of recall memory; and development of metacognition and metamemory.

sensory memory the structure of memory first encountered by sensory input. Information is maintained in sensory memory for only a fraction of a second

sensory register another term for sensory memory

working memory the structure of memory that can hold a sensory stimulus for up to 30 seconds after the trace decays

encode to transform sensory input into a form that is more readily processed

rehearsing repeat—in this case, mentally

long-term memory the memory structure capable of relatively permanent storage of information

elaborative strategy a method for increasing retention of new information by relating it to well-known information

metacognition awareness of and control of one's cognitive abilities

metamemory knowledge of the functions and processes involved in one's storage and retrieval of information

12-4 **Describe intellectual development in middle childhood, focusing on theories of intelligence.** Intelligence is usually perceived as a child's underlying competence or *learning ability*, whereas achievement involves a child's acquired competencies or *performance*. Factor theorists view intelligence as consisting of one or more major mental abilities. Sternberg proposed a three-part theory of intelligence (see Figure 12.7). Gardner theorized that intelligence reflected more than academic achievement, with nine different categories of intelligence, or "talents." The Wechsler and SBIS scales have been developed to measure intelligence. Many psychologists and educational specialists have developed culture-free tests to avoid cultural biases they feel are present in the Wechsler and SBIS. About half of children score between 90 and 110 on IQ tests. Those who score below 70 are labeled "intellectually deficient" and above 130 are labeled "gifted." Most tests indicate only a moderate relationship between IQ scores and creativity. Intelligence tests usually rely on convergent thinking, and creativity is generally based on divergent thinking.

intelligence a general mental capability that involves the ability to reason, plan, solve problems, think abstractly, comprehend complex ideas, learn quickly, and learn from experience

achievement that which is attained by one's efforts and presumed to be made possible by one's abilities

intelligence quotient (IQ) (1) a ratio obtained by dividing a child's mental age on an intelligence test by his or her chronological age; (2) a score on an intelligence test

mental age (MA) the intellectual level at which a child is functions, based on the typical performance of a child of a certain age

chronological age (CA) a person's age

cultural bias a factor hypothesized to be present in intelligence tests that provides an advantage for test takers from certain cultural backgrounds

culture-free descriptive of a test in which cultural biases have been removed

cultural–familial disability substandard intellectual performance stemming from lack of opportunity to acquire knowledge and skills

creativity a trait characterized by flexibility, ingenuity, and originality

convergent thinking a thought process that attempts to focus on the single best solution to a problem

divergent thinking free and fluent association to the elements of a problem

heritability the degree to which the variations in a trait from one person to another can be attributed to genetic factors

12-5 **Describe language development in middle childhood, including reading and bilingualism.** Children's language ability grows more sophisticated in middle childhood. Children learn to read as well. Table 12.4 illustrates literacy rates in various regions around the world. Approximately 47 million Americans live in homes where a language other than English is spoken.

word-recognition method a method for learning to read in which children come to recognize words through repeated exposure to them

phonetic method a method for learning to read in which children decode the sounds of words based on their knowledge of the sounds of letters and letter combinations

sight vocabulary words that are immediately recognized on the basis of familiarity with their overall shapes, rather than decoded

bilingual using or capable of using two languages with nearly equal or equal facility

13-1 **Explain theories of social and emotional development in middle childhood.** Freud viewed middle childhood as the latency stage; Erikson saw it as the stage of industry versus inferiority. Social cognitive theorists note that children now depend less on external rewards and punishments and increasingly regulate their own behavior. Cognitive-developmental theory notes that concrete operations enhance social development. In middle childhood, children become more capable of taking the role or perspective of another person. Selman theorizes that children move from egocentricity to seeing the world through the eyes of others in five stages.

In early childhood, children's self-concepts focus on external traits. In middle childhood, children begin to include abstract internal traits. Social relationships and group membership assume importance. In middle childhood, competence and social acceptance contribute to self-esteem, but self-esteem tends to decline because the self-concept becomes more

realistic. Authoritative parenting fosters self-esteem. Children with "learned helplessness" tend not to persist in the face of failure.

latency stage in psychoanalytic theory, the fourth stage of psychosexual development, characterized by repression of sexual impulses and development of skills

industry versus inferiority a stage of psychosocial development in Erikson's theory occurring in middle childhood. Mastery of tasks leads to a sense of industry, whereas failure produces feelings of inferiority

social cognition development of children's understanding of the relationship between the self and others

learned helplessness an acquired (hence, learned) belief that one is unable to control one's environment

TABLE 13.1 LEVELS OF PERSPECTIVE TAKING

Level	Approximate Age (Years)	What Happens
0	3–6	Children are egocentric and do not realize that other people have perspectives different from their own. A child of this age will typically say that Holly will save the kitten because she likes kittens and that her father will be happy because he likes kittens too. The child assumes that everyone feels as she does.
1	5–9*	Children understand that people in different situations may have different perspectives. The child still assumes that only one perspective is "right." A child might say that Holly's father would be angry if he did not know why she climbed the tree. But if she told him why, he would understand. The child recognizes that the father's perspective may differ from Holly's because of lack of information. But once he has the information, he will assume the "right" (i.e., Holly's) perspective.
2	7–12*	The child understands that people may think or feel differently because they have different values or ideas. The child also recognizes that others are capable of understanding the child's own perspective. Therefore, the child is better able to anticipate reactions of others. The typical child of this age might say that Holly knows that her father will understand why she climbed the tree and that he therefore will not punish her.
3	10–15*	The child finally realizes that both she and another person can consider each other's point of view at the same time. The child may say something similar to this reasoning: Holly's father will think that Holly shouldn't have climbed the tree. But now that he has heard her side of the story, he would feel that she was doing what she thought was right. Holly realizes that her father will consider how she felt.
4	12 and above*	The child realizes that mutual perspective taking does not always lead to agreement. The perspectives of the larger social group also must be considered. A child of this age might say that society expects children to obey their parents and therefore that Holly should realize why her father might punish her.

*Ages may overlap.
Source: Selman (1976).

13-2 **Discuss the influences of the family on social development in middle childhood.** In middle childhood, the family continues to play a key role in socialization. Parent–child interactions focus on school-related issues, chores, and peers. Parents do less monitoring of children; "coregulation" develops. Children of lesbian and gay parents by and large develop as well as children of heterosexual parents. The sexual orientation of these children is generally heterosexual. Divorce disrupts children's lives and usually lowers the family's financial status. Children are likely to greet divorce with sadness, shock, and disbelief. Children of divorce fare better when parents cooperate on child rearing. Children appear to suffer as much from marital conflict as from divorce. Having both parents in the workforce can lead to lack of supervision, but there is little evidence that maternal employment

per se harms children. Maternal employment fosters greater independence and flexibility in gender-role stereotypes.

coregulation a gradual transferring of control from parent to child, beginning in middle childhood

transgender referring to people who feel as though they are persons of the other sex who are 'trapped' in the body of the wrong sex. Some transgender individuals (also called 'trans') are content to adopt the clothing and cosmetic appearance of people of the other sex; others undergo hormone treatments and surgery to achieve the body shape and external physical traits of persons of the other sex

13-3 **Discuss the influences of peers on social development in middle childhood.** Peers take on increasing importance in middle childhood and exert pressure to conform. Peers afford practice in social skills, sharing, relating to leaders, and coping with aggressive impulses. Popular children tend to be attractive and mature for their age. Early in middle childhood, friendships are based on proximity. Between the ages of 8 and 11, children become more aware of the value of friends as meeting each other's needs and having traits such as loyalty. At this age, peers tend to discourage contact with members of the other sex.

cyberbullying the use of electronic devices such as cellphones, computers, and tablets to transmit threatening and taunting messages

TABLE 13.2	STAGES IN CHILDREN'S CONCEPTS OF FRIENDSHIP		
Stage	Name	Approximate Age (Years)	What Happens
0	Momentary physical interaction	3–6	Children remain egocentric. Their concept of a friend is one who likes to play with the same things and lives nearby.
1	One-way assistance	5–9*	Children are less egocentric but view a friend as someone who does what they want.
2	Fair-weather cooperation	7–12*	Friends are viewed as doing things for one another, but the focus remains on self-interest.
3	Intimate and mutual sharing	10–15*	The focus is on the relationship rather than on the individuals separately. Friendship is viewed as providing mutual support over a long period of time.
4	Autonomous interdependence	12 and above*	Children (adolescents, and adults) understand that friendships grow and change as people change and that they may need different friends to satisfy different needs.

*Ages can overlap

Source: Selman (1980).

13-4 **Describe the influence of the school on social development in middle childhood.** Schools make demands for mature behavior and nurture positive physical, social, and cognitive development. Readiness for school is related to children's early life experiences, individual differences in development and learning, and the schools' expectations. An effective school has an orderly atmosphere, empowers teachers and students, holds high expectations of children, and has solid academics. Teachers' expectations can become self-fulfilling prophecies. Many girls suffer from sexism and sexual harassment in school. Math and science are still often stereotyped as masculine, and language arts as feminine.

Pygmalion effect a positive self-fulfilling prophecy in which an individual comes to display improved performance because of the positive expectation of the people with whom he or she interacts

self-fulfilling prophecy an event that occurs because of the behavior of those who expect it to occur

sexism discrimination or bias against people based on their gender

sexual harassment unwelcome verbal or physical conduct of a sexual nature

13-5 **Discuss social and emotional problems that tend to develop in middle childhood.** There may be a genetic component to conduct disorders, but sociopathic models in the family, deviant peers, and inconsistent discipline contribute. Depressed children tend to complain of poor appetite, insomnia, lack of energy, and feelings of worthlessness. They blame themselves excessively for shortcomings. Psychotherapy focuses on cognitive errors; antidepressants are sometimes helpful but controversial. Separation anxiety disorder (SAD) is diagnosed when separation anxiety is persistent and excessive and interferes with daily life. Children with SAD tend to cling to parents and might refuse to attend school. Children might also refuse school because they find it to be unpleasant or hostile. The central aspect of treatment of school refusal is to insist that the child attend school.

conduct disorder marked by persistent breaking of the rules and violations of the rights of others

attributional style the way in which one is disposed toward interpreting outcomes (successes or failures), as in tending to place blame or responsibility on oneself or on external factors

serotonin a neurotransmitter that is involved in mood disorders such as depression

generalized anxiety disorder (GAD) an anxiety disorder in which anxiety appears to be present continuously and is unrelated to the situation

phobia an irrational, excessive fear that interferes with one's functioning

separation anxiety disorder (SAD) an extreme form of otherwise normal separation anxiety that is characterized by anxiety about separating from parents; SAD often takes the form of refusal to go to school

school phobia fear of attending school, marked by extreme anxiety at leaving parents

14-1 **Discuss growth in adolescence, focusing on the growth spurt and asynchronous growth.** G. Stanley Hall believed that adolescence is marked by "storm and stress." Current views challenge the idea that storm and stress are normal or beneficial. Puberty is a stage of physical development that is characterized by reaching sexual maturity. Sex hormones trigger the development of primary and secondary sex characteristics. Girls undergo a growth spurt earlier than boys do. Boys tend to spurt up to 4 inches per year, and girls, up to 3 inches per year. During their growth spurts, boys catch up with girls and grow taller and heavier. Boys' shoulders become broader, and girls develop broader and rounder hips. More of a male's body weight is made of muscle. Adolescents may look gawky because of asynchronous growth. Boys typically ejaculate by age 13 or 14. Female sex hormones regulate the menstrual cycle.

The effects of early maturation are generally positive for boys and often negative for girls. Early-maturing boys tend to be more popular. Early-maturing girls become conspicuous, often leading to sexual approaches, deviant behavior, and a poor body image. Girls are generally more dissatisfied with their bodies than boys are. By age 18, dissatisfaction tends to decline.

puberty the biological stage of development characterized by changes that lead to reproductive capacity

feedback loop a system in which glands regulate each other's functioning through a series of hormonal messages

primary sex characteristics the structures that make reproduction possible

secondary sex characteristics physical indicators of sexual maturation—such as changes to the voice and growth of bodily hair—that do not directly involve reproductive structures

asynchronous growth unbalanced growth, such as the growth that occurs during the early part of adolescence and causes many adolescents to appear gawky

secular trend a historical trend toward increasing adult height and earlier puberty

semen the fluid that contains sperm and substances that nourish and help transport sperm

nocturnal emission emission of seminal fluid while asleep

gynecomastia enlargement of breast tissue in males

epiphyseal closure the process by which the cartilage that separates the long end of a bone from the main part of the bone turns to bone

menarche the onset of menstruation

| FIG.14.1 | SPURTS IN GROWTH |

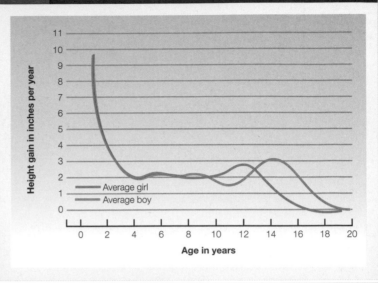

Girls begin the adolescent growth spurt about two years earlier than boys. Girls and boys reach their periods of peak growth about two years after the spurt begins.

| FIG.14.4 | THE DECLINE IN AGE AT MENARCHE |

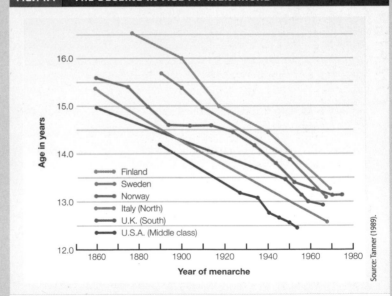

Source: Tanner (1989).

The age at menarche has been declining since the mid-1800s among girls in Western nations, apparently because of improved nutrition and health care.

14-2

Describe the biological events of puberty and discuss gender differences in the effects of maturing early or late. Teenagers are at particular risk for STIs. Sexually active adolescents have higher rates of STIs than any other age group. Chlamydia, a bacterial infection of the vagina or urinary tract that can result in sterility, is the most commonly occurring STI in adolescents, followed by gonorrhea, genital warts, genital herpes, syphilis, and HIV/AIDS.

14-3

Discuss health in adolescence, focusing on causes of death and nutritional needs. Most adolescent health problems stem from their lifestyles. Accidents, suicide, and homicide account for aboutthree in four deaths among adolescents. To fuel the adolescent growth spurt, the average girl needs 1,800 to 2,400 calories per day, and the average boy needs 2,200 to 3,200 calories. Adolescents need high quantities of calcium, iron, zinc,

14-4

Discuss the eating disorders anorexia nervosa and bulimia nervosa, including their origins. The stage of formal operations is Piaget's final stage of development. Many children reach this stage during adolescence, but not all. The formal operational stage is characterized by the individual's increased ability to classify objects and ideas, engage in logical thought, hypothesize, and demonstrate a sophisticated use of symbols.

Adolescents show a new egocentrism in which they comprehend the ideas of other people, but have difficulty sorting out those things that concern other people from the things that concern themselves.

Eating disorders include anorexia nervosa and bulimia nervosa. Eating disorders mainly afflict females. Some psychoanalysts suggest that anorexia represents efforts to remain prepubescent.

14-5

Discuss adolescent substance use and abuse. Alcohol and cigarettes are the most widely used substances by adolescents. Marijuana has increased in popularity. Substance use disorders may develop with repeated use of a substance, leading to changes in "brain circuitry" that are connected with impaired control over use of the substance, social problems, risky behavior, and biological factors suggestive of addiction. Some substances can lead to physical addiction, so that when the dosage is lowered, withdrawal symptoms, also known as abstinence syndrome, occur.

Depressants slow the activity of the nervous system and include alcohol, narcotics, and sedatives. Stimulants speed up the heartbeat and other bodily functions. Nicotine, cocaine, and amphetamines are the most common stimulants. Hallucinogenics give rise to perceptual distortions called hallucinations, which sometimes can be so strong as to be confused with reality. Marijuana, Ecstasy, LSD, and PCP are hallucinogenic drugs.

substance use disorder a persistent pattern of use of a substance characterized by frequent intoxication; impairment of physical, social, or emotional well-being; and possible physical addiction

abstinence syndrome a characteristic cluster of symptoms that results from a sudden decrease in the level of usage of a substance

hallucinogenics drugs that give rise to hallucinations

HIV/AIDS Human immunodefi ciency virus (HIV) is the cause of acquired immunodeficiency syndrome (AIDS), a condition that cripples the immune system.

magnesium, and nitrogen. Adolescents usually need more vitamins than they get from what they usually eat, but less sugar, fat, protein, and sodium.

osteoporosis a condition involving progressive loss of bone tissue

One risk factor for eating disorders in adolescent females is a history of child abuse. Eating disorders might develop because of fear of gaining weight resulting from cultural idealization of the slim female. Genetic factors might connect eating disorders with perfectionistic personality styles.

anorexia nervosa an eating disorder characterized by irrational fear of weight gain, distorted body image, and severe weight loss

bulimia nervosa an eating disorder characterized by cycles of binge eating and purging as a means of controlling weight gain

TABLE 14.3 HAVE YOU USED ____ IN YOUR ____?

Percent saying "Yes"

	Lifetime	Last year	Last 30 days
Alcohol	45.2	39.9	21.8
Amphetamines	9.1	6.2	2.7
Cigarettes	21.1	N/A	7.0
E-cigarettes	N/A	N/A	13.2
Cocaine	2.7	1.7	0.8
Ecstasy	3.5	2.2	0.8
Heroin	0.7	0.4	0.2
LSD	2.8	1.9	0.7
Marijuana	30.0	23.7	14.0

Source: Johnston, L. D., O'Malley, P. M., Miech, R. A., Bachman, J. G., & Schulenberg, J. E. (2016). Monitoring the Future national survey results on drug use, 1975–2015: Overview, key findings on adolescent drug use. Ann Arbor: Institute for Social Research, The University of Michigan.

Notes: Drug use increases from the 8th grade through the 12th grade. Use of e-cigarettes has surpassed use of tobacco cigarettes among adolescents. Finally, results reflect usage only among adolescents in school; dropouts are not included.

15-1 **Discuss adolescent cognitive development and the key events of Piaget's stage of formal operations.** In Western societies, formal operational thought begins at about the time of puberty. The major achievements of the stage involve classification, logical thought (deductive reasoning), and the ability to hypothesize. Adolescent egocentrism is shown in the concepts of the imaginary audience and the personal fable.

formal operations the fourth stage in Piaget's cognitive-developmental theory, characterized by the capacity for flexible, reversible operations concerning abstract ideas and concepts, such as symbols, statements, and theories

imaginary audience the belief that others around us are as concerned with our thoughts and behaviors as we are; one aspect of adolescent egocentrism

personal fable the belief that our feelings and ideas are special and unique and that we are invulnerable; one aspect of adolescent egocentrism

15-2 **Describe gender differences in cognitive abilities.** The stage of formal operations is Piaget's final stage of development. Many children reach this stage during adolescence, but not all. The formal operational stage is characterized by the individual's increased ability to classify objects and ideas, engage in logical thought, hypothesize, and demonstrate a sophisticated use of symbols.

Adolescents show a new egocentrism in which they comprehend the ideas of other people, but have difficulty sorting out those things that concern other people from the things that concern themselves.

FIG.15.1 EXAMPLES OF TESTS USED TO MEASURE VISUAL–SPATIAL ABILITY

Mental-rotation test. If you mentally rotate the figure on the left, which of the five figures on the right would you obtain?

1.   a   b   c   d   e

2.   a   b   c   d   e

No gender differences are found on the spatial visualization tasks. The gender difference is greatest on the mental rotation tasks. What are some possible reasons for these differences?

15-3 **Discuss Kohlberg's theory of moral development in adolescence.** Females tend to excel in verbal ability. Males tend to excel in visual–spatial ability. Females and males show equal ability in math. Boys are more likely than girls to have reading problems. Gender differences in cognitive abilities have been linked to biological factors and to gender stereotypes.

postconventional level according to Kohlberg, a period during which moral judgments are derived from moral principles and people look to themselves to set moral standards

---

TABLE 15.1 KOHLBERG'S POSTCONVENTIONAL LEVEL OF MORAL DEVELOPMENT

Stage	Examples of Moral Reasoning That Support Heinz's Stealing the Drug	Examples of Moral Reasoning That Oppose Heinz's Stealing the Drug
Stage 5: Contractual, legalistic orientation: One must weigh pressing human needs against society's need to maintain social order.	This thing is complicated because society has a right to maintain law and order, but Heinz has to take the drug to save his wife.	I can see why Heinz feels he has to take the drug, but laws exist for the benefit of society as a whole and cannot simply be cast aside.
Stage 6: Universal ethical principles orientation: People must follow universal ethical principles and their own consciences, even if it means breaking the law.	In this case, the law comes into conflict with the principle of the sanctity of human life. Heinz must take the drug because his wife's life is more important than the law.	If Heinz truly believes that stealing the drug is worse than letting his wife die, he should not take it. People have to make sacrifices to do what they think is right.

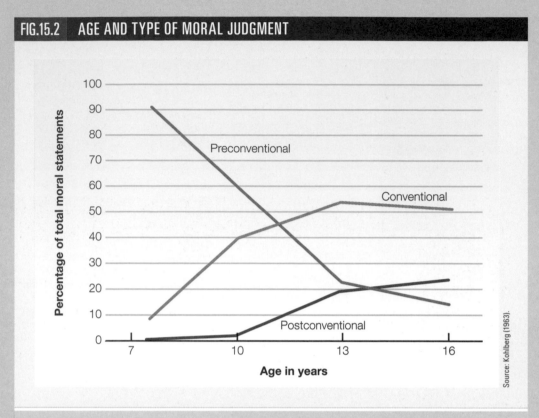

FIG. 15.2   AGE AND TYPE OF MORAL JUDGMENT

Source: Kohlberg (1963).

The incidence of preconventional reasoning declines from more than 90% of moral statements at age 7 to less than 20% of statements at age 16. Conventional moral statements increase with age between the ages of 7 and 13 but then level off to account for 50% to 60% of statements at ages 13 and 16. Postconventional moral statements are all but absent at ages 7 and 10 but account for about 20% to 25% of statements at ages 13 and 16.

15-4 **Discuss the roles of the school in adolescence, focusing on dropping out.** In the postconventional level, according to Kohlberg, moral reasoning is based on the person's own moral standards. In Kohlberg's scheme, males reason at higher levels of moral development than females do, but Gilligan argues that this gender difference reflects patterns of socialization, with girls being encouraged to take a more "caring" orientation.

15-5 **Discuss adolescent work experiences and career choices.** The transition to middle, junior high, or high school generally involves a shift from a smaller neighborhood elementary school to a larger, more impersonal setting. The transition is often accompanied by a decline in grades and a drop in self-esteem. High school dropouts are more likely to be unemployed and earn lower salaries. Dropouts are more likely to show delinquent behaviors. Truancy and reading below grade level predict school dropout.

Psychologists have devised approaches to matching personality traits with careers to predict adjustment in a given career. Holland's (1997) RIASEC method, as used in his Vocational Preference Inventory, matches six personality types to various kinds of careers: realistic, investigative, artistic, social, enterprising, and conventional (see Figure 15.3).

self-efficacy expectations beliefs that we will be able to successfully meet the requirements of our situations

16-1

Discuss the formation of identity in adolescence.
Erikson's adolescent stage of psychosocial development is ego identity versus role diffusion. The primary task of this stage is for adolescents to develop a sense of who they are and what they stand for. Marcia's identity statuses represent the four combinations of the dimensions of exploration and commitment: identity diffusion, foreclosure, moratorium, and identity achievement. Development of identity is more complicated for adolescents who belong to ethnic minority groups. Minority adolescents are faced with two sets of cultural values and might need to reconcile and incorporate elements of both.

Researchers propose a three-stage model of the development of ethnic identity: unexamined ethnic identity, an ethnic identity search, and an achieved ethnic identity. As minority youth move through adolescence, they are increasingly likely to explore and achieve ethnic identity.

Erikson proposed that interpersonal relationships are more important to women's identity than occupational and ideological issues, bur research suggests that U.S. adolescent females and males are equally concerned about careers. Adolescents incorporate psychological traits and social relationships into their self-descriptions. Self-esteem tends to decline as the child progresses from middle childhood into early adolescence, perhaps because of increasing recognition of the disparity between the ideal self and the real self. Then, self-esteem gradually improves.

TABLE 16.1   THE FOUR IDENTITY STATUSES OF JAMES MARCIA

Commitment		Exploration	
		Yes	**No**
Yes		**Identity Achievement** • Most developed in terms of identity • Has experienced a period of exploration • Has developed commitments • Has a sense of personal well-being, high self-esteem, and self-acceptance • Cognitively flexible • Sets goals and works toward achieving them	**Foreclosure** • Makes commitments without considering alternatives • Commitments based on identification with parents, teachers, or other authority figures • Often authoritarian and inflexible
No		**Moratorium** • Actively exploring alternatives • Attempting to make choices with regard to occupation, ideological beliefs, and so on • Often anxious and intense • Ambivalent feelings toward parents and authority figures	**Identity Diffusion** • Least developed in terms of identity • Lacks commitments • Not trying to form commitments • May be carefree and uninvolved or unhappy and lonely • May be angry, alienated, rebellious

ego identity vs. role diffusion Erikson's fifth life crisis, during which adolescents develop a firm sense of who they are and what they stand for (ego identity), or they do not develop a sense of who they are and tend to be subject to the whims of others

psychological moratorium a period when adolescents experiment with different roles, values, beliefs, and relationships

identity crisis a turning point in development during which one examines one's values and makes decisions about life roles

Identity diffusion an identity status that characterizes those who have no commitments and who are not in the process of exploring alternatives

foreclosure an identity status that characterizes those who have made commitments without considering alternatives

moratorium an identity status that characterizes those who are actively exploring alternatives in an attempt to form an identity

Identity achievement an identity status that characterizes those who have explored alternatives and have developed commitments

ethnic identity a sense of belonging to an ethnic group

unexamined ethnic identity the first stage of ethnic identity development; similar to the diffusion or foreclosure identity statuses

ethnic identity search the second stage of ethnic identity development; similar to the moratorium identity status

achieved ethnic identity the final stage of ethnic identity development; similar to the identity achievement status

16-2

Describe relationships with parents and peers during adolescence. During adolescence, children spend much less time with parents than during childhood. Although adolescents become more independent of their parents, they generally continue to love and respect them. The role of peers increases markedly during the teen years. Adolescents are more likely than younger children to stress intimate self-disclosure and

mutual understanding in friendships. The two major types of peer groups are cliques and crowds. Adolescent peer groups also include peers of the other gender. Romantic relationships begin to appear during early and middle adolescence. Dating is a source of fun, prestige, and experience in relationships. Dating is also a preparation for adult courtship.

cliques a group of five to ten individuals who hang around together and who share activities and confidences

crowds a large, loosely organized group of people who may or may not spend much time together and who are identified by the activities of the group

16-3 **Discuss sexuality during adolescence, focusing on sexual orientation, sexual behavior, and teenage pregnancy.** Some adolescents have a homosexual orientation. The process of "coming out" can be a long and painful struggle. Masturbation is the most common sexual outlet in adolescence. Adolescents today start dating earlier than past generations. Teens who date earlier are

- more likely to engage in sexual activity
- less likely to use contraception
- more likely to become pregnant

Early onset of puberty is connected with earlier sexual activity. Adolescents who have close relationships with parents are less likely to initiate sexual activity early. Peer pressure is a powerful contributor to sexual activity.

Many girls who become pregnant have received little advice about how to resist sexual advances. Most of them do not have access to contraception. Most misunderstand reproduction or miscalculate the odds of

conception. Teenage mothers are more likely to have medical complications during pregnancy and birth, largely because of inadequate medical care. The babies are more likely to be premature and to have low birth weight. Teenage mothers have a lower standard of living and a greater need for public assistance. Their children have more academic and emotional problems.

FIG.16.1 NEVER-MARRIED TEENAGERS, AGED 15–19, WHO HAVE HAD SEXUAL INTERCOURSE

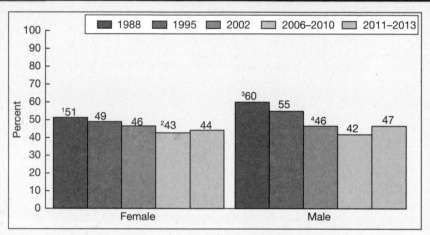

Source: Martinez, G., & Abma, J. C. (2015). Sexual activity, contraceptive use, and childbearing of teenagers aged 15–19 in the United States. U.S. Department of Health and Human Services, National Center for Health Statistics. NCHS Data Brief, No. 209, Figure 1.

masturbation sexual self-stimulation

petting kissing and touching the breasts and genitals

homosexual referring to an erotic orientation toward members of one's own gender

bisexual attracted to individuals of both genders

transgendered psychologically belonging to the other gender—that is, the gender that is inconsistent with one's sexual anatomy

LGBT acronym for lesbian, gay, bisexual, and transgender

sexual identity the label a person uses to signal who she or he is as a sexual being, especially concerning her or his sexual orientation

16-4 **Discuss the characteristics of juvenile delinquents.** Behaviors, such as drinking, that are considered illegal when performed by minors are called status offenses. Boys are more apt to commit crimes of violence, whereas girls are more likely to commit status offenses. Risk factors associated with juvenile delinquency include poor school performance, delinquent friends, early aggressive or hyperactive behavior, substance abuse, low verbal IQ, low self-esteem, impulsivity,

and immature moral reasoning. The parents and siblings of delinquents have frequently engaged in antisocial behavior themselves.

juvenile delinquency conduct in a child or adolescent characterized by illegal activities

16-5 **Discuss risk factors in adolescent suicide.** Suicide is the third leading cause of death among adolescents. Most suicides among adolescents and adults are linked to stress, feelings of

depression, identity problems, impulsivity, and social problems. Girls are more likely to attempt suicide, whereas boys are more likely to "succeed."